VOCATIONAL-TECHNICAL
MATHEMATICS

VOCATIONAL-TECHNICAL
MATHEMATICS

ROBERT D. SMITH

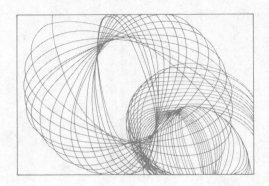

For information address Delmar Publishers Inc.
2 Computer Drive-W, Box 15-015
Albany, New York 12212

10 9 8 7 6

LIBRARY OF CONGRESS CATALOG CARD NUMBER: 81-70966
ISBN: 0-8273-1882-0

PRINTED IN THE UNITED STATES OF AMERICA
PUBLISHED SIMULTANEOUSLY IN CANADA
BY NELSON CANADA,
A DIVISION OF INTERNATIONAL THOMSON LIMITED

Vocational-Technical Mathematics is dedicated to my wife, Kathy, and children, Dawn, Arline, and Eric. Their understanding, patience, and co-operation are gratefully acknowledged.

NOTICE TO THE READER

Vocational-Technical Mathematics

PREFACE

Vocational-Technical Mathematics is written to provide practical vocational and technical applications of mathematical concepts. Presentation of concepts is followed by applied examples and problems which have been drawn from diverse occupational fields.

Both content and method are those used by the author in teaching related vocational-technical mathematics on both the secondary and post-secondary levels. Each unit is developed as a learning experience based on preceding units. The applied examples and problems progress from the simple to those whose solutions are relatively complex. Many problems require the student to work with illustrations such as are found in trade and technical manuals, handbooks, and drawings.

The book was written from material developed for classroom use and it is designed for classroom purposes. However, the text is also very appropriate for self-instruction use. Great care has been taken in presenting explanations clearly and in giving easy to follow procedural steps in solving examples. One or more examples are given for each mathematical concept presented. Throughout the book, practical application examples from various occupations are shown to illustrate the actual on-the-job uses of the mathematical concept. Students often ask, "Why do we have to learn this material and of what actual practical value is it?" This question was constantly kept in mind in writing the book and every effort was made to continuously provide an answer.

An understanding of mathematical concepts is emphasized in all topics. Much effort was made to avoid the mechanical *plug in* approach often found in vocational related textbooks. A practical rather than an academic approach to mathematics is taken. Derivations and formal proofs are not presented; instead, understanding of concepts followed by the application of concepts in real situations is stressed.

Section I, Fundamentals of General Mathematics contains the prerequisites for the subsequent sections. It is assumed that students using this book have previously studied the topics presented in Section I; therefore the material in Section I is structured differently than that of the rest of the text. The approach taken is that of treating the topics entirely as review material. Mathematical procedures are not presented in this section, rather an example of the concept is given followed by student exercises and problems. It is felt that the topics, exercises, and problems presented in Section I are of value to the instructor and students for diagnostic and placement testing purposes.

Student exercises and applied problems immediately follow the presentation of concept and examples. In addition, exercises and occupationally related problems are included at the end of each unit. The book contains a sufficient number of exercises and problems to permit the instructor to selectively plan assignments.

The Solutions and Tests Booklet contains the complete solutions to many problems, the answers to all problems, and a set of section achievement reviews developed for each of the six sections. The achievement reviews are comprehensive and are designed to measure students' achievement of all of the unit objectives contained within each section.

Illustrations, examples, exercises, and practical problems expressed in metric units of measure are a basic part of the content of the entire text. Emphasis is placed on the ability of the student to think and to work with equal ease with both the English and the metric systems. Tables of equivalent units of measure are contained in the Appendix.

An analytical approach to problem solving is emphasized in the plane geometry, computed measure, and trigonometry sections. The approach is that which is used in actual on-the-job trade and technical occupations applications. Integration of algebraic and geometric principles with trigonometry by careful sequencing and treatment of material also helps the student in solving occupationally related problems.

About the Author

The author, Robert D. Smith, is presently a faculty member in the Vocational-Technical Education Department at Central Connecticut State College, New Britain, Connecticut. Mr. Smith has had experience in the manufacturing industry as tool designer, quality control engineer, and chief manufacturing engineer. He has also been active in teaching applied mathematics, physics, and industrial materials and processes on the secondary school level. He is the author of Delmar's MATHEMATICS FOR MACHINE TECHNOLOGY and APPLIED GENERAL MATHEMATICS.

Mr. Smith has been involved in several professional organizations in his field of interest, including The American Technical Education Association and The Society of Manufacturing Engineers.

CONTENTS

SECTION 2 FUNDAMENTALS OF ALGEBRA

SECTION 3 FUNDAMENTALS OF PLANE GEOMETRY

SECTION 5   COMPUTED MEASURE

SECTION 6 FUNDAMENTALS OF TRIGONOMETRY

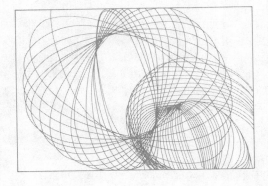

SECTION 1
Fundamentals of General Mathematics

UNIT 1
Whole
Numbers

OBJECTIVE

After studying this unit you should be able to

- solve whole number problems by applying the principles of whole numbers.

ADDING WHOLE NUMBERS

Example.   Add and check. 55 907 + 12 + 7 785 079 + 3 986

```
  7 844 984  Ck
     55 907
         12
  7 785 079
+     3 986
  7 844 984  Ans
```

Exercise 1-1

Add and check.

1. 73 + 24

2. 876 + 97

3. 4 397 + 8 512

4. 8 677 + 12 393 + 155 071

5. 64 + 178 + 9 766

SUBTRACTING WHOLE NUMBERS

Example.   Subtract and check. 5 532 006 − 3 350 078

```
   5 532 006          2 181 928
 − 3 350 078        + 3 350 078
   2 181 928  Ans     5 532 006  Ck
```

Exercise 1-2

Subtract and check.

1. 87 − 23

2. 978 − 349

3. 7 833 − 626

4. 30 092 − 28 398

5. 438 078 − 29 066

ADDING AND SUBTRACTING WHOLE NUMBERS IN PRACTICAL APPLICATIONS

Exercise 1-3

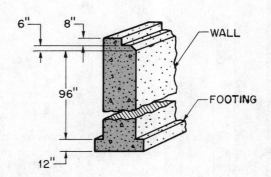

Fig. 1-1

1. A section of concrete wall and footing is shown in figure 1-1. What is the total height of the wall and footing?

2. During the first week of April, a print shop used the following paper stock: 5 570 sheets on Monday, 7 855 sheets on Tuesday, 7 236 sheets on Wednesday, 6 867 sheets on Thursday, and 6 643 sheets on Friday. During the following week, 4 050 more sheets are used than during the first week. Find the total sheets used during the first two weeks of April.

3. The duplicating machine operator of a manufacturing company makes copies of printed material for various departments within the company. A log is kept to record the number of copies made for each department. The monthly log is shown in figure 1-2.

	NUMBER OF COPIES			
	WEEK 1	WEEK 2	WEEK 3	WEEK 4
DEPARTMENT				
Production	853	712	956	1 088
Engineering and Design	1 050	936	277	732
Personnel	2 756	1 935	2 080	993
Accounting	830	0	344	130
Sales	1 202	555	3 859	2 444
Data Processing	85	53	0	187
Purchasing	1 932	1 637	767	845
Inspection	177	286	53	0
Receiving and Shipping	538	613	423	778

Fig. 1-2

a. Find the total number of copies made in week 1.

b. Find the total number of copies made in week 2.

c. Find the total number of copies made in week 3.

d. Find the total number of copies made in week 4.

e. Find the total number of copies made for the month.

4. An automobile body shop charges $465 for repairs on a customer's car. The charges for labor are $196. Paint and materials cost $67 and replacement parts cost $110. How much profit is made on the job?

5. A machinist must know dimensions A and B in order to finish grind surfaces F and G of the casting shown in figure 1-3. All dimensions are in millimetres.

   a. Find, in millimetres, dimension A.
   b. Find, in millimetres, dimension B.

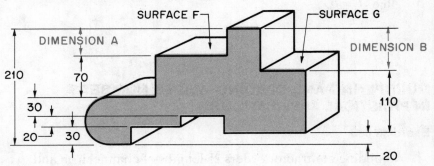

Fig. 1-3

6. A baker makes a batch of cookie mix which weighs 48 pounds. Pastry flour and other ingredients are used to make the mix. The weights of the other ingredients are 13 pounds of almond paste, 12 pounds of margarine, 5 pounds of egg whites, and 7 pounds of granulated sugar. How many pounds of pastry flour are used?

MULTIPLYING WHOLE NUMBERS

Example. Multiply and check. 706 × 315

```
      315              706
    × 706            × 315
    1 890            3 530
  220 50             7 06
  222 390 Ans      211 8
                   222 390 Ck
```

Exercise 1-4

Multiply and check.

1. 84 × 76
2. 59 × 898
3. 305 × 8 756
4. 403 × 6 007
5. 6 959 × 27 877

DIVIDING WHOLE NUMBERS

Example. Divide and check. 476 947 ÷ 646

```
           738 R199 Ans          738
    646) 476 947                × 646
         452 2                   4 428
          24 74                 29 52
          19 38                442 8
           5 367              476 748
           5 168
             199             476 748
                           +     199
                           476 947 Ck
```

Exercise 1-5

Divide and check.

1. 365 ÷ 5
2. 4 800 ÷ 16
3. 46 877 ÷ 5

4. 56 107 ÷ 79
5. 58 218 ÷ 836

MULTIPLYING AND DIVIDING WHOLE NUMBERS IN PRACTICAL APPLICATIONS

Exercise 1-6

1. A building contractor orders 25 lengths of channel iron and 18 lengths of I beam as shown in figure 1-4. What is the total length of channel iron and I beam ordered?

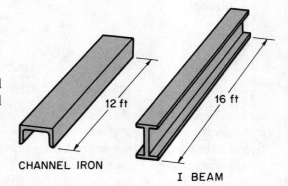

CHANNEL IRON   I BEAM

Fig. 1-4

2. The invoice shown in figure 1-5 is mailed to the Center Sports Shop by a billing clerk of the M & N Sports Equipment Manufacturing Company. (An invoice is a bill sent to a retailer by a manufacturer or wholesaler for merchandise purchased by the retailer.) The extension shown in the last column of the invoice is the product of the number (quantity) of units multiplied by the price of one unit. Find the extension amount for each item on the invoice and add the extensions to determine total cost.

	QUANTITY	UNIT	UNIT PRICE	DESCRIPTION	EXTENSION
a.	15	dozen	$ 2	Floats	$30
b.	24	each	$11	Fishing rods	
c.	1	box	$18	Spools of line	
d.	18	each	$ 7	Reels	
e.	36	each	$ 5	Baseball bats	
f.	5	box	$36	Baseballs	
g.	24	package	$ 6	Golfballs	
h.	15	each	$14	Putters	
i.				Total Cost	_____

Fig. 1-5

3. The drill jig shown in figure 1-6 is laid out by a machine drafter. All dimensions are in centimetres.

    a. Find, in centimetres, dimension A.

    b. Find, in centimetres, dimension B.

    c. Find, in centimetres, dimension C.

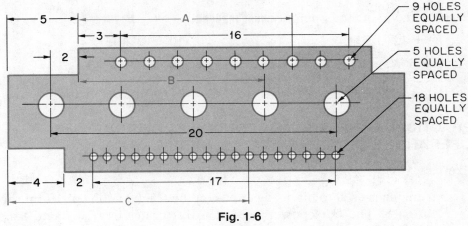

Fig. 1-6

4. Figure 1-7 shows the front view of a wooden counter that is to be built for a clothing store. All pieces of the counter except the top and back are to be made of the same thickness and width of lumber. How many total feet $(1' = 12'')$ of lumber should be ordered for this job? Do not include the top or back. Allow 6 feet for waste.

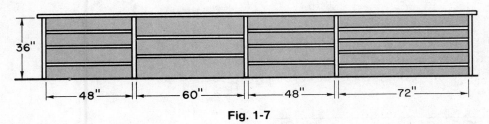

Fig. 1-7

5. An 8-pound cut of roast beef is to be medium roasted at 350°F. Total roasting time is determined by allowing 15 minutes roasting time for each pound of beef. If the roast is placed in a preheated oven at 2:00 PM, at what time should it be removed?

6. A designer fashions a dress which is 46 inches long from the neck to the hem. The first button is placed one inch from the top; the last button is placed 3 inches from the hem. The buttons are placed 2 inches apart. How many buttons are required?

COMBINED OPERATIONS IN ARITHMETIC EXPRESSIONS

Order of Operations

- First, do all operations within grouping symbols. Grouping symbols are parentheses ( ), brackets [ ], and braces { }.

   Next, do multiplication and division operations in order from left to right.

- Last, do addition and subtraction operations in order from left to right.

Example . Find the value of $(15 + 6) \times 3 - 28 \div 7$.

$$(15 + 6) \times 3 - 28 \div 7$$
$$21 \times 3 - 28 \div 7$$
$$63 - 4$$
59 *Ans*

Exercise 1-7

Perform the indicated operations.

1. $9 + 12 - 5$
2. $35 + 30 \div 5$
3. $(35 + 30) \div 5$
4. $(10 \times 8) \div (5 \times 4)$
5. $(240 - 80) \times 15 \div 3$

PRACTICAL APPLICATIONS REQUIRING COMBINED OPERATIONS OF ARITHMETIC EXPRESSIONS

Exercise 1-8

1. An engine is used to lift heavy crates on the truck loading platform shown in figure 1-8. The horsepower needed to lift crates can be found using this formula.

$$hp = (f \times d \div t) \div 550$$

where hp = horsepower
f = force in pounds
d = distance in feet
t = time in seconds

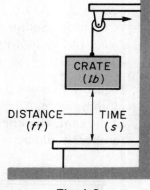

Fig. 1-8

The force is equal to the weight of a crate. The distance is the number of feet a crate is lifted. The time is the number of seconds needed to lift the crate a certain distance. Find the number of horsepower needed to lift each of the crates listed in figure 1-9.

CRATE	WEIGHT OF CRATE	DISTANCE LIFTED	TIME	HORSE-POWER
A	660 lb	10 ft	4 s	
B	1 100 lb	12 ft	6 s	
C	1 650 lb	14 ft	7 s	
D	3 300 lb	8 ft	16 s	
E	2 640 lb	10 ft	8 s	

Fig. 1-9

2. The accountant for a small manufacturing firm computes the annual depreciation of each piece of tooling, equipment, and machinery in the company. From a detailed itemized list, the accountant groups all items together that have the same life expectancy (number of years of usefulness) as shown in figure 1-10. Find the annual depreciation for each group and the total annual depreciation of all tooling, equipment and machinery, using the straight line formula.

Annual Depreciation = (cost − final value) ÷ number of years of usefulness.

	GROUP	COST	FINAL VALUE	NUMBER OF YEARS OF USEFULNESS	ANNUAL DEPRECIATION
a.	Tooling	$14 500	$1 200	5 years	
b.	Equipment	$28 350	$3 750	6 years	
c.	Equipment	$17 900	$2 040	10 years	
d.	Machinery	$67 700	$7 940	8 years	
e.	Machinery	$80 300	$10 600	10 years	
f.				Total Annual Depreciation	

Fig. 1-10

3. A landscaper contracts to provide topsoil and to seed and lime the parcel of land shown in figure 1-11. In order to determine labor and material costs, the landscaper must first know the total area of the land. Find the total area in square feet.

   Total Area (square feet) $= l \times w + (a \times b) \div 2$

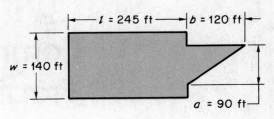

Fig. 1-11

4. The formula called Young's Rule is used in the health field to determine a child's dose of medicine.

   Child's dose = (Age of child) ÷ (Age of child + 12) × average adult dose

   What dose (number of milligrams) of morphine sulfate should be given to a 3-year-old child if the adult dose is 10 milligrams?

UNIT 2
Common
Fractions

OBJECTIVE

After studying this unit you should be able to

- solve common fraction problems by applying the principles of common fractions.

EQUIVALENT FRACTIONS

Example. Express $\frac{23}{7} = \frac{?}{168}$ as an equivalent fraction as indicated.

$\frac{23}{7} = \frac{552}{168}$ *Ans*

Exercise 2-1

Express each fraction as an equivalent fraction as indicated.

1. $\frac{3}{8} = \frac{?}{16}$ 2. $\frac{13}{15} = \frac{?}{75}$ 3. $\frac{9}{13} = \frac{?}{78}$ 4. $\frac{9}{4} = \frac{?}{20}$

EXPRESSING FRACTIONS IN LOWEST TERMS

Example. Express $\frac{148}{36}$ as a fraction in lowest terms.

$\frac{148}{36} = \frac{37}{9}$ *Ans*

Exercise 2-2

Express each fraction as a fraction in lowest terms.

1. $\frac{3}{6}$ 2. $\frac{5}{30}$ 3. $\frac{6}{16}$ 4. $\frac{180}{15}$ 5. $\frac{21}{49}$

EXPRESSING MIXED NUMBERS AS FRACTIONS

Example. Express $372\frac{3}{8}$ as a fraction.

$372\frac{3}{8} = \frac{2\,979}{8}$ *Ans*

Exercise 2-3

Express each mixed number as a common fraction.

1. $2\frac{1}{2}$ 2. $4\frac{2}{3}$ 3. $9\frac{4}{5}$ 4. $2\frac{17}{32}$ 5. $54\frac{7}{16}$

EXPRESSING FRACTIONS AS MIXED NUMBERS

Example.   Express $\dfrac{812}{25}$ as a mixed number.

$$\dfrac{812}{25} = 32\dfrac{12}{25} \; Ans$$

Exercise 2-4

Express each common fraction as a mixed number.

1. $\dfrac{7}{2}$ 2. $\dfrac{19}{5}$ 3. $\dfrac{87}{4}$ 4. $\dfrac{133}{64}$ 5. $\dfrac{411}{32}$

LOWEST COMMON DENOMINATORS

Example.   Find the lowest common denominator for this set of fractions.

$$\dfrac{5}{6}, \quad \dfrac{3}{20}, \quad \dfrac{2}{5}, \quad \dfrac{3}{4}$$

Factor each denominator into prime factors. $6 = 2 \times 3$
Multiply the different prime factors. The $20 = 2 \times 2 \times 5$
number of times each factor is multiplied $5 = 5 \times 1$
is equal to the largest number of times $4 = 2 \times 2$
it appears in any denominator. $2 \times 2 \times 3 \times 5 = \mathbf{60} \; Ans$

Exercise 2-5

Determine the lowest common denominators of each set of fractions.

1. $\dfrac{1}{4}, \quad \dfrac{3}{16}, \quad \dfrac{5}{8}$ 3. $\dfrac{9}{15}, \quad \dfrac{1}{3}, \quad \dfrac{3}{5}, \quad \dfrac{7}{10}$

2. $\dfrac{3}{4}, \quad \dfrac{1}{3}, \quad \dfrac{7}{8}$ 4. $\dfrac{3}{10}, \quad \dfrac{1}{7}, \quad \dfrac{1}{2}, \quad \dfrac{1}{3}$

ADDING FRACTIONS

Example.   Add $\dfrac{1}{12} + \dfrac{19}{32} + \dfrac{1}{6} + \dfrac{6}{7}$ and express the answer in lowest terms.

$$\dfrac{1}{12} = \dfrac{56}{672}$$

$$\dfrac{19}{32} = \dfrac{399}{672}$$

$$\dfrac{1}{6} = \dfrac{112}{672}$$

$$+ \; \dfrac{6}{7} = \dfrac{576}{672}$$

$$\dfrac{1\,143}{672} = 1\dfrac{471}{672} \; Ans$$

Exercise 2-6

Add these fractions. Express the answers in lowest terms.

1. $\dfrac{3}{16} + \dfrac{7}{16}$ 3. $\dfrac{1}{2} + \dfrac{5}{6} + \dfrac{11}{12}$ 5. $\dfrac{9}{32} + \dfrac{1}{4} + \dfrac{5}{24}$

2. $\dfrac{5}{8} + \dfrac{3}{8} + \dfrac{1}{8}$ 4. $\dfrac{3}{10} + \dfrac{1}{5} + \dfrac{3}{4}$ 6. $\dfrac{2}{3} + \dfrac{7}{9} + \dfrac{11}{12}$

ADDING FRACTIONS, MIXED NUMBERS, AND WHOLE NUMBERS

Example.   Add $3\dfrac{3}{16} + 9 + 14\dfrac{27}{64}$ and express the answer in lowest terms.

$$3\dfrac{3}{16} = 3\dfrac{12}{64}$$
$$9 = 9$$
$$+ 14\dfrac{27}{64} = 14\dfrac{27}{64}$$
$$\overline{\phantom{+ 14\dfrac{27}{64} = }26\dfrac{39}{64}} \; Ans$$

Exercise 2-7

Add these values. Express the answers in lowest terms.

1. $7 + \dfrac{7}{8}$ 2. $10\dfrac{1}{16} + \dfrac{7}{16}$ 3. $4\dfrac{3}{16} + 12\dfrac{3}{8}$ 4. $23\dfrac{1}{8} + 36\dfrac{7}{32}$

SUBTRACTING FRACTIONS

Example.   Subtract $\dfrac{13}{15} - \dfrac{9}{20}$ and express the answer in lowest terms.

$$\dfrac{13}{15} = \dfrac{52}{60}$$
$$- \dfrac{9}{20} = \dfrac{27}{60}$$
$$\overline{\phantom{- \dfrac{9}{20} = }\dfrac{25}{60} = \dfrac{5}{12}} \; Ans$$

Exercise 2-8

Subtract these fractions as indicated. Express the answers in lowest terms.

1. $\dfrac{7}{10} - \dfrac{3}{10}$ 3. $\dfrac{15}{16} - \dfrac{2}{3}$ 5. $\dfrac{1}{3} - \dfrac{3}{16}$

2. $\dfrac{9}{16} - \dfrac{1}{16}$ 4. $\dfrac{19}{20} - \dfrac{4}{5}$ 6. $\dfrac{5}{8} - \dfrac{1}{6}$

SUBTRACTING FRACTIONS, MIXED NUMBERS, AND WHOLE NUMBERS

Example.   Subtract $33\frac{7}{10} - 17\frac{3}{4}$ and express the answer in lowest terms.

$$33\frac{7}{10} = 33\frac{14}{20} = 32\frac{34}{20}$$

$$-17\frac{3}{4} = 17\frac{15}{20} = 17\frac{15}{20}$$

$$15\frac{19}{20} \; Ans$$

Exercise 2-9

Subtract these values as indicated. Express the answers in lowest terms.

1. $21 - \frac{9}{16}$

2. $107 - \frac{5}{9}$

3. $312 - 297\frac{7}{12}$

4. $828 - 682\frac{51}{64}$

5. $9\frac{3}{8} - \frac{1}{8}$

6. $27\frac{31}{32} - \frac{7}{8}$

7. $53\frac{17}{28} - 12\frac{3}{7}$

8. $111\frac{1}{4} - \frac{13}{16}$

ADDING AND SUBTRACTING FRACTIONS IN PRACTICAL APPLICATIONS

Exercise 2-10

1. A baker prepares a cake mix which weighs 100 pounds. The cake mix consists of shortening and other ingredients. The weights of the other ingredients are $20\frac{1}{2}$ pounds of flour, $29\frac{3}{4}$ pounds of sugar, $18\frac{1}{8}$ pounds of milk, 16 pounds of whole eggs, and a total of $5\frac{1}{4}$ pounds of flavoring, salt, and baking powder. How many pounds of shortening are used in the mix?

2. Determine dimensions A, B, C, D, and E of the machined part shown in figure 2-1.

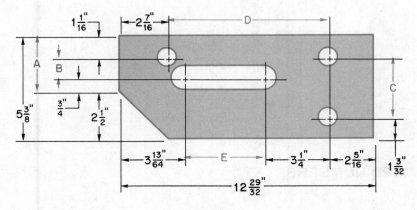

Fig. 2-1

3. Before starting a wiring job, an electrician takes an inventory of materials and finds that 4 550 feet of BX cable are in stock. The following lengths of cable are removed from stock for the job: $275\frac{1}{4}$ feet, 482 feet, $56\frac{1}{2}$ feet, $212\frac{3}{4}$ feet, and 148 feet. Upon completion of the job, $87\frac{1}{4}$ feet are left over and returned to stock. How many feet of cable are in stock after completing the job?

4. A truck is loaded at a structural steel supply house for a delivery to a construction site. The order calls for 125 feet of channel iron which weighs $3\frac{3}{4}$ tons, 140 feet of I beam which weighs $4\frac{3}{10}$ tons, and 80 feet of angle iron which weighs $2\frac{1}{5}$ tons. The maximum legal tonnage permitted to be hauled by the truck is $9\frac{1}{2}$ tons. All of the channel iron and I beam are loaded. Only part of the angle iron is loaded so that the maximum legal tonnage is met but not exceeded. By how many tons of angle iron will the delivery be short of the order?

MULTIPLYING FRACTIONS

Example.   Multiply $\frac{11}{15} \times \frac{3}{4} \times \frac{9}{22} \times \frac{1}{2}$ and express the answer in lowest terms.

$$\frac{\overset{1}{\cancel{11}}}{\underset{5}{\cancel{15}}} \times \frac{3}{4} \times \frac{\overset{3}{\cancel{9}}}{\underset{2}{\cancel{22}}} \times \frac{1}{2} = \frac{9}{80} \; Ans$$

Exercise 2-11

Multiply these fractions as indicated. Express the answers in lowest terms.

1. $\frac{1}{8} \times \frac{1}{2}$

2. $\frac{3}{5} \times \frac{5}{8}$

3. $\frac{4}{5} \times \frac{7}{8}$

4. $\frac{5}{8} \times \frac{5}{16}$

5. $\frac{1}{6} \times \frac{11}{12}$

6. $\frac{5}{6} \times \frac{2}{5}$

7. $\frac{5}{7} \times \frac{14}{25}$

8. $\frac{1}{3} \times \frac{3}{4} \times \frac{8}{9}$

9. $\frac{19}{20} \times \frac{10}{11} \times \frac{2}{9}$

10. $\frac{7}{12} \times \frac{1}{6} \times \frac{18}{23}$

MULTIPLYING FRACTIONS, MIXED NUMBERS, AND WHOLE NUMBERS

Example.   Multiply $7\frac{2}{3} \times 12 \times \frac{11}{12}$ as indicated. Express the answer in lowest terms.

$$7\frac{2}{3} \times 12 \times \frac{11}{12} = \frac{23}{3} \times \frac{\overset{1}{\cancel{12}}}{1} \times \frac{11}{\underset{1}{\cancel{12}}} = \frac{253}{3} = \; 84\frac{1}{3} \; Ans$$

Exercise 2-12

Multiply these values as indicated. Express the answers in lowest terms.

1. $\dfrac{3}{8} \times 12$

2. $10 \times \dfrac{7}{15}$

3. $\dfrac{5}{9} \times 21$

4. $\dfrac{3}{4} \times 4\dfrac{1}{3}$

5. $3\dfrac{7}{9} \times \dfrac{3}{10}$

6. $\dfrac{7}{15} \times 9\dfrac{13}{32}$

7. $3\dfrac{1}{5} \times 6\dfrac{25}{32}$

8. $20\dfrac{2}{3} \times 5\dfrac{1}{8}$

9. $79\dfrac{3}{4} \times 2\dfrac{1}{9}$

10. $\dfrac{3}{8} \times 24 \times 5\dfrac{1}{2}$

DIVIDING FRACTIONS

Example. Divide $\dfrac{3}{100}$ by $\dfrac{99}{120}$ and express the answer in lowest terms.

$$\frac{3}{100} \div \frac{99}{120} = \frac{\cancel{3}^{1}}{\cancel{100}_{5}} \times \frac{\cancel{120}^{\,2}_{}}{\cancel{99}_{33}^{}} = \frac{2}{55} \; Ans$$

Exercise 2-13

Divide these fractions as indicated. Express the answers in lowest terms.

1. $\dfrac{5}{6} \div \dfrac{4}{6}$

2. $\dfrac{1}{12} \div \dfrac{5}{12}$

3. $\dfrac{3}{5} \div \dfrac{9}{10}$

4. $\dfrac{3}{10} \div \dfrac{11}{15}$

5. $\dfrac{7}{9} \div \dfrac{3}{7}$

6. $\dfrac{5}{11} \div \dfrac{19}{44}$

7. $\dfrac{14}{15} \div \dfrac{7}{25}$

8. $\dfrac{18}{21} \div \dfrac{5}{8}$

9. $\dfrac{4}{15} \div \dfrac{8}{45}$

10. $\dfrac{6}{7} \div \dfrac{18}{23}$

DIVIDING FRACTIONS, MIXED NUMBERS, AND WHOLE NUMBERS

Example. Divide $10\dfrac{3}{11}$ by $2\dfrac{12}{55}$ and express the answer in lowest terms.

$$10\frac{3}{11} \div 2\frac{12}{55} = \frac{113}{11} \div \frac{122}{55} = \frac{113}{\cancel{11}_{1}} \times \frac{\cancel{55}^{\,5}}{122} = \frac{565}{122} = 4\frac{77}{122} \; Ans$$

Exercise 2-14

Divide these values as indicated. Express the answers in lowest terms.

1. $14 \div \frac{2}{3}$

2. $\frac{2}{3} \div 14$

3. $\frac{7}{9} \div 14$

4. $\frac{32}{35} \div 16$

5. $\frac{7}{8} \div 5\frac{1}{16}$

6. $3\frac{2}{3} \div \frac{11}{24}$

7. $2\frac{19}{32} \div \frac{3}{64}$

8. $\frac{1}{150} \div 14\frac{7}{75}$

9. $15\frac{7}{25} \div 6$

10. $3\frac{1}{2} \div 7\frac{5}{6}$

MULTIPLYING AND DIVIDING FRACTIONS IN PRACTICAL APPLICATIONS

Exercise 2-15

1. Horticulture is the science of cultivating plants. A horticultural assistant prepares a soil mixture for house plants using the materials shown on the chart in figure 2-2. The amounts indicated on the chart are added to a soilless mix in order to prepare one bushel of potting soil.

		1 BUSHEL	a. $1\frac{1}{2}$ BUSHELS	b. $2\frac{1}{2}$ BUSHELS
(1)	Ammonium nitrate	$3\frac{1}{2}$ tablespoons		
(2)	Garden fertilizer	6 tablespoons		
(3)	Superphosphate	$2\frac{1}{2}$ tablespoons		
(4)	Ground limestone	9 tablespoons		
(5)	Bone meal	$1\frac{1}{2}$ tablespoons		
(6)	Potassium nitrate	$2\frac{1}{2}$ tablespoons		
(7)	Calcium nitrate	2 tablespoons		

Fig. 2-2

a. Determine the amount of each material needed to prepare $1\frac{1}{2}$ bushels of soil.

b. Determine the amount of each material needed to prepare $2\frac{1}{2}$ bushels of soil.

2. As the speed of an automobile increases, the amount of gasoline that is used also increases. The table shown in figure 2-3 lists the gasoline mileage (miles per gallon) at various speeds for a particular 6-cylinder automobile. Determine

the total number of gallons of gasoline used when the automobile travels the speeds and times indicated.

a. 30 mi/h for $1\frac{1}{3}$ hours.

b. 40 mi/h for $3\frac{3}{4}$ hours.

c. 50 mi/h for $\frac{7}{10}$ hour.

d. 55 mi/h for $3\frac{1}{5}$ hours.

MILES PER HOUR	MILES PER GALLON
30	30
35	$27\frac{1}{2}$
40	25
45	23
50	21
55	20

Fig. 2-3

3. When two or more different metals are melted together, a new material called an alloy is formed. Most metals that are used are alloys rather than pure metals. The physical properties, such as hardness and strength, are improved by making an alloy. A metallurgist determines the composition of alloys and their chemical and physical properties. Three types of bronze castings are listed on the table shown in figure 2-4. The fractions listed give the fractional part of each metal in the alloy. Use the table in figure 2-5 to find the weight, in pounds, of each metal for each of the 3 casting alloys.

CASTING ALLOYS	FRACTIONAL PARTS						
	Copper	Zinc	Manganese	Tin	Lead	Phosphorus	Other
Manganese Bronze	$\frac{11}{20}$	$\frac{2}{5}$	$\frac{3}{100}$	$\frac{1}{125}$	$\frac{1}{250}$	0	$\frac{1}{125}$
Phosphor Bronze	$\frac{4}{5}$	$\frac{1}{200}$	0	$\frac{1}{10}$	$\frac{9}{100}$	$\frac{1}{400}$	$\frac{1}{400}$
Hard Bronze	$\frac{22}{25}$	$\frac{1}{50}$	0	$\frac{9}{100}$	$\frac{1}{500}$	0	$\frac{1}{125}$

Fig. 2-4

CASTING ALLOYS	NUMBER OF POUNDS						
	(1) Copper	(2) Zinc	(3) Manganese	(4) Tin	(5) Lead	(6) Phosphorus	(7) Other
a. $3\frac{3}{8}$ Tons of Manganese Bronze							
b. $3\frac{3}{4}$ Tons of Phosphor Bronze							
c. $2\frac{5}{8}$ Tons of Hard Bronze							

Fig. 2-5

NOTE: The last item, "Other" means the fractional part of all the other metals or impurities in the alloy.

4. To determine the mathematical ability of an applicant, some firms require the applicant to take a preemployment test. Usually the test is given before the applicant is interviewed. An applicant that fails the test is often not considered for the job. The following problem is taken from a preemployment test given by a large retail firm:

> What is the total cost of the following items?
>
> $6\frac{2}{3}$ boxes of Item A at \$$3\frac{1}{4}$ per box
>
> $\frac{1}{3}$ yard of Item B at \$$4\frac{1}{2}$ per yard
>
> 8 pieces of Item C at \$$15\frac{3}{4}$ per dozen pieces

Find the total cost of the items listed.

ORDER OF OPERATIONS

- Do all the work in parentheses first. Parentheses are used to group numbers. In a problem expressed in fractional form, the numerator and the denominator are each considered as being enclosed in parentheses.

$$\frac{2\frac{5}{8} - \frac{3}{4}}{15 + 7\frac{9}{16}} = (2\frac{5}{8} - \frac{3}{4}) \div (15 + 7\frac{9}{16})$$

If an expression contains parentheses within brackets, do the work within the innermost parentheses first.

- Do multiplication and division next in order from left to right.
- Last, do addition and subtraction in order from left to right.

Example.   Find the value of $\dfrac{84\frac{3}{5} - 18\frac{7}{10} \times 3}{1\frac{8}{9} + 20\frac{2}{3} \div 2\frac{2}{5}} - 1\frac{4}{7}.$

$(84\frac{3}{5} - 18\frac{7}{10} \times 3) \div (1\frac{8}{9} + 20\frac{2}{3} \div 2\frac{2}{5}) - 1\frac{4}{7}$

$28\frac{1}{2} \div 10\frac{1}{2} - 1\frac{4}{7}$

$2\frac{5}{7} - 1\frac{4}{7} = 1\frac{1}{7}$ *Ans*

Exercise 2-16

Perform the indicated operations.

1. $\dfrac{7}{8} + \dfrac{5}{16} - \dfrac{3}{4}$

2. $(\dfrac{5}{9} + \dfrac{2}{3}) \div \dfrac{1}{3}$

3. $\dfrac{5}{9} + \dfrac{2}{3} \div \dfrac{1}{3}$

4. $\dfrac{\dfrac{3}{25} - \dfrac{1}{10} + \dfrac{4}{5}}{\dfrac{10}{11}}$

5. $(\dfrac{7}{8} \times 14) \div (\dfrac{3}{8} \times 6)$

6. $\dfrac{7\frac{1}{8} \times (6\frac{7}{8} - 4\frac{3}{16})}{4\frac{3}{4}}$

7. $\dfrac{15}{2\frac{2}{3}} + \dfrac{25\frac{1}{5}}{4}$

8. $(1\frac{3}{4} + 3\frac{3}{8} \times 6) \div 18 + \frac{1}{2}$

9. $\dfrac{1}{4} \times 20 \times \dfrac{3}{5} + 120\frac{1}{10} \div 14 - 7\frac{1}{5}$

10. $10\frac{9}{10} \times [15\frac{7}{16} \times (\frac{2}{3} + \frac{5}{6}) - 3\frac{3}{10}] \div 2\frac{1}{2}$

PRACTICAL APPLICATIONS REQUIRING COMBINED OPERATIONS OF ARITHMETIC EXPRESSIONS

Exercise 2-17

1. A building contractor acquires three parcels of land as shown in figure 2-6. The contractor plans to subdivide the 3 parcels into 9 building lots of equal area (square footage). Use this formula to determine the total area of the 3 parcels.

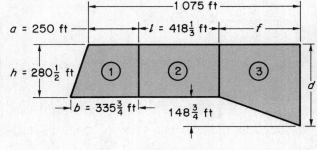

Fig. 2-6

Total area of 3 parcels =
$$\dfrac{(a + b) \times h}{2} + h \times l + \dfrac{(h + d) \times f}{2}$$

a. Find, to the nearer square foot, the number of square feet in the three parcels of land.

b. Find, to the nearer square foot, the number of square feet in each building lot.

2. The fuel oil tank shown in figure 2-7 is to be constructed by a steel fabricator. The specifications call for a 4-foot diameter. The tank must hold a minimum of 2 057 gallons of fuel oil. Determine the required length of the tank.

$$L = \dfrac{G}{\pi \times \dfrac{D}{2} \times \dfrac{D}{2} \times 7\frac{12}{25}}$$

where L = length of tank in feet
G = number of gallons the tank is to hold (capacity)
D = tank diameter in feet

Use $\pi = 3\frac{1}{7}$

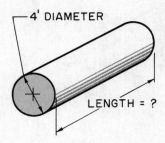

Fig. 2-7

3. In estimating the cost of building the table shown in figure 2-8, a cabinetmaker must find the number of board feet of lumber needed. One board foot of lumber is the equivalent of a piece of lumber 1 foot wide, 1 foot long, and 1 inch thick. Use this formula to find the number of board feet of lumber.

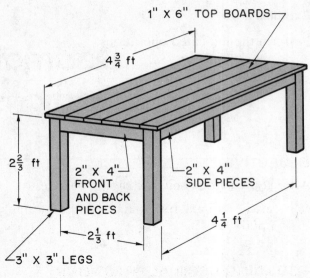

$$bd\,ft = \frac{T'' \times W'' \times L'}{12}$$

where T'' = thickness in inches
W'' = width in inches
L' = length in feet

Fig. 2-8

Different sizes of lumber are required for the table. These sizes are the measurement of the lumber before finishing. Use these measurements to find the board feet needed.

a. Find the number of board feet of $1'' \times 6''$ lumber needed.
b. Find the number of board feet of $3'' \times 3''$ lumber needed.
c. Find the number of board feet of $2'' \times 4''$ lumber needed.
d. Find the total number of board feet needed.

UNIT 3
Decimal
Fractions

OBJECTIVE

After studying this unit you should be able to

- solve decimal fraction problems by applying the principles of decimal fractions.

ROUNDING DECIMAL FRACTIONS

Example.   Round 0.738 62 inch to 3 decimal places.

0.73<u>8</u> ⑥2″ ≈ **0.739″** *Ans*

Exercise 3-1

Round each number to the indicated number of decimal places.

1. 0.784   (2 places)   5. 3.805   (2 places)

2. 0.085 5   (3 places)   6. 76.899 9   (3 places)

3. 0.006 3   (2 places)   7. 139.006 2   (2 places)

4. 0.057   (1 place)   8. 33.019 97   (4 places)

EXPRESSING COMMON FRACTIONS AS DECIMAL FRACTIONS

Example.   Express $\frac{3}{8}$ as a decimal fraction.

$$8)\overline{3.000}^{\,\underline{0.375}\ Ans}$$

Exercise 3-2

Express each common fraction as a decimal fraction. Where necessary, round the answers to 3 decimal places.

1. $\frac{7}{8}$ 3. $\frac{19}{20}$ 5. $\frac{17}{21}$

2. $\frac{2}{9}$ 4. $\frac{5}{12}$ 6. $\frac{23}{24}$

EXPRESSING DECIMAL FRACTIONS AS COMMON FRACTIONS

Example.   Express 0.065 as a common fraction.

$0.065 = \frac{65}{1\,000} = \frac{13}{200}$ *Ans*

Exercise 3-3

Express each decimal fraction as a common fraction in lowest terms.

1. 0.8   3. 0.062   5. 0.335
2. 0.375   4. 0.006   6. 0.084

DECIMAL FRACTIONS IN PRACTICAL APPLICATIONS

Exercise 3-4

Determine the decimal fraction answer for each of these problems. Where necessary, round to 2 decimal places.

1. A mechanic determines the total cost of a repair job as $560. Labor costs are $350. What decimal fraction of the total cost is the labor cost?

2. An inspector checks 175 pieces of a lot containing 615 pieces. What decimal fraction of the lot has not been inspected?

3. Three pieces are cut from the length of angle iron shown in figure 3-1. What decimal fraction of the original length of angle iron (36″) is the length of angle iron remaining? Include all $\frac{1}{16}″$ cuts in the computations.

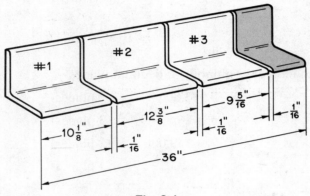

Fig. 3-1

ADDING DECIMAL FRACTIONS

Example.   Add. 8.75 + 23.1 + 23

$$\begin{array}{r} 8.75 \\ 23.10 \\ + 23.00 \\ \hline 54.85 \ Ans \end{array}$$

Exercise 3-5

Add these numbers.

1. 0.317 + 0.029

2. 8.036 + 16 + 0.7

3. 83.712 + 0.056 + 35

4. $0.073\,2 + \frac{7}{16} + 0.232\,3$

5. 12.002 + 0.018 + 0.003 + 0.017

6. $305.1 + 43.95 + 0.014 + \frac{1}{8}$

SUBTRACTING DECIMAL FRACTIONS

Example.   Subtract. 44.6 − 27.368

$$\begin{array}{r} 44.600 \\ -\ 27.368 \\ \hline 17.232 \ \mathit{Ans} \end{array}$$

Exercise 3-6

Subtract these numbers.

1. 0.877 − 0.304
2. 3.062 − 1.956
3. 0.009 − 0.008 6
4. 26.009 − 25.999
5. $46\frac{3}{10}$ − 33.912
6. 10.002 − 0.199 9

ADDING AND SUBTRACTING DECIMAL FRACTIONS IN PRACTICAL APPLICATIONS

Exercise 3-7

1. A salesclerk totals the following amounts for purchased items: $2.73, $0.75, $2.00, $5.19, and $4.38. The items are paid for with a $20 bill. How much change does the salesclerk return to the customer?

2. In a parallel circuit, the total circuit current equals the sum of the individual currents. The total circuit current of the parallel circuit shown in figure 3-2 is 17.5 amperes when all lamps and appliances are operating. Find the current (amperes) of the refrigerator in the parallel circuit shown.

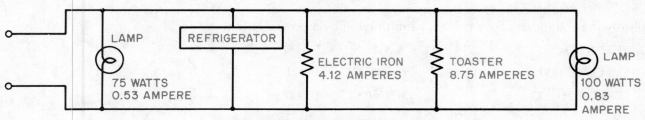

Fig. 3-2 Parallel Circuit

3. A part of the structure of a building is shown in figure 3-3. Find the thickness of the girder in inches.

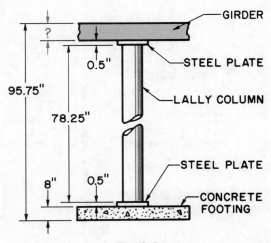

Fig. 3-3

MULTIPLYING DECIMAL FRACTIONS

Example.   Multiply. 60.412×0.53

$$
\begin{array}{r}
60.412 \\
\times\ 0.53 \\
\hline
1\ 81236 \\
30\ 2060 \\
\hline
32.01836
\end{array}
$$

32.018 36 *Ans*

Exercise 3-8

Multiply these numbers. Round to 4 decimal places where necessary.

1. 0.9×0.5
2. 0.8×29
3. 0.63×0.16
4. $7.22 \times \dfrac{3}{8}$
5. 0.025×0.09
6. $0.42 \times 11 \times 0.4$
7. $0.009 \times 120 \times 6.7$
8. $1\dfrac{9}{16} \times 0.33 \times 4.27$

MULTIPLYING BY POWERS OF TEN

Example.   Multiply 0.085 by 10 000.

$0.085 \times 10\ 000 = 0.0850 =$ **850** *Ans*

Exercise 3-9

Multiply these numbers. Use rules for multiplying by a power of ten.

1. 0.31×10
2. $0.042 \times 1\ 000$
3. $37.37 \times 10\ 000$
4. 12.8×0.1
5. 17.023×0.001
6. $66\ 913 \times 0.000\ 1$

DIVIDING DECIMAL FRACTIONS

Example.   Divide. $0.338 \div 0.52$

$$
\begin{array}{r}
0.65\ Ans \\
0\ 52.\overline{)0\ 33.80} \\
31\ 2 \\
\hline
2\ 60 \\
2\ 60 \\
\hline
\end{array}
$$

Exercise 3-10

Divide these numbers. Round to 3 decimal places where necessary.

1. $0.8 \div 0.2$
2. $6.3 \div 0.3$
3. $1.44 \div 0.08$
4. $18.750 \div \dfrac{3}{4}$
5. $0.002 \div 0.91$
6. $153.73 \div 14.27$
7. $0.008\ 4 \div 3.094$
8. $3\ 876.5 \div 5.125$

DIVIDING BY POWERS OF TEN

Example.   Divide 732.4 by 10 000.

$$732.4 \div 10\ 000 = 0\ 073\ 2.4 = \mathbf{0.073\ 24}\ \textit{Ans}$$

Exercise 3-11

Divide these numbers. Use the rules for dividing by a power of ten.

1. $0.37 \div 10$
2. $9.69 \div 100$
3. $298.05 \div 1\ 000$
4. $0.95 \div 0.1$
5. $0.026 \div 0.000\ 1$
6. $432.07 \div 0.000\ 01$

MULTIPLYING AND DIVIDING DECIMAL FRACTIONS IN PRACTICAL APPLICATIONS

Exercise 3-12

1. A certain 6-cylinder automobile engine produces 0.63 brake horsepower for each cubic inch of piston displacement. Each piston displaces 34.75 cubic inches. Find the total brake horsepower of the engine to one decimal place.

2. The part shown in figure 3-4 is to be made by a machinist. Twenty equally spaced holes are drilled along the length of the part. Find, in centimetres, the total length of material needed.

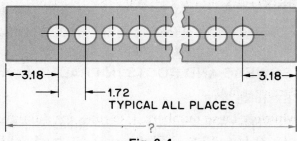

Fig. 3-4

3. Plywood sheets are purchased by a carpenter in the quantities and for the costs shown in figure 3-5. Some of the purchased plywood is used on two jobs. The following number of sheets are used.

   Job A: 12 sheets of $\frac{3}{8}''$, 15 sheets of $\frac{1}{2}''$, and 8 sheets of $\frac{5}{8}''$.

   Job B: 14 sheets of $\frac{3}{8}''$, 9 sheets of $\frac{1}{2}''$, and 5 sheets of $\frac{5}{8}''$.

   a. Find the total cost of plywood that is charged against Job A.

   b. Find the total cost of plywood that is charges against Job B.

TYPE OF PLYWOOD	NUMBER OF SHEETS PURCHASED	TOTAL COST OF PURCHASED QUANTITIES
$\frac{3}{8}''$ thick	40 sheets	$260.00
$\frac{1}{2}''$ thick	25 sheets	$181.25
$\frac{5}{8}''$ thick	30 sheets	$246.60

Fig. 3-5

POWERS OF NUMBERS

Example.   Find the indicated power. 0.8^3

$$0.8^3 = 0.8 \times 0.8 \times 0.8 = \mathbf{0.512}\ \textit{Ans}$$

Exercise 3-13

Raise these values to the indicated powers.

1. 11^2
2. 2.8^2
3. 0.5^2
4. 3^4
5. 4.2^3
6. 0.017^2
7. 0.8^3
8. 220.83^2
9. $(0.04 \times 6)^2$

ROOTS OF NUMBERS

Example.   Find the indicated root. $\sqrt[4]{256}$

$\sqrt[4]{256} = \sqrt[4]{4 \times 4 \times 4 \times 4} = $ **4** *Ans*

Exercise 3-14

Determine the whole number roots of these values as indicated.

1. $\sqrt{81}$ 5. $\sqrt[3]{27}$ 9. $\sqrt{87.9 - 23.9}$

2. $\sqrt{121}$ 6. $\sqrt[4]{16}$ 10. $\sqrt{\dfrac{60.8}{3.8}}$

3. $\sqrt[5]{1}$ 7. $\sqrt{2.5 \times 19.6}$ 11. $\sqrt[3]{320 \times 0.2}$

4. $\sqrt{196}$ 8. $\sqrt{0.93 + 8.07}$ 12. $\sqrt[3]{3.993 + 4.007}$

Exercise 3-15

Determine the square roots of these numbers to the indicated number of decimal places.

1. 392   (2 places)   4. 35.921 (3 places)   7. 0.000 7 (2 places)

2. 4.807   (3 places)   5. 505.08 (2 places)   8. 18 944 (1 place)

3. 0.931 6 (4 places)   6. 0.030 3 (4 places)   9. 3.105 1 (3 places)

POWERS AND ROOTS IN PRACTICAL APPLICATIONS

Exercise 3-16

1. The lengths of the sides of squares and cubes are given in the table shown in figure 3-6. Find the areas ($A = s^2$) and the volumes ($V = s^3$) to the nearer hundredth.

	LENGTHS OF SIDES (s)	AREAS OF FRONT SURFACES (A)	VOLUMES OF CUBES (V)
a.	3.2 ft		
b.	18.7 mm		
c.	0.5 m		
d.	9.8 in		

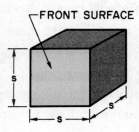

Fig. 3-6

2. In the table shown in figure 3-7 the areas of squares and the volumes of cubes are given. Find the lengths of sides of squares ($s = \sqrt{A}$) and the lengths of sides of cubes ($s = \sqrt[3]{V}$) to the nearer hundredth.

	AREAS OF FRONT SURFACES (A)	VOLUMES OF CUBES (V)	LENGTHS OF SIDES (s)
a.	56.85 sq ft	–	
b.	–	27 m³	
c.	172.9 cm²	–	
d.	–	125 cu ft	

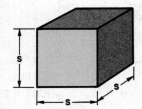

Fig. 3-7

3. A carton in the shape of a cube is designed to contain 8 cubic metres. What is the maximum height of an object that can be packaged in the carton? $s = \sqrt[3]{V}$.

4. A landscaper is to landscape the shaded area of land around the office building shown in figure 3-8. The landscaper charges $0.07 per square foot for this job. Find the price charged to complete the job. All dimensions are in feet. $A = s^2$

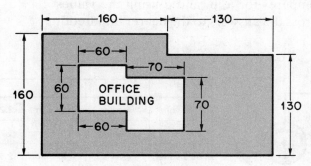

Fig. 3-8

COMBINED OPERATION EXPRESSIONS

Exercise 3-17

Solve the following combined operations expressions. Round the answers to 2 decimal places.

1. $9.03 + 2.75 \times 0.9$

2. $1.31 \times 6 - 8.2 \div 3.4$

3. $12.4 \times (13.88 - 0.07 \times 0.5)$

PRACTICAL APPLICATIONS REQUIRING COMBINED OPERATIONS OF ARITHMETIC EXPRESSIONS

Exercise 3-18

1. An inspector checks a 60° groove which has been machined in the fixture shown in figure 3-9. The groove is checked by placing a pin in the groove and measuring the distance (H) between the top of the fixture and the top of the pin. Find H to the nearer thousandth centimetre.
$H = 1.5 \times D - 0.866 \times W$

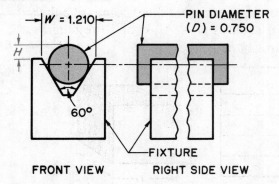

FRONT VIEW   RIGHT SIDE VIEW

Fig. 3-9

2. Four cells are connected in series in an electrical circuit shown in figure 3-10. A technician finds the amount of current (I), in amperes, in the circuit.

$$I = \frac{E \times ns}{r \times ns + R}$$ where E = volts of one cell
ns = number of cells in circuit
r = internal resistance of one cell in ohms
R = external resistance of circuit in ohms

Find the amount of current (I) in amperes for a, b, and c using the values given on the table in figure 3-11. Express the answers to the nearer hundredth ampere.

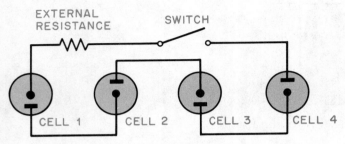

Fig. 3-10

E	ns	r	R	I
3.25 volts	4 cells	0.85 ohm	2.2 ohms	a.
2.5 volts	4 cells	0.67 ohm	1.75 ohms	b.
5.75 volts	4 cells	1.13 ohms	2.65 ohms	c.

Fig. 3-11

3. A steel fabricating firm is contracted to construct the fuel storage tank shown in figure 3-12. The specifications call for a tank height of 22 feet. The tank must hold 25 000 gallons (G) of fuel.

$$D = \sqrt{\frac{4 \times G}{3.141\,6 \times H \times 7.479}}$$

Find the diameter to the nearer hundredth foot.

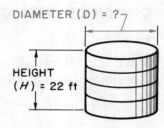

Fig. 3-12

4. Main Street, Second Avenue, and Maple Street intersect as shown in figure 3-13. The shaded triangular portion of land between the streets is to be used as a small park. In finding the cost of converting the parcel of land to a park, a city planning assistant computes the area of the parcel. The sides (a, b, c) of the parcel are measured. Find the area to the nearer whole square metre.

Area (number of square metres) $= \dfrac{b}{2} \times \sqrt{a^2 - \left(\dfrac{c^2 - a^2 - b^2}{2 \times b}\right)^2}$

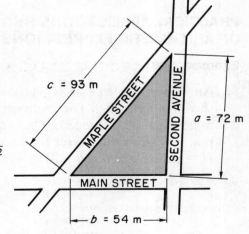

Fig. 3-13

UNIT 4
Percents, Statistical Measure, and Graphs

OBJECTIVE

After studying this unit you should be able to

- solve percentage, statistical measures, and graphing problems by applying the principles of percentage, statistical measures, and graphs.

EXPRESSING PERCENTS AS DECIMAL OR COMMON FRACTIONS

Example. Express $37\frac{1}{2}\%$ as a decimal fraction and as a common fraction.

$$37\frac{1}{2}\% = 37.5 \div 100 = \mathbf{0.375} = \frac{375}{1\,000} = \frac{3}{8} \; Ans$$

Exercise 4-1

1. Express each percent as a decimal fraction or mixed decimal.

   a. 23%   b. 5.9%   c. 218.7%   d. $3\frac{1}{2}\%$ e. $110\frac{3}{10}\%$

2. Express each percent as a common fraction or mixed number.

   a. 40%   b. 3%   c. 170%   d. 8.5%   e. $205\frac{2}{5}\%$

EXPRESSING DECIMAL AND COMMON FRACTIONS AS PERCENTS

Example. Express $\frac{7}{8}$ as a percent.

$$\frac{7}{8} = 0.875 = 0.875 \times 100\% = \mathbf{87.5\%} \; Ans$$

Exercise 4-2

Express each value as a percent.

1. 0.83   2. 0.08   3. 3.158   4. $\frac{1}{4}$ 5. $1\frac{3}{4}$

DETERMINING PERCENTAGE, PERCENT (RATE), OR BASE

Example 1.   Find 15% of 60.

   $60 \times 0.15 = 9$ *Ans*

Example 2.   What percent of 60 is 9?

   $\dfrac{9}{60} = \dfrac{3}{20} = 0.15 = 15\%$ *Ans*

Example 3.   9 is 15% of what number?

   $\dfrac{9}{0.15} = 60$ *Ans*

Exercise 4-3

Solve for each. Round the answers to 2 decimal places when necessary.

1. Find 25% of 80.
2. Find 115% of 54.
3. 82 is 70% of what number?
4. Find 40% of 60.
5. Find 18.5% of 150.
6. What percent of 87 is 95?
7. 34 is 95% of what number?
8. What percent of 63 is 44.2?
9. Find $3\frac{1}{2}$% of 120.
10. Find 22% of 164.
11. What percent of 19.4 is 8?
12. Find 0.8% of 2.
13. Find 52% of 230.
14. Find 14% of 46.6.
15. What percent of 298 is 420?
16. Find 13% of 78.
17. What percent of 2.3 is 1.7?
18. 814 is 105% of what number?
19. What percent of 40 is 13.1?
20. Find $88\frac{1}{2}$% of 136.

PERCENTAGES IN PRACTICAL APPLICATIONS

Exercise 4-4

Solve for each. Round to 2 decimal places when necessary.

1. A carpenter estimates that a job requires 550 board feet of lumber. An additional 15% is allowed for waste. How many board feet are allowed for waste?

2. If $6\frac{1}{2}$ acres of a 15-acre orchard are harvested, what percent of the orchard is harvested?

3. A machine produces 76 pieces when operating at 80% of its capacity. How many pieces can be produced when the machine is operating at full capacity?

4. It is estimated that a company's earnings next year will be 125% of this year's earnings. If the company earned $650 000 this year, what are next year's estimated earnings?

5. A baker prepares a 130-pound batch of bread dough and uses 120 pounds of the dough. What percent of the batch is used?

6. In an electrical circuit, a certain resistor takes 16% of the total voltage. How many volts are taken by the resistor in a 230-volt circuit?

7. A welder orders 150 square metres of steel plate. If 85 square metres are delivered, what percent of the order is received?

8. A laboratory technician prepares 85% of a total required amount of solution. If the total amount of solution required is 2.8 litres, how many litres are prepared?

9. A mason lays 72 feet of sidewalk which represents 40% of the total job. What is the total length, in feet, of the completed sidewalk?

10. Before stretching, a spring measures 5.84 centimetres. The spring is stretched an additional 1.22 centimetres. What percent of the original length is the amount of stretch?

11. By installing new machinery, a firm increases production by 25%. An average of 1 800 units are produced per day with the new machinery. Determine the average daily production before installation of the new machinery.

12. A retailer purchased merchandise wholesale for $1 050. The wholesale cost is 35% less than the retail price. What is the retail price?

13. A building contractor has 4 250 feet of $2'' \times 4''$ lumber at the start of a job. At the end of the first week of the job, 32% of the lumber is used. At the end of the second week 40% of the stock that remained at the end of the first week is used. How many feet of lumber remain unused at the end of the second week?

14. A resistor is rated at 1 600 ohms with a tolerance of ± 4%. The resistor is checked and found to have an actual resistance of 1 510 ohms. By how many ohms is the resistor below the acceptable resistance low limit?

15. Brazing solder contains 51.2% copper, 48.3% zinc, 0.1% iron, and lead. How many pounds of lead are required to make 2 000 pounds of solder?

16. The manager of a clothing store computes semiannual monthly profits as follows: July, $6 250; August, $5 700; September, $7 100; October, $6 000; November, $5 200; and December, $11 050. What percent of the entire semi-annual profit is the December profit?

17. A landscaper estimates that 72 cubic metres of topsoil is required for a job. After the job is completed, it is found that the amount of topsoil estimated was 20% more than what was actually used. How many cubic metres of topsoil were used on the job?

18. In a given volume of solution, 50 millilitres of acid makes up 20% of the solution. For the same volume solution, how many millilitres of acid are required to produce a 28% acid solution?

19. On Monday, a manufacturing firm produced a total of 1 100 units with 3% of the units defective. On Tuesday, the firm produced a total of 1 000 units with $5\frac{1}{2}$% of the units defective. How many more acceptable units were produced on Monday than on Tuesday?

20. A length of copper wire measures 20 feet $6\frac{1}{2}$ inches before being heated. When heated, the wire measures 20 feet $7\frac{3}{4}$ inches. What is the percent of increase in length?

MEASURES OF CENTRAL TENDENCY

Example.   Find the mean, median, and mode of 23.6, 22.8, 23.0, 24.5, 25.3, 24.3, 23.2 and 24.5.

22.8   Mean: $\dfrac{191.2}{8} = 23.9 \; Ans$

23.0

23.2

23.6   Median: $\dfrac{23.6 + 24.3}{2} = 23.95 \; Ans$

24.3

24.5

24.5   Mode: **24.5** *Ans*

25.3

Exercise 4-5

1. Determine the mean of 21, 28, 24, 19, 26, 23, 27.

2. Determine the median of 3.9, 3.5, 4.2, 3.0, 3.8, 4.1, 3.7.

3. Determine the mode of 35.3, 34.7, 36.9, 35.2, 34.8, 34.7, 35.2, 36.6, 34.4, 36.1, 34.7, 36.0, 34.5.

4. Determine the mean, median and mode of the following set of numbers: 10.62, 11.55, 10.76, 11.05, 10.87, 10.73, 11.05, 10.95, 11.24.

5. Determine the mean, median and mode of the following set of numbers: 0.519, 0.498, 0.502, 0.489, 0.511, 0.492, 0.507, 0.502.

MEASURES OF CENTRAL TENDENCY PRACTICAL APPLICATIONS

Exercise 4-6

1. In order to determine fuel consumption for a new model car, a manufacturer tested six identical cars. Each car traveled the same number of highway miles. Highway fuel consumption in miles per gallon for each car is recorded on the table in figure 4-1. Determine the mean (average) fuel consumption for the six cars to the nearer 0.1 mile per gallon.

CAR	#1	#2	#3	#4	#5	#6
HIGHWAY FUEL CONSUMPTION IN MILES PER GALLON	31.4	30.7	30.2	31.9	30.6	31.7

Fig. 4-1

2. A materials laboratory technician made tensile stress (tension) tests on 12 samples of lumber. The test data are recorded in the table in figure 4-2. The recorded figures show the amount of force which was required to pull apart each of the samples. For example, 2 950 pounds of force per square inch of cross sectional area was required to pull apart sample number 1.

SAMPLE NUMBER	TENSION STRENGTH (lb/sq in)	SAMPLE NUMBER	TENSION STRENGTH (lb/sq in)	SAMPLE NUMBER	TENSION STRENGTH (lb/sq in)
1	2 950	5	2 940	9	3 040
2	2 910	6	3 010	10	2 980
3	2 970	7	2 980	11	2 920
4	3 000	8	3 020	12	3 000

Fig. 4-2

a. What is the median tension value of the 12 samples?

b. What is the mode?

3. Temperatures in degrees Celsius for a 10-hour period are shown in the table in figure 4-3.

TIME	TEMPERATURE	TIME	TEMPERATURE	TIME	TEMPERATURE
12:00 noon	21.0°C	3:00 PM	25.0°C	7:00 PM	21.0°C
1:00 PM	22.5°C	4:00 PM	24.6°C	8:00 PM	20.5°C
2:00 PM	23.2°C	5:00 PM	23.0°C	9:00 PM	18.2°C
		6:00 PM	22.4°C	10:00 PM	17.0°C

Fig. 4-3

a. What is the mean temperature, to the nearer tenth, during the 10-hour period?

b. What is the median temperature during the 10-hour period?

4. A time study technician observed and recorded the production times shown in the table in figure 4-4.

	PRODUCTION TIME IN MINUTES							
OPERATOR 1	4.2	4.0	4.6	4.1	4.8	4.7	4.8	4.6
	4.9	4.4	4.3	4.0	4.6	4.2	4.9	4.3
OPERATOR 2	4.5	3.8	4.2	4.3	5.0	3.8	3.8	4.5
	4.1	3.9	4.6	4.5	3.8	4.6	4.6	4.1
OPERATOR 3	4.7	4.7	4.8	4.1	4.3	5.0	4.0	3.8
	4.6	5.0	4.9	4.2	4.8	4.7	4.3	4.9

Fig. 4-4

a. Make a table of the data showing the number of times each production time occurs.

b. Find the mode of all production times.

c. Find the median of all production times.

MEASURES OF SPREAD (DISPERSION)

Example.   Find the range and the mean deviation for this set of numbers.

12, 10, 8, 13, 10, 11, 8, 7, 12, 9

Range: $13 - 7 = 6$ *Ans*

Mean deviation: $12 + 10 + 8 + 13 + 10 + 11 + 8 + 7 + 12 + 9 = 100$

$$\frac{100}{10} = 10$$

$$2 + 0 + 2 + 3 + 0 + 1 + 2 + 3 + 2 + 1 = 16$$

$$\frac{16}{10} = 1.6 \; Ans$$

Exercise 4-7

1. Determine both the range and mean deviation of each of the following sets of numbers.

   a. 13, 11, 12, 10, 12, 14, 13, 11.

   b. 0.098, 0.100, 0.102, 0.097, 0.105, 0.102, 0.096.

2. An inspector selects 5 pieces from a machining process as a sample of one hour's production. The following measurements are made: 48.002 millimetres, 47.996 millimetres, 47.994 millimetres, 48.000 millimetres, and 47.998 millimetres. Compute the range and mean deviation of the 5-piece sample.

3. Certain air valves are designed to open at 25 pounds ± 0.5 pound pressure per square inch. The table in figure 4-5 lists the pressure readings of 8 tested valves. Determine the range and mean deviation of the tested valves.

VALVE NUMBER	1	2	3	4	5	6	7	8
PRESSURE TEST READINGS IN POUNDS PER SQUARE INCH	25.1	25.5	24.4	25.2	24.6	24.9	24.5	25.0

Fig. 4-5

READING GRAPHS

Exercise 4-8

1. A wholesale distributor maintains area offices and warehouses in five parts of the country. The bar graph in figure 4-6 shows the domestic and foreign sales made by each area office for one year.

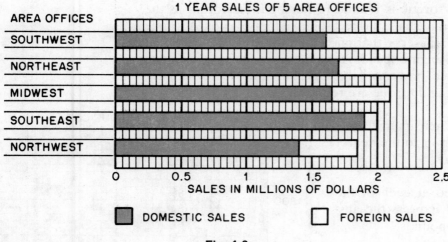

Fig. 4-6

a. What is the amount of the firm's total foreign and domestic sales for the year?

b. What is the amount of the firm's total foreign sales for the year?

c. What percent of the total sales is foreign sales? Round the answer to 1 decimal place.

d. What percent of the total sales is made by the southwest office? Round the answer to 1 decimal place.

2. The percent of defective pieces for a production run for 10 consecutive work days is indicated on the graph in figure 4-7.

a. What is the percent of defective pieces for each of the dates shown on the graph?

b. The total production on May 1 is 1 500 pieces. How many pieces are defective?

c. What is the mean daily percent of defective pieces over the 10-day period?

d. What is the percent of defective range over the 10-day period?

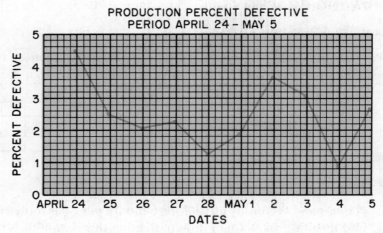

Fig. 4-7

3. Internal combustion engine torque is related to horsepower. Torque is the twisting force of an engine's crankshaft. It is measured in foot-pounds. A torque curve is plotted in figure 4-8. Observe that maximum torque is developed at a speed below the maximum engine speed. At high engine speeds the engine parts absorb a greater amount of power and the engine breathes less efficiently. Therefore, both horsepower and torque are reduced.

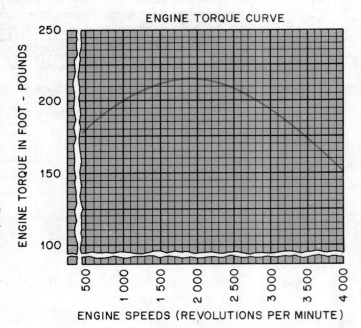

Fig. 4-8

a. At what engine speed is the maximum torque attained? Express the answer to the nearer 100 revolutions per minute.

b. What torque is developed at each of the following engine speeds? Express the answers to the nearer 5 foot-pounds.

   (1.)   700 r/min   (3.)   3 200 r/min
   (2.)   1 200 r/min   (4.)   3 800 r/min

c. What percent of the maximum torque is the torque at 4 000 revolutions per minute? Express the answer to the nearer whole percent.

DRAWING GRAPHS

Exercise 4-9

1. The total value of United States exports for six consecutive years is shown in figure 4-9. Draw and label a vertical bar graph to indicate this data.

YEAR	1	2	3	4	5	6
EXPORTS IN BILLIONS OF DOLLARS	29.5	31.0	34.0	37.5	42.5	44.0

Fig. 4-9

2. A company's monthly profit for a 6-month period is shown in figure 4-10. Draw and label a broken line graph indicating this data.

MONTH	July	Aug	Sept	Oct	Nov	Dec
MONTHLY PROFIT	$19 200	$20 000	$19 500	$19 700	$21 600	$22 500

Fig. 4-10

3. The formula for determining the surface or rim speed of a wheel in metres per minute is:

    surface speed = 3.14 times wheel diameter in metres times revolutions per minute

    surface speed (m/min) = 3.14 × Dia (m) × r/min

    Draw and label a straight-line graph showing the relation of surface speeds and wheel diameters at a constant speed of 180 revolutions per minute. Use wheel diameters of 0.2, 0.4, 0.6, 0.8, and 1.0 metre. Note: It is helpful to make a table of the values to be graphed.

4. The formula for determining the volume of a cube, given the length of a side, is:

    volume = length of side cubed

    $V = s^3$

    Draw and label a curved-line graph showing the relation of volumes and lengths of sides of cubes. Use cube side lengths of 1, 2, 3, 4, 5, and 6 feet. Volume is in units of cubic feet. Note: It is helpful to make a table of the values to be graphed.

UNIT 5
Measure

After studying this unit you should be able to

- solve measure problems by applying the principles of measure. (Tables for equivalent units of measure are found in the Appendix.)

EQUIVALENT ENGLISH UNITS OF LINEAR MEASURE

Example 1. Express 76.5 inches as feet.

$76.5 \div 12 = 6.375$
$\qquad 76.5 \text{ in} = 6.375 \text{ ft } \textit{Ans}$

Example 2. Express 6.375 feet as inches.

$6.375 \times 12 = 76.5$
$\qquad 6.375 \text{ ft} = 76.5 \text{ in } \textit{Ans}$

Exercise 5-1

Express each length as indicated. Round the answers to 3 decimal places when necessary.

1. $25\frac{1}{2}$ inches as feet
2. 16.25 feet as yards
3. 3 960 feet as miles
4. 78 inches as feet and inches
5. 47 feet as yards and feet
6. $7\frac{1}{4}$ feet as inches

7. $12\frac{2}{3}$ yards as feet
8. 0.6 mile as feet
9. $2\frac{1}{4}$ yards as inches
10. $5\frac{1}{2}$ yards as feet and inches
11. $\frac{1}{12}$ mile as yards and feet
12. 6.2 yards as feet and inches

ARITHMETIC OPERATIONS WITH ENGLISH COMPOUND NUMBERS

Exercise 5-2

Perform the indicated arithmetic operation. Express the answer in the same units as those given in the exercise. Regroup the answer when necessary.

1. 5 ft 7 in + 6 ft 8 in
2. 4 yd 2 ft + 5 yd 2 ft
3. 6 ft $9\frac{1}{2}$ in + 3 ft $4\frac{1}{4}$ in

4. 10 ft 7 in − 3 ft 4 in
5. 14 yd $\frac{1}{2}$ ft − 11 yd 2 ft
6. 6 ft $1\frac{3}{4}$ in − 4 ft $8\frac{1}{4}$ in

7. 4 ft 2 in × 5

8. 6 ft $8\frac{1}{2}$ in × 3

9. 3 yd 2 ft 7 in × 4

10. 20 ft 10 in ÷ 5

11. 11 yd 2 ft ÷ 3

12. 3 yd 2 ft 4 in ÷ 2

PRACTICAL APPLICATIONS USING ENGLISH UNITS OF LINEAR MEASURE

Exercise 5-3

1. The first-floor plan of a ranch house is shown in figure 5-1. Determine distances A, B, C, and D in feet and inches.

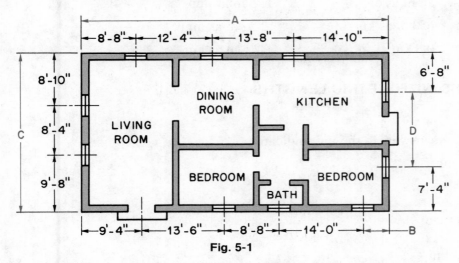

Fig. 5-1

2. A bolt of fabric contains $80\frac{1}{2}$ yards of fabric. The following lengths of fabric are sold: 2 lengths each 5 yards 2 feet long, 3 lengths each 8 yards $1\frac{1}{2}$ feet long, and 5 lengths each 6 yards 2 feet long. What length of fabric does the bolt now contain? Express the answer in yards and feet.

3. A surveyor subdivides a parcel of land into 4 building lots as shown in figure 5-2. Determine the number of feet in distances A and B of lot #1.

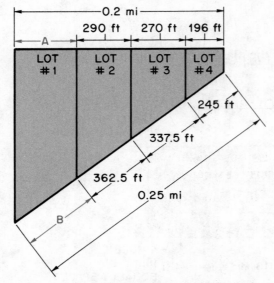

Fig. 5-2

EQUIVALENT METRIC UNITS OF LINEAR MEASURE

Example 1.   Express 0.378 metre as millimetres.

0.378 m = 0.378 mm = **378 mm** *Ans*

Example 2.   Express 378 millimetres as metres.

378 mm = 0 378. m = **0.378 m** *Ans*

Exercise 5-4

Express each value in the unit indicated.

1. 30 mm as cm
2. 8 cm as mm
3. 2 460 mm as m

4. 23 m as cm
5. 650 m as km
6. 0.8 km as m

7. 0.75 m as mm
8. 12.2 cm as mm
9. 372.5 m as km

ARITHMETIC OPERATIONS WITH METRIC LENGTHS

Exercise 5-5

Solve each exercise. Express the answers in the unit indicated.

1. 6.3 cm + 13.6 mm = ? mm
2. 1.7 m − 92 cm = ? cm
3. 18 × 4.3 m = ? m
4. 8.46 dm ÷ 6 = ? dm
5. 0.02 km + 370 m + 18.5 hm = ? m
6. 723.2 cm − 5.1 m = ? cm
7. 70.6 dm + 127 mm + 4.7 m = ? dm
8. 41.8 cm + 4.3 dm + 77.7 mm + 0.03 m = ? cm

PRACTICAL APPLICATIONS USING METRIC UNITS OF LINEAR MEASURE

Exercise 5-6

1. Determine dimensions A, B, C, and D of the plate shown in figure 5-3. Round the answers to 2 decimal places.

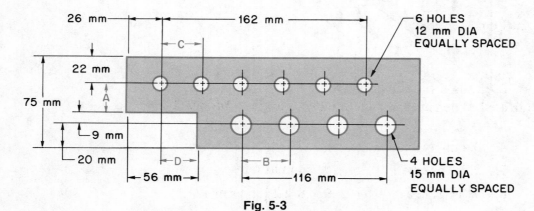

Fig. 5-3

2. Determine the total length, in metres, of the wall section shown in figure 5-4.

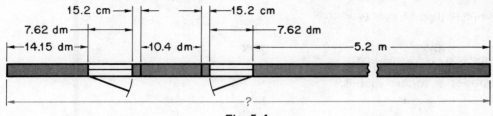

Fig. 5-4

3. A car travels from Town A to Town C by way of Town B. The car travels 135 kilometres. The trip takes 2.25 hours. It takes 0.8 hour to get from Town A to Town B. Assuming the same speed is maintained for the entire trip, how many kilometres apart are Town A and Town B?

EXPRESSING METRIC UNITS AS ENGLISH UNITS OF LINEAR MEASURE

Example. Express 5.2 centimetres as inches. Express the answer to 3 decimal places.

5.2 cm = 5.2 × 0.393 7 in = **2.047 in** *Ans*

Exercise 5-7

Express each length as indicated. When necessary, round the answers to 3 decimal places.

1. 0.4 m as in	4. 0.18 km as ft	7. 4.6 m as yd
2. 12 mm as in	5. 0.75 m as ft	8. 78 cm as ft
3. 4.5 m as ft	6. 286 km as mi	9. 9.8 cm as in

EXPRESSING ENGLISH UNITS AS METRIC UNITS OF LINEAR MEASURE

Example. Express 2.047 inches as centimetres. Express the answer to 1 decimal place.

2.047 in = 2.047 × 2.54 cm = **5.2 cm** *Ans*

Exercise 5-8

Express each length as indicated. When necessary, round the answers to 2 decimal places.

1. 8 in as mm	4. 3.4 mi as km	7. 3 872 ft as km
2. 23 in as cm	5. 2.7 ft as cm	8. $\frac{3}{4}$ in as mm
3. 5.8 ft as m	6. 71 in as m	9. 8 ft $2\frac{1}{4}$ in as m

EQUIVALENT ENGLISH UNITS OF AREA MEASURE

Example 1.   Express 720 square inches as square feet.

$720 \div 144 = 5$

720 sq in = 5 sq ft *Ans*

Example 2.   Express 5 square feet as square inches.

$5 \times 144 = 720$

5 sq ft = 720 sq in *Ans*

Exercise 5-9

Express each English area measure in the indicated unit. Round the answer to 2 decimal places.

1.	504 sq in as sq ft	6.	2.6 acres as sq ft
2.	128 sq ft as sq yd	7.	5.3 sq yd as sq ft
3.	4.2 sq ft as sq in	8.	0.2 sq mi as acres
4.	2 400 acres as sq mi	9.	0.08 sq yd as sq in
5.	217 800 sq ft as acres	10.	0.01 sq mi as sq ft

EQUIVALENT METRIC UNITS OF AREA MEASURE

Example 1.   Express 46 square centimetres as square millimetres.

$46 \text{ cm}^2 = 46.00 \text{ mm}^2 = 4\,600 \text{ mm}^2$ *Ans*

Example 2.   Express 4 600 square millimetres as square centimetres.

$4\,600 \text{ mm}^2 = 46\,00. \text{ cm}^2 = 46 \text{ cm}^2$ *Ans*

Exercise 5-10

Express each metric area measure in the indicated unit. Round the answer to 3 decimal places.

1.	530 mm² as cm²	6.	2.84 m² as cm²
2.	23 dm² as m²	7.	0.009 km² as m²
3.	14 600 cm² as m²	8.	173 000 m² as km²
4.	53 cm² as mm²	9.	28 000 mm² as m²
5.	6 m² as dm²	10.	0.7 dm² as mm²

PRACTICAL APPLICATIONS USING UNITS OF AREA MEASURE

Exercise 5-11

Round the answers to 2 decimal places.

1. How many strips, each having an area of 36 square inches, can be sheared from a sheet of aluminum which measures 12 square feet?

2. A painter computes the total interior wall surface of a building as 330 square yards after allowing for windows and doors. Two coats of paint are required for the job. One gallon of paint covers 500 square feet. How many gallons of paint are required?

3. An assembly consists of five metal plates. The respective areas of the plates are 650 cm², 800 cm², 16.3 dm², 12 dm², and 0.12 m². Determine the total surface measure, in square metres, of the five plates.

4. A roll of fabric has a surface measure of 12 square metres. How many pieces, each requiring 1 800 square centimetres of fabric, can be cut from the roll? Make an allowance of 10% for waste.

EXPRESSING METRIC UNITS AS ENGLISH UNITS OF AREA MEASURE

Example.   Express 3 square metres as square feet.

$3 \text{ m}^2 = 3 \times 10.764 \text{ sq ft} = $ **32.292 sq ft** *Ans*

Exercise 5-12

Express each area measure in the indicated unit. Round the answers to 3 decimal places.

1. 20 cm² as sq in
2. 0.6 m² as sq ft
3. 620 mm² as sq in
4. 0.6 km² as acres

EXPRESSING ENGLISH UNITS AS METRIC UNITS OF AREA MEASURE

Example.   Express 32.292 square feet to the nearer square metre.

$32.292 \text{ sq ft} = 32.292 \times 0.092\ 9 \text{ m}^2 = $ **3 m²** *Ans*

Exercise 5-13

Express each area measure in the indicated unit. Round the answers to 3 decimal places.

1. 14 sq in as cm²
2. 6.3 sq yd as m²
3. 2.5 sq mi as km²
4. 510 acres as km²

EQUIVALENT ENGLISH UNITS OF VOLUME MEASURE

Example 1.   Express 4 320 cubic inches as cubic feet.

$4\ 320 \div 1\ 728 = 2.5$

$4\ 320 \text{ cu in} = $ **2.5 cu ft** *Ans*

Example 2.   Express 2.5 cubic feet as cubic inches.

$2.5 \times 1\ 728 = 4\ 320$

$2.5 \text{ cu ft} = $ **4 320 cu in** *Ans*

Exercise 5-14

Express each volume in the unit indicated. Round the answers to 2 decimal places.

1.   4 700 cu in as cu ft
2.   216 cu ft as cu yd
3.   0.70 cu ft as cu in
4.   12.34 cu yd as cu ft

5.   0.63 cu ft as cu in
6.   19.80 cu ft as cu yd
7.   20 000 cu in as cu yd
8.   0.03 cu yd as cu in

EQUIVALENT METRIC UNITS OF VOLUME MEASURE

Example 1.   Express 450 cubic millimetres as cubic centimetres.

$450 \text{ mm}^3 = 0\ 450.\ \text{cm}^3 = $ **0.450 cm^3** *Ans*

Example 2.   Express 0.450 cubic centimetres as cubic millimetres.

$0.450 \text{ cm}^3 = 0.450\ \text{mm}^3 = $ **450 mm^3** *Ans*

Exercise 5-15

Express each volume in the unit indicated. Round the answers to 2 decimal places.

1.   2 400 mm^3 as cm^3
2.   1 700 cm^3 as dm^3
3.   7 dm^3 as cm^3
4.   15 cm^3 as mm^3

5.   3.8 m^3 as dm^3
6.   420 dm^3 as m^3
7.   60 000 cm^3 as m^3
8.   0.004 8 dm^3 as mm^3

EQUIVALENT ENGLISH-METRIC VOLUME MEASURES

Example 1.   Express 4.5 cubic metres as cubic yards.

$4.5 \text{ m}^3 = 4.5 \times 1.308 \text{ cu yd} = $ **5.886 cu yd** *Ans*

Example 2.   Express 5.886 cubic yards as cubic metres. Round the answer to 1 decimal place.

$5.886 \text{ cu yd} = 5.886 \times 0.764\ 5 \text{ m}^3 = $ **4.5 m^3** *Ans*

Exercise 5-16

Express each volume in the unit indicated. Round the answers to 3 decimal places.

1.   6.3 m^3 as cu ft
2.   14 m^3 as cu yd
3.   8.5 cu in as cm^3

4.   32 cu yd as m^3
5.   176 cm^3 as cu in
6.   940 cu ft as m^3

PRACTICAL APPLICATIONS USING UNITS OF VOLUME MEASURE

Exercise 5-17

Solve each volume problem. Round the answers to 2 decimal places.

1. Hot air passes through a duct at the rate of 800 cubic inches per second. Compute the number of cubic feet of hot air that passes through the duct in one minute.

2. A cord is a unit of measure of cut fuel wood equal to 128 cubic feet. If wood is burned at the rate of $\frac{1}{2}$ cord per week, how many weeks would a stack of wood measuring 12 cubic yards last?

3. A total of 340 pieces are punched from a strip of stock which has a volume of 20 cubic centimetres. Each piece has a volume of 22 cubic millimetres. How many cubic centimetres of strip stock are wasted after the pieces are punched?

4. Twenty concrete support bases are required for a construction job. Seventy-five cubic decimetres of concrete are used for each base. Compute the total number of cubic metres of concrete required for the 20 bases.

5. Common brick weighs 112 pounds per cubic foot. How many cubic yards of brick can be carried by a truck whose maximum carrying load is rated at 10 short tons?

EQUIVALENT ENGLISH UNITS OF CAPACITY MEASURE

Example 1.   Express 20 ounces as pints.

$20 \div 16 = 1.25$

$20 \text{ oz} = $ **1.25 pt** *Ans*

Example 2.   Express 1.25 pints as ounces

$1.25 \times 16 = 20$

$1.25 \text{ pt} = $ **20 oz** *Ans*

Exercise 5-18

Express each capacity in the unit indicated. Round the answers to 2 decimal places.

1. 15 gal as qt
2. 30 oz as pt
3. 6.5 pt as qt
4. 26 qt as gal
5. 1.8 gal as cu in
6. 84 cu ft as gal
7. 0.2 gal as pt
8. 1.4 qt as oz

EQUIVALENT METRIC UNITS OF CAPACITY MEASURE

Example 1.   Express 2.4 litres as millilitres.

$2.4 \text{ L} = 2.400 \text{ mL} = $ **2 400 mL** *Ans*

Example 2.   Express 2 400 millilitres as litres.

$2\,400 \text{ mL} = 2\,400. \text{ L} = $ **2.4 L** *Ans*

Exercise 5-19

Express each metric capacity in the unit indicated. Round the answer to 2 decimal places.

1. 1.3 L as mL
2. 2 100 mL as L
3. 93.4 mL as cm^3
4. 5 210 cm^3 as L
5. 542 L as m^3
6. 3.17 dm^3 as L
7. 0.06 L as mL
8. 19 000 mL as L

EQUIVALENT ENGLISH-METRIC CAPACITY MEASURES

Example 1. Express 2.5 ounces as millilitres. Round the answer to 2 decimal places.

2.5 oz = 2.5 × 29.563 mL = **73.91 mL** *Ans*

Example 2. Express 73.91 millilitres as ounces. Round the answer to 1 decimal place.

73.91 mL = 73.91 × 0.034 oz = **2.5 oz** *Ans*

Exercise 5-20

Express each capacity in the unit indicated. Round the answers to 3 decimal places.

1. 10.4 L as qt	4. 75 mL as oz	7. 0.67 L as pt
2. 4.2 oz as mL	5. 1.75 qt as L	8. 21 oz as L
3. 8 gal as L	6. 513 L as gal	

EQUIVALENT ENGLISH UNITS OF WEIGHT MEASURE

Example 1. Express 200 ounces as pounds.

200 ÷ 16 = 12.5

200 oz = **12.5 lb** *Ans*

Example 2. Express 12.5 lb as ounces.

12.5 × 16 = 200
12.5 lb = **200 oz** *Ans*

Exercise 5-21

Express each weight in the unit indicated. Round the answers to 2 decimal places.

1. 34 oz as lb	4. 9 700 lb as short tons
2. 0.6 lb as oz	5. 0.66 short tons as lb
3. 48 000 lb as long tons	6. 1.08 long tons as lb

EQUIVALENT METRIC UNITS OF WEIGHT MEASURE

Example 1. Express 5 400 g as kilograms.

5 400 g = 5 400. kg = **5.4 kg** *Ans*

Example 2. Express 5.4 kg as grams.

5.4 kg = 5.400 g = **5 400 g** *Ans*

Exercise 5-22

Express each metric weight in the unit indicated. Round the answers to 2 decimal places.

1. 1 880 g as kg	4. 4.75 g as mg
2. 730 mg as g	5. 0.21 kg as g
3. 2.7 metric tons as kg	6. 310 000 kg as metric tons

EQUIVALENT ENGLISH-METRIC WEIGHT MEASURES

Example 1.   Express 35 pounds as kilograms.

   35 lb = 35 × 0.454 kg = **15.89 kg** *Ans*

Example 2.   Express 15.89 kg as pounds. Round the answer to the nearer whole pound.

   15.89 kg = 15.89 × 2.205 lb = **35 lb** *Ans*

Exercise 5-23

Express each weight in the unit indicated. Round the answers to 3 decimal places.

1.   154 kg as lb
2.   0.9 oz as g
3.   220 g as oz
4.   964.8 lb as kg
5.   3.07 metric tons as lb
6.   40.4 short tons as metric tons

PRACTICAL APPLICATIONS USING UNITS OF CAPACITY AND WEIGHT MEASURE

Exercise 5-24

Round the answers to 2 decimal places.

1.   The liquid intake of a hospital patient during a specified period of time is as follows: 275 mL, 150 mL, 325 mL, 275 mL, 175 mL, 200 mL, and 300 mL. What is the total litre intake of liquid for the time period?

2.   A water tank which has a volume of 4 500 cubic feet is $\frac{3}{4}$ full. How many gallons of water are contained in the tank?

3.   A solution contains 5% acid and 95% water. How many quarts of the solution can be made with 4 ounces of acid?

4.   A truck is to deliver 8 prefabricated concrete wall sections to a job site. Each wall section has a volume of 0.6 cubic metre. One cubic metre of concrete weighs 2 300 kilograms. How many metric tons is carried on this delivery?

5.   An assembly housing weighs 7.50 pounds. The weight of the housing is to be reduced to 5.25 pounds by drilling holes in the housing. How many holes must be drilled if each drilled hole removes 1.5 ounce of material?

6.   An engine running at a constant speed uses 140 millilitres of gasoline per minute. How many litres of gasoline are used in 7 hours?

7.   Air-dried commercial white fir lumber weighs 27 pounds per cubic foot. What is the weight, in long tons, of 500 cubic feet of white fir?

8.   A bottle contains 1.750 litres of solution. A laboratory technician takes 20 samples from the bottle. Each sample contains 40 millilitres of solution. How many litres of solution remain in the bottle?

SECTION 2
Fundamentals of Algebra

UNIT 6
Introduction to Algebra

OBJECTIVES

After studying this unit you should be able to

- express word statements as algebraic expressions.
- express diagram values as algebraic expressions.
- evaluate algebraic expressions by substituting given numbers for letter values.
- solve formulas by substituting numbers for letters, word statements, and diagram values.

Algebra is a branch of mathematics that uses letters to represent numbers; it is an extension of arithmetic. The rules and procedures which apply to arithmetic also apply to algebra.

By the use of letters, general rules called *formulas* can be stated mathematically. The expression, $°C = \frac{5(°F - 32°)}{9}$ is an example of a formula that is used to express degrees Fahrenheit as degrees Celsius. Many operations in shop, construction, and industrial work are expressed as formulas. Business, finance, transportation, agriculture, and health occupations require the employee to understand and apply formulas.

A knowledge of algebra fundamentals is necessary in a wide range of occupations. Algebra is often used in solving on-the-job geometry and trigonometry problems. The basic principles of algebra presented in this text are intended to provide a practical background for diverse occupational applications.

SYMBOLISM

Symbols are the language of algebra. Both arithmetic and literal numbers are used in algebra.

Arithmetic numbers are numbers which have definite numerical values, such as 2, 8.5, and $\frac{1}{4}$.

Literal numbers are letters which represent arithmetic numbers, such as *x, y, a, A,* and *T.* Depending on how it is used, a literal number can represent one particular arithmetic number, a wide range of numerical values, or all numerical values.

Customarily, the multiplication sign ($\times$) is not used in algebra because it can be misinterpreted as the letter *x*. When a literal number (letter) is multiplied by a numerical value, or when two or more literal numbers are multiplied, no sign of operation is required. For example, $2 \times a$ is written $2a$; $b \times c$ is written bc, $4 \times L \times W$ is written $4LW$. When two or more arithmetic numbers are multiplied, parentheses ( ) are used in place of the multiplication sign. For example, 3 times 5 can be written as (3)5, 3(5), or (3)(5).

ALGEBRAIC EXPRESSIONS

An *algebraic expression* is a word statement put into mathematical form by using literal numbers, arithmetic numbers, and signs of operation. Generally, part of a word statement contains an unknown quantity. The unknown quantity is indicated by a symbol. The symbol usually used is a single letter, such as *x, y, a, V, P,* etc.

A variety of words and phrases indicate mathematical operations in word statements. Some of the many words and phrases which indicate the mathematical operations of addition, subtraction, multiplication and division are listed.

Addition: The operation symbol (+) is substituted for words and phrases such as add, sum, plus, increase, greater than, heavier than, larger than, exceeded by, and gain of.

Subtraction: The operation symbol (−) is substituted for words and phrases such as subtract, minus, decreased by, reduced by, less than, smaller than, shorter than, lighter than, and loss of.

Multiplication: No sign of operation is required for the product of all literal numbers or the product of a literal number and a numerical value. Otherwise, the symbol ( ) is substituted for words such as multiply, times, and product of.

Division: The operation symbols ($\div$) and (-) in fractional form as in $\frac{a}{b}$ are substituted for words and phrases, such as divide by and quotient of.

Examples of Algebraic Expressions

Example 1.   The statement "add 5 to *x*" is expressed algebraically as $x + 5$.

Example 2.   The statement "12 is decreased by *b*" is expressed algebraically as $12 - b$.

Example 3.   The cost, in dollars, of one pound of grass seed is *d*. The cost of 6 pounds of seed is expressed as $6d$.

Example 4.   The weight, in pounds, of ten gallons of gasoline is *W*. The weight of one gallon is expressed as $W \div 10$ or $\frac{W}{10}$.

Example 5.   The length of a spring, in millimetres, is *l*. The spring is stretched to 3 times its original length plus 0.4 millimetre. The stretched spring length is expressed as $3l + 0.4$.

Example 6. A patio is shown in figure 6-1. Length A is expressed in feet as x. Length B is $\frac{1}{2}$ of Length A or $\frac{1}{2}x$. Length C is twice Length A or $2x$. The total length of the patio is expressed as $x + \frac{1}{2}x + 2x$.

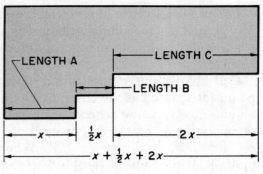

Fig. 6-1

Example 7. A plate with 2 drilled holes is shown in figure 6-2. The total length of the plate is 14 centimetres. The distance, in centimetres, from the left edge of the plate to the center of hole 1 is c. The distance, in centimetres, from the right edge of the plate to hole 2 is b. The distance between holes, in centimetres, is expressed as $14 - c - b$, or $14 - (c + b)$.

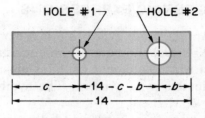

Fig. 6-2

Example 8. Perimeter (P) is the distance around an object. The perimeter of a rectangle equals twice its length plus twice its width. The perimeter of a rectangle expressed as a formula is $P = 2l + 2w$.

Exercise 6-1

Express each exercise as an algebraic expression.

1. Add 3 to a
2. Subtract 7 from d
3. Subtract d from 7
4. Multiply 8 times m
5. Multiply x times y
6. Divide 25 by b
7. Divide b by 25
8. Square x
9. Increase e by 12
10. The product of r and s
11. Divide 20 by n
12. Reduce 75 by y
13. Reduce y by 75
14. The sum of e and f reduced by g

15. Increase a by the square of b.
16. The square root of x plus 6.8
17. Three times V minus 12
18. The product of c and d increased by e
19. One-half x minus four times y
20. The sum of $4\frac{1}{4}$ and b reduced by c.
21. The product of 9 and m increased by the product of 2 and n.
22. The cube root of h times the square of p.
23. Divide x by the product of 25 and y.
24. Take the square root of r, add s, and subtract the product of 2 and t.

Express each problem as an algebraic expression.

25. Refer to figure 6-3. All values are in inches.

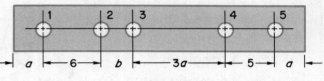

Fig. 6-3

   a. Express the distance from the left edge of the part to the center of hole 3.

   b. Express the distance from the center of hole 1 to the center of hole 4.

   c. Express the distance from the center of hole 2 to the center of hole 5.

   d. Express the distance from the right edge of the part to the center of hole 2.

26. A machine produces P parts per hour. Express the number of parts produced in h hours.

27. The length of a board, in metres, is L. The board is cut into N number of equal pieces. Express the length of each piece.

28. A cross-sectional view of a pipe is shown in figure 6-4.

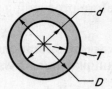

Fig. 6-4

   a. The pipe wall thickness (T) is equal to the difference between the outside diameter (D) and the inside diameter (d) divided by 2. Express the wall thickness.

   b. The inside diameter (d) is equal to the outside diameter (D) minus twice the wall thickness (T). Express the inside diameter.

29. A person has a checkbook balance represented as B. A check is made out for an amount represented as C. The amount deposited in the account is represented as D. Express the new account balance.

30. A series circuit is shown in figure 6-5. The total resistance (R_T) of the circuit is equal to the sum of the individual resistance R_1, R_2, and R_3. The circuit has a total resistance of 200 ohms. Express the resistance of R_1.

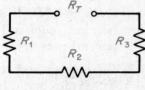

Fig. 6-5

31. The total piston displacement of an engine is determined by computing the product of 0.785 4 times the square of the cylinder bore (D) times the length of the piston stroke (L) times the number of cylinders (N). Express the total piston displacement.

32. A stairway is shown in figure 6-6. The actual number of steps is shown.

   a. The stairway run is x. Express the run per step.

   b. The stairway rise is y. Express the rise per step.

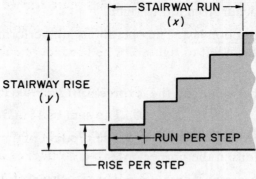

Fig. 6-6

33. Impedance (Z) of the circuit shown in figure 6-7 is computed by adding the square of resistance (R) to the square of reactance (X), then taking the square root of the sum. Express the circuit impedance.

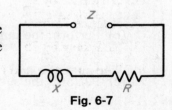

Fig. 6-7

34. Refer to figure 6-8. Express the distances between the following points:

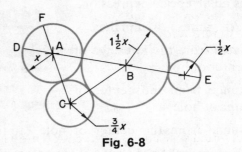

Fig. 6-8

   a. point A to point B.

   b. point F to point C.

   c. point B to point C.

   d. point D to point E.

EVALUATION OF ALGEBRAIC EXPRESSIONS

Certain problems in this text involve the use of formulas. Some problems require substituting numerical values for letter values. The problems are solved by applying the order of operations of arithmetic. Review the order of operations before proceeding to solve the exercises and problems which follow.

Order of Operations for Combined Operations of Addition, Subtraction, Multiplication, Division, Powers, and Roots

1. <u>Do all the work in parentheses first</u>. Parentheses are used to group numbers. In a problem expressed in fractional form, two or more numbers in the dividend (numerator) and/or divisor (denominator) may be considered as being enclosed in parentheses. For example, $\frac{4.87 + 0.34}{9.75 - 8.12}$ may be considered as $(4.87 + 0.34) \div (9.75 - 8.12)$. If an expression contains parentheses within parentheses or brackets, such as $[5.6 \times (7 - 0.09) + 8.8]$ do the work within the innermost parentheses first.

2. <u>Do powers and roots next</u>. The operations are performed in the order in which they occur from left to right. If a root consists of two or more operations within the radical sign, perform all the operations within the radical sign, then extract the root.

3. <u>Do multiplication and division next</u>. The operations are performed in the order in which they occur from left to right.

4. <u>Do addition and subtraction last</u>. The operations are performed in the order in which they occur from left to right.

Example 1. What is the value of the expression $25 - x(xy - m)$, when $x = 8, y = 3$, and $m = 22$?

Substitute the numerical values for $x, y,$ and m. $25 - 8[8(3) - 22]$

Perform the operations in the proper order.

(a) Perform the operations within parentheses or brackets.

   $8(3) = 24$ $25 - 8(24 - 22)$

   $24 - 22 = 2$ $25 - 8(2)$

(b) Perform the multiplication.

   $8(2) = 16$ $25 - 16$

(c) Perform the subtraction.

   $25 - 16 = 9$ *9 Ans*

Example 2. The total resistance (R_T) of the circuit shown in figure 6-9 is computed using this formula.

$$R_T = R_1 + \frac{R_2 R_3}{R_2 + R_3}$$

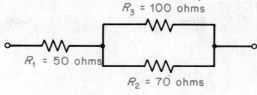

R_3 = 100 ohms

R_1 = 50 ohms

R_2 = 70 ohms

Fig. 6-9

The values of the individual resistances (R_1, R_2, R_3) are given in the figure. Determine the total resistance (R_T) of the circuit to the nearer tenth ohm. The symbol for ohm is Ω.

Substitute the numerical values for R_1, R_2, and R_3.

$$R_T = 50\ \Omega + \frac{70\ \Omega (100\ \Omega)}{70\ \Omega + 100\ \Omega}$$

Perform the operations in the proper order.

(a) Consider the numerator and the denominator as being enclosed within parentheses. Perform the operations within parentheses.

$70\ \Omega (100\ \Omega) = 7\,000\ \Omega^2$

$70\ \Omega + 100\ \Omega = 170\ \Omega$

$$R_T = 50\ \Omega + \frac{7\,000\ \Omega^2}{170\ \Omega}$$

(b) Perform the division.

$7\,000\ \Omega^2 \div 170\ \Omega = 41.2\ \Omega$ $R_T = 50\ \Omega + 41.2\ \Omega$

(c) Perform the addition.

$50\ \Omega + 41.2\ \Omega = 91.2\ \Omega$ $R_T =$ **91.2 Ω** *Ans*

Example 3. To determine the center-to-center hole distance (c) shown in figure 6-10, an inspector uses the formula $c = \sqrt{a^2 + b^2}$. Compute the value of c.

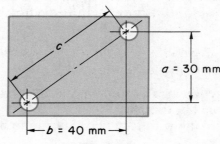

c

a = 30 mm

b = 40 mm

Fig. 6-10

Substitute the numerical values for a and b.

$$c = \sqrt{(30\text{ mm})^2 + (40\text{ mm})^2}$$

Perform the operations in the proper order.

(a) Perform the operations within the radical sign.

$(30\text{ mm})^2 = 900\text{ mm}^2$

$(40\text{ mm})^2 = 1\,600\text{ mm}^2$

$900\text{ mm}^2 + 1\,600\text{ mm}^2 = 2\,500\text{ mm}^2$

$$c = \sqrt{900\text{ mm}^2 + 1\,600\text{ mm}^2}$$

$$c = \sqrt{2\,500\text{ mm}^2}$$

(b) Extract the square root.

$\sqrt{2\,500\text{ mm}^2} = 50\text{ mm}$ $c =$ **50 mm** *Ans*

Exercise 6-2

Substitute the given numbers for letters and compute the value of each expression.

1. If $a = 5$ and $b = 3$, find

   a. $4a - 2$
   b. $5 + b - a$
   c. $6a \div b$
   d. $b(a + b)$
   e. $3a - (2 + a)$

4. If $m = 8$, $s = 4$ and $t = 2$, find

   a. $\frac{m}{s} + t - 1$
   b. $ms(5 + 2s - 3t)$
   c. $12s(m + 5 - t)$
   d. $\frac{3m - s + 4t}{22 - st}$
   e. $\frac{12s}{t} - [3m - (s + t) + 4]$

2. If $x = 6$ and $y = 2$, find

   a. $2xy - y$
   b. $(x + y)(x - y)$
   c. $\frac{x + y}{x - y}$
   d. $2x - x \div 3$
   e. $2x + xy - 4y$

5. If $x = 10$, $y = 6$ and $w = 12$, find

   a. $20 - \frac{w}{y} + 12x$
   b. $(x + w) \div (2y - x)$
   c. $\frac{xy + 4}{2x - 2y}$
   d. $\sqrt{x + 5y - (w + 3)}$
   e. $\frac{4x^2}{\sqrt{6w - 8}}$

3. If $e = 8$ and $f = 4$, find

   a. $3ef + 9$
   b. $5f + (ef)$
   c. $5e + f(\frac{e}{4})$
   d. $\frac{10e - 6f}{8}$
   e. $12e \div (2f + 2)$

6. If $p = 5$, $h = 4$ and $k = 3$, find

   a. $p + ph^2 - k^3$
   b. $(h + 2)^2(p - k)^2$
   c. $\left[\frac{(hk)^2}{2} - hk\right] + p^3$
   d. $\frac{h^3 + 3h - 12}{p^2 + 15}$
   e. $\frac{k^3}{3h - 9} + p^2 (ph - 6k)^2$

Each problem requires working with formulas. Substitute numerical values for letters and solve.

7. A drill revolving at 300 revolutions per minute has a feed of 0.025 inch per revolution. Determine the cutting time required to drill through a workpiece 3.60 inches thick. Use this formula for finding cutting time. Round the answer to 1 decimal place.

   $$T = \frac{L}{FN}$$

   where T = time in minutes
   L = length of cut in the work-piece in inches
   F = feed in inches per revolution
   N = speed in revolutions per minute

8. The constant value for the resistance of a circular-mil foot of copper wire at 75°F is 10.5 ohms. Compute the resistance of a copper wire 21 mils in diameter and 250 feet long. Use this formula for determining resistance. Round the answer to 1 decimal place.

$$R = \frac{KL}{d^2}$$ where R = resistance in ohms
  K = constant (10.5 Ω/CM-ft)
  L = length in feet
  d = diameter in mils

9. The resistance of an aluminum wire is 10 ohms. The constant value for the resistance of a circular-mil foot of aluminum wire at 75°F is 17.7 ohms. Compute the wire diameter, to the nearer whole mil, for a wire 500 feet long.

$$d = \sqrt{\frac{KL}{R}}$$ where d = diameter in mils
  K = constant (17.7 Ω/CM-ft)
  L = length in feet
  R = resistance in ohms

10. Express 75°F as degrees Celsius using this formula. Round the answer to the nearer whole degree.

$$°C = \frac{5(°F - 32°)}{9}$$

11. Express 12°C as degrees Fahrenheit using this formula. Round the answer to the nearer whole degree.

$$°F = \frac{9}{5}(°C) + 32°$$

12. An orginial principal of $2 500 is deposited in a compound interest savings account. The money is left on deposit for 2 compounding periods with an interest rate of 3% per period. Determine the amount of money in the account at the end of the 2 periods. Use this formula and express the answer to the nearer cent.

$$A = P(1 + R)^n$$ where A = accumulated principal
  P = original principal
  R = rate per period
  n = number of periods

13. An engine is turning at the rate of 1 500 revolutions per minute. The piston has a diameter (d) of 3 inches and a stroke length of 4 inches. The mean effective pressure on the piston is 60 lb/sq in. Find the horsepower developed by this engine. Round the answer to 1 decimal place.

$$hp = \frac{PLAN}{33\,000}$$ where P = mean effective pressure
  L = length of stroke in inches
  A = piston cross-sectional area in sq in (0.785 4 d^2)
  N = number of revolutions per minute

14. A tapered plug is shown in 2 views in figure 6-11. Compute the taper per millimetre, to the nearer hundredth, using this formula.

$$T = \frac{D - d}{L}$$

    where T = taper per millimetre
               D = diameter of larger end in millimetres
               d = diameter of smaller end in millimetres
               L = length in millimetres

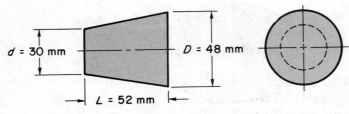

Fig. 6-11

15. Find the area (A) of the plot of land shown in figure 6-12 using this formula.

$$A = \frac{(H + h)b + ch + aH}{2}$$

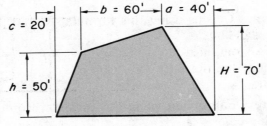

Fig. 6-12

16. A cabinetmaker cuts a piece of plywood to the form and dimensions shown in figure 6-13. Use this formula to determine the radius (r) of the circle from which the piece is cut.

$$r = \frac{c^2 + 4h^2}{8h}$$

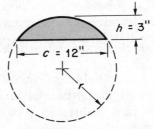

Fig. 6-13

17. Pulley dimensions are given in figure 6-14. Compute the length (L) of the belt required using this formula. Round the answer to 2 decimal places.

$$L = 2c + \frac{11D + 11d}{7} + \frac{(D - d)^2}{4c}$$

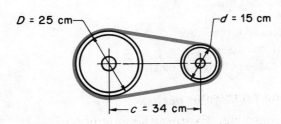

Fig. 6-14

18. The total resistance (R_T) of the parallel circuit shown in figure 6-15 is computed using this formula. Compute the total circuit resistance in ohms.

$$R_T = \cfrac{1}{\cfrac{1}{R_1} + \cfrac{1}{R_2} + \cfrac{1}{R_3} + \cfrac{1}{R_4} + \cfrac{1}{R_5}}$$

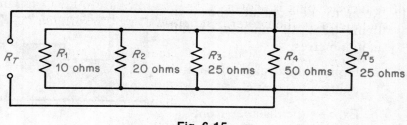

Fig. 6-15

19. An ellipse is shown in figure 6-16. Compute the perimeter (P) of the ellipse using this formula. Round the answer to 1 decimal place.

$$P = 3.14 \sqrt{2(a^2 + b^2)}$$

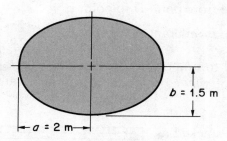

Fig. 6-16

20. A cross-sectional view of an I beam is shown in figure 6-17. Compute the cross-sectional area (A) of the beam using this formula.

$$A = dt + 2a(s + n)$$

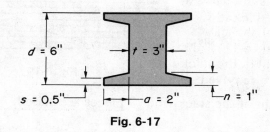

Fig. 6-17

UNIT EXERCISE AND PROBLEM REVIEW

Exercise 6-3

WRITING ALGEBRAIC EXPRESSIONS

Express each of these exercises as an algebraic expression.

1. Six times x plus 12

2. The sum of a and b minus c

3. One-quarter m times R

4. The square of V reduced by the product of 3 and P.

5. Divide d by the product of 14 and f.

6. The cube of x increased by the square root of y.

7. Twice M decreased by one-third R.

8. The sum of a and b divided by the difference between a and b

9. Square F, add G, and divide the sum by H.

10. Multiply x and y, take the square root of the product, and subtract 5.

WRITING ALGEBRAIC EXPRESSIONS

Express each of these problems as an algebraic expression.

11. A car averages C miles per gallon of gasoline. Express the number of gallons of gasoline used when the car travels M miles.

12. Refer to the template shown in figure 6-18. All values are given in millimetres.

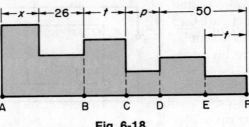

Fig. 6-18

   a. Express the distance from point A to point C.

   b. Express the distance from point B to point F.

   c. Express the distance from point D to point E.

   d. Express the distance from point A to point E.

13. Three pumps are used to drain water from a construction site. Each pump discharges G gallons of water per hour. How much water is drained from the site in H hours?

14. Sheets of plywood are stacked as shown in figure 6-19. The actual number of sheets is shown. All sheets are the same thickness.

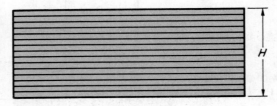

Fig. 6-19

   a. Express the thickness of 1 sheet.

   b. Express the height of the stack when 4 sheets are removed.

   c. Express the height of the stack when 7 pieces are added.

15. A piece of property is going to be enclosed by a fence with 2 gates. The property is in the shape of a square with each side S feet long. Each gate is G feet in length. Express the total number of feet of fencing required.

SUBSTITUTING VALUES IN EXPRESSIONS

Substitute the given numbers for letters and compute the value of each expression.

16. If $x = 12$ and $y = 9$, find

   a. $15 + x - y$

   b. $y(3 + x)$

   c. $\frac{1}{2}x - (y - 6)$

   d. $x + y\left(\frac{x}{3}\right)$

17. If $c = 3$ and $d = 2$, find

   a. $4c - 5d \div 2$

   b. $10cd - (c + d)$

   c. $(c - d)(c + d)$

   d. $\frac{cd + 14}{5c - 5d}$

18. If $h = 6$, $m = 3$ and $s = 8$, find

   a. $hm(2s + 1 + 0.5h)$

   b. $(3s - 2m) \div (6m - 2h)$

   c. $s^2 + 5m^2 - h^2$

   d. $\frac{2m^3}{0.5s^2 - 5h + 7}$

19. If $x = 2$, $y = 4$ and $t = 5$, find

   a. $100 - [8t - (x + y)]$

   b. $\frac{(xy)^2}{y} + xyt - \frac{2t^2}{5x}$

   c. $\sqrt{2xy}(xy - t)$

   d. $y\left(\frac{x^2t}{y}\right) + \sqrt{2x^4 + t - 12}$

SOLVING FORMULAS

Each problem requires working with formulas. Substitute numerical values for letters and solve.

20. Three cells are connected as shown in figure 6-20. In each cell the internal resistance is 2.2 ohms and the voltage is 1.5 volts. The resistance of the external circuit is 2.5 ohms. Use this formula to determine the circuit current to the nearer tenth ampere.

$$I = \frac{En}{rn + R}$$

where I = current in amperes
E = voltage of each cell in volts
n = number of cells
r = internal resistance of each cell in ohms
R = external resistance in ohms

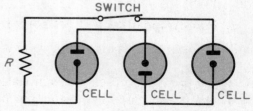

Fig. 6-20

21. A cylindrical tank is shown in figure 6-21. Compute the capacity, to the nearer tenth gallon, of the tank using this formula.

$$C = \frac{0.785\,4D^2H}{231}$$

where C = capacity in gallons
D = diameter in inches
H = height in inches

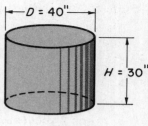

Fig. 6-21

22. A shaft with a 3-inch diameter is turned in a lathe at 180 revolutions per minute. The cutting speed is the number of feet that the shaft travels past the cutting tool in 1 minute. Determine the cutting speed, to the nearer foot per minute, using this formula.

$$C = \frac{3.141\,6DN}{12}$$

where C = cutting speed in feet per minute
D = diameter in inches
N = revolutions per minute

23. A tapered pin is shown in figure 6-22. Compute the length of the side, to the nearer tenth millimetre, using this formula.

$$S = \sqrt{\left(\frac{D}{2} - \frac{d}{2}\right)^2 + L^2}$$

where S = side in millimetres
L = length in millimetres
D = diameter of larger end in millimetres
d = diameter of smaller end in millimetres

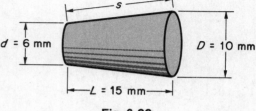

Fig. 6-22

24. The top view of a concrete platform is shown in figure 6-23. Determine the area (A), in square feet, of the platform using this formula.

$$A = c[b + 2(a - c)]$$

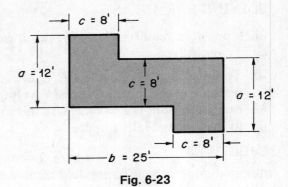

Fig. 6-23

UNIT 7
Signed
Numbers

OBJECTIVES

After studying this unit you should be able to

- express word statements as signed numbers.
- write signed number values using a number scale.
- add and subtract signed numbers.
- multiply and divide signed numbers.
- compute powers and roots of signed numbers.
- solve combined operations of signed number expressions.
- solve signed number problems.

MEANING OF SIGNED NUMBERS

Plus and minus signs which you have worked with so far in this book have been *signs of operation*. These are the signs used in arithmetic, with the plus sign (+) indicating the operation of addition and the minus sign (−) indicating the operation of subtraction.

In algebra, plus and minus signs are used to indicate both operation and direction from a reference point or zero. A *positive number* is indicated either with no sign or with a plus sign (+) preceding the number. A *negative number* is indicated with a minus sign (−) preceding the number. Positive and negative numbers are called *signed numbers* or *directed numbers*.

Signed numbers are common in everyday use as well as in occupational applications. For example, a Celsius temperature reading of 20 degrees above zero is written as +20°C or 20°C. A temperature reading of 20 degrees below zero is written as −20°C as shown in figure 7-1.

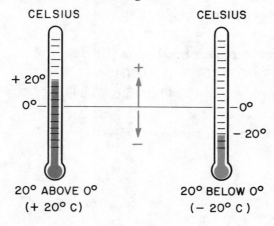

Fig. 7-1

Signed numbers are often used to indicate direction and distance from a reference point. Opposites, such as up and down, left and right, north and south, and clockwise and counterclockwise, may be expressed using positive and negative signs. For example, 100 feet above sea level may be expressed as +100 feet and 100 feet below sea level as −100 feet. Sea level in this case is the zero reference point.

The automobile ammeter shown in figure 7-2 indicates whether a battery is charging (+) or discharging (−). In business applications, a profit of $1 000 is expressed as +$1 000 while a loss of $1 000 is expressed as −$1 000. Closing prices for stocks are indicated as up (+) or down (−) from the previous day's closing prices.

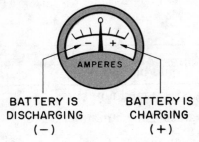

BATTERY IS
DISCHARGING
(−)

BATTERY IS
CHARGING
(+)

Fig. 7-2

Signed numbers are used in programming operations for numerical control machines. From a reference point, machine movements are expressed as + and − directions.

Exercise 7-1

Express the answer to each of the following problems as a signed number.

1. A speed increase of 12 miles per hour is expressed as +12 mi/h. Express a speed decrease of 8 miles per hour.

2. Traveling 50 kilometres west is expressed as −50 km. How is traveling 75 kilometres east expressed?

3. A wage increase of $25 is expressed at +$25. Express a wage decrease of $18.

4. The reduction of a person's daily calorie intake by 400 calories is expressed as −400 calories. Express a daily intake increase of 350 calories.

5. A company's assets of $73 600 are expressed as +$73 600. Express company liabilities of $48 000.

6. An increase of 30 pounds per square inch of pressure is expressed as +30 lb/sq in. Express a pressure decrease of 28 pounds per square inch.

7. A circuit voltage loss of 7.5 volts is expressed as −7.5 volts. Express a voltage gain of 9 volts.

8. A manufacturing department's production increase of 500 parts per day is expressed as +500 parts. Express a production decrease of 175 parts.

9. A savings account deposit of $140 is expressed at +$140. Express a withdrawal of $280.

10. A 0.75 percent contraction of a length of wire is expressed as −0.75%. Express a 1.2 percent expansion.

THE NUMBER SCALE

The number scale in figure 7-3 shows the relationship between positive and negative numbers. The scale shows both distance and direction between numbers. Considering a number as a starting point and counting to a number to the right represents a positive (+) direction with numbers increasing in value. Counting to the left represents negative (−) direction with numbers decreasing in value.

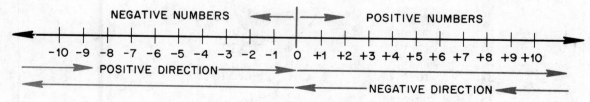

Fig. 7-3

Example 1. Starting at 0 and counting to the right to +5 represents 5 units in a positive (+) direction; **+5 is 5 units greater than 0.**

Example 2. Starting at 0 and counting to the left to −5 represents 5 units in a negative (−) direction; **−5 is 5 units less than 0.**

Example 3. Starting at −4 and counting to the right to +3 represents 7 units in a positive (+) direction; **+3 is 7 units greater than −4.**

Example 4. Starting at +3 and counting to the left to −4 represents 7 units in a negative (−) direction; **−4 is 7 units less than +3.**

Example 5. Starting at −2 and counting to the left to −10 represents 8 units in a negative (−) direction; **−10 is 8 units less than −2.**

Example 6. Starting at −9 and counting to the right to 0 represents 9 units in a positive (+) direction; **0 is 9 units greater than −9.**

Exercise 7-2

Refer to the number scale shown in figure 7-4. Give the direction (+ or −) and the number of units counted going from the first to the second number.

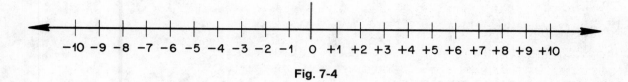

Fig. 7-4

1. 0 to +6	8. +6 to −6	15. −3 to −7
2. 0 to −6	9. −10 to −4	16. −9 to −4
3. −2 to 0	10. +9 to +1	17. +4 to +10
4. +2 to 0	11. +10 to −10	18. +7 to +2
5. −3 to +5	12. −10 to +10	19. −4 to +7
6. −7 to +1	13. +6 to −5	20. +6 to −4
7. +8 to −3	14. −9 to +8	

Refer to the number scale shown in figure 7-5. Give the direction (+ or −) and the number of units counted going from the first to the second number.

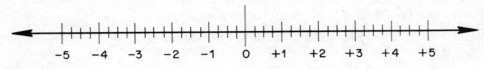

Fig. 7-5

21. -2 to $+3\frac{1}{2}$	25. $+3$ to -4.25	29. -0.75 to -3
22. -5 to $-4\frac{1}{4}$	26. $+4\frac{1}{2}$ to $+1$	30. $+2\frac{1}{4}$ to $-3\frac{3}{4}$
23. $+1.5$ to -2	27. $+3\frac{1}{4}$ to $+\frac{1}{2}$	31. $+4.75$ to 0.5
24. -2.75 to 0	28. -4.25 to -4.5	32. -1.5 to $+4.25$

Select the greater of each of the 2 signed numbers and indicate the number of units by which it is greater.

33. $+3, -2$	38. $+18, +14$	43. $+18.3, -20.6$
34. $-6, 0$	39. $-18, -14$	44. $-23\frac{1}{4}, -15\frac{3}{8}$
35. $-5, +1$	40. $+10, -12$	45. $+1\frac{1}{16}, -1\frac{7}{8}$
36. $-12, -4$	41. $-2.5, +2.5$	46. $-50.23, -41.76$
37. $-28, -73$	42. $-86\frac{3}{4}, 0$	47. $+\frac{3}{16}, -\frac{9}{32}$

List each set of signed numbers in order of increasing value, starting with the smallest value.

48. $+14, -25, +25, 0, +7, -7, -10$

49. $0, -18, +4, -22, -1, +2, +16$

50. $-2, -19, -21, +13, +27, 0, -5$

51. $-15, +17, +3, -3, +15, 0, -8$

52. $-13.9, 0, +12, -3.2, +1, -12.6$

53. $+17.8, +2.3, -1, +1, -1.1, -0.4$

54. $+4\frac{3}{8}, -6, -12\frac{7}{8}, 0, -12\frac{13}{16}, -\frac{1}{4}$

55. $0, -1\frac{1}{2}, -6\frac{5}{32}, -6\frac{1}{4}, -1\frac{15}{32}, -1\frac{7}{16}$

OPERATIONS USING SIGNED NUMBERS

In order to solve problems in algebra, you must be able to perform basic operations using signed numbers. The operations of addition, subtraction, multiplication, division, powers, and roots with both positive and negative numbers are presented.

ABSOLUTE VALUE

The procedure for performing certain operations of signed numbers are based on an understanding of absolute value. The *absolute value* of a number is the number without regard to its sign. The absolute value of a number is indicated by placing the number between a pair of vertical bars. The absolute values of +8 and −8 is written as follows.

$$|+8| = 8 \qquad\qquad |-8| = 8$$

The absolute values of +8 and −8 are the same value. The absolute values of −15 and +5 is written as follows.

$$|-15| = 15 \qquad\qquad |+5| = 5$$

The absolute value of −15 is 10 greater than the absolute value of 5.

Exercise 7-3.

Express each of the pairs of signed numbers as absolute values. Subtract the smaller absolute value from the larger absolute value.

1. +15, −10	6. +9, 0	11. $+6\frac{1}{4}, -8\frac{3}{4}$
2. −15, +10	7. −23, +22	12. $-3\frac{1}{2}, -12\frac{7}{8}$
3. −6, +2	8. +18, −18	13. +12.7, −9.8
4. −14, +14	9. +18, +18	14. +10.54, −12.46
5. −9, 0	10. −18, −18	15. −0.03, −0.007

ADDITION OF SIGNED NUMBERS

Procedure for Adding Two or More Positive Numbers

• Add the numbers as in arithmetic.

Example 1. $4 + 8 = 12$ *Ans*

Example 2. $(+25\frac{1}{2}) + (+10) = +35\frac{1}{2}$ or $35\frac{1}{2}$ *Ans*

Example 3. $9 + 5.6 + 2.1 = 16.7$ *Ans*

Example 4. $6 + (+2) + (+7) = +15$ or 15 *Ans*

Procedure for Adding Two or More Negative Numbers

• Add the absolute values of the numbers.
• Prefix a minus sign to the sum.

Example 1.   Add −6 and −14.

   The absolute value of −6 is 6.

   The absolute value of −14 is 14.

   Add. $6 + 14 = 20$

   Prefix a minus sign to the sum. $(-6) + (-14) = -20$ *Ans*

Example 2. $(-2) + (-5) + (-8) + (-10) = -25$ *Ans*

Example 3. $(-4) + (-12) = -16$ *Ans*

Example 4. $-2.5 + (-3) + (-0.2) + (-5.8) = -11.5$ *Ans*

Procedure for Adding a Positive and a Negative Number

- Subtract the smaller absolute value from the large absolute value.
- Prefix the sign of the number having the larger absolute value to the difference.

Example 1. Add $+10$ and -4.

The absolute value of $+10$ is 10.

The absolute value of -4 is 4.

Subtract. $10 - 4 = 6$

Prefix the plus sign to the difference. $\qquad (+10) + (-4) = +6$ or 6 *Ans*

Example 2. Add -10 and $+4$.

The absolute value of -10 is 10.

The absolute value of -4 is 4.

Subtract. $10 - 4 = 6$

Prefix the minus sign to the difference. $\qquad (-10) + (+4) = -6$ *Ans*

Example 3. $15.8 + (-2.4) = +13.4$ or 13.4 *Ans*

Example 4. $6\frac{1}{4} + (-10\frac{3}{4}) = -4\frac{1}{2}$ *Ans*

Example 5. $-20 + (+20) = 0$ *Ans*

Procedure for Adding Combinations of Two or More Positive and Negative Numbers

- Add all the positive numbers.
- Add all the negative numbers.
- Add their sums following the procedure for adding signed numbers.

Example 1. $-12 + 7 + 3 + (-5) + 20 = +13$ or 13 *Ans*

Example 2. $6 + (-10) + (-5) + 8 + 2 + (-7) = -6$ *Ans*

Example 3. $-2 + (-5) + 1 + 3 + (-7) + 12 + (-6) + 4 = 0$ *Ans*

Exercise 7-4

Add the signed numbers as indicated.

1. $+6 + (+9)$
2. $+15 + (+8)$
3. $4 + 20$
4. $7 + (+18) + 2$
5. $0 + (+25)$
6. $-12 + (-7)$
7. $-8 + (-15)$
8. $0 + (-16)$
9. $-14 + (-4) + (-11)$
10. $-3 + (-6) + (-17)$

11. $+12 + (-5)$
12. $+18 + (-26)$
13. $-20 + (+17)$
14. $46 + (-14)$
15. $-23 + 17$
16. $25 + (-3)$
17. $-25 + 3$
18. $-18 + (-25)$
19. $-4 + (-31)$
20. $+27 + (-27)$

21. $-15.3 + (-3.5)$

22. $-15.3 + (+3.5)$

23. $-16.4 + (-2.7)$

24. $+37.9 + (-40.4)$

25. $-9\frac{1}{4} + (-3\frac{3}{4})$

26. $18\frac{5}{8} + (-21\frac{3}{4})$

27. $-13 + (-\frac{3}{16})$

28. $-13 + (+\frac{3}{16})$

29. $-4.25 + (-7) + (-3.22)$

30. $18.07 + (-17.64)$

31. $16 + (-4) + (-11)$

32. $-21 + (-6) + 14 + 12$

33. $30 + (-7) + (-8) + 3$

34. $-10.2 + (-9) + (-7.6) + 14.7$

35. $8 + 16.7 + (-4.1) + 9.5$

36. $1\frac{1}{4} + (-2\frac{1}{2}) + (-\frac{3}{4}) + (4\frac{1}{2})$

SUBTRACTION OF SIGNED NUMBERS

Procedure for Subtracting Signed Numbers

- Change the sign of the number subtracted (subtrahend) to the opposite sign.
- Follow the procedure for addition of signed numbers.

NOTE: When the sign of the subtrahend is changed, the problem becomes one in addition. Therefore, subtracting a negative number is the same as adding a positive number. Subtracting a positive number is the same as adding a negative number.

Example 1. Subtract 8 from 5. $5 - 8$

Change the sign of the subtrahend to the opposite sign. Change 8 or $+8$ to -8.

Follow the procedure for the addition $5 + (-8) = -3$ *Ans*
of signed numbers.

Example 2. $4 - (-10) = 4 + (+10) = +14$ or 14 *Ans*

Example 3. $-7 - (-12) = -7 + (+12) = +5$ or 5 *Ans*

Example 4. $10.6 - (-7.2) = 10.6 + (+7.2) = +17.8$ or 17.8 *Ans*

Example 5. $-10.6 - (+7.2) = -10.6 + (-7.2) = -17.8$ *Ans*

Example 6. $0 - (-14) = 0 + (+14) = +14$ or 14 *Ans*

Example 7. $0 - (+14) = 0 + (-14) = -14$ *Ans*

Example 8. $-20 - (-20) = -20 + (+20) = 0$ *Ans*

Example 9. $(18 - 4) - (-20 + 3) = 14 - (-17) = 14 + 17 = 31$ *Ans*

NOTE: Following the proper order of operations, the operations enclosed within parentheses must be done first.

Exercise 7-5

Subtract the signed numbers as indicated.

1. $-10 - (-8)$

2. $+10 - (+8)$

3. $+5 - (-13)$

4. $+5 - (+13)$

5. $-22 - (-14)$

6. $+17 - (+8)$

7. $+3 - (-19)$

8. $+26 - (+31)$

9. $+40 - (+40)$

10. $-40 - (-40)$

11. $-40 - (+40)$

12. $-25 - 0$

13. $0 - (+7)$

14. $0 - (-7)$

15. $36 - (+41)$

16. $-52 - (-8)$

17. $-8 - (-52)$

18. $34 - (+17)$

19. $16.5 - (+14.3)$

20. $16.5 - (-14.3)$

21. $-16.5 - (-14.3)$

22. $-50.2 - (+51)$

23. $+50.2 - (-51)$

24. $0.03 - (+0.05)$

25. $10\frac{1}{2} - (+7\frac{1}{4})$

26. $-10\frac{1}{2} - (-7\frac{1}{4})$

27. $5\frac{7}{8} - (-4\frac{1}{8})$

28. $\frac{9}{32} - (+\frac{11}{32})$

29. $(6 + 10) - (-7 + 8)$

30. $(-12 + 9) - (-2 + 6)$

31. $(-14 + 5) - (2 - 10)$

32. $(2.7 - 5.6) - (18.4 - 6.3)$

33. $(7.23 - 6.81) - (-10.73)$

34. $(9\frac{3}{8} + 1\frac{1}{2}) - (8 - 9\frac{1}{4})$

35. $[3 - (-7)] - [14 - (-6)]$

36. $[-8 + (-5)] - [12 - (-1)]$

MULTIPLICATION OF SIGNED NUMBERS

Procedure for Multiplying Two or More Signed Numbers

- Multiply the absolute values of the numbers.
- Count the number of negative signs.

    If there is an odd number of negative signs, the product is negative.

    If there is an even number of negative signs, the product is positive.

    If all numbers are positive, the product is positive.

It is not necessary to count the number of positive values in an expression consisting of both positive and negative numbers. Count only the number of negative values to determine the sign of the product.

Example 1.   Multiply. $3(-5)$

Multiply the absolute values.

There is one negative sign.
Since one is an odd number,
the product is negative. $3(-5) = -15$ *Ans*

Example 2.   Multiply. $-3(-5)$

Multiply the absolute values.

There are two negative signs.
Since two is an even number,
the product is positive. $-3(-5) = +15$ or **15** *Ans*

Example 3. $(-3)(-1)(-2)(-3)(-2)(-1) = +36$ or **36** *Ans*

Example 4. $(-3)(+1)(-2)(-3)(-2)(-1) = -36$ *Ans*

Example 5. $(3)(-1)(-2)(3)(2)(-1) = -36$ *Ans*

Example 6. $(-3)(-1)(-2)(3)(-2)(1) = +36$ or 36 *Ans*

Example 7. $(3)(1)(2)(3)(2)(1) = +36$ or 36 *Ans*

NOTE: The product of any number or numbers and 0 equals 0. For example,
$0(4) = 0$; $0(-4) = 0$; $(7)(-4)(0)(3) = 0$.

Exercise 7-6

Multiply the signed numbers as indicated.

1. $(-4)(6)$
2. $(+4)(-6)$
3. $(-4)(-6)$
4. $(4)(6)$
5. $(+10)(-2)$
6. $(-10)(-2)$
7. $(-5)(7)$
8. $(-2)(-14)$
9. $0(16)$
10. $0(-16)$
11. $(6.5)(-2)$
12. $(-3.2)(-0.1)$
13. $(+8)(-1.4)$
14. $(-0.06)(-0.60)$
15. $(1\frac{1}{2})(-\frac{1}{2})$
16. $(-2\frac{1}{8})(-1\frac{1}{2})$
17. $\frac{1}{4}(0)$
18. $(-\frac{1}{4})(0)$
19. $(-2)(-2)(-2)$
20. $(-2)(+2)(+2)$
21. $(-2)(+2)(-2)$
22. $(-3)(-2)(1)(-1)(2)(1)$
23. $(8)(-2)(3)(0)(-1)$
24. $(-6)(-0.5)(2)(-1)(-0.5)$
25. $(1)(1)(-1)(1)(1)(1)(1)$
26. $(1)(1)(-1)(1)(1)(-1)(1)$
27. $(-4)(-0.25)(-2)(-0.5)$
28. $(-0.03)(-100)(-0.10)$
29. $(+\frac{1}{4})(-8)(\frac{1}{2})(2\frac{3}{8})$
30. $(-\frac{1}{4})(-8)(\frac{1}{2})(-2\frac{3}{8})$

DIVISION OF SIGNED NUMBERS

Procedure for Dividing Signed Numbers

- Divide the absolute values of the numbers.
- Determine the sign of the quotient.

  If both numbers have the same sign (both negative or both positive) the quotient is positive.

  If the two numbers have unlike signs (one positive and one negative) the quotient is negative.

Example 1.   Divide -20 by -4.

Divide the absolute values.

There are two negative signs.

The quotient is positive. $-20 \div (-4) = +5$ or 5 *Ans*

Example 2. Divide 24 by -8.

Divide the absolute values.

The signs are unlike.

The quotient is negative. $\qquad 24 \div (-8) = -3 \; Ans$

Example 3. $30 \div 15 = +2$ or $2 \; Ans$

Example 4. $-24 \div 3 = -8 \; Ans$

NOTE: Zero divided by any number equals 0. For example, $0 \div (+9) = 0$; $0 \div (-9) = 0$

Exercise 7-7

Divide the signed numbers as indicated.

1. $-10 \div (-5)$
2. $-10 \div (+5)$
3. $+10 \div (-5)$
4. $+18 \div (+9)$
5. $-21 \div 3$
6. $12 \div (-4)$
7. $-30 \div (-5)$
8. $+48 \div (-6)$
9. $-48 \div (-6)$
10. $-35 \div 7$
11. $\dfrac{-16}{-4}$
12. $\dfrac{0}{-10}$

13. $\dfrac{+30}{-10}$
14. $\dfrac{-40}{-8}$
15. $\dfrac{-36}{6}$
16. $\dfrac{39}{13}$
17. $\dfrac{-60}{-0.5}$
18. $\dfrac{-20}{-2.5}$
19. $\dfrac{+6}{-8}$
20. $\dfrac{-17.92}{3.2}$
21. $+\dfrac{1}{2} \div (-2)$
22. $-\dfrac{1}{2} \div (-\dfrac{1}{2})$

23. $-15 \div 1\dfrac{1}{4}$
24. $-3 \div \dfrac{3}{4}$
25. $4\dfrac{1}{3} \div (-2\dfrac{2}{3})$
26. $0 \div (-\dfrac{7}{8})$
27. $-29.96 \div 5.35$
28. $-4.125 \div (-1.5)$
29. $-20.4 \div 5$
30. $-41.87 \div 7.9$

POWERS OF SIGNED NUMBERS

Procedure for Determining Values with Positive Exponents

- Apply the procedure for multiplying signed numbers to raising signed numbers to powers.

Example 1. $2^3 = (2)(2)(2) = +8$ or $8 \; Ans$

Example 2. $2^4 = (2)(2)(2)(2) = +16$ or $16 \; Ans$

Example 3. $(-4)^2 = (-4)(-4) = +16$ or $16 \; Ans$

Example 4. $(-4)^3 = (-4)(-4)(-4) = -64 \; Ans$

Example 5. $(-2)^4 = (-2)(-2)(-2)(-2) = +16$ or $16 \; Ans$

Example 6. $(-2)^5 = (-2)(-2)(-2)(-2)(-2) = -32 \; Ans$

NOTE:
- A positive number raised to any power is positive.
- A negative number raised to an even power is positive.
- A negative number raised to an odd power is negative.

Procedure for Determining Values with Negative Exponents

- Invert the number.
- Change the negative exponent to a positive exponent.

Example 1. Find the value of 5^{-2}

Invert the number.

Change the negative exponent to
a positive exponent. $\qquad 5^{-2} = \frac{1}{5^2} = \frac{1}{(5)(5)} = \frac{1}{25}$ *Ans*

Example 2. $2^{-3} = \frac{1}{2^3} = \frac{1}{(2)(2)(2)} = \frac{1}{8}$ *Ans*

Example 3. $(-5)^{-2} = \frac{1}{(-5)^2} = \frac{1}{(-5)(-5)} = \frac{1}{+25} = \frac{1}{25}$ *Ans*

Example 4. $(-4)^{-3} = \frac{1}{(-4)^3} = \frac{1}{(-4)(-4)(-4)} = \frac{1}{-64} = -\frac{1}{64}$ *Ans*

Exercise 7-8

Raise each signed number to the indicated power.

1. $(+2)^2$	13. $(-2)^6$	23. $(-\frac{3}{4})^3$
2. $(-2)^2$	14. $(-1.5)^2$	24. -2^{-2}
3. 2^3	15. $(-1.2)^3$	25. -2^{-1}
4. $(-2)^3$	16. $(-0.3)^2$	26. $+4^{-2}$
5. $(-3)^3$	17. $(-0.3)^3$	27. -3^{-3}
6. $(+3)^3$	18. $+0.3^3$	28. $(-5)^{-2}$
7. 2^4	19. $(-\frac{1}{2})^2$	29. $(-5)^{-3}$
8. $(-2)^4$	20. $(-\frac{1}{2})^3$	30. 6^{-2}
9. $(-2)^5$	21. $(+\frac{1}{2})^3$	31. 2^{-5}
10. $(-5)^2$	22. $(-\frac{3}{4})^2$	32. 1.5^{-2}
11. $(-5)^3$		33. -2.1^{-3}
12. $(-5)^1$		

ROOTS OF SIGNED NUMBERS

A *root* of a number is a quantity which is taken two or more times as an equal factor of the number. The expression $\sqrt[3]{64}$ is called a radical. A *radical* is an indicated root of a number. The symbol $\sqrt{}$ is called a *radical sign* and indicates a root of a number. The digit 3 is called the index. An *index* indicates the number of times that a root is to be taken as an equal factor to produce the given number. The given number 64 is called a *radicand*.

When either a positive number or a negative number are squared, a positive number results. For example, $3^2 = 9$ and $(-3)^2 = 9$. Therefore, every positive number has two square roots, one positive root and one negative root. The square roots of 9 are $+3$ and -3. The expression $\sqrt{9}$ is used to indicate the positive or *principal root*, $+3$ or 3. The expression $-\sqrt{9}$ is used to indicate the negative root, -3. The expression $\pm\sqrt{9}$ indicates both the positive and negative square roots, ± 3. The principal cube root of 8 is 2. The principal cube root of -8 is -2.

$$\sqrt[3]{8} = 2 \qquad \sqrt[3]{-8} = -2$$

Example 1. $\sqrt{36} = \sqrt{(6)(6)} = 6 \ Ans$

Example 2. $\sqrt[4]{16} = \sqrt[4]{(2)(2)(2)(2)} = 2 \ Ans$

Example 3. $\sqrt[3]{(-8)} = \sqrt[3]{(-2)(-2)(-2)} = -2 \ Ans$

Example 4. $\sqrt[5]{32} = \sqrt[5]{(2)(2)(2)(2)(2)} = 2 \ Ans$

Example 5. $\sqrt[3]{\dfrac{-8}{27}} = \sqrt[3]{\dfrac{(-2)(-2)(-2)}{(3)(3)(3)}} = \dfrac{-2}{3} = -\dfrac{2}{3} \ Ans$

NOTE: The square root of a negative number has no solution in the real number system.

Exercise 7-9

Determine the indicated root of each signed number.

1. $\sqrt{+9}$

2. $\sqrt[3]{+64}$

3. $\sqrt[3]{-64}$

4. $\sqrt{64}$

5. $\sqrt[3]{-27}$

6. $\sqrt[3]{-1\,000}$

7. $\sqrt[4]{+81}$

8. $\sqrt[5]{-32}$

9. $\sqrt[3]{-125}$

10. $\sqrt[3]{125}$

11. $\sqrt[7]{-128}$

12. $\sqrt[5]{+32}$

13. $\sqrt{1}$

14. $\sqrt[3]{+1}$

15. $\sqrt[3]{-1}$

16. $\sqrt[5]{-1}$

17. $\sqrt[6]{+1}$

18. $\sqrt[9]{-1}$

19. $\sqrt[4]{81}$

20. $\sqrt[3]{-216}$

21. $\sqrt[3]{\dfrac{8}{27}}$

22. $\sqrt[3]{\dfrac{-8}{+27}}$

23. $\sqrt[3]{\dfrac{+8}{-27}}$

24. $\sqrt[4]{\dfrac{+1}{+16}}$

25. $\sqrt[5]{\dfrac{-1}{+32}}$

26. $\sqrt[3]{\dfrac{+64}{-125}}$

27. $\dfrac{\sqrt{16}}{4}$

28. $\dfrac{16}{\sqrt{4}}$

29. $\dfrac{\sqrt[3]{-27}}{8}$

30. $\dfrac{27}{\sqrt[3]{-8}}$

EXPRESSING NUMBERS WITH FRACTIONAL EXPONENTS AS RADICALS

Procedure for Simplifying Numbers with Fractional Exponents

*   Write the numerator or the fractional exponent as the power of the radicand.

*   Write the denominator of the fractional exponent as the root index of the radicand.

*   Simplify.

Example 1.   Determine the value of $25^{\frac{1}{2}}$.

Write the numerator 1 as the exponent of 25 and the denominator 2 as the root index of 25.

$$25^{\frac{1}{2}} = \sqrt[2]{25^1}$$

Simplify.

$$25^{\frac{1}{2}} = \sqrt{25} = \sqrt{(5)(5)} = 5 \ Ans$$

Example 2.   Determine the value of $8^{\frac{2}{3}}$.

Write the numerator 2 as the exponent of 8 and the denominator 3 as the root index of 8.

$$8^{\frac{2}{3}} = \sqrt[3]{8^2}$$

Simplify.

$$8^{\frac{2}{3}} = \sqrt[3]{8^2} = \sqrt[3]{64} = 4 \; Ans$$

Example 3. $36^{-\frac{1}{2}} = \dfrac{1}{36^{\frac{1}{2}}} = \dfrac{1}{\sqrt{36}} = \dfrac{1}{6} \; Ans$

Exercise 7-10

Determine the value of each.

1. $4^{\frac{1}{2}}$

2. $81^{\frac{1}{2}}$

3. $144^{\frac{1}{2}}$

4. $8^{\frac{1}{3}}$

5. $27^{\frac{1}{3}}$

6. $-8^{\frac{1}{3}}$

7. $16^{\frac{1}{4}}$

8. $81^{\frac{1}{4}}$

9. $-125^{\frac{1}{3}}$

10. $125^{\frac{1}{3}}$

11. $8^{\frac{2}{3}}$

12. $4^{-\frac{1}{2}}$

13. $8^{-\frac{1}{3}}$

14. $-64^{-\frac{1}{3}}$

15. $8^{-\frac{2}{3}}$

COMBINED OPERATIONS OF SIGNED NUMBERS

Expressions consisting of two or more operations of signed numbers are solved using the same order of operations as in arithmetic.

Order of Operations

- First, do all operations within grouping symbols. Grouping symbols are parentheses ( ), brackets [ ], and braces { }.

- Second, do powers and roots.

- Next, do multiplication and division operations in order from left to right.

- Last, do addition and subtraction operations in order from left to right.

Example 1.   Find the value of $50 + (-2)[6 + (-2)^3(4)]$

Perform the operations within brackets in the proper order.

$$50 + (-2)[6 + (-2)^3(4)]$$

Raise to a power.
$-2^3 = -8$

$$50 + (-2)[6 + (-8)(4)]$$

Multiply.
$(-8)(4) = -32$

$$50 + (-2)[6 + (-32)]$$

Add.
$6 + (-32) = -26$

$$50 + (-2)(-26)$$

Multiply.
$(-2)(-26) = +52$

$$50 + 52$$

Add.
$50 + 52 = 102$

102 *Ans*

Example 2. Find the value of $\dfrac{-37 - \sqrt{b^3 - (-8)c + (-7)}}{-3a^2 - b}$ when

$a = -2$, $b = -4$, and $c = 10$.

Substitute for *a, b,* and *c* in the expression.	$\dfrac{-37 - \sqrt{(-4)^3 - (-8)(10) + (-7)}}{-3(-2)^2 - (-4)}$

Perform the operations within the radical sign.

Raise to a power. $(-4)^3 = -64$	$\dfrac{-37 - \sqrt{-64 - (-8)(10) + (-7)}}{-3(-2)^2 - (-4)}$
Multiply. $(-8)(10) = -80$	$\dfrac{-37 - \sqrt{-64 - (-80) + (-7)}}{-3(-2)^2 - (-4)}$
Subtract. $-64 - (-80) = 16$	$\dfrac{-37 - \sqrt{16 + (-7)}}{-3(-2)^2 - (-4)}$
Add. $16 + (-7) = 9$	$\dfrac{-37 - \sqrt{9}}{-3(-2)^2 - (-4)}$
Take the square root. $\sqrt{9} = 3$	$\dfrac{-37 - 3}{-3(-2)^2 - (-4)}$

Complete the operations in the numerator. $-37 - 3 = -40$	$\dfrac{-40}{-3(-2)^2 - (-4)}$

Complete the operations in the denominator.

Raise to a power. $(-2)^2 = 4$	$\dfrac{-40}{-3(4) - (-4)}$
Multiply. $-3(4) = -12$	$\dfrac{-40}{-12 - (-4)}$
Subtract. $-12 - (-4) = -8$	$\dfrac{-40}{-8}$

Divide.

$-40 \div -8 = +5$ or 5   *5 Ans*

Exercise 7-11

Solve each of the combined operation signed number exercises. Use the proper order of operations.

1. $6(-5) + (2)(7) - (-3)(-4)$

2. $\dfrac{2(-1)(-3) - (6)(5)}{3(7) - 9}$

3. $[4 + (2)(-5)]^2 + (-3)$

4. $4(-2) + 3(10 - 4)$

5. $\dfrac{3(5 + 1)}{4(9 - 7) - 2}$

6. $[4^2 + (2)(5)(-3)]^2 + 2(-3)^3$

7. $(-2)^3 + \sqrt{16} - (5)(3)(4)$

8. $\dfrac{2(-5)^2}{2(5)} - \dfrac{(-4)^3}{18 + (-2)}$

9. $(-2)^3 + \sqrt{(-3)(-10) - (-6)} - \sqrt[3]{-8}$

10. $10^{-2} + [43 + (9)(-2)]^{\frac{1}{2}}$

Substitute the given numbers for letters in these expressions and solve. Use the proper order of operations.

11. $6xy + 15 - xy$; $x = -2, y = 5$

12. $\dfrac{-3ab - 2bc}{abc - 35}$; $a = -3, b = 10, c = -4$

13. $rst(2r - 5st)$; $r = -1, s = 4, t = 6$

14. $(x - y)(3x - 2y)$; $x = -5, y = -7$

15. $\dfrac{p(2m - 2w)}{m(p + w) + 8}$; $m = 8, p = -4, w = -2$

16. $\dfrac{d^3 + 4f - fh}{h^2 - (2 + d)}$; $d = -2, f = -3, h = 4$

17. $\dfrac{x^2}{n} - \dfrac{21 + y^3}{xy}$; $n = 5, x = -5, y = -1$

18. $\sqrt{6(ab - 6)} - (b)^3$; $a = -6, b = -2, c = 1$

19. $5\sqrt[3]{e} + (ef - d) - (d)^3$; $d = -10, e = 8, f = -7$

20. $\dfrac{(mpt + pt + 19)^{\frac{1}{2}}}{t^2 + 2p - 7}$; $m = 2, p = -2, t = -5$

UNIT EXERCISE AND PROBLEM REVIEW

Exercise 7-12

WORD EXPRESSIONS AS SIGNED NUMBERS

Express the answer to each of these problems as a signed number.

1. A business profit of $15 000 is expressed as +$15 000. Express a business loss of $20 000.

2. A force of 600 pounds which pulls an object to the left is expressed as −600 pounds. Express a force of 780 pounds which pulls the object to the right.

3. A certain decrease of the cost of wholesale merchandise to a retailer is expressed as −15%. Express a wholesale cost increase of 18%.

4. A circuit current increase of 4.5 amperes is expressed as +4.5 amperes. Express a current decrease of 5.6 amperes.

THE NUMBER SCALE

5. Refer to the number scale shown in figure 7-6. Give the direction (+ or −) and the number of units counted going from the first to the second number.

   a. −3 to +6   c. +4.8 to −4.4   e. −0.8 to −3.2   g. −5.8 to +5.8

   b. −5.4 to 0   d. −0.6 to +0.2   f. +3.4 to +0.6   h. +2.6 to −3.2

Fig. 7-6

6. List each set of signed numbers in order of increasing value starting with the smallest value.

    a. $-5, -23, +8.0, +1, -18, +7.9$

    b. $-7.5, 0, +7.5, -2.3, +0.5, -0.3$

    c. $+21.3, 0, +20.6, -4.6, -7, -23.4$

    d. $+3\frac{1}{2}, -3, +6\frac{3}{4}, -6\frac{7}{8}, -6\frac{13}{16}$

ADDITION AND SUBTRACTION OF SIGNED NUMBERS

Add or subtract the signed numbers as indicated.

7. $-6 + (-13)$

8. $+14 + (-6)$

9. $-25 + (+18)$

10. $50 + (-23)$

11. $+21 + (-21)$

12. $-14.7 + (-3.4)$

13. $-7.2 + (+2.5)$

14. $-10\frac{3}{8} + (-2\frac{3}{4})$

15. $+18 - (+7)$

16. $+5 - (-22)$

17. $-37 - (-31)$

18. $-23 - 0$

19. $0 - (-23)$

20. $-30.7 - (+5.5)$

21. $+0.9 - (-10.6)$

22. $-12\frac{1}{2} - (-4\frac{1}{8})$

23. $15 + (-8) + (-15) + (-10)$

24. $-20 + 12 + (-3) + 36$

25. $-2.9 + 1.6 + 3.2 + 7.5$

26. $2\frac{1}{2} + (-3\frac{3}{4}) + (-\frac{1}{8}) + \frac{3}{8}$

27. $(5 + 9) - (-3 + 6)$

28. $(-13 - 6) - (4 + 7)$

29. $(6.48 - 5.32) - (4 - 8.31)$

30. $(8 - 10\frac{1}{2}) - (9\frac{5}{8} + 2\frac{1}{4})$

MULTIPLICATION AND DIVISION OF SIGNED NUMBERS

Multiply or divide the signed numbers as indicated.

31. $(-5)(3)$

32. $(+10)(-7)$

33. $(-9)(-3)$

34. $(-16)(0)$

35. $(5.6)(-3)$

36. $(-1.2)(-2.1)$

37. $(-0.5)(+0.3)$

38. $(-3)(-3)(-3)$

39. $(-3)(-3)(-3)(-3)$

40. $(1\frac{1}{4})(-2)$

41. $(-3\frac{1}{2})(-2\frac{1}{4})$

42. $(-\frac{1}{4})(-\frac{1}{4})(\frac{1}{4})$

43. $(-5)(-0.2)(3)(-1.8)$

44. $(-0.01)(50)(-2)(0.2)$

45. $-8 \div (-2)$

46. $12 \div (-3)$

47. $\frac{-24}{-3}$

48. $\frac{-21}{7}$

49. $\frac{-5}{0.2}$

50. $\frac{0.8}{-0.1}$

51. $0 \div 12\frac{1}{2}$

52. $-2\frac{1}{2} \div (-1\frac{1}{4})$

53. $\frac{-16.8}{4}$

54. $-3.03 \div (-6)$

POWERS AND ROOTS OF SIGNED NUMBERS

Raise to a power or determine a root as indicated.

55. $(-4)^2$

56. $(-4)^3$

57. $(+4)^3$

58. $(-2)^4$

59. $(-2)^5$

60. $(-2.5)^2$

61. $(-0.2)^3$

62. $(-\frac{1}{4})^2$

63. $(\frac{1}{2})^3$

64. $(-\frac{1}{2})^3$

65. 10^{-2}

66. $(-2)^{-3}$

67. $(-64)^{\frac{1}{3}}$

68. $(16)^{-\frac{1}{2}}$

69. $\sqrt[3]{-27}$

70. $\sqrt[5]{-32}$

71. $\sqrt[4]{81}$

72. $\sqrt[7]{-1}$

73. $\sqrt[3]{-125}$

74. $\sqrt[3]{\dfrac{+27}{-64}}$

75. $\sqrt[5]{\dfrac{1}{+32}}$

76. $\dfrac{\sqrt[3]{-64}}{5}$

COMBINED OPERATIONS OF SIGNED NUMBERS

Solve each combined operation signed number exercise. For exercises 83-88, substitute given numbers for letters, then solve. Use the proper order of operations.

77. $8(-4) + (-1)(6) - (-2)(3)$

78. $\dfrac{4(5 + 1)}{8(9 - 7) - 4}$

79. $[5^2 - (3)(-1)(-4)]^2 + 3(-2)^3$

80. $(-3)^2 + \sqrt[3]{-27} - (3)(-4)(2)$

81. $\sqrt{(-5) - (-6)(+5)} + (4)^2 - (-4)^3$

82. $[64 - (-8)(-6)]^{\frac{1}{2}} - (2)^{-2}$

83. $abc(3a - 4bc);\ a = -2, b = 4, c = 6$

84. $(m - p)(4m - 3p);\ m = -5, p = -8$

85. $\dfrac{x^3 + 2y - ys}{s^2 - (x + 2)};\ x = -2, y = -3, s = 4$

86. $b^3 + \sqrt{8 + (ab - 4)};\ a = -8, b = -4, c = 2$

87. $(-3)\sqrt[3]{d} + (fh - d) - (h)^3;\ d = 8, f = -10, h = -3$

88. $\dfrac{(17 + 2xyt - 2t)^{\frac{1}{2}}}{2y + t^3 - 2};\ x = -3, y = 5, t = -1$

SIGNED NUMBER PROBLEMS

Express the answers as signed numbers for each problem.

89. The daily closing price net changes of a certain stock for one week are shown in figure 7-7. What is the average daily net change in price?

DAY	MON.	TUES.	WED.	THUR.	FRI.
NET CHANGE	$-1\frac{1}{4}$	$+\frac{1}{4}$	$+\frac{7}{8}$	$-\frac{1}{4}$	$+1\frac{5}{8}$

Fig. 7-7

90. An hourly temperature report in degrees Celsius is given in figure 7-8.

a. What is the temperature change for each time period listed?

TIME	TEMPERATURE	TIME	TEMPERATURE
12 Noon	−1.0°C	6 PM	0.4°C
1 PM	1.2°C	7 PM	−1.0°C
2 PM	3.6°C	8 PM	−3.8°C
3 PM	5.8°C	9 PM	−4.4°C
4 PM	3.2°C	10 PM	−6.6°C
5 PM	0°C	11 PM	−8.0°C

Fig. 7-8

   (1)   12 Noon to 3 PM

   (2)   2 PM to 6 PM

   (3)   4 PM to 9 PM

   (4)   3 PM to 11 PM

b. What is the mean or average temperature to 1 decimal place during each time period listed?

   (1)   12 Noon to 5 PM   (3)   6 PM to 11 PM

   (2)   4 PM to 9 PM   (4)   12 Noon to 11 PM

91. During an 8-year period a company experiences profits some years and losses other years. Company annual profits (+) and losses (−) are shown in figure 7-9.

YEAR	1976	1977	1978	1979	1980	1981	1982	1983
Profit (+) or Loss (−)	+$20 000	+$60 000	+$10 000	−$30 000	−$45 000	−$70 000	−$20 000	+$30 000

Fig. 7-9

a. What is the total dollar change for the years listed?

   (1)   1976 to 1977   (3)   1978 to 1979   (5)   1981 to 1982

   (2)   1977 to 1978   (4)   1979 to 1980   (6)   1982 to 1983

b. What is the average annual profit or loss for the years listed?

   (1)   1976 to 1980   (2)   1980 to 1983   (3)   1976 to 1983

92. Holes are drilled in a plate as shown in figure 7-10. The holes are drilled in the sequence shown, that is, hole 1 is drilled first, hole 2 is drilled second, etc. Movement to the left from one hole to the next is expressed as negative (−) direction. Movement to the right from one hole to the next is expressed as positive (+) direction. Express the distance and direction (+ or −) when moving from the holes listed.

a. Hole 1 to hole 2

b. Hole 2 to hole 3

c. Hole 3 to hole 4

d. Hole 4 to hole 5

e. Hole 5 to hole 6

f. Hole 3 to hole 6

g. Hole 6 to hole 3

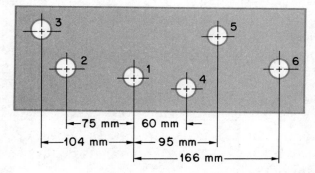

Fig. 7-10

UNIT 8
Basic Algebraic
Operations

OBJECTIVES

After studying this unit you should be able to

- add and subtract single and multiple literal terms.
- multiply and divide single and multiple literal terms.
- compute powers of single and multiple literal terms.
- compute roots of single literal terms.
- remove parentheses which are preceded by plus or minus signs.
- simplify combined operations of literal term expressions.
- solve literal term problems.

A knowledge of basic operations is required in order to solve certain algebraic expressions. In solving trade applied problems, it is sometimes necessary to perform operations with literal or letter values. Formulas given in trade handbooks cannot always be used directly as given, but must be rearranged. Operations are performed to rearrange a formula so that it can be used for a particular occupational application.

DEFINITIONS

It is important that you understand the following definitions in order to apply procedures which are required for solving problems involving basic operations.

A *term* of an algebraic expression is that part of the expression which is separated from the rest by a plus or minus sign. There are five terms in this expression.

$$6x + \frac{xy}{2} - 20 + 2ab - dhx \sqrt[3]{c}$$

A *factor* is one of two or more literal and/or numerical values of a term that are multiplied. For example, 6 and x are each factors of $6x$; 2, a^2 and b are each factors of $2a^2b$; d, h, x^3, and $\sqrt{c}$ are each factors of $dhx^3 \sqrt{c}$.

It is absolutely necessary that you distinguish between factors and terms.

A *numerical coefficient* is the number factor of a term. The letter factors of a term are called *literal factors*. For example, in the term $7xy$, 7 is the numerical coefficient; x and y are the literal factors.

Like terms are terms that have identical literal factors, including exponents. The numerical coefficients do not have to be the same. For example, $3a$ and $10a$ are like terms; $2x^2y$ and $5x^2y$ are like terms.

Unlike terms are terms which have different literal factors or exponents. For example, $8x$ and $8y$ are unlike terms. The terms $12xy$, $4x^2y$, and $5xy^2$ are unlike terms. Although the literal factors are x and y in each of the terms, they are raised to different powers.

ADDITION

Only like terms can be added. The addition of unlike terms can only be indicated. As in arithmetic, like things can be added, but unlike things cannot be added. For example, 2 inches and 3 inches = 5 inches. Both values are like units of measure. Both are inches, therefore, they can be added. It can be readily seen that 2 inches and 3 pounds cannot be added. Inches and pounds are unlike units of measure.

Procedure for Adding Like Terms

- Add the numerical coefficients applying the procedure for addition of signed numbers.
- Leave the literal factors unchanged.

NOTE: If a term does not have numerical coefficient, the coefficient 1 is understood. For example, $x = 1x$; $axy = 1axy$; $c^3dy^2 = 1c^3dy^2$.

Example 1. Add $5x$ and $10x$.

Both terms have the identical literal factor, x. These terms are like terms.

Add the numerical coefficients.

$5 + 10 = 15$

Leave the literal factor unchanged. $5x + 10x =$ **$15x$** *Ans*

Example 2. $R + (-12R) =$ **$-11R$** *Ans*

Example 3. $-7xy + 7xy =$ **0** *Ans*

Example 4. $-14a^2b^3 + (-6a^2b^3) =$ **$-20a^2b^3$** *Ans*

Example 5. $3CD + (-5CD) + 8CD =$ **$6CD$** *Ans*

Procedure for Adding Unlike Terms

The addition of unlike terms can only be indicated.

Example 1.   Add 13 and x.

The literal factors are not identical. These terms are unlike. Indicate the addition. **$13 + x$** *Ans*

Example 2.   Add $12M$ and $8P$

$12M + 8P$ *Ans*

Example 3.   Add $4W$ and $-9W^2$

$4W + (-9W^2)$ *Ans*

Example 4.   Add $-7a$, $-5b$, and $10ab$.

$-7a + (-5b) + 10ab$ *Ans*

Procedure for Adding Expressions that Consist of Two or More Terms

- Group like terms in the same column.

- Add like terms and indicate the addition of the unlike terms.

Example 1.   Add $7x + (-xy) + 5xy^2$ and $-2x + 3xy + (-6xy^2)$.

Group like terms in the same column. $\qquad$ $7x + (-xy) + \quad 5xy^2$
Add the like terms. $\qquad\qquad\qquad\qquad$ $\underline{-2x + \quad 3xy \quad + (-6xy^2)}$
Indicate the addition of the $\qquad\qquad\qquad\quad$ $5x + \quad 2xy \quad + \ (-xy^2)\, Ans$
unlike terms.

Example 2.   Add $[3c + (-4d)], [c + 10d + (-4cd)],$ and $[-12c + (-5cd) + cd^2]$.

$$3c + (\ -4d)$$
$$c + \quad 10d \ + (-4cd)$$
$$\underline{-12c \qquad\qquad\quad + (-5cd) + cd^2}$$
$$-8c + \quad\ 6d \ + (-9cd) + cd^2 \text{ Ans}$$

Exercise 8-1

These expressions consist of groups of single terms. Add these terms.

1. $4a, 7a$
2. $6b, 12b$
3. $-7x, 3x$
4. $7x, -3x$
5. $20y, y$
6. $15xy, 7xy$
7. $-15xy, -7xy$
8. $25m^2, -m^2$
9. $-5x^2y, 5x^2y$
10. $4c^3, 0$
11. $-7pt, -pt$
12. $0.4x, -0.8x$
13. $8.3a^2b, 6.9a^2b$
14. $-0.02y, 0.07y$
15. $\frac{1}{2}xy, \frac{3}{4}xy$
16. $2\frac{7}{8}c^2d, -3\frac{1}{8}c^2d$
17. $-2.06gh^3, -0.85gh^3$
18. $-50.6abc, 50.5abc$
19. $4P, -6P, P, 7P$
20. $-0.3dt^2, -1.7dt^2, -dt^2$
21. $\frac{1}{4}xy, \frac{7}{8}xy, xy, -4xy$
22. $20.06D, -19.97D, -0.9D$
23. $6M, 0.6M, 0.06M, 0.006M$
24. $-\frac{3}{8}C, -C, 2C, -\frac{1}{16}C$

These expressions consist of groups of two or more terms. Group like terms and add.

25. $(6x + 8y), (7x + 10y)$
26. $(2a + 6b + 3c), (a + 5b + 4c)$
27. $(x + 4xy + 3y), (9x + 3xy + y)$
28. $[6a + (-10ab)], [(-a) + 12ab]$
29. $[3x + (-9xy) + y], [x + 8xy + (-y)]$
30. $[(-8cd) + 7c^2d + 14cd^2], [7cd + (-12c^2d) + (-17cd^2)]$

31. $[3x^2y + 4xy^2 + (-15x^2y^2)], [(-2x^2y) + (-5xy^2)]$

32. $[1.3M + (-3N)], [(-8M) + 0.5N], [20M + (-0.7N)]$

33. $[c + 3.6cd + (-5.7d)], [(-1.4c) + 8.6d]$

34. $[0.5T + (-2.8T^2) + (-T^3)], [5.5T^2 + 0.7T^3]$

35. $[b^4 + 4b^3c + 3b^2c], [5b^4 + (-4b^3c) + (-9b^2c)]$

36. $[1\frac{1}{2}P + (-\frac{1}{2}V) + (\frac{1}{4}PV)], [\frac{3}{4}P + \frac{3}{4}V + (-2PV) + (-P^2V)]$

Determine the literal value answers for these problems.

37. Six stamping machines produce the same product. The number of pieces per hour produced by each machine is shown in figure 8-1. What is the total number of pieces produced per hour by all six machines?

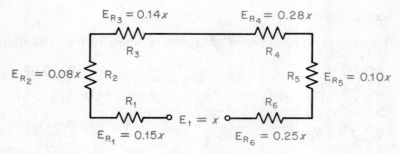

MACHINE	#1	#2	#3	#4	#5	#6
NUMBER OF PIECES PRODUCED PER HOUR	x	0.8x	1.3x	0.6x	1.5x	1.2x

Fig. 8-1

38. The total voltage (E_t), in volts, of the circuit shown in figure 8-2 is represented as x. The amount of voltage taken by each of the 6 resistors is given as E_{R_1} - E_{R_6}. What is the sum of the voltage taken by the resistors listed?

    a. R_1 and R_2

    b. R_3 and R_4

    c. R_4, R_5, and R_6

    d. all six resistors

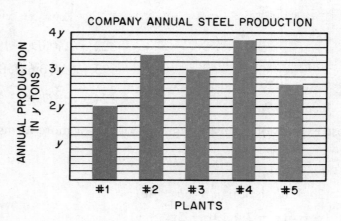

Fig. 8-2

39. A checking account has a balance represented as B. The following deposits are made: $\frac{1}{2}B$, $\frac{3}{4}B$, $\frac{1}{4}B$, and $2B$. No checks are issued during this time. What is the new balance?

40. A steel manufacturing company has 5 plants. The annual production, in tons, given in terms of y is shown in figure 8-3. How many tons are produced by the plants listed?

    a. plants 1 and 2

    b. plants 3 and 4

    c. plants 2, 3, and 4

    d. all 5 plants

41. The machined plate distances shown in figure 8-4 are dimensioned, in millimetres, in terms of x. Determine dimensions A-G.

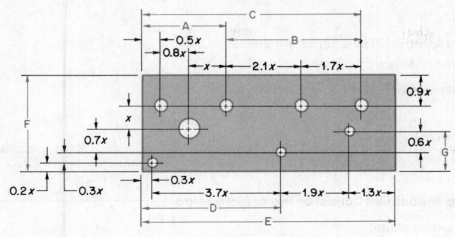

Fig. 8-4

SUBTRACTION

As in addition, only like terms can be subtracted. The subraction of unlike
terms can only be indicated. The same principles apply in arithmetic. For example,
7 metres − 5 metres = 2 metres. Both values are like units of measure. Both are
metres, therefore, they can be subtracted. The values 7 metres and 5 litres cannot
be subtracted. Metres and litres are unlike units of measure.

Procedures for Subtracting Like Terms

- Subtract the numerical coefficients applying the procedure for subtraction
  of signed numbers.
- Leave the literal factors unchanged.

Example 1. $14xy - (-6xy)$

Both terms have identical literal factors, xy. These terms are like terms.

Subtract the numerical coeffients.

$14 - (-6) = 20$

Leave the literal factor unchanged. $14xy - (-6xy) = 20xy$ *Ans*

Example 2. $16H - 13H = 3H$ *Ans*

Example 3. $ab - 10ab = -9ab$ *Ans*

Example 4. $-4L^2 - 7L^2 = -11L^2$ *Ans*

Example 5. $-15x^2y - (-15x^2y) = 0$ *Ans*

Procedure for Subtracting Unlike Terms

- The subtraction of unlike terms can only be indicated.

Example 1.   Subtract $3b$ from $4a$.

The literal factors are not identical. These terms are unlike.

Indicate the subtraction. $4a - 3b$ *Ans*

Example 2.   Subtract $5xy^2$ from $-16xy$.

$-16xy - 5xy^2$ *Ans*

Example 3.   Subtract $-2P$ from $-PT$

$-PT - (-2P)$ or $-PT + 2P$ *Ans*

Procedure for Subtracting Expressions that Consist of Two or More Terms

- Group like terms in the same column.
- Subtract like terms and indicate the subtractions of the unlike terms.

NOTE: Each term of the subtrahend is subtracted following the procedure for subtraction of signed numbers.

Example 1.   Subtract $6a + 8b - 5c$ from $9a - 13b + 7c$.

Group like terms in the same column.

$$9a - 13b + 7c$$
$$- \quad (6a + \ 8b - 5c)$$

Change the sign of each term in the subtrahend and follow the procedure for addition of signed numbers.

$$9a - 13b + 7c$$
$$+ (-6a - \ 8b + 5c)$$
$$\overline{3a - 21b + 12c} \ Ans$$

Example 2.   Subtract. $(4x^2 + 6x - 15xy) - (9x^2 - x - 2y + 5y^2)$

$$4x^2 + 6x - 15xy \qquad = \quad 4x^2 + 6x - 15xy$$
$$- (9x^2 - \ x \qquad - 2y + 5y^2) \quad = -9x^2 + \ x \qquad + 2y - 5y^2$$
$$\overline{-5x^2 + 7x - 15xy + 2y - 5y^2} \ Ans$$

Exercise 8-2

These expressions consist of groups of single terms. Subtract terms as indicated.

1. $5x - 3x$

2. $5x - (-3x)$

3. $-7a - a$

4. $-6ab - (-4ab)$

5. $3y^2 - 11y^2$

6. $10xy - (-10xy)$

7. $-10xy - (-10xy)$

8. $-12c^2 - c^2$

9. $-12c^2 - (-c^2)$

10. $0 - 16M$

11. $0 - (-16M)$

12. $0.5x^2y - 1.2x^2y$

13. $-18.7P - (-12.6P)$

14. $-ax^3 - 2ax^3$

15. $0.025D - (-0.075D)$

16. $8.12n - 8.82n$

17. $\frac{1}{2}c^2d - (-\frac{1}{2}c^2d)$

18. $-\frac{1}{2}c^2d - (-\frac{1}{2}c^2d)$

19. $1\frac{3}{4}H - \frac{3}{8}H$

20. $\frac{3}{8}H - 1\frac{3}{4}H$

21. $-2.7xy - 3.4xy$

22. $2.03F - (-0.08F)$

23. $0 - (-g^2h)$

24. $-3\frac{3}{16}G - 5\frac{5}{8}G$

These expressions consist of groups of two or more terms. Group like terms and subtract.

25. $(3P^2 - 2P) - (6P^2 - 7P)$

26. $(5x + 9xy) - (2x + 6xy)$

27. $(10y^2 + 2) - (10y^2 - 2)$

28. $(10y^2 - 2) - (10y^2 - 2)$

29. $(3N + 12NS) - (4N + NS)$

30. $(ab - a^2b + ab^2) - 0$

31. $0 - (ab - a^2b + ab^2)$

32. $(0.5y - 0.7y^2) - (y - 0.2y^2)$

33. $(-x^3 + x^2 - x) - (-6x^3 + 2x)$

34. $(15L - 12H) - (-12L + 6H - 4)$

35. $(-\frac{1}{2}x + \frac{1}{4}x^2 - \frac{1}{8}x^3) - (-\frac{1}{4}x + \frac{1}{4}x^3)$

36. $(\frac{3}{8}R - \frac{1}{8}D + 2\frac{1}{4}) - (\frac{3}{8}D - 3\frac{5}{8})$

37. $(11.09e + 14.76f) - (e - f - 10.03)$

38. $(-20T + 8.5T^2 - 0.3T^3) - (T^3 + 4.4)$

Determine the literal value answers for these problems.

39. The support bracket dimensions shown in figure 8-5 are given, in inches, in terms of x. Determine dimensions A-F.

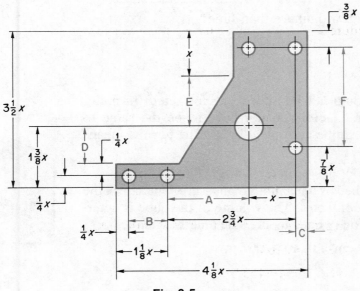

Fig. 8-5

40. An employee earns a gross wage represented as W. The employee's payroll deductions are shown in figure 8-6. What is the employee's net wage?

TYPE OF DEDUCTION	FEDERAL INCOME TAX	SOCIAL SECURITY	HEALTH AND ACCIDENT INSURANCE	RETIREMENT	MISCELLANEOUS
AMOUNT OF DEDUCTION	0.18W	0.065W	0.05W	0.04W	0.035W

Fig. 8-6

41. A field is shown in figure 8-7. The perimeter of the field, in metres, is $10x$.
    What is the length of side A of the field?

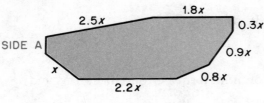

2.5x   1.8x
0.3x
SIDE A
0.9x
x
0.8x
2.2x

Fig. 8-7

42. A company's monthly earnings for a 6-month
    period are shown in the graph in figure 8-8.

    a. How much less are the earnings in February
       than January?

    b. How much less are the earnings in April
       than March?

    c. How much less are the earnings in April
       than February?

    d. How much less are the earnings in May
       than June?

    e. How much less are the earnings in March
       than May?

    f. How much less are the earnings in January than June?

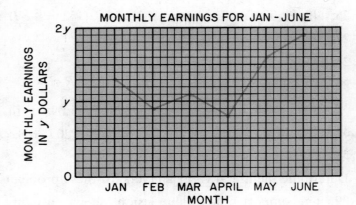

Fig. 8-8

MULTIPLICATION

It was shown that unlike terms could not be added or subtracted. In multiplication, the exponents of the literal factors do not have to be the same to multiply the values. For example, x^2 can be multiplied by x^4. The term x^2 means $(x)(x)$. The term x^4 means $(x)(x)(x)(x)$.

$$(x^2)(x^4) = (x)(x)(x)(x)(x)(x) = x^{2+4} = x^6$$

Area units of measure can be multiplied by linear units of measure. One side of the cube shown in figure 8-9 has an area of 9 cm^2. The volume of the cube is determined by multiplying the area of a side (9 cm^2) by the side length (3 cm).

$$\text{Volume} = (9 \text{ cm}^2)(3 \text{ cm}) = 27 \text{ cm}^3$$

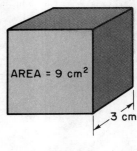

Fig. 8-9

Procedure for Multiplying Two or More Terms

- Multiply the numerical coefficients following the procedure for multiplication of signed numbers.

- Add the exponents of the same literal factors.

- Show the product as a combination of all numerical and literal factors.

Example 1. Multiply. $(2xy^2)(-3x^2y^3)$

Multiply the numerical coefficients following the procedure for multiplication of signed numbers. $(2)(-3) = -6$

Add the exponents of the same literal factors.

$(x^1)(x^2) = x^{1+2} = x^3$

$(y^2)(y^3) = y^{2+3} = y^5$

Show the product as a combination of all numerical and literal factors.

$(2xy^2)(-3x^2y^3) = -6x^3y^5$ *Ans*

Example 2. $(-4a^2b^3)(-5a^2b^4) = (-4)(-5)(a^{2+2})(b^{3+4}) = 20a^4b^7$ *Ans*

Example 3. $(-2)(3a)(-5b^2c^2)(-2ac^3d^3) = (-2)(3)(-5)(-2)(a^{1+1})(b^2)(c^{2+3})(d^3)$
$= -60a^2b^2c^5d^3$ *Ans*

It is sometimes necessary to multiply expressions that consist of more than one term within an expression, such as $3a(6 + 4a)$ and $(2x - 4y)(-x + 5y)$.

Procedure for Multiplying Expressions that Consist of More than One Term within an Expression

- Multiply each term of one expression by each term of the other expression.
- Combine like terms.

Before applying the procedure to algebraic expressions, two examples are given to show that the procedure is consistent with arithmetic.

Arithmetic Example 1. Multiply. $2(3 + 4)$

From arithmetic: $2(3 + 4) = 2(7) = 14$ *Ans*

From algebra:

Multiply each term of one expression by each term of the other expression.

$2(3 + 4) = 2(3) + 2(4) = 6 + 8$

Combine like terms. $6 + 8 = 14$ *Ans*

Arithmetic Example 2. Multiply. $(5 + 3)(2 + 4)$

From arithmetic: $(5 + 3)(2 + 4) = (8)(6) = 48$ *Ans*

From algebra:

Multiply each term of one expression by each term of the other expression.

Step 1	Step 2	Step 3	Step 4	
↓	↓	↓	↓	
$5(2)$ +	$5(4)$ +	$3(2)$ +	$3(4)$ =	
10 +	20 +	6 +	12	

Combine like terms. $10 + 20 + 6 + 12 = 48$ *Ans*

Algebra Example 1.   Multiply: $3a(6 + 2a^2)$

Multiply each term of one expression by each term of the other expression.

$3a(6 + 2a^2) = (3a)(6) + 3a(2a^2) = 18a + 6a^3$

Combine like terms. Since $18a$ and $6a^3$ are unlike terms, they cannot be combined. The answer is $\mathbf{18a + 6a^3}$. *Ans*

Algebra Example 2.   Multiply: $(3c + 5d^2)(4d^2 - 2c)$

Multiply each term of one expression by each term of the other expression.

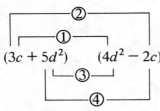

Step 1		Step 2		Step 3		Step 4
$\downarrow$		$\downarrow$		$\downarrow$		$\downarrow$
$3c(4d^2)$	$+$	$3c(-2c)$	$+$	$5d^2(4d^2)$	$+$	$5d^2(-2c)$ $=$
$12cd^2$	$+$	$(-6c^2)$	$+$	$20d^4$	$+$	$(-10cd^2)$

Combine like terms.

$\overline{\text{COMBINE}}$

$12cd^2 + (-6c^2) + 20d^4 + (-10cd^2) =$

$2cd^2 + (-6c^2) + 20d^4$ or

$\mathbf{2cd^2 - 6c^2 + 20d^4}$ *Ans*

Exercise 8-3

These expressions consist of single terms. Multiply these terms as indicated.

1. $(x)(2x^2)$
2. $(4ab)(6a^2b^2)$
3. $(2c^2)(-5c^3)$
4. $(-10x)(-7x^2)$
5. $(9ab^2c)(3a^2bc^4)$
6. $(-5x^2y^2)(x^3y^3)$
7. $(6cd^2)(2c^4d)$
8. $(-15M)(0)$
9. $(-12P^5N^4)(-P^3)$
10. $(-12P^5N^4)(-P^3)(-1)$
11. $(2.5x^4y)(0.5y^3)$
12. $(0.2ST^2)(-0.3S^4)$
13. $(15V^2)(0)(-2V)$

14. $(\frac{1}{2}x^3)(\frac{1}{4}x^2y)$
15. $(-\frac{3}{4}x^2y)(-\frac{5}{8}x^3y^2)$
16. $(-6)(-LW^2)(W)$
17. $(a^2b)(bc)(d)$
18. $(-a^2b)(bc)(d)$
19. $(0.6F)(3F^2G)(G^2)$
20. $(-4.2m^2n)(-5m^3)(-m)$
21. $(10xy)(-2xy^3)(-4p)$
22. $(-\frac{1}{3}B)(\frac{1}{2}C^2D)(-BD^2)$
23. $(x^3y^2)(-x^2y)(-x)$
24. $(0.06H^2L^2)(-1)(5L)$

These expressions consist of groups of two or more terms. Multiply as indicated and combine like terms where possible.

25. $2x(3x + y)$

26. $a^2(a + b + b^2)$

27. $3M(M^2 - MN)$

28. $-6x^3(-x - x^2y)$

29. $10c^2d(3cd^3 - 4d)$

30. $-2(PV + V^2 - 6)$

31. $r^2t^3s(-r^2s^2 + s - r^3t)$

32. $-0.3 L^2H(-0.4H^3 - L + 4H^2)$

33. $-1(f^2g - 9fg^2 + 12fh)$

34. $-1(-f^2g + 9fg^2 - 12fh)$

35. $(x + y)(x + y)$

36. $(x - y)(x + y)$

37. $(x - y)(x - y)$

38. $(A + F)(A - 20)$

39. $(4a + 5)(a^3 + 6)$

40. $(2m^2 - n^3)(-3m^3 + 6n)$

41. $(3ax^2 + cx)(7a^2x^3 - c^2)$

42. $(-0.1S^3T - 10)(0.5T^2 - 0.2S^2)$

43. $(4x^2y^3 - 6xy)(4x^2y^3 + 6xy)$

44. $(-4x^2y^3 + 6xy)(-4x^2y^3 + 6xy)$

Determine the literal value answers for these problems.

45. A gear speed is measured in revolutions per minute (r/min). The speed of a gear is represented by N.

   a. How many revolutions does the gear turn in 15 minutes?

   b. When the gear speed is reduced by 20 revolutions per minute, the speed is $N - 20$ r/min. How many revolutions does the gear turn in $6\frac{1}{2}$ minutes at the reduced speed?

46. A rectangle is shown in figure 8-10. The area of a rectangle equals its length times its width.

   a. What is the area of the rectangle?

   b. What is the area of the rectangle if the width is increased by 3 inches?

   c. What is the area of the rectangle if the width is increased by 5 inches and the length is decreased by 6 inches?

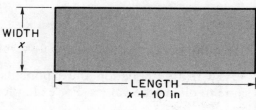

WIDTH
x

LENGTH
$x + 10$ in

Fig. 8-10

47. Power (watts) is equal to the product of current (amperes) and voltage (volts). In the electrical circuit shown in figure 8-11, the current received by each of the resistors R_1-R_5 is $3y$ and the voltage is $0.2x$. The amperes received by each of the resistors R_6-R_9 is $5y$ and the voltage is $0.25x$.

   a. What is the power, in watts, of each of the resistors R_1-R_5?

   b. What is the power, in watts, of each of the resistors R_6-R_9?

   c. What is the total power, in watts, of resistors R_1-R_5?

   d. What is the total power, in watts, of resistors R_6-R_9?

   e. What is the total power, in watts, of the complete circuit?

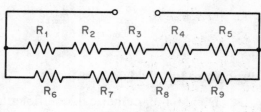

Fig. 8-11

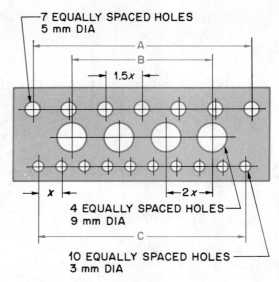

48. The distances, in millimetres, are given between 2 consecutive holes for each of the 3 sets of holes in the face plate
shown in figure 8-12.

    a. Determine distance A, distance B, and distance C.

    b. The distance between 2 consecutive 5-mm diameter holes
        is decreased by 0.7 mm. Determine distance A.

    c. The distance between 2 consecutive 9-mm diameter holes
        is increased by 1.08 mm. Determine distance B.

Fig. 8-12

49. The diameter, in metres, of the storage tank shown in figure 8-13 is x and
the height is $0.5x$. The approximate volume (number of cubic metres) of the
storage tank is computed by multiplying 0.785 4 times the square of the
diameter times the height.

    a. Determine the volume (number of cubic metres) of the tank when the tank
        is full.

    b. Determine the volume (number of cubic metres) in the tank when the tank
        is filled to a height 6 metres below the top of the tank.

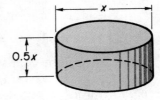

Fig. 8-13

DIVISION

As with multiplication, the exponents of the literal factors do not have to be the
same to divide the values. For example, x^4 can be divided by x.

$$\frac{x^4}{x} = \frac{(x)(x)(x)(x)}{x} = x^{4-1} = x^3$$

Volume units of measure can be divided by linear units of measure. The container
shown in figure 8-14 has a volume of 480 cm³ and a height of 6 cm. The area of
the container top is determined by dividing the volume by the height.

$$\text{Top Area} = \frac{480 \text{ cm}^3}{6 \text{ cm}} = 80 \text{ cm}^2$$

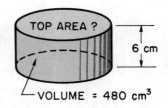

Fig. 8-14

Procedure for Dividing Two Terms

-   Divide the numerical coefficients following the procedure for division
    of signed numbers.

-   Subtract the exponents of the literal factors of the divisor from the exponents
    of the same letter factors of the dividend.

-   Combine numerical and literal factors.

Example 1.   Divide $-12a^3$ by $3a$.

Divide the numerical coefficients following the procedure for signed numbers.

$-12 \div 3 = -4$

Subtract the exponents of the literal factors in the divisor from the exponents of the same letter factors in the dividend.

$a^3 \div a = a^{3-1} = a^2$

Combine the numerical and literal factors.

$\dfrac{-12a^3}{3a} = -4a^2 \; Ans$

Example 2.   Divide. $(-20a^3x^5y^2) \div (-2ax^2)$

Divide the numerical coefficients following the procedure for signed numbers.

$-20 \div -2 = 10$

Subtract the exponents of the literal factors in the divisor from the exponents of the same letter factors in the dividend.

$a^{3-1} = a^2$

$x^{5-2} = x^3$

$y^2 = y^2$

Combine. $\dfrac{-20a^3x^5y^2}{-2ax^2} = 10a^2x^3y^2 \; Ans$

In arithmetic, any number except 0 divided by itself equals 1. For example, $5 \div 5 = 1$. Applying the division procedure $5 \div 5 = 5^{1-1} = 5^0$. Therefore, $5^0 = 1$. Any number except 0 raised to the zero power equals 1.

Example 1. $\dfrac{6^2}{6^2} = 6^{2-2} = 6^0 = 1 \; Ans$

Example 2. $\dfrac{a^3b^2c}{a^3b^2c} = (a^{3-3})(b^{2-2})(c^{1-1}) = a^0b^0c^0 = (1)(1)(1) = 1 \; Ans$

Example 3. $\dfrac{4P}{P} = 4P^{1-1} = 4P^0 = 4(1) = 4 \; Ans$

Procedure for Dividing when the Dividend Consists of More than One Term

- Divide each term of the dividend by the divisor following the procedure for division of signed numbers.

- Combine terms.

Before applying the procedure to algebraic expressions an example is given to show that the procedure is consistent with arithmetic.

Arithmetic Example.

From arithmetic: $(12 + 8) \div 4 = 20 \div 4 = 5 \; Ans$

From algebra:

Divide each term of the dividend by the divisor.

$\dfrac{12 + 8}{4} = \dfrac{12}{4} + \dfrac{8}{4} = 3 + 2$

Combine terms. $3 + 2 = 5 \; Ans$

Algebra Example.   Divide. $\dfrac{-16x^2y + 8x^3y^2 + 24x^5y^3z}{-8x^2y}$

Divide each term of the dividend by the divisor.

$-16x^2y \div -8x^2y = 2x^{2-2}y^{1-1} = 2x^0y^0 = 2(1)(1) = 2$

$+8x^3y^2 \div -8x^2y = -1x^{3-2}y^{2-1} = -1xy = -xy$

$+24x^5y^3z \div -8x^2y = -3x^{5-2}y^{3-1}z^{1-0} = -3x^3y^2z$

Combine. $2 - xy - 3x^3y^2z$ *Ans*

Exercise 8-4.

These exercises require division of single terms. Divide terms as indicated.

1. $4x^2 \div 2x$

2. $21a^4 \div 7a$

3. $10T^2 \div 5T^2$

4. $-16a^4b^5 \div 4ab^3$

5. $25x^3y^4 \div 5x^2$

6. $FS^2 \div (-FS^2)$

7. $-FS^2 \div (-FS^2)$

8. $0 \div 14mn$

9. $(-42a^5d^2) \div (-7a^2d^2)$

10. $(-3.6H^2P) \div (0.6HP)$

11. $DM^2 \div (-1)$

12. $-DM^2 \div (-1)$

13. $2.6ab \div ab$

14. $0.8PV^2 \div (-0.2V)$

15. $1\frac{1}{4}c^2d^3 \div \frac{1}{4}cd^2$

16. $(-\frac{1}{2}x^3y^3) \div \frac{1}{8}x^3$

17. $-6g^3h^2 \div (-\frac{3}{4}gh)$

18. $-24x^2y^5 \div (-0.5x^2y^4)$

19. $x^2y^3z^4 \div xy^3z$

20. $18a^2bc^2y \div (-a^2)$

21. $\frac{1}{4}P^2V \div \frac{1}{16}$

22. $-0.08xy \div 0.4y$

23. $-9.6x^2yz \div (-1.2x)$

24. $\frac{3}{4}FS^3 \div (-3S)$

These exercises consist of expressions in which the dividends have two or more terms. Divide as indicated.

25. $(6x^3 + 10x^2) \div 2x$

26. $(6x^3 - 10x^2) \div (-2x)$

27. $(12x^3y^3 - 8x^2y^2) \div 4xy$

28. $(35a^2 + 15a^3) \div (-a)$

29. $(14M - 12MN) \div (-1)$

30. $(21b - 24c) \div 3$

31. $(-36a^2b^5 - 27a^3b^4) \div (-9ab^4)$

32. $(15TF^2 - 45T^2F + 30) \div (-15)$

33. $(0.6x^4y^5 + 0.2x^3y^4) \div 2x^3y^2$

34. $(0.5D^2 - 1.5D^2H - 2.5D^3) \div 10D^2$

35. $(-x^3y^3z + x^2z^4 + x^3y) \div (-x^2)$

36. $(5MN^3P^2 - 2M^3N^3P) \div 0.01MN^2P$

37. $(\frac{1}{2}a^2c - \frac{3}{4}a^3c^2 - ac^3) \div \frac{1}{8}ac$

38. $(-2.5e^2f - 0.5ef^2 + e^2f^2) \div 0.5f$

39. $(\frac{3}{10}EG^2 + \frac{7}{10}E^2G^3 - \frac{9}{10}E^3GH) \div (-\frac{1}{10}EG)$

40. $(0.8x^2y^3z - 0.6xy^2z^2 + 0.4y^2) \div (0.2y^2)$

Determine the literal value answers for the following problems.

41. A concrete slab is shown in figure 8-15. The thickness of a slab is determined by dividing the slab volume by the face area. The face area is determined by dividing the volume by the thickness. Dimensions of 6 slabs of different sizes are given in the table in figure 8-16. Determine either the thickness or face area as required.

Fig. 8-15

	VOLUME (cubic metres)	FACE AREA (square metres)	THICKNESS (metres)		VOLUME (cubic feet)	FACE AREA (square feet)	THICKNESS (feet)
a.	$1\,000x^3$	$500x^2$	?	d.	$2\,400x^3$	?	$0.25x$
b.	$750x^3$	$1\,500x^2$	?	e.	$2\,100x^3$	?	$1.4x$
c.	$1\,920x^3$	$1\,600x^2$	?	f.	$360x^3$	?	$0.09x$

Fig. 8-16

42. Twenty loaves of bread are made from a batch of dough. The weight, in pounds, of the dough is represented by x.

a. What is the weight of each of the 20 loaves?

b. If the batch of dough is increased by an additional 5 pounds of dough, what is the weight of each of the 20 loaves?

c. If the batch of dough is decreased by $0.2x$, what is the weight of each of the 20 loaves?

43. If x represents a number of inches, a sheet of stock is $x + 8$ inches wide and $2x + 4$ inches long as shown in figure 8-17. A sheet metal technician shears the stock into 100 pieces of equal size as shown.

a. What is the width of each sheared piece?

b. What is the length of each sheared piece?

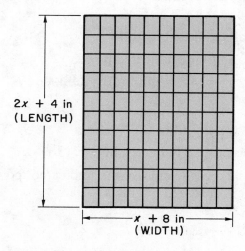

$2x + 4$ in
(LENGTH)

$x + 8$ in
(WIDTH)

Fig. 8-17

44. The daily sales amounts of a company for one week are shown in the chart in figure 8-18. Determine the average daily sales amount when x represents a number of dollars.

DAY	MONDAY	TUESDAY	WEDNESDAY	THURSDAY	FRIDAY
AMOUNT	$4x + \$180$	$5x + \$120$	$3x + \$200$	$5x$	$3x + \$250$

Fig. 8-18

45. Refer to the drill jig shown in figure 8-19 and determine, in millimetres, distances A, B, C, and D. The values of x and y represent a number of millimetres.

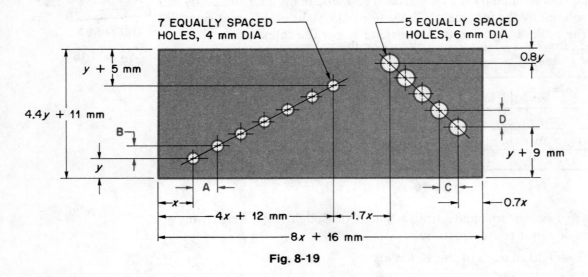

Fig. 8-19

POWERS

Procedure for Raising a Single Term to a Power

- Raise the numerical coefficients to the indicated power following the procedure for powers of signed numbers.

- Multiply each of the literal factor exponents by the exponent of the power to which it is raised.

- Combine numerical and literal factors.

Arithmetic Example.   Raise to the indicated power. $(2^2)^3$

From arithmetic: $(2^2)^3 = (4)^3 = (4)(4)(4) = 64$ *Ans*

From algebra:

$(2^2)^3 = 2^{2(3)} = 2^6 = (2)(2)(2)(2)(2)(2) = 64$ *Ans*

Algebra Example 1.   Raise to the indicated power. $(5x^3)^2$

Raise the numerical coefficient to the indicated power following the procedure for powers of signed numbers.

$5^2 = 25$

Multiply each literal factor exponent by the exponent of the power to which it is to be raised.

$$(x^3)^2 = x^{3(2)} + x^6$$

Combine numerical and literal factors. $(5x^3)^2 = 25x^6$ *Ans*

NOTE: $(x^3)^2$ is not the same as x^3x^2.

$$(x^3)^2 = (x^3)(x^3) = (x)(x)(x)(x)(x)(x) = x^6$$
$$x^3x^2 = (x)(x)(x)(x)(x) = x^5$$

Algebra Example 2.   Solve. $(-4x^2y^4z)^3$

Raise the numerical coefficient to the indicated power.

$$(-4)^3 = (-4)(-4)(-4) = -64$$

Multiply the exponents of the literal factors by the indicated power.

$$(x^2y^4z)^3 = x^{2(3)}y^{4(3)}z^{1(3)} = x^6y^{12}z^3$$

Combine. $(-4x^2y^4z)^3 = -64x^6y^{12}z^3$ *Ans*

Algebra Example 3.   Solve. $[-\frac{1}{4}a^3(bc^2)^3d^4]^2$

Perform the correct order of operations. $[-\frac{1}{4}a^3(bc^2)^3d^4]^2 =$

$$(bc^2)^3 = b^3c^6 \qquad\qquad\qquad [-\frac{1}{4}a^3b^3c^6d^4]^2 =$$

Apply the power procedure.

$$(-\frac{1}{4})^2 = \frac{1}{16}$$
$$(a^3)^2 = a^6$$
$$(b^3)^2 = b^6$$
$$(c^6)^2 = c^{12}$$
$$(d^4)^2 = d^8$$

Combine. $\frac{1}{16}a^6b^6c^{12}d^8$ *Ans*

Procedure for Raising Two or More Terms to a Power

• Apply the procedure for multiplying expressions that consist of more than one term.

Example.   Solve. $(3a + 5b^3)^2$

	Step 1	Step 2	Step 3	Step 4
$(3a + 5b^3)(3a + 5b^3)$	$= 3a(3a)$	$+\ 3a(5b^3)$	$+\ 5b^3(3a)$	$+\ 5b^3(5b^3)$
	$9a^2$	$+\ 15ab^3$	$+\ 15ab^3$	$+\ 25b^6$

$$9a^2 + 30ab^3 + 25b^6 \ Ans$$

Exercise 8-5

These exercises consist of expressions with single terms. Raise terms to the indicated powers.

1. $(ab)^2$
2. $(DF)^3$
3. $(3ab)^2$
4. $(-4xy)^2$
5. $(2x^2y)^3$
6. $(4a^4b^3)^2$
7. $(-3c^3d^2e^4)^3$
8. $(2MS^2)^4$
9. $(-7x^4y^5)^2$
10. $(-3N^2P^2T^3)^4$
11. $(a^2bc^3)^3$
12. $(-2a^2bc^3)^3$
13. $(-x^4y^5z)^3$

14. $(9C^4F^2H)^2$
15. $(0.4x^3y)^3$
16. $(-0.5c^2d^3e)^3$
17. $(3.2M^3NP^2)^2$
18. $(\frac{1}{2}x^3y^2z)^2$
19. $(\frac{3}{4}abc^3)^3$
20. $[-8(a^2b^3)^2c]^2$
21. $[-3x^2(y^2)^2z^3]^3$
22. $[0.6d^3(ef^2)^3]^2$
23. $[\frac{5}{8}(a^2bc^3)^2]^2$
24. $[(-2x^2y)^2(xy^2)^2]^3$

These exercises consist of expressions of more than one term. Raise these expressions to the indicated powers and combine like terms where possible.

25. $(a + b)^2$
26. $(a - b)^2$
27. $(x^2 + y)^2$
28. $(D^3 + G^4)^2$
29. $(2x^2 - 3y^3)^2$
30. $(6m^2 - 5n^2)^2$

31. $(x^2y^3 + xy^2)^2$
32. $(0.9c^3e^2 - 0.2e)^2$
33. $(4.5M^2P - P^4)^2$
34. $(\frac{3}{4}d^2h + \frac{1}{4}dh^2)^2$
35. $[(a^2)^3 - (b^3)^2]^2$
36. $[(-x^4y)^2 + (x^2y)^3]^2$

Determine the literal value answers for the following problems.

37. The area of the square shown in figure 8-20 is computed by squaring the length of a side ($A = s^2$). Express the areas of squares for each of the side lengths given in figure 8-21.

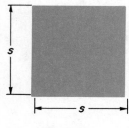

Fig. 8-20

	LENGTH OF SIDE (s)	AREA (A)
a.	7x	?
b.	0.25x	?
c.	$3\frac{1}{4}x$	?
d.	x + 3 m	?
e.	2x + 6 in	?

Fig. 8-21

38. The volume of a cube shown in figure 8-22 is computed by cubing the length of a side ($V = s^3$). Express the volumes of cubes for each of the side lengths given in figure 8-23.

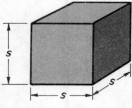

Fig. 8-22

	LENGTH OF SIDE (s)	VOLUME (V)
a.	$5x$	?
b.	$0.2x$	?
c.	$10\frac{1}{2}x$	?
d.	$1.8x$	?

Fig. 8-23

39. The approximate area of the circle shown in figure 8-24 is computed by multiplying 3.14 times the square of the radius ($A = 3.14R^2$). Express the areas of circles for each radius given in figure 8-25.

Fig. 8-24

	LENGTH OF RADIUS (R)	AREA (A)
a.	$4x$	?
b.	$0.2x$	?
c.	$7.1x$	?
d.	$x + 2$ ft	?
e.	$3x + 1$ mm	?

Fig. 8-25

40. The approximate volume of the sphere shown in figure 8-26 is computed by multiplying 0.52 times the cube of the diameter ($V = 0.52D^3$). Express the volumes of spheres for each diameter given in figure 8-27.

Fig. 8-26

	LENGTH OF DIAMETER (D)	VOLUME (V)
a.	$2x$	?
b.	$0.5x$	?
c.	$1.1x$	?
d.	x	?

Fig. 8-27

ROOTS

Procedures for Extracting the Root of a Term

- Determine the root of the numerical coefficient following the procedure for roots of signed numbers.
- The roots of the literal factors are determined by dividing the exponent of each literal factor by the index of the root.
- Combine the numerical and literal factors.

Arithmetic Example. $\sqrt{2^6}$

From Arithmetic:

$\sqrt{2^6} = \sqrt{(2)(2)(2)(2)(2)(2)} = \sqrt{64} = 8 \; Ans$

From algebra:

$\sqrt{2^6} = 2^{6 \div 2} = 2^3 = (2)(2)(2) = 8 \; Ans$

Algebra Example 1. Solve. $\sqrt{36x^4y^2z^6}$

Determine the root of the numerical coefficient. $\sqrt{36} = 6$

Determine the roots of the literal factors by dividing the exponents of each literal factor by the index of the root.

$\sqrt{x^4} = x^{4 \div 2} = x^2$

$\sqrt{y^2} = y^{2 \div 2} = y$

$\sqrt{z^6} = z^{6 \div 2} = z^3$

Combine. $\sqrt{36x^4y^2z^6} = 6x^2yz^3 \; Ans$

Algebra Example 2. Solve. $\sqrt[3]{-27ab^6c^2}$

Determine the cube root of -27.

$\sqrt[3]{-27} = -3$

Divide the exponent of each literal factor by the index 3.

$\sqrt[3]{a} = \sqrt[3]{a}$

$\sqrt[3]{b^6} = b^{6 \div 3} = b^2$

$\sqrt[3]{c^2} = \sqrt[3]{c^2}$

Combine. $\sqrt[3]{-27ab^6c^2} = -3b^2\sqrt[3]{ac^2} \; Ans$

NOTE: Roots of expressions that consist of two or more terms <u>cannot</u> be extracted by this procedure. For example, $\sqrt{x^2 + y^2}$, consists of two terms and does <u>not</u> equal $\sqrt{x^2} + \sqrt{y^2}$. This mistake, commonly made by students, must be avoided. This fact is consistent with arithmetic.

$\sqrt{3^2 + 4^2} = \sqrt{9 + 16} = \sqrt{25} = 5 \; Ans$

$\sqrt{3^2 + 4^2} \neq \sqrt{3^2} + \sqrt{4^2}$

$\sqrt{3^2 + 4^2} \neq 3 + 4$

$\sqrt{3^2 + 4^2} \neq 7$

Exercise 8-6

Determine the roots of these terms.

1. $\sqrt{4a^2b^2c^2}$
2. $\sqrt{4x^2y^4}$
3. $\sqrt{16c^2d^6}$
4. $\sqrt[3]{64x^3y^9}$
5. $\sqrt[3]{-64x^3y^9}$

6. $\sqrt{m^4n^2s^6}$
7. $\sqrt{25f^2g^8}$
8. $\sqrt{81x^8y^6}$
9. $\sqrt{49c^2d^6e^{10}}$
10. $\sqrt[3]{8p^6t^3w^9}$

11. $\sqrt[3]{-27x^6y^{12}}$
12. $\sqrt{0.25h^4y^2}$
13. $\sqrt{0.64a^6c^8f^2}$
14. $\sqrt{25ab^2}$
15. $\sqrt{100xy}$

16. $\sqrt[3]{64ab^3}$

17. $\sqrt{144mp^4s}$

18. $\sqrt{\frac{4}{9}a^2b^4c^6}$

19. $\sqrt{\frac{1}{16}xy^4}$

20. $\sqrt[3]{\frac{8}{27}m^3n^6}$

21. $\sqrt[3]{-64d^6t^9}$

22. $\sqrt[3]{-8ef^2}$

23. $\sqrt[3]{27d^2ef^6}$

24. $\sqrt[4]{16x^4y^2}$

25. $\sqrt[5]{32h^{10}}$

26. $\sqrt[5]{-32a^2b^5}$

27. $\sqrt[3]{c^2dt^6}$

28. $\sqrt[3]{-n^2xy^3}$

29. $\sqrt{\frac{4}{9}a^4bc^6}$

30. $\sqrt[3]{-\frac{1}{64}x^2y^3z}$

Determine the literal value answers for these problems.

31. The length of a side of the square shown in figure 8-28 is computed by taking the square root of the area ($s = \sqrt{A}$). Express the length of sides for each of the square areas given in figure 8-29.

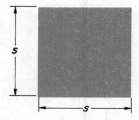

Fig. 8-28

	AREA (A)	LENGTH OF EACH SIDE (s)
a.	$100x^2$	?
b.	$0.36x^2$	?
c.	$1.44x^2$	?
d.	$\frac{1}{4}x^2$	?

Fig. 8-29

32. The length of a side of the cube shown in figure 8-30 is computed by taking the cube root of the volume ($s = \sqrt[3]{V}$). Express the lengths of sides for each of the cube volumes given in figure 8-31.

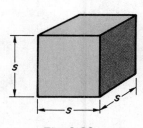

Fig. 8-30

	VOLUME (V)	LENGTH OF EACH SIDE (s)
a.	$125x^3$	?
b.	$0.008x^3$	?
c.	$\frac{1}{8}x^3$	?
d.	$\frac{27}{64}x^3$	?

Fig. 8-31

33. The approximate radius of the circle shown in figure 8-32 is computed by dividing the area by 3.14 and taking the square root of the quotient ($R = \sqrt{\frac{A}{3.14}}$). Express the radius for each of the circle areas given in figure 8-33.

Fig. 8-32

	AREA (A)	RADIUS (R)
a.	$12.56x^2$	?
b.	$50.24x^2$	?
c.	$0.1256x^2$	?
d.	$0.2826x^2$	?

Fig. 8-33

34. The approximate diameter of the sphere shown in figure 8-34 is computed by multiplying the cube root of the volume by 1.24 ($D = 1.24\sqrt[3]{V}$). Express the diameters of each of the volumes given in figure 8-35.

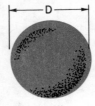

D

Fig. 8-34

	VOLUME (V)	DIAMETER (D)
a.	$64x^3$	?
b.	$1\,000x^3$	?
c.	$0.027x^3$	?
d.	$0.125x^3$	?

Fig. 8-35

REMOVAL OF PARENTHESES

In certain expressions, terms are enclosed within parentheses which are preceded by a plus or minus sign. In order to combine like terms, it is necessary to first remove parentheses.

Procedure for Removal of Parentheses Preceded by a Plus Sign

- Remove the parentheses without changing the signs of any terms within the parentheses.
- Combine like terms.

Example. $3x + (5x - 8 + 6y) = 3x + 5x - 8 + 6y =$ **$8x - 8 + 6y$** *Ans*

Procedure for Removal of Parentheses Preceded by a Minus Sign

- Remove the parentheses and change the sign of each term within the parentheses.
- Combine like terms.

Example 1. $8x - (4y - 6a + 7) =$ **$8x - 4y + 6a - 7$** *Ans*

Example 2. $-(7a^2 + b - 3) + 12 - (-b + 5) =$
$$-7a^2 - b + 3 + 12 + b - 5 =$$
$$\mathbf{-7a^2 + 10}\ Ans$$

Exercise 8-7

Remove parentheses and combine like terms where possible.

1. $4a + (3a - 2a^2 + a^3)$
2. $4a - (3a - 2a^2 + a^3)$
3. $9b - (15b^2 - c + d)$
4. $15 + (x^2 - 10)$
5. $3y^2 - (-5 - y^2)$
6. $-7m + (3m + m^2)$
7. $xy^2 - (xy + xy^2)$
8. $-(ab + a^2b - 6a)$

9. $-10c^3 - (-8c^3 - d + 12)$

10. $-10c^3 + (-8c^3 - d + 12)$

11. $-(16 + xy - x) + (-x)$

12. $15 - (r^2 + r) + (r^2 - 14)$

13. $-(a^2 + b^2) + (a^2 + b^2)$

14. $-(3x + xy - 6) + 12 + (x + xy)$

15. $20 + (cd - c^2d + d) + 14 - (cd + d)$

16. $20 - (cd - c^2d + d) - 14 + (cd + d)$

COMBINED OPERATIONS

Expressions which consist of two or more different operations are solved by applying the proper order of operations.

Order of Operations

- First, do all operations within grouping symbols. Grouping symbols are parentheses ( ), brackets [ ] and braces { }.

- Second, do powers and roots.

- Next, do multiplication and division operations in order from left to right.

- Last, do addition and subtraction operations in order from left to right.

Example 1.   Simplify. $5b + 4b(5 + a - 2b^2)$

Multiply. $5b + 4b(5 + a - 2b^2)$

$4b(5 + a - 2b^2) = 20b + 4ab - 8b^3$ $5b + 20b + 4ab - 8b^3$

Combine like terms.

$5b + 20b = 25b$ $\mathbf{25b + 4ab - 8b^3 \ Ans}$

Example 2.   Simplify. $18 + \sqrt{\dfrac{32x^3}{2x}} + 3(7x + 6y) - 2y$

Perform the division under the radical symbol. $18 + \sqrt{\dfrac{32x^3}{2x}} + 3(7x + 6y) - 2y$

$\dfrac{32x^3}{2x} = 16x^2$ $18 + \sqrt{16x^2} + 3(7x + 6y) - 2y$

Take the square root.

$\sqrt{16x^2} = 4x$ $18 + 4x + 3(7x + 6y) - 2y$

Multiply.

$3(7x + 6y) = 21x + 18y$ $18 + 4x + 21x + 18y - 2y$

Combine like terms.

$4x + 21x = 25x$

$18y - 2y = 16y$ $\mathbf{18 + 25x + 16y \ Ans}$

Example 3. Simplify. $15a^6b^3 + (2a^2b)^3 - \dfrac{a^7(b^3)^2}{ab^3}$

Raise to the indicated powers. $\qquad\qquad 15a^6b^3 + (2a^2b)^3 - \dfrac{a^7(b^3)^2}{ab^3}$

$(2a^2b)^3 = 8a^6b^3$

$a^7(b^3)^2 = a^7b^6$ $\qquad\qquad\qquad\qquad 15a^6b^3 + 8a^6b^3 - \dfrac{a^7b^6}{ab^3}$

Divide.

$\dfrac{a^7b^6}{ab^3} = a^6b^3$ $\qquad\qquad\qquad\qquad 15a^6b^3 + 8a^6b^3 - a^6b^3$

Combine like terms.

$15a^6b^3 + 8a^6b^3 - a^6b^3 = 22a^6b^3$ $\qquad\qquad$ **$22a^6b^3$ Ans**

Exercise 8-8

These expressions consist of combined operations. Simplify.

1. $14 + 4(3a) + a$
2. $18 - 6(-2x) - 3x$
3. $20 - 2(5xy)^2 + x^2y^2$
4. $7 + 4(M^2N^2) - (MN)^2$
5. $6(c^2 - d) + c^2 - 3d$
6. $(10 - P^2)(4 + P^2) + P$
7. $(2 + H^2)(3 + H^2) - 4H^4$
8. $-7(x^2 + 5)^2 + (10x)^2$
9. $(xy \div x) - (x^2y \div x) + 5x$
10. $(6 - 10L + 14L^2) \div 2 + 3L^2$

11. $(8ab^8) \div (4ab^2) - (b^2)^3 + 12$
12. $\sqrt{36x^4y^2} - 5y(2x)^2$
13. $\sqrt{(64D^6) \div 4} \div D^2$
14. $(20x^6 + 12x^4) \div (2x)^2 + x^4$
15. $5a[-6 + (ab^2)^3 - 10]$
16. $[9 - (xy^2)^2]^2$
17. $-c[-12 + (c^2d)^2 - 4c] + 8c$
18. $(M + 3N)^2 + (M - 3N)^2 - 5M^2$
19. $x(x - 4y)^2 - x(x + 4y)^2$
20. $(10f^6 + 12f^4h) \div \sqrt{4f^4}$

UNIT EXERCISE AND PROBLEM REVIEW

Exercise 8-9

ADDITION OF SINGLE TERMS

These expressions consist of groups of single terms. Add these terms.

1. $-8x, 5x$
2. $10m^2, -m^2$
3. $7MP, MP$
4. $0.6xy, 0.9xy$
5. $7.4a^2c, 7.3a^2c$
6. $-0.07F, -0.02F$
7. $\frac{1}{4}x^2y^3, -\frac{7}{8}x^2y^3$

8. $3\frac{1}{2}V, -3\frac{1}{2}V$
9. $5x, -6x, -x, 8x$
10. $-0.4HL, -3.6HL, -0.3HL$
11. $\frac{1}{4}ab, -\frac{3}{8}ab, ab, \frac{1}{2}ab$
12. $5.5N, 0.55N, -0.055N$

ADDITION OF GROUPS OF TWO OR MORE TERMS

These expressions consist of groups of two or more terms. Group like terms and add.

13. $(5a + 6b), (4a + 8b)$

14. $(4x + 3y + 52), (x + 7y + 22)$

15. $[7m + (-3mn)], [(-m) + 6mn]$

16. $[8P + (-7PT)], [P + (-5PT) + (-T)]$

17. $[2.4F + (-4G)], [(-7.6F) + 0.3G], [0.9F + (-1.2G)]$

18. $[1\frac{3}{4}x + (-\frac{1}{4}y) + \frac{3}{8}xy], [\frac{1}{2}x + \frac{7}{8}y + (-3xy) + (-xy^2)]$

SUBTRACTION OF SINGLE TERMS

These expressions consist of groups of single terms. Subtract terms as indicated.

19. $1P - 7P$

20. $9ab - (-3ab)$

21. $-14x^2y - (-14x^2y)$

22. $0 - (-15E)$

23. $0.7x^2 - 1.4x^2$

24. $-cd - 5.7cd$

25. $0.09H - (-0.15H)$

26. $\frac{1}{4}fg^2 - \frac{3}{16}fg^2$

27. $-\frac{5}{16}B - (-\frac{5}{8}B)$

28. $2.06M - 3.74M$

29. $0 - cd^2$

30. $-4\frac{1}{8}x^2y - 3\frac{7}{16}x^2y$

SUBTRACTION OF GROUPS OF TWO OR MORE TERMS

These expressions consist of groups of two or more terms. Group like terms and subtract.

31. $(6R - 5R^2) - (4R - 8R^2)$

32. $(12x^2 - 3) - (12x^2 - 3)$

33. $(2T + 9TW) - (T + TW)$

34. $0 - (x^2y - xy^2 + x^2y^2)$

35. $(-y^3 - y^2 - y) - (-5y^2 + 3y)$

36. $(7.5M + 9.6N) - (3.4M - N + 3.2)$

37. $(\frac{1}{2}c - \frac{1}{4}d + 1\frac{3}{4}) - (\frac{7}{8}c - 2\frac{1}{2} + cd)$

38. $(-15L + 6.1L^2) - (9.3L + 0.6L^2 - L^3)$.

MULTIPLICATION OF SINGLE TERMS

These expressions consist of single terms. Multiply these terms as indicated.

39. $(6xy)(10x^2y^2)$

40. $(-12a)(-5a^2)$

41. $(5c^2de^2)(-4cd^2e^3)$

42. $(-7M^4N)(-N^2)$

43. $(4.3x^4y)(0.6y^2)$

44. $(0.06S^3T)(4S^2)$

45. $(-\frac{3}{4}a^2b)(-\frac{3}{8}a^2b^2c)$

46. $(-10)(-FH^3)(F^2)$

47. $(c^2d)(b^2c)(d^2)$

48. $(-5.6M^2N)(-M^3)(-MN^2)$

49. $(\frac{1}{5}P)(\frac{1}{2}PS^3)(-P^2)$

50. $(0.1x^3y)(-y)(-3x^2z)$

MULTIPLICATION OF TWO OR MORE TERMS

These expressions consist of groups of two or more terms. Multiply as indicated and combine like terms where possible.

51. $7D^2(D^3 - DH)$

52. $-5x^2(-x - x^2y)$

53. $a^2b^3c^4(-a^2c^2 + b - cb^2)$

54. $-0.9A^2E(-0.2E^2 - A + 3A^2E)$

55. $(4m^2 - 3n^3)(-5m^2 + 7n^3)$

56. $(2.4by^2 + ax)(0.2b^3 - x^2)$

57. $(-0.8P^3S - 12)(-0.8S^2 - 0.5P)$

58. $(6e^2f^3 - 8ef)(-7ef + 3e^2f^3)$

DIVISION OF SINGLE TERMS

These exercises require division of single terms. Divide terms as indicated.

59. $16y^2 \div 8y$

60. $-10a^5b^4 \div 2a^2b^3$

61. $C^2D \div (-CD)$

62. $0 \div x^2y$

63. $(-35m^5n^2) \div (-5m^2n^2)$

64. $0.6BF^2 \div (-0.2F^2)$

65. $5.2a^3b \div a$

66. $-\frac{1}{4}x^4y^3 \div \frac{1}{8}x^4y$

67. $-9E^3F^2 \div (-\frac{3}{4}E^2F)$

68. $0.06x^5y^3 \div (-0.5x^3y^2)$

69. $\frac{3}{8}ab^3 \div 3b$

70. $-10.5NS^4 \div (-0.2S)$

DIVISION OF TWO OR MORE TERMS

These exercises consist of expressions in which the dividends have two or more terms. Divide as indicated.

71. $(12x^3 - 8x^2) \div 4x$

72. $(9a^3b^2 - 6a^2b) \div 3ab$

73. $(-40C^2D^5 - 32C^3D^4) \div (-8CD)$

74. $(25xy^2 - 35x^2y + 50) \div (-5)$

75. $(0.8F^3G^4 + 0.4F^4G^3) \div 4F^2G^2$

76. $(-3.5c^2d - 0.5cd^2 + c^2d^2) \div (0.5c)$

77. $(\frac{1}{2}x^2y - \frac{3}{4}x^3y^2 - 2xy^3) \div \frac{1}{4}xy$

78. $(\frac{3}{5}HM^3 - \frac{1}{5}H^2M^2 + \frac{4}{5}H^2M^3) \div (-2M^2)$

RAISING SINGLE TERMS TO POWERS

These exercises consist of expressions with single terms. Raise terms to the indicated powers.

79. $(5ab)^2$

80. $(-7xy)^2$

81. $(3M^4P^2)^2$

82. $(-2a^3b^2c)^3$

83. $(-3M^3P^2T^4)^4$

84. $(0.5x^3y)^3$

85. $(6.1d^3fh^2)^2$

86. $(\frac{3}{4}a^3bc^2)^2$

87. $[-7(x^2b^3)^2c]^2$

88. $[-3d^2(e^2)^2f^3]^3$

89. $[0.4m^3(ns^2)^3]^2$

90. $[(-2C^2D)^3(CD^2)^2]^2$

RAISING EXPRESSIONS CONSISTING OF MORE THAN ONE TERM TO POWERS

These exercises consist of expressions of more than one term. Raise these expressions to the indicated powers and combine like terms where possible.

91. $(x^2 + y)^2$

92. $(E^2 - F^3)^2$

93. $(3a^2 + 2b)^2$

94. $(c^2d^2 - cd)^2$

95. $(0.8P^2T^3 - 0.4T)^2$

96. $(\frac{1}{2}x^2y + \frac{1}{2}xy^2)^2$

97. $[(F^3)^2 - (H^2)^3]^2$

98. $[(ab^2)^3 + (-a^2b)^3]^2$

EXTRACTING ROOTS OF TERMS

Determine the roots of these terms.

99. $\sqrt{9x^2y^4z^2}$

100. $\sqrt{25a^4b^2c^6}$

101. $\sqrt[3]{8M^3P^6T^9}$

102. $\sqrt[3]{-27d^6e^3f^3}$

103. $\sqrt{0.16F^4H^2}$

104. $\sqrt{0.36a^4b^8c^2}$

105. $\sqrt{100xy^2}$

106. $\sqrt{\frac{1}{4}C^2D^6}$

107. $\sqrt[3]{-64d^2e}$

108. $\sqrt[4]{81x^4y^8z^2}$

109. $\sqrt[5]{-32a^{10}b^5c^2}$

110. $\sqrt[3]{-\frac{8}{27}G^3HL^2}$

REMOVING PARENTHESES

Remove parentheses and combine like terms where possible.

111. $-(3a^2 + b - c^2)$

112. $+(18x^2y - y^2 - x)$

113. $x^2y - (xy + x^2y)$

114. $7C^2 + (-8C^2 - D + 4)$

115. $20 - (P^2 + P) + (P^2 - 7)$

116. $-(E^2 + F^3) + (E^2 + F^3)$

117. $17 + (mr - m^2r + r) + 8 - (mr - r)$

118. $17 - (mr - m^2r + r) - 8 + (mr - r)$

COMBINED OPERATIONS

These expressions consist of combined operations. Simplify.

119. $18 + 5(6x) + x$

120. $26 - 8(-3a) - 4a$

121. $4(M^2 - P) + P - 2M^2$

122. $-10(C^2 + 4)^2 + (5C^2)^2$

123. $(12 - 8D + 6D^2) \div 2 + D$

124. $\sqrt{25f^2g^4} - 3f(4f)^2$

125. $-x[-6 + (x^2y)^2 - 2x] + 4y$

126. $[7 - (a^2b)^2]^2$

127. $m(m - 3t)^2 - m(m + 3t)^2$

128. $(20R^4 - 24R^2T) \div \sqrt{16R^4}$

LITERAL PROBLEMS

Determine the literal value answers for these problems.

129. The total voltage (E_t) in volts, of the circuit shown in figure 8-36 is represented as x. The amount of voltage taken by 5 of the 6 resistors is given as E_{R_1}-E_{R_5}.

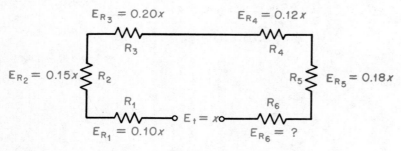

$E_{R_3} = 0.20x$ $E_{R_4} = 0.12x$

R_3 R_4

$E_{R_2} = 0.15x$ R_2 R_5 $E_{R_5} = 0.18x$

R_1 R_6

$E_t = x$

$E_{R_1} = 0.10x$ $E_{R_6} = ?$

Fig. 8-36

a. What is the sum of the voltage taken by R_1, R_2, R_3, R_4, and R_5?

b. What is the average resistor voltage for resistors R_1-R_5?

c. What voltage is taken by R_6?

130. A corporation's annual profits and losses for a 6-year period are shown in the graph in figure 8-37.

    a. What is the increase or decrease in profits for the years listed?

       (1) the 1st to the 2nd year

       (2) the 2nd to the 4th year

       (3) the 3rd to the 5th year

       (4) the 4th to the 6th year

    b. What is the total dollar amount lost by the corporation from the 3rd through the 5th year?

    c. What is the net profit or loss for the 6-year period?

    d. What is the average annual profit or loss for the 6-year period?

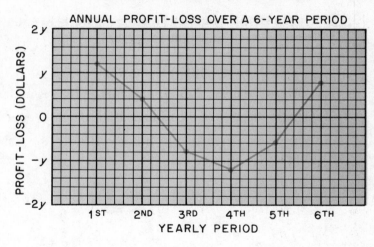

Fig. 8-37

131. The daily sales amounts of a retail firm for one week are shown in the chart in figure 8-38.

DAY	MONDAY	TUESDAY	WEDNESDAY	THURSDAY	FRIDAY
AMOUNT	5x + $150	4x + $60	6x + $100	5x + $50	7x + $200

Fig. 8-38

    a. What is the sales amount increase on the days listed?

       (1) Monday over Tuesday

       (2) Wednesday over Tuesday

       (3) Friday over Monday

    b. What is the total amount of sales for the week?

    c. What is the average daily amount of sales during the week?

132. Refer to the bracket shown in figure 8-39 and determine distances A-G.

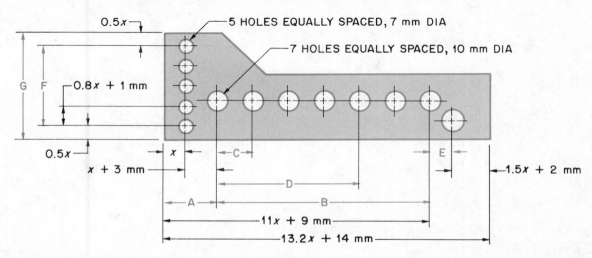

Fig. 8-39

133. The area of the triangle shown in figure 8-40 equals one-half the product of the base and the height $(A = \frac{1}{2}bh)$.

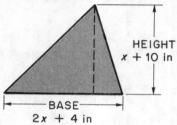

a. What is the area of the triangle?

b. What is the area of the triangle if the base is increased by 2 inches?

c. What is the area of the triangle if the height is decreased by 4 inches?

d. What is the area of the triangle if both the base and height are doubled?

Fig. 8-40

UNIT 9
Simple
Equations

OBJECTIVES

After studying this unit you should be able to

- express word problems as equations.
- express problems given in graphic form as equations.
- solve equations using the six fundamental principles of equality.
- solve problems by writing equations and determining the values of unknowns.
- substitute values in formulas and solve for the unknowns.

EXPRESSION OF EQUALITY

An *equation* is a mathematical statement of equality between two or more quantities. An equation always contains an equal sign (=). The value of all the quantities on the left side of the equal sign equals the value of all quantities on the right side of the equal sign. A *formula* is a particular type of an equation which states a mathematical rule.

Because it expresses the equality of the quantities on the left and on the right of the equal sign, an equation is a balanced mathematical statement. An equation may be considered similar to a balanced scale as illustrated in figure 9-1. The total weight on the left side of the scale equals the total weight on the right side.

$$3 \text{ lb} + 5 \text{ lb} + 2 \text{ lb} = 4 \text{ lb} + 6 \text{ lb}$$
$$10 \text{ lb} = 10 \text{ lb} \text{ (The scale is balanced.)}$$

Fig. 9-1

Figure 9-2 shows that when the 2-pound weight is removed from the scale, the scale is no longer in balance.

$$3 \text{ lb} + 5 \text{ lb} \neq 4 \text{ lb} + 6 \text{ lb}$$
$$8 \text{ lb} \neq 10 \text{ lb} \text{ (The scale is \underline{not} balanced.)}$$

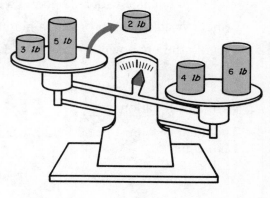

Fig. 9-2

In general, an equation is solved to determine the value of an unknown quantity. Although any letter or symbol can be used to represent the unknown quantity, the letter x is commonly used.

The first letter of the unknown quantity is sometimes used to represent a quantity. These are some common letter designations used to represent specific quantities.

L to represent length P to represent pressure V to represent volume

A to represent area W to represent weight h to represent height

t to represent time D to represent diameter

WRITING EQUATIONS FROM WORD STATEMENTS

It is important to develop the ability to express word statements as mathematical symbols, or equations. A problem must be fully understood before it can be written as an equation.

Whether the word problem is simple or complex, a definite logical procedure should be followed to analyze the problem. A few or all of the following steps may be required, depending on the complexity of the particular problem.

- Carefully read the entire problem, several times if necessary.

- Break the problem down into simpler parts.

- It is sometimes helpful to draw a simple picture as an aid in visualizing the various parts of the problem.

- Identify and list the unknowns. Give each unknown a letter name, such as x.

- Decide where the equal sign should be, and group the parts of the problem on the proper side of the equal sign.

- Check. Are the statements on the left equal to the statements on the right of the equal sign?

- Check the answer against the original problem, step-by-step.

The following examples illustrate the method of writing equations from given word statements. After each equation is written the value of the unknown quantity is obtained. No specific procedures are given at this time in solving for the unknown. The unknown quantity values are determined by logical reasoning.

Example 1.   What weight must be added to a 12-pound weight so that it will be in balance with a 20-pound weight?

To help visualize the problem, a picture is shown in figure 9-3.

Identify the unknown.   Let $x =$ the number of pounds of the unknown weight

Write the equation. $12 + x = 20$

The number 8 must be added to 12 to equal 20.
$12 + 8 = 20$ $x = 8$

8 pounds *Ans*

Check the answer by substituting 8 for x in the equation. $12 + 8 = 20$

Perform the indicated operation.
$12 + 8 = 20$ $20 = 20$ ck

Fig. 9-3

The equation is balanced since the left side of the equation equals the right side. Figure 9-4 shows that 8 pounds must be added to 12 pounds to equal 20 pounds and make the scale balance.

Fig. 9-4

Example 2. A $14\frac{1}{2}$-inch length of board is needed. How many inches must be cut from a board 18 inches long to obtain the required board? (Make no allowance for the saw cut.)

A picture of the problem is shown in figure 9-5.

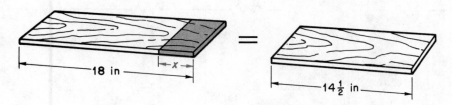

Fig. 9-5

Identify the unknown.   Let x = the number of inches cut off.

Write the equation. $18 - x = 14\frac{1}{2}$

The number $3\frac{1}{2}$ must be subtracted from 18 to equal $14\frac{1}{2}$.

$18 - 3\frac{1}{2} = 14\frac{1}{2}$ $x = 3\frac{1}{2}$

$3\frac{1}{2}$ inches *Ans*

Check the answer by substituting $18 - 3\frac{1}{2} = 14\frac{1}{2}$
$3\frac{1}{2}$ for x in the equation.

Perform the indicated operation.

$18 - 3\frac{1}{2} = 14\frac{1}{2}$ $14\frac{1}{2} = 14\frac{1}{2}$ ck

The equation is balanced since the left side of the equation equals the right side. Figure 9-6 shows that $3\frac{1}{2}$ inches must be cut off 18 inches to equal $14\frac{1}{2}$ inches.

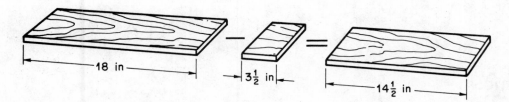

Fig. 9-6

Example 3. In a series circuit, the sum of the individual voltages equals the applied line voltage. A certain series circuit with 3 resistors has an applied line voltage (E_t) of 120 volts. The voltage across R_2 (E_{R_2}) is twice the voltage across R_1 (E_{R_1}). The voltage across R_3 (E_{R_3}) is three times the voltage across R_1. What is the voltage across each resistor?

Identify the unknown.

$$\text{Let } x = \text{number of volts across } R_1$$
$$2x = \text{number of volts across } R_2$$
$$3x = \text{number of volts across } R_3$$

A picture of the problem is shown in figure 9-7.

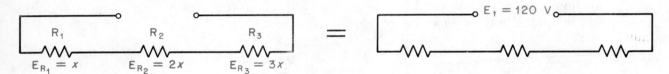

Fig. 9-7

Write the equation. $x + 2x + 3x = 120$

Simplify the equation. $6x = 120$

The number 6 must be multiplied by 20 to equal 120.

$6(20) = 120$

$$x = 20$$
$$2x = 40$$
$$3x = 60$$
$$E_{R_1} = 20 \text{ volts } Ans$$
$$E_{R_2} = 40 \text{ volts } Ans$$
$$E_{R_3} = 60 \text{ volts } Ans$$

Check the answers by substituting the answers. $20 + 40 + 60 = 120$

Perform the indicated operations.

$20 + 40 + 60 = 120$ $120 = 120 \text{ ck}$

The equation is balanced since the left side of the equation equals the right side. Figure 9-8 shows the resistor voltages equal the applied voltage.

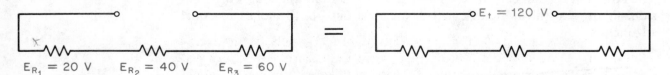

Fig. 9-8

CHECKING THE EQUATION

In the final step in each of the preceding examples, the value found for the unknown was substituted in the original equation to prove that it was the correct value. If an equation is properly written and if both sides of the equation are equal, the equation is balanced and the solution is correct.

It is important that you check your computations. When working with equations for actual on-the-job applications, checking your work is essential. Errors in computation can often be costly in terms of time, labor, and materials.

Exercise 9-1

Express each of these word problems as an equation. Let the unknown number equal x and solve for the value of the unknown. Check the equation by comparing it to the word problem. Does the equation state mathematically what the problem states in words? Check whether the equation is balanced by substituting the value of the unknown in the equation.

1. A number plus 20 equals 35.

2. A number less 12 equals 18.

3. Four times a number equals 40.

4. A number divided by 2 equals 14.

5. Twenty divided by a number equals 5.

6. A number plus twice the number equals 45.

7. Five times a number, plus the number, equals 36.

8. Four times a number, minus the number, equals 21.

9. Six times a number divided by 3 equals 12.

10. Twice a number, plus three times the number, equals 20.

11. Ten times a number, minus four times the number, equals 42.

12. Three subtracted from three times a number, plus twice the number, equals 27.

13. Four added to five times a number, minus twice the number, equals 34.

14. Sixty multiplied by three times a number equals 360.

15. A length of lumber 12 feet long is cut into two unequal lengths. One piece is three times as long as the other.

    a. Find the length of the shorter piece.

    b. Find the length of the longer piece.

16. A building contractor estimates labor cost for a job will be $25 000 more than material cost. The total labor and material cost is $95 000.

    a. What is the estimated material cost?

    b. What is the estimated labor cost?

17. A plot of land which has an area of 65 000 square feet is subdivided into 4 building lots. Lot 2 and Lot 3 each have twice the area of Lot 1. Lot 4 is 5 000 square feet greater in area than Lot 1. Find the area (number of square feet) of each lot listed.

    a. Lot 1   c. Lot 3
    b. Lot 2   d. Lot 4

18. In two cuts, the total amount of stock milled off an aluminum casting is 7.5 millimetres. The first cut (roughing cut) is 6.5 millimetres greater than the second cut (finish cut). How much stock is removed on the finish cut?

19. A hospital dietician computes the daily calorie intake for a patient as 2 550 calories. The calories allowed for lunch are twice the calories allowed for breakfast. The calories allowed for dinner are one and one-half the calories allowed for lunch. The allowance for an evening snack is 150 calories. How many calories are allowed for each meal listed?

a. Breakfast   b. Lunch   c. Dinner

20. Five holes are drilled in a steel plate as shown in figure 9-9. There are 300 degrees between hole 1 and hole 5. The number of degrees between any two consecutive holes doubles in going from hole 1 to hole 5. Find the number of degrees between the holes listed.

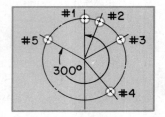

Fig. 9-9

a. Hole 1 and hole 2   c. Hole 3 and hole 4

b. Hole 2 and hole 3   d. Hole 4 and hole 5

For each of these problems, refer to the corresponding figure. Write an equation and solve for x. Check the equation.

21. Let x = a given number of inches

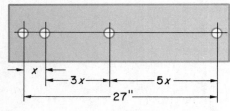

Fig. 9-10

22. Let x = a given number of degrees

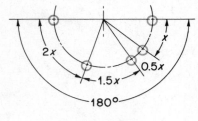

Fig. 9-11

23. Let x = a given number of centimetres

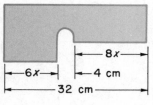

Fig. 9-12

24. Let x = a given number of inches

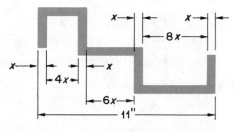

Fig. 9-13

25. Let x = a given number of degrees

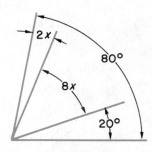

Fig. 9-14

26. Let x = a given number of millimetres

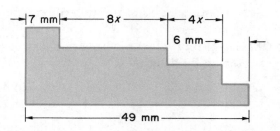

Fig. 9-15

For each of these problems write an equation. Solve for the unknown and check the equation.

27. In the series circuit shown in figure 9-16, the sum of the voltages across each of the individual resistors is equal to the applied line voltage of 120 volts. Find the number of volts for each voltage listed.

Let x = volts across R_1

  a. E_{R_1}

  b. E_{R_2}

  c. E_{R_3}

  d. E_{R_4}

  e. E_{R_5}

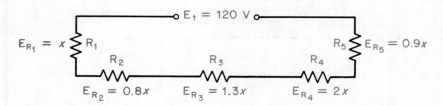

Fig. 9-16

28. Refer to figure 9-17. Determine the distances between these holes.

Let l = a given number of millimetres

  a. Hole 1 to hole 2

  b. Hole 2 to hole 3

  c. Hole 3 to hole 4

  d. Hole 4 to hole 5

  e. Hole 1 to hole 5

  f. Hole 2 to hole 6

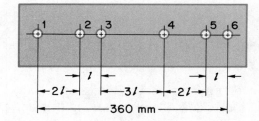

Fig. 9-17

29. Refer to figure 9-18. Determine the value for these angles.

        Let y = number of degrees in $\angle 1$
           $2y$ = number of degrees in $\angle 2$
  $3y - 20°$ = number of degrees in $\angle 3$
  $4y - 40°$ = number of degrees in $\angle 4$

  a. $\angle 1$

  b. $\angle 2$

  c. $\angle 3$

  d. $\angle 4$

  e. $\angle 1 + \angle 2$

  f. $\angle 2 + \angle 3 + \angle 4$

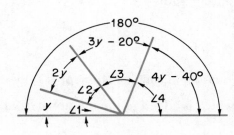

Fig. 9-18

30. Refer to figure 9-19. Determine the distance between these points.

Let h = a given number of inches

a. A and B

b. C and D

c. E and F

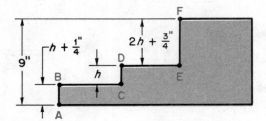

Fig. 9-19

PRINCIPLES OF EQUALITY

In actual practice, equations cannot always be solved by inspection or common sense. There are specific procedures for solving equations using the fundamental principles of equality. The principles of equality which will be presented are those of addition, subtraction, multiplication, division, powers, and roots. Equations are solved directly and efficiently by the application of these principles.

SOLUTION OF EQUATIONS BY THE SUBTRACTION PRINCIPLE OF EQUALITY

The subtraction principle of equality states that if the same number is subtracted from both sides of an equation, the sides remain equal and the equation remains balanced. The subtraction principle is used to solve an equation in which a number is added to the unknown, such as $x + 4 = 10$.

Figure 9-20 shows a balanced scale. If 4 pounds are removed from the left side only, the scale is not in balance, as shown in figure 9-21. If 4 pounds are removed from both the left and right sides, the scale remains in balance as shown in figure 9-22.

$$6 \text{ lb} + 4 \text{ lb} = 10 \text{ lb}$$
$$6 \text{ lb} + 4 \text{ lb} - 4 \text{ lb} \neq 10 \text{ lb}$$
$$6 \text{ lb} \neq 10 \text{ lb}$$
$$6 \text{ lb} + 4 \text{ lb} - 4 \text{ lb} = 10 \text{ lb} - 4 \text{ lb}$$
$$6 \text{ lb} = 6 \text{ lb}$$

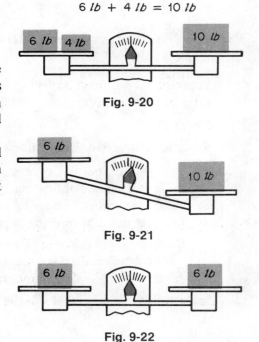

Fig. 9-20

Fig. 9-21

Fig. 9-22

Procedure for Solving an Equation in which a Number is Added to the Unknown

- Subtract the number which is added to the unknown from both sides of the equation.

- Check.

Example 1. Solve for x.

$$x + 5 = 12$$

In the equation, the number 5 is added to x. To solve the equation, subtract 5 from both sides of the equation.

$$\begin{array}{r} x + 5 = 12 \\ -5 = -5 \\ \hline x = 7 \ Ans \end{array}$$

Check. Substitute 7 for x in the original equation.

$$x + 5 = 12$$
$$7 + 5 = 12$$
$$12 = 12 \ ck$$

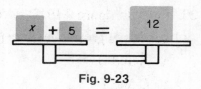

Fig. 9-23

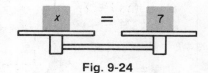

Fig. 9-24

Example 2. Solve for T.

$$-12°C = T + 4°C$$

In the equation, $4°C$ is added to T. To solve the equation, subtract $4°C$ from both sides of the equation.

$$\begin{array}{r} -12°C = T + 4°C \\ -\ 4°C = -\ 4°C \\ \hline -16°C = T \ Ans \end{array}$$

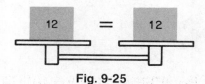

Fig. 9-25

Check.

$$-12°C = T + 4°C$$
$$-12°C = -16°C + 4°C$$
$$-12°C = -12°C \ ck$$

Example 3. Determine dimension D of the plate shown in figure 9-26.

Write the equation.

$$5.2 \text{ cm} + D = 16.8 \text{ cm}$$

Subtract 5.2 cm from both sides of the equation.

$$\begin{array}{r} -5.2 \text{ cm} = -5.2 \text{ cm} \\ \hline D = 11.6 \text{ cm } Ans \end{array}$$

Check.

$$5.2 \text{ cm} + D = 16.8 \text{ cm}$$
$$5.2 \text{ cm} + 11.6 \text{ cm} = 16.8 \text{ cm}$$
$$16.8 \text{ cm} = 16.8 \text{ cm } ck$$

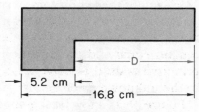

Fig. 9-26

Example 4. The 2.4-volt cell shown in figure 9-27 has an internal resistance (r) of 0.5 ohm. The total circuit resistance (R) is 1.8 ohms. The external resistance is expressed as R_L. Using the formula $R = r + R_L$, determine the external resistance.

Substitute the given values in the formula.

$$R = r + R_L$$
$$1.8 \ \Omega = 0.5 \ \Omega + R_L$$

Subtract 0.5 Ω from both sides of the equation.

$$\begin{array}{r} -0.5 \ \Omega = -0.5 \ \Omega \\ \hline 1.3 \ \Omega = R_L \ Ans \end{array}$$

Check.

$$1.8 \ \Omega = 0.5 \ \Omega + R_L$$
$$1.8 \ \Omega = 0.5 \ \Omega + 1.3 \ \Omega$$
$$1.8 \ \Omega = 1.8 \ \Omega \ ck$$

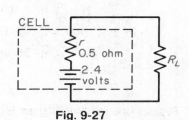

Fig. 9-27

Exercise 9-2

Solve each of these equations using the subtraction principle of equality. Check all answers.

1. $P + 15 = 25$
2. $x + 18 = 27$
3. $M + 24 = 43$
4. $y + 50 = 82$
5. $13 = T + 9$
6. $37 = D + 2$
7. $55 = a + 19$
8. $y + 16 = 15$
9. $C + 34 = 12$
10. $x + 6 = -11$
11. $y + 30 = -23$
12. $x + 63 = 17$
13. $10 + R = 44$
14. $51 = 48 + E$
15. $-36 = 14 + x$
16. $H + 7.6 = 15.2$

17. $22.5 = L + 3.7$
18. $-36.2 = y + 6.2$
19. $86.04 = x + 61.95$
20. $F + 0.007 = 1.006$
21. $T + 9.07 = 9.07$
22. $H + 3\frac{1}{4} = 7\frac{1}{2}$
23. $-\frac{7}{8} = x + \frac{3}{4}$
24. $20\frac{3}{16} = A + 17\frac{1}{8}$
25. $39\frac{5}{8} = y + 42\frac{7}{8}$
26. $1\frac{7}{16} = W + \frac{9}{16}$
27. $x + 13\frac{1}{8} = -10$
28. $0.015 = 1.009 + H$
29. $-14.067 = 3.034 + x$
30. $20.863 = D + 25.942$

For each of these problems write an equation. Solve for the unknown and check.

31.

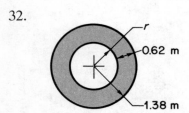

Fig. 9-28

32.

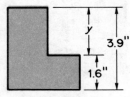

Fig. 9-29

33.

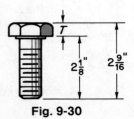

Fig. 9-30

34.

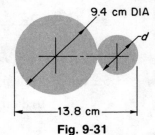

Fig. 9-31

35.

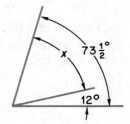

Fig. 9-32

36.

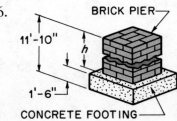

Fig. 9-33

37. The retail selling price of merchandise is $367.50. The retail markup is $172.75. What is the cost (C) of the merchandise to the retailer?

38. A shaft rotates in a bearing. The bearing is 0.375 0 inch in diameter. The total clearance between the shaft and bearing is 0.000 8 inch. Find the diameter (d) of the shaft.

39. Three holes are drilled in a housing. The center distance between the first hole and the second hole is 17.54 centimetres. The center-to-center distance between the first hole and the third hole is 24.76 centimetres. Find the distance, (D) between the second hole and the third hole.

40. A savings account balance (amount) is $3 835. The principal deposited is $3 572. What is the amount of earned interest (I)?

For each of these problems, substitute the given values in the formula and solve for the unknown. Check.

41. Using the formula $P_T = P_1 + P_2$, determine P_1 when $P_2 = 150$ watts and $P_T = 225$ watts.

42. On a company's balance sheet, assets equal liabilities plus net worth. $A = L + NW$. Determine L when $NW = \$56\ 200$ and $A = \$127\ 370$.

43. One of the formulas used in computing spur gear dimensions is $D_o = D + 2a$. Determine D when $a = 0.142\ 9$ inch and $D_o = 4.714\ 4$ inches.

44. A sheet metal formula used in computing the size of a stretchout is $LS = 4s + W$. Determine W when $s = 3$ inches and $LS = 12\frac{1}{8}$ inches.

45. A formula used to compute the dimensions of a ring is $D = d + 2T$. Determine d when $D = 5.2$ centimetres and $T = 0.86$ centimetre.

SOLUTION OF EQUATIONS BY THE ADDITION PRINCIPLE OF EQUALITY

The addition principle of equality states that if the same number is added to both sides of an equation, the sides remain equal and the equation remains balanced. The addition principle is used to solve an equation in which a number is subtracted from the unknown, such as $x - 6 = 24$.

Procedure for Solving an Equation in which a Number is Subtracted from the Unknown

- Add the number, which is subtracted from the unknown, to both sides of the equation.

- Check.

Example 1.   Solve for y.

$$y - 7 = 10$$

In the equation, the number 7 is subtracted from y. To solve the equation, add 7 to both sides of the equation.

$$\begin{array}{r} y - 7 = \quad 10 \\ + 7 = + \ 7 \\ \hline y = \quad 17 \ Ans \end{array}$$

Check.

$$y - 7 = 10$$
$$17 - 7 = 10$$
$$10 = 10 \ ck$$

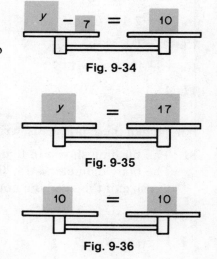

Fig. 9-34

Fig. 9-35

Fig. 9-36

Example 2.   A $5\frac{1}{4}$-inch length is cut from a block as shown in figure 9-37. The remaining block is $6\frac{3}{4}$ inches high. What was the original height, H, of the block?

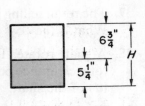

Fig. 9-37

Write the equation.

$$H - 5\frac{1}{4}'' = 6\frac{3}{4}''$$

Add $5\frac{1}{4}''$ to both sides of the equation.

$$+ 5\frac{1}{4}'' = +5\frac{1}{4}''$$

$$\overline{H = 12'' \; Ans}$$

Check.

$$H - 5\frac{1}{4}'' = 6\frac{3}{4}''$$

$$12'' - 5\frac{1}{4}'' = 6\frac{3}{4}''$$

$$6\frac{3}{4}'' = 6\frac{3}{4}'' \; ck$$

Exercise 9-3

Solve each of these equations using the addition principle of equality. Check all answers.

1. $T - 12 = 28$
2. $x - 9 = -19$
3. $B - 4 = 9$
4. $P - 50 = 87$
5. $y - 23 = -20$
6. $16 = M - 12$
7. $-35 = E - 21$
8. $47 = R - 36$
9. $h - 8 = 12$
10. $T - 19 = -6$
11. $-22 = x - 31$
12. $39 = F - 39$
13. $W - 16 = 33$
14. $N - 2.4 = 6.9$
15. $A - 0.8 = 0.5$
16. $x - 10.09 = -13.78$
17. $4.93 = r - 3.07$

18. $-30.003 = x - 29.998$
19. $91.96 = L - 13.74$
20. $P - 0.02 = 0.07$
21. $G - 59.875 = 49.986$
22. $x - 8.12 = -13.01$
23. $D - \frac{1}{2} = \frac{1}{2}$
24. $y - \frac{7}{8} = -\frac{3}{4}$
25. $15\frac{5}{8} = H - 2\frac{7}{8}$
26. $-46\frac{3}{32} = x - 29\frac{15}{16}$
27. $C - 5\frac{7}{16} = -5\frac{7}{16}$
28. $W - 10.003\,9 = 9.058\,3$
29. $-14\frac{15}{32} = y - 14\frac{7}{16}$
30. $E - 29.893\,6 = 18.305\,9$

For each of these problems, write an equation and solve for the unknown. Check.

31. The bushing shown in figure 9-38 has a body diameter of 44.17 millimetres. The body diameter is 14.20 millimetres less than the head diameter. What is the size of the head diameter (D)?

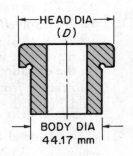

HEAD DIA
(D)

BODY DIA
44.17 mm

Fig. 9-38

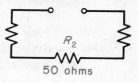

32. A series circuit is shown in figure 9-39. R_2 is 50 ohms. R_2 is 125 ohms less than the total circuit resistance, R_T. What is total circuit resistance (R_T)?

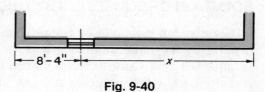

Fig. 9-39

33. A wall section is shown in figure 9-40. The distance from the left edge of the wall to the center of a window is 8'-4". This is 9'-6" less than the distance from the right edge of the wall to the center of the window (x). What is the distance from the right edge of the wall to the center of the window?

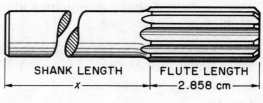

Fig. 9-40

34. The flute length of the reamer shown in figure 9-41 is 2.858 centimetres, which is 8.572 centimetres less than the shank length. How long is the shank (x)?

Fig. 9-41

35. A cross-sectional view of an I Beam is shown in figure 9-42. The web thickness is 0.798 inch. The web thickness is 7.250 inches less than the flange width. What is the width (W) of the flange?

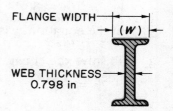

Fig. 9-42

For each of these problems, substitute the given values in the formula and solve for the unknown. Check.

36. A retailer's net profit (NP) on the sale of merchandise is determined by subtracting overhead (O) expenses from the merchandise markup (M): $NP = M - O$. Determine M when $NP = \$122$ and $O = \$74$.

37. The total taper of a shaft equals the diameter of the large end minus the diameter of the small end: $T = D - d$. Determine D when $T = 22.5$ millimetres and $d = 30.8$ millimetres.

38. A formula often used for computing total weekly salaries of salespeople is total salary (TS) minus flat salary (FS) equals commission (C): $TS - FS = C$. Determine the total salary of a salesperson whose flat salary is \$150 and commission is \$178.

39. The net change of stock equals the closing price of stock on the day of the stock quotation minus the closing price of the stock on the previous day: $NC = CP - PCP$. The closing price of the stock on the previous day is $27\frac{1}{4}$ (\$27.25). If the net change is $-1\frac{1}{2}$ (−\$1.50), what is the closing price on the day of the stock quotation?

40. The spur gear formula is $D_R = D - 2d$. Compute the pitch diameter (D) when the root diameter (D_R) = 3.011 8 inches and the dedendum (d) = 0.160 8 inch.

41. A sheet metal formula is $W = LS - 4S$. Determine the length size (LS) when $W = 38.2$ centimetres and $S = 10.6$ centimetres.

42. The formula for computing straight-line depreciation of equipment book value is book value (BV) equals original cost (OC) minus the number of years depreciated (n) times the annual depreciation (AD): $BV = OC - n(AD)$. Determine the original cost of the equipment when $BV = \$2\,400$, $n = 3$, and $AD = \$350$.

SOLUTION OF EQUATIONS BY THE DIVISION PRINCIPLE OF EQUALITY

The division principle of equality states that if both sides of an equation are divided by the same number, the sides remain equal and the equation remains balanced. The division principle is used to solve an equation in which a number is multiplied by the unknown such as $3x = 18$.

Procedure for Solving an Equation in which the Unknown is Multiplied by a Number

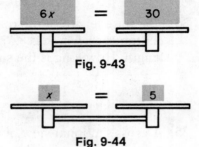

Fig. 9-43

Fig. 9-44

- Divide both sides of the equation by the number which multiplies the unknown.
- Check.

Example 1.   Solve for x.

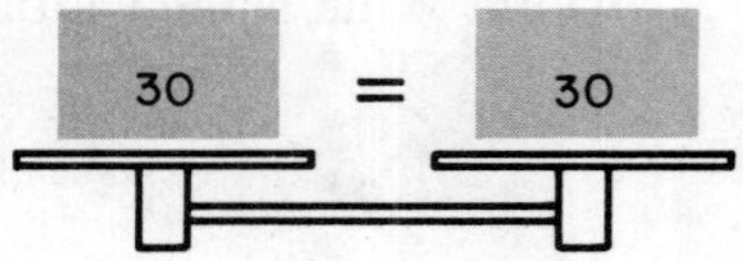

$$6x = 30$$

In the equation, x is multiplied by 6.

To solve the equation, divide both sides by 6.

$$\frac{6x}{6} = \frac{30}{6}$$

$$x = 5\ Ans$$

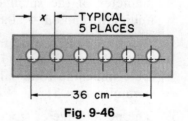

Fig. 9-45

Check.

$$6x = 30$$
$$6(5) = 30$$
$$30 = 30\ ck$$

Example 2.   A plate with equally spaced holes is shown in figure 9-46. Find the center-to-center distance between the holes as represented by x.

Write the equation. $5x = 36$ cm

Divide both sides of the equation by 5. $\dfrac{5x}{5} = \dfrac{36\ \text{cm}}{5}$

$$x = 7.2\ \text{cm}\ Ans$$

TYPICAL
5 PLACES

36 cm

Fig. 9-46

Check. $5x = 36$ cm
$$5(7.2\ \text{cm}) = 36\ \text{cm}$$
$$36\ \text{cm} = 36\ \text{cm}\ ck$$

Exercise 9-4

Solve each of these equations using the division principle of equality. Check all answers.

1. $4D = 32$	4. $54 = 9P$	7. $10y = 0.80$
2. $7x = -21$	5. $-27 = 3y$	8. $18T = 41.4$
3. $15M = 60$	6. $30 = 6x$	9. $-12x = 42$

10. $-x = 19$

11. $0 = 7H$

12. $-5C = 0$

13. $7.1E = 42.6$

14. $0.6L = 12$

15. $-2.7x = 23.76$

16. $0.1y = -0.09$

17. $13.2W = 0$

18. $-x = -19.75$

19. $0.125P = 0.875$

20. $9.37R = 103.07$

21. $-0.66x = 4.752$

22. $\frac{1}{4}D = 8$

23. $24 = \frac{3}{8}B$

24. $-\frac{1}{2}y = 36$

25. $1\frac{5}{8}L = 8\frac{1}{8}$

26. $-48\frac{3}{8} = 10\frac{3}{4}x$

27. $-\frac{7}{16} = -\frac{7}{16}y$

28. $50.98W = 10.196$

29. $-0.002x = 4.938$

30. $-\frac{3}{16} = -1\frac{1}{16}y$

For each of these problems write an equation and solve for the unknown. Check.

31.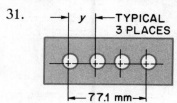

Fig. 9-47

32.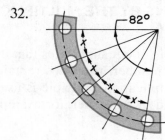

Fig. 9-48

33.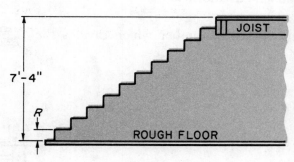

Fig. 9-49

34. The feed of a drill is the depth of material that the drill penetrates in one revolution. The total depth of penetration equals the product of the number of revolutions and the feed. A drill is shown in figure 9-50. Compute the feed (F) of a drill which cuts to a depth of 2.400 inches while turning 400 revolutions.

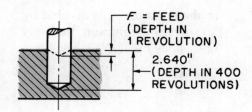

Fig. 9-50

For each of these problems substitute the given values in the formula and solve for the unknown. Check.

35. The perimeter of a square equals 4 times the length of a side of the square, $p = 4s$. Determine s when $p = 63.2$ feet.

36. The circumference of a circle equals π (approximately 3.14) times the diameter of the circle, $C = \pi d$. Determine d when $C = 3.768$ metres.

37. Power, in watts, is equal to the product of current, in amperes, and voltage, in volts: $P_W = IE$. Determine E when $P_W = 4\,600$ watts and $I = 20$ amperes.

38. Power, in watts, is also equal to the product of the square of the current, in amperes, and the total line resistance, in ohms, $P_W = I^2R$. Determine R when $P_W = 120$ watts and $I = 20$ amperes.

39. Power, in kilowatts, is equal to 0.001 times the voltage, in volts, times the current, in amperes: $P_{kW} = 0.001EI$. Determine I when $P_{kW} = 2.415$ kilowatts and $E = 230$ volts.

40. The length of cut, in inches, of a workpiece in a lathe is equal to the product of the cutting time, in minutes, the tool feed, in inches per revolution, and the number of revolutions per minute of the workpiece, $L = TFN$. Determine N when $L = 18$ inches, $T = 3$ minutes, and $F = 0.050$ inch per revolution.

41. Simple annual interest earned on money loaned is equal to the product of the principal, the rate of interest, and the time, in years, $i = prt$. Determine t when $i = \$1\ 260$, $p = \$4\ 500$, and $r = 8\%$.

SOLUTION OF EQUATIONS BY THE MULTIPLICATION PRINCIPLE OF EQUALITY

The multiplication principle of equality states that if both sides of an equation are multiplied by the same number, the sides remain equal and the equation remains balanced. The multiplication principle is used to solve an equation in which the unknown is divided by a number, for example, $\frac{y}{7} = 42$.

Procedure for Solving an Equation in which the Unknown is Divided by a Number

- Multiply both sides of the equation by the number which divides the unknown.

- Check.

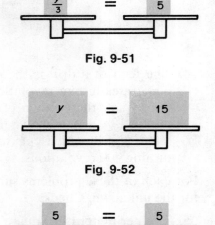

Fig. 9-51

Fig. 9-52

Fig. 9-53

Example 1.   Solve for y.

$$\frac{y}{3} = 5$$

In the equation, y is divided by 3. To solve the equation, multiply both sides by 3.

$$\frac{3}{1}(\frac{y}{3}) = (\frac{5}{1})\frac{3}{1}$$

$$y = 15\ Ans$$

Check.

$$\frac{y}{3} = 5$$

$$\frac{15}{3} = 5$$

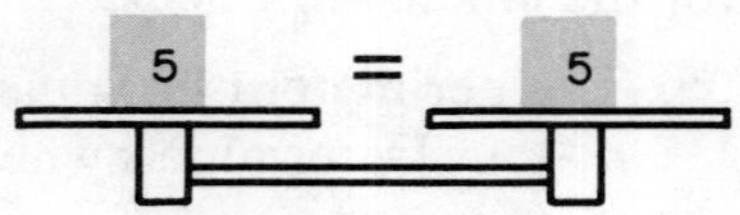

$$5 = 5\ ck$$

Example 2. Six strips of equal width are sheared from the piece of flat stock shown in figure 9-54. Each strip is $1\frac{3}{4}$ inches wide. The original width (W) of the piece of stock can be expressed in the equation $\frac{W}{6} = 1\frac{3}{4}''$. Solve for W.

Multiply both sides of the equation by 6. $\qquad \frac{6}{1}\left(\frac{W}{6}\right) = \left(1\frac{3}{4}''\right)\frac{6}{1}$

$$W = 10'' \; Ans$$

Check.

$$\frac{W}{6} = 1\frac{3}{4}''$$

$$\frac{10\frac{1}{2}''}{6} = 1\frac{3}{4}''$$

$$1\frac{3}{4}'' = 1\frac{3}{4}'' \; ck$$

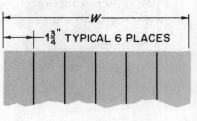

Fig. 9-54

Exercise 9-5

Solve each of these equations using the multiplication principle of equality. Check all answers.

1. $\dfrac{P}{5} = 4$

2. $\dfrac{M}{12} = 5$

3. $D \div 9 = 7$

4. $3 = L \div 6$

5. $3 = W \div 9$

6. $\dfrac{N}{12} = -2$

7. $\dfrac{C}{14} = 0$

8. $\dfrac{x}{-10} = 7$

9. $\dfrac{E}{-2} = -18$

10. $13 = y \div (-4)$

11. $\dfrac{F}{3.6} = 5$

12. $\dfrac{A}{-0.5} = 24$

13. $S \div (7.8) = 3$

14. $x \div (-0.4) = 16$

15. $-20 = \dfrac{y}{0.3}$

16. $\dfrac{T}{-1.8} = 2.4$

17. $0 = H \div (-3.8)$

18. $M \div 9.5 = -10$

19. $\dfrac{y}{-0.1} = -0.01$

20. $\dfrac{R}{12.6} = 0.002$

21. $1.04 = \dfrac{H}{0.08}$

22. $\dfrac{B}{\frac{1}{2}} = 7$

23. $V \div 1\frac{1}{4} = 3$

24. $\dfrac{x}{\frac{3}{8}} = -\dfrac{1}{2}$

25. $D \div \left(-\dfrac{1}{16}\right) = -32$

26. $4 = y \div \left(-\dfrac{7}{8}\right)$

27. $\dfrac{1}{4} = \dfrac{T}{1\frac{1}{2}}$

28. $H \div (-2) = 7\frac{9}{16}$

29. $\dfrac{M}{0.009} = 100$

30. $x \div (6.004) = -0.17$

For each of these problems write an equation. Solve for the unknown and check.

31.

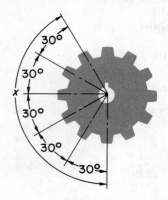

Fig. 9-55

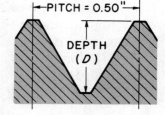

Fig. 9-56

32. The depth of an American Standard thread divided by 0.649 5 is equal to the pitch. Compute the depth of the thread shown in figure 9-56.

33. The width of a rectangle is equal to its area divided by its length. Compute the area of the rectangular patio shown in figure 9-57.

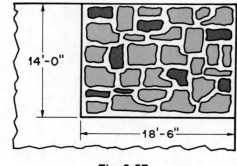

Fig. 9-57

34. The grade of a road is expressed as a percent. It is equal to the amount of rise divided by the horizontal distance. Compute the rise of the road shown in figure 9-58.

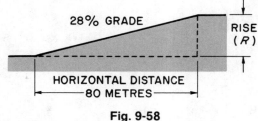

Fig. 9-58

For each of these problems, substitute the given values in the formula and solve for the unknown. Check.

35. The average rate of speed of a vehicle, in miles per hour, is computed by dividing distance, in miles, by time, in hours: $R = \frac{D}{T}$. Determine D when $T = 0.8$ hour and $R = 55$ miles per hour.

36. The pitch (P) of a spur gear equals the number (N) of gear teeth divided by the pitch diameter (D): $P = \frac{N}{D}$. Determine N when $P = 5$ and $D = 5.600\ 0$ inches.

37. Ohm's Law states that current, in amperes (I), equals voltage, in volts (E), divided by resistance, in ohms (R): $I = \frac{E}{R}$. Determine E when $I = 1.5$ amperes and $R = 8$ ohms.

38. The diameter of a circle equals the circle circumference divided by 3.141 6: $D = \frac{C}{3.141\ 6}$. Determine C when $D = 10$ centimetres.

39. In mechanical energy applications, force, in pounds (F), equals work in foot-pounds (W), divided by distance, in feet (D): $F = \frac{W}{D}$. Determine W when $F = 150$ pounds and $D = 7.5$ feet.

40. In electrical energy applications, power, in watts (W), equals energy, in watt-hour (Wh), divided by time, in hours (T): $W = \frac{Wh}{T}$. Determine Wh when $W = 250$ watts and $T = 3.2$ hours.

SOLUTION OF EQUATIONS BY THE ROOT PRINCIPLE OF EQUALITY

The root principle of equality states that if the same root of both sides of an equation is taken, the sides remain equal and the equation remains balanced. The root principle is used to solve an equation that contains an unknown which is raised to a power, for example, $s^2 = 36$.

Procedure for Solving an Equation in which the Unknown is Raised to a Power

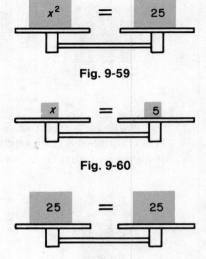

* Extract the root of both sides of the equation which leaves the unknown with an exponent of one.

* Check.

Fig. 9-59

Example 1.   Solve for x.

$$x^2 = 25$$

In the equation, x is squared. To solve the equation, extract the square root of both sides.

$$x^2 = 25$$
$$\sqrt{x^2} = \sqrt{25}$$
$$x = 5 \; Ans$$

Fig. 9-60

Check.

$$x^2 = 25$$
$$5^2 = 25$$
$$25 = 25 \; ck$$

Fig. 9-61

Example 2.   The volume of the cube shown in figure 9-62 equals 8 cubic centimetres. Expressed as an equation $s^3 = 8 \text{ cm}^3$. Solve for s.

Extract the cube root of both sides of the equation.

$$s^3 = 8 \text{ cm}^3$$
$$\sqrt[3]{s^3} = \sqrt[3]{8 \text{ cm}^3}$$
$$s = 2 \text{ cm} \; Ans$$

Check.

$$s^3 = 8 \text{ cm}^3$$
$$(2 \text{ cm})^3 = 8 \text{ cm}^3$$
$$8 \text{ cm}^3 = 8 \text{ cm}^3 \; ck$$

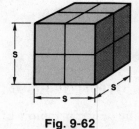

Fig. 9-62

Exercise 9-6

Solve each of these equations using the root principle of equality. Check all answers.

1. $S^2 = 16$
2. $P^2 = 36$
3. $81 = M^2$
4. $49 = B^2$
5. $D^3 = 27$
6. $x^3 = -27$
7. $144 = F^2$
8. $-64 = y^3$
9. $L^3 = 125$
10. $T^3 = 0$
11. $10\,000 = L^2$
12. $-125 = x^3$

13. $\dfrac{4}{9} = W^2$

14. $C^2 = \dfrac{1}{16}$

15. $P^2 = \dfrac{9}{25}$

16. $M^3 = \dfrac{1}{8}$

17. $-\dfrac{1}{8} = y^3$

18. $D^3 = \dfrac{64}{27}$

19. $G^3 = \dfrac{64}{125}$

20. $x^3 = \dfrac{-64}{125}$

21. $E^2 = 0.09$

22. $0.64 = H^2$

23. $W^2 = 2.25$

24. $0.000\ 1 = R^2$

25. $N^3 = 0.064$

26. $-0.125 = x^3$

27. $7.84 = F^2$

28. $T^2 = 88.36$

29. $y^3 = 0.027$

30. $-0.027 = y^3$

31. The area of a square equals the length of a side (s) squared. Given the areas of squares in figure 9-64, write an equation for each, solve for s, and check.

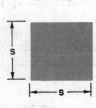

Fig. 9-63

	AREA	EQUATION	s
a.	49 square feet		
b.	81 square millimetres		
c.	$\dfrac{25}{64}$ square inch		
d.	6.25 square metres		
e.	0.36 square yard		

Fig. 9-64

32. The volume of a cube equals the length of a side (s) cubed. Given the volumes of cubes in figure 9-66, write an equation for each, solve for s, and check.

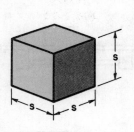

Fig. 9-65

	VOLUME	EQUATION	s
a.	125 cubic centimetres		
b.	0.064 cubic yard		
c.	$\dfrac{8}{27}$ cubic foot		
d.	0.027 cubic metre		
e.	$\dfrac{1}{8}$ cubic inch		

Fig. 9-66

SOLUTION OF EQUATIONS BY THE POWER PRINCIPLE OF EQUALITY

The power principle of equality states that if both sides of an equation are raised to the same power, the sides remain equal and the equation remains balanced. The power principle is used to solve an equation that contains a root of the unknown, for example, $\sqrt{A} = 8$.

Procedure for Solving an Equation which Contains a Root of the Unknown

- Raise both sides of the equation to the power which leaves the unknown with an exponent of one.

- Check.

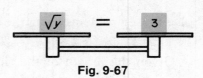

Fig. 9-67

Example 1. Solve for y.

$$\sqrt{y} = 3$$

In the equation, y is expressed as a square root. To solve the equation, square both sides.

$$\sqrt{y} = 3$$
$$(\sqrt{y})^2 = 3^2$$
$$y = 9 \ Ans$$

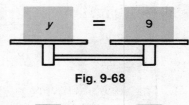

Fig. 9-68

Check.

$$\sqrt{y} = 3$$
$$\sqrt{9} = 3$$
$$3 = 3 \ \text{ck}$$

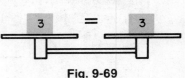

Fig. 9-69

Example 2. The length of each side of the cube shown in figure 9-70 equals 4 centimetres. The volume (V) of the cube can be expressed as the equation $\sqrt[3]{V} = 4$ cm. Solve for V.

Cube both sides of the equation.

$$\sqrt[3]{V} = 4 \text{ cm}$$
$$(\sqrt[3]{V})^3 = (4 \text{ cm})^3$$
$$V = 64 \text{ cm}^3 \ Ans$$

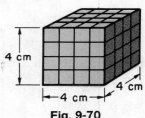

Fig. 9-70

Check.

$$\sqrt[3]{V} = 4 \text{ cm}$$
$$\sqrt[3]{64 \text{ cm}^3} = 4 \text{ cm}$$
$$4 \text{ cm} = 4 \text{ cm ck}$$

Exercise 9-7

Solve each of these equations using the power principle of equality. Check all answers.

1. $\sqrt{C} = 8$
2. $\sqrt{T} = 12$
3. $\sqrt{P} = 1.2$
4. $0.7 = \sqrt{M}$
5. $0.82 = \sqrt{F}$
6. $\sqrt[3]{V} = 3$
7. $\sqrt[3]{H} = 2.3$
8. $\sqrt[3]{x} = -4$
9. $-0.1 = \sqrt[3]{y}$
10. $\sqrt[4]{M} = 2$
11. $\sqrt{A} = 0$
12. $\sqrt[5]{N} = 1$

13. $-2 = \sqrt[5]{y}$
14. $0.2 = \sqrt[4]{D}$
15. $\sqrt[3]{x} = -0.6$
16. $\sqrt[4]{P} = 0.1$
17. $0.1 = \sqrt[3]{B}$
18. $\frac{1}{2} = \sqrt{A}$
19. $\sqrt{R} = \frac{3}{8}$
20. $\sqrt[3]{V} = \frac{2}{3}$
21. $\sqrt[4]{F} = \frac{1}{2}$
22. $-\frac{3}{5} = \sqrt[3]{y}$

23. $\frac{5}{8} = \sqrt{H}$
24. $\sqrt{P} = 1\frac{1}{4}$
25. $\sqrt[3]{B} = 2\frac{1}{2}$
26. $\sqrt[5]{x} = -\frac{1}{2}$
27. $1\frac{3}{4} = \sqrt[3]{y}$
28. $-1\frac{3}{4} = \sqrt[3]{y}$
29. $\sqrt[3]{x} = -\frac{3}{10}$
30. $\sqrt[5]{x} = -0.2$

Solve these problems using the power principle of equality.

31. The length of a side of a square equals the square root of the area (*A*). Given the length of the sides of squares in figure 9-72, write an equation for each, solve for area (*A*) and check.

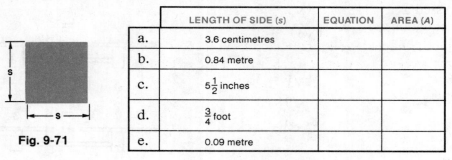

	LENGTH OF SIDE (s)	EQUATION	AREA (A)
a.	3.6 centimetres		
b.	0.84 metre		
c.	$5\frac{1}{2}$ inches		
d.	$\frac{3}{4}$ foot		
e.	0.09 metre		

Fig. 9-71

Fig. 9-72

32. The length of a side of a cube equals the cube root of the volume (*V*). Given the lengths of the sides of cubes in figure 9-74, write an equation for each, solve for volume (*V*), and check.

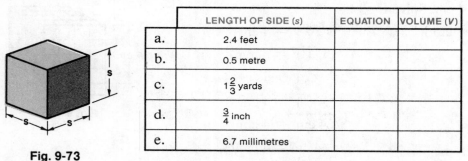

	LENGTH OF SIDE (s)	EQUATION	VOLUME (V)
a.	2.4 feet		
b.	0.5 metre		
c.	$1\frac{2}{3}$ yards		
d.	$\frac{3}{4}$ inch		
e.	6.7 millimetres		

Fig. 9-73

Fig. 9-74

TRANSPOSITION

With your instructor's permission, an alternate method of solving certain equations may be used. The alternate method is called transposition. *Transposition* or transposing a term means that a term is moved from one side of an equation to the opposite side with the sign changed.

Transposition is not a mathematical process although it is based on the addition and subtraction principles of equality. Transposition should only be used after the principles of equality are fully understood and applied.

Transposition is a quick and convenient means of solving equations in which a term is added to or subtracted from the unknown. The purpose of using transposition is the same as that of using the addition and subtraction principles of equality. Both methods involve getting the unknown term to stand alone on one side of the equation in order to determine the value of the unknown.

The next two examples are solved by applying both the addition or subtraction principles of equality and transposition. Notice that when applying the addition or subtraction principles of equality, a term is eliminated on one side of the equation and appears on the other side with the sign changed.

Example 1.   Solve for *x*.

$$x + 15 = 25$$

METHOD 1.   The Subtraction Principle of Equality

$x + 15 =$ 25

$\underline{- 15 = -15}$

$\quad\quad x =$ $25 - 15$ ← Observe that +15 is eliminated from the left side of
$\quad\quad x =$ 10 *Ans*   the equation and appears as −15 on the right side.

METHOD 2.   Transposition

$x + 15 = 25$

$x \boxed{+ 15} = 25 - 15$

$\quad\quad x = 25 - 15$ ← Observe that this expression is identical to the
$\quad\quad x = 10$ *Ans*   expression obtained when applying the subtraction
                              principle of equality.

Example 2.   Solve for *y*.

$$y - 8 = 32$$

METHOD 1.   The Addition Principle of Equality

$y - 8 =$ 32

$\underline{+ 8 = + 8}$

$\quad\quad y =$ $32 + 8$ ← Observe that −8 is eliminated from the left side of
$\quad\quad y =$ 40 *Ans*   the equation and appears as +8 on the right side.

METHOD 2.   Transposition

$y - 8 = 32$

$y \boxed{- 8} = 32 + 8$ Observe that this expression is identical to the
$\quad\quad y = 40$ *Ans*   expression obtained when applying the addition
                                  principle of equality.

- Transposition should only be used with the permission of your instructor.

- Before using transposition, solving equations by the principles of equality should be fully understood and applied.

- Transposition is not a mathematical process. It is a mechanical short cut method based on the addition and subtraction principles of equality.

UNIT EXERCISE AND PROBLEM REVIEW

Exercise 9-8

EXPRESSING WORD PROBLEMS AS EQUATIONS

Express each of these word problems as an equation. Let the unknown number equal *x* and solve for the value of the unknown. Check the equation by comparing it to the word problem. Does the equation state mathematically what the problem states in words? Check whether the equation is balanced by substituting the value of the unknown in the equation.

1. Five times a number, minus the number, equals 24.

2. Three times a number, divided by 6, equals $\frac{1}{2}$.

3. Two added to four times a number, minus three times the number, equals 5.

4. A length of tubing 40 inches long is cut into two unequal lengths. One piece is four times as long as the other.

   a. Find the length of the shorter piece.

   b. Find the length of the longer piece.

5. A company's profit for the second half year is $150 000 greater than the profit for the first half year. The total annual profit is $850 000. What is the profit for the first half year?

6. Four holes are drilled along a straight line in a plate. The distance between Hole 1 and Hole 4 is 35 centimetres. The distance between Hole 2 and Hole 3 is twice the distance between Hole 1 and Hole 2. The distance between Hole 3 and Hole 4 is the same as the distance between Hole 2 and Hole 3. What is the distance between Hole 1 and Hole 3?

7. In a series circuit, the sum of the voltages across each of the individual resistors is equal to the applied line voltage. In a 120-volt circuit with 3 resistors, the voltage across R_2 is 20 volts greater than the voltage across R_1. The voltage across R_3 is 20 volts greater than the voltage across R_2. What is the voltage across R_3?

EQUATIONS INVOLVING ADDITION OR SUBTRACTION

Solve each of these equations. Check all answers.

8. $M + 7 = 22$

9. $16 = P + 12$

10. $T - 18 = 9$

11. $y - 7 = -20$

12. $x + 13 = -20$

13. $25 = D - 8$

14. $25 = D + 8$

15. $-17 = T - 15$

16. $y - 36 = -18$

17. $x + 10 = -2$

18. $H + 9.3 = 14.8$

19. $A - 0.6 = 0.4$

20. $-22 = L - 26.1$

21. $2.6 = F + 3.7$

22. $M + 0.03 = 2.05$

23. $R - 4.52 = 5.48$

24. $29.197 = x + 31.093$

25. $y - 14.69 = -10.05$

26. $D - \frac{3}{4} = \frac{3}{4}$

27. $H + 2\frac{1}{2} = 6\frac{1}{4}$

28. $27\frac{3}{8} = B + 19\frac{1}{8}$

29. $y - \frac{5}{8} = -\frac{1}{2}$

30. $6\frac{9}{16} = F - 8\frac{11}{16}$

31. $x + 14\frac{13}{16} = -10\frac{7}{8}$

EQUATIONS INVOLVING MULTIPLICATION OR DIVISION

Solve each of these equations. Check all answers.

32. $5L = 55$

33. $9x = -63$

34. $\dfrac{D}{7} = 42$

35. $H \div 4 = 8$

36. $50 = -10x$

37. $\dfrac{A}{-6} = 54$

38. $\dfrac{B}{-3} = -27$

39. $9M = 0$

40. $-12E = -48$

41. $-y = 17$

42. $26 = \dfrac{H}{2.5}$

43. $0.66 = 0.3F$

44. $-7.5x = 24$

45. $\dfrac{W}{11.4} = 0.2$

46. $\dfrac{y}{0.1} = -0.06$

47. $8.73B = 29.682$

48. $-20 = M \div 18.85$

49. $P \div (-5.6) = -10.3$

50. $-0.073x = 0.584$

51. $\dfrac{1}{2}E = 6$

52. $V \div 2\dfrac{3}{4} = 8$

53. $\dfrac{x}{\frac{3}{8}} = -\dfrac{1}{4}$

54. $-\dfrac{5}{16} = -2\dfrac{1}{2}F$

55. $y \div \left(-\dfrac{3}{4}\right) = 3\dfrac{1}{2}$

EQUATIONS INVOLVING POWERS OR ROOTS

Solve each of these equations. Check all answers.

56. $B^2 = 64$

57. $x^3 = 64$

58. $x^3 = -64$

59. $\sqrt{M} = 11$

60. $15 = \sqrt{D}$

61. $H^3 = 125$

62. $\sqrt[3]{V} = 6$

63. $\sqrt{P} = 0$

64. $-8 = y^3$

65. $\sqrt{E} = 0.7$

66. $\sqrt[4]{L} = 0.1$

67. $x^3 = -0.125$

68. $0.2 = \sqrt[3]{F}$

69. $0.09 = B^2$

70. $\sqrt[3]{y} = -2.2$

71. $x^3 = 0.027$

72. $T^2 = 43.56$

73. $\sqrt[5]{M} = -1$

74. $E^2 = \dfrac{4}{9}$

75. $G^3 = \dfrac{-1}{27}$

76. $\sqrt{A} = \dfrac{3}{4}$

77. $\sqrt[3]{V} = \dfrac{2}{5}$

78. $y^3 = \dfrac{-8}{125}$

79. $\sqrt[3]{x} = -2\dfrac{3}{4}$

PROBLEMS: WRITING AND SOLVING EQUATIONS

For each of the following problems write an equation, solve for the unknown, and check.

80.

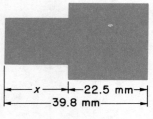

x ⟶ 22.5 mm
39.8 mm

Fig. 9-75

81.

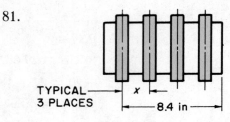

TYPICAL ⟶ x
3 PLACES   8.4 in

Fig. 9-76

82.

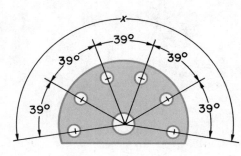

x

39° 39° 39° 39° 39° 39°

Fig. 9-77

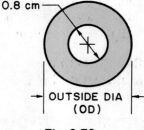

0.8 cm

OUTSIDE DIA
(OD)

Fig. 9-78

83. The inside diameter of the washer shown in figure 9-78 is 0.8 centimetre, which is 1.7 centimetres less than the outside diameter. What is the outside diameter (OD)?

84. Power, in watts, is equal to the product of the square of the current, in amperes, and the total line resistance, in ohms. Determine the line resistance (R) when power equals 400 watts and current equals 40 amperes.

85. The book value of equipment using the straight-line depreciation method is equal to the original cost minus the product of number of years depreciated and the annual depreciation. Determine the original cost (OC) when the book value equals \$3 200, the annual depreciation is \$400, and the depreciation is over a five-year period.

PROBLEMS: SUBSTITUTING VALUES IN FORMULAS

For each of these problems, substitute the given values in the formula and solve for the unknown. Check.

86. The spur gear formula is $D_R = D - 2d$. Determine the pitch diameter (D) when the root diameter (D_R) = 76.50 millimetres and the dedendum (d) = 4.08 millimetres.

87. Power, in kilowatts (P_{kW}), is equal to 0.001 times voltage, in volts (E), times current, in amperes (I): $P_{kW} = 0.001EI$. Determine E when $P_{kW} = 3.6$ kilowatts and $I = 30$ amperes.

88. The area of a triangle is equal to $\frac{1}{2}$ times the base times the height: $A = \frac{1}{2}bh$. Determine h when $A = 3\frac{1}{2}$ square feet and $b = 1\frac{3}{4}$ feet.

89. The volume of a cube equals the length of a side cubed: $V = s^3$. Determine s when $V = 125$ cubic centimetres.

90. The distance traveled (D) by a vehicle, in miles, is computed by multiplying the average rate of speed (R), in miles per hour, by the time (T), in hours: $D = RT$. Determine T when $D = 116.4$ miles and $R = 48.5$ miles per hour.

91. The annual rate (r) of simple interest on money loaned is equal to the interest earned (i) divided by the product of the principal (p) and the time (t) in years: $r = \frac{i}{pt}$. Determine i when $r = 12\%$, $p = \$2\,700$ and $t = 3\frac{1}{2}$ years.

UNIT 10
Complex Equations

After studying this unit you should be able to

- solve equations consisting of combined operations.
- substitute values in formulas and solve for unknowns.
- rearrange formulas to solve for any letter value.

EQUATIONS CONSISTING OF COMBINED OPERATIONS

Often in actual occupational applications, formulas are used and equations are developed which are complex. These equations require the use of two or more principles of equality for their solutions. For example, the equation $0.13x - 4.73(x + 6.35) = 5.06x - 2.87$ requires a definite step-by-step procedure in determining the value of x. Use of proper procedure results in the unknown standing alone on one side of the equation with its value on the other.

Procedure for Solving Equations Consisting of Combined Operations

It is essential that the steps used in solving an equation be taken in this order. Some or all of these steps may be used, depending upon the particular equation.

- Remove parentheses.
- Combine like terms on each side of the equation.
- Apply the addition and subtraction principle of equality to get all unknown terms on one side of the equation and all known terms on the other side.
- Combine like terms.
- Apply the multiplication and division principles of equality.
- Apply the power and root principles of equality.

NOTE: Always solve for a positive unknown. A positive unknown may equal a negative value, but a negative unknown is not a solution. For example, $x = -10$ is correct, but $-x = 10$ is incorrect.

Example 1. Solve for x.

$$8x + 12 = 52$$

In the equation, the operations involved are multiplication and addition. First subtract 12 from both sides of the equation.

$$
\begin{aligned}
8x + 12 &= 52 \\
-12 &= -12 \\
\hline
\frac{8x}{8} &= \frac{40}{8}
\end{aligned}
$$

Next divide both sides of the equation by 8.

$$x = 5 \; Ans$$

Check.

$$8x + 12 = 52$$
$$8(5) + 12 = 52$$
$$40 + 12 = 52$$
$$52 = 52 \; ck$$

Example 2. Solve for D.

$$6D + 4D = 3D - 5D + 19 + 5$$

Combine like terms on each side of the equation.

$$6D + 4D = 3D - 5D + 19 + 5$$
$$10D = -2D + 24$$

Add $2D$ to both sides of the equation.

$$
\begin{aligned}
+2D &= +2D \\
\hline
\frac{12D}{12} &= \frac{24}{12}
\end{aligned}
$$

Divide both sides of the equation by 12.

$$D = 2 \; Ans$$

Check.

$$6D + 4D = 3D - 5D + 19 + 5$$
$$6(2) + 4(2) = 3(2) - 5(2) + 19 + 5$$
$$12 + 8 = 6 - 10 + 19 + 5$$
$$20 = 20 \; ck$$

Example 3. Solve for y.

$$14y - 6(y - 3) = 22$$

Remove the parentheses.

$$14y - 6(y - 3) = 22$$
$$14y - 6y + 18 = 22$$

Combine like terms.

$$8y + 18 = 22$$

Subtract 18 from both sides of the equation.

$$
\begin{aligned}
-18 &= -18 \\
\hline
\frac{8y}{8} &= \frac{4}{8}
\end{aligned}
$$

Divide both sides of the equation by 8.

$$y = \frac{1}{2} \; Ans$$

Check.

$$14y - 6(y - 3) = 22$$
$$14\left(\tfrac{1}{2}\right) - 6\left(\tfrac{1}{2} - 3\right) = 22$$
$$14\left(\tfrac{1}{2}\right) - 6\left(-2\tfrac{1}{2}\right) = 22$$
$$7 + 15 = 22$$
$$22 = 22 \; ck$$

Example 4.   Solve for x.

$$\frac{x^2}{6} - 36.5 = -35$$

Add 36.5 to both sides of the equation.

$$\frac{x^2}{6} - 36.5 = -35$$
$$\underline{ + 36.5 = +36.5}$$

Multiply both sides of the equation by 6.

$$\frac{6}{1}\left(\frac{x^2}{6}\right) = (1.5)6$$

$$x^2 = 9$$

Extract the square root of both sides of the equation.

$$x = 3 \; Ans$$

Check.

$$\frac{x^2}{6} - 36.5 = -35$$
$$\frac{3^2}{6} - 36.5 = -35$$
$$\frac{9}{6} - 36.5 = -35$$
$$1.5 - 36.5 = -35$$
$$-35 = -35 \; \text{ck}$$

Example 5.   Solve for P.

$$6\sqrt[3]{P} = 4(\sqrt[3]{P} + 1.5)$$

Remove parentheses.

$$6\sqrt[3]{P} = 4(\sqrt[3]{P} + 1.5)$$
$$6\sqrt[3]{P} = 4\sqrt[3]{P} + 6$$

Subtract $4\sqrt[3]{P}$ from both sides of the equation.

$$\underline{-4\sqrt[3]{P} = -4\sqrt[3]{P}}$$

Divide both sides of the equation by 2.

$$\frac{2\sqrt[3]{P}}{2} = \frac{6}{2}$$

Raise both sides of the equation to the third power.

$$\sqrt[3]{P} = 3$$

$$P = 27 \; Ans$$

Check.

$$6\sqrt[3]{P} = 4(\sqrt[3]{P} + 1.5)$$
$$6\sqrt[3]{27} = 4(\sqrt[3]{27} + 1.5)$$
$$6(3) = 4(3 + 1.5)$$
$$6(3) = 4(4.5)$$
$$18 = 18 \; \text{ck}$$

Exercise 10-1

Solve for the unknown and check each of these combined operations equations.

1. $5x - 33 = 7$

2. $10M + 5 + 4M = 89$

3. $8E - 14 = 2E + 28$

4. $4B - 7 = B + 14$

5. $7T - 14 = 0$

6. $6N + 4 = 84 + N$

7. $2.5A + 8 = 15 - 6.5$

8. $12 - (-x + 8) = 18$

9. $3H + (2 - H) = 20$

10. $6 = -(2 + C) - (4 + 2C)$

11. $-5(R + 6) = 10(R - 2)$

12. $0.29E = 9.39 - 0.01E$

13. $7.2F + 5(F - 8.1) = 0.6F + 15.18$

14. $\frac{P}{7} + 8 = 5.9$

15. $\frac{1}{4}W + (W - 8) = \frac{3}{4}$

16. $\frac{1}{8}D - 3(D - 7) = 5\frac{1}{8}D - 3$

17. $0.58y = 18.78 - 0.02y$

18. $2H^2 - 20 = (H + 4)(H - 4)$

19. $4A^2 + 3A + 36 = 8A^2 + 3A$

20. $x(3 + x) + 20 = x^2 - (x - 5)$

21. $(\frac{b}{2})^3 + 34 = 42$

22. $3F^3 + F(F + 8) = 8F + F^2 + 81$

23. $9 + y^2 = (y - 4)(y - 1)$

24. $\frac{1}{4}(2B - 12) + B^2 = \frac{1}{2}B + 22$

25. $-4(y - 3) = 2\sqrt{y} - 4y$

26. $14\sqrt{x} = 6(\sqrt{x} + 8) + 16$

27. $8P^2 + 6P + 72 = 16P^2 + 6P$

28. $7\sqrt{x} = 3(\sqrt{x} + 8) - 4$

29. $\sqrt{B^2} - 2B = -2(B - 3)$

30. $(2y)^3 - 2.8(5 + 3y) = -22 - 8.4y$

SUBSTITUTING VALUES AND SOLVING FORMULAS

Occupational applications often require solving formulas in which all but one numerical value for letter values are known. The unknown letter value can appear anywhere within the formula. To determine the numerical value of the unknown, write the original formula, substitute the known number values for their respective letter values, and simplify. Then follow the procedure given for solving equations consisting of combined operations.

Example 1.   An open belt pulley system is shown in figure 10-1. The number of inches between the pulley centers is represented by x. The larger pulley diameter (D) is 6 inches and the smaller pulley diameter (d) is

4 inches. The belt length (L) is 56 inches. This formula is found in a trade handbook.

$$L = 3.14(0.5D + 0.5d) + 2x$$

Use this formula to compute x.

Write the formula.	$L = 3.14(0.5D + 0.5d) + 2x$
Substitute the known numerical values for their respective letter values and simplify.	56 in $= 3.14[0.5(6\ \text{in}) + 0.5(4\ \text{in})] + 2x$ 56 in $= 3.14(5\ \text{in}) + 2x$ 56 in $= 15.70\ \text{in} + 2x$
Subtract 15.70 inches from both sides.	56.00 in $= 15.70\ \text{in} + 2x$ $-15.70\ \text{in} = -15.70\ \text{in}$

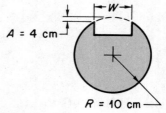

BELT

$D = 6"$ x $d = 4"$

Fig. 10-1

Divide both sides by 2.	$\dfrac{40.30\ \text{in}}{2} = \dfrac{2x}{2}$
	$x = 20.15\ \text{in}$ *Ans*
Check.	$L = 3.14(0.5D + 0.5d) + 2x$ 56 in $= 3.14[0.5(6\ \text{in}) + 0.5(4\ \text{in})] + 2(20.15\ \text{in})$ 56 in $= 15.70\ \text{in} + 40.30\ \text{in}$ 56 in $= 56\ \text{in}$ ck

Example 2. A slot is cut in the circular piece shown in figure 10-2. The piece has a radius (R) of 10 centimetres. The number of centimetres in the width is represented by W. Dimension A is 4 centimetres. This formula is found in a trade handbook.

$$A = R - \sqrt{R^2 - 0.25W^2}$$

Find dimension W.

Write the formula.	$A = R - \sqrt{R^2 - 0.25W^2}$
Substitute the known numerical values for their respective letter values and simplify.	4 cm $= 10\ \text{cm} - \sqrt{(10\ \text{cm})^2 - 0.25W^2}$ 4 cm $= 10\ \text{cm} - \sqrt{100\ \text{cm}^2 - 0.25W^2}$
Subtract 10 cm from both sides.	$-10\ \text{cm} = -10\ \text{cm}$ $-6\ \text{cm} = \sqrt{100\ \text{cm}^2 - 0.25W^2}$

$A = 4$ cm W

$R = 10$ cm

Fig. 10-2

Observe that both terms, 100 cm² and 0.25W² are enclosed within radical sign. Neither term can be removed until the radical sign is eliminated.

Square both sides	36 cm² $= 100\ \text{cm}^2 - 0.25W^2$
Subtract 100 cm² from both sides.	$-100\ \text{cm}^2 = -100\ \text{cm}^2$
Divide both sides by -0.25.	$\dfrac{-64\ \text{cm}^2}{-0.25} = \dfrac{-0.25W^2}{-0.25}$
	256 cm² $= W^2$
Take the square root of both sides.	$W = 16\ \text{cm}$ *Ans*

Check.

$$A = R - \sqrt{R^2 - 0.25W^2}$$

$$4 \text{ cm} = 10 \text{ cm} - \sqrt{(10 \text{ cm})^2 - 0.25(16 \text{ cm})^2}$$

$$4 \text{ cm} = 10 \text{ cm} - \sqrt{100 \text{ cm}^2 - 64 \text{ cm}^2}$$

$$4 \text{ cm} = 10 \text{ cm} - \sqrt{36 \text{ cm}^2}$$

$$4 \text{ cm} = 10 \text{ cm} - 6 \text{ cm}$$

$$4 \text{ cm} = 4 \text{ cm ck}$$

Exercise 10-2

The formulas for this set of problems have been taken from various technical fields. Substitute the given numerical values for letter values and solve for the unknown. Calculate answers to 3 decimal places where necessary.

1. This is the formula for finding the area of a triangle.

   $$A = \frac{ab}{2}$$ where A = area

                                 a = altitude

                                 b = base

   Solve for a when A = 24 sq ft and b = 8 ft.

2. The inductive reactance is found using this formula.

   $$X_L = 2\pi fL$$ where X_L = inductive reactance, in ohms

                                 π = 3.14

                                 f = frequency in hertz

                                 L = inductance in henrys

   Solve for L when f = 60 Hz and X_L = 82 ohms.

3. In a power transformer the ratio of the primary and the secondary voltages is directly proportional to the number of turns on the primary and the secondary.

   $$\frac{E_p}{E_s} = \frac{T_p}{T_s}$$

   Solve for T_s when E_p = 440 volts, E_s = 2 200 volts and T_p = 150 turns.

4. This formula is used to express a temperature in degrees Celsius as a temperature in degrees Fahrenheit.

   $$^\circ F = \frac{9}{5}(^\circ C) + 32^\circ$$

   Solve for $^\circ C$ when the temperature is 28°F.

5. The area of a trapezoid is found using this formula.

   $$A = \frac{h}{2}(b + b')$$ where A = area

                                 h = height

                                 b = first base

                                 b' = second base

   Solve for b when A = 108 sq ft, h = 8 ft and b' = 12 ft.

6. The accumulated amount in a savings account is found using this formula.

$A = p + prt$ where A = amount at end of period

p = principal invested

r = rate

t = time

Solve for t when $p = \$1\ 800$, $r = 7\%$, and $A = \$3\ 312$.

7. The sum of an arithmetic progression is found using this formula.

$S = \frac{n}{2}(a + l)$ where S = sum

n = number of terms

a = first term

l = last term

Solve for l when $S = 150$, $n = 6$, and $a = 5$.

8. There are 4 cells connected in a series circuit. The internal resistance of each cell is 5 ohms. The external circuit resistance is 8 ohms. The current in the circuit is 4 amperes. Find the voltage of each cell.

$I = \dfrac{nE}{R + nr}$ where I = current in amperes

n = number of cells

E = voltage of one cell

r = internal resistance of one cell

R = resistance of external circuit

9. This is the formula for finding horsepower.

$\text{hp} = \dfrac{IE(Eff)}{746}$ where hp = horsepower

E = voltage in volts

I = current in amperes

Eff = efficiency

Solve for I when hp = 12 horsepower, $E = 220$ volts, and $Eff = 87\%$.

10. This formula is used to find the impedance of a circuit.

$Z = \sqrt{R^2 + X^2}$ where Z = impedance in ohms

R = resistance in ohms

X = reactance in ohms

Solve for X when $R = 8$ ohms and $Z = 60$ ohms.

REARRANGING FORMULAS

A formula that is used to find a particular value must sometimes be rearranged to solve for another value. Consider the letter to be solved for as the unknown term and the other letters in the formula as the known values. The formula must be rearranged so that the unknown term is on one side of the equation and all other values are on the other side. A formula is rearranged using the same procedure that is used for solving equations consisting of combined operations.

Example 1. The area of a triangle shown in figure 10-3 is computed using this formula.

$$A = \frac{ab}{2}$$
where A = area

a = altitude

b = base

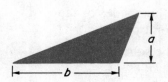

Rearrange the formula and solve for b.

Multiply both sides of the equation by 2.

$$A = \frac{ab}{2}$$

$$2(A) = (\frac{ab}{2})\frac{2}{1}$$

Fig. 10-3

Divide both sides of the equation by a.

$$\frac{2A}{a} = \frac{ab}{a}$$

$$b = \frac{2A}{a}\ Ans$$

Example 2. A screw thread is checked using a micrometer and 3 wires as shown in figure 10-4. The measurement is checked using this formula.

$$M = D - 1.515\,5p + 3w$$
where M = measurement over the wires

D = major diameter

p = pitch

w = wire size

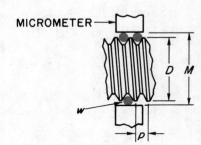

Solve the formula for w.

Subtract D from both sides of the equation.

$$M = D - 1.515\,5p + 3w$$
$$-D = -D$$

$$M - D = -1.515\,5p + 3w$$

Add $1.515\,5p$ to both sides of the equation.

$$+1.515\,5p = +1.515\,5p$$

Fig. 10-4

Divide both sides of the equation by 3.

$$\frac{M - D + 1.515\,5p}{3} = \frac{3w}{3}$$

$$w = \frac{M - D + 1.515\,5p}{3}\ Ans$$

Example 3.   The area of a ring shown in figure 10-5 is computed using this formula.

$$A = \pi(R^2 - r^2)$$ where A = area

Fig. 10-5

π = pi

R = outside radius

r = inside radius

Solve for R.

Remove parentheses.	$A = \pi(R^2 - r^2)$
Add πr^2 to both sides of the equation.	$A = \pi R^2 - \pi r^2$
	$\underline{+\ \pi r^2 =\qquad\quad +\ \pi r^2}$
Divide both sides of the equation by π.	$\dfrac{A + \pi r^2}{\pi} = \dfrac{\pi R^2}{\pi}$
Take the square root of both sides.	$\dfrac{A + \pi r^2}{\pi} = R^2$

$$R = \sqrt{\dfrac{A + \pi r^2}{\pi}} \quad Ans$$

Exercise 10-3

The formulas for this set of problems are found in various occupational handbooks and manuals. Rearrange each and solve for the designated letter.

1. Solve for b.

    $A = ab$

2. Solve for l.

    $p = 2l + 2w$

3. Solve for E.

    $I = \dfrac{E}{R}$

4. Solve for w.

    $V = lwh$

5. Solve for $\angle C$.

    $\angle A + \angle B + \angle C = 180°$

6. Solve for M.

    $hp = 0.000\ 016MN$

7. Solve for T.

    $S = T - \dfrac{1.732}{N}$

8. Solve for r.

    $E = I(R + r)$

9. Solve for C.

    $C_a = S(C - F)$

10. Solve for $P.F.$

    $P = 2EI(P.F.)$

11. Solve for I.

    $P = \dfrac{EI}{1\ 000}$

12. Solve for K.

    $R = \dfrac{KL}{d^2}$

13. Solve for E_x.

    $I = \dfrac{E_x - E_c}{R}$

14. Solve for D.

    $CM = \dfrac{KIND}{c}$

15. Solve for E.

    $P = \dfrac{E^2}{R}$

16. Solve for I.

$$kW = \frac{2IE(PE)}{1\,000}$$

17. Solve for C.

$$D_o = 2C - d + 2a$$

18. Solve for P.

$$M = D - 1.515\,5P + 3W$$

19. Solve for P.

$$I = \sqrt{\frac{P}{R}}$$

20. Solve for F.

$$C_x = B_y(F - 1)$$

21. Solve for E.

$$M \doteq E - 0.866P + 3W$$

22. Solve for D.

$$hp = \frac{D^2N}{2.5}$$

23. Solve for d.

$$L = 3.14(0.5D + 0.5d) + 2x$$

24. Solve for D.

$$C = \frac{0.785\,4D^2L}{231}$$

25. A windlass is shown in figure 10-6. The formula used to find the required force is given.

$$F = \frac{Wr}{R}$$

where F = force

W = weight

r = smaller radius

R = larger radius

a. Solve for W.

b. Solve for r.

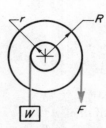

Fig. 10-6

26. A differential pulley is shown in figure 10-7. This formula is used to find the pulling force.

$$P = \frac{W(R - r)}{2R}$$

where P = pulling force

R = larger pulley

r = smaller pulley

a. Solve for W.

b. Solve for r.

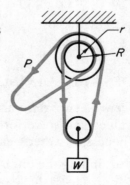

Fig. 10-7

27. The area shown in figure 10-8 is computed using this formula.

$$A = \frac{a(H + h) + bh + cH}{2}$$

a. Solve for b.

b. Solve for a.

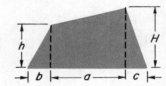

Fig. 10-8

UNIT EXERCISE AND PROBLEM REVIEW

Exercise 10-4

SOLVING COMBINED OPERATIONS EQUATIONS

Solve for the unknown and check each of these combined operations equations.

1. $8F - 7 + 5F = 45$

2. $12P - 9 = 39$

3. $3.6M - 6 = 26.2 - M$

4. $20 - (-B + 14) = 32$

5. $-14 = 3 - C + (9 + 5C)$

6. $15(E - 3) = -10(E + 2)$

7. $0.34T = 3.45 - 0.12T$

8. $6.8R + 2(R - 3.1) = 0.3R + 32.9$

9. $\frac{M}{6} + 5.3 = 7.4$

10. $\frac{1}{2}D + 2(D - \frac{1}{4}) = 5\frac{1}{2}$

11. $\frac{3}{8}N + 5(N - 6) = 1\frac{7}{8}N - 2$

12. $6A^2 - 54 = (A + 3)(A - 3)$

13. $28 + x^2 = (x - 6)(x - 2)$

14. $10\sqrt{B} = 4(\sqrt{B} + 12)$

15. $W + 5\sqrt{W} = -7\sqrt{W} + (W + 6)$

16. $3.7(4y - 2) + y^3 = 14.8y + 0.6$

SUBSTITUTING VALUES AND SOLVING FORMULAS

These formulas have been taken from various technical fields. Substitute the given values for letter values and solve for the unknown. Calculate answers to 3 decimal places where necessary. Check each answer.

17. This is the formula for finding the circumference of a circle.

$$C = 2\pi r \qquad \text{where } C = \text{circumference}$$
$$\pi = 3.141\ 6$$
$$r = \text{radius}$$

Solve for r when $C = 13$ inches.

18. Use this formula and solve for the $°F$ when the temperature is $-12°C$.

$$°F = \frac{9}{5}(°C) + 32°$$

19. The current for a motor is found using this formula.

    $$I = \frac{E_x}{R} - \frac{E_c}{R}$$

    where I = current in amperes

    R = resistance in ohms

    E_x = impressed voltage

    E_c = counter voltage

    Solve for E_c when I = 6 amperes, R = 0.3 ohm, and E_x = 250 volts.

20. This is the formula for finding the hypotenuse of a right triangle.

    $$c = \sqrt{a^2 + b^2}$$

    where c = hypotenuse

    a = first side

    b = second side

    Solve for b when c = 50 mm and a = 16 mm.

REARRANGING FORMULAS

These formulas are found in various occupational handbooks and manuals. Rearrange each and solve for the designated letter.

21. Figure 10-9 shows the inscribed and circumscribed circles for a regular hexagon.

    a. Solve for r.

       $R = 1.155r$

    b. Solve for R.

       $A = 2.598R^2$

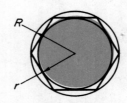

Fig. 10-9

22. Use this formula for the area shown in figure 10-10.

    $A = dt + 2a(s + n)$

    a. Solve for t.

    b. Solve for n.

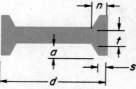

Fig. 10-10

23. Use this formula for the length of the diagonal shown in figure 10-11.

    $d = \sqrt{a^2 + b^2}$

    a. Solve for a.

    b. Solve for b.

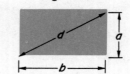

Fig. 10-11

24. Use this formula for the area shown in figure 10-12.

    $A = \pi(ab - cd)$

    a. Solve for b.

    b. Solve for d.

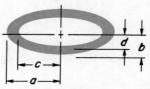

Fig. 10-12

25. Use this formula for the distance shown in figure 10-13.

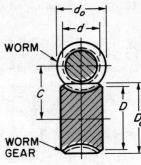

$$D_o = 2C - d + 2a$$

a. Solve for a.

b. Solve for C.

Fig. 10-13

26. Use this formula for the area shown in figure 10-14.

$$A = \frac{\pi(R^2 - r^2)}{2}$$

a. Solve for R.

b. Solve for r.

Fig. 10-14

27. Use this formula for the volume shown in figure 10-15.

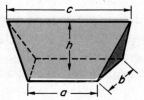

$$V = \frac{bh(2a + c)}{6}$$

a. Solve for c.

b. Solve for a.

Fig. 10-15

28. Refer to figure 10-16.

a. Solve for h.

$$V = 1.05(R^2 + Rr + r^2)h$$

b. Solve for h.

$$S = \sqrt{(R - r)^2 + h^2}$$

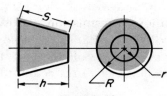

Fig. 10-16

UNIT 11
Ratio and Proportion

OBJECTIVES

After studying this unit you should be able to

- write comparisons as ratios.
- solve applied ratio problems.
- solve for the missing terms of given proportions.
- solve proportion problems by substituting values in formulas.
- analyze problems to determine whether they are direct or inverse proportions, set up proportions, and solve for unknowns.

The ability to solve applied problems using ratio and proportion is a requirement of many occupations. A knowledge of ratio and proportion is necessary in solving many everyday food service occupation problems. Proportions are used to solve many problems in medications in the health occupations.

Ratio and proportion are widely used in manufacturing applications, such as computing gear speeds and sizes, tapers, and machine cutting times. Electrical resistance, wire sizes, and material requirements are determined using proportions. The building trades apply ratios in determining roof pitches and pipe capacities. Compression ratios, transmission ratios, and rear axle ratios are commonly used by automobile mechanics. Employees in the business field compute selling price to cost ratios, profit to cost ratios, and dividend to cost ratios. In agricultural applications, fertilizer requirements are often determined by proportions.

DESCRIPTION OF RATIOS

Ratio is the comparison of two <u>like</u> quantities. For example, the compression ratio of an engine is the comparison between the amount of space in a cylinder when the piston is at the bottom of the stroke, and the amount of space when the piston is at the top of the stroke. A compression ratio of 8 to 1 is shown in figure 11-1.

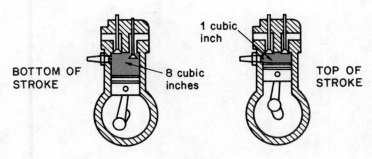

BOTTOM OF STROKE   8 cubic inches   1 cubic inch   TOP OF STROKE

Fig. 11-1

147

An automobile pulley system is shown in figure 11-2. The comparison of the fan pulley size to the alternator pulley size is expressed as the ratio of 3 to 4. The comparison of the alternator pulley size to the crankshaft pulley size is expressed as the ratio of 4 to 5. The comparison of the fan pulley size to the crankshaft pulley size is expressed as the ratio of 3 to 5.

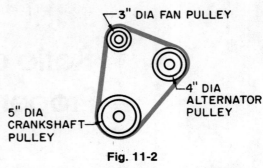

Fig. 11-2

The *terms* of a ratio are the two numbers that are compared. **Both terms must be expressed in the same units.** For example, the width and length of the strip of stock shown in figure 11-3 cannot be compared as a ratio until the 9-centimetre length is expressed as 90 millimetres. Both terms must be in the same units. The width and length are in the ratio of 13 to 90.

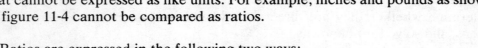

Fig. 11-3

It is impossible to express two quantities as ratios if the terms have unlike units that cannot be expressed as like units. For example, inches and pounds as shown in figure 11-4 cannot be compared as ratios.

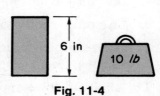

Fig. 11-4

Ratios are expressed in the following two ways:

1. With a colon between the two terms, such as 4:9. The ratio 4:9 is read 4 to 9.

2. With a division sign separating the two numbers, such as $4 \div 9$ or as a fraction, $\frac{4}{9}$.

ORDER OF TERMS OF RATIOS

The terms of a ratio must be compared in the order in which they are given. The first term is the numerator of a fraction and the second term is the denominator. A ratio should be expressed in lowest fractional terms.

The ratio 2 to 10 $= 2 \div 10 = \frac{2}{10} = \frac{1}{5}$

The ratio 10 to 2 $= 10 \div 2 = \frac{10}{2} = \frac{5}{1}$

Examples.   Express each ratio in lowest terms.

1. $5{:}15 = \frac{5}{15} = \frac{1}{3} \, Ans$

2. $21{:}6 = \frac{21}{6} = \frac{7}{2} \, Ans$

3. $\frac{3}{8}{:}\frac{9}{16} = \frac{3}{8} \div \frac{9}{16} = \frac{3}{8} \times \frac{16}{9} = \frac{2}{3} \, Ans$

4. $10{:}\frac{5}{6} = 10 \div \frac{5}{6} = \frac{10}{1} \times \frac{6}{5} = \frac{12}{1} \, Ans$

5. $4xy{:}6x = \frac{4xy}{6x} = \frac{2y}{3} \, Ans$

6. $18a^3b^2{:}9a^2b = \frac{18a^3b^2}{9a^2b} = \frac{2ab}{1} \, Ans$

Exercise 11-1

Express these ratios in lowest fractional form.

1. 3:7
2. 7:3
3. 12:24
4. 24:12
5. 8:30
6. 39:26
7. 12 in:46 in
8. 35 lb:10 lb
9. 9 cm:22 cm
10. 83 ft:100 ft
11. 52 m:16 m
12. $x^2:x$
13. x to x^2
14. $6M^2P$ to $2M$

15. $5D^3E$ to $7D^3E$
16. $13y$ to $26y$
17. $26y$ to $13y$
18. $15FG^3$ to $7G$
19. $\frac{2}{3}$ to $\frac{1}{2}$
20. $\frac{1}{2}$ to $\frac{2}{3}$
21. 8 to $\frac{3}{4}$
22. 8 to $\frac{4}{3}$
23. $\frac{a}{b}$ to $\frac{a}{c}$
24. $\frac{x}{y}$ to x
25. 4 in to 2 ft
26. 23 mm to 3 cm

27. 3 cm to 23 mm
28. 3 ft to 2 yd
29. 18 in to 1 yd
30. 16 min to 2 h
31. 20 cm to 0.5 m
32. 6 min to $\frac{1}{4}$ h
33. 3 pt to 2 qt
34. $\frac{1}{2}$ gal to 5 qt
35. 200 m to 0.4 km
36. 0.4 km to 200 m

37. Four field rheostats are shown in figure 11-5. Determine each ratio.

   a. R_1 to R_2

   b. R_3 to R_4

   c. R_4 to R_2

   d. R_3 to R_1

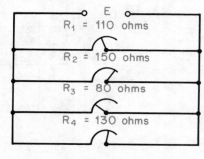

Fig. 11-5

38. Refer to the data given in the table in figure 11-6. Determine the compression ratios of the engines listed.

	AMOUNT OF SPACE WHEN THE PISTON IS AT THE:		COMPRESSION RATIO
	BOTTOM OF THE STROKE	TOP OF THE STROKE	
a.	27 cubic inches	3 cubic inches	?
b.	280 cubic centimetres	35 cubic centimetres	?
c.	22 cubic inches	2 cubic inches	?
d.	294 cubic centimetres	42 cubic centimetres	?

Fig. 11-6

39. In the building trades, the terms pitch, rise, run, and span are used in the layout and construction of roofs. In the gable roof shown in figure 11-7, the span is twice the run. Pitch is the ratio of the rise to the span.

$$\text{Span} = 2 \times \text{run} \qquad \text{Pitch} = \frac{\text{rise}}{\text{span}}$$

Determine the pitch of these gable roofs.

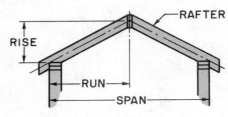

a. 12 ft rise, 30 ft span

b. 8 ft rise, 24 ft span

c. 4 m rise, 10 m span

d. 3 m rise, 9 m span

e. 6 m rise, 8 m run

f. 10 ft rise, 12 ft run

g. 15'-0" rise, 17'-6" run

h. 5 m rise, 7.5 m run

Fig. 11-7

40. Refer to the hole locations given for the plate shown in figure 11-8. Determine each ratio.

a. A to B

b. A to C

c. B to C

d. B to D

e. C to D

f. D to A

g. C to B

h. D to C

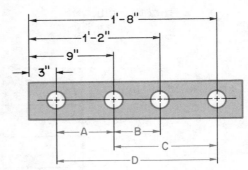

Fig. 11-8

DESCRIPTION OF PROPORTIONS

A proportion is an expression that states the equality of two ratios. Proportions are expressed in the following two ways:

1. 3:4 = 6:8 which is read as, "3 is to 4 as 6 is to 8."

2. $\frac{3}{4} = \frac{6}{8}$ which is the equation form. Proportions are generally written as equations in on-the-job applications.

A proportion consists of four terms. The first and the fourth terms are called *extremes* and the second and third terms are called *means*. In the proportion, 3:4 = 6:8, 3 and 8 are the extremes; 4 and 6 are the means. In the proportion, $\frac{4}{5} = \frac{12}{15}$, 4 and 15 are the extremes; 5 and 12 are the means. **The product of the means equals the product of the extremes.** If the terms are cross multiplied, their products are equal.

Example 1. $\frac{2}{3} = \frac{4}{6}$

Cross multiply.

$$\frac{2}{3} = \frac{4}{6}$$

$$\frac{2}{3} \times \frac{4}{6}$$

$$2 \times 6 = 3 \times 4$$

$$12 = 12$$

Example 2. $\frac{a}{b} = \frac{c}{d}$

Cross multiply.

$$\frac{a}{b} = \frac{c}{d}$$

$$\frac{a}{b} \times \frac{c}{d}$$

$$ad = bc$$

The method of cross multiplying is used in solving many practical occupational problems. The value of the unknown term can be determined when the values of three terms are known. Since a proportion is an equation, the principles used for solving equations are applied in determining the value of the unknown after the terms have been cross multiplied.

Example 1.   Solve for x.

$$\frac{2}{5} = \frac{x}{20}$$

$$\frac{2}{5} = \frac{x}{20}$$

Cross multiply. $5x = 2(20)$

Divide both sides of
the equation by 5. $\frac{5x}{5} = \frac{40}{5}$

$$x = 8 \; Ans$$

Check. Substitute 8 for x. $\frac{2}{5} = \frac{x}{20}$
Divide to simplify the fractions. $\frac{2}{5} = \frac{8}{20}$

$$0.4 = 0.4 \; ck$$

Example 2.   Solve for F.

$$\frac{F}{6.2} = \frac{9.8}{21.7}$$

$$\frac{F}{6.2} = \frac{9.8}{21.7}$$

Cross multiply. $21.7F = 6.2(9.8)$

Divide both sides of the
equation by 21.7. $\frac{21.7F}{21.7} = \frac{60.76}{21.7}$

$$F = 2.8 \; Ans$$

Check. $\frac{F}{6.2} = \frac{9.8}{21.7}$

$$\frac{2.8}{6.2} = \frac{9.8}{21.7}$$

$$0.451\,612\,9 = 0.451\,612\,9 \; ck$$

Example 3. Solve for V'.

$$\frac{V}{V'} = \frac{P'}{P}$$

$$\frac{V}{V'} = \frac{P'}{P}$$

Cross multiply.

$$VP = V'P'$$

Divide both sides of the equation by P'.

$$\frac{VP}{P'} = \frac{V'P'}{P'}$$

$$V' = \frac{VP}{P'} \; Ans$$

Check.

$$\frac{V}{V'} = \frac{P'}{P}$$

$$\frac{V}{\frac{VP}{P'}} = \frac{P'}{P}$$

$$V \div \frac{VP}{P'} = \frac{P'}{P}$$

$$\frac{V}{1} \times \frac{P'}{VP} = \frac{P'}{P}$$

$$\frac{P'}{P} = \frac{P'}{P} \; ck$$

Example 4. The proportion $\frac{R_1}{R_2} = \frac{l_1}{l_2}$ is used in electrical trades. R_1 and R_2 are the resistances of two wires and l_1 and l_2 are the lengths of the wires. Determine R_1 when R_2 is 20 ohms, l_1 is 60 feet, and $l_2 = 150$ feet.

Substitute the given values for letters.

$$\frac{R_1}{20 \, \Omega} = \frac{60 \, ft}{150 \, ft}$$

Cross multiply.

$$150R_1 = 20 \, \Omega (60)$$

Divide both sides of the equation by 150.

$$\frac{150R_1}{150} = \frac{1\,200 \, \Omega}{150}$$

$$R_1 = 8 \, \Omega \; Ans$$

Check.

$$\frac{R_1}{R_2} = \frac{l_1}{l_2}$$

$$\frac{8 \, \Omega}{20 \, \Omega} = \frac{60 \, ft}{150 \, ft}$$

$$0.4 = 0.4 \; ck$$

Example 5. This formula relates to the circuit shown in figure 11-9.

$$I = \frac{nE}{R + nr}$$ where I = circuit current

n = number of cells

E = voltage of one cell

R = external resistance

r = internal resistance of one cell

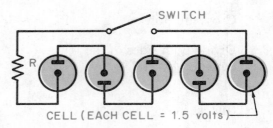

Fig. 11-9

There are five 1.5 volt cells connected in series each with an internal resistance of 1.8 ohms. The circuit current is 0.8 ampere. Find the external resistance in ohms.

Substitute the given values for the letters.	$\dfrac{0.8}{1} = \dfrac{5(1.5)}{R + 5(1.8)}$

Cross multiply. $0.8[R + 5(1.8)] = 5(1.5)$

Remove parentheses. $0.8(R + 9) = 7.5$

Subtract 7.2 from both sides of the equation. $0.8R + 7.2 = 7.5$

$$-7.2 = -7.2$$

Divide both sides of the equation by 0.8.

$$\frac{0.8R}{0.8} = \frac{0.3}{0.8}$$

$$R = 0.375 \text{ ohm } Ans$$

Check.

$$I = \frac{nE}{R + nr}$$

$$0.8 = \frac{5(1.5)}{0.375 + 5(1.8)}$$

$$0.8 = \frac{7.5}{9.375}$$

$$0.8 = 0.8 \text{ ck}$$

Exercise 11-2

Solve for the unknown value in each of these proportions. Check each answer.

1. $\dfrac{x}{4} = \dfrac{6}{24}$

2. $\dfrac{3}{A} = \dfrac{15}{30}$

3. $\dfrac{7}{9} = \dfrac{E}{45}$

4. $\dfrac{6}{13} = \dfrac{24}{y}$

5. $\dfrac{15}{c} = \dfrac{5}{4}$

6. $\dfrac{P}{18} = \dfrac{1}{3}$

7. $\dfrac{6}{7} = \dfrac{15}{F}$

8. $\dfrac{12}{H} = \dfrac{4}{25}$

9. $\dfrac{T}{6.6} = \dfrac{7.5}{22.5}$

10. $\dfrac{2.4}{3} = \dfrac{M}{0.8}$

11. $\dfrac{4}{4.1} = \dfrac{8}{L}$

12. $\dfrac{3.4}{y} = \dfrac{1}{-7}$

13. $\dfrac{A}{5} = \dfrac{3.2}{A}$

14. $\dfrac{\frac{3}{8}}{N} = \dfrac{\frac{1}{2}}{4}$

15. $\dfrac{3}{\frac{1}{2}} = \dfrac{5}{F}$

16. $\dfrac{G}{\frac{1}{4}} = \dfrac{\frac{7}{8}}{\frac{3}{8}}$

17. $\dfrac{7}{\frac{-1}{8}} = \dfrac{x}{\frac{9}{16}}$

18. $\dfrac{4}{R} = \dfrac{2R}{12.5}$

19. $\dfrac{11}{8} = \dfrac{E + 3}{6}$

20. $\dfrac{M - 5}{12} = \dfrac{15}{9}$

21. $\dfrac{8.5}{2} = \dfrac{16.15}{7.6F}$

22. $\dfrac{5}{x + 9.2} = \dfrac{10}{13}$

23. $\dfrac{D + 8}{-4} = \dfrac{7}{D - 8}$

24. $\dfrac{6}{3H^2 - 12} = \dfrac{5}{12.5}$

Solve these proportion problems. Substitute the known values in the formulas and determine the values of the unknowns.

25. Both roofs shown in figure 11-10 have the same pitch. Using the given values in the table in figure 11-11, determine the unknown rise or span of either roof.

$$\frac{R_1}{R_2} = \frac{S_1}{S_2}$$

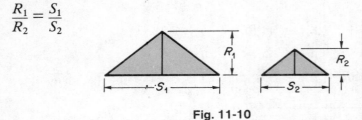

Fig. 11-10

	R_1	R_2	S_1	S_2
a.	?	12 ft	48 ft	36 ft
b.	10 ft	?	30 ft	12 ft
c.	5 m	4 m	?	8 m
d.	1.8 m	1.2 m	6.6 m	?
e.	?	9'-9"	41'-0"	30'-9"

Fig. 11-11

26. A lever is an example of a simple machine. A lever is a rigid bar that is free to turn about its supporting point. The supporting point is called a fulcrum. Levers have a great many practical uses. Scissors, shovels, brooms, and bottle openers are a few common examples of levers. There are three classes of levers. A diagram of a first-class lever is shown in figure 11-12. F_1 and F_2 are forces and D_1 and D_2 are distances. Using the given values in the table in figure 11-13, compute the missing values.

$$\frac{F_1}{F_2} = \frac{D_2}{D_1}$$

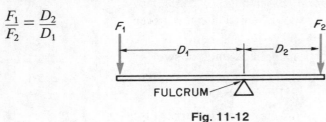

Fig. 11-12

	F_1	F_2	D_1	D_2
a.	? lb	150 lb	8 ft	6 ft
b.	72 lb	? lb	15 ft	2.5 ft
c.	175 lb	1050 lb	? ft	$6\frac{3}{4}$ ft
d.	32.8 lb	393.6 lb	8.4 ft	? ft

Fig. 11-13

27. Compute the radius (r) of the circular segment shown in figure 11-14. Round the answer to 1 decimal place.

$$\alpha = \frac{57.3l}{r}$$

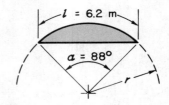

Fig. 11-14

28. The impressed voltage (E_x) across a motor armature is 230 volts. The counter voltage (E_c) is 223 volts and the current (I) is 14 amperes. What is the armature resistance (R) in ohms?

$$I = \frac{E_x - E_c}{R}$$

29. A tapered shaft is shown in figure 11-15. Find the taper in inches per foot of length (t/ft) using this formula. Round the answer to 3 decimal places.

$$L = \frac{12(D - d)}{t/ft}$$

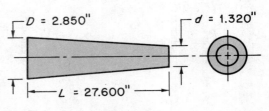

Fig. 11-15

30. A cell which has a voltage (E) of 2.6 volts and an internal resistance (r) of 0.08 ohm is connected to an electromagnet. The electromagnet receives a current (I) of 1.7 amperes. Find the resistance (R) to 2 decimal places.

$$I = \frac{E}{R + r}$$

DIRECT PROPORTIONS

In actual practice, word statements or other data must be expressed as proportions. When setting up a proportion the terms of the proportion must be placed in their proper positions. A problem which is set up and solved as a proportion must first be analyzed in order to determine where the terms are placed. Depending upon the positions of the terms, proportions are either direct or inverse.

Two quantities are *directly proportional* if a change in one produces a change in the other in the same direction. If an increase in one produces an increase in the other, or if a decrease in one produces a decrease in the other, the two quantities are directly proportional. The proportions discussed will be those that change at the same rate. An increase or decrease in one quantity produces the same rate of increase or decrease in the other quantity.

When setting up a direct proportion in fractional form, the numerator of the first ratio must correspond to the numerator of the second ratio. The denominator of the first ratio must correspond to the denominator of the second ratio.

Example 1.   A machine produces 280 pieces in 3.5 hours. How long does it take to produce 720 pieces?

Analyze the problem. An increase in the number of pieces produced (from 280 pieces to 720 pieces) requires an increase in time. Time increases as production increases; therefore, the proportion is direct.

Set up the proportion. Let x represent the time required to produce 720 pieces.

$$\frac{280 \text{ pieces}}{720 \text{ pieces}} = \frac{3.5 \text{ hours}}{x}$$

Notice that the numerator of the first ratio corresponds to the numerator of the second ratio; 280 pieces corresponds with 3.5 hours. The denominator of the first ratio corresponds to the denominator of the second ratio; 720 pieces corresponds with x.

Solve for x.

$$\frac{280 \text{ pieces}}{720 \text{ pieces}} = \frac{3.5 \text{ hours}}{x}$$

$$280x = 3.5 \text{ hours } (720)$$

$$\frac{280x}{280} = \frac{2\,520 \text{ hours}}{280}$$

$$x = 9 \text{ hours } Ans$$

Check.

$$\frac{280 \text{ pieces}}{720 \text{ pieces}} = \frac{3.5 \text{ hours}}{x}$$

$$\frac{280 \text{ pieces}}{720 \text{ pieces}} = \frac{3.5 \text{ hours}}{9 \text{ hours}}$$

$$0.3\overline{8} = 0.3\overline{8} \text{ ck}$$

Example 2.   A sheet metal cone is shown in figure 11-16. The cone is 35 centimetres high with a 38-centimetre diameter base. Determine the diameter 14 centimetres from the top of the cone.

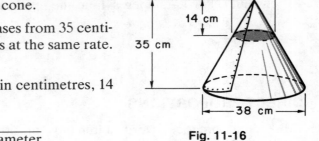

Fig. 11-16

Analyze the problem. As the height of the cone decreases from 35 centimetres to 14 centimetres, the diameter also decreases at the same rate. The proportion is direct.

Set up the proportion. Let x represent the diameter in centimetres, 14 centimetres from the top.

$$\frac{14 \text{ centimetres in height}}{35 \text{ centimetres in height}} = \frac{x}{38 \text{ centimetres in diameter}}$$

Notice that the numerator of the first ratio corresponds to the numerator of the second ratio; the 14-centimetre height corresponds to the x. The denominator of the first ratio corresponds to the denominator of the second ratio; the 35-centimetre height corresponds to the 38-centimetre diameter.

Solve for x.
$$\frac{14 \text{ cm}}{35 \text{ cm}} = \frac{x}{38 \text{ cm}}$$
$$35x = 14(38 \text{ cm})$$
$$\frac{35x}{35} = \frac{532 \text{ cm}}{35}$$
$$x = 15.2 \text{ cm } Ans$$

Check.
$$\frac{14 \text{ cm}}{35 \text{ cm}} = \frac{x}{38 \text{ cm}}$$
$$\frac{14 \text{ cm}}{35 \text{ cm}} = \frac{15.2 \text{ cm}}{38 \text{ cm}}$$
$$0.4 = 0.4 \text{ ck}$$

INVERSE PROPORTIONS

Two quantities are *inversely or indirectly proportional* if a change in one produces a change in the other in the opposite direction. If an increase in one produces a decrease in the other, or if a decrease in one produces an increase in the other, the two quantities are inversely proportional. For example, if one quantity increases by 4 times its original value, the other quantity decreases by 4 times or is $\frac{1}{4}$ of its original value. Notice 4 or $\frac{4}{1}$ inverted is $\frac{1}{4}$.

When setting up an inverse proportion in fractional form, the numerator of the first ratio must correspond to the denominator of the second ratio. The denominator of the first ratio must correspond to the numerator of the second ratio.

Example 1.   Five identical machines produce the same parts at the same rate. The five machines complete the required number of parts in 1.8 hours. How many hours does it take 3 machines to produce the same number of parts?

Analyze the problem. A decrease in the number of machines (from 5 to 3 machines) requires an increase in time. Time increases as the number of machines decreases; therefore, the proportion is inverse.

Set up the proportion. Let x represent the time required by 3 machines to produce the parts.

$$\frac{5 \text{ machines}}{3 \text{ machines}} = \frac{x}{1.8 \text{ hours}}$$

Notice that the numerator of the first ratio corresponds to the denominator of the second ratio; 5 machines corresponds with 1.8 hours. The denominator of the first ratio corresponds to the numerator of the second ratio; 3 machines correspond with x.

Solve for x.

$$\frac{5}{3} = \frac{x}{1.8 \text{ hours}}$$

$$3x = 5(1.8 \text{ hours})$$

$$\frac{3x}{3} = \frac{9 \text{ hours}}{3}$$

$$x = \textbf{3 hours } Ans$$

Check.

$$\frac{5}{3} = \frac{x}{1.8 \text{ hours}}$$

$$\frac{5}{3} = \frac{3 \text{ hours}}{1.8 \text{ hours}}$$

$$1.\overline{6} = 1.\overline{6} \text{ ck}$$

Example 2.   Two gears are in mesh as shown in figure 11-17. The driver gear has 40 teeth and revolves at 360 revolutions per minute. Determine the number of revolutions per minute of a driven gear with 16 teeth.

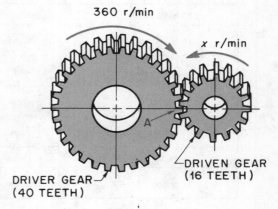

360 r/min

x r/min

DRIVER GEAR (40 TEETH)

DRIVEN GEAR (16 TEETH)

Fig. 11-17

Analyze the problem. When the driver turns one revolution, 40 teeth pass point A. The same number of teeth on the driven gear must pass point A. Therefore, the driven gear turns more than one revolution for each revolution of the driver gear. The gear with 16 teeth (driven gear) revolves at greater revolutions per minute than the gear with 40 teeth (driver gear). A decrease in the number of teeth produces an increase in revolutions per minute. The proportion is inverse.

Set up the proportion. Let x represent the revolutions per minute of the gear with 16 teeth.

$$\frac{40 \text{ teeth}}{16 \text{ teeth}} = \frac{x}{360 \text{ r/min}}$$

Notice that the numerator of the first ratio corresponds to the denominator of the second ratio; the gear with 40 teeth corresponds with 360 r/min. The denominator of the first ratio corresponds to the numerator of the second ratio; the gear with 16 teeth corresponds with x.

Solve for x.

$$\frac{40}{16} = \frac{x}{360 \text{ r/min}}$$

$$16x = 40(360 \text{ r/min})$$

$$\frac{16x}{16} = \frac{14\ 400 \text{ r/min}}{16}$$

$$x = \textbf{900 r/min } Ans$$

Check.

$$\frac{40}{16} = \frac{x}{360 \text{ r/min}}$$

$$\frac{40}{16} = \frac{900 \text{ r/min}}{360 \text{ r/min}}$$

$$2.5 = 2.5 \text{ ck}$$

Exercise 11-3

Analyze each of these problems to determine whether the problem is a direct or an inverse proportion. Set up the proportion and solve.

1. An engine uses 6 gallons of gasoline when it runs for $7\frac{1}{2}$ hours. If it runs at the same speed, how many gallons will be used in 10 hours?

2. In excavating the foundation of a building to a 4-foot depth, 1 800 cubic yards of soil are removed. How many cubic yards are removed when excavating to a 9-foot depth?

3. In the health field, both the metric and the apothecaries' systems of measure are used in calculating dosages and mixing solutions. Metric units of liquid and dry measure with their equivalent apothecaries' units are given in the table in figure 11-18. Using the equivalents in figure 11-18, express the quantities in the table in figure 11-19 from one system to the other as indicated.

METRIC		APOTHECARIES'
0.030 millilitre	=	0.5 minim
10 millilitres	=	$2\frac{1}{2}$ fluidrams
100 millilitres	=	$3\frac{1}{3}$ fluidounces
100 millilitres	=	$\frac{1}{5}$ pint
0.5 gram	=	$7\frac{1}{2}$ grains
15 grams	=	4 drams
10 grams	=	$\frac{1}{3}$ ounce

Fig. 11-18

	METRIC		APOTHECARIES'
a.	0.180 millilitre	=	? minim
b.	? millilitres	=	$5\frac{3}{4}$ fluidrams
c.	? millilitres	=	$\frac{1}{2}$ fluidounce
d.	250 millilitres	=	? pint
e.	? grams	=	$52\frac{1}{2}$ grains
f.	20 grams	=	? drams
g.	? grams	=	$\frac{3}{4}$ ounce

Fig. 11-19

4. Of the two gears that mesh as shown in figure 11-20, the one which has the greater number of teeth is called the gear, and the one which has the fewer teeth is called the pinion. Refer to the table in figure 11-21 and determine x in each problem.

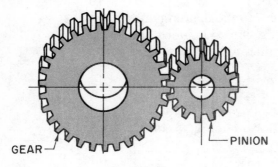

GEAR — PINION

Fig. 11-20

	NUMBER OF TEETH ON GEAR	NUMBER OF TEETH ON PINION	GEAR (r/min)	PINION (r/min)
a.	48	20	120	x
b.	32	24	x	210
c.	35	x	160	200
d.	x	15	150	250
e.	54	28	80	x

Fig. 11-21

5. Six bakers take 7 hours to produce the daily bread requirements of a bakery. Working at the same rate, how many bakers are required to produce the same quantity of bread in $5\frac{1}{4}$ hours?

6. A home owner pays $860 in taxes on property assessed at $46 400. After improvements are made, the property is assessed at $68 700. Using the same tax rate, what are the taxes on the $68 700 assessment?

7. The tank shown in figure 11-22 contains 7 200 litres of water when completely full. How many litres does it contain when filled to these heights (H)?

   a. 2 metres

   b. 3.4 metres

   c. 1.86 metres.

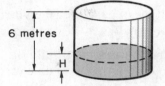

Fig. 11-22

8. A balanced lever is shown in figure 11-24. Observe that the heavier weight is closer to the fulcrum than the lighter weight. An increase in the distance from the fulcrum produces a decrease in weight required to balance the lever. Refer to the table in figure 11-23 and determine the unknown values.

	W_1	W_2	D_1	D_2
a.	76.8 lb	24 lb	3.5 ft	? ft
b.	? lb	$\frac{3}{4}$ lb	$\frac{1}{4}$ ft	$2\frac{1}{2}$ ft
c.	96.32 lb	60.2 lb	? ft	7.4 ft
d.	175 lb	? lb	$1\frac{1}{2}$ ft	$7\frac{1}{2}$ ft

Fig. 11-23

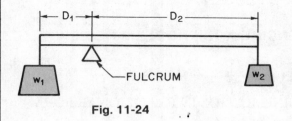

Fig. 11-24

9. The crankshaft speed of a car is 2 900 r/min when the car is traveling 55 mi/h. What is the crankshaft speed when the car is traveling 42 mi/h?

10. Two forgings are made of the same stainless steel alloy. A forging which weighs 170 pounds contains 0.8 pound of chromium. How many pounds of chromium does the second forging contain if it weighs 255 pounds?

11. A three pulley system is shown in figure 11-25. Using the data given in the table in figure 11-26, compute the missing values.

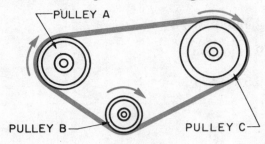

Fig. 11-25

	PULLEY A		PULLEY B		PULLEY C	
	DIAMETER	r/min	DIAMETER	r/min	DIAMETER	r/min
a.	12 cm	360	5 cm	?	16 cm	?
b.	? cm	510	8 cm	918	? cm	306
c.	9 cm	?	? cm	720	13.5 cm	400
d.	? cm	625	12 cm	?	21 cm	500

Fig. 11-26

12. A template is shown in figure 11-27. A drafter makes an enlarged drawing of the template as shown in figure 11-28. The original length of 1.80 inches on the enlarged drawing is 3.06 inches as shown. Determine the lengths of A, B, C, and D.

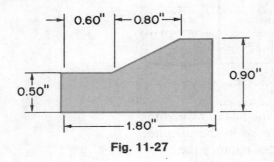

Fig. 11-27

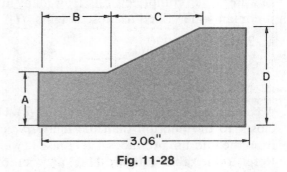

Fig. 11-28

UNIT EXERCISE AND PROBLEM REVIEW

Exercise 11-4

EXPRESSING RATIOS IN FRACTIONAL FORM

Express these ratios in lowest fractional form.

1. 15:32
2. 46:12
3. 12:46
4. 27 mm:45 mm
5. 14 ft: 32 ft
6. M^2:M
7. $10x^2y$ to $2xy$
8. $38PV^2$ to $8PV^2$
9. $\frac{1}{4}$ to $\frac{1}{2}$
10. 16 to $\frac{2}{3}$
11. $\frac{D}{F}$ to $\frac{D}{H}$
12. $\frac{M}{R}$ to M
13. 25 cm to 50 mm
14. 2 ft to 8 in
15. $\frac{1}{2}$ h to 20 min
16. 3 min to 45 sec
17. 9 in to $\frac{1}{3}$ yd
18. 0.5 km to 100 m

RATIO PROBLEMS

Solve these ratio problems. Express the answers in lowest fractional form.

19. The cost and selling price of merchandise are listed in the table in figure 11-29. Determine the cost to selling price ratio and the cost to profit ratio.

    Profit = selling price − cost

	COST	SELLING PRICE	RATIO OF COST TO SELLING PRICE	RATIO OF COST TO PROFIT
a.	$ 60	$ 96	?	?
b.	$105	$180	?	?
c.	$ 18	$ 33	?	?
d.	$204	$440	?	?

Fig. 11-29

20. Bronze is an alloy of copper, zinc, and tin with small amounts of other elements. Two types of bronze castings are listed in the table in figure 11-30 with the percent composition of copper, tin, and zinc in each casting. Determine the ratios called for in the table.

	TYPE OF CASTING	PERCENT COMPOSITION			RATIOS		
		COPPER	TIN	ZINC	COPPER TO TIN	TIN TO ZINC	COPPER TO ZINC
a.	Manganese Bronze	58	1	40	?	?	?
b.	Hard Bronze	86	10	2	?	?	?

Fig. 11-30

SOLVING FOR UNKNOWNS IN GIVEN PROPORTIONS

Solve for the unknown value in each of these proportions. Check each answer.

21. $\dfrac{M}{8} = \dfrac{3}{12}$

22. $\dfrac{7}{E} = \dfrac{4}{32}$

23. $\dfrac{5}{20} = \dfrac{C}{96}$

24. $\dfrac{11}{13.2} = \dfrac{88}{T}$

25. $\dfrac{x}{-8.1} = \dfrac{3}{5.4}$

26. $\dfrac{10}{P} = \dfrac{P}{4.9}$

27. $\dfrac{4}{\frac{1}{2}} = \dfrac{B}{7}$

28. $\dfrac{\frac{3}{4}}{\frac{1}{8}} = \dfrac{\frac{1}{2}}{W}$

29. $\dfrac{6D}{15} = \dfrac{6}{10}$

30. $\dfrac{14}{L+4} = \dfrac{5}{8}$

31. $\dfrac{34.2}{12} = \dfrac{x-3.6}{4}$

32. $\dfrac{H+7}{-3} = \dfrac{8}{H-7}$

SOLVING PROPORTIONS GIVEN AS FORMULAS

Solve these proportion problems. Substitute the known values in the formulas and determine the values of the unknowns.

33. The volume of gas decreases as pressure increases. The relationship between pressure and volume of a confined gas is graphed in figure 11-31. Using the given values in the table in figure 11-32, compute the missing values.

$$\dfrac{P_1}{P_2} = \dfrac{V_2}{V_1}$$

where P_1 = the original pressure

V_1 = the original volume

P_2 = the new pressure

V_2 = the new volume

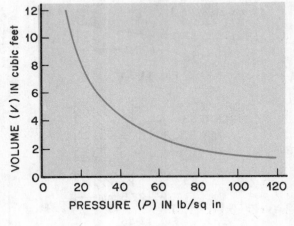

Fig. 11-31

	P_1 (lb/sq in)	P_2 (lb/sq in)	V_1 (cu ft)	V_2 (cu ft)
a.	?	30	4	6
b.	15	?	12	2
c.	180	60	?	3
d.	1.5	9	1.2	?

Fig. 11-32

34. The tool feed (*F*), in inches per revolution, of a lathe may be computed using this formula.

$$T = \frac{L}{FN}$$

where *T* = cutting time per cut in minutes

L = length of cut in inches

N = r/min of revolving workpiece

	T (min)	L (in)	N (r/min)	F (in/r)
a.	4.8	20	2 100	?
b.	12.5	37	610	?
c.	3	8	335	?
d.	5.2	17	1 200	?

Fig. 11-33

Compute *F* to three decimal places using the table in figure 11-33.

SETTING UP AND SOLVING DIRECT AND INVERSE PROPORTIONS

Analyze each of these problems to determine whether the problem is a direct or an inverse proportion. Set up the proportion and solve.

35. An annual interest of $110.25 is received on a savings deposit of $2 100. At the same rate, how much annual interest is received on a deposit of $2 520?

36. A piece of lumber 2.8 metres long weighs 24.5 kilograms. A piece 0.8 metre long is cut from the 2.8-metre length. Determine the weight of the 0.8-metre piece.

37. The amount of taper is the difference between diameters at each end of a tapered part. A tapered plug gage is shown in figure 11-34. The plug gage taper is 9 millimetres (17 mm - 8 mm) along a 27.5-millimetre length. The plug gage is shown in a tapered hole in a workpiece in figure 11-35. Given workpiece thicknesses in the table in figure 11-36, determine the amount of taper in each workpiece.

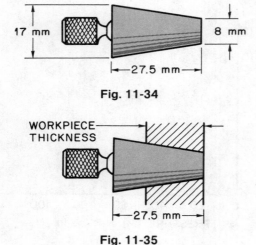

Fig. 11-34

Fig. 11-35

	WORKPIECE THICKNESS	TAPER IN WORKPIECE
a.	22 mm	? mm
b.	8.25 mm	? mm
c.	16.5 mm	? mm
d.	24.75 mm	? mm
e.	19.25 mm	? mm

Fig. 11-36

38. Two sump pumps working at the same rate drain a flooded basement in $5\frac{1}{2}$ hours. How long does it take 3 pumps working at the same rate to drain the basement?

39. A solution contains $\frac{1}{4}$ ounce acid and $8\frac{1}{2}$ ounces of water. For the same strength solution, how much acid should be mixed with $12\frac{3}{4}$ ounces of water?

40. A compound gear train is shown in figure 11-37. Gears B and C are keyed (connected) to the same shaft; therefore, they turn at the same rate. Gear A and gear C are the driving gears. Gear B and gear D are the driven gears. Compute the missing values in the table in figure 11-38.

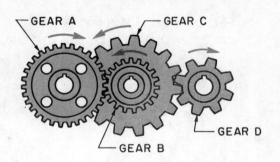

Fig. 11-37

	NUMBER OF TEETH				REVOLUTIONS PER MINUTE			
	GEAR A	GEAR B	GEAR C	GEAR D	GEAR A	GEAR B	GEAR C	GEAR D
a.	80	30	50	20	120	?	?	?
b.	60	?	45	?	100	300	?	450
c.	?	24	60	36	144	?	?	280
d.	55	25	?	15	?	?	175	350

Fig. 11-38

SECTION 3
Fundamentals of Plane Geometry

UNIT 12
Introduction to Plane Geometry

OBJECTIVES

After studying this unit you should be able to

- identify axioms and postulates that apply to geometric statements.
- write geometric statements in symbol form.
- illustrate geometric statements.

Geometry is the branch of mathematics in which the properties of points, lines, surfaces, and solids are studied. Many geometric principles were first recognized by the early Babylonians and Egyptians more than 5 000 years ago. The Egyptians used geometry for land surveying. This is the earliest known use of geometry. Throughout the centuries geometry has been used in many ways that have greatly influenced modern living.

Much of the environment has been affected by the use of geometric principles. Practically everything in modern living is dependent upon geometry. Geometric applications are used in building houses, apartments, offices, and shops where people live and work. Roads, bridges, and airports could not be constructed without the use of geometry. Automobiles, airplanes, and ships could not be designed and produced without the application of geometric principles. The manufacture of clothes and the processing and distribution of food depend on geometric applications.

Many occupations require a knowledge of geometry and the ability to apply this knowledge to practical on-the-job uses. Carpentry, plumbing, machining, drafting, and auto body repair are but a few of the occupations in which geometry is used regularly.

In addition to occupational uses, a knowledge of geometry is also of value in daily living. It is used, for example, to estimate the amount of paint or wall paper required for a room, to determine the number of bags of fertilizer needed for a lawn, and to compute the number of feet of lumber needed for a home project.

PLANE GEOMETRY

Plane geometry deals with points, lines, and various figures that are made of combinations of points and line segments. The figures lie on a flat surface or *plane*. Examples of common plane figures which are discussed in this book are shown in figure 12-1.

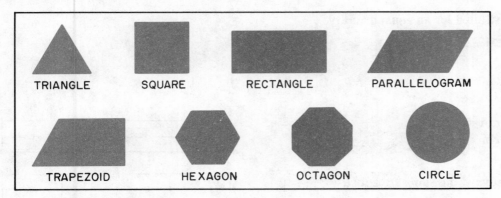

Fig. 12-1

Since geometry is used in many occupational and nonoccupational applications, it is essential that the definitions and terms of geometry be understood. It is even more important to be able to apply geometric principles in problem solving. The methods and procedures used in problem solving are the same as those required in actual occupational situations.

Procedure for Solving Geometry Problems

- Study the figure.
- Relate the figure to the principle or principles that are needed for the solution.
- Base all conclusions on given information and geometric principles.
- <u>Do not</u> assume that something is true because of its appearance or the way it is drawn.

AXIOMS AND POSTULATES

In the study of plane geometry certain basic statements called axioms or postulates are accepted as true without requiring proof. Axioms or postulates may be compared to the rules of a game. Some axioms and postulates are listed. Others will be given as they are required for problem solving.

- **Quantities equal to the same quantities or to equal quantities are equal to each other.**

Example.   Refer to figure 12-2.

    Given: a = 15 cm
              d = 15 cm

    Conclusion: **a = d**

• **A quantity may be substituted for an equal quantity.**

Example.   Refer to figure 12-2.

    Given: a = 15 cm
              b = 5 cm
              c = a + b

    Conclusion: c = 15 cm + 5 cm
                     c = 20 cm

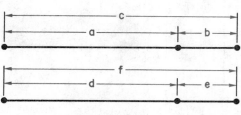

• **If equals are added to equals, the sums are equal.**

Example.   Refer to figure 12-2.

    Given: a = d
              b = e

    Conclusion: a + b = d + e
                    c = f

Fig. 12-2

• **If equals are subtracted from equals, the remainders are equal.**

Example.   Refer to figure 12-2.

    Given: c = f
            a = d

    Conclusion: c − a = f − d
                   b = e

• **If equals are multiplied by equals, the products are equal.**

Example.   Refer to figure 12-3.

    Given: a = c

    Conclusion: 2a = 2c
                b = d

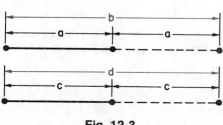

• **If equals are divided by equals, the quotients are equal.**

Example.   Refer to figure 12-3.

    Given: 2a = 2c

    Conclusion: 2a ÷ 2 = 2c ÷ 2
                  a = c

Fig. 12-3

- **The whole is equal to the sum of all its parts.**

Example.   Refer to figure 12-4.

$$e = a + b + c + d$$

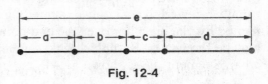
Fig. 12-4

- **The whole is greater than any of its parts.**

Example.   Refer to figure 12-4.

The whole, e, is greater than a or b or c or d.

- **One and only one straight line can be drawn between two given points.**

Example.   In figure 12-5, only one straight line can be drawn between point A and point B.

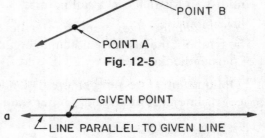
POINT B
POINT A
Fig. 12-5

- **Through a given point, one and only one line can be drawn parallel to a given straight line.**

Example.   In figure 12-6, lines a and b will never touch or cross.

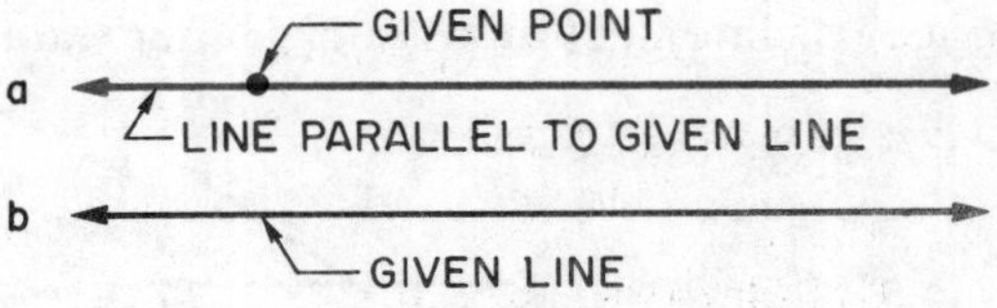

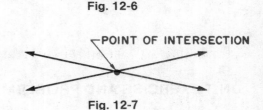
GIVEN POINT
LINE PARALLEL TO GIVEN LINE
GIVEN LINE
Fig. 12-6

- **Two straight lines can intersect at only one point.**

Example.   In figure 12-7, the lines cross at only one point.

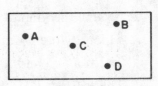
POINT OF INTERSECTION
Fig. 12-7

POINTS AND LINES

A *point* is shown as a dot. It is usually named by a capital letter as shown in figure 12-8. A point has no size or form; it has location only. For example, points on a map locate places; they do not show size or shape.

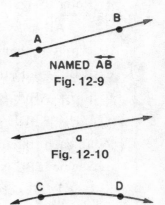
Fig. 12-8

As used in this book, a *line* always means a straight line. A line other than a straight line, such as a curved line, is identified. A line extends without end in two directions. A line has no width; it is an infinite number of points. Arrowheads are used in drawing a line to show that there are no end points. A line is usually named by two points on the line. A double-headed arrow is placed over the letters that name the line, figure 12-9. A line can also be named by a single lowercase letter, figure 12-10.

NAMED $\overleftrightarrow{AB}$
Fig. 12-9

A *curved line* is a line no part of which is straight, figure 12-11.

a
Fig. 12-10

C   D
Fig. 12-11

A *line segment* is that part of a line which lies between two definite points, figure 12-12. When we speak of a definite distance on a line we are dealing with a line segment. A line segment is usually referred to as simply a segment. Line segments are often named by placing a bar over the end point letters. Segment AB may be shown as $\overline{AB}$. In this book, segments are shown without a bar. Segment AB is shown as AB.

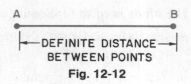

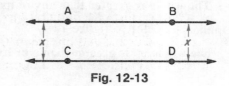

Fig. 12-12

Parallel lines do not meet regardless of how far they are extended. They are the same distance apart (equidistant) at all points. The symbol $\parallel$ means parallel. In figure 12-13 line AB is parallel to line CD ($\overleftrightarrow{AB} \parallel \overleftrightarrow{CD}$). Therefore, $\overleftrightarrow{AB}$ and $\overleftrightarrow{CD}$ are equidistant (distance x) at all points.

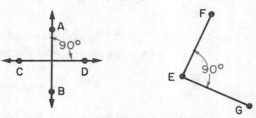

Fig. 12-13

Perpendicular lines meet or intersect at a right or 90° angle. The symbol $\perp$ means perpendicular. Figure 12-14 shows examples of perpendicular lines. $\overleftrightarrow{AB} \perp \overleftrightarrow{CD}$ and $EF \perp EG$.

Oblique lines are neither parallel nor perpendicular. They meet or intersect at an angle other than 90°, figure 12-15.

Fig. 12-14

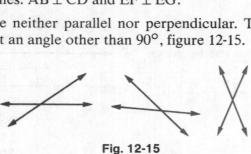

Fig. 12-15

UNIT EXERCISE AND PROBLEM REVIEW

Exercise 12-1

1. Define geometry.

2. Name the kind of surface used in plane geometry.

3. Identify the postulate that applies to each of these statements.

   a. If a = 5 and b = 5, then a = b.

   b. If EF = GH, then EF − KL = GH − KL.

   c. Refer to figure 12-16.

   x = AB + BC + CD

   d. If m = p, then m + 8 = p + 8.

   e. If BC = DE, then 15BC = 15DE.

   f. If e = AB + BC + CD, then e − g = AB + BC + CD − g.

   g. If HK − 4DE = 25, and 2LM + ST = 25, then HK − 4DE = 2LM + ST.

4. Write each statement using symbols.

   a. Segment BC is parallel to segment DE.

   b. Line FG is perpendicular to line HK.

   c. Segment AB is parallel to line CD.

Fig. 12-16

5. Sketch each of the following statements.

   a. Line MP is parallel to line RS and the distance between the two lines is represented by x.

   b. Segment AB is perpendicular to segment CD and point C lies on segment AB.

   c. Oblique lines EF and GH intersect at point R.

   d. $\overleftrightarrow{AB} \perp CD$ and $\overleftrightarrow{AB}$ intersects CD at point M.

   e. $\overleftrightarrow{EF} \parallel \overleftrightarrow{GH}$ and $\overleftrightarrow{EF} \perp \overleftrightarrow{LM}$ at point P.

UNIT 13
Angular
Measure

OBJECTIVES

After studying this unit you should be able to

- add, subtract, multiply, and divide angles given in degrees, minutes, and seconds.

- solve problems which require combinations of two or more arithmetic operations on angles.

- express decimal degrees as degrees, minutes, and seconds.

- construct and measure angles with a simple protractor.

- construct circle graphs from given data.

- read vernier protractor scale settings.

- compute complements and supplements of angles.

The ability to compute and measure angles is required in a wide range of occupations. A plumber computes pipe lengths by making pipe diagrams using fitting angles of various degrees. A cabinetmaker determines angles and adjusts table saw miter gages to assure proper angular fits of stock. A land surveyor measures angles and distances to points from transit stations. A sheet metal technician computes and measures angles required in bending material.

Angular measure is required when working on many of our home projects and hobbies as well as for occupational uses.

An *angle* is a figure made by two lines which intersect. An *angle* is also described as the union of two rays having a common endpoint. The two rays are called the *sides* of the angle and their common endpoint is called a *vertex*. A *ray* starts with an endpoint and continues indefinitely as shown in figure 13-1. An example of an angle is shown in figure 13-2. The symbol for angle is ∠. The size of an angle is determined by the number of degrees one side is rotated from the other. The size of an angle does *not* depend on the length of its sides.

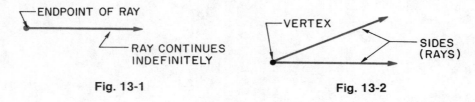

Fig. 13-1   Fig. 13-2

UNITS OF ANGULAR MEASURE

In order to measure the size of angles, the early Babylonians divided a circle into 360 parts. Each part was called one degree. The degree is still the basic unit of angular measure. The symbol ° means degree.

A circle may be thought of as a ray with a fixed endpoint; the ray is rotated. One rotation makes a complete circle or 360°, figure 13-3.

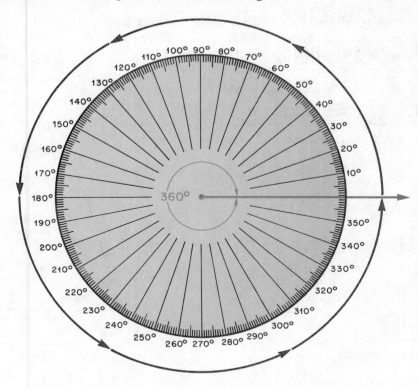

Fig. 13-3

The degree of precision required in computing and measuring angles depends on how the angle is used. In woodworking, measuring to the nearer whole degree is often close enough. An automobile mechanic is required to make caster and camber adjustments to within $\frac{1}{2}°$ or $\frac{1}{4}°$. Some manufactured parts are designed and processed to a very high degree of precision.

In metric calculations, the decimal degree is generally the preferred unit of measurement. In the English system, angular measure is expressed in these ways.

- As decimal degrees, such as 6.5 degrees and 108.274 degrees.

- As fractional degrees, such as $12\frac{1}{4}$ degrees and $53\frac{1}{10}$ degrees.

- As degrees, minutes, and seconds, such as 37 degrees, 18 minutes and 123 degrees, 46 minutes, 53 seconds.

Decimal and fractional degrees are added, subtracted, multiplied, and divided the same as any other numbers.

UNITS OF ANGULAR MEASURE IN DEGREES, MINUTES, AND SECONDS

A degree is divided in 60 equal parts called *minutes*. The symbol for minute is '. A minute is divided in 60 equal parts called *seconds*. The symbol for second is ". The relationship between degrees, minutes, and seconds is shown in figure 13-4.

1 Circle = 360 Degrees (°)	1 Degree (°) = $\frac{1}{360}$ of a Circle
1 Degree (°) = 60 Minutes (')	1 Minute (') = $\frac{1}{60}$ Degree (°)
1 Minute (') = 60 Seconds (")	1 Second (") = $\frac{1}{60}$ Minute (')

Fig. 13-4

ARITHMETIC OPERATIONS ON ANGULAR MEASURE IN DEGREES, MINUTES, AND SECONDS

The division of minutes and seconds permit very precise computations and measurements. For example, precise measurements are made in land surveying. In machining operations, dimensions at times are computed to seconds in order to assure the proper functioning of parts.

When computing with degrees, minutes, and seconds, it is sometimes necessary to exchange units. When exchanging units, keep in mind 1 degree equals 60 minutes and 1 minute equals 60 seconds. These examples illustrate adding, subtracting, multiplying, and dividing angles in degrees, minutes, and seconds.

ADDING ANGLES

Example 1.   Refer to figure 13-5 and determine ∠1.

$$\angle 1 = 16°35' + 57°16'$$

$$\begin{array}{r} 16°35' \\ + \ 57°16' \\ \hline 73°51' \ \textit{Ans} \end{array}$$

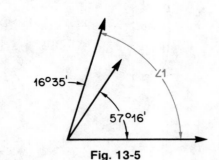

Fig. 13-5

Example 2.   Refer to figure 13-6 and determine ∠2.

$$\angle 2 = 68°50' + 67°42'$$

$$\begin{array}{r} 68°50' \\ + \ 67°42' \\ \hline 135°92' \end{array}$$

Express 92' as degrees and minutes.
$$92' = 60' + 32' = 1°32'$$

Add.
135° + 1°32'   =**136°32'** *Ans*

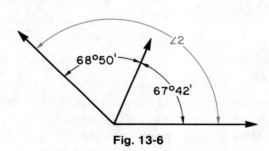

Fig. 13-6

Example 3.   Refer to figure 13-7 and determine ∠3.

$$\angle 3 = 59°43'35'' + 77°31'48''$$

$$\begin{array}{r} 59°43'35'' \\ + \ 77°31'48'' \\ \hline 136°74'83'' \end{array}$$

Express 83'' as minutes and seconds.
$$83'' = 60'' + 23'' = 1'23''$$

Add.
136°74' + 1'23''   =**136°75'23''**

Express 75' as degrees and minutes.
$$75' = 60' + 15' = 1°15'$$

Add.
136°0'23'' + 1°15'   =**137°15'23''** *Ans*

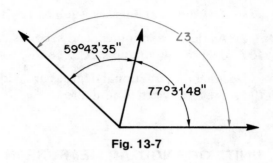

Fig. 13-7

SUBTRACTING ANGLES

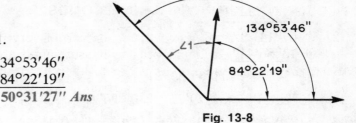

Fig. 13-8

Example 1.   Refer to figure 13-8 and determine ∠1.

∠1 = 134°53′46″ − 84°22′19″

$$
\begin{array}{r}
134°53′46″ \\
-\ \ 84°22′19″ \\
\hline
50°31′27″\ Ans
\end{array}
$$

Example 2.   Refer to figure 13-9 and determine ∠2.

∠2 = 79°15′ − 31°46′

$$
\begin{array}{r}
79°15′ \\
-\ 31°46′
\end{array}
$$

Since 46′ cannot be subtracted from 15′,
1° is exchanged for 60 minutes.

$$
\begin{array}{r}
79°15′ = 78°75′ \\
-\ 31°46′ = 31°46′ \\
\hline
47°29′\ Ans
\end{array}
$$

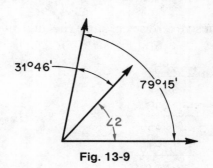

Fig. 13-9

Example 3.   Refer to figure 13-10 and determine ∠3.

∠3 = 74°10′18″ − 47°28′35″

$$
\begin{array}{r}
74°10′18″ \\
-\ 47°28′35″
\end{array}
$$

Since 28′ cannot be subtracted from
10′, and 35″ cannot be subtracted
from 18″, units are exchanged.

$$
\begin{array}{r}
74°10′18″ = 73°70′18″ = 73°69′78″ \\
-\ 47°28′35″ = 47°28′35″ = 47°28′35″ \\
\hline
26°41′43″\ Ans
\end{array}
$$

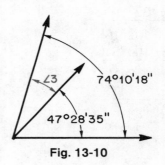

Fig. 13-10

Exercise 13-1

These exercises require the addition of angles. Determine the value of each.

1. $\begin{array}{r} 23° \\ +\ 59° \end{array}$

2. $\begin{array}{r} 128° \\ +\ \ 43° \end{array}$

3. $\begin{array}{r} 17°18′ \\ +\ \ 9°31′ \end{array}$

4. $\begin{array}{r} 27°44′ \\ +\ 88°15′ \end{array}$

5. $\begin{array}{r} 72°26′ \\ +\ 12°48′ \end{array}$

6. $\begin{array}{r} 21°50′ \\ +\ \ 7°17′ \end{array}$

7. $\begin{array}{r} 42°12′14″ \\ +\ 33°17′25″ \end{array}$

8. $\begin{array}{r} 70°19′55″ \\ +\ 42°\ \ 0′\ \ 2″ \end{array}$

9. $\begin{array}{r} 6°25′18″ \\ +\ 13°48′16″ \end{array}$

10. $\begin{array}{r} 41°13′20″ \\ +\ 19°58′12″ \end{array}$

11.   108°48′28″
     + 24° 0′47″

12.   67°14′29″
     + 13°56′44″

13. 90°54′33″ + 11°17′33″

14. 23°20′14″ + 31°19′22″ + 14°36′49″

15. 51°19′28″ + 0°43′27″ + 12°9′ + 33°0′14″

These exercises require the subtraction of angles. Determine the value of each.

16.   67°
     − 28°

17.   116°
     − 99°

18.   − 74°27′
     − 67°16′

19.   48°17′
     − 32° 9′

20.   102°16′
     − 100°54′

21.   61°41′
     − 7°47′

22.   88°
     − 22°31′

23.   44°14′54″
     − 41°27′13″

24.   31° 0′12″
     − 27°28′ 4″

25.   70° 1′3″
     − 66°59′2″

26.   120°17′44″
     − 112°48′53″

27.   6°16′
     − 4°18′19″

28. 93°0′6″ − 87°10′15″

29. 55°30′29″ − 23°32′50″

30. 68° − 67°59′59″

These problems require the addition or subtraction of angles.

Determine the value of each.

31. Refer to figure 13-11 and determine ∠1.

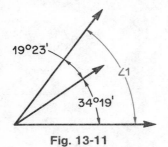

Fig. 13-11

33. Refer to figure 13-13 and determine ∠3.

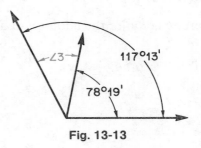

Fig. 13-13

32. Refer to figure 13-12 and determine ∠2.

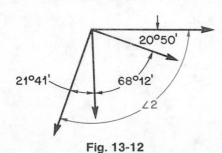

Fig. 13-12

34. Refer to figure 13-14 and determine ∠4.

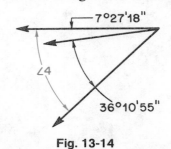

Fig. 13-14

35. Refer to figure 13-15 and determine the value of ∠5 − ∠6.

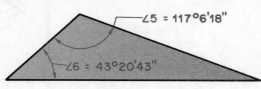

Fig. 13-15

36. Refer to figure 13-16. Determine the value of ∠1 + ∠2 + ∠3.

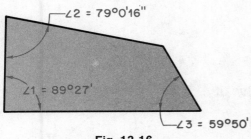

Fig. 13-16

37. Refer to figure 13-17. Determine the value of ∠1.

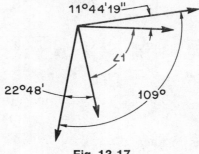

Fig. 13-17

38. Refer to figure 13-18. If ∠1 + ∠2 + ∠3 + ∠4 + ∠5 + ∠6 = 720°, what is the value of ∠6?

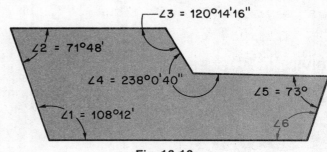

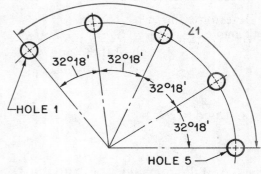

Fig. 13-18

MULTIPLYING ANGLES

Example 1. Five holes are drilled on a circle as shown in figure 13-19. The angular measure between two consecutive holes is 32°18'. Determine the angular measure, ∠1, between hole 1 and hole 5.

∠1 = 4 × (32°18')

$$\begin{array}{r} 32°18' \\ \times\ 4 \\ \hline 128°72' \end{array}$$

Express 72' as degrees and minutes.

72' = 60' + 12' = 1°12'

Add.

128° + 1°12'   = **129°12' Ans**

Fig. 13-19

Example 2. Refer to figure 13-20 and determine ∠2 when
∠a = 43°28′45″.

∠2 = 5 × (43°28′45″)

$$\begin{array}{r} 43°28'45'' \\ \times\ 5 \\ \hline 215°140'225'' \end{array}$$

Express 225″ as minutes
and seconds.
225″ = 3 × 60″ + 45″ = 3′45″

Add.
215°140′ + 3′45″   = 215°143′45″

Express 143′ as degrees
and minutes.
143′ = 2 × 60′ + 23′ = 2°23′

Add.
215°0′45″ + 2°23′   = 217°23′45″ *Ans*

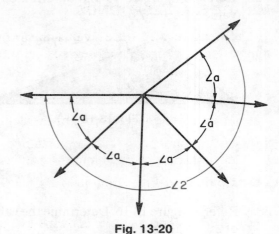

Fig. 13-20

DIVIDING ANGLES

Example 1.   In figure 13-21, ∠1 equals ∠2. Determine the value of ∠1.

∠1 = (78°31′) ÷ 2

$$\begin{array}{r} 39°15.5' \\ 2\overline{)\ 78°31'} \end{array}$$

Express 15.5 minutes as minutes
and seconds.
0.5 × 60″ = 30″

Add.
39°15′ + 30″   = 39°15′30″ *Ans*

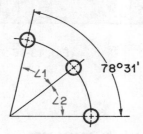

Fig. 13-21

Example 2.   Refer to figure 13-22. If ∠1, ∠2, and ∠3 are equal, determine the value
of each of these angles.

∠1 = ∠2 = ∠3 = (128°37′21″) ÷ 3   3)‾128°37′21″‾

Divide 128° by 3.

$$\begin{array}{r} 42° \\ 3\overline{)\ 128°} \\ 126° \\ \hline 2° \end{array}$$

Add the remainder of 2° to the 37′.
2° = 120′
120′ + 37′ = 157′

Divide 157′ by 3.

$$\begin{array}{r} 52' \\ 3\overline{)\ 157'} \\ 156' \\ \hline 1' \end{array}$$

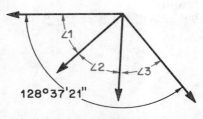

128°37′21″

Fig. 13-22

Add the remainder of 1′ to the 21″.
1′ = 60″
60″ + 21″ = 81″

Divide 81″ by 3.

$$\begin{array}{r} 27'' \\ 3\overline{)\ 81''} \end{array}$$

Combine.   42°52′27″ *Ans*

EXPRESSING DECIMAL DEGREES AS DEGREES, MINUTES, AND SECONDS

The measure of an angle given in the form of decimal degrees, such as 53.276 2°, must often be expressed as degrees, minutes, and seconds.

Procedure for Expressing Decimal Degrees as Degrees, Minutes and Seconds

- Multiply the decimal part of the degrees by 60 minutes to obtain minutes.
- If the number of minutes obtained is not a whole number, multiply the decimal part of the minutes by 60 seconds to obtain seconds.
- Combine degrees, minutes, and seconds.

Example 1. Express 53.45° as degrees, minutes, and seconds.

Multiply the decimal part of the degrees by 60 minutes to obtain minutes.

$$0.45 \times 60' = 27'$$

Combine degrees and minutes.

$$53.45° = \textbf{53°27'} \textit{Ans}$$

Example 2. Express 28.276 3° as degrees, minutes, and seconds.

Multiply the decimal part of the degrees by 60 minutes to obtain minutes.

$$0.276\ 3 \times 60' = 16.578'$$

Multiply the decimal part of the minutes by 60 seconds to obtain seconds.

$$0.578 \times 60'' = 34.68'' = 35'' \text{ (rounded to the nearer whole second)}.$$

Combine degrees, minutes, and seconds.

$$28.276\ 3° = \textbf{28°16'35''} \textit{Ans}$$

Exercise 13-2

These exercises require multiplication of angles. Determine the value of each.

1. $6 \times 18°$	6. $4 \times (42°23')$	11. $2 \times (47°24'37'')$
2. $14 \times 9°$	7. $9 \times (6°14')$	12. $7 \times (2°8'12'')$
3. $2 \times (15°19')$	8. $3 \times (20°14'10'')$	13. $4 \times (10°21'12'')$
4. $5 \times (21°7')$	9. $12 \times (7°2'4'')$	14. $8 \times (9°23'15'')$
5. $2 \times (36° 54')$	10. $5 \times (15°11'8'')$	15. $6 \times (45°52'49'')$

These exercises require division of angles. Determine the value of each.

16. $56° \div 2$	21. $(46°12') \div 4$	26. $(78°25'35'') \div 5$
17. $(27°18') \div 3$	22. $(123°43') \div 5$	27. $(278°5'57'') \div 3$
18. $(51°30') \div 5$	23. $(56°42'21'') \div 7$	28. $(0°59'42'') \div 6$
19. $(73°8') \div 4$	24. $(132°12'48'') \div 12$	29. $(333°5'30'') \div 15$
20. $(19°3') \div 6$	25. $(97°30'50'') \div 2$	30. $(116°49'48'') \div 9$

These problems require multiplication or division of angles. Some problems may also require the addition or subtraction of angles. Determine the value of each.

31. Refer to figure 13-23 and determine ∠1 when ∠A = 32°43′.

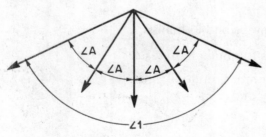

Fig. 13-23

34. Refer to figure 13-26 and detemine ∠D.

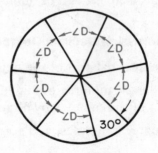

Fig. 13-26

32. Refer to figure 13-24 and determine ∠B.

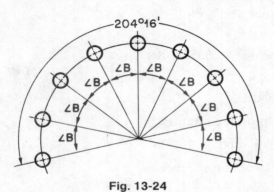

Fig. 13-24

35. Refer to figure 13-27 and determine ∠E when ∠A = 43°16′22″.

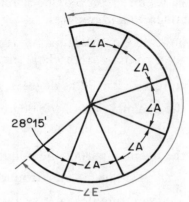

Fig. 13-27

33. Refer to figure 13-25 and determine ∠C.

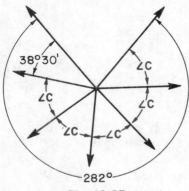

Fig. 13-25

36. Refer to figure 13-28 and determine ∠B.

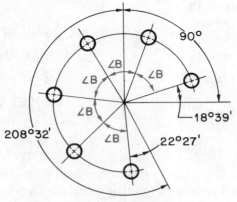

Fig. 13-28

37. Refer to figure 13-29 and determine ∠A and ∠B if ∠A = 2∠B.

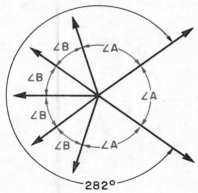

Fig. 13-29

38. Refer to figure 13-30 and determine ∠1. The sum of all angles = 1 440°.
∠1 = ∠2 = ∠3 = ∠4 = ∠5 = ∠6.
∠7 = ∠8 = ∠9 = ∠10 = 211°14′24″.

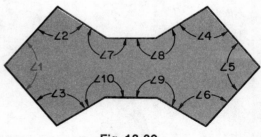

Fig. 13-30

These exercises require expressing decimal degrees as degrees and minutes or as degrees, minutes, and seconds.

39. Express these decimal degrees as degrees and minutes. Where necessary round minutes to the nearer whole minute.

a.	48.50°	f.	29.90°	k.	134.66°
b.	18.35°	g.	66.10°	l.	19.29°
c.	106.20°	h.	72.86°	m.	7.02°
d.	57.05°	i.	93.08°	n.	31.77°
e.	5.75°	j.	2.83°	o.	25.08°

40. Express these decimal degrees as degrees, minutes, and seconds. Where necessary, round seconds to the nearer whole second.

a.	32.520°	e.	68.450 5°	i.	9.300 3°
b.	86.925°	f.	106.892 8°	j.	213.729 3°
c.	17.865°	g.	22.078 8°	k.	99.987 6°
d.	44.035°	h.	59.631 7°	l.	172.445 8°

SIMPLE SEMICIRCULAR PROTRACTOR

Protractors are used for measuring, drawing, and laying out angles. Various types of protractors are available, such as the simple semicircular protractor, swinging blade protractor, and bevel protractor. The type of protractor used depends on its application and the degree of precision required. Protractors have wide occupational use, particularly in the metal and woodworking trades.

A simple semicircular protractor has two scales, each graduated from 0° to 180° so that it can be read from either the left or right side. The vertex of the angle to be measured or drawn is located at the center of the base of the protractor. A simple semicircular protractor is shown in figure 13-31.

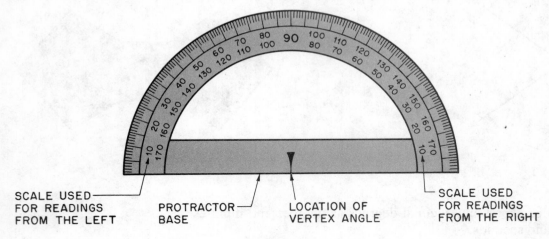

SCALE USED
FOR READINGS
FROM THE LEFT

PROTRACTOR
BASE

LOCATION OF
VERTEX ANGLE

SCALE USED
FOR READINGS
FROM THE RIGHT

Fig. 13-31

Procedure for Drawing or Laying Out an Angle

- Draw a baseline.

- On the baseline mark a point as the vertex.

- Place the protractor base on the baseline with the protractor center on the vertex.

- If the angle rotates from the right, choose the scale which has a zero degree reading on the right side of the protractor. If the angle rotates from the left, choose the scale which has a zero degree reading on the left side of the protractor. At the scale reading for the angle being drawn, mark a point.

- Remove the protractor and connect the two points.

Example.   Lay out an angle of 105°.

Draw baseline AB as shown in figure 13-32.

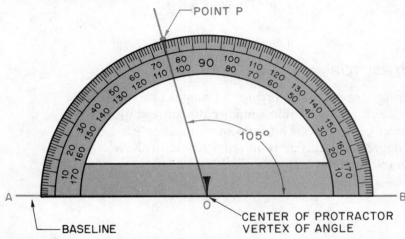

POINT P

105°

A

O

B

BASELINE

CENTER OF PROTRACTOR
VERTEX OF ANGLE

Fig. 13-32

On AB mark point O as the vertex.

Place the protractor base on AB with the protractor center on point O.

The angle is rotated from the right. The inside scale has a zero degree reading on the right side of the protractor. Use the inside scale and mark a point at the scale reading of 105°.

Remove the protractor and connect points P and O.

Procedure for Measuring an Angle

- Place the protractor base on one side of the angle with the protractor center on the angle vertex.

- If the angle rotates from the right, choose the scale which has the zero degree reading on the right side of the protractor. If the angle rotates from the left, choose the scale which has the zero degree reading on the left side of the protractor. Read the measurement where the side crosses the protractor scale.

Example 1. Measure ∠1 shown in figure 13-33.

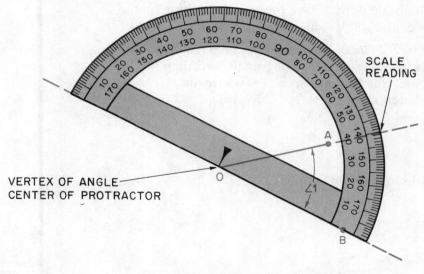

Fig. 13-33

Extend the sides OA and OB of ∠1 as shown.

Place the protractor base on side OB with the protractor center on the angle vertex, point O.

Angle 1 is rotated from the right. The angle measurement is read from the inside scale since the inside scale has a zero degree (0°) reading on the right side of the protractor base. Read the measurement where the extension of the side OA crosses the protractor scale. **Angle 1 = 40° Ans**

Example 2.   Measure ∠2 shown in figure 13-34.

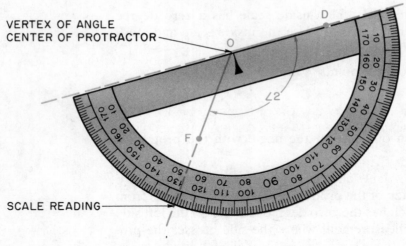

Fig. 13-34

Extend the side OD and OF of ∠2 as shown.

The protractor is positioned upside down. Place the protractor base on the side OD with the protractor center on the angle vertex, point O.

Angle 2 is rotated from the right. The angle measurement is read from the outside scale since the outside scale has a zero degree (0°) reading on the right side of the protractor base. Read the measurement where the extension of side OF crosses the protractor scale. **Angle 2 = 125° Ans**

Exercise 13-3

1. Write the values of angles A-J shown in figure 13-35.

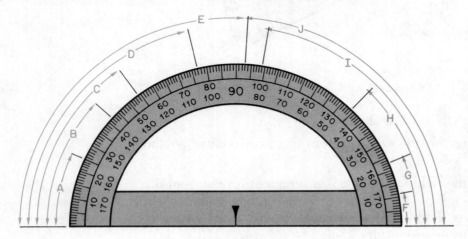

Fig. 13-35

Using a protractor, draw each of these angles.

2. 35°   7. 77°

3. 62°   8. 93°

4. 14°   9. 115°

5. 88°   10. 146°

6. 6°   11. 178°

12. Draw a 3-sided closed figure (triangle) of any size containing angles of 53° and 108°. Measure the third angle. How many degrees are contained in the third angle?

13. Draw a 4-sided closed figure (quadrilateral) of any size containing angles of 97°, 64°, and 132°. Measure the fourth angle. How many degrees are contained in the fourth angle?

14. Using a protractor, measure each of these angles, ∠1-∠18, to the nearer degree. Depending on the size of your protractor, it may be necessary to extend the sides of the angles.

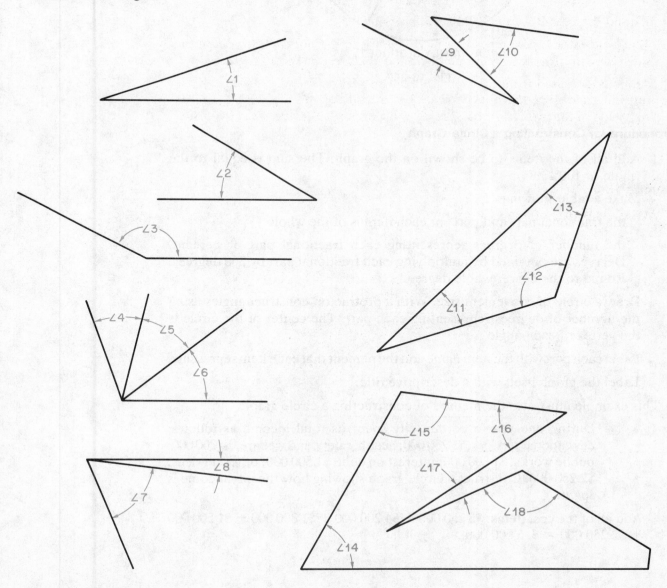

CIRCLE GRAPHS

A common use of the protractor is in the construction of a circle graph. A *circle graph* shows the comparison of parts to each other and to the whole. It compares quantities by means of angles constructed from the center of the circle. A circle graph is shown in figure 13-36.

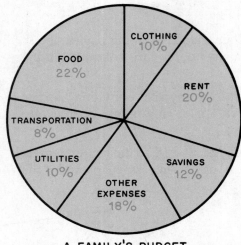

A FAMILY'S BUDGET

Fig. 13-36

Procedure for Constructing a Circle Graph

- Add all of the items to be shown on the graph. The sum is equal to the whole or 100%.

- Make a table showing:

    the fractional part and percent each item is of the whole.

    the number of degrees representing each fractional part or percent. Degrees are obtained by multiplying each fractional part by 360 degrees. Round to the nearer whole degree.

- Draw a circle of convenient size. With a protractor, construct angles using the number of degrees representing each part. The center of the circle is the vertex of each angle.

- Label each part with the item name and the percent that each item represents.

- Label the graph itself with a descriptive title.

This example illustrates the method of constructing a circle graph.

Example. During one year a certain city spent its total income as follows: educational services, $5 250 000; health, safety, and welfare, $4 200 000; public works, $1 800 000; interest on debt, $1 500 000; other services, $2 250 000. Construct a circle graph showing how the city income is spent.

Add all of the cost items: $5 250 000 + $4 200 000 + $1 800 000 + $1 500 000 + $2 250 000 = $15 000 000.

Make a table (figure 13-37) showing the fractional part and percent each cost item is of the whole, and the number of degrees represented by each.

	EDUCATIONAL SERVICES	HEALTH, SAFETY, AND WELFARE	PUBLIC WORKS	INTEREST ON DEBT	OTHER SERVICES
a.	$\dfrac{\$5\ 250\ 000}{\$15\ 000\ 000} =$ 0.35 = 35%	$\dfrac{\$4\ 200\ 000}{\$15\ 000\ 000} =$ 0.28 = 28%	$\dfrac{\$1\ 800\ 000}{\$15\ 000\ 000} =$ 0.12 = 12%	$\dfrac{\$1\ 500\ 000}{\$15\ 000\ 000} =$ 0.10 = 10%	$\dfrac{\$2\ 250\ 000}{\$15\ 000\ 000} =$ 0.15 = 15%
b.	0.35 x 360° = 126°	0.28 x 360° = 100.8° = 101°	0.12 x 360° = 43.2° = 43°	0.10 x 360° = 36°	0.15 x 360° = 54°

Fig. 13-37

Draw a circle and construct the respective angles. The center of the circle is the vertex of each angle. See figure 13-38.

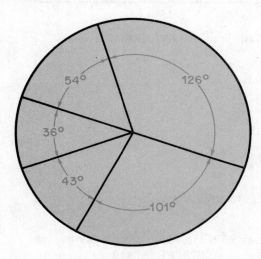

Fig. 13-38

Label each part with the cost item name and the percent that each item represents. Identify the graph with a descriptive title. See figure 13-39.

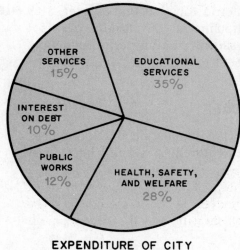

EXPENDITURE OF CITY ANNUAL INCOME

Fig. 13-39

Exercise 13-4

1. In producing a certain product, a company had the following manufacturing costs: material costs, $136 800; labor costs, $167 200; overhead expenses, $76 000. Construct a circle graph showing these manufacturing costs.

2. World motor vehicle production for a certain year is shown in the following table. Construct a circle graph using this data.

COUNTRY	UNITED STATES	JAPAN	WEST GERMANY	FRANCE	UNITED KINGDOM	ITALY	OTHER
NUMBER OF MOTOR VEHICLES PRODUCED IN MILLIONS	12.6	6.8	4.1	3.5	2.7	1.8	0.6

3. A firm's operating expenses for the first half year are as follows:

    SALARIES, $620 000

    UTILITIES, $100 000

    MAINTENANCE, $125 000

    ADVERTISING, $55 000

    DELIVERY, $70 000

    DEPRECIATION, $140 000

    Construct a circle graph showing these operating expenses.

4. An employee has a net or take-home pay of $255. These deductions are made from the employee's gross wage: income tax, $28; FICA, $13; retirement, $5; insurance, $9; other, $7. Construct a circle graph showing net pay and deductions.

5. The quarterly United States production of iron ore during a certain year is as follows: first-quarter, 16.8 million metric tons; second-quarter, 18.9 million metric tons; third-quarter, 17.5 million metric tons; last-quarter, 15.4 million metric tons. Construct a circle graph showing the quarterly production.

BEVEL PROTRACTOR WITH VERNIER SCALE

The bevel protractor with a vernier scale is used in many occupations where precision measuring and layout of angles are required. A vernier bevel protractor is shown in figure 13-40.

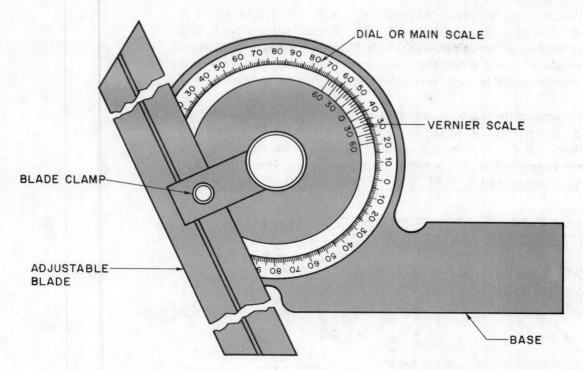

Fig. 13-40

A vernier bevel protractor consists of a fixed dial or main scale. The main scale is divided into four sections, each from 0° to 90°. The vernier scale rotates within the main scale. A blade which can be adjusted to required positions is rotated to a desired angle. Measuring an angle with a bevel protractor is shown in figure 13-41.

(Courtesy: The L.S. Starrett Company)

Fig. 13-41

The vernier scale permits accurate readings to $\frac{1}{12}$ degree or 5 minutes. The vernier scale is divided into 24 units, with 12 units on each side of zero. The divisions on the vernier scale are in minutes. Each division is equal to 5 minutes.

The left vernier scale is used when the vernier zero is to the left of the dial zero. The right vernier scale is used when the vernier zero is to the right of the dial zero.

An example of a vernier protractor reading of 30°35′ is shown in figure 13-42. The zero mark on the vernier scale is just to the right of the 30° division of the dial scale. The vernier zero is to the right of the dial zero; therefore, the right vernier scale is read. The 35′ vernier graduation coincides with a dial graduation. The protractor reading is 30°35′.

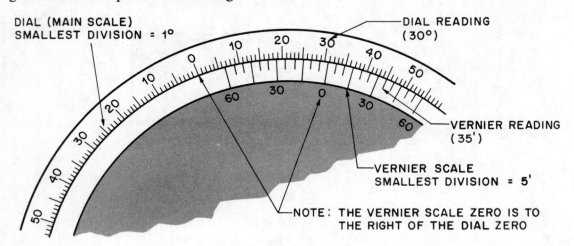

Fig. 13-42

COMPLEMENTS AND SUPPLEMENTS OF SCALE READINGS

When measuring with a bevel protractor, the user must determine whether the desired angle of the object measured is the actual reading on the protractor or the complement or supplement of the protractor reading. Particular caution must be taken when measuring angles close to 45° and 90°.

Two angles are *complementary* when their sum is 90°. For example, in figure 13-43, 42° + 48° = 90°. Therefore, 42° is the complement of 48°, and 48° is the complement of 42°.

Two angles are *supplementary* when their sum is 180°. For example, in figure 13-44, 87° + 93° = 180°. Therefore, 87° is the supplement of 93°, and 93° is the supplement of 87°.

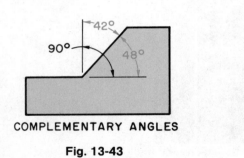

COMPLEMENTARY ANGLES

Fig. 13-43

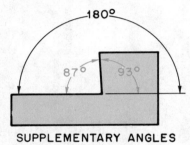

SUPPLEMENTARY ANGLES

Fig. 13-44

Exercise 13-5

Write the values of the settings on these vernier protractor scales.

1.

4.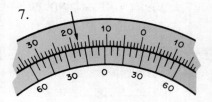

7.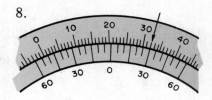

2.

5.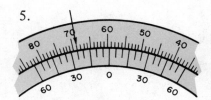

8.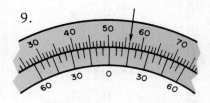

3.

6.

9.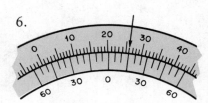

Write the complements of these angles.

10. 59°   14. 56°18′   18. 49°0′58″

11. 12°   15. 44°59′   19. 89°59′59″

12. 46°   16. 73°18′27″

13. 1°   17. 0°43′19″

Write the supplements of these angles.

20. 84°   24. 65°36′   28. 90°1′2″

21. 19°   25. 179°59′   29. 0°3′12″

22. 97°   26. 2°43′20″

23. 129°   27. 89°57′50″

UNIT EXERCISE AND PROBLEM REVIEW

Exercise 13-6

ADDING AND SUBTRACTING ANGLES

Add or subtract each of these exercises as indicated.

1.   34°   3.   43°38′
     + 97°   + 16°51′

2.   14°27′   4.   50°19′20″
     + 66°15′   + 28°30′14″

5. 5°43'18" + 13°40'26"

6. 17°27'53" + 92°56'27"

7. 20°34'19" + 44°0'27" + 16°54'49"

8.   94°
      − 67°

9.   68°26'
      − 54°17'

10.   74°19'
      − 68°34'

11.   53°41'18"
      − 17°22' 7"

12. 114°26'43" − 107°43'16"

13. 55°9'18" − 51°57'30"

14. 64°0'8" − 9°41'17"

15. 90° − 59°58'57"

MULTIPLYING AND DIVIDING ANGLES

Multiply or divide each of these exercises as indicated.

16. 12 × 23°

17. 6 × (18°7')

18. 4 × (34°26')

19. 3 × (53°19'12")

20. 5 × (34°15'6")

21. 9 × (12°5'23")

22. 7 × (28°16'25")

23. 107° ÷ 4

24. (35°42') ÷ 7

25. (53°28') ÷ 5

26. (192°56'40") ÷ 8

27. (89°36'42") ÷ 3

28. (103°44'18") ÷ 6

29. (47°18'27") ÷ 9

Each of these problems requires two or more arithmetic operations on angles for its solution. Determine the value of each.

30. Refer to figure 13-45. Determine the value of ∠4 if ∠1 + ∠2 + ∠3 + ∠4 = 360°.

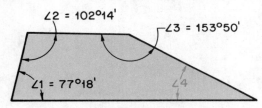

Fig. 13-45

31. Refer to figure 13-46 and determine ∠A.

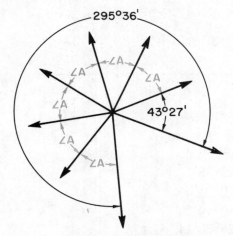

Fig. 13-46

32. Refer to figure 13-47. Determine ∠C when ∠B = 51°17′.

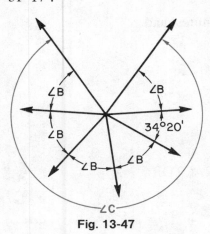

Fig. 13-47

35. Refer to figure 13-50. Determine ∠A and ∠B if ∠A = 3∠B.

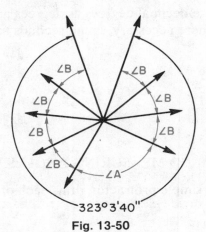

Fig. 13-50

33. Refer to figure 13-48. The sum of all angles = 540°. ∠1 = ∠5 = 118°46′. ∠2 = ∠4 = 27°14′. Determine ∠3.

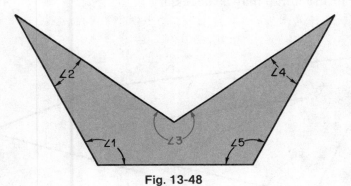

Fig. 13-48

36. Refer to figure 13-51. The sum of all angles = 720°. ∠1 = ∠3 = ∠4 = ∠6. ∠2 = ∠5 = 280°24′10″. Determine ∠1.

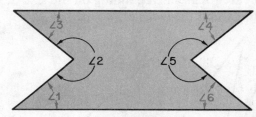

Fig. 13-51

34. Refer to figure 13-49 and determine ∠A.

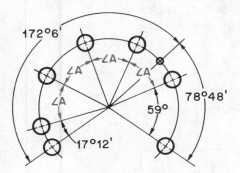

Fig. 13-49

EXPRESSING DECIMAL DEGREES AS DEGREES,
MINUTES, AND SECONDS

Express these decimal degrees as degrees and minutes or degrees, minutes, and
seconds. Where necessary, round seconds to the nearer whole second.

37. 66.20°

38. 117.05°

39. 8.85°

40. 49.62°

41. 216.83°

42. 153.107°

43. 60.083°

44. 88.679 4°

DRAWING AND MEASURING ANGLES WITH A SIMPLE PROTRACTOR

45. Using a simple protractor, draw each of the following angles.

a. 53°

b. 19°

c. 96°

d. 78°

e. 129°

46. Using a protractor, measure each of the following angles, ∠1 - ∠11, to the
nearer degree. Depending on the size of your protractor, it may be necessary
to extend the sides of the angles.

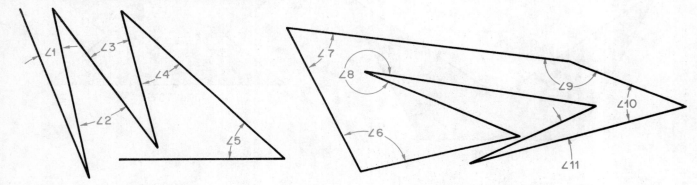

47. Draw a 4-sided closed figure (quadrilateral) of any size containing angles
of 38°, 165°, and 57°. Measure the fourth angle. How many degrees are
contained in the fourth angle?

CIRCLE GRAPHS

48. A family's annual expenses are shown in figure 13-52. Construct a circle
graph showing these expenses.

EXPENSE	FOOD	CLOTHING	RENT	UTILITIES	TRANSPORTATION	OTHER EXPENSES
AMOUNT	$5 250	$2 940	$4 620	$2 730	$1 890	$3 570

Fig. 13-52

49. A wholesale distributor maintains area offices and warehouses in five parts
of the country. The annual sales of each area are as follows: Northeast,
$2 400 000; Southeast, $1 800 000; Midwest, $3 000 000; Southwest, $2 200 000;
Northwest, $1 400 000. Construct a circle graph showing the distributor's
annual area sales.

VERNIER PROTRACTOR

Write the values of the settings on these vernier protractor scales.

50.

51.

52.

ANGLE COMPLEMENTS AND SUPPLEMENTS

53. Write the complements of these angles.

    a. 63°

    b. 18°27′

    c. 86°19′48″

    d. 45°2′7″

    e. 44°3′4″

54. Write the supplements of these angles.

    a. 78°

    b. 109°56′

    c. 89°13′32″

    d. 178°9′21″

    e. 2°0′59″

UNIT 14
Angular
Geometric Principles

OBJECTIVES

After studying this unit you should be able to

- identify different types of angles.

- identify pairs of adjacent, alternate interior, corresponding, and vertical angles.

- determine values of angles in geometric figures applying theorems of opposite, alternate interior, and corresponding angles.

- determine values of angles in geometric figures applying theorems of angular parallel and perpendicular corresponding sides.

NAMING ANGLES

Angles are named by a number, a letter or three letters. When an angle is named with three letters, the vertex must be the middle letter. For example, the angle shown in figure 14-1 can be called $\angle 1$, $\angle C$, $\angle ACB$, or $\angle BCA$.

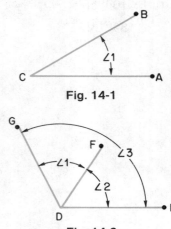
Fig. 14-1

In cases where a point is the vertex of more than one angle, a single letter cannot be used to name an angle. In figure 14-2, the single letter D cannot be used in naming an angle since point D is the vertex of three different angles. Each of the three angles is named $\angle 1$, $\angle FDG$, or $\angle GDF$; $\angle 2$, $\angle FDE$, or $\angle EDF$; $\angle 3$, $\angle GDE$, or $\angle EDG$.

Fig. 14-2

TYPES OF ANGLES

An *acute angle* is an angle that is less than 90°. Angle 1 shown in figure 14-3 is acute.

A *right angle* is an angle of 90°. Angle A shown in figure 14-4 is a right angle.

An *obtuse angle* is an angle greater than 90° and less than 180°. Angle ABC shown in figure 14-5 is an obtuse angle.

A *straight angle* is an angle of 180°. A straight line is a straight angle. Line segment DBC shown in figure 14-5 is a straight angle.

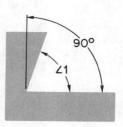
Fig. 14-3

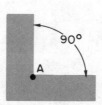
Fig. 14-4

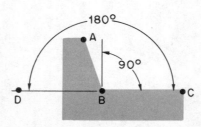
Fig. 14-5

194

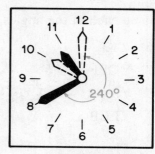

Fig. 14-6

A *reflex angle* is an angle greater than 180° and less than 360°. For example, in figure 14-6, the clock shows a time change from 10:00 to 10:40. The minute hand moves from the 12 to the 8. Since the minute hand moves through 30° (360° ÷ 12 = 30°) for each 5 minutes of time, it moves through 8 × 30° or 240°. The 240° moved by the minute hand is a reflex angle.

Two angles are *adjacent* if they have a common vertex and a common side. Angle 1 and angle 2 shown in figure 14-7 are adjacent since they both contain the common vertex B and the common side BC.

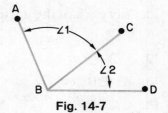

Fig. 14-7

ANGLES FORMED BY A TRANSVERSAL

A *transversal* is a line that intersects (cuts) two or more lines. Line EF shown in figure 14-8 is a transversal since it cuts lines AB and CD.

Alternate interior angles are pairs of interior angles on opposite sides of a transversal. The angles have different vertices. In figure 14-8, angles 3 and 5 and angles 4 and 6 are pairs of alternate interior angles.

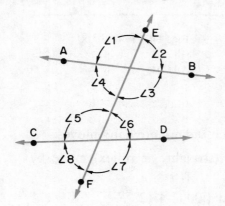

Fig. 14-8

Corresponding angles are pairs of angles, one interior and one exterior. Both angles are on the same side of the transversal with different vertices. In figure 14-8, angles 1 and 5, 2 and 6, 3 and 7, and 4 and 8 are pairs of corresponding angles.

Exercise 14-1

Name each of the angles shown in figure 14-9 in three additional ways.

1. ∠1
2. ∠2
3. ∠D
4. ∠DEF
5. ∠F

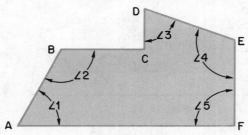

Fig. 14-9

Name each of the angles shown in figure 14-10 in two additional ways.

6. ∠1

7. ∠CBF

8. ∠3

9. ∠ECB

10. ∠5

11. ∠BCD

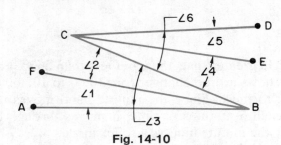

Fig. 14-10

Identify each of the angles shown in figure 14-11 as acute, right, obtuse, straight, or reflex.

12. ∠B

13. ∠ACB

14. ∠CDE

15. ∠BAF

16. ∠ABC

17. ∠BCD

18. ∠1

19. ∠EFG

20. ∠EFA

21. ∠EDF

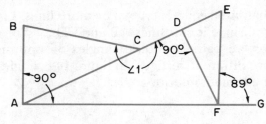

Fig. 14-11

For each of the time changes in problems 22-30:

a. determine the number of degrees through which the minute hand moves.

b. write the type of angle (acute, right, obtuse, straight, or reflex) made by the movement of the minute hand.

22. from 8:00 to 8:25

23. from 11:00 to 11:55

24. from 6:30 to 6:45

25. from 5:50 to 6:20

26. from 3:15 to 4:05

27. from 4:00 to 4:12

28. from 2:22 to 2:54

29. from 7:18 to 7:48

30. from 1:39 to 2:26

31. Name all pairs of adjacent angles shown in figure 14-12.

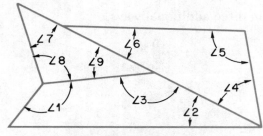

Fig. 14-12

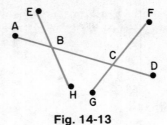

Refer to figure 14-13 for problems 32-33.

32. Name all pairs of alternate interior angles.

33. Name all pairs of corresponding angles.

Fig. 14-13

THEOREMS AND COROLLARIES

Based on postulates, other statements about points, lines, and planes can be proved. A statement in geometry which can be proved is called a *theorem*. Theorems which are proved can then be used with postulates and definitions in proving other theorems.

A *corollary* is a statement which is based on a theorem. A corollary is often a special case of the theorem which it follows and can be proved by applying the theorem.

In this book, theorems and corollaries are not proved. They are used as the geometric rules for problem solving.

If two lines intersect, the opposite or vertical angles are equal.

Example.   Refer to figure 14-14.

Given: Lines $\overleftrightarrow{AB}$ and $\overleftrightarrow{CD}$ intersect and angles 1 and 3 and angles 2 and 4 are pairs of opposite or vertical angles.

Conclusion: $\angle 1 = \angle 3$ and $\angle 2 = \angle 4$

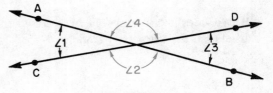

Fig. 14-14

If two parallel lines are intersected by a transversal, the alternate interior angles are equal.

Example.   Refer to figure 14-15.

Given: $\overleftrightarrow{AB} \parallel \overleftrightarrow{CD}$

Conclusion: $\angle 1 = \angle 4$ and $\angle 2 = \angle 3$

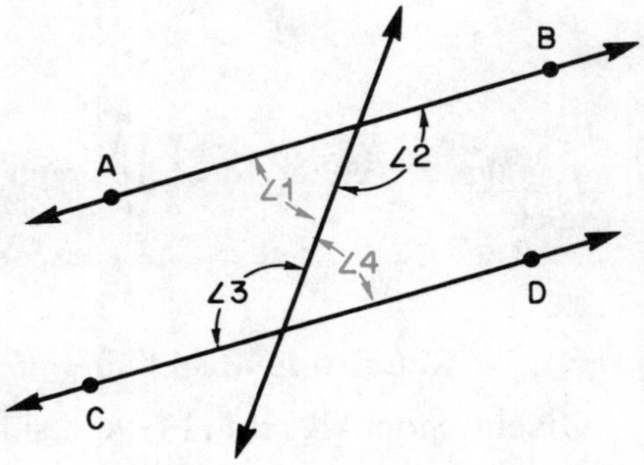

Fig. 14-15

If two lines are intersected by a transversal and a pair of alternate interior angles are equal, the lines are parallel.

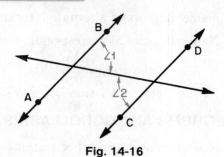

Fig. 14-16

Example.   Refer to figure 14-16.

Given: $\angle 1 = \angle 2$

Conclusion: $\overleftrightarrow{AB} \parallel \overleftrightarrow{CD}$

If two parallel lines are intersected by a transversal, the corresponding angles are equal.

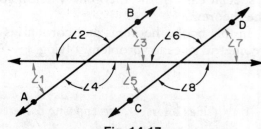

Fig. 14-17

Example.   Refer to figure 14-17.

Given: $\overleftrightarrow{AB} \parallel \overleftrightarrow{CD}$

Conclusion: $\angle 1 = \angle 5$; $\angle 2 = \angle 6$; $\angle 3 = \angle 7$; and $\angle 4 = \angle 8$

If two lines are intersected by a transversal and a pair of corresponding angles are equal, the lines are parallel.

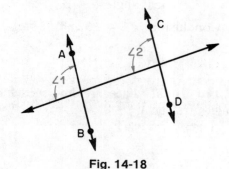

Fig. 14-18

Example.   Refer to figure 14-18.

Given: $\angle 1 = \angle 2$

Conclusion: $\overleftrightarrow{AB} \parallel \overleftrightarrow{CD}$

Two angles are either equal or supplementary if their corresponding sides are parallel.

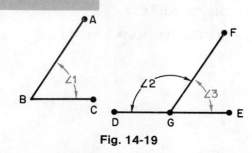

Fig. 14-19

Example.   Refer to figure 14-19.

Given: Side AB $\parallel$ side FG and side BC $\parallel$ side DE

Conclusion: $\angle 1 = \angle 3$

$\angle 1 + \angle 2 = 180°$

Two angles are either equal or supplementary if their corresponding sides are perpendicular.

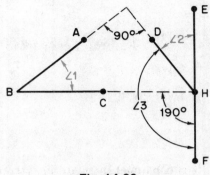

Example.   Refer to figure 14-20.

Given: Side AB ⊥ side DH and side BC ⊥ EF

Conclusion: ∠1 = ∠2

∠1 + ∠3 = 180°

Fig. 14-20

This example illustrates methods of solution for angular measure problems.

Example.   Refer to figure 14-21.

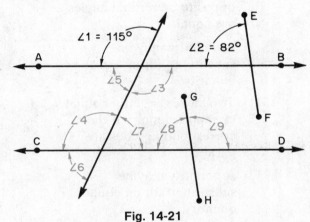

Fig. 14-21

Given: $\overleftrightarrow{AB} \parallel \overleftrightarrow{CD}$, $EF \parallel GH$,
∠1 = 115°, and ∠2 = 82°

Determine the values of ∠3 through ∠9.

a. (1) ∠3 = ∠1

(2) ∠3 = 115° *Ans*

b. (1) ∠4 = ∠3

(2) ∠4 = 115° *Ans*

a. (1) If two lines intersect, the opposite or vertical angles are equal.

(2) A quantity may be substituted for an equal quantity.

b. (1) If two parallel lines are intersected by a transversal, the alternate interior angles are equal.

(2) A quantity may be substituted for an equal quantity.

c. (1) $\angle 5 + \angle 1 = 180°$

   (2) $\angle 5 + 115° = 180°$

   (3) $\angle 5 = 180° - 115° = 65°$ *Ans*

d. (1) $\angle 6 = \angle 5$

   (2) $\angle 6 = 65°$ *Ans*

e. (1) $\angle 7 = \angle 6$

   (2) $\angle 7 = 65°$ *Ans*

f. (1) $\angle 8 = \angle 2$

   (2) $\angle 8 = 82°$ *Ans*

g. (1) $\angle 8 + \angle 9 = 180°$

   (2) $\angle 9 = 180° - \angle 8$

   (3) $\angle 9 = 180° - 82° = 98°$ *Ans*

c. (1) A straight angle is an angle of 180°.

   (2) A quantity may be substituted for an equal quantity.

   (3) If equals are subtracted from equals, the differences are equal.

d. (1) If two parallel lines are intersected by a transversal, the corresponding angles are equal.

   (2) A quantity may be substituted for an equal quantity.

e. (1) If two lines intersect, the opposite or vertical angles are equal.

   (2) A quantity may be substituted for an equal quantity.

f. (1) Two angles are either equal or supplementary if their corresponding sides are parallel.

   (2) A quantity may be substituted for an equal quantity.

g. (1) A straight angle equals 180°.

   (2) If equals are subtracted from equals, the differences are equal.

   (3) A quantity may be substituted for an equal quantity.

Exercise 14-2

Solve these problems.

1. Refer to figure 14-22 and determine the values of angles 1-5.

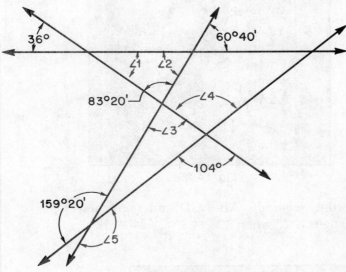

Fig. 14-22

2. **Refer to figure 14-23. Determine the values of angles 2, 3, and 4 for these values of angle 1.**

    a. ∠1 = 31°

    b. ∠1 = 29°53′

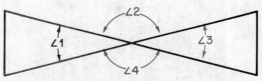

Fig. 14-23

3. Refer to figure 14-24. $\overleftrightarrow{AB} \parallel \overleftrightarrow{CD}$. Determine the values of angles 2-8 for these values of angle 1.

    a. ∠1 = 59°

    b. ∠1 = 63°18′

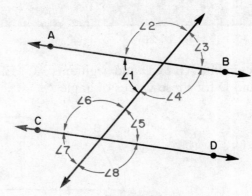

Fig. 14-24

4. Refer to figure 14-25. Hole centerline segments EF ‖ GH and segments MP ‖ KL. Determine the values of angles 1-15 for these values of angle 16.

   a. ∠16 = 77°
   b. ∠16 = 81°13′

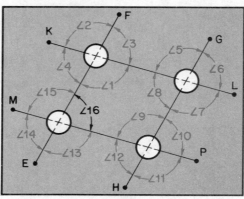

Fig. 14-25

5. Refer to figure 14-26. Hole centerline segments AB ‖ CD and segments EF ‖ GH. Determine the values of angles 1-22 when ∠23 = 95°, ∠24 = 32°, and ∠25 = 104°.

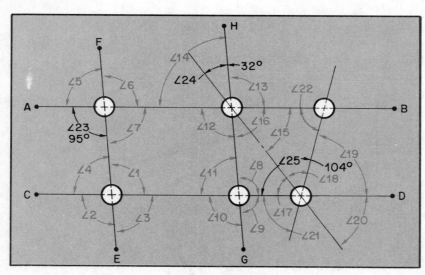

Fig. 14-26

6. Refer to figure 14-27. Segments AB ‖ CD and segments AC ‖ ED. Determine the values of angles C and D for these values of angle A.

   a. ∠A = 64°
   b. ∠A = 70°27′

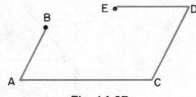

Fig. 14-27

7. Refer to figure 14-28. Segments FH ∥ GS ∥ KM and segments FG ∥ HK. Determine the values of angles F, G, and H for these values of angle K.

    a. ∠K = 86°
    b. ∠K = 79°19′

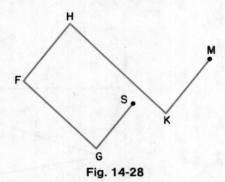

Fig. 14-28

8. Refer to figure 14-29. Segments AE ⊥ FD and segments AD ⊥ CE. Determine the values of ∠D and ∠DBE for these values of ∠E and ∠CBD.

    a. ∠E = 52° and ∠CBD = 38°
    b. ∠E = 50°19′ and ∠CBD = 39°41′

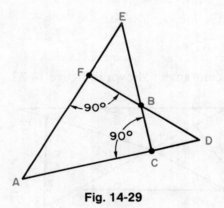

Fig. 14-29

UNIT EXERCISE AND PROBLEM REVIEW

Exercise 14-3

NAMING ANGLES

Name each of the angles shown in figure 14-30 in two additional ways.

1. ∠CBA
2. ∠4
3. ∠HFD
4. ∠EDF
5. ∠1
6. ∠5

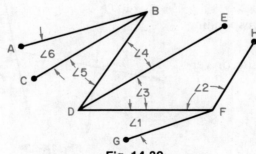

Fig. 14-30

TYPES OF ANGLES

Identify each of the angles shown in figure 14-31 as acute, right, obtuse, straight, or reflex.

7. $\angle 2$

8. $\angle DCA$

9. $\angle ACB$

10. $\angle DCB$

11. $\angle 3$

12. $\angle 1$

13. $\angle D$

14. $\angle DAC$

15. $\angle AFB$

16. $\angle AEF$

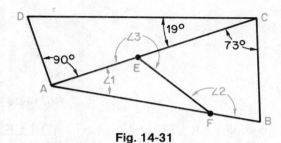

Fig. 14-31

ADJACENT ANGLES

17. Name all pairs of adjacent angles shown in figure 14-32.

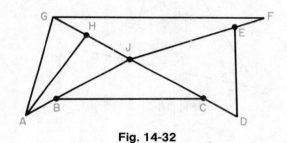

Fig. 14-32

ANGLES FORMED BY A TRANSVERSAL, VERTICAL ANGLES

Refer to figure 14-33 for problems 18-20.

18. Name all pairs of alternate interior angles.

19. Name all pairs of corresponding angles.

20. Name all pairs of opposite or vertical angles.

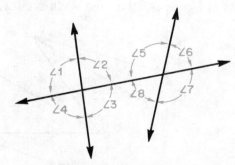

Fig. 14-33

ANGULAR PROBLEMS

Solve these problems.

21. Refer to figure 14-34 and determine the values of angles 1-10.

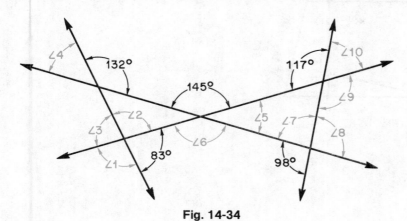

Fig. 14-34

22. Refer to figure 14-35. $\overleftrightarrow{AB} \parallel \overleftrightarrow{CD}$. Determine the values of angles 1-5.

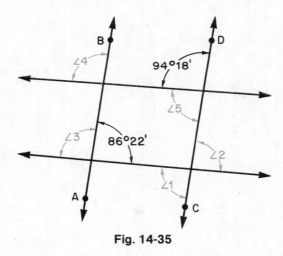

Fig. 14-35

23. Refer to figure 14-36. Hole centerline segments AB ∥ CD and EF ∥ GH. Determine the values of angles 1-10.

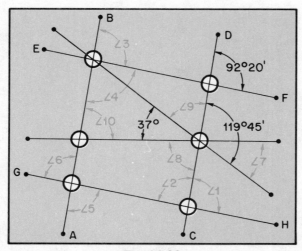

Fig. 14-36

24. Refer to figure 14-37. Segments AB ∥ CD and AC ∥ BD; segments AF ⊥ AC and GE ⊥ CD. Determine the value of ∠B, ∠D, and ∠AEG.

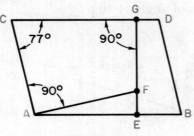

Fig. 14-37

UNIT 15
Triangles

OBJECTIVES

After studying this unit you should be able to

- make figures rigid by applying the fact that a triangle is a rigid figure.

- identify types of triangles by sides or angles.

- apply triangle theorems in determining unknown angles of a triangle.

- informally prove pairs of triangles are congruent and determine unknown angles and sides.

- solve practical applied problems.

- compute unknown sides of right triangles by applying the Pythagorean Theorem.

A *polygon* is a closed plane figure formed by three or more line segments.

A *triangle* is a three-sided polygon. It is the simplest kind of polygon. The symbol △ means triangle. Triangles are used in art, manufacturing, surveying, navigation, astronomy, architecture, and engineering. The triangle is the basic figure in many designs and structures.

A triangle is a rigid figure. The rigidity of a triangle is illustrated by this simple example. Three strips of wood are fastened to form a triangular frame with one nail at each vertex, figure 15-1. The size and shape of the frame cannot be changed without bending or breaking the strips. The triangular frame is said to be rigid.

A figure with more than three sides is not rigid. The frame made of four strips of wood fastened with one nail at each vertex is not rigid, figure 15-2. The sides can be readily moved without bending or breaking to change its shape, figure 15-3.

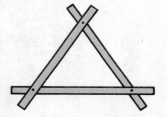

Fig. 15-1 A rigid triangular frame

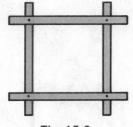

Fig. 15-2

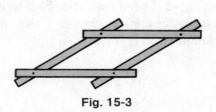

Fig. 15-3

The four-sided frame can be made rigid by adding a cross brace, figure 15-4. Observe that the addition of the brace divides the figure into two triangles.

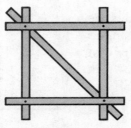

Fig. 15-4

The design and construction of many structures such as buildings and bridges are based on a system of triangles. Cross bridging is used between joists to reinforce floors, figure 15-5. A roof truss gives support and rigidity to a roof, figure 15-6. Notice the truss is made up of a combination of triangles.

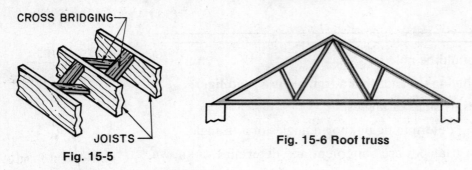

Fig. 15-5

Fig. 15-6 Roof truss

Many objects used in the home are made rigid by means of triangles. The step ladder and shelf brackets show common applications of triangles, figures 15-7 and 15-8.

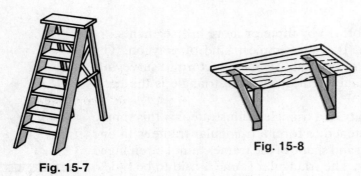

Fig. 15-8

Fig. 15-7

The designer, drafter, sheet metal technician, welder, and structural steel worker are some of the many occupations which require a knowledge of triangles in laying out work. Plumbers and pipefitters compute pipe lengths in diagonal pipe assemblies using triangular relationships. Auto body technicians apply principles of triangles when measuring and repairing automobile frames. Carpenters make use of triangular relationships when checking the squareness of wall corners and computing rafter lengths.

TYPES OF TRIANGLES

An *equilateral triangle* has three equal sides. It also has three equal angles. In the equilateral triangle ABC shown in figure 15-9, sides AB = AC = BC and ∠A = ∠B = ∠C.

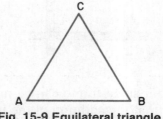

Fig. 15-9 Equilateral triangle

An *isosceles triangle* has two equal sides. The equal sides are called *legs*. The third side is called the *base*. The base angles of an isosceles triangle are equal. *Base angles* are the angles that are opposite the legs. In the isosceles triangle DEF shown in figure 15-10, leg DF = leg EF. Since ∠D is opposite leg EF and ∠E is opposite leg DF, ∠D and ∠E are base angles.

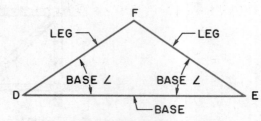

Fig. 15-10 Isosceles triangle

A *scalene triangle* has three unequal sides. It has three unequal angles. Triangle ABC shown in figure 15-11 is scalene. Sides AB, AC, and BC are unequal and angles A, B, and C are unequal.

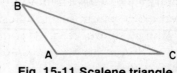

Fig. 15-11 Scalene triangle

A *right triangle* has a right or 90° angle. The symbol for a right angle is ⌐ which is shown at the vertex of the angle. The side opposite the right angle is called the hypotenuse. The other two sides are called legs. Figure 15-12 shows a right triangle with the right angle at D and the hypotenuse EF.

An *acute triangle* has three acute angles. An example of an acute triangle is shown in figure 15-13.

An *obtuse triangle* has one obtuse angle and two acute angles. An example of an obtuse triangle is shown in figure 15-14.

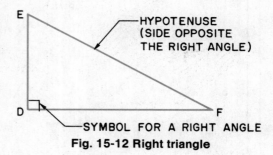

Fig. 15-12 Right triangle

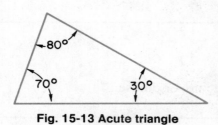

Fig. 15-13 Acute triangle

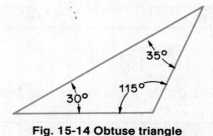

Fig. 15-14 Obtuse triangle

Exercise 15-1

1. Make a sketch of each shape shown in figure 15-15. Show how each shape can be made rigid using a minimum number of braces.

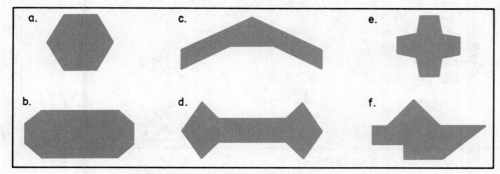

Fig. 15-15

2. Make a list of at least five examples of practical uses of triangles as rigid figures found in and around your home.

3. Identify each of the triangles in figure 15-16 as scalene, isosceles, or equilateral.

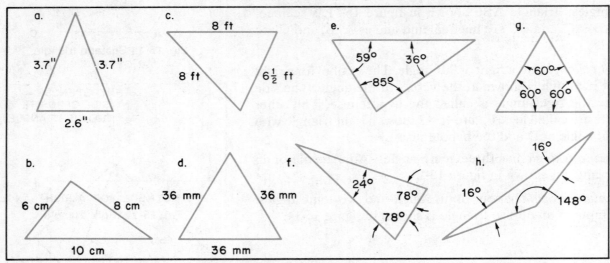

Fig. 15-16

4. Identify each of the triangles in figure 15-17 as right, acute, or obtuse.

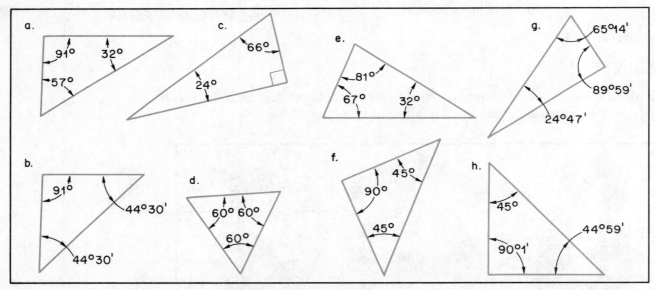

Fig. 15-17

ANGLES OF A TRIANGLE

In every triangle the sum of the three angles is always the same.

The sum of the angles of any triangle is equal to 180°.

The sum of the angles in a triangle is used in many practical applications.

Example 1. In figure 15-18, angles A, B, and C are centerline angles. Angle A equals 48°35′ and angle C = 87°10′. Find angle B.

∠B = 180° − (48°35′ + 87°10′)

∠B = **44°15′** *Ans*

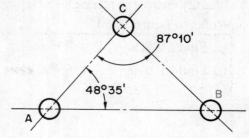

Fig. 15-18

Example 2. A roof truss is shown in figure 15-19. Determine ∠4.

The sum of the angles in a triangle is equal to 180°.

∠AED = 180° − (43° + 90°)
∠AED = 47°

A straight angle equals 180°.

∠CEF = 180° − (47° + 58°)
∠CEF = 75°

The sum of the angles in a triangle is equal to 180°.

∠4 = 180° − (64° + 75°)
∠4 = **41°** *Ans*

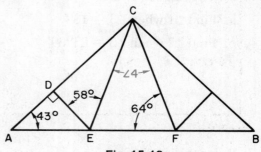

Fig. 15-19

Exercise 15-2

Solve these problems.

1. Refer to figure 15-20. Determine the value of ∠A + ∠B + ∠C.

Fig. 15-20

2. Refer to figure 15-21.

   a. Find ∠3 when ∠1 = 68° and ∠2 = 85°

   b. Find ∠1 when ∠2 = 81° and ∠3 = 33°

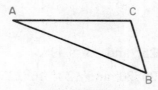

Fig. 15-21

3. Refer to figure 15-22.

   a. Find ∠6 when ∠4 = 31°23′ and ∠5 = 122°16′.

   b. Find ∠4 when ∠5 = 124°57′ and ∠6 = 27°15′.

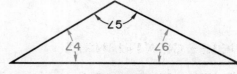

Fig. 15-22

4. Refer to figure 15-23.

   a. Find ∠B when ∠A = 21°36′.

   b. Find ∠A when ∠B = 64°19′27″.

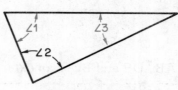

Fig. 15-23

5. Refer to figure 15-24.

   a. Find ∠G when ∠E = 83°.

   b. Find ∠F when ∠G = 85°22′.

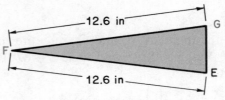

Fig. 15-24

6. Refer to figure 15-25.

   a. Find ∠1 when ∠3 = 18°.

   b. Find ∠2 when ∠3 = 23°39′.

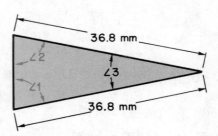

Fig. 15-25

7. Refer to figure 15-26.

   a. Find ∠1.

   b. Find ∠2.

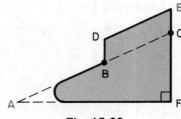

Fig. 15-26

8. Refer to figure 15-27.

   a. Find ∠2 when ∠1 = 25° and ∠3 = 49°.

   b. Find ∠3 when ∠1 = 28°30′ and ∠2 = 16°22′.

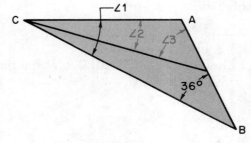

Fig. 15-27

9. Refer to figure 15-28. AB∥DE and BC is an extension of AB.

   a. Find ∠A when ∠E = 65°17′.

   b. Find ∠E when ∠A = 21°46′.

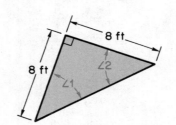

Fig. 15-28

10. Refer to figure 15-29. Hole centerline AB ∥ CD.

    a. Find ∠2 when ∠1 = 87°51′.

    b. Find ∠1 when ∠2 = 68°29′.

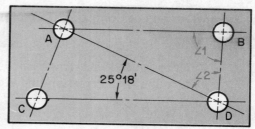

Fig. 15-29

11. Refer to the roof truss shown in figure 15-30.

    a. Determine the value of ∠1.

    b. Determine the value of ∠2.

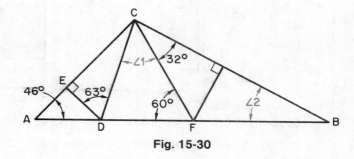

Fig. 15-30

CONGRUENT TRIANGLES

Two triangles are *congruent* if they are identical in size and shape. If one triangle is placed on the other, the congruent triangles coincide or fit exactly. The symbol ≅ means congruent.

Corresponding parts of congruent triangles are equal.

The corresponding parts of triangles are corresponding sides and corresponding angles. If congruent triangles are placed one on the other (superimposed), the parts which fit exactly are corresponding.

Corresponding Sides of Congruent Triangles

The sides which lie opposite equal angles are *corresponding sides*.

Example.   Refer to figure 15-31. Triangles ABC and DEF are congruent triangles. Determine the corresponding equal sides.

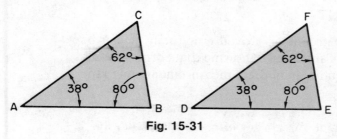

Fig. 15-31

AB and DE both lie opposite 62° angles. AB = DE *Ans*

BC and EF both lie opposite 38° angles. BC = EF *Ans*

AC and DF both lie opposite 80° angles. AC = DF *Ans*

Corresponding Angles of Congruent Triangles

The angles which lie opposite equal sides are *corresponding angles*.

Example.   Refer to figure 15-32. Triangles MNP and RST are congruent triangles. Determine the corresponding equal angles.

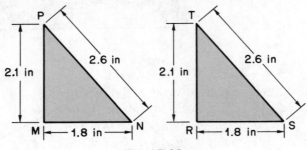

Fig. 15-32

∠M and ∠R both lie opposite 2.6-inch sides. **∠M = ∠R** *Ans*

∠N and ∠S both lie opposite 2.1-inch sides. **∠N = ∠S** *Ans*

∠P and ∠T both lie opposite 1.8-inch sides. **∠P = ∠T** *Ans*

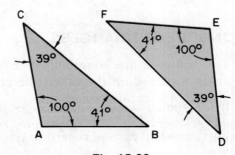

It is important to remember that corresponding parts of congruent triangles are *not* determined by the positions of the triangles. For example, with the congruent triangles shown in figure 15-33, sides AC and DF are not corresponding. They do not lie opposite equal angles. Sides AC and ED are corresponding and equal since they both lie opposite 41° angles.

Fig. 15-33

Congruent triangles are often marked as shown in figure 15-34 to indicate corresponding sides and angles. When side AB is given one mark, corresponding side DE is also given one mark. Angle C which is opposite AB and angle F which is opposite DE are also given one mark. The same procedure is used to mark the other corresponding sides and angles.

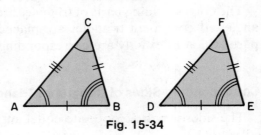

Fig. 15-34

PROVING TRIANGLES CONGRUENT

If two triangles are known to be congruent or proved congruent, it can be concluded that their corresponding parts are equal. Knowing that corresponding parts are equal has wide practical application in indirect measurement and in the duplication of parts.

> **If three sides of one triangle are equal to three sides of another triangle, the triangles are congruent. (Abbreviated SSS)**

Example.   Refer to △ABC and △DEF shown in figure 15-35.

Given: AB = DE

BC = EF

AC = DF

Conclusion: △ABC ≅ △DEF

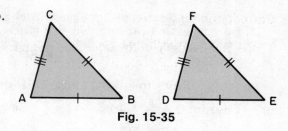

Fig. 15-35

Practical Application

A duplicate of the plate shown in figure 15-36 is made. The hole pattern must be the same. The three distances (AB, BC, and AC) are measured in the original plate. The respective distances (A′B′, B′C′, and A′C′) are laid out on the plate, figure 15-37. A hole is drilled at each vertex of the triangle which was laid out. The hole patterns of the two plates are identical since the triangles in the original plate and the duplicated plate are congruent.

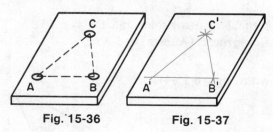

Fig. 15-36   Fig. 15-37

If two sides and the included angle of one triangle are equal to two sides and the included angle of the other, the triangles are congruent. (Abbreviated SAS)

Example.   Refer to △ABC and △DEF shown in figure 15-38.

Given: AB = DE

∠A = ∠D

AC = DF

Conclusion: △ABC ≅ △DEF

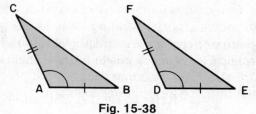

Fig. 15-38

NOTE: ∠A is <u>included</u> between sides AC and AB. ∠D is <u>included</u> between sides DE and DF.

Practical Application

The distance between points A and B shown in figure 15-39 must be determined. Since an obstruction lies between the two points, a direct measurement cannot be made. If the ground in the area is flat with no further obstructions, distance AB can be determined. Drive a stake at a convenient point C. Sight along AC and extend AC. Measure off CE equal to AC and drive a stake at point E. Sight along BC and extend BC. Measure off CD equal to BC and drive a stake at point D. Vertical angles DCE and ACB are equal. Triangles ACB and DCE are congruent (SAS). Since AB and DE are corresponding sides, AB = DE. Measure distance DE. Distance AB is equal to the measured distance.

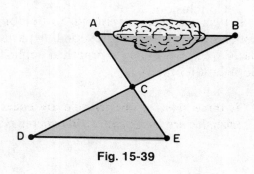

Fig. 15-39

If two angles and the included side of one triangle are equal to two angles and the included side of the other, the triangles are congruent. (Abbreviated ASA)

Example.   Refer to △ABC and △DEF shown in figure 15-40.

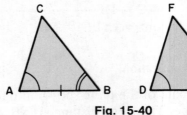

Given: ∠A = ∠D

AB = DE

∠B = ∠E

Conclusion: △ABC ≅ △DEF

Fig. 15-40

NOTE: Side AB is included between ∠A and ∠B. Side DE is included between ∠D and ∠E.

If two angles and a side of one triangle are equal to two angles and the corresponding side of the other, the triangles are congruent. (Abbreviated AAS)

Example.   Refer to △ABC and △DEF shown in figure 15-41.

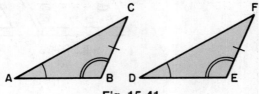

Given: ∠A = ∠D

∠B = ∠E

BC = EF

Conclusion: △ABC ≅ △DEF

Fig. 15-41

NOTE: Side BC is <u>not</u> included between ∠A and ∠D. Side EF is <u>not</u> included between ∠D and ∠E.

If the hypotenuse and a leg of one right triangle are equal to the hypotenuse and a leg of another right triangle, the triangles are congruent. (Abbreviated HL)

Example.   Refer to right △ABC and right △DEF shown in figure 15-42.

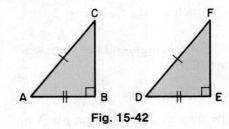

Given: AC = DF

AB = DE

Triangles ABC and DEF are right triangles.

Conclusion: △ABC ≅ △DEF

Fig. 15-42

Exercise 15-3

1. Three pairs of congruent triangles are shown in figure 15-43. Identify the pairs of corresponding sides in problems a, b, and c.

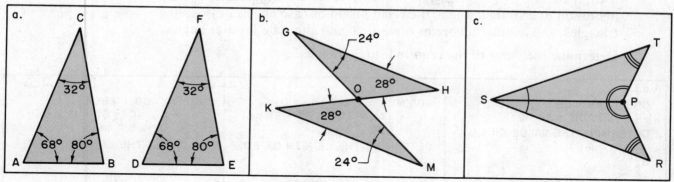

Fig. 15-43

2. Three pairs of congruent triangles are shown in figure 15-44. Identify the pairs of corresponding angles in problems a, b, and c.

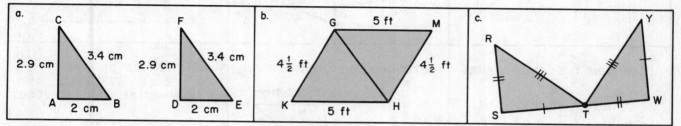

Fig. 15-44

3. Six pairs of congruent triangles are shown in figure 15-45. Identify the congruency theorem (SSS, SAS, ASA, AAS, or HL) which applies to each of the problems a-f.

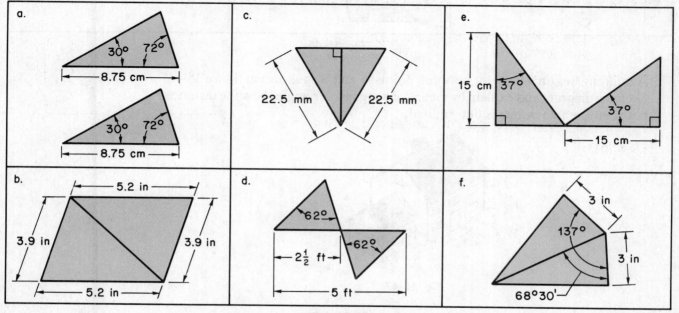

Fig. 15-45

4. For each of the following problems, a–f, shown in figure 15-46, do the following:

   (1) Informally prove that pairs of triangles are congruent. Each pair must meet the requirements of one of the five congruency theorems (SSS, SAS, ASA, AAS, or HL). Certain problems require the application of the definition of a straight angle, the relationship of base angles of isosceles triangles, and angular theorems of vertical and alternate interior angles.

   (2) Determine the value of the required side or angle.

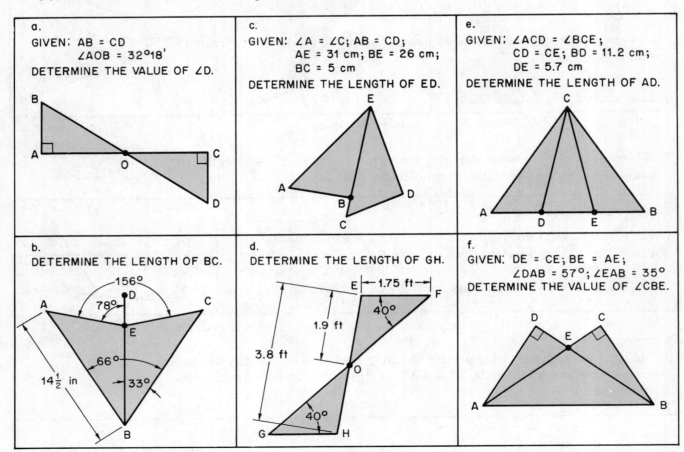

a.
GIVEN: AB = CD
        ∠AOB = 32°18'
DETERMINE THE VALUE OF ∠D.

b.
DETERMINE THE LENGTH OF BC.

c.
GIVEN: ∠A = ∠C; AB = CD;
        AE = 31 cm; BE = 26 cm;
        BC = 5 cm
DETERMINE THE LENGTH OF ED.

d.
DETERMINE THE LENGTH OF GH.

e.
GIVEN: ∠ACD = ∠BCE;
        CD = CE; BD = 11.2 cm;
        DE = 5.7 cm
DETERMINE THE LENGTH OF AD.

f.
GIVEN: DE = CE; BE = AE;
        ∠DAB = 57°; ∠EAB = 35°
DETERMINE THE VALUE OF ∠CBE.

Fig. 15-46

5. A building lies on a level lot between points A and B as shown in figure 15-47. Sketch a diagram and explain by means of congruent triangles how the distance between the two points is determined.

Fig. 15-47

THE PYTHAGOREAN THEOREM

The Pythagorean Theorem deals with the relationship of the sides of a right triangle. The application of the Pythagorean Theorem permits accurate indirect measure. If the lengths of the sides of a triangle are known, it can be determined if the triangle contains a right angle.

If two sides of a right triangle are known, the third side can be calculated. The theorem is the basis of many formulas used in diverse occupational fields such as construction, metal fabrication, woodworking, electrical, and electronics.

In a right triangle, the square of the hypotenuse is equal to the sum of the squares of the legs.

Example.   Refer to right triangle ABC shown in figure 15-48.

Side c is the hypotenuse.

$c^2 = a^2 + b^2$

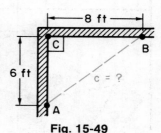

Fig. 15-48

Practical Applications

1. Carpenters and masons often apply the Pythagorean Theorem in squaring-up corners of buildings. Squaring-up means making corner walls at right angles. A 6-foot length is marked off on one wall at point A, figure 15-49. An 8-foot length is marked off on the other wall at point B. For the corner to be square, what should the measurement be from point A to point B (length c):

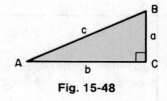

Fig. 15-49

Solution: The 6-foot and 8-foot legs are given and the hypotenuse is determined.

$c^2 = (6 \text{ ft})^2 + (8 \text{ ft})^2$

$c^2 = 36 \text{ sq ft} + 64 \text{ sq ft}$

$c^2 = 100 \text{ sq ft}$

$c = 10 \text{ ft } Ans$

2. Rafters 18 feet long are used on an equally pitched roof with a 24-foot span, figure 15-50. Determine the rise, FG, of the roof.

Solution: Since △DEF is an isosceles triangle, the rise, FG is an altitude to the base (24 ft span).

$DG = 24 \text{ ft} \div 2$

$DG = 12 \text{ ft}$

$DF = 18 \text{ ft} - 2 \text{ ft}$

$DF = 16 \text{ ft}$

$(16 \text{ ft})^2 = (FG)^2 + (12 \text{ ft})^2$

$256 \text{ sq ft} = (FG)^2 + 144 \text{ sq ft}$

$(FG)^2 = 112 \text{ sq ft}$

$FG = 10.583 \text{ ft (rounded)}$

$10.583 \text{ ft} = 10 \text{ ft 7 in } Ans$

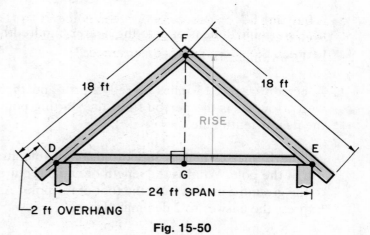

Fig. 15-50

Exercise 15-4

Apply the Pythagorean Theorem in solving problems 1-6, figure 15-51. Refer to the right triangle shown in figure 15-52. Where necessary, express the answers to 2 decimal places.

	SIDE a	SIDE b	SIDE c
1.	15 in ·	20 in	?
2.	6 m	7.5 m	?
3.	18 mm	?	30 mm
4.	?	12.5 ft	16 ft
5.	45 mm	?	75 mm
6.	?	10.2 in	14.6 in

Fig. 15-51

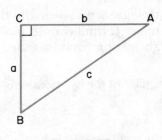

Fig. 15-52

Solve these practical problems. In addition to the Pythagorean Theorem, certain problems require the application of other triangle theorems.

7. A machined piece is shown in figure 15-53.

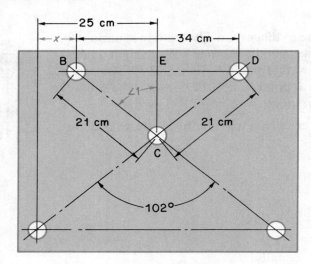

Fig. 15-53

    a. Determine dimension x to the nearer hundredth centimetre.

    b. Determine $\angle 1$.

8. A person travels 15 miles directly north and then travels 7 miles directly west. How far is the person from the starting point? Express the answer to the nearer tenth mile.

9. A pole 15 metres high is supported by a cable attached 2 metres from the top of the pole. What is the length of cable required if the cable is fastened to the ground 6 metres from the foot of the pole? Assume the ground is level. Express the answer to 2 decimal places.

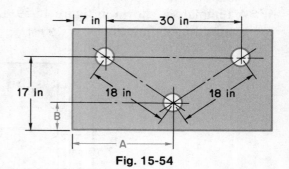

Fig. 15-54

10. Three holes are drilled in a plate as shown in figure 15-54. Determine dimensions A and B to 1 decimal place.

11. In remodeling a house, a carpenter checks the squareness of a wall and floor. A $4\frac{1}{2}$-foot length is marked off on the wall (point A) and a 6-foot length is marked off on the floor (point B) as shown in figure 15-55. The measurement from point A to point B is 7'-9″. Are the wall and floor square? Show your computations.

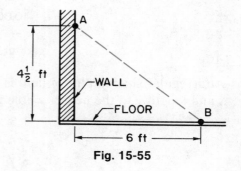

Fig. 15-55

12. Can the piece shown in figure 15-56 be sheared (cut) from the sheet shown in figure 15-57? Show your computations.

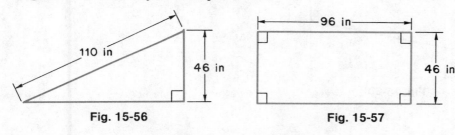

Fig. 15-56   **Fig. 15-57**

13. Two cars start from the same point at the same time. One car travels south at 60 kilometres per hour. The other car travels east at 50 kilometres per hour. How far apart to the nearer tenth kilometre are the cars after 1.5 hours?

14. A landscaper is contracted to plant shrubs around the sides (perimeter) of the plot of land shown in figure 15-58. A shrub is planted in each corner. The shrubs are planted 5 feet apart. How many shrubs are needed for the job?
NOTE: The number of shrubs shown is not the actual required number.

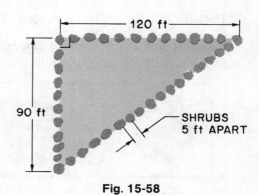

Fig. 15-58

15. A template is shown in figure 15-59. Determine dimension x to the nearer hundredth centimetre.

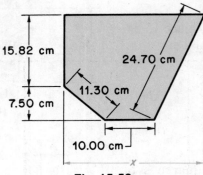

Fig. 15-59

16. An irregular shaped plot of land is shown in figure 15-60. Determine length x and length y to the nearer whole metre.

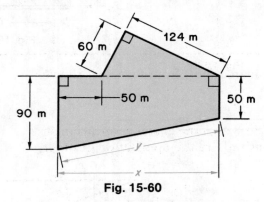

Fig. 15-60

UNIT EXERCISE AND PROBLEM REVIEW ═══════════════

Exercise 15-5

MAKING FIGURES RIGID BY BRACING

1. Make a sketch of each shape shown in figure 15-61. Show how each shape can be made rigid using a minimum number of braces.

Fig. 15-61

TYPES OF TRIANGLES

2. Identify each of the triangles in figure 15-62 in these two ways:

   (1) as scalene, isosceles, or equilateral.

   (2) as right, acute, or obtuse.

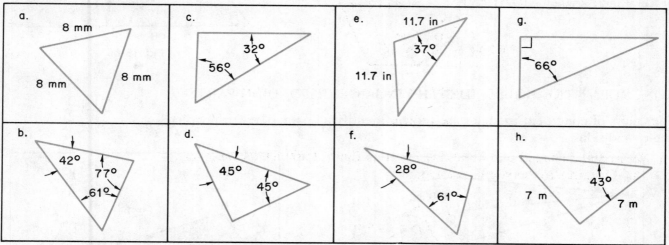

Fig. 15-62

APPLICATIONS OF THEOREMS

Solve these problems applying the theorem "The sum of the angles of any triangle is equal to 180°." In addition, certain problems require the application of other angular and triangular facts and theorems.

3. Refer to figure 15-63.

   a. Find ∠3 when ∠1 = 19°37′.

   b. Find ∠2 when ∠3 = 142°36′.

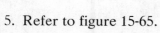

Fig. 15-63

4. Refer to figure 15-64. Line AB ∥ line CD.

   a. Find ∠3 when ∠1 = 110°.

   b. Find ∠4 when ∠2 = 146°.

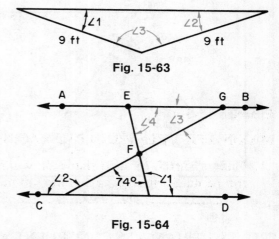

Fig. 15-64

5. Refer to figure 15-65.

   a. Find ∠2 when ∠1 = 18° and ∠3 = 41°.

   b. Find ∠3 when ∠1 = 31°17′ and ∠2 = 19°52′.

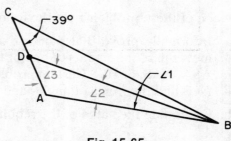

Fig. 15-65

6. Refer to figure 15-66. Segment AC = segment BC.

   a. Find ∠1 when ∠2 = 66°.

   b. Find ∠2 when ∠1 = 27°30′.

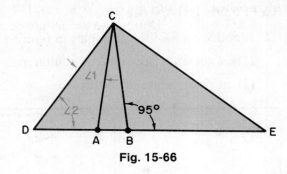

Fig. 15-66

CONGRUENT TRIANGLES: IDENTIFYING CORRESPONDING PARTS

Four pairs of congruent triangles are shown. Identify all pairs of corresponding angles and sides.

7.
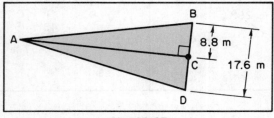

Fig. 15-67

9.
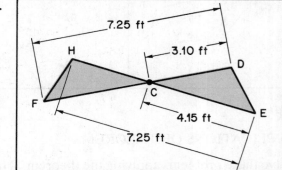

Fig. 15-69

8.
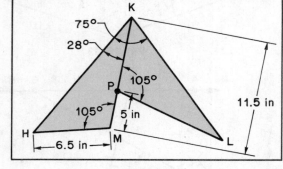

Fig. 15-68

10.
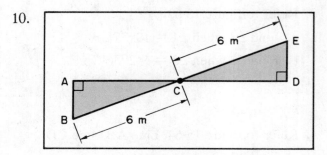

Fig. 15-70

PROVING TRIANGLES CONGRUENT AND DETERMINING VALUES

For each of these problems, do the following:

   a. Informally prove that pairs of triangles are congruent. Each pair must meet the requirements of one of the five congruency theorems (SSS, SAS, ASA, AAS, or HL). Certain problems require the application of additional facts and theorems of angles and triangles.

   b. Determine the value of the required side or angle.

11. Refer to figure 15-71. ∠D = ∠B, DE = BC, AE = 23.7″, EB = 5.9″, and AD = 29.6″. Determine the length of AC.

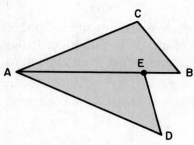

Fig. 15-71

12. Refer to figure 15-72. ∠KMP = ∠KPM = 81°, ∠HKM = 14°, and HM = PJ. Determine the value of ∠J.

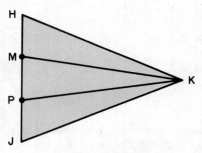

Fig. 15-72

13. Refer to figure 15-73. KG ⊥ FH, FK = HK, ∠FKP = ∠HKP, ∠KFG = 41°, and ∠KFP = 23°. Determine the value of ∠HPG.

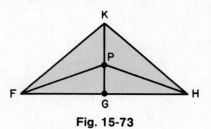

Fig. 15-73

PYTHAGOREAN THEOREM

14. In a right triangle, a and b represent the legs and c represents the hypotenuse. Determine the unknown side. Express the answer to 1 decimal place where necessary.

    a. $a = 12$ ft and $b = 16$ ft, find c.

    b. $a = 1.5$ m and $c = 2.5$ m, find b.

    c. $b = 8$ in and $c = 11$ in, find a.

    d. $a = 10.5$ cm and $b = 14.2$ cm, find c.

15. A mason checks the squareness of a building foundation. From a corner, a 9-foot length is marked off on one wall and a 12-foot length is marked off on the adjacent wall. A measurement of 15 feet is made between the two markings. Is the foundation wall square? Show your computations.

16. Town B is 6.6 miles directly north of town A. Town C is directly east of town B. If the distance between town A and town C is 11 miles, what is the distance from town B to town C?

17. A beam is set on the tops of two vertical support columns which are 30 feet apart. One column is 10 feet high. The other column is 18 feet high. If the beam extends an additional 2 feet beyond each column, what length beam, to the nearer whole foot, is required?

18. Determine distance x of the parcel of land shown in figure 15-74. Express the answer to the nearer whole metre.

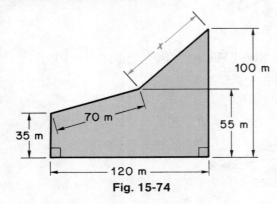

Fig. 15-74

19. Two trucks start from the same place at the same time. One travels directly south at an average rate of speed of 50 miles per hour. The other truck travels directly west. After each truck travels for 7 hours, the trucks are 437.5 miles apart. What is the average rate of speed of the truck traveling west?

UNIT 16
Similar
Figures

OBJECTIVES

After studying this unit you should be able to

- identify similar pairs of polygons.

- compute lengths of sides and perimeters of similar polygons.

- determine whether given pairs of triangles are similar.

- informally prove that pairs of triangles are similar and determine unknown sides and angles.

- apply isosceles and equilateral triangle theorems in computing triangle sides and angles.

- solve practical applied problems using theorems discussed in this unit.

SIMILAR FIGURES

Stated in a general way, *similar figures* mean figures that are alike in shape but different in size. The idea of similarity is constantly experienced in our daily activities. For example, a road map is similar to the territory that it represents and a photograph is similar to the object which is photographed.

Scale drawings, which are commonly used in a great variety of occupations, are examples of similar figures. Often scale drawings are in the form of similar polygons or combinations of similar polygons. *Similar polygons* have the same number of sides, equal corresponding angles, and proportional corresponding sides. The symbol ~ means similar.

Corresponding angles of similar polygons are equal.

Corresponding sides of similar polygons are proportional.

Example.   Refer to similar polygons shown in figure 16-1.

Given: ABCDEF ~ A'B'C'D'E'F'

Conclusion: The corresponding angles are equal.

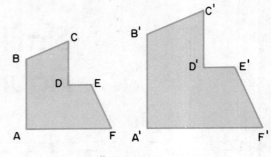

Fig. 16-1

$\angle A = \angle A'$	$\angle D = \angle D'$
$\angle B = \angle B'$	$\angle E = \angle E'$
$\angle C = \angle C'$	$\angle F = \angle F'$

The corresponding sides are proportional.

$$\frac{AB}{A'B'} = \frac{BC}{B'C'} = \frac{CD}{C'D'} = \frac{DE}{D'E'} = \frac{EF}{E'F'} = \frac{FA}{F'A'}$$

The distance around a polygon, or the sum of all sides is called the *perimeter*. In figure 16-1,

$$P = AB + BC + CD + DE + EF + FA$$

$$P' = A'B' + B'C' + C'D' + D'E' + E'F' + F'A'$$

The perimeters of two similar polygons have the same ratio as any two corresponding sides. For example in figure 16-1,

$$\frac{P}{P'} = \frac{AB}{A'B'}$$

Except in the case of triangles, if two polygons have equal corresponding angles, it does <u>not</u> necessarily follow that the corresponding sides are proportional. This fact is illustrated in figure 16-2.

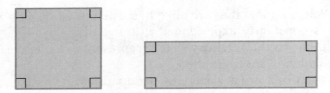

Corresponding angles are equal.
Corresponding sides are <u>not</u> proportional.
Fig. 16-2

Except in the case of triangles, if two polygons have proportional corresponding sides, it does <u>not</u> necessarily follow that the corresponding angles are equal. This fact is illustrated in figure 16-3.

Corresponding sides are proportional.
Corresponding angles are <u>not</u> equal.
Fig. 16-3

Exercise 16-1

1. Identify which of the 6 pairs of polygons in figure 16-4 are similar. For each pair of polygons, state the reason why the polygons are similar or why the polygons are not similar.

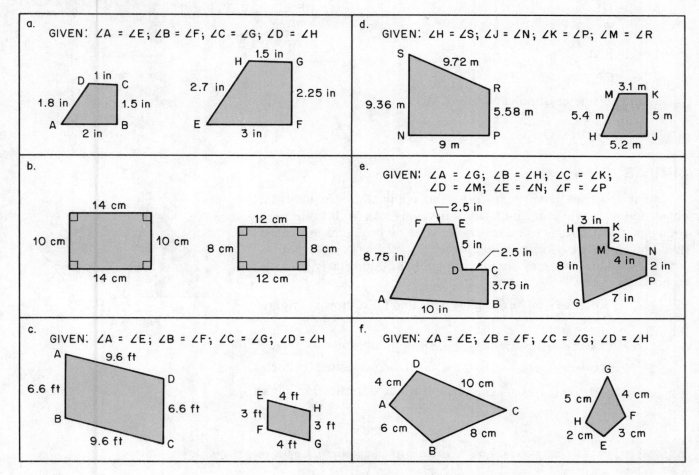

Fig. 16-4

2. Refer to figure 16-5. The two polygons are similar. ∠A = ∠A′; ∠B = ∠B′; ∠C = ∠C′; ∠D = ∠D′. Determine these values.

   a. side A′B′

   b. side B′C′

   c. side C′D′

   d. the perimeter of polygon A′B′C′D′

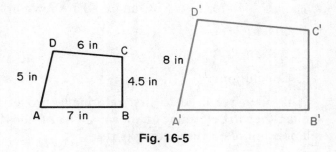

Fig. 16-5

3. Refer to figure 16-6. The two polygons are similar. ∠A =∠A′; ∠B = ∠B′; ∠C = ∠C′; ∠D = ∠D′; ∠E = ∠E′. Determine these values.

   a. side BC

   b. side CD

   c. side DE

   d. side AE

   e. the perimeter of polygon ABCDE

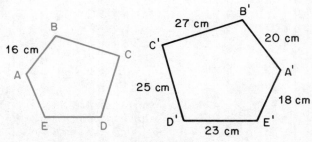

Fig. 16-6

4. Refer to figure 16-7. The two polygons are similar.
∠A = ∠G; ∠B = ∠H; ∠C = ∠J; ∠D = ∠K; ∠E = ∠M;
∠F = ∠N. Determine these values.

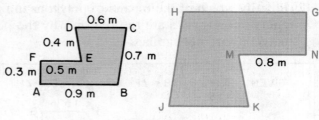

a. side GH

b. side HJ

c. side JK

d. side KM

e. side GN

f. the perimeter of polygon GHJKMN

Fig. 16-7

SIMILAR TRIANGLES

Similar triangles have many practical applications in industry, construction, navigation, and land surveying. As with congruent triangles, the solutions to many similar triangle problems are based on a knowledge of corresponding parts.

Corresponding sides of similar triangles lie opposite equal corresponding angles.

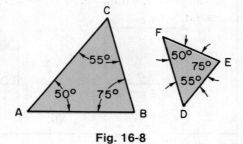

Fig. 16-8

Example.   Refer to similar triangles ABC and DEF shown in figure 16-8.

AB and EF are corresponding sides. Both lie opposite 55° angles.

BE and DE are corresponding sides. Both lie opposite 50° angles.

AC and DF are corresponding sides. Both lie opposite 75° angles.

If two angles of a triangle are equal to two angles of another triangle, the triangles are similar.

Example.   Refer to △ABC and △DEF shown in figure 16-9.

Given: ∠A = ∠D

∠B = ∠E

Conclusion: △ABC ∼ △DEF

It is often required to first informally prove triangles are similar, then to determine unknown angles or sides based on the relationship of corresponding parts.

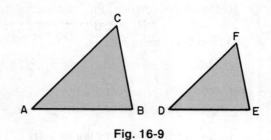

Fig. 16-9

Practical Application

Five holes are located on a piece as shown in figure 16-10. Determine distance AB.

Solution: $\angle A = \angle C$

$\angle AEB = \angle CED$ (Vertical angles are equal)

$\therefore \triangle ABE \sim \triangle CDE$

Determine AB.

$$\frac{7 \text{ in}}{10.5 \text{ in}} = \frac{AB}{9 \text{ in}}$$

$AB = 6 \text{ in } Ans$

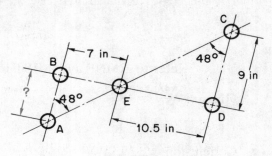

Fig. 16-10

If the corresponding sides of two triangles are proportional, the triangles are similar.

Example.   Refer to $\triangle ABC$ and $\triangle DEF$ shown in figure 16-11.

Given: $\dfrac{AB}{DE} = \dfrac{BC}{EF} = \dfrac{AC}{DF}$

Conclusion: $\triangle ABC \sim \triangle DEF$

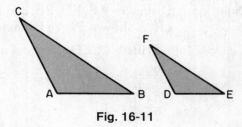

Fig. 16-11

Practical Application

Determine $\angle 1$ shown in figure 16-12.

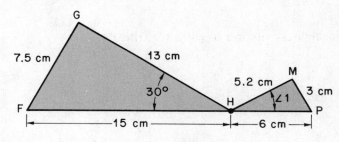

Fig. 16-12

Solution: First determine whether the corresponding sides are proportional.

$\dfrac{6 \text{ cm}}{15 \text{ cm}} = 0.4$

$\dfrac{3 \text{ cm}}{7.5 \text{ cm}} = 0.4$

$\dfrac{5.2 \text{ cm}}{13 \text{ cm}} = 0.4$

The sides are proportional.

$\therefore \triangle FGH \sim \triangle PMH$

Determine $\angle 1$.

$\angle 1 = \angle FHG$

$\angle 1 = 30° \ Ans$

> **If two sides of a triangle are proportional to two sides of another triangle and if the angles included between these sides are equal, the triangles are similar.**

Example.   Refer to △MNP and △RST in figure 16-13.

Given: $\dfrac{MN}{RS} = \dfrac{MP}{RT}$

$\angle M = \angle R$

Conclusion: △MNP ~ △RST

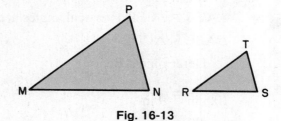

Fig. 16-13

Practical Application

An obstruction lies between points A and B as shown in figure 16-14. Distance AB can be determined by making sides AD and BE proportional to sides DE and CE.

Solution: Distances AE, ED, BE, and EC are measured and marked off as shown. Prove triangles AEB and CED similar.

$\angle AEB = \angle CED$ (Vertical angles are equal)

$\dfrac{90\ ft}{30\ ft} = 3$ (The sides are proportional)

$\dfrac{75\ ft}{25\ ft} = 3$

∴ △AEB ~ △CED

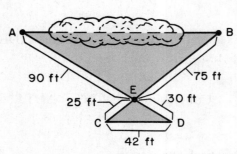

Fig. 16-14

Distance CD is measured; CD measures 42 feet. Determine distance AB.

$\dfrac{AB}{CD} = \dfrac{AE}{ED}$

$\dfrac{AB}{42\ ft} = \dfrac{90\ ft}{30\ ft}$

AB = 126 ft *Ans*

> **Within a triangle, if a line is parallel to one side and intersects the other two sides, the triangle formed and the given triangle are similar.**

Example.   Refer to △PNM shown in figure 16-15.

Given: RS ∥ PN

Conclusion: △RSM ~ △PNM

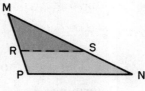

Fig. 16-15

Practical Application

A design change is made in a building. A roof span is changed from 36 feet to 30 feet as shown in figure 16-16. The roof pitch and rafter overhang are to remain unchanged. The changed rafter, GE is parallel to the original rafter, FC. Compute the changed rafter length, GE.

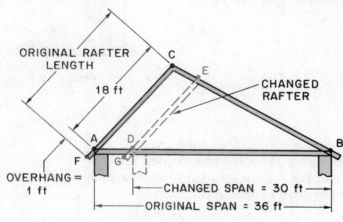

Fig. 16-16

Solution: $\triangle ACB \sim \triangle DEB$

$$\frac{DE}{AC} = \frac{DB}{AB}$$

$$\frac{DE}{18 \text{ ft}} = \frac{30 \text{ ft}}{36 \text{ ft}}$$

$$DE = 15 \text{ ft}$$

$$GE = 15 \text{ ft} + 1 \text{ ft} = \textbf{16 ft } \textit{Ans}$$

If the corresponding sides of two triangles are respectively parallel or perpendicular, the triangles are similar.

Example 1. Refer to $\triangle ABC$ and $\triangle EDF$ shown in figure 16-17.

Given: $AB \parallel DE$

$AC \parallel FE$

$CB \parallel DF$

Conclusion: $\triangle ABC \sim \triangle EDF$

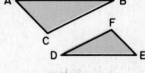

Fig. 16-17

Example 2. Refer to $\triangle MNP$ and $\triangle RST$ in figure 16-18.

Given: $RS \perp MN$

$RT \perp MP$

$ST \perp PN$

Conclusion: $\triangle RSM \sim \triangle PNM$

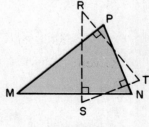

Fig. 16-18

An *altitude* is a line segment drawn from a vertex perpendicular to the side opposite the vertex.

If the altitude is drawn to the hypotenuse of a right triangle, the two triangles formed are similar to each other and to the given triangle.

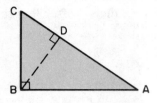

Fig. 16-19

Example.   Refer to the right △ABC shown in figure 16-19.

Given: BD ⊥ AC

Conclusion: △ADB ∼ △BDC ∼ △ABC

Practical Application

A plot of land, right △MSP, shown in figure 16-20 is to be divided into two building lots. Lot 1 is shown as △MTS and Lot 2 is shown as △STP. Determine the frontage, MT and PT, of each lot to the nearer whole foot.

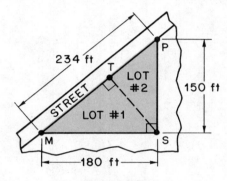

Fig. 16-20

Solution: Since ST is ⊥ to the hypotenuse MP of △MSP, ST is the altitude to the hypotenuse. △MTS ∼ △STP ∼ △MSP. Determine the length of MT.

$$\frac{MT}{MS} = \frac{MS}{MP}$$

$$\frac{MT}{180 \text{ ft}} = \frac{180 \text{ ft}}{234 \text{ ft}}$$

$$MT = 138 \text{ ft } Ans$$

$$PT = 234 \text{ ft} - 138 \text{ ft} = 96 \text{ ft } Ans$$

Exercise 16-2

1. Eight pairs of similar triangles are shown in figure 16-21. Write the similar triangle theorem which applies to each problem.

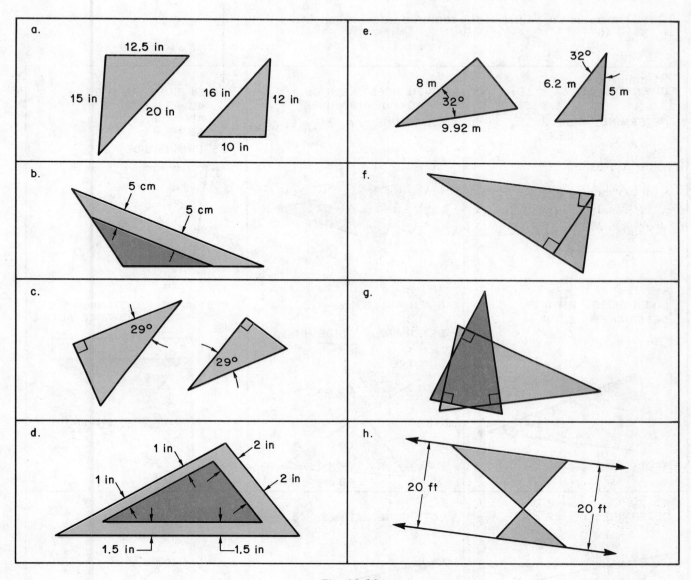

Fig. 16-21

2. For each of the problems in figure 16-22, do the following:

(1) Informally prove that pairs of triangles are similar. Each pair must meet the requirements of one of the similar triangle theorems. Certain problems also require the application of angle theorems.

(2) Determine the values of the required sides and angles.

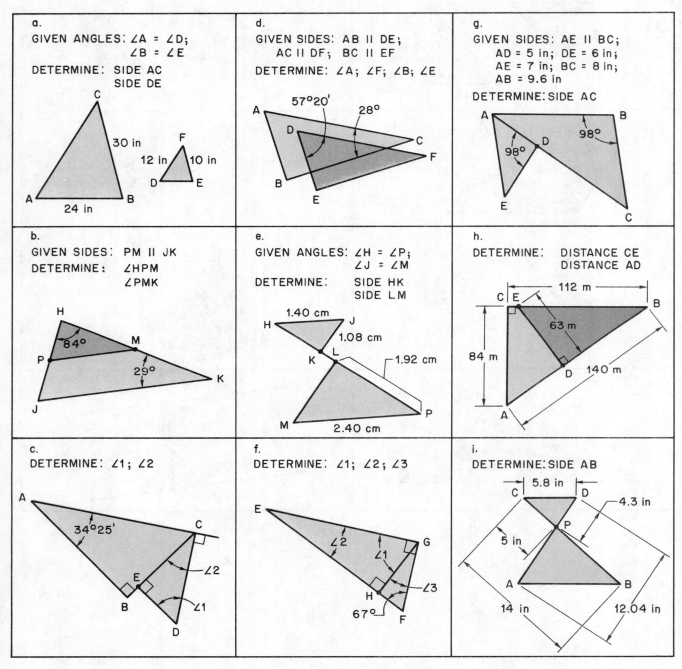

Fig. 16-22

3. A cluster of 5 holes is drilled in a casting as shown in figure 16-23. Determine missing dimensions x and y to 2 decimal places.

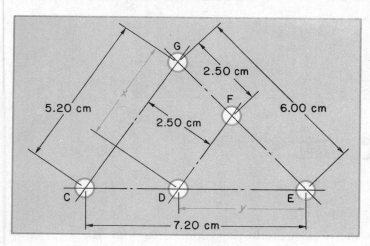

Fig. 16-23

4. Two triangular grooves are machined in a piece as shown in figure 16-24. Sides AB and CB of the small groove are parallel respectively to sides DE and FE of the larger groove. Dimensions x and y are inspected. What are the values of dimensions x and y? Express the answers to 3 decimal places.

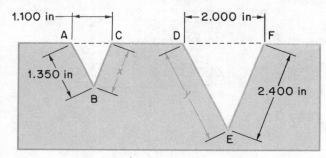

Fig. 16-24

5. A drawing of a house roof and an attached garage roof is shown in figure 16-25. Both roofs have the same pitch. The front rafters of the house and the garage are parallel. The house and garage overhang are the same. Determine the length of the garage front rafter.

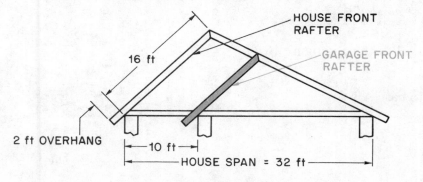

Fig. 16-25

6. A highway ramp with a 12% grade is shown in figure 16-26. A 12% grade means that for 100 feet of horizontal distance there is a vertical rise of 12 feet.

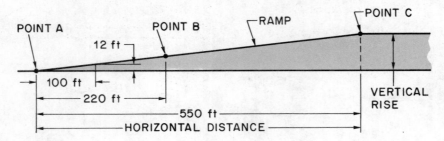

Fig. 16-26

a. How much higher is point C than point B?

b. A car travels 221.6 feet from the foot of the ramp (point A) to point B. How far does the car travel from point B to the end of the ramp (point C)?

7. The side view of a tapered shaft is shown in figure 16-27. Since the taper is uniform, △ABC and △DEF are congruent. Compute the shaft diameter at point R.

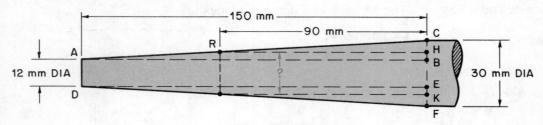

Fig. 16-27

ISOSCELES AND EQUILATERAL TRIANGLES

The *vertex angle* is the angle opposite the base. To *bisect* means to divide into two equal parts.

> **In an isosceles triangle, an altitude to the base bisects the base and the vertex angle.**

Example.   Refer to isosceles △ABC shown in figure 16-28.

Given: AC = BC

CD is an altitude to base AB.

Conclusion: **AD = BD**

$\angle 1 = \angle 2$

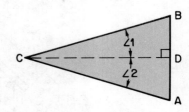

Fig. 16-28

Practical Application

Sides DE and EF of the triangular frame DEF shown in figure 16-29 are equal. Piece EG is to be fastened to the frame for additional support. Determine ∠1, ∠2, and distance DG.

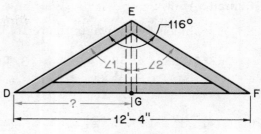

Fig. 16-29

Solution: Since EG ⊥ DF, EG is an altitude to the base. EG bisects ∠DEF (116°) and base DE (12'-4").

$$\angle 1 = \angle 2 = 116° \div 2 = 58° \; Ans$$
$$DG = 12'\text{-}4'' \div 2 = 6'\text{-}2'' \; Ans$$

In an equilateral triangle, an altitude to any side bisects the side and the vertex angle.

Example.   Refer to equilateral △ABC shown in figure 16-30.

Given: BD is an altitude to side AC.

Conclusion: AD = DC
$$\angle 1 = \angle 2$$

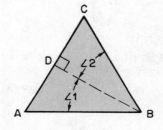

Fig. 16-30

Practical Application

Three holes are equally spaced on a circle as shown in figure 16-31. The centerlines between holes form equilateral △MPT. Determine ∠1 and distance MW.

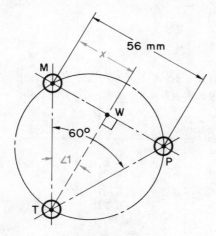

Fig. 16-31

Solution: Since TW ⊥ MP, TW is an altitude to side MP. TW bisects MP (56 mm) and ∠MTP (60°),

$$MW = 56 \text{ mm} \div 2 = 28 \text{ mm} \; Ans$$
$$\angle 1 = 60° \div 2 = 30° \; Ans$$

Exercise 16-3

Solve problems 1-6 shown in figure 16-32.

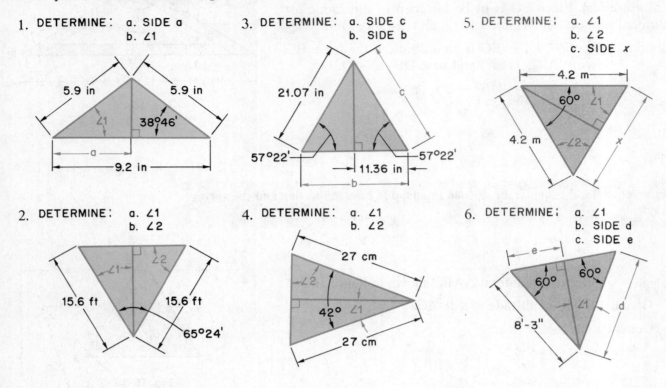

Fig. 16-32

UNIT EXERCISE AND PROBLEM REVIEW

Exercise 16-4

SIMILAR POLYGONS

1. Identify which of the 2 pairs of polygons in figure 16-33 are similar. For each pair of polygons state the reason why the polygons are similar or why the polygons are not similar.

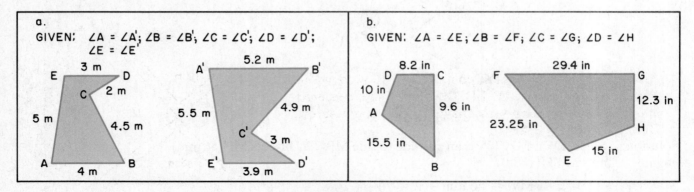

Fig. 16-33

2. Refer to figure 16-34. The two polygons are similar. ∠A = ∠F; ∠B = ∠G; ∠C = ∠H; ∠D = ∠J; ∠E = ∠K. Determine each value.

   a. side FG

   b. side GH

   c. side JK

   d. side FK

   e. the perimeter of polygon FGHJK

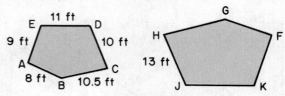

Fig. 16-34

SIMILAR TRIANGLES

3. For each of the problems shown in figure 16-35, do the following:

   (1) Informally prove that pairs of triangles are similar. Each pair must meet the requirements of one of the similar triangle theorems. Certain problems also require the application of angle theorems.

   (2) Determine the values of the required sides or angles.

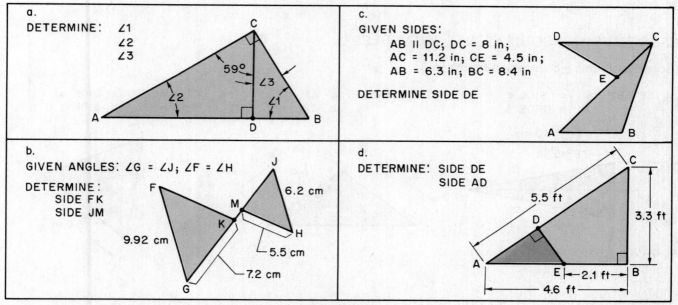

a.
DETERMINE: ∠1
∠2
∠3
59°

b.
GIVEN ANGLES: ∠G = ∠J; ∠F = ∠H
DETERMINE:
SIDE FK
SIDE JM
6.2 cm
9.92 cm
5.5 cm
7.2 cm

c.
GIVEN SIDES:
AB ∥ DC; DC = 8 in;
AC = 11.2 in; CE = 4.5 in;
AB = 6.3 in; BC = 8.4 in

DETERMINE SIDE DE

d.
DETERMINE: SIDE DE
SIDE AD
5.5 ft
3.3 ft
2.1 ft
4.6 ft

Fig. 16-35

4. An obstruction lies between points A and B as shown in figure 16-36. Distances AE, ED, BE, and EC are measured and marked off as shown. Distance CD is measured. Determine distance AB.

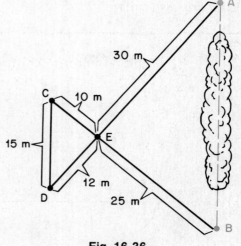

30 m
10 m
15 m
12 m
25 m

Fig. 16-36

5. Vertical braces A and B are added to the frame shown in figure 16-37. Determine dimensions E, F, G, and H in feet and inches.

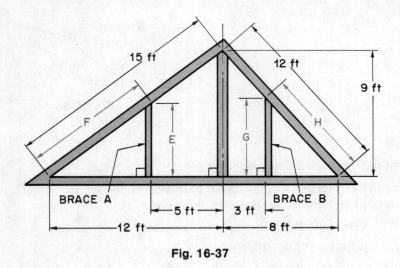

Fig. 16-37

ISOSCELES AND EQUILATERAL TRIANGLES

Solve problems 6-8 shown in figure 16-38.

6. DETERMINE: a. SIDE c
                b. SIDE b

7. DETERMINE: a. ∠1
                b. ∠2

8. DETERMINE: a. SIDE s
                b. SIDE p

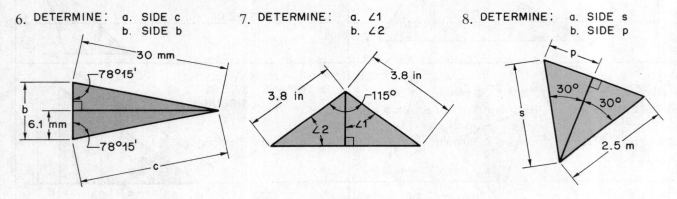

Fig. 16-38

UNIT 17
Polygons

After studying this unit you should be able to

- identify various types of polygons.

- determine unknown sides and angles of quadrilaterals.

- compute interior and exterior angles of polygons by applying polygon angle theorems.

- apply parallelogram and trapezoid theorems in computing lengths.

- solve practical applied problems using theorems discussed in this unit.

As previously stated, a *polygon* is a closed plane figure formed by three or more straight-line segments. Examples of polygons are shown in figure 17-1.

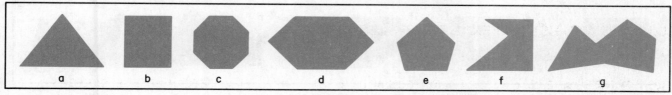

Fig. 17-1

A *convex polygon* is a polygon in which no side, if extended, cuts inside the polygon. In figure 17-1, polygons a-e are convex. In this book, unless otherwise stated, the word polygon means convex polygon.

A *concave polygon* is a polygon in which two or more sides, if extended, cut inside the polygon. In figure 17-1, polygons f and g are concave.

An *equilateral polygon* is a polygon with all sides equal. In figure 17-2, polygon a is equilateral.

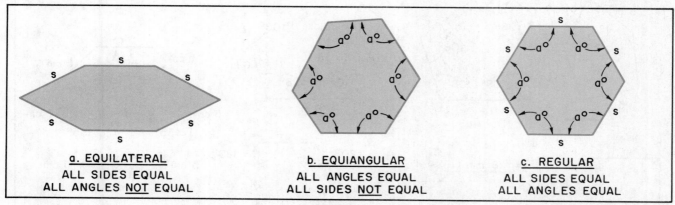

a. EQUILATERAL
ALL SIDES EQUAL
ALL ANGLES **NOT** EQUAL

b. EQUIANGULAR
ALL ANGLES EQUAL
ALL SIDES **NOT** EQUAL

c. REGULAR
ALL SIDES EQUAL
ALL ANGLES EQUAL

Fig. 17-2

An *equiangular polygon* is a polygon with all angles equal. In figure 17-2, polygon b is equiangular.

A *regular polygon* is a polygon that is both equilateral and equiangular; all sides and all angles are equal. In figure 17-2, polygon c is regular.

Except in the case of triangles, a polygon can be equilateral without being equiangular and equiangular without being equilateral. This fact is shown by polygons a and b in figure 17-2.

Polygons are often classified according to their number of sides. In addition to the triangle, the following polygons are the most common.

A *quadrilateral* is a polygon with four sides.

A *pentagon* is a polygon with five sides.

A *hexagon* is a polygon with six sides.

An *octagon* is a polygon with eight sides.

Exercise 17-1

1. Of the figures shown in figure 17-3, which are polygons? Identify the polygons as convex or concave.

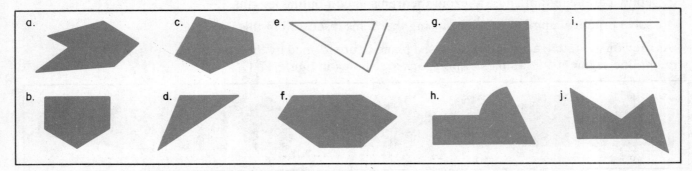

Fig. 17-3

2. Identify each of the polygons shown in figure 17-4 as:

    (1) equilateral, equiangular, or regular.

    (2) a quadrilateral, a pentagon, a hexagon, or an octagon.

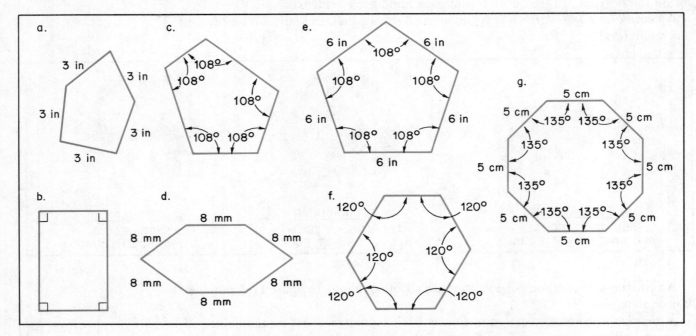

Fig. 17-4

TYPES OF QUADRILATERALS

A *parallelogram* is a quadrilateral whose opposite sides are parallel and equal. Opposite angles of a parallelogram are equal. In the parallelogram shown in figure 17-5, AB∥DC; AB = DC; AD∥BC; AD = BC; ∠A = ∠C; ∠B = ∠D.

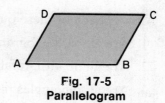

Fig. 17-5
Parallelogram

A *rectangle* is a special type of parallelogram whose angles each equal 90°. In the rectangle shown in figure 17-6, EF∥GH; EF = GH; EG∥FH; EG = FH; ∠E = ∠F = ∠G = ∠H = 90°.

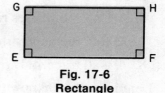

Fig. 17-6
Rectangle

A *square* is a special type of rectangle whose sides are all equal. In the square shown in figure 17-7, AB∥CD; AC∥BD; AB = BD = CD = AC; ∠A = ∠B = ∠C = ∠D = 90°.

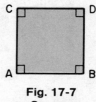

Fig. 17-7
Square

A *rhombus* is a special type of parallelogram whose sides are all equal, but whose angles are not all equal. In the rhombus shown in figure 17-8, EF∥GH; EG∥FH; EF = FH = GH = EG; ∠E = ∠H; ∠G = ∠F.

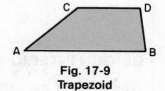

Fig. 17-8
Rhombus

A *trapezoid* is a quadrilateral which has only two sides parallel. In the trapezoid shown in figure 17-9, AB∥CD. An *isosceles trapezoid* is a trapezoid in which the legs are equal. The legs are the sides which are <u>not</u> parallel. The base angles of an isosceles trapezoid are equal. The parallel sides of a trapezoid are called *bases*. In the isosceles trapezoid shown in figure 17-10, EF∥GH; EG = FH; ∠E = ∠F; ∠G = ∠H.

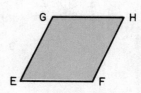

Fig. 17-9
Trapezoid

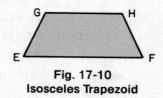

Fig. 17-10
Isosceles Trapezoid

Exercise 17-2

Answer each of these questions.

1. Are all parallelograms quadrilaterals? Explain.

2. Are all quadrilaterals parallelograms? Explain.

3. Are all rectangles parallelograms? Explain.

4. Are all parallelograms rectangles? Explain.

5. Are all squares parallelograms? Explain.

6. Are all rhombuses rectangles? Explain.

7. Are all rectangles rhombuses? Explain.

8. Are all trapezoids rhombuses? Explain.

Determine the unknown sides or angles of the quadrilaterals shown in figure 17-11.

9. DETERMINE THESE VALUES.
   a. SIDE AB
   b. SIDE AC
   c. ∠A
   d. ∠C

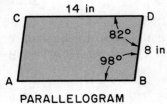

PARALLELOGRAM

11. DETERMINE THESE VALUES.
    a. SIDE AC
    b. ∠B
    c. ∠C

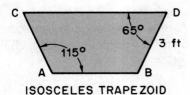

ISOSCELES TRAPEZOID

10. DETERMINE THESE VALUES.
    a. SIDE EF
    b. SIDE FH
    c. ∠E

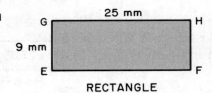

RECTANGLE

12. DETERMINE THESE VALUES.
    a. SIDE CD
    b. ∠A
    c. ∠B

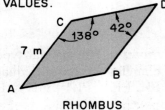

RHOMBUS

Fig. 17-11

POLYGON INTERIOR AND EXTERIOR ANGLES

The fields of navigation, land surveying, and manufacturing use the sum of the interior and exterior angles of polygons in many practical applications.

A *diagonal* is a line segment which connects two nonadjacent vertices. If diagonals are drawn in a polygon from any one vertex, there are two less triangles (n − 2) formed than the number of sides (n) of the polygon.

Example. A quadrilateral is shown in figure 17-12. Find the sum of the interior angles.

A diagonal is drawn from vertex D to vertex B. Two triangles, ABD and DBC, are formed. Since the sum of the angles of a triangle equals 180°, the sum of the angles in quadrilateral ABCD = 2(180°) = 360°. *Ans*

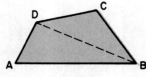

Fig. 17-12

The sum of the interior angles of a polygon of n sides is equal to (n − 2) times 180°.

Example. An octagon is shown in figure 17-13. Find the sum of the interior angles.

The sum of angles in an octagon = (n − 2)180°

$$= (8 - 2)180°$$

$$= 1\ 080°\ \textit{Ans}$$

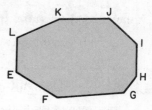

Fig. 17-13

Practical Applications

1. A survey map of a piece of property is shown in figure 17-14. The surveyor's transit stations are shown by the small triangles at each vertex. The interior angular measurements made at each station are recorded on the survey map. Check the angular measurements using the sum of the interior angles of a polygon.

   Solution: The sum of the interior angles = (n − 2)180°

   $$= (6 - 2)180°$$

   $$= 720°$$

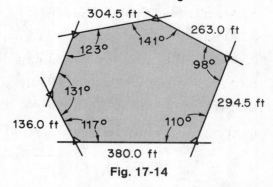

Fig. 17-14

   Add the angles recorded at each station on the map.

   $$117° + 131° + 123° + 141° + 98° + 110° = 720°$$

   The angular measurement made and recorded are correct. *Ans*

2. In laying out the piece shown in figure 17-15, a sheet metal technician marks off and scribes angles and lengths at each vertex. The angular value at vertex A is not given on the drawing. Determine the angle at vertex A.

   Solution: The sum of the interior angles = (n − 2)180°

   $$= (5 - 2)180°$$

   $$= 540°$$

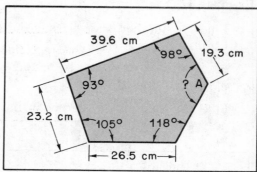

Fig. 17-15

   Add the 4 angles given on the drawing.

   $$93° + 98° + 105° + 118° = 414°$$

   The angle at vertex A = 540° − 414° = 126° *Ans*

   If a side of a polygon is extended, the angle between the extended side and the adjacent side of the polygon is an *exterior angle*. For example, in figure 17-16, angles 1, 2, 3, 4, and 5 are exterior angles.

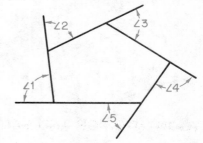

Fig. 17-16

Example. A polygon is shown in figure 17-17. Find the sum of the exterior angles.

From a point inside the polygon, lines are drawn parallel to the sides of the polygon. The respective angles are equal to the exterior angles of the polygon and equal to a complete revolution or a full circle. The sum of the angles equals 360°. *Ans*

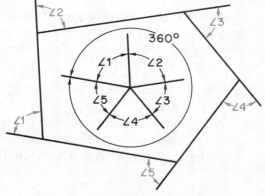

Fig. 17-17

The sum of the exterior angles of any polygon, formed as each side is extended in succession, is equal to 360°.

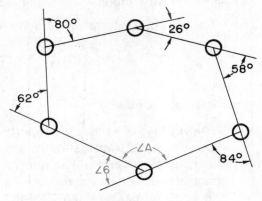

Example   Determine ∠A of the polygon in figure 17-18.

Compute exterior ∠6.

$62° + 80° + 26° + 58° + 84° + ∠6 = 360°$

$∠6 = 360° - 310°$

$∠6 = 50°$

∠6 and ∠A are supplementary.

$∠A = 180° - ∠6 = 130°$ *Ans*

Fig. 17-18

Exercise 17-3

1. Find the number of degrees in the sum of the interior angles of each figure listed.

   a. quadrilateral   b. pentagon   c. hexagon   d. octagon

2. Find the number of degrees in the unknown interior angle in each of the polygons in figure 17-19.

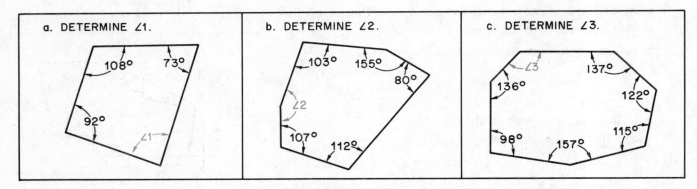

Fig. 17-19

3. Find the number of degrees in each interior angle of the regular figures listed.

   a. pentagon   b. hexagon   c. octagon   d. polygon of 12 sides

4. Find the number of degrees in the unknown exterior angles in each of the polygons shown in figure 17-20.

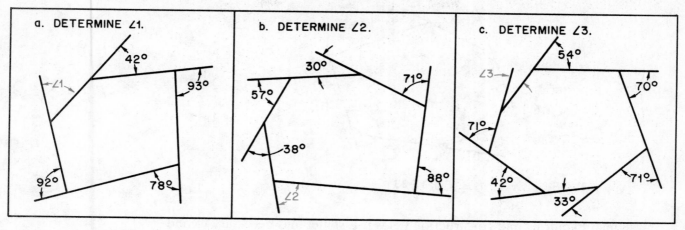

Fig. 17-20

5. Find the number of degrees in each exterior angle of the regular figures listed.

   a. pentagon   b. hexagon   c. octagon   d. polygon of 16 sides

6. Find the number of sides for each regular polygon having these exterior angles.

   a. 60°   b. 24°   c. 45°   d. 7°30'

7. Each interior angle of a regular polygon of n sides equals $\frac{(n-2)180°}{n}$. Find the number of sides for each regular polygon having these interior angles.

   a. 120°   b. 135°   c. 108°   d. 140°

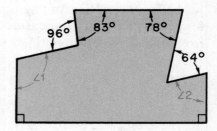

8. Refer to the template shown in figure 17-21.

   a. Determine ∠1 when ∠2 = 83°.

   b. Determine ∠2 when ∠1 = 114°30'.

Fig. 17-21

9. Refer to the drill jig shown in figure 17-22. Determine ∠1.

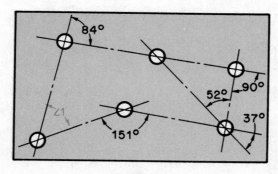

Fig. 17-22

10. A survey map of a piece of property is shown in figure 17-23. Determine ∠1.

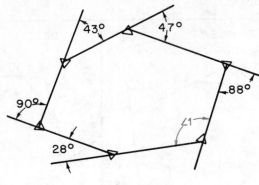

Fig. 17-23

In the manufacturing and construction fields it is sometimes necessary to find unknown lengths.

The diagonals of a parallelogram bisect each other.

In the parallelogram ABCD shown in figure 17-24, diagonals AC and BD bisect each other at point P.

$$AP = PC \text{ and } DP = PB$$

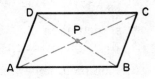

Fig. 17-24

Practical Application

A drafter receives a sketch as shown in figure 17-25 from a designer. The sketch shows hole locations of an assembly piece in which AB ∥ CD, AB = CD and AC ∥ BD, AC = BD. Among other dimensions, the drafter in drawing the piece for production, must dimension the location of hole E vertically and horizontally from hole A as shown in figure 17-26. Find these working dimensions, m and p.

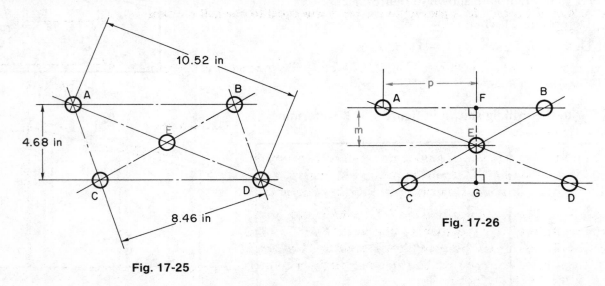

Fig. 17-25

Fig. 17-26

Solution:

Diagonals AD and CB bisect each other at point E.

AD = ED and CE = EB

Project line segment EF ⊥ AB and EG ⊥ CD as shown in figure 17-26.

AE = DE

∠A = ∠D (Equal alternate interior angles)

∠AFE = ∠EGD

Right △AFE ≅ right △DGE (AAS)

FE = EG (Corresponding parts of congruent triangles are equal)

FE = 4.68 in ÷ 2 = 2.34 in

m = FE

m = **2.34 in** *Ans*

In rt. △AFE: AE = 10.52 in ÷ 2 = 5.26 in

FE = 2.34 in

Determine AF using the Pythagorean Theorem.

$$(AE)^2 = (AF)^2 + (FE)^2$$
$$(5.26 \text{ in})^2 = (AF)^2 + (2.34 \text{ in})^2$$
$$27.667\ 6 \text{ sq in} = (AF)^2 + 5.475\ 6 \text{ sq in}$$
$$AF = \sqrt{22.192 \text{ sq in}}$$
$$AF = 4.71 \text{ in (rounded)}$$
$$p = AF$$
$$p = \textbf{4.71} \textit{ Ans}$$

A *median* of a trapezoid is a line which joins the midpoints of the nonparallel sides (legs).

> **The median of a trapezoid is parallel to the bases and equal to one-half the sum of the bases.**

In the trapezoid shown in figure 17-27, CD ∥ AB and EF is the median. Therefore, EF ∥ CD ∥ AB and EF = ½(AB + CD).

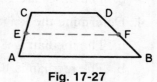

Fig. 17-27

Practical Applications

1. A support column (column B) is located midway between the 7'-6" and 10'-6" high columns shown in the rear view of a carport in figure 17-28. Determine the height of column B.

   Solution: The figure made by the 7'-6" column, the 10'-6" column, the roof, and the floor is a trapezoid. The 7'-6" and 10'-6" columns are the bases of the trapezoid and column B is midway between the bases. The required height of column B = ½(7'-6" + 10'-6") or **9'** *Ans*

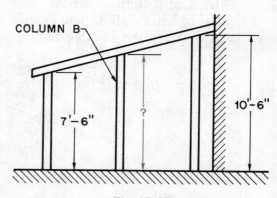

Fig. 17-28

2. The plot of land shown in figure 17-29 is in the shape of a trapezoid with AB∥CD. Stakes have been driven at corners A, B, C, and D of the plot. Measurements are made between stakes. Distances AB, BD, and AC are measured and recorded as shown. The section of land between stakes C and D is heavily wooded and a direct measurement CD cannot be made. Find distance CD.

Solution: One-half of AC (115') and one-half of BD (154') are measured and stakes are driven at points E and F. Distance EF is measured as 258'.

$$EF = \tfrac{1}{2}(AB + CD)$$
$$258' = \tfrac{1}{2}(326' + CD)$$
$$CD = \mathbf{190'} \; Ans$$

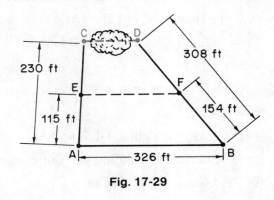

Fig. 17-29

Exercise 17-4

1. A parallelogram is shown in figure 17-30. Determine the lengths of AP, PC, DP, and PB for these given lengths.

   a. AC = 23 cm and DB = 29.4 cm

   b. AC = 4'-6'' and DB = 5'-8''

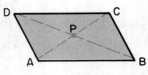

Fig. 17-30

2. A rectangle is shown in figure 17-31. Determine these values.

   a. HO when HE = 6 m and HG = 8 m

   b. HE when HO = 15 ft and HG = 24 ft

   c. EF when FG = $7\frac{1}{2}$ in and GO = $6\frac{1}{4}$ in

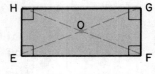

Fig. 17-31

3. Determine the length of the median of these trapezoids.

   a. The bases are 13 cm and 21 cm.

   b. The bases are 12'-4'' and 20'-8''.

   c. The bases are 25.3 m and 47.9 m.

4. Determine the length of the other base of each trapezoid listed.

   a. The median is 9 in and one base is 14 in.

   b. The median is 17.4 mm and one base is 11.6 mm.

5. In the hole pattern shown in figure 17-32, line segments connecting the centers of holes A, B, C, and D form parallelogram ABCD. Determine, to 2 decimal places, the working dimensions x and y to hole P.

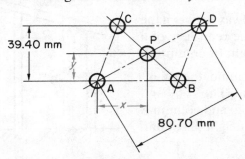

Fig. 17-32

6. The sheet stock in the shape of a trapezoid shown in figure 17-33 is sheared into four pieces of equal length as shown by the broken lines. Determine widths A, B, and C.

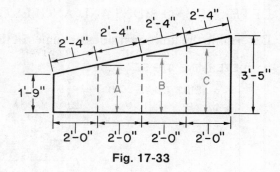

Fig. 17-33

7. The frame ABCD shown in figure 17-34 is in the form of a trapezoid. Cross member EF is located midway on side AD and side BC. If vertical member EG is added to the frame, how far should it be located horizontally from vertex A (Distance AG)?

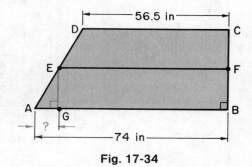

Fig. 17-34

UNIT EXERCISE AND PROBLEM REVIEW

Exercise 17-5

IDENTIFYING POLYGONS

1. Of the figures shown in figure 17-35, which are polygons? Identify the polygons as convex or concave.

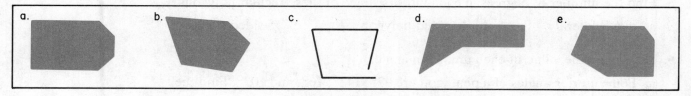

Fig. 17-35

2. Identify each of the polygons shown in figure 17-36 as:

   (1) equilateral, equiangular, or regular.

   (2) a quadrilateral, a pentagon, a hexagon, or an octagon.

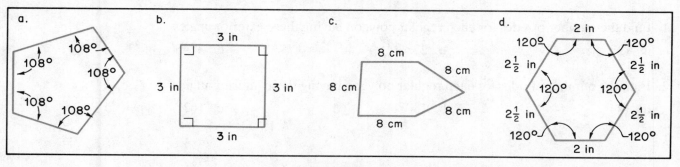

Fig. 17-36

DETERMINING SIDES AND ANGLES OF QUADRILATERALS

Determine the unknown sides or angles of the quadrilaterals shown in figure 17-37.

3. DETERMINE THESE VALUES.

    a. SIDE CB
    b. ∠B
    c. ∠C

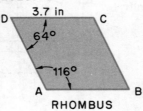

RHOMBUS

5. DETERMINE THESE VALUES.

    a. ∠M
    b. ∠STP
    c. ∠SPM

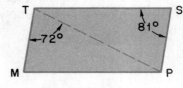

PARALLELOGRAM

4. DETERMINE THESE VALUES.

    a. SIDE EF
    b. ∠EFH
    c. ∠GFH

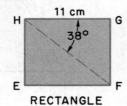

RECTANGLE

6. DETERMINE THESE VALUES.

    a. ∠1
    b. ∠A
    c. ∠B

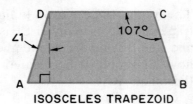

ISOSCELES TRAPEZOID

Fig. 17-37

POLYGON INTERIOR AND EXTERIOR ANGLES

7. Find the number of degrees in the sum of the interior angles of each polygon.

    a. hexagon   b. 9-sided polygon   c. 12-sided polygon

8. Find the number of degrees in each interior angle of these regular polygons.

    a. quadrilateral   b. 10-sided polygon   c. 15-sided polygon

9. Determine the value of each unknown angle.

    a. Four interior angles of a pentagon are 97°, 142°, 76°, and 103°. Find the fifth angle.

    b. Seven interior angles of an octagon are 94°, 157°, 132°, 119°, 163°, 170°, and 127°. Find the eighth angle.

10. Find the number of degrees in each exterior angle of these regular polygons.

    a. quadrilateral   b. 9-sided polygon   c. 25-sided polygon

11. Find the number of sides for each regular polygon having these exterior angles.

    a. 12°   b. 22°30′   c. 3°45′

12. Find the number of sides for each regular polygon having these interior angles.

    a. 144°   b. 150°   c. 162°

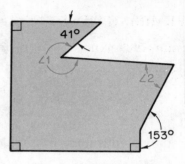

13. Refer to the pattern shown in figure 17-38.

    a. Determine ∠1 when ∠2 = 67°.

    b. Determine ∠2 when ∠1 = 322°.

Fig. 17-38

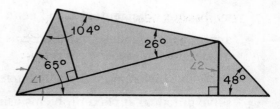

14. Refer to the truss shown in figure 17-39.

    a. Determine ∠1.

    b. Determine ∠2.

Fig. 17-39

PARALLELOGRAM AND TRAPEZOID PROBLEMS

15. In the parallelogram shown in figure 17-40, determine the lengths of BE, ED, AE, and EC using these values.

    a. AC = 9 m and BD = 7.4 m

    b. AC = 8'-3" and BD = 6'-7"

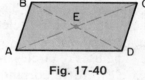

Fig. 17-40

16. Determine the length of the median of these trapezoids.

    a. Bases of 21.6 cm and 36.2 cm

    b. Bases of 14'-9" and 20'-7"

17. Determine the length of the other base of these trapezoids.

    a. Median of $14\frac{3}{16}$ in and one base of $21\frac{1}{16}$ in

    b. Median of 8.36 m and one base of 0.78 m

18. The frame shown in figure 17-41 is in the form of an isosceles trapezoid ABCD. Cross member EF is located midway on sides AB and CD.

    a. Determine distances AG and HD.

    b. Determine lengths AB and CD to the nearer inch.

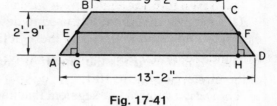

Fig. 17-41

19. In the parallelogram shown in figure 17-42, diagonal LJ = 130 mm and diagonal HK = 160 mm. Determine length A to 1 decimal place.

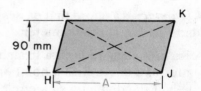

Fig. 17-42

UNIT 18
Circles

OBJECTIVES

After studying this unit you should be able to

- identify lines and angles used in describing the properties of circles.

- apply circumference and arc length formulas in computations.

- apply chord, tangent, arc, and central angle theorems in computations.

- apply tangent and secant theorems in computing arcs and angles formed inside, on, and outside a circle.

- apply internally and externally tangent circles theorems in computations.

- solve practical applied problems using theorems discussed in this unit.

A *circle* is a closed curve of which every point on the curve is equally distant from a fixed point called the center. A circle is also defined as the set of all points in a plane that are at a given distance from a given point in the plane.

The circle is the simplest of all closed curves. Circles are easily drawn with a compass and their basic properties are readily understood. Students become acquainted with circles early in their education in making simple designs and constructions.

The uses of circles in everyday living and in occupations are almost unlimited. Circles are important in art, architecture, construction, and manufacturing. Circular designs are often used to create artistic effects. Machines operate by the use of combinations of gears and pulleys. Circular forms are widely found in nature. The earth and most plants have a circular cross section.

The relation of lines to circles are presented in this unit. Radii, diameters, chords, secants, and tangents have wide practical application.

DEFINITIONS

These terms are commonly used to describe the properties of circles. It is necessary to know and understand these definitions.

The *circumference* is the length of the curved line which forms the circle. See figure 18-1.

A *chord* is a straight line segment that joins two points on the circle. In figure 18-1, AB is a chord.

A *diameter* is a chord that passes through the center of a circle. In figure 18-1, CD is a diameter.

A *radius* (plural radii) is a straight line segment that connects the center of a circle with a point on the circle. A radius is equal to one-half the diameter of a circle. In figure 18-1, OE is a radius.

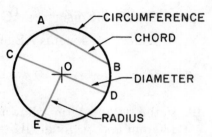

Fig. 18-1

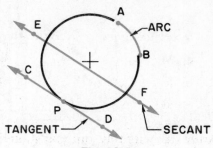

Fig. 18-2

An *arc* is that part of a circle between any two points on the circle. The symbol ⌢ written above the letters means arc. In figure 18-2, ⌢AB is an arc.

A *tangent* is a straight line that touches the circle at only one point. The point on the circle touched by the tangent is called the point of tangency. In figure 18-2 ↔CD is a tangent and point P is the point of tangency.

A *secant* is a straight line passing through a circle and intersecting the circle at two points. In figure 18-2, ↔EF is a secant.

A *segment* is a figure formed by an arc and the chord joining the end points of the arc. In figure 18-3, the shaded figure ABC is a segment.

A *sector* is a figure formed by two radii and the arc intercepted by the radii. In figure 18-3, the shaded figure EOF is a sector.

A *central angle* is an angle whose vertex is at the center of the circle and whose sides are radii. In figure 18-4, ∠MON is a central angle.

An *inscribed angle* is an angle in a circle whose vertex is on the circle and whose sides are chords. In figure 18-4, ∠SRT is an inscribed angle.

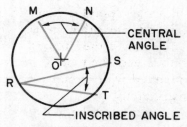

Fig. 18-3

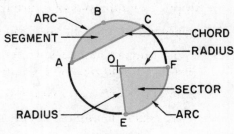

Fig. 18-4

Exercise 18-1

These problems require the identification of terms used to describe the properties of circles.

1. Refer to figure 18-5. Write the word that identifies each of the following.

    a. AB

    b. CD

    c. EO

    d. Point O

Fig. 18-5

2. Refer to figure 18-6. Write the word that identifies each of the following.

    a. ↔HK

    b. ⌢GF

    c. GF

    d. ↔LM

    e. Point P

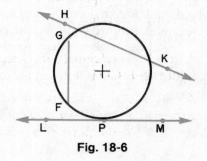

Fig. 18-6

3. Refer to figure 18-7. Write the word that identifies each of the following.

a. M

b. P

c. SO

d. RW

e. R̂W

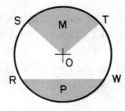

Fig. 18-7

4. Refer to figure 18-8. Write the word that identifies each of the following.

a. ∠1

b. ∠2

c. ĈE

d. CE

e. CD

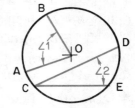

Fig. 18-8

CIRCUMFERENCE FORMULA

A polygon is *inscribed* in a circle when each vertex of the polygon is a point of the circle. In figure 18-9, regular polygons are inscribed in circles. As the number of sides increases, the perimeter increases and approaches the circumference.

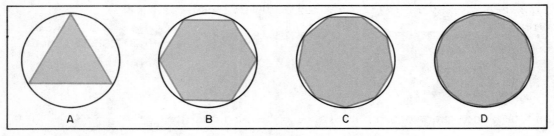

Fig. 18-9

An important relationship exists between the circumference and the diameter of a circle. As the number of sides of an inscribed polygon increases, the perimeter approaches a certain number times the diameter. This number is called *pi* and has a value of 3.141 6 to four decimals places. The symbol for pi is π. No matter how many sides an inscribed polygon has, the value of π cannot be expressed exactly with digits. Pi is called an irrational number.

The value of π used in computations depends on the type of problem to be solved and the degree of precision required. For example, a welder working to the nearer tenth inch would compute using a value of π of 3.14. However, a tool and die maker, when working to the nearer ten-thousandth inch, would use a more precise value of π, such as 3.141 59. The most commonly used approximations for π are $3\frac{1}{7}$, 3.14, and 3.141 6.

> The circumference of a circle is equal to pi times the diameter or two pi times the radius.

Expressed as a formula where C is the circumference, d is the diameter, and r is the radius:

$$C = \pi d \text{ or } C = 2\pi r$$

Example 1. What is the circumference of a circle if the diameter equals 14.5 inches?

Solution: Since the diameter is given to only 1 decimal place, use 3.14 for the value of π. Substitute values.

$$C = \pi d$$
$$C = 3.14(14.5 \text{ in})$$
$$C = 45.5 \text{ in } Ans$$

Example 2. What is the circumference of a circle if the radius equals 23.764 centimetres?

Solution: Since the radius is given to 3 decimal places, use 3.141 6 for the value of π. Substitute values.

$$C = 2\pi r$$
$$C = 2(3.141\ 6)\ (23.764 \text{ cm})$$
$$C = 149.314 \text{ cm } Ans$$

Example 3. Determine the radius of a circle which has a circumference of 18.4 metres.

Solution: Substitute values.

$$C = 2\pi r$$
$$18.4 \text{ m} = 2(3.14)r$$
$$18.4 \text{ m} = (6.28)r$$
$$r = 2.9 \text{ m } Ans$$

ARC LENGTH FORMULA

There are the same number of degrees in the arc of a central angle as there are in the central angle itself. In figure 18-10, if central $\angle 1 = 62°$, then $\overset{\frown}{AB} = 62°$ and if $\overset{\frown}{CD} = 150°$, then $\angle 2 = 150°$.

When computing lengths of arcs, consider a complete circle as an arc of 360°. The ratio of the number of degrees of an arc to 360° gives the fractional part of the circumference for the arc.

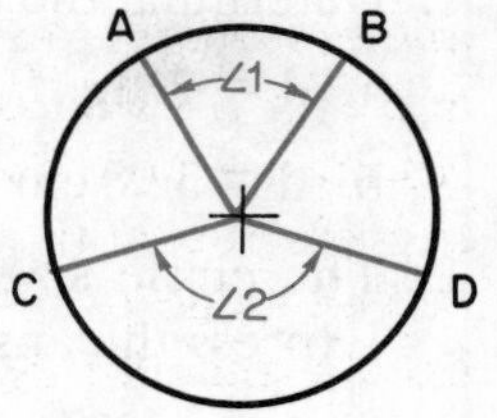

Fig. 18-10

> The length of an arc equals the ratio of the number of degrees of the arc to 360° times the circumference.

Expressed as a formula:

$$\text{Length of Arc} = \frac{\text{Arc Degrees}}{360°} (2\pi r) \text{ or}$$

$$\text{Length of Arc} = \frac{\text{Central Angle}}{360°} (2\pi r)$$

Example 1.   Determine the length of a 65° arc on a circle with a 4.2-inch radius.

Solution: Substitute values in the formula.

$$\text{Length of Arc} = \frac{\text{Arc Degrees}}{360°}(2\pi r)$$

$$= \frac{65°}{360°}[2(3.14)(4.2 \text{ in})]$$

$$= 4.8 \text{ in } Ans$$

Example 2.   Determine the radius of the circle shown in figure 18-11.

Solution: Substitute values in the formula.

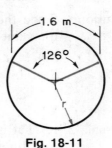

Fig. 18-11

$$\text{Length of Arc} = \frac{\text{Central Angle}}{360°}(2\pi r)$$

$$1.6 \text{ m} = \frac{126°}{360°}(2)(3.14)r$$

$$1.6 \text{ m} = 2.20r$$

$$r = 0.7 \text{ m } Ans$$

Example 3.   Determine the central angle which cuts off an arc length of 2.8 inches on a circle with a 5-inch radius.

Solution: Substitute values in the formula.

$$\text{Length of Arc} = \frac{\text{Central Angle}}{360°}(2\pi r)$$

$$2.8 \text{ in} = \frac{\text{Central Angle}}{360°}[2(3.14)(5 \text{ in})]$$

$$(2.8 \text{ in})(360°) = \text{Central Angle } (31.4 \text{ in})$$

$$\text{Central Angle} = 32.1° \text{ Ans}$$

Exercise 18-2

For these exercises and problems use 3.14 for the value of π. Express the answers to 1 decimal place unless otherwise specified.

1. Determine the circumference of each circle.

   a. d = 28 in   c. d = 7.5 ft   e. r = 17.7 in

   b. d = 32.8 cm   d. r = 3.1 m   f. r = 35.6 mm

2. The circle size and the arc degrees are given. Determine the arc length. Express the answer to 1 decimal place.

   a. 6-in radius; 45° arc   d. 5-m diameter; 108° arc

   b. 14.6-cm radius; 62° arc   e. 40-cm diameter; 15° arc

   c. 2-ft radius; 130° arc

3. Find the radius of a circle which has a circumference of 38 inches.

4. Determine the central angle which cuts off an arc length of 1.2 metres on a circle with a 3-metre radius.

5. Find the radius of a circle in which a 50° central angle cuts off an arc length of 6.3 inches.

6. Determine the length of belt required to connect the two pulleys shown in figure 18-12.

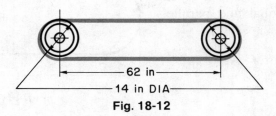

Fig. 18-12

7. A circular walk is 1.5 metres wide as shown in figure 18-13. If the outer circumference is 72 metres, what is the inside diameter of the walk?

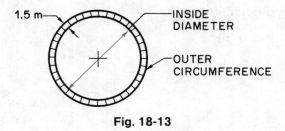

Fig. 18-13

8. Determine the length of wire in feet in a coil of 50 turns if the average diameter of the coil is 32 inches.

9. An automobile wheel has an outside tire diameter of 27 inches. In going one mile, how many revolutions does the wheel make?

10. A spur gear is shown in figure 18-14. Pitch circles of spur gears are the imaginary circles of meshing gears that make contact with each other. A pitch diameter is the diameter of a pitch circle. Circular pitch is the length of the arc measured on the pitch circle between the centers of two adjacent teeth. Determine the circular pitch of a spur gear which has 26 teeth and a pitch diameter of 4.125 0 inches. Use 3.141 59 for the value of π. Express the answer to 4 decimal places.

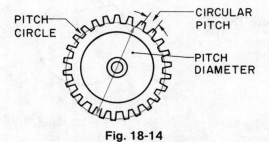

Fig. 18-14

11. The flywheel of a machine has an 0.8-metre diameter and revolves 240 times per minute. How many metres does a point on the outside of the flywheel rim travel in 5 minutes?

12. A 1 000-metre track is shown in figure 18-15. The track consists of two semicircles and two equal and parallel straightaways, AB and CD.

   a. Find the length of each straightaway.

   b. Find distance L.

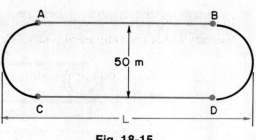

Fig. 18-15

13. Determine the total distance around (perimeter) the patio shown in figure 18-16.

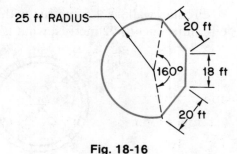

Fig. 18-16

CIRCLES

· All radii of the same circle, or of equal circles, are equal.

· A diameter of a circle bisects the circle and the surface enclosed by the circle; if a line bisects a circle, it is a diameter.

· The diameter of a circle is longer than any other chord of that circle.

· A straight line passing through a point within a circle intersects the circle in two and only two points.

In the same circle or in equal circles, equal chords subtend (cut off) equal arcs.

Example.   Refer to the circles shown in figure 18-17.

   Given: Circle A = circle B

   CD = EF = GH = MS

   Conclusion: $\overset{\frown}{CD} = \overset{\frown}{EF} = \overset{\frown}{GH} = \overset{\frown}{MS}$

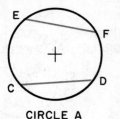

CIRCLE A

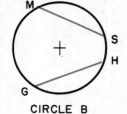

CIRCLE B

Fig. 18-17

In the same circle or in equal circles, equal central angles subtend (cut off) equal arcs.

Example.   Refer to the circles shown in figure 18-18.

   Given: Circle D = circle E

   $\angle 1 = \angle 2 = \angle 3 = \angle 4$

   Conclusion: $\overset{\frown}{AB} = \overset{\frown}{GF} = \overset{\frown}{HK} = \overset{\frown}{MP}$

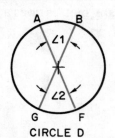

CIRCLE D

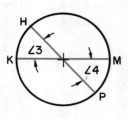

CIRCLE E

Fig. 18-18

In the same circle or in equal circles, two central angles have the same ratio as the arcs which are subtended (cut off) by the angles.

Example.   Refer to the circles shown in figure 18-19.

a. Find $\widehat{EF}$.

b. Find $\angle GOH$.

Given: Circle A = circle B

$\angle COD = 75°$

$\angle EOF = 42°$

$\widehat{CD} = 18''$

$\widehat{GH} = 24''$

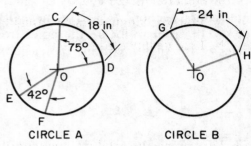

CIRCLE A   CIRCLE B

Fig. 18-19

Solution:

a. Set up a proportion with $\widehat{CD}$, $\widehat{EF}$, and their respective central angles.

$$\frac{75°}{42°} = \frac{18''}{\widehat{EF}}$$

$\widehat{EF} = \mathbf{10.08''}$ *Ans*

b. Set up a proportion with $\widehat{CD}$, $\widehat{GH}$, and their respective central angles.

$$\frac{18''}{24''} = \frac{75°}{\angle GOH}$$

$\angle GOH = \mathbf{100°}$ *Ans*

A diameter perpendicular to a chord bisects the chord and the arcs subtended (cut off) by the chord; the perpendicular bisector of a chord passes through the center of the circle.

Example.   Refer to the circle in figure 18-20.

Given: Diameter $DE \perp AB$ at C.

Conclusion: $\mathbf{AC = CB}$

$\mathbf{\widehat{AD} = \widehat{DB}}$

$\mathbf{\widehat{AE} = \widehat{EB}}$

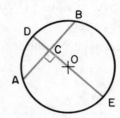

Fig. 18-20

Practical Application

Holes A, B, and C are to be drilled in the plate shown in figure 18-21. The centers of holes A and C lie on a circle with a diameter of 28 cm. The center of hole B lies on the intersection of chord AC and segment OB which is perpendicular to AC. In order to locate the holes from the left and bottom edges of the plate, working dimensions F, G, and H must be computed.

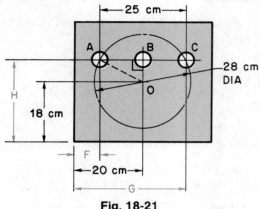

Fig. 18-21

Solution:

Compute F.

AB = 25 cm ÷ 2 = 12.5 cm

F = 20 cm − 12.5 cm = *7.5 cm Ans*

Compute G. BC = AB = 12.5 cm

G = 20 cm + 12.5 cm = *32.5 cm Ans*

Compute H. In rt. △ABO, AB = 12.5 cm and AO = 14 cm. Using the Pythagorean Theorem, determine OB.

$(OB)^2 = (14 \text{ cm})^2 + (12.5 \text{ cm})^2$

$(14 \text{ cm})^2 = (OB)^2 + (12.5 \text{ cm})^2$

$(OB)^2 = 39.75 \text{ cm}^2$

$OB = 6.3 \text{ cm (rounded)}$

H = 18 cm + 6.3 cm = *24.3 cm Ans*

Exercise 18-3

Solve these problems. Express the answers to 1 decimal place unless otherwise specified. Certain problems require the application of two or more theorems in the solutions.

1. Refer to figure 18-22. △ABC is equilateral. Determine the length of these arcs.

   a. $\overarc{AB}$

   b. $\overarc{BC}$

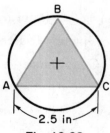

Fig. 18-22

2. Refer to figure 18-23. AC and DB are diameters. Determine the length of these arcs.

   a. $\overarc{AB}$

   b. $\overarc{BC}$

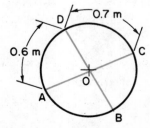

Fig. 18-23

3. Refer to figure 18-24. Determine the length of these arcs.

   a. $\overset{\frown}{HP}$ when $\overset{\frown}{EF}$ = 2.8″

   b. $\overset{\frown}{EF}$ when $\overset{\frown}{HP}$ = 5.9″

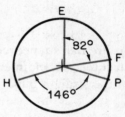

Fig. 18-24

4. Refer to figure 18-25. Determine these values.

   a. ∠1 when $\overset{\frown}{SW}$ = 7.5 cm and $\overset{\frown}{TM}$ = 10 cm

   b. ∠1 when $\overset{\frown}{TM}$ = 56 mm and $\overset{\frown}{SW}$ = 29 mm

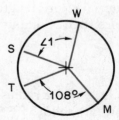

Fig. 18-25

5. Refer to figure 18-26. Determine these lengths.

   a. DB and $\overset{\frown}{ACB}$ when AB = 0.8 m and $\overset{\frown}{AC}$ = 0.6 m

   b. AB and $\overset{\frown}{CB}$ when DB = 1.2 m and $\overset{\frown}{ACB}$ = 2.7 m

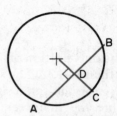

Fig. 18-26

6. Refer to figure 18-27. Determine the length of $\overset{\frown}{HK}$ when $\overset{\frown}{EF}$ = 8.4 in.

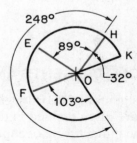

Fig. 18-27

7. Refer to figure 18-28. Determine these values.

   a. The length of $\overset{\frown}{ABC}$ when ∠1 = 236°

   b. ∠1 when $\overset{\frown}{ABC}$ = 2.5 ft

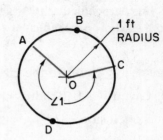

Fig. 18-28

8. Refer to figure 18-29. The circumference of the circle is 160 mm. Determine these values.

   a. The length of $\overset{\frown}{AB}$ when ∠1 = 42°

   b. ∠1 when $\overset{\frown}{AB}$ = 34 mm

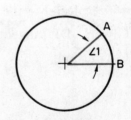

Fig. 18-29

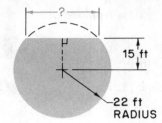
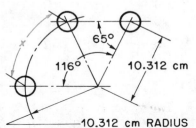

9. A circular shaped concrete slab with one straight edge is to be constructed to the dimensions shown in figure 18-30. Determine the length
of the straight edge.

Fig. 18-30

10. Determine arc length x between the centers of two holes shown in
figure 18-31. Compute the answer to the nearer thousandth centimetre.

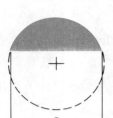

11. A circle with a radius OE of 5.6 metres has a chord EF 8.4 metres long.
How far is chord EF from the center O of the circle? Note: It is helpful
to sketch and label this problem.

Fig. 18-31

12. The only portion of an old table top which remains is a segment as shown
in figure 18-32. The segment is less than a semicircle. In order to make a
new top the same size as the original, a furniture restorer must determine the diameter of the original top. Describe how the required
diameter is determined.

Fig. 18-32

CIRCLE TANGENTS AND CHORD SEGMENTS

Tangents and chord segments are used to compute unknown lengths and angles
and are often applied in design, layout, and problem solving in the construction
and manufacturing occupations.

> **A line perpendicular to a radius at its extremity is tangent to the circle; a tangent
> to a circle is perpendicular to the radius at the tangent point.**

Example 1.   Refer to the circle in figure 18-33.

    Given: AB ⊥ radius OC at point C.

    Conclusion: AB is tangent to the circle at point C.

Example 2.   Refer to the circle in figure 18-33.

    Given: DE tangent to the circle at point F.

    Conclusion: DE ⊥ radius OF

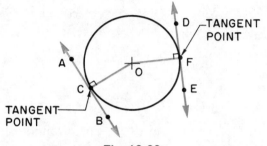

Fig. 18-33

Practical Application

In figure 18-34, AC is tangent to circle O at point C. Determine distance AO.

Solution:

AC ⊥ radius CO at point C

△AOC is a right triangle

$(AO)^2 = (9 \text{ m})^2 + (7 \text{ m})^2$

$(AO)^2 = 130 \text{ m}^2$

   AO = **11.4 m** (rounded) *Ans*

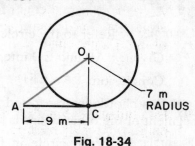

Fig. 18-34

> **Two tangents drawn to a circle from a point outside the circle are equal and make equal angles with the line joining the point to the center.**

Example.   Refer to the circle in figure 18-35.

   Given: Tangents AP and BP are drawn to circle O from point P. Line PO is drawn from point P to center point O.

   Conclusion: **AP = BP**

   ∠APO = ∠BPO

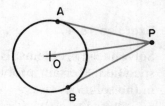

Fig. 18-35

Practical Application

A drawing of a proposed park flower garden is shown in figure 18-36. PA and PB are tangent to circle O. A walk is to be made along the complete lengths of PA and PB. Determine the total length of walk required.

Solution:

PA ⊥ radius OA

△PAO is a right triangle.

$(50 \text{ ft})^2 = (PA)^2 + (35 \text{ ft})^2$

   $(PA)^2 = 1\ 275 \text{ ft}$

   PA = **35.7 ft**

PB = PA

PB = 35.7 ft

35.7 ft + 35.7 ft = **71.4 ft** *Ans*

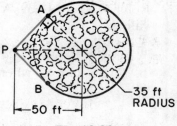

Fig. 18-36

If two chords intersect inside a circle, the product of the two segments of one chord is equal to the product of the two segments of the other chord.

Example.   Refer to the circle in figure 18-37.

    Given: AB and CD intersect at point E.

    Conclusion: **AE(EB) = CE(ED)**

If two chords intersect and both segments of one chord are known and one segment of the other chord is known, the second segment can be determined.

Example. : In the circle in figure 18-37, CE = 15 cm, ED = 3.4 cm, and AE = 4.5 cm. Find EB.

$$(4.5 \text{ cm})(EB) = (15 \text{ cm})(3.4 \text{ cm})$$

$$EB = 11.3 \text{ cm (rounded)} \; Ans$$

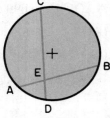

Fig. 18-37

Exercise 18-4

Solve these problems. Express the answers to 2 decimal places unless otherwise specified. Certain problems require the application of two or more theorems in the solution.

1. Refer to figure 18-38. Point P is a tangent point and ∠1 = 109°26′. Determine these values.

    a. ∠E and ∠F when ∠2 = 44°18′

    b. ∠2 when ∠E = 46°20′

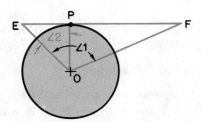

Fig. 18-38

2. Refer to figure 18-39. AB and BC are tangents. Determine these values.

    a. ∠1 and BC when AB = 2.78 in and ∠ABC = 65°

    b. ∠ABC and AB when BC = 3.93 in and ∠1 = 36°47′

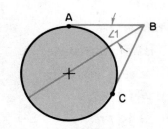

Fig. 18-39

3. Refer to figure 18-40. Points E, G, and F are tangent points. Determine these values.

    a. ∠2

    b. ∠3 when ∠1 = 125°31′

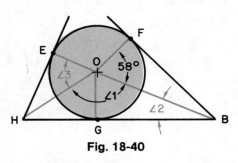

Fig. 18-40

4. Refer to figure 18-41. Determine these values.

   a. GK when EK = 6.80 m

   b. EK when GK = 5.10 m

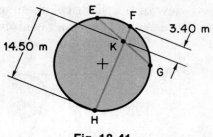

Fig. 18-41

5. In the layout shown in figure 18-42, determine dimension *x* to 3 decimal places.

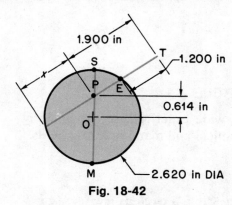

Fig. 18-42

6. In the layout shown in figure 18-43, points E, F, and G are tangent points. Determine lengths OA, OB, and OC.

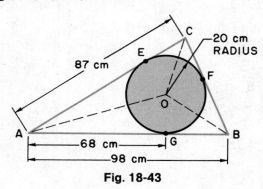

Fig. 18-43

7. A circular railing is installed around a portion of the platform shown in figure 18-44. The railing extends around the circumference from point A to point B (ACB). Determine the length of railing required.

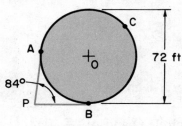

Fig. 18-44

8. The front view of a cylindrical shaft setting in the V-groove of a block is shown in figure 18-45. The center of circular cross section (point O) is directly above vertex B. Determine dimension x to 3 decimal places.

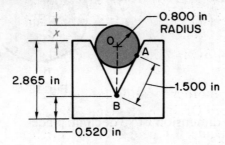

Fig. 18-45

ANGLES FORMED INSIDE AND ON A CIRCLE

Arcs and angles inside and on circles have wide practical use, particularly in design and layout in the architectural, mechanical and manufacturing fields.

Angles Inside a Circle

An angle formed by two chords which intersect within a circle is measured by one-half the sum of its two intercepted arcs.

Example 1. Refer to the circle in figure 18-46.

Given: Chords CD and EF intersect within circle O at point P.

Conclusion: $\angle EPD = \frac{1}{2}(\overset{\frown}{CF} + \overset{\frown}{DE})$

Example 2. In figure 18-46, $\overset{\frown}{CF} = 104°$ and $\overset{\frown}{DE} = 38°$.

Determine $\angle EPD$.

$\angle EPD = \frac{1}{2}(104° + 38°)$

$\angle EPD = 71°$ *Ans*

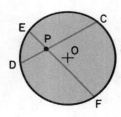

Fig. 18-46

Example 3. In figure 18-46, $\angle EPD = 68°$ and $\overset{\frown}{CF} = 96°$.

Determine the number of degrees in $\overset{\frown}{DE}$.

$68° = \frac{1}{2}(96° + \overset{\frown}{DE})$

$\overset{\frown}{DE} = 40°$ *Ans*

Angles on a Circle

An inscribed angle is measured by one-half its intercepted arc.

Example. In figure 18-47, vertex B is a point on circle O and $\overset{\frown}{AC} = 103°$.

$\angle ABC = \frac{1}{2}(103°)$

$\angle ABC = 51.5° = 51°30'$ *Ans*

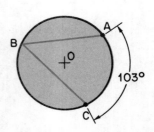

Fig. 18-47

Practical Application

The center of the disc shown in figure 18-48 is located as follows:

- Place the vertex of the carpenter's square anywhere on the circle, such as point A. The outside edges of the square intersect the circle at points B and C. Draw a line, BC, connecting these points. Since ∠A of the carpenter's square is 90°, $\widehat{BC}$ is twice 90° or 180°. Chord BC is a diameter since it cuts off an arc of 180° or a semicircle.

- Place the vertex of the carpenter's square at another location on the circle, such as point D. Connect points E and F. Chord DF is also a diameter.

- The intersection of diameters BC and EF locate the center of the circle, point O.

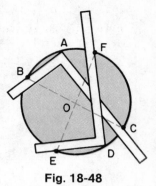

Fig. 18-48

> An angle formed by a tangent and a chord at the tangent point is measured by one-half its intercepted arc.

Example. Refer to the circle in figure 18-49.

Given: Tangent CD meets chord AB at tangent point A.
$\widehat{AEB} = 110°$

Conclusion: $\angle CAB = \frac{1}{2}\widehat{AEB} = \frac{1}{2}(110°) = 55°$

$\widehat{AFB} = 360° - 110° = 250°$

$\angle DAB = \frac{1}{2}\widehat{DFB} = \frac{1}{2}(250°) = 125°$

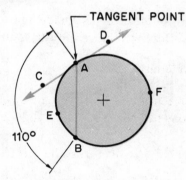

Fig. 18-49

Practical Application

Refer to figure 18-50. The centers of 3 holes lie on line AC. Line AC is tangent to circle O at hole center point B. The center D of a fourth hole lies on the circle. Determine ∠ABD.

Solution: $\widehat{DEB}$ = Central ∠DOB = 132°

$\angle ABD = \frac{1}{2}\widehat{DEB} = \frac{1}{2}(132°) = 66°$ *Ans*

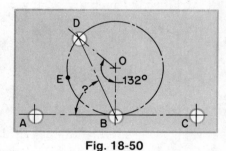

Fig. 18-50

Exercise 18-5

Solve these problems. Express the answers to the nearer minute. Certain problems require the application of two or more theorems in the solution.

1. Refer to figure 18-51. Determine these values.

   a. ∠1

   b. ∠2

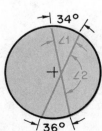

Fig. 18-51

2. Refer to figure 18-52. Determine the number of degrees in these arcs.

a. $\overset{\frown}{AB}$ when $\overset{\frown}{DC} = 30°$

b. $\overset{\frown}{DC}$ when $\overset{\frown}{AB} = 135°$

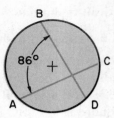

Fig. 18-52

3. Refer to figure 18-53. Determine the number of degrees for each arc or angle.

a. $\overset{\frown}{EF}$ and $\angle 4$ when $\angle 3 = 49°$ and $\overset{\frown}{GH} = 84°$

b. $\overset{\frown}{GH}$ and $\angle 3$ when $\angle 4 = 18°50'$ and $\overset{\frown}{EF} = 105°$

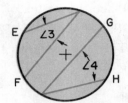

Fig. 18-53

4. Refer to figure 18-54. Determine the number of degrees in these arcs.

a. $\overset{\frown}{PT}$

b. $\overset{\frown}{KT}$

c. $\overset{\frown}{MP}$

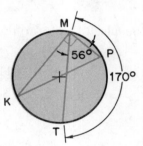

Fig. 18-54

5. Refer to figure 18-55. When $\overset{\frown}{AB} = 122°$, determine the number of degrees for each arc or angle.

a. $\angle 1$

b. $\angle 2$

c. $\overset{\frown}{BC}$

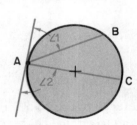

Fig. 18-55

6. Refer to figure 18-56. Determine the number of degrees for each arc or angle.

a. $\angle 1$

b. $\overset{\frown}{ADC}$

c. $\angle 2$

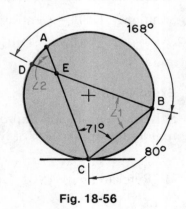

Fig. 18-56

7. A triangle is inscribed in a circle. Two angles of the triangle cut off arcs of 56° and 108° respectively. Determine the third angle of the triangle.

8. In a circle, an inscribed angle and a central angle cut off the same arc. How do these two angles compare in size?

9. If the end points of two diameters of a circle are connected, what kind of a quadrilateral is formed? Explain your answer.

10. Describe how the carpenter's square is used to check the accuracy of the semicircular cutout in the trim piece shown in figure 18-57.

Fig. 18-57

11. In figure 18-58, $\angle CAD = 38°$, $\angle BEC = 40°$, $\overset{\frown}{ABC} = 130°$, and $\overset{\frown}{CDE} = 134°$. Determine angles 1 through 10.

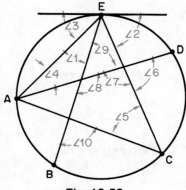

Fig. 18-58

ANGLES OUTSIDE A CIRCLE

An angle formed outside a circle by two secants, two tangents, or a secant and a tangent is measured by one-half the difference of the intercepted arcs.

Two Secants

Example 1.   Refer to the circle in figure 18-59.

Given: Secant ABP and DCP meet at point P and intercept $\overset{\frown}{BC}$ and $\overset{\frown}{AD}$.

Conclusion: $\angle P = \frac{1}{2}(\overset{\frown}{AD} - \overset{\frown}{BC})$

Example 2.   In figure 18-59, $\overset{\frown}{AD} = 109°$ and $\overset{\frown}{BC} = 43°$.
Determine $\angle P$.

$\angle P = \frac{1}{2}(109° - 43°) = 33°$ *Ans*

Example 3.   In figure 18-59, $\angle P = 28°$ and $\overset{\frown}{BC} = 40°$.
Determine $\overset{\frown}{AD}$.

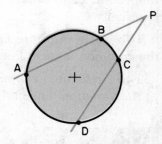

Fig. 18-59

$28° = \frac{1}{2}(\overset{\frown}{AD} - 40°)$

$\overset{\frown}{AD} = 96°$ *Ans*

Two Tangents

Example 1.   Refer to figure 18-60.

> Given: Tangents DP and EP meet at point P and intercept $\overset{\frown}{DE}$ and $\overset{\frown}{DCE}$.
>
> Conclusion: $\angle P = \frac{1}{2}(\overset{\frown}{DCE} - \overset{\frown}{DE})$

Example 2.   In figure 18-60, $\overset{\frown}{DCE} = 247°$. Determine $\angle P$.

$$\overset{\frown}{DE} = 360° - 247° = 113°$$

$$\angle P = \frac{1}{2}(247° - 113°) = 67° \; Ans$$

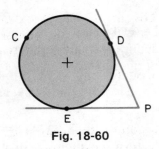

Fig. 18-60

A Tangent and a Secant

Example 1.   Refer to figure 18-61.

> Given: Tangent AP and secant CBP meet at point P and intercept $\overset{\frown}{AC}$ and $\overset{\frown}{AB}$.
>
> Conclusion: $\angle P = \frac{1}{2}(\overset{\frown}{AC} - \overset{\frown}{AB})$

Example 2.   In figure 18-61, $\overset{\frown}{AC} = 135°$ and $\overset{\frown}{AB} = 74°$. Determine $\angle P$.

$$\angle P = \frac{1}{2}(135° - 74°) = 30.5° = 30°30' \; Ans$$

Example 3.   In figure 18-61, $\overset{\frown}{AC} = 126°38'$ and $\angle P = 28°50'$. Determine the number of degrees in $\overset{\frown}{AB}$.

$$28°50' = \frac{1}{2}(126°38' - \overset{\frown}{AB})$$

$$\overset{\frown}{AB} = 68°58' \; Ans$$

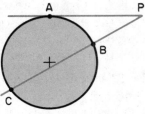

Fig. 18-61

INTERNALLY AND EXTERNALLY TANGENT CIRCLES

Two circles that are tangent to the same line at the same point are tangent to each other. Circles may be either tangent internally or externally.

Two circles are *internally tangent* if both are on the same side of the common tangent line as shown in figure 18-62.

Two circles are *externally tangent* if the circles are on opposite sides of the common tangent line as shown in figure 18-63.

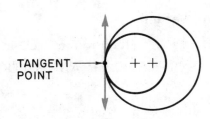

**Fig. 18-62
Internally tangent circles**

> **If two circles are either internally or externally tangent, a line connecting the centers of the circles passes through the point of tangency and is perpendicular to the tangent line.**

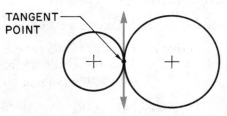

**Fig. 18-63
Externally tangent circles**

Internally Tangent Circles

Example.   Refer to figure 18-64.

> Given: Circle D and circle E are internally tangent at point C. D is the center of circle D. E is the center of circle E and line AB is tangent to both circles at point C.

> Conclusion: **Line DE, which connects centers D and E, passes through tangent point C and line CDE is ⊥ to tangent line AB.**

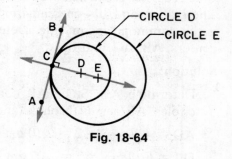

Fig. 18-64

Computing dimensions of objects on which two or more radii blend to give a smooth curved surface is illustrated by this practical application.

Practical Application

A sheet metal section is to be fabricated as shown in figure 18-65. The proper location of the two radii results in a smooth curve from point A to point B. Note that the curve from A to B is <u>not</u> an arc of one circle. It is made up of arcs of two different size circles. In order to lay out the section, the location to the center of the 12-inch radius (dimension x) must be determined.

Solution: (Refer to figure 18-66.)

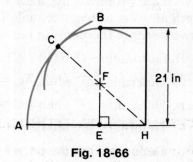

Fig. 18-65

- The 12″ radius arc and the 25″ radius arc are internally tangent. A line connecting centers F and H of the arcs passes through the point of tangency, point C.

- Since tangent point C is the end point of the 25″ radius, CFH = 25″. Also, since point C is the end point of the 12″ radius, CF = 12″.

  FH = 25″ − 12″ = 13″

- Since BFE is vertical and AEH is horizontal, ∠FEH is a right angle. △FEH is a right triangle.

- In right △FEH,

  FH = 13″

  FE = 21″ − 12″ = 9″

  Compute EH using the Pythagorean Theorem.

  $(13'')^2 = (\ H)^2 + (9'')^2$

  EH = 9.38″ (rounded)

  EH = x = 9.38″ *Ans*

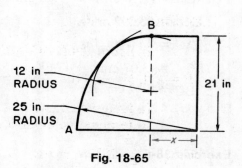

Fig. 18-66

Externally Tangent Circles

Example.   Refer to figure 18-67.

> Given: Circle D and circle E are externally tangent at point C. D is the center of circle D. E is the center of circle E and line AB is tangent to both circles at point C.

> Conclusion: **Line DE, which connects centers D and E, passes through tangent point C and line DCE is ⊥ to tangent line AB at point C.**

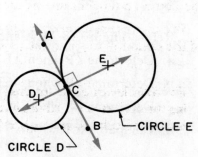

Fig. 18-67

Practical Application

Three holes are to be bored in a metal plate as shown in figure 18-68. The 4.20-cm and 6.14-cm diameter holes are tangent at point D and CD is the common tangent line. Determine the distances between hole centers, AB, AC, and BC.

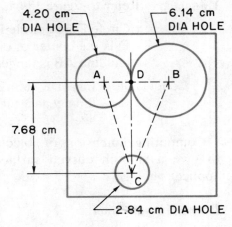

Solution:

- Determine AB: Since AB connects the centers of two tangent circles, AB passes through tangent point D.

  AD = 4.20 cm ÷ 2 = 2.10 cm

  DB = 6.14 cm ÷ 2 = 3.07 cm

  AB = 2.10 cm + 3.07 cm = **5.17 cm** *Ans*

- Determine AC and BC: Since AB connects the centers of two tangent circles, AB is ⊥ to tangent line DC. Therefore, ∠ADC and ∠BDC are both right angles.

  $(AC)^2 = (2.10 \text{ cm})^2 + (7.68 \text{ cm})^2$

  $(AC)^2 = 63.392 \text{ cm}^2$

  AC = **7.96 cm** *Ans*

  $(BC)^2 = (3.07 \text{ cm})^2 + (7.68 \text{ cm})^2$

  BC = **8.27 cm** *Ans*

Fig. 18-68

Exercise 18-6

Solve these problems. Express angular value answers to the nearer minute and length answers to two decimal places. Certain problems require the application of two or more theorems in the solution.

1. Refer to figure 18-69.

   a. Determine ∠P when $\overset{\frown}{AC} = 58°$ and $\overset{\frown}{BD} = 32°$.

   b. Determine ∠P when $\overset{\frown}{AC} = 63°$ and $\overset{\frown}{BD} = 28°$.

   c. Determine the arc degrees for $\overset{\frown}{BD}$ when ∠P = 16° and $\overset{\frown}{AC} = 64°$.

   d. Determine the arc degrees for $\overset{\frown}{AC}$ when ∠P = 37° and $\overset{\frown}{BD} = 30°$.

   e. Determine ∠P when $\overset{\frown}{CAB} = 178°$, $\overset{\frown}{CD} = 157°$, and $\overset{\frown}{AC} = 52°$.

   f. Determine the arc degrees for $\overset{\frown}{AC}$ when $\overset{\frown}{CD} = 140°$, $\overset{\frown}{CAB} = 193°$, and ∠P = 39°.

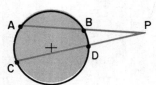

Fig. 18-69

2. Refer to figure 18-70. A and B are tangent points.

   a. Determine ∠P when $\overset{\frown}{AB} = 120°$.

   b. Determine ∠P when $\overset{\frown}{ACB} = 231°$.

   c. Determine ∠P when $\overset{\frown}{AC} = 160°$ and $\overset{\frown}{CB} = 88°$.

   d. Compare $\overset{\frown}{ACB}$ with $\overset{\frown}{AB}$ when ∠P is a very small value.

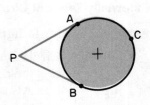

Fig. 18-70

3. Refer to figure 18-71. A is a tangent point.

    a. Determine $\angle P$ when $\overset{\frown}{AC} = 120°$ and $\overset{\frown}{BA} = 70°$.

    b. Determine $\angle P$ when $\overset{\frown}{AC} = 113°$ and $\overset{\frown}{BA} = 66°$.

    c. Determine the arc degrees for $\overset{\frown}{AC}$ when $\angle P = 25°$ and $\overset{\frown}{BA} = 58°$.

    d. Determine the arc degrees for $\overset{\frown}{BA}$ when $\angle P = 37°$ and $\overset{\frown}{AC} = 85°$.

    e. Determine $\angle P$ when $\overset{\frown}{BC} = 160°$ and $\overset{\frown}{AC} = 112°$.

    f. Determine $\angle P$ when $\overset{\frown}{BC} = 150°$ and $\overset{\frown}{AC} = 2\overset{\frown}{BA}$.

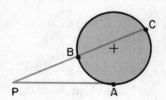

Fig. 18-71

4. Refer to figure 18-72. A and D are tangent points. Determine $\angle 1$, $\angle 2$, and $\angle 3$ when $\overset{\frown}{AB} = 72°$ and $\overset{\frown}{CD} = 50°$.

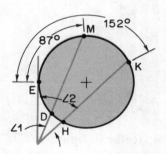

Fig. 18-72

5. Refer to figure 18-73. E is a tangent point.

    a. Find the arc degrees for $\overset{\frown}{DH}$ and $\overset{\frown}{EDH}$ when $\angle 1 = 26°$ and $\angle 2 = 63°$.

    b. Find the arc degrees for $\overset{\frown}{HK}$ when $\angle 2 = 50°$.

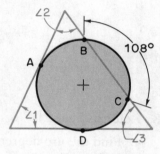

Fig. 18-73

6. Refer to figure 18-74. A is a tangent point.

    a. Find x when Dia A = 41.25 in and Dia B = 23.65 in.

    b. Find Dia A when $x = 9.83$ in and Dia B = 11.58 in.

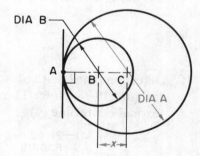

Fig. 18-74

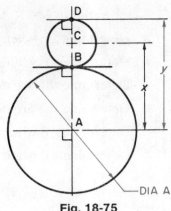

Fig. 18-75

7. Refer to figure 18-75.

    a. Find Dia A when $x = 9.82$ cm and $y = 11.94$ cm.

    b. Find y when Dia A $= 30.36$ cm and $x = 23.72$ cm.

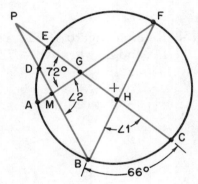

Fig. 18-76

8. Refer to figure 18-76.

    a. Find the arc degrees for $\overset{\frown}{AB}$ and $\overset{\frown}{DE}$ when $\angle 1 = 71°$ and $\angle 2 = 97°$.

    b. Find the arc degrees for $\overset{\frown}{AB}$ and $\overset{\frown}{DE}$ when $\angle 1 = 66°$ and $\angle 2 = 92°$.

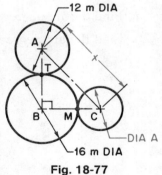

Fig. 18-77

9. Refer to figure 18-77. T and M are tangent points.

    a. Find x when Dia A $= 10$ m.

    b. Find Dia A when $x = 18$ m.

10. Determine the length of stock, dimension L, required to make the gage shown in figure 18-78. Note: The gage is symmetrical (identical) on each side of the vertical centerline (℄).

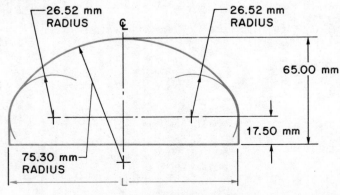

Fig. 18-78

11. Three posts are mounted on the fixture shown in figure 18-79. Each post is tangent to the arc made by the 0.650-inch radius. Determine dimension A and dimension B to 3 decimal places. Note: The fixture is symmetrical (identical) on each side of the horizontal centerline (℄).

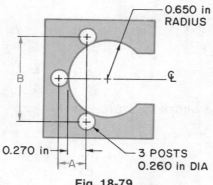

Fig. 18-79

12. Three holes are to be located on the layout shown in figure 18-80. The 7.24-cm and 3.08-cm diameter holes are tangent at point T and TA is the common tangent line between the two holes. Determine dimension C and dimension D.

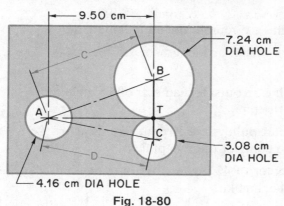

Fig. 18-80

UNIT EXERCISE AND PROBLEM REVIEW

Exercise 18-7

IDENTIFYING PARTS

These problems require the identification of terms.

1. Refer to figure 18-81. Write the word that identifies each of the following.

   a. AB

   b. CD

   c. OD

   d. $\overset{\frown}{AC}$

   e. $\overleftrightarrow{EF}$

   f. point G

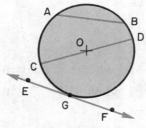

Fig. 18-81

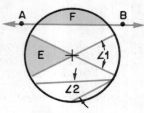

Fig. 18-82

2. Refer to figure 18-82. Write the word that identifies each of the following.

   a. $\overleftrightarrow{AB}$ d. E

   b. $\angle 1$ e. F

   c. $\angle 2$

CIRCUMFERENCE AND ARC LENGTH

For these exercises and problems use 3.14 for the value of π. Express the answers to 1 decimal place unless otherwise specified.

3. Determine the circumference of each circle.

   a. d = 32 cm   b. d = 5.2 in   c. r = 0.8 m

4. The circle size and the arc degrees are given. Determine the arc length.

   a. 8-in radius; 60° arc

   b. 6-m diameter; 120° arc

   c. 3-ft diameter; 25° arc

5. Determine the radius of a circle which has a circumference of 15 metres.

6. Determine the central angle which cuts off an arc length of 7.5 feet on a circle with a 4-foot radius.

7. A pipe with a wall thickness of 0.20 inch has an outside diameter of 3.5 inches. Determine the inside circumference of the pipe.

8. The centers of two 15-centimetre diameter pulleys are 50 centimetres apart. Determine the length of belt required to connect the two pulleys.

9. A truck wheel has an outside tire diameter of 45 inches. In going one-half mile, how many revolutions does the wheel make?

CHORD, ARC, AND CENTRAL ANGLE APPLICATIONS

Solve these problems. Express answers to 1 decimal place unless otherwise specified. Certain problems require the application of two or more theorems in the solution.

10. Refer to figure 18-83. ABCDEF is a regular hexagon. Determine the number of degrees in each arc or angle.

    a. $\overarc{BC}$ b. $\overarc{CDE}$ c. $\angle 1$

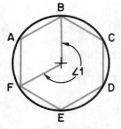

Fig. 18-83

11. Refer to figure 18-84.

    a. Find the length of $\overarc{MH}$ when $\overarc{EF} = 1.5$ m.

    b. Find the length of $\overarc{EF}$ when $\overarc{MH} = 3.2$ m.

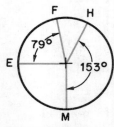

Fig. 18-84

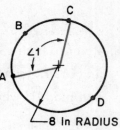

Fig. 18-85

12. Refer to figure 18-85.

   a. Find the length of $\overset{\frown}{ABC}$ when $\angle 1 = 115°$.

   b. Find $\angle 1$ when $\overset{\frown}{ADC} = 32$ in.

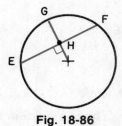

Fig. 18-86

13. Refer to figure 18-86.

   a. Find the length of EH and $\overset{\frown}{EGF}$ when EF = 23 cm and $\overset{\frown}{EG}$ = 14 cm.

   b. Find the length of $\overset{\frown}{EGF}$ and HF when EF = 35 cm and $\overset{\frown}{GF}$ = 20 cm.

14. Circle O has a diameter AB of 14.50 feet and a chord CD of 8 feet. Chord CD is perpendicular to diameter AB. How far is chord CD from the center O of the circle? Express the answer to 2 decimal places. Note: It is helpful to sketch and label this problem.

15. A flat is cut on a circular piece as shown in figure 18-87. Determine the distance from the center of the circle to the flat, dimension x.

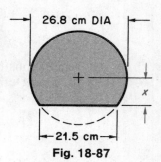

Fig. 18-87

TANGENT AND CHORD SEGMENT APPLICATIONS

Solve these problems. Express the answers to 1 decimal place unless otherwise specified. Certain problems require the application of two or more theorems in the solution.

16. Refer to figure 18-88. AT and BT are tangents.

   a. Find $\angle 1$ and AT when BT = 5'-3" and $\angle BTA = 59°20'$.

   b. Find $\angle ATB$ and BT when $\angle 1 = 31°14'$ and AT = 8'-4".

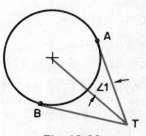

Fig. 18-88

17. Refer to figure 18-89. Points C, D, and E are tangent points.

   a. Find $\angle 1$.   b. Find $\angle 2$.

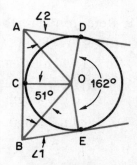

Fig. 18-89

18. Refer to figure 18-90.

    a. Find FM when MH = 0.8 m.

    b. Find MH when FM = 1.3 m.

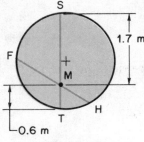

Fig. 18-90

19. Refer to figure 18-91.

    Determine dimension *x*.

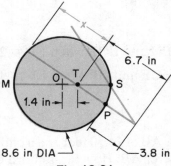

Fig. 18-91

20. A sidewalk is constructed along distance ABCD of the parcel of land shown in figure 18-92. Determine the total length of sidewalk required.

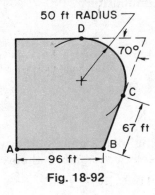

Fig. 18-92

ANGLES FORMED INSIDE, ON, AND OUTSIDE A CIRCLE

Solve these problems. Certain problems require the application of two or more theorems in the solution. Express answers to the nearer minute.

21. Refer to figure 18-93. Find the number of degrees in each arc or angle.

    a. $\angle 1$ when $\overset{\frown}{BC} = 62°$ and $\overset{\frown}{AD} = 57°$

    b. $\overset{\frown}{AD}$ when $\angle 1 = 42°$ and $\overset{\frown}{BC} = 50°$

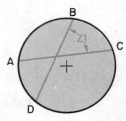

Fig. 18-93

22. Refer to figure 18-94.

    Find the number of degrees in each angle.

    a. ∠1 when $\widehat{JH} = 86°$

    b. ∠2 when $\widehat{FGHJK} = 198°$

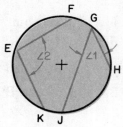

Fig. 18-94

23. Refer to figure 18-95.

    Find the number of degrees in each arc.

    a. $\widehat{BC}$

    b. $\widehat{DC}$

    c. $\widehat{AB}$

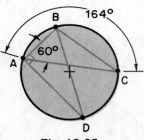

Fig. 18-95

24. Refer to figure 18-96. When $\widehat{BCA} = 255°$, find the number of degrees in each angle.

    a. ∠1

    b. ∠2

    c. ∠3

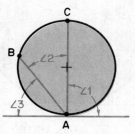

Fig. 18-96

25. Refer to figure 18-97.

    a. Determine ∠P when $\widehat{AD} = 28°$ and $\widehat{BC} = 60°$.

    b. Determine the arc degrees for $\widehat{BC}$ when ∠P = 34° and $\widehat{AD} = 20°$.

    c. Determine the arc degrees for $\widehat{AD}$ when $\widehat{AB} = 94°$, $\widehat{ABC} = 195°$ and ∠P = 35°.

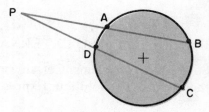

Fig. 18-97

26. Refer to figure 18-98. E and F are tangent points.

    a. Determine ∠P when $\widehat{EF} = 156°$.

    b. Determine ∠P when $\widehat{EGF} = 221°$.

    c. Determine ∠P when $\widehat{EGF} = 3\widehat{EF}$.

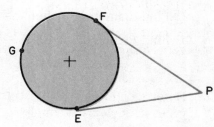

Fig. 18-98

27. Refer to figure 18-99. C is a tangent point.

a. Determine $\angle P$ when $\widehat{BC} = 64°$ and $\widehat{AC} = 114°$.

b. Determine the arc degrees for $\widehat{AC}$ when $\angle P = 59°$ and $\widehat{BC} = 80°$.

c. Determine $\angle P$ when $\widehat{BA} = 120°$ and $\widehat{BC} = \frac{1}{2}\widehat{AC}$.

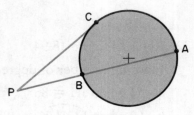

Fig. 18-99

28. A quadrilateral is inscribed in a circle. Three vertex angles of the quadrilateral cut off arcs of 180°, 170°, and 230° respectively. Determine the fourth vertex angle of the quadrilateral.

29. In figure 18-100, points A and C are tangent points, DC is a diameter, $\widehat{AHC} = 116°$, $\widehat{EFC} = 140°$, $\widehat{EF} = 64°$, and $\widehat{CH} = 42°$. Determine angles 1-10.

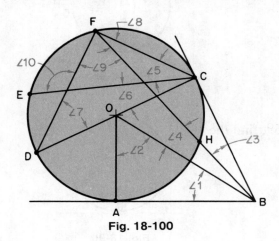

Fig. 18-100

INTERNALLY AND EXTERNALLY TANGENT CIRCLES

Solve these problems. Certain problems require the application of two or more theorems in the solution. Express answers to 2 decimal places.

30. Refer to figure 18-101.

a. Find diameter A when $x = 3.60$ inches and $y = 5.10$ inches.

b. Find t when diameter A = 8.76 inches and $x = 10.52$ inches.

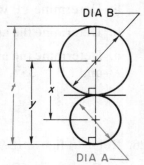

Fig. 18-101

31. Refer to figure 18-102.

a. Find diameter M when diameter H = 7.20 m, diameter T = 5.80 m, $e = 4.70$ m and $d = 4.10$ m.

b. Find dimension f when diameter T = 3.60 m, diameter H = 5.60 m, $e = 7.80$ m, and $d = 6.20$ m.

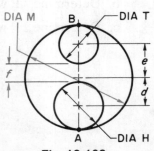

Fig. 18-102

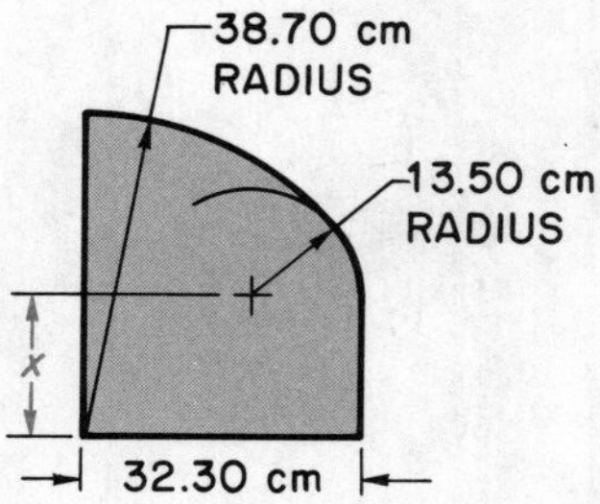

38.70 cm
RADIUS

13.50 cm
RADIUS

x

32.30 cm

Fig. 18-103

32. A pattern is made as shown in figure 18-103. Determine the distance from the base of the pattern to the center of the 13.50-cm radius arc, dimension x.

33. Three cutouts are to be laid out as shown in figure 18-104. Find diameter A.

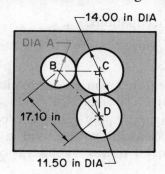

14.00 in DIA

DIA A

B   C

17.10 in

D

11.50 in DIA

Fig. 18-104

UNIT 19
Geometric
Constructions

OBJECTIVES

After studying this unit you should be able to

- make constructions which are basic to many occupations.

- lay out practical applied problems typical of those required in the metal and woodworking occupations.

A knowledge of basic geometric constructions is required in many occupations. Work is often laid out using a compass or dividers and a straightedge.

Architectural and mechanical drafters and designers apply geometric construction methods. Principles of geometric construction are widely used in the graphic arts. In the fields of woodworking and metal trades, geometric constructions are applied in laying out work.

Marking tools are available for laying out pieces in the metal trades. A sheet-metal worker uses scratch awls, scribers, dividers, and trammels to scribe straight lines, circles, and arcs on metal sheets. Hole centers may be located using a prick punch or a center punch. Sheets may then be accurately cut to the finely scribed lines. Some common marking tools are shown in figures 19-1 through 19-4.

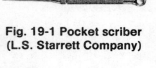

**Fig. 19-1 Pocket scriber
(L.S. Starrett Company)**

**Fig. 19-2 Center punch
(L.S. Starrett Company)**

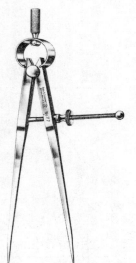

**Fig. 19-3 Dividers
(L.S. Starrett Company)**

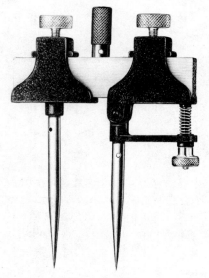

**Fig. 19-4 Trammels
(L.S. Starrett Company)**

286

There are many geometric constructions, some of which are relatively complex. The constructions presented in this book are those which are most basic and common to a wide range of practical applications.

CONSTRUCTION 1. TO CONSTRUCT A PERPENDICULAR BISECTOR OF A LINE SEGMENT

Required: Construct a perpendicular bisector to line segment AB shown in figure 19-5.

Procedure:

* With endpoint A as a center and using a radius equal to more than half AB, draw arcs above and below AB, figure 19-5.

* With endpoint B as a center and with the same radius used at A, draw arcs above and below AB, intersecting the first pair of arcs, figure 19-6.

* Draw a connecting line between the intersection of the arcs above and below AB. Line CD is perpendicular to AB and point O is the midpoint of AB, figure 19-7.

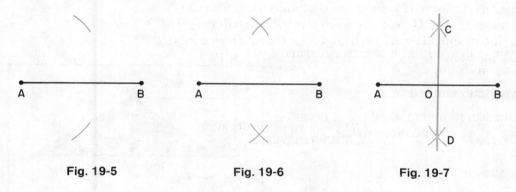

Fig. 19-5   Fig. 19-6   Fig. 19-7

Practical Application

Locate the center of the circle shown in figure 19-8.

Solution:

The perpendicular bisector of a chord passes through the center of the circle. The center of a circle is located by drawing two chords and constructing a perpendicular bisector to each chord. The intersection of the two perpendicular bisectors locates the center of the circle. The construction lines are shown in figure 19-8.

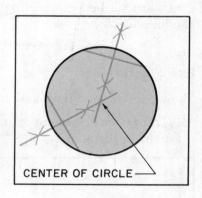

Fig. 19-8

CONSTRUCTION 2.   TO CONSTRUCT A PERPENDICULAR TO A LINE SEGMENT AT A GIVEN POINT ON THE LINE SEGMENT

Required: Construct a perpendicular at point O on line segment AB shown in figure 19-9.

Procedure:

- With given point O as a center, and with a radius of any convenient length, draw arcs intersecting AB at points C and D, figure 19-9.

- With C as a center, and with a radius greater than OC, draw an arc. With D as a center, and with the same radius used at C, draw an arc which intersects the first arc at E, figure 19-10.

- Draw a line connecting point E and point O. Line EO is perpendicular to line AB at point O, figure 19-11.

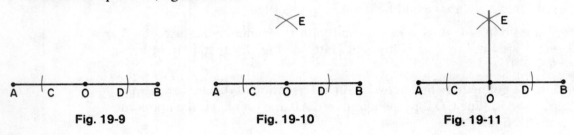

Fig. 19-9   **Fig. 19-10**   **Fig. 19-11**

Practical Application

The triangular piece shown in figure 19-12 is to be scribed and sheared. The piece is laid out as follows:

The 22-inch base is measured and marked off.

The $10\frac{7}{64}$-inch distance is measured and marked off at point A on the baseline. From point A, a perpendicular to the baseline is constructed.

The construction lines are shown.

The $7\frac{1}{2}$-inch distance is measured and marked off at point B on the constructed perpendicular.

Lines are scribed connecting vertex B with the endpoints of the baseline.

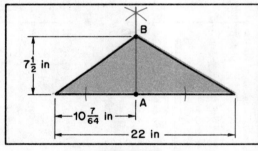

Fig. 19-12

Exercise 19-1

Show construction lines and arcs for each of these problems.

1. Trace each line segment in figure 19-13 and construct perpendicular bisectors to each segment.

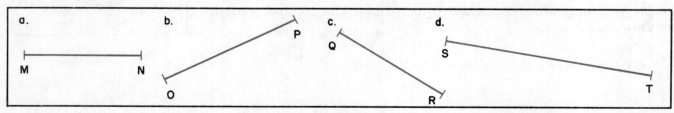

Fig. 19-13

2. Trace each line in problems a-c, figure 19-14, and construct perpendiculars to each line at the given points on the lines.

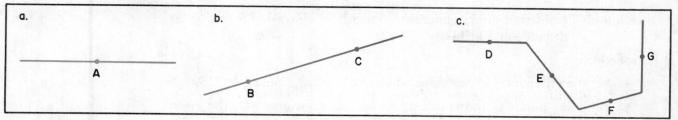

a.

A

b.

B

C

c.

D

E

F

G

Fig. 19-14

3. With a compass, draw a circle 2 inches in diameter. By construction, locate the center of the circle.

4. Trace the equilateral triangle shown in figure 19-15 and construct a perpendicular bisector to each side of the triangle. Extend the bisectors so they intersect within the triangle. Draw an inscribed circle whose center is the point of intersection of the bisectors. An inscribed circle is a circle in which each side of the triangle touches the circle at only one point (the tangent point).

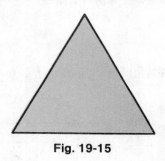

Fig. 19-15

5. Lay out a figure as follows:

   a. Draw a horizontal line and mark off a distance of $2\frac{1}{2}$ inches. Label the left endpoint of the $2\frac{1}{2}$-inch line segment point A and label the right endpoint point D.

   b. From point A and above point A, construct a perpendicular to AD. Mark off a distance of $1\frac{7}{8}$ inches on the perpendicular from point A. Label the top endpoint point B.

   c. From point B and to the right of point B, construct a perpendicular to AB. Mark off a distance of $2\frac{1}{2}$ inches on the perpendicular from point B. Label the right endpoint point C.

   d. From point C and below point C, construct a perpendicular to BC. Mark off a distance of $1\frac{7}{8}$ inches on the perpendicular from point C. If your constructions are accurate the $1\frac{7}{8}$-inch distance marked off coincides with point D.
   What kind of a figure is formed by this construction?

CONSTRUCTION 3.   TO CONSTRUCT A LINE PARALLEL TO A GIVEN LINE AT A GIVEN DISTANCE

Required: Construct a line parallel to line AB in figure 19-16 at a given distance of 1 inch.

Procedure:

- Set the compass to the required distance (1 inch), figure 19-17.

- With any points C and D as centers on AB, draw arcs with the given distance (1 inch) as the radius as shown in figure 19-18.

- Draw a line, EF, that touches each arc at one point (the tangent point) as shown in figure 19-19. Line EF is parallel to line AB and EF is 1 inch from AB.

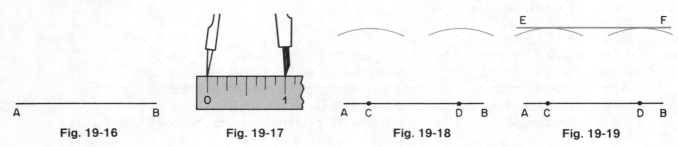

| Fig. 19-16 | Fig. 19-17 | Fig. 19-18 | Fig. 19-19 |

Practical Application

The cutout shown in the drawing, figure 19-20, is laid out on a sheet as follows: (Refer to figure 19-21).

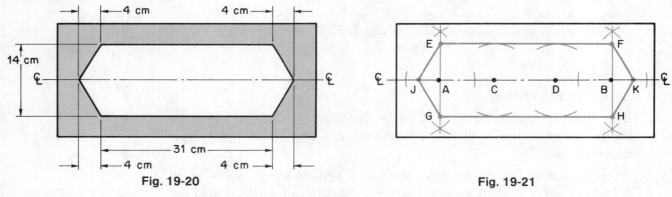

Fig. 19-20   Fig. 19-21

The centerline (℄) is scribed and the 31-cm distance is marked off. Points A and B are the endpoints of the 31-cm segment.

From points A and B perpendiculars are constructed. The perpendiculars are extended more than 7 cm (14 cm ÷ 2) above and below AB.

With points C and D as centers on AB, 7-cm radius arcs are drawn above and below AB. A line is scribed above and a line is scribed below AB touching the pairs of arcs. The lines are extended to intersect the perpendiculars constructed. The points of intersection are E, F, G, and H.

From point A and from point B on AB, 4-cm distances are marked off. Point J and point K are the endpoints.

Lines are scribed connecting J to E and G and connecting K to F and H. Scribed figure JEFKHG is the required cutout.

CONSTRUCTION 4.   TO BISECT A GIVEN ANGLE

Required: Bisect ∠ABC in figure 19-22.

Procedure:

- With point B as the center, draw an arc intersecting sides BA and BC at points D and E as shown in figure 19-22.

- With D as the center, and with a radius equal to more than half the distance DE, draw an arc. With E as the center, and with the same radius, draw an arc. The intersection of the two arcs is point F as shown in figure 19-23.

- Draw a line from point B to point F. Line BF is the bisector of ∠ABC as shown in figure 19-24.

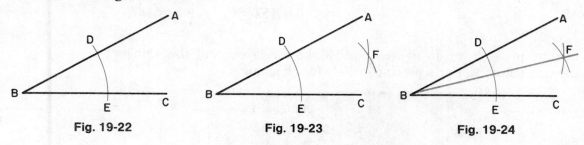

Fig. 19-22   Fig. 19-23   Fig. 19-24

Practical Application

The centers of the three $\frac{1}{2}$-inch diameter holes in the mounting plate shown in figure 19-25 are located and center punched. Two $\frac{1}{4}$-inch diameter holes are located by constructing the bisector of ∠ABC as shown, and marking and centerpunching the $1\frac{3}{8}$-inch and $4\frac{1}{4}$-inch hole center locations on the bisector.

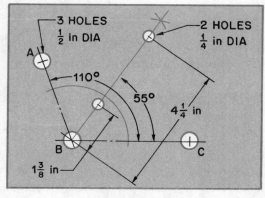

Fig. 19-25

Exercise 19-2

Show construction lines and arcs for each of these problems.

1. Trace each of the lines in figure 19-26 and construct a line parallel to the line at a distance of $1\frac{1}{2}$ inches.

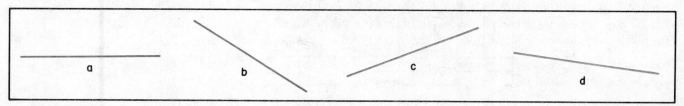

Fig. 19-26

2. Trace each of the angles and construct a bisector to each angle shown in figure 19-27.

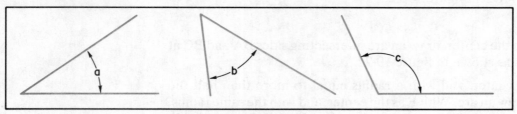

Fig. 19-27

3. Lay out these angles by construction. Check the angle with a protractor, but do not lay out angles with a protractor.

   a. 45°   b. 22°30′   c. 67°30′   d. $157\frac{1}{2}°$ e. $168\frac{3}{4}°$

4. Lay out the plate shown in figure 19-28. Make the layout full size using construction methods. Use a protractor only for checking.

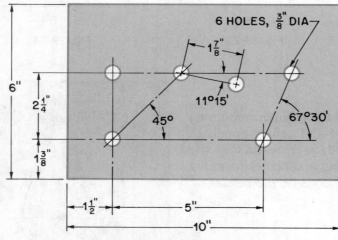

Fig. 19-28

5. Lay out the gage shown in figure 19-29. Make the layout full size using construction methods. Use a protractor only for checking.

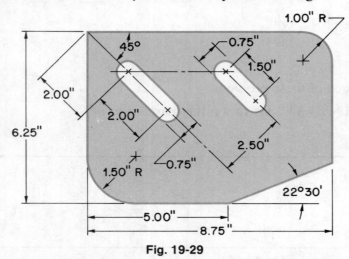

Fig. 19-29

CONSTRUCTION 5.   TO CONSTRUCT TANGENTS TO A CIRCLE FROM AN OUTSIDE POINT

Required: Construct tangents to given circle O from given outside point P shown in figure 19-30.

Procedure:

* Draw a line segment connecting center O and point P. Bisect OP. Point A is the midpoint of OP, figure 19-30.

* With point A as the center and AP as a radius, draw arcs intersecting circle O at points B and C. Points B and C are tangent points, figure 19-31.

* Connect points B and P, and C and P. Line segments BP and CP are tangents, figure 19-32.

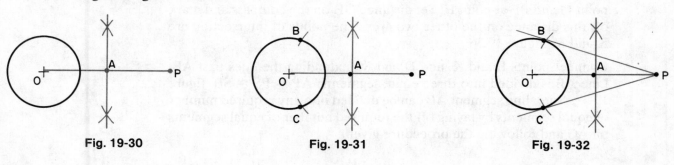

Fig. 19-30   Fig. 19-31   Fig. 19-32

Practical Application

A piece is made as shown in the drawing, figure 19-33.

The piece is laid out as follows: (Refer to figure 19-34.)

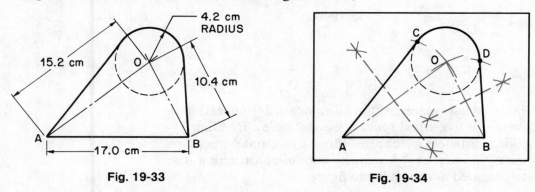

Fig. 19-33   Fig. 19-34

A baseline is scribed and AB (17.0 cm) is marked off.

Distance OA (15.2 cm) is set on dividers and with OA as the radius, an arc is scribed. Distance OB (10.4 cm) is set on dividers and with OB as the radius, an arc is scribed to intersect with the OA radius arc. The intersection of the arcs locates center O of the 4.2-cm radius circle.

Dividers are set to the 4.2-cm radius dimension, and the circle is scribed from center O.

Tangents to the circle from points A and B are constructed resulting in tangent points C and D and tangent line segments AC and BD. The piece is now laid out and ready to be cut to the scribed lines.

CONSTRUCTION 6.   TO DIVIDE A LINE SEGMENT INTO A GIVEN NUMBER OF EQUAL PARTS

Required: Divide line segment AB shown in figure 19-35 into three equal parts.

Procedure:

- From point A, draw line AC forming any convenient angle with AB, figure 19-35.

- On AC, with a compass, lay off any three equal segments, AD, DE, and EF, figure 19-35.

- Connect point F with point B. With centers at points F, E, and D, draw arcs of equal radii. The arc with a center at point F intersects AC at point G and BF at point H. Set distance GH on the compass and mark off this distance on the other two arcs. The points of intersection are K and M, figure 19-36.

- Connect points E and K, and D and M, extending the lines past AB. Line AB is divided into three equal segments; AP = PS = SB, figure 19-37. Note: line segment AB can be divided into any required number of equal segments by laying off the required number of equal segments on AC and following the procedure given.

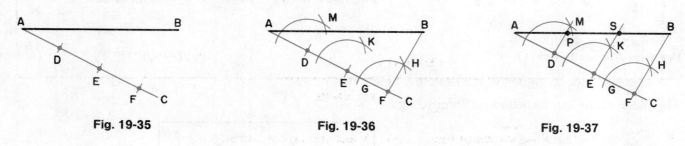

Fig. 19-35   Fig. 19-36   Fig. 19-37

Practical Application

In figure 19-38, six holes are equally spaced within a distance of $2\frac{11}{16}$ inches. Since six holes are required, there are five equal spaces between holes. Dividing $2\frac{11}{16}$ inches by 5 results in fractional distances which are difficult to accurately measure or transfer, such as $\frac{8.6}{16}$ inch, $\frac{17.2}{32}$ inch, or $\frac{34.4}{64}$ inch. By careful construction, the hole centers are accurately located as shown in the figure.

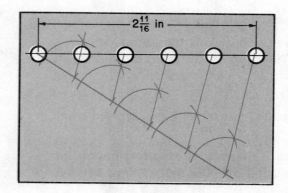

Fig. 19-38

Exercise 19-3

Show construction lines and arcs for each of these problems.

1. Trace each circle and point in figure 19-39 and construct tangents to the circles from the given points.

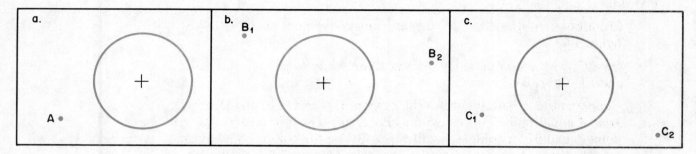

Fig. 19-39

2. Refer to figure 19-40. Trace each line segment of problems a, b, and c. Divide the given lines into the designated number of segments by means of construction.

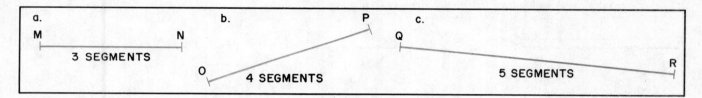

Fig. 19-40

3. Lay out the template shown in figure 19-41. Make the layout full size using construction methods.

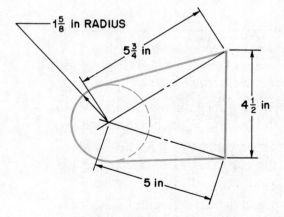

Fig. 19-41

4. Lay out the cutout shown in figure 19-42. Make the layout full size using construction methods.

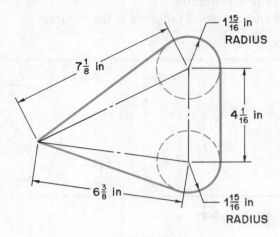

Fig. 19-42

5. Trace the plate shown in figure 19-43. Lay out three sets of holes by construction. Follow the given directions.

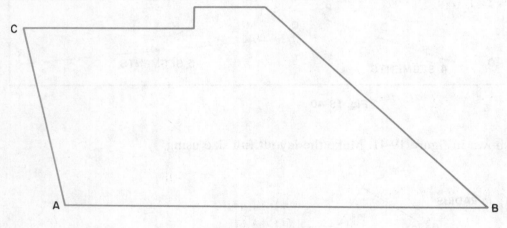

Fig. 19-43

Directions:

- Bisect ∠A and construct 4 equally spaced $\frac{3}{16}$-inch diameter holes. Make the first hole $\frac{7}{8}$ inch from point A and the last hole $2\frac{7}{16}$ inches from point A.

- Bisect ∠B and construct 8 equally spaced $\frac{1}{4}$-inch diameter holes. Make the first hole $\frac{3}{4}$ inch from point B and the last hole $3\frac{11}{16}$ inches from the first hole.

- Bisect ∠C and construct 4 equally spaced $\frac{3}{16}$-inch diameter holes. Make the first hole $\frac{9}{16}$ inch from point C and last hole $2\frac{11}{16}$ inches from point C.

UNIT EXERCISE AND PROBLEM REVIEW

Exercise 19-4

Trace each line, line segment, angle, point, or circle and construct as directed. Show construction lines and arcs for each problem.

1. Construct the perpendicular bisector to MN, figure 19-44.

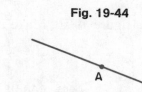

Fig. 19-44

2. Refer to figure 19-45. Construct the perpendicular to the line at the given point A on the line.

Fig. 19-45

3. Refer to figure 19-46. Construct a line parallel to line g at a distance of $1\frac{1}{4}$ inches.

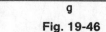

g

Fig. 19-46

4. Construct the bisector of ∠J, figure 19-47.

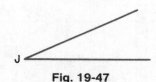

Fig. 19-47

5. Construct the tangent to the circle shown in figure 19-48 at point L.

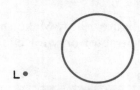

Fig. 19-48

6. Refer to figure 19-49. Divide line segment MN into 3 equal segments.

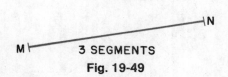

3 SEGMENTS

Fig. 19-49

Lay out these angles by construction. Check the angles with a protractor, but do not lay out angles with a protractor. Show construction lines and arcs.

7. 67°30′   8. $11\frac{1}{4}$°   9. $112\frac{1}{2}$°

Lay out these problems by means of construction. Show construction lines and arcs.

10. With a compass, draw a $2\frac{1}{2}$-inch diameter circle. By construction, locate the center of the circle.

11. Lay out a piece as follows:

    • Construct a rectangle $2\frac{1}{2}$ inches wide and $3\frac{1}{4}$ inches long.

    • Bisect the lower left vertex angle of the rectangle.

    • Bisect the lower right vertex angle of the rectangle.

    • Draw a $1\frac{3}{4}$-inch diameter circle whose center is the point of intersection of the angle bisectors.

12. Lay out the baseplate shown in figure 19-50. Make the layout full size. Use construction methods.

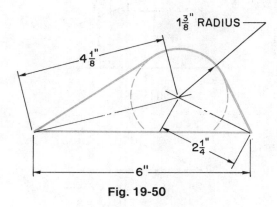

Fig. 19-50

13. Lay out the gage shown in figure 19-51. Make the layout full size. Use construction methods. Use a protractor only for checking.

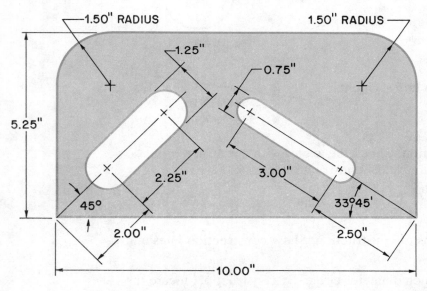

Fig. 19-51

14. Lay out the support bracket shown in figure 19-52. Make the layout full size. Use construction methods.

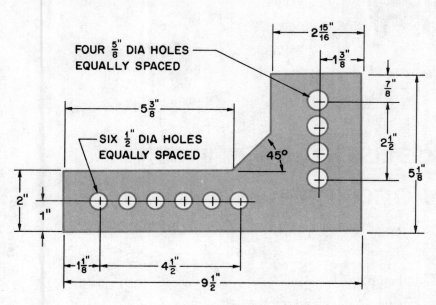

Fig. 19-52

SECTION 4
Measurement

UNIT 20
Degree of Precision, Tolerance, Clearance, and Interference

OBJECTIVES

After studying this unit you should be able to

- determine the degree of precision of any given number.

- compute the greatest possible error of English and metric unit lengths.

- compute total tolerance, maximum limits, and minimum limits of English and metric unit lengths.

- compute maximum and minimum clearances of bilateral and unilateral tolerance dimensioned parts (English and metric).

- compute maximum and minimum interferences of bilateral and unilateral tolerance dimensioned parts (English and metric).

- express unilateral tolerances as bilateral tolerances (English and metric).

- solve practical applied problems involving tolerances, limits, clearances and interferences (English and metric).

DEGREE OF PRECISION

The exact length of an object cannot be measured. All measurements are approximations. By increasing the number of graduations on a measuring instrument, the degree of precision is increased. Increasing the number of graduations enables the user to get closer to the exact length. The precision of a measurement depends on the measuring instrument used. The degree of precision of a measuring instrument depends on the smallest graduated unit of the instrument.

The degree of precision necessary in different trades varies. In building construction, generally $\frac{1}{16}$-inch or 2-millimetre precision is adequate. Sheet metal technicians often work to $\frac{1}{32}$-inch or 1-millimetre precision. Machinists and automobile mechanics usually work to 0.001-inch or 0.02-millimetre precision. In the manufacture of some products, very precise measurements to 0.000 01 inch or 0.000 3 millimetre and 0.000 001 inch or 0.000 03 millimetre are sometimes required.

Various measuring instruments have different limitations on the degree of precision possible. The accuracy achieved in measurement does not only depend

300

on the limitations of the measuring instrument. Accuracy can also be affected by errors of measurement. Errors can be caused by defects in the measuring instruments and by environmental changes such as differences in temperature. Perhaps the greatest cause of error is the inaccuracy of the person using the measuring instrument.

COMMON LINEAR MEASURING INSTRUMENTS

Tape Measure. Tape measures, figure 20-1, are commonly used by garment makers and tailors. English tape measures are generally 5 feet long with $\frac{1}{8}$ inch the smallest graduation. Therefore, the degree of precision is $\frac{1}{8}$ inch. Metric tape measures are generally 2 metres long with 1 millimetre the smallest graduation. The degree of precision for a metric tape measure is 1 millimetre.

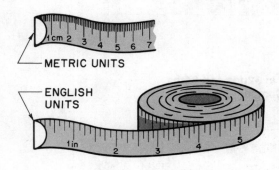

Fig. 20-1 Tape measure

Folding Rule. Folding rules, figure 20-2, are used by construction workers such as carpenters, cabinetmakers, electricians, and masons. English rules are generally 6 feet long and fold to 6 inches. The smallest graduation is usually $\frac{1}{16}$ inch. The smallest graduation on metric rules is generally 1 millimetre. English units and metric units are available on the same rule. The English units are on one side of the rule and the metric units are on the opposite side.

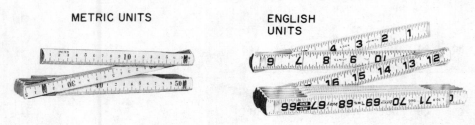

Fig. 20-2 Folding rule
(The Cooper Group, Lufkin Measuring Tools)

Steel Tape. Steel tapes, figure 20-3, are used by contractors, construction workers, and surveyors. English steel tapes are available in 25-foot, 50-foot, and 100-foot lengths. Generally, the smallest graduation is $\frac{1}{8}$ inch. Metric tapes are available in 10-metre, 15-metre, 20-metre, and 30-metre lengths. Generally, the smallest graduation is 1 millimetre. English units and metric units are also available on the same tape. English units are on one side of the tape and metric units are on the opposite side.

Fig. 20-3 Steel tape
(The L.S. Starrett Company)

Steel Rules. Steel rules, figures 20-4, 20-5, and 20-6, are widely used in manufacturing industries by machine operators, machinists, and sheet metal technicians. English steel rules are available in sizes from 1 inch to 144 inches; 6 inches is the most common length. English rules are available in both fractional and decimal-inch graduations. The smallest graduation on fractional rules is 64ths inch; the smallest graduation on a decimal-inch is 0.01 inch. Metric measure steel rules are available in a range from 150 millimetres to 1 000 millimetres (1 metre) in length. The smallest graduation is 0.5 millimetre.

Fig. 20-4
English rule with graduations in 32nds and 64ths
(The L.S. Starrett Company)

Fig. 20-5
English rule with decimal graduations in 50ths and 100ths
(The L.S. Starrett Company)

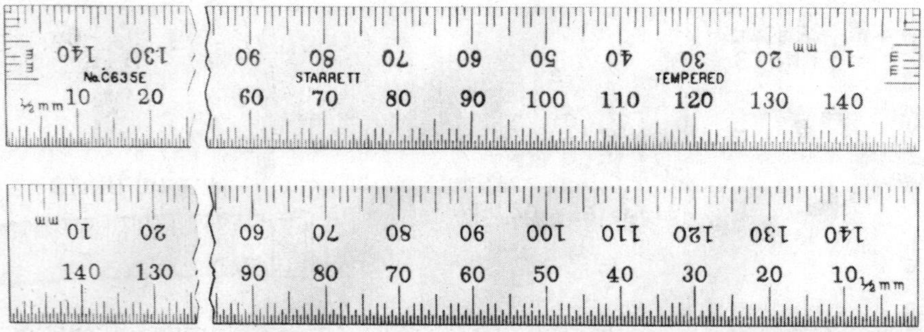

Fig. 20-6 Metric rule
(The L.S. Starrett Company)

Vernier and Dial Calipers. Vernier calipers, figure 20-7, and dial calipers, figure 20-8, are widely used in the metal trades. The most common English unit lengths are 6 inches and 12 inches, although calipers are available in up to 72-inch lengths. The smallest unit that can be read is 0.001 inch. Metric measure rules are available in lengths from 150 millimetres to 600 millimetres. The smallest unit that can be read is 0.02 millimetre. Some vernier calipers are designed with both English and metric unit scales on the same instrument.

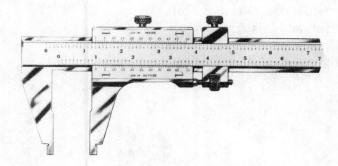

**Fig. 20-7 Vernier caliper
(The L.S. Starrett Company)**

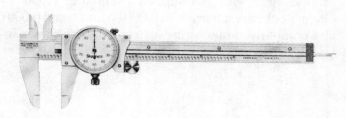

**Fig. 20-8 Dial caliper
(The L.S. Starrett Company)**

Micrometers. Micrometers, figures 20-9 and 20-10, are used by tool and die makers, automobile mechanics, and inspectors. Micrometers are used when relatively high precision measurements are required. There are many different types and sizes of micrometers. English outside micrometers are available in sizes from 0.5 inch to 60 inches. The smallest graduation is 0.000 1 inch with a vernier attachment. Metric outside micrometers are available in sizes up to 600 millimetres. The smallest graduation is 0.002 millimetre with a vernier attachment.

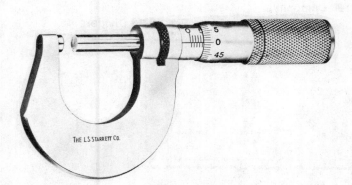

**Fig. 20-9 Metric outside micrometer
(The L.S. Starrett Company)**

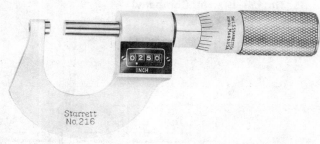

**Fig. 20-10 English digital outside micrometer
(The L.S. Starrett Company)**

TRANSFER AND COMPARISON MEASUREMENT

Tapes, rules, calipers, and micrometers are direct measurement instruments. Measured lengths are read directly on these instruments. It is sometimes not practical or possible to read a measurement directly. Measurements can then be made by transfer or comparison instruments.

Calipers, dividers, and trammels are transfer measuring instruments. Dial indicators, gage blocks, and high amplification comparators (mechanical, optical, pneumatic, and electronic) are comparison measuring instruments. These instruments are available in a variety of types and dial graduations. Dial indicators are available with graduations as small as 0.000 05 inch and 0.002 millimetre. Gage blocks are accurate to 0.000 002 inch and 0.000 06 millimetre. Some transfer and comparison measuring instruments are shown in figures 20-11 through 20-16.

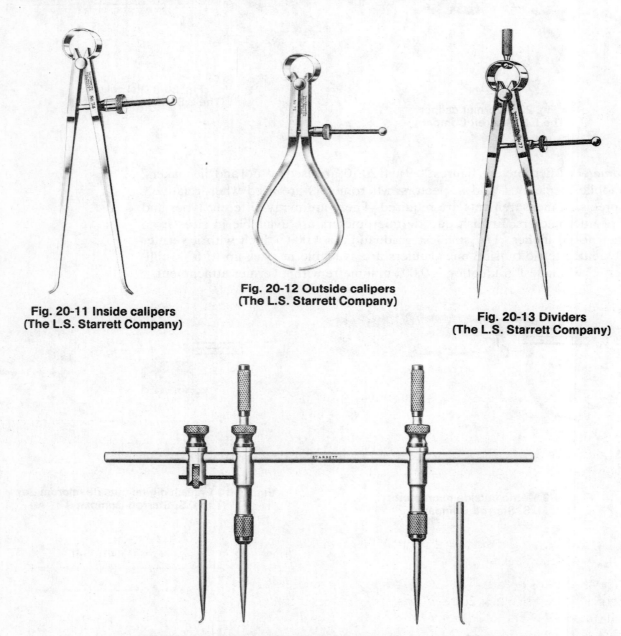

**Fig. 20-11 Inside calipers
(The L.S. Starrett Company)**

**Fig. 20-12 Outside calipers
(The L.S. Starrett Company)**

**Fig. 20-13 Dividers
(The L.S. Starrett Company)**

Fig. 20-14 Steel beam trammels (The L.S. Starrett Company)

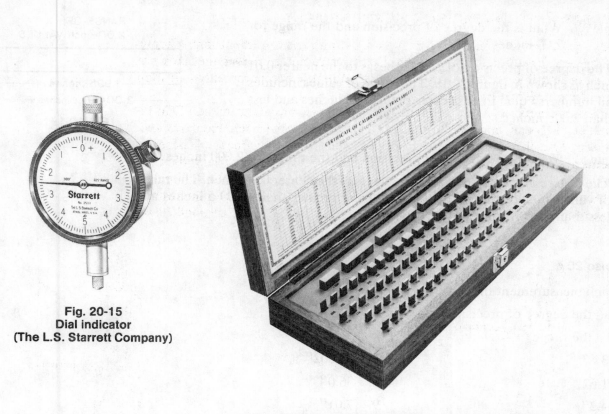

**Fig. 20-15
Dial indicator
(The L.S. Starrett Company)**

Fig. 20-16 Gage block set (Brown & Sharpe Mfg. Co.)

DEGREE OF PRECISION OF NUMBERS

The degree of precision of a number or measurement depends upon the number of decimal places used. The number becomes more precise as the number of decimal places increases. The range includes all of the values which are represented by the number.

Example 1.   What is the degree of precision and the range for 2 inches?

The degree of precision of 2 inches is to the nearer inch as shown in figure 20-17. The range of values includes all numbers equal to or greater than 1.5 inches or less than 2.5 inches.

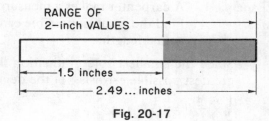

Fig. 20-17

Example 2.   What is the degree of precision and the range for 2.0 inches?

The degree of precision of 2.0 inches is to the nearer 0.1 inch as shown in figure 20-18. The range of values includes all numbers equal to or greater than 1.95 inches and less than 2.05 inches.

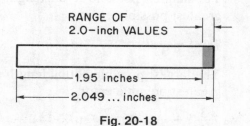

Fig. 20-18

Example 3.   What is the degree of precision and the range for 2.00 inches?

The degree of precision of 2.00 inches is to the nearer 0.01 inch as shown in figure 20-19. The range of values includes all numbers equal to or greater than 1.995 inches and less than 2.005 inches.

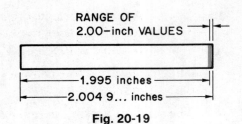

Fig. 20-19

Example 4.   What is the degree of precision and the range for 2.000 inches?

The degree of precision of 2.000 inches is to the nearer 0.001 inch. The range of values includes all numbers equal to or greater than 1.999 5 inches and less than 2.000 5 inches.

Exercise 20-1

For each measurement find

    a. the degree of precision

    b. the range

1.	3.6″	7.	12.002″
2.	1.62″	8.	36.0″
3.	4.3″	9.	7.01″
4.	7.08″	10.	23.00″
5.	15.885″	11.	9.1″
6.	9.183 7″	12.	14.010 70″

GREATEST POSSIBLE ERROR

The *greatest possible error* of a measurement is one-half the smallest graduated unit of the measuring instrument used to make the measurement. Therefore, the greatest possible error is equal to $\frac{1}{2}$ or 0.5 of the degree of precision.

Example 1.   A carpenter makes a measurement of $7\frac{3}{16}$ inches with a folding rule. Find the greatest possible error and the smallest and largest possible actual length.

Since the smallest rule graduation is $\frac{1}{16}$ inch, the precision is $\frac{1}{16}$ inch. The greatest possible error is $\frac{1}{2}$ of the degree of precision.

$$\frac{1}{2} \times \frac{1}{16}'' = \frac{1}{32}'' \ Ans$$

The smallest possible actual length is equal to the measured length minus the greatest possible error.

$$7\frac{3}{16}'' - \frac{1}{32}'' = 7\frac{5}{32}'' \ Ans$$

The largest possible actual length is equal to the measured length plus the greatest possible error.

$$7\frac{3}{16}'' + \frac{1}{32}'' = 7\frac{7}{32}'' \ Ans$$

Example 2. A metal fabricator reads a measurement of 24 millimetres on a steel rule. Find the greatest possible error and the smallest and largest possible actual length.

The greatest possible error is 0.5 of the degree of precision.
0.5×1 mm = **0.5 mm** *Ans*

The smallest possible actual length is equal to the measured length minus the greatest possible error.
24 mm − 0.5 mm = **23.5** *Ans*

The largest possible actual length is equal to the measured length plus the greatest possible error.
24 mm + 0.5 mm = **24.5 mm** *Ans*

Example 3. A tool and die maker makes a measurement of 0.375 8 inch with a vernier micrometer. Find the greatest possible error and the smallest and largest possible actual length.

The greatest possible error is 0.5 of the degree of precision.
$0.5 \times 0.000\ 1'' =$ **0.000 05″** *Ans*

The smallest possible actual length is equal to the measured length minus the greatest possible error.
$0.375\ 8'' - 0.000\ 05'' =$ **0.375 75″** *Ans*

The largest possible actual length is equal to the measured length plus the greatest possible error.
$0.375\ 8'' + 0.000\ 05'' =$ **0.375 85″** *Ans*

Exercise 20-2

For each of the exercises in the tables in figures 20-20 and 20-21 the measurement made and the smallest graduation of the measuring instrument used is given. Determine the greatest possible error and the smallest and largest possible actual length for each exercise.

English System Exercises

	MEASUREMENT MADE (inches)	SMALLEST GRADUATION OF MEASURING INSTRUMENT USED (inches)	GREATEST POSSIBLE ERROR (inches)	ACTUAL LENGTH	
				SMALLEST POSSIBLE (inches)	LARGEST POSSIBLE (inches)
1.	$23\frac{7}{16}$	(folding rule) $\frac{1}{16}$			
2.	$5\frac{7}{8}$	(tape measure) $\frac{1}{8}$			
3.	15.68	(steel rule) 0.02			
4.	8.30	(steel rule) 0.05			
5.	0.753	(vernier caliper) 0.001			
6.	0.936 9	(vernier micrometer) 0.000 1			

Fig. 20-20

Metric System Exercises

	MEASUREMENT MADE (millimetres)	SMALLEST GRADUATION OF MEASURING INSTRUMENT USED (millimetres)	GREATEST POSSIBLE ERROR (millimetres)	ACTUAL LENGTH	
				SMALLEST POSSIBLE (millimetres)	LARGEST POSSIBLE (millimetres)
7.	75	(tape measure) 2			
8.	105	(steel rule) 0.5			
9.	362	(steel tape) 1			
10.	96.5	(steel rule) 0.5			
11.	58.26	(vernier caliper) 0.02			
12.	12.778	(vernier micrometer) 0.002			

Fig. 20-21

TOLERANCE (LINEAR)

Tolerance is the amount of variation permitted for a given length. Tolerance is equal to the difference between the maximum and minimum limits of a given length.

Example 1. The maximum permitted length (limit) of the tapered shaft shown in figure 20-22 is 134.2 millimetres. The minimum permitted length (limit) is 133.4 millimetres. Find the tolerance.

The tolerance equals the maximum limit minus the minimum limit.
134.2 mm − 133.4 mm = **0.8 mm** *Ans*

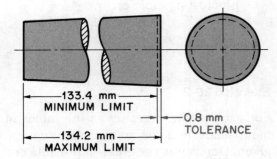

Fig. 20-22 Tapered shaft

Example 2. The maximum permitted depth (limit) of the dado joint shown in figure 20-23 is $\frac{21}{32}$ inch. The tolerance is $\frac{1}{16}$ inch. Find the minimum permitted depth (limit).

The minimum limit equals the maximum limit minus the tolerance.

$$\frac{21}{32}'' - \frac{1}{16}'' = \frac{19}{32}'' \ Ans$$

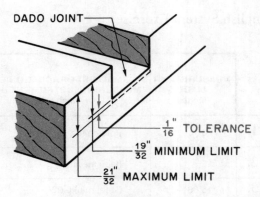

Fig. 20-23 Dado joint

Exercise 20-3

Refer to the tables in figures 20-24 and 20-25 and determine the tolerance, maximum limit, or minimum limit as required for each exercise.

English System Exercises

	TOLERANCE	MAXIMUM LIMIT	MINIMUM LIMIT
1.		$5\frac{7}{16}''$	$5\frac{13}{32}''$
2.		$7'-9\frac{1}{16}''$	$7'-8\frac{15}{16}''$
3.	0.02″	16.76″	
4.	0.007″		0.904″
5.		1.700 1″	1.699 8″
6.	0.005″		10.999″

Fig. 20-24

Metric System Exercises

	TOLERANCE	MAXIMUM LIMIT	MINIMUM LIMIT
7.		50.7 mm	49.8 mm
8.		26.8 cm	26.6 cm
9.	0.04 mm		258.03 mm
10.	0.12 mm	80.09 mm	
11.	0.006 cm		12.731 cm
12.		4.01 mm	3.98 mm

Fig. 20-25

UNILATERAL TOLERANCE

A *basic dimension* is the standard size from which the maximum and minimum limits are made. *Unilateral tolerance* means that the total tolerance is taken in only one direction from the basic dimension. *Clearance* is the distance between two surfaces. For circular section objects, clearance is the difference between the two diameters.

A shaft requires a hole clearance such that the diameter of the hole is larger than the diameter of the shaft regardless of how the tolerances are combined. These examples are applications of unilateral tolerances where clearances are required between shafts and holes.

Example 1. Refer to figure 20-26 and determine the following:

a. Maximum shaft diameter

    1.385″ + 0.000″ = **1.385″** *Ans*

b. Minimum shaft diameter

    1.385″ − 0.002″ = **1.383″** *Ans*

c. Maximum hole diameter

    1.387″ + 0.002″ = **1.389″** *Ans*

d. Minimum hole diameter

    1.387″ − 0.000″ = **1.387″** *Ans*

e. Maximum clearance equals maximum hole diameter minus minimum shaft diameter

    1.389″ − 1.383″ = **0.006″** *Ans*

f. Minimum clearance equals minimum hole diameter minus maximum shaft diameter

    1.387″ − 1.385″ = **0.002″** *Ans*

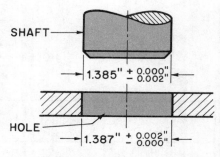

SHAFT

$1.385'' \begin{array}{l} + \ 0.000'' \\ - \ 0.002'' \end{array}$

HOLE

$1.387'' \begin{array}{l} + \ 0.002'' \\ - \ 0.000'' \end{array}$

BASIC SHAFT DIA = 1.385″
BASIC HOLE DIA = 1.387″

Fig. 20-26

Example 2.   Refer to figure 20-27 and determine the following:

a. Maximum shaft diameter

   53.97 mm + 0.00 mm = **53.97 mm** *Ans*

b. Minimum shaft diameter

   53.97 mm − 0.07 mm = **53.90 mm** *Ans*

c. Maximum hole diameter

   54.05 mm + 0.07 mm = **54.12 mm** *Ans*

d. Minimum hole diameter

   54.05 mm − 0.00 mm = **54.05 mm** *Ans*

e. Maximum clearance equals maximum hole diameter minus minimum shaft diameter

   54.12 mm − 53.90 mm = **0.22 mm** *Ans*

f. Minimum clearance equals minimum hole diameter minus maximum shaft diameter

   54.05 mm − 53.97 mm = **0.08 mm** *Ans*

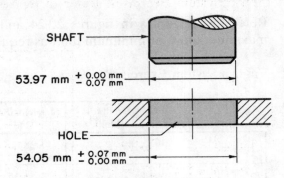

53.97 mm $\pm$ 0.00 mm / 0.07 mm

54.05 mm $\pm$ 0.07 mm / 0.00 mm

BASIC SHAFT DIA = 53.97 mm
BASIC HOLE DIA = 54.05 mm

Fig. 20-27

Exercise 20-4

These exercises require computations with unilateral tolerance clearance fits between mating parts. Given dimensions A and B, compute the missing values in the tables.

English System Exercises. Refer to figure 20-28 to determine the table values in figure 20-29. The values for exercise 1 are given.

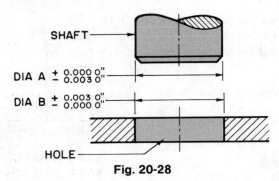

DIA A $\pm$ 0.000 0" / 0.003 0"

DIA B $\pm$ 0.003 0" / 0.000 0"

Fig. 20-28

		BASIC DIMENSION (inches)	MAXIMUM DIAMETER (inches)	MINIMUM DIAMETER (inches)	MAXIMUM CLEARANCE (inches)	MINIMUM CLEARANCE (inches)
1.	DIA A	1.458 0	1.458 0	1.455 0	0.009 0	0.003 0
	DIA B	1.461 0	1.464 0	1.461 0		
2.	DIA A	0.934 5				
	DIA B	0.936 5				
3.	DIA A	2.105 3				
	DIA B	2.107 8				
4.	DIA A	0.687 2				
	DIA B	0.688 0				
5.	DIA A	0.999 6				
	DIA B	1.000 7				

Fig. 20-29

Metric System Exercises. Refer to figure 20-30 to determine the table values in figure 20-31.

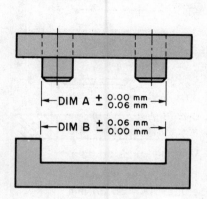

←DIM A $\pm$ 0.00 mm / 0.06 mm→

←DIM B $\pm$ 0.06 mm / 0.00 mm→

Fig. 20-30

		BASIC DIMENSION (millimetres)	MAXIMUM DIMENSION (millimetres)	MINIMUM DIMENSION (millimetres)	MAXIMUM CLEARANCE (millimetres)	MINIMUM CLEARANCE (millimetres)
6.	DIM A	26.25				
	DIM B	26.32				
7.	DIM A	40.12				
	DIM B	40.18				
8.	DIM A	14.97				
	DIM B	15.01				
9.	DIM A	56.73				
	DIM B	56.75				
10.	DIM A	18.99				
	DIM B	19.02				

Fig. 20-31

BILATERAL TOLERANCE

Bilateral tolerance means that tolerance is divided partly above (+) and partly below (−) the basic dimension. This example shows bilateral tolerances where clearance is required between shaft and hole.

Example.   Refer to figure 20-32 and determine the following:

a. Maximum shaft diameter

   0.750 2″ + 0.000 8″ = **0.751 0″** *Ans*

b. Minimum shaft diameter

   0.750 2″ − 0.000 8″ = **0.749 4″** *Ans*

c. Maximum hole diameter

   0.753 6″ + 0.000 8″ = **0.754 4″** *Ans*

d. Minimum hole diameter

   0.753 6″ − 0.000 8″ = **0.752 8″** *Ans*

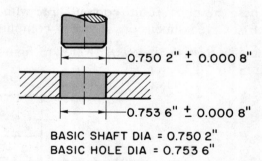

—0.750 2″ $\pm$ 0.000 8″

—0.753 6″ $\pm$ 0.000 8″

BASIC SHAFT DIA = 0.750 2″
BASIC HOLE DIA = 0.753 6″

Fig. 20-32

e. Maximum clearance equals maximum hole diameter minus minimum shaft diameter

   0.754 4″ − 0.749 4″ = **0.005 0″** *Ans*

f. Minimum clearance equals minimum hole diameter minus maximum shaft diameter

   0.752 8″ − 0.751 0″ = **0.001 8″** *Ans*

Figure 20-33 shows a pin which is to be pressed into a hole. This is an example of a forced or interference fit. A *forced or interference fit* means that the hole diameter is smaller than the pin diameter regardless of how the tolerances are combined. This example shows bilateral tolerance where an interference fit is required between pin and hole.

Example.   Refer to figure 20-33 and determine the following:

a. Maximum pin diameter

   35.28 mm + 0.01 mm = **35.29 mm** *Ans*

b. Minimum pin diameter

   35.28 mm − 0.01 mm = **35.27 mm** *Ans*

c. Maximum hole diameter

   35.24 mm + 0.01 mm = **35.25 mm** *Ans*

d. Minimum hole diameter

   35.24 mm − 0.01 mm = **35.23 mm** *Ans*

e. Maximum interference equals maximum pin diameter minus minimum hole diameter

   35.29 mm − 35.23 mm = **0.06 mm** *Ans*

f. Minimum interference equals minimum pin diameter minus maximum hole diameter

   35.27 mm − 35.25 mm = **0.02 mm** *Ans*

35.28 mm ± 0.01 mm

35.24 mm ± 0.01 mm

BASIC PIN DIA = 32.28 mm
BASIC HOLE DIA = 35.24 mm

Fig. 20-33

Exercise 20-5

These exercises require computations with bilateral clearance fits between mating parts. Given dimensions A and B, compute the missing values in the tables.

English System Exercises. Refer to figure 20-34 to determine the table values in figure 20-35.

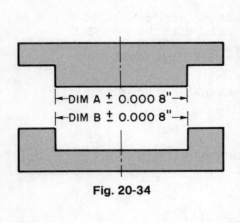

←DIM A ± 0.000 8"→
←DIM B ± 0.000 8"→

Fig. 20-34

		BASIC DIMENSION (inches)	MAXIMUM DIMENSION (inches)	MINIMUM DIMENSION (inches)	MAXIMUM CLEARANCE (inches)	MINIMUM CLEARANCE (inches)
1.	DIM A	0.839 2	0.840 0	0.838 4	0.003 6	0.000 4
	DIM B	0.841 2	0.842 0	0.840 4		
2.	DIM A	2.137 7				
	DIM B	2.140 5				
3.	DIM A	0.999 5				
	DIM B	1.002 0				
4.	DIM A	2.055 4				
	DIM B	2.058 0				
5.	DIM A	1.439 2				
	DIM B	1.441 2				

Fig. 20-35

Metric System Exercises. Refer to figure 20-36 to determine the table values in figure 20-37.

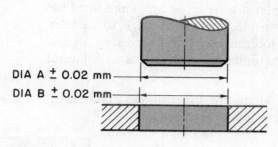

DIA A ± 0.02 mm
DIA B ± 0.02 mm

Fig. 20-36

		BASIC DIMENSION (millimetres)	MAXIMUM DIAMETER (millimetres)	MINIMUM DIAMETER (millimetres)	MAXIMUM INTERFERENCE (millimetres)	MINIMUM INTERFERENCE (millimetres)
6.	DIA A	20.73				
	DIA B	20.68				
7.	DIA A	32.07				
	DIA B	32.01				
8.	DIA A	10.82				
	DIA B	10.75				
9.	DIA A	47.02				
	DIA B	46.97				
10.	DIA A	26.73				
	DIA B	26.65				

Fig. 20-37

MEAN DIMENSION

A *mean dimension* is a value which is midway between the maximum and minimum limits. Where bilateral dimensioning is used and the plus and minus tolerances are the same, the mean dimension is equal to the basic dimension. This example shows a method commonly used in actual practice in determining mean dimensions.

Example. What is the mean dimension of a part if the maximum dimension (limit) is 38.65 mm and the minimum dimension (limit) is 38.57 mm?

Subtract: 38.65 mm − 38.57 mm = 0.08 mm

Divide: 0.08 mm ÷ 2 = 0.04 mm

Subtract: 38.65 mm − 0.04 mm = **38.61 mm** *Ans*

Notice that 38.61 mm is midway between 38.65 mm and 38.57 mm.

(Mean Dimension) 38.61 mm $\begin{array}{l} + \ 0.04 \text{ mm} = 38.65 \text{ mm (Max Limit)} \\ - \ 0.04 \text{ mm} = 38.57 \text{ mm (Min Limit)} \end{array}$

EXPRESSING UNILATERAL TOLERANCE AS BILATERAL TOLERANCE

In the manufacture of a part, given unilateral tolerances are sometimes expressed as bilateral tolerances. A technician may prefer to work to a mean dimension and take equal plus and minus tolerances while processing a part. This example shows the steps in expressing unilateral tolerances as bilateral tolerances.

Example. Figure 20-38 shows mating parts which are dimensioned unilaterally. Express the unilateral tolerances as bilateral tolerances.

Top piece

Divide the total tolerance by 2.

$0.002\ 8'' \div 2 = 0.001\ 4''$

Determine the mean dimension.

$1.258\ 0'' - 0.001\ 4'' = 1.256\ 6''$

Show as a bilateral tolerance.

1.256 6″ ± 0.001 4″ Ans

Bottom piece

Divide total tolerance by 2.

$0.002\ 8'' \div 2 = 0.001\ 4''$

Determine the mean dimension.

$1.259\ 0'' + 0.001\ 4'' = 1.260\ 4''$

Show as a bilateral tolerance.

1.260 4″ ± 0.001 4″ Ans

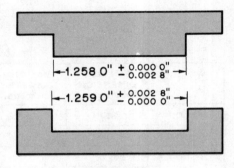

$\leftarrow 1.258\ 0'' \ {}^{+\ 0.000\ 0''}_{-\ 0.002\ 8''} \rightarrow$

$\leftarrow 1.259\ 0'' \ {}^{+\ 0.002\ 8''}_{-\ 0.000\ 0''} \rightarrow$

Fig. 20-38

Exercise 20-6

Given the maximum and minimum limits, determine the mean dimension in each exercise in the tables in figure 20-39 and figure 20-40.

English System

	MAXIMUM LIMIT	MINIMUM LIMIT	MEAN DIMENSION
1.	3.783″	3.775″	
2.	0.537 0″	0.536 4″	
3.	$9\frac{7}{8}''$	$9\frac{27}{32}''$	
4.	18.020″	17.990″	
5.	$7'-5\frac{1}{2}''$	$7'-5\frac{3}{8}''$	
6.	0.201 0″	0.198 0″	

Fig. 20-39

Metric System

	MAXIMUM LIMIT	MINIMUM LIMIT	MEAN DIMENSION
7.	16.8 mm	16.2 mm	
8.	5.03 cm	4.97 cm	
9.	1.006 3 m	1.005 7 m	
10.	126.2 mm	125.9 mm	
11.	7.316 cm	7.315 cm	
12.	89.95 mm	89.92 mm	

Fig. 20-40

Express each of these unilateral tolerances as bilateral tolerances having equal plus and minus values.

English System

13. $0.738'' \begin{array}{l} + 0.010'' \\ - 0.000'' \end{array}$

14. $0.738'' \begin{array}{l} + 0.000'' \\ - 0.010'' \end{array}$

15. $2.000'' \begin{array}{l} + 0.000'' \\ - 0.002'' \end{array}$

16. $3.485'' \begin{array}{l} + 0.006'' \\ - 0.000'' \end{array}$

17. $0.193\,0'' \begin{array}{l} + 0.003\,0'' \\ - 0.000\,0'' \end{array}$

18. $1.001\,2'' \begin{array}{l} + 0.000\,0'' \\ - 0.007\,4'' \end{array}$

19. $0.999\,8'' \begin{array}{l} + 0.001\,8'' \\ - 0.000\,0'' \end{array}$

20. $0.008\,0'' \begin{array}{l} + 0.000\,0'' \\ - 0.001\,2'' \end{array}$

21. $4.467\,3'' \begin{array}{l} + 0.000\,0'' \\ - 0.001\,0'' \end{array}$

22. $3.569\,0'' \begin{array}{l} + 0.005\,4'' \\ - 0.000\,0'' \end{array}$

23. $0.387\,3'' \begin{array}{l} + 0.000\,0'' \\ - 0.003\,0'' \end{array}$

24. $10.366\,9'' \begin{array}{l} + 0.002\,2'' \\ - 0.000\,0'' \end{array}$

Metric System

25. $38.6 \text{ mm} \begin{array}{l} + 0.2 \text{ mm} \\ - 0.0 \text{ mm} \end{array}$

26. $25.1 \text{ mm} \begin{array}{l} + 0.0 \text{ mm} \\ - 0.2 \text{ mm} \end{array}$

27. $10.06 \text{ mm} \begin{array}{l} + 0.00 \text{ mm} \\ - 0.08 \text{ mm} \end{array}$

28. $64.89 \text{ mm} \begin{array}{l} + 0.06 \text{ mm} \\ - 0.00 \text{ mm} \end{array}$

29. $104.1 \text{ mm} \begin{array}{l} + 0.0 \text{ mm} \\ - 0.2 \text{ mm} \end{array}$

30. $9.9 \text{ mm} \begin{array}{l} + 0.6 \text{ mm} \\ - 0.0 \text{ mm} \end{array}$

31. $37.98 \text{ mm} \begin{array}{l} + 0.90 \text{ mm} \\ - 0.00 \text{ mm} \end{array}$

32. $5.2 \text{ mm} \begin{array}{l} + 0.0 \text{ mm} \\ - 0.4 \text{ mm} \end{array}$

33. $66.66 \text{ mm} \begin{array}{l} + 0.10 \text{ mm} \\ - 0.00 \text{ mm} \end{array}$

34. $250.8 \text{ mm} \begin{array}{l} + 0.6 \text{ mm} \\ - 0.0 \text{ mm} \end{array}$

35. $43.091 \text{ mm} \begin{array}{l} + 0.000 \text{ mm} \\ - 0.030 \text{ mm} \end{array}$

36. $79.97 \text{ mm} \begin{array}{l} + 0.12 \text{ mm} \\ - 0.00 \text{ mm} \end{array}$

UNIT EXERCISE AND PROBLEM REVIEW

Exercise 20-7

DEGREE OF PRECISION OF NUMBERS

For each measurement find

   a. the degree of precision
   b. the range

1. $5.3''$

2. $2.78''$

3. $1.834''$

4. $12.9''$

5. $19.001''$

6. $19.1''$

7. $29.0''$

8. $6.108\,8''$

GREATEST POSSIBLE ERROR

For each of the exercises in the tables in figures 20-41 and 20-42, the measurement made and the smallest graduation of the measuring instrument used is given. Determine the greatest possible error and the smallest and largest possible actual length for each exercise.

9. English System Exercises

	MEASUREMENT MADE (inches)	SMALLEST GRADUATION OF MEASURING INSTRUMENT USED (inches)	GREATEST POSSIBLE ERROR (inches)	ACTUAL LENGTH	
				SMALLEST POSSIBLE (inches)	LARGEST POSSIBLE (inches)
a.	$18\frac{3}{4}$	(folding rule) $\frac{1}{16}$			
b.	3.25	(steel rule) 0.05			
c.	11.028	(vernier caliper) 0.001			
d.	0.803 1	(vernier micrometer) 0.000 1			

Fig. 20-41

10. Metric System Exercises

	MEASUREMENT MADE (millimetres)	SMALLEST GRADUATION OF MEASURING INSTRUMENT USED (millimetres)	GREATEST POSSIBLE ERROR (millimetres)	ACTUAL LENGTH	
				SMALLEST POSSIBLE (millimetres)	LARGEST POSSIBLE (millimetres)
a.	419	(steel tape) 1			
b.	62	(steel rule) 0.5			
c.	76.44	(vernier caliper) 0.02			
d.	23.086	(vernier micrometer) 0.002			

Fig. 20-42

TOLERANCE

Refer to the tables in figures 20-43 and 20-44 and determine the tolerance, maximum limit, or minimum limit as required for each exercise.

11. English System Exercises

	TOLERANCE	MAXIMUM LIMIT	MINIMUM LIMIT
a.		$7\frac{3}{16}''$	$7\frac{1}{8}''$
b.	$\frac{1}{64}''$	$18\frac{1}{4}''$	
c.	0.006''		2.775''
d.		0.620 1''	0.619 0''

Fig. 20-43

12. Metric System Exercises

	TOLERANCE	MAXIMUM LIMIT	MINIMUM LIMIT
a.		40.3 mm	39.7 mm
b.	0.008 cm		6.502 cm
c.	0.18 mm	78.84 mm	
d.		34.02 cm	33.95 cm

Fig. 20-44

UNILATERAL TOLERANCE

These exercises require computation with unilateral tolerance clearance fits between mating parts. Given dimensions A and B, compute the missing values in the tables.

13. English System Exercises. Refer to figure 20-45 to determine the table values in figure 20-46.

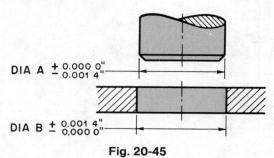

DIA A $\pm^{+\ 0.000\ 0"}_{-\ 0.001\ 4"}$

DIA B $\pm^{+\ 0.001\ 4"}_{-\ 0.000\ 0"}$

Fig. 20-45

		BASIC DIMENSION (inches)	MAXIMUM DIAMETER (inches)	MINIMUM DIAMETER (inches)	MAXIMUM CLEARANCE (inches)	MINIMUM CLEARANCE (inches)
a.	DIA A	1.712 0				
	DIA B	1.713 6				
b.	DIA A	0.296 2				
	DIA B	0.297 0				
c.	DIA A	2.806 4				
	DIA B	2.807 5				

Fig. 20-46

14. Metric System Exercises. Refer to figure 20-47 to determine the table values in figure 20-48.

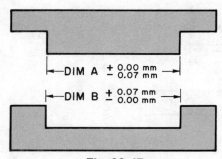

DIM A $\pm^{+\ 0.00\ mm}_{-\ 0.07\ mm}$

DIM B $\pm^{+\ 0.07\ mm}_{-\ 0.00\ mm}$

Fig. 20-47

		BASIC DIMENSION (millimetres)	MAXIMUM DIMENSION (millimetres)	MINIMUM DIMENSION (millimetres)	MAXIMUM CLEARANCE (millimetres)	MINIMUM CLEARANCE (millimetres)
a.	DIM A	61.13				
	DIM B	61.19				
b.	DIM A	23.75				
	DIM B	23.77				
c.	DIM A	120.98				
	DIM B	121.01				

Fig. 20-48

BILATERAL TOLERANCE

These exercises require computations with bilateral tolerances of mating parts. Given dimensions A and B, compute the missing values in the tables.

15. English System Clearance Fit Exercises. Refer to figure 20-49 to determine the table values in figure 20-50.

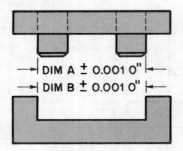

DIM A ± 0.001 0"

DIM B ± 0.001 0"

Fig. 20-49

		BASIC DIMENSION (inches)	MAXIMUM DIMENSION (inches)	MINIMUM DIMENSION (inches)	MAXIMUM CLEARANCE (inches)	MINIMUM CLEARANCE (inches)
a.	DIM A	3.142 5				
	DIM B	3.147 5				
b.	DIM A	5.903 5				
	DIM B	5.906 4				
c.	DIM A	8.076 0				
	DIM B	8.080 6				

Fig. 20-50

16. Metric System Interference Fit Exercises. Refer to figure 20-51 to determine the table values in figure 20-52.

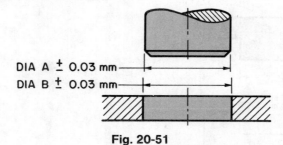

DIA A ± 0.03 mm

DIA B ± 0.03 mm

Fig. 20-51

		BASIC DIMENSION (millimetres)	MAXIMUM DIAMETER (millimetres)	MINIMUM DIAMETER (millimetres)	MAXIMUM INTERFERENCE (millimetres)	MINIMUM INTERFERENCE (millimetres)
a.	DIA A	78.78				
	DIA B	78.70				
b.	DIA A	9.94				
	DIA B	9.85				
c.	DIA A	130.03				
	DIA B	129.96				

Fig. 20-52

MEAN DIMENSION

Given the maximum and minimum limits, determine the mean dimension in each exercise in the tables in figures 20-53 and 20-54.

17. English System

	MAXIMUM LIMIT	MINIMUM LIMIT	MEAN DIMENSION
a.	6.052″	6.044″	
b.	2.326 0″	2.319 0″	
c.	$10\frac{13}{32}″$	$10\frac{3}{8}″$	
d.	$5'-3\frac{1}{64}″$	$5'-2\frac{63}{64}″$	

Fig. 20-53

18. Metric System

	MAXIMUM LIMIT	MINIMUM LIMIT	MEAN DIMENSION
a.	81.7 mm	80.3 mm	
b.	2.01 cm	1.95 cm	
c.	95.640 cm	95.590 cm	
d.	121.030 mm	120.920 mm	

Fig. 20-54

EXPRESSING UNILATERAL TOLERANCES AS BILATERAL TOLERANCES

Express each of these unilateral tolerances as bilateral tolerances having equal plus and minus values.

19.   English System

a. $1.903''\begin{smallmatrix} +\ 0.008'' \\ -\ 0.000'' \end{smallmatrix}$

b. $1.903''\begin{smallmatrix} +\ 0.000'' \\ -\ 0.008'' \end{smallmatrix}$

c. $0.875''\begin{smallmatrix} +\ 0.010'' \\ -\ 0.000'' \end{smallmatrix}$

d. $0.062\ 5''\begin{smallmatrix} +\ 0.003\ 0'' \\ -\ 0.000\ 0'' \end{smallmatrix}$

e. $5.001''\begin{smallmatrix} +\ 0.000\ 0'' \\ -\ 0.001\ 2'' \end{smallmatrix}$

f. $0.999''\begin{smallmatrix} +\ 0.018'' \\ -\ 0.000'' \end{smallmatrix}$

g. $12.560\ 3''\begin{smallmatrix} +\ 0.000\ 0'' \\ -\ 0.001\ 0'' \end{smallmatrix}$

h. $0.601\ 0''\begin{smallmatrix} +\ 0.000\ 0'' \\ -\ 0.000\ 6'' \end{smallmatrix}$

i. $3.999\ 0''\begin{smallmatrix} +\ 0.001\ 4'' \\ -\ 0.000\ 0'' \end{smallmatrix}$

20.   Metric System

a. $80.9\ \text{mm}\begin{smallmatrix} +\ 0.4\ \text{mm} \\ -\ 0.0\ \text{mm} \end{smallmatrix}$

b. $7.7\ \text{mm}\begin{smallmatrix} +\ 0.0\ \text{mm} \\ -\ 0.2\ \text{mm} \end{smallmatrix}$

c. $25.97\ \text{mm}\begin{smallmatrix} +\ 0.08\ \text{mm} \\ -\ 0.00\ \text{mm} \end{smallmatrix}$

d. $133.20\ \text{mm}\begin{smallmatrix} +\ 0.00\ \text{mm} \\ -\ 0.06\ \text{mm} \end{smallmatrix}$

e. $56.31\ \text{mm}\begin{smallmatrix} +\ 0.000\ \text{mm} \\ -\ 0.070\ \text{mm} \end{smallmatrix}$

f. $9.8\ \text{mm}\begin{smallmatrix} +\ 0.4\ \text{mm} \\ -\ 0.0\ \text{mm} \end{smallmatrix}$

g. $203.09\ \text{mm}\begin{smallmatrix} +\ 0.30\ \text{mm} \\ -\ 0.00\ \text{mm} \end{smallmatrix}$

h. $47.870\ \text{mm}\begin{smallmatrix} +\ 0.030\ \text{mm} \\ -\ 0.000\ \text{mm} \end{smallmatrix}$

i. $55.030\ \text{mm}\begin{smallmatrix} +\ 0.000\ \text{mm} \\ -\ 0.090\ \text{mm} \end{smallmatrix}$

PRACTICAL APPLIED PROBLEMS

21. Spacers are manufactured to the mean dimension and tolerance shown in figure 20-55. An inspector measures 10 bushings and records the following thicknesses:

0.372″	0.379″	0.370″	0.377″	0.373″
0.376″	0.375″	0.373″	0.378″	0.380″

Which spacers are defective (above the maximum limit or below the minimum limit)?

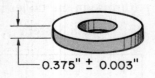

0.375″ ± 0.003″

Fig. 20-55

22. A drafter draws and dimensions the length of the tapered shaft shown in figure 20-56. The maximum permissible length is 150.06 millimetres. The minimum permissible length is 149.98 millimetres. Express the shaft length using bilateral dimensioning with the mean dimension as the basic dimension.

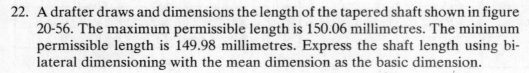

SHAFT LENGTH

Fig. 20-56

23. A cabinetmaker saws a board as shown in figure 20-57. What are the maximum and minimum permissible values of length A?

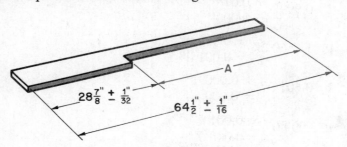

$28\frac{7}{8}'' \pm \frac{1}{32}''$ $64\frac{1}{2}'' \pm \frac{1}{16}''$ A

Fig. 20-57

24. A tool and die maker grinds a pin to an 18.25-millimetre diameter as shown in figure 20-58. The pin is to be pressed (an interference fit) in a hole. The minimum interference allowed is 0.03 millimetre. The maximum interference allowed is 0.07 millimetre. Determine the mean diameter of the hole.

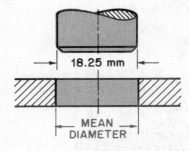

18.25 mm

MEAN DIAMETER

Fig. 20-58

25. A sheet metal technician lays out a job to the dimensions and tolerances shown in figure 20-59. Determine the maximum permissible value of length A.

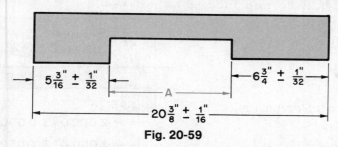

Fig. 20-59

26. Determine the maximum and minimum permissible wall thickness of the steel sleeve shown in figure 20-60.

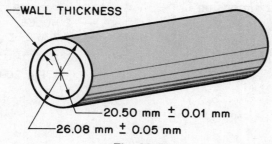

Fig. 20-60

27. The drawing in figure 20-61 gives the locations with tolerances of 6 holes that are to be drilled in a length of angle iron. An ironworker drills the holes then checks them for proper locations from edge A. The actual locations of the drilled holes are shown in figure 20-62. Which holes are drilled out of tolerance (located incorrectly)?

Fig. 20-61

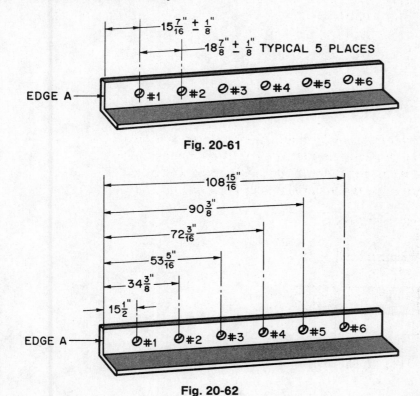

Fig. 20-62

28. Mating parts are shown in figure 20-63. The pins in the top piece fit into the holes in the bottom piece. Determine the following:

   a. The mean pin diameters.

   b. The mean hole diameters.

   c. The maximum dimension A.

   d. The minimum dimension A.

   e. The maximum dimension B.

   f. The minimum dimension B.

   g. The maximum total clearance between dimension C and dimension D.

   h. The minimum total clearance between dimension C and dimension D.

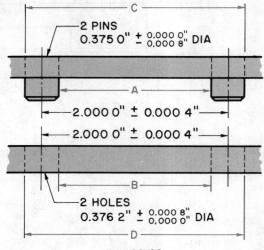

Fig. 20-63

UNIT 21

Steel Rules and Gage Blocks

OBJECTIVES

After studying this unit you should be able to

- read measurements on an English rule graduated in 32nds and 64ths.
- measure given lengths with an English rule to the nearer 32nd inch.
- read measurements on an English rule graduated in 50ths and 100ths.
- measure given lengths with an English rule to the nearer 20th inch.
- read measurements on a metric rule with 1-millimetre and 0.5-millimetre graduations.
- measure given lengths with a metric rule to the nearer millimetre.
- determine combinations of English or metric gage blocks for given dimensions.

TYPES OF STEEL RULES

Steel rules are widely used in the metal trades and in certain woodworking occupations. There are many different types of rules designed for specific job requirements. Steel rules are available in various English and metric graduations. Rules can be obtained in a wide range of lengths, widths, and thicknesses. A few of the many types of steel rules are shown in figures 21-1 through 21-6.

Fig. 21-1 English rule
with graduations in 32nds and 64ths
(The L.S. Starrett Company)

Fig. 21-2 English rule
with decimal graduations in 50ths and 100ths
(The L.S. Starrett Company)

Fig. 21-3 Narrow spring
tempered rule
(The L.S. Starrett Company)

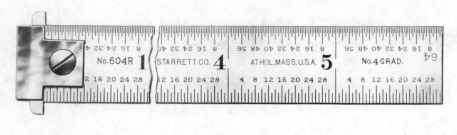

Fig. 21-4 Adjustable steel hook rule
(The L.S. Starrett Company)

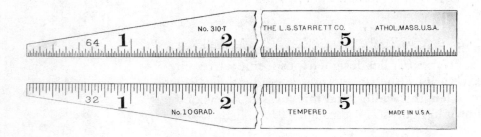

Fig. 21-5 Tapered-end rule
(The L.S. Starrett Company)

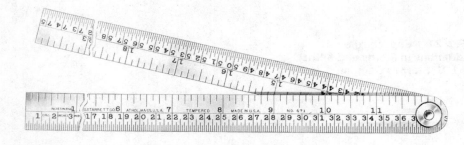

Fig. 21-6 Folding rule
(The L.S. Starrett Company)

CORRECT PROCEDURE IN THE USE OF STEEL RULES

The end of a rule receives more wear than the rest of the rule. Therefore, the end should not be used as a reference point unless it is used with a knee (a straight block), figure 21-7.

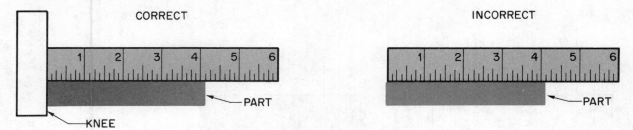

Fig. 21-7

If a knee is not used, the 1-inch graduation of English measure rules should be used as the reference point, figure 21-8. The 1 inch must be subtracted from the English measurement obtained. For metric measure rules, use the 10 millimetre-graduation as the reference point. The 10 millimetres must be subtracted from the metric measurement obtained.

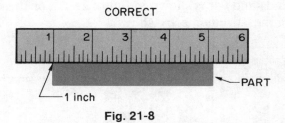

Fig. 21-8

A parallax error is caused by the scale and the part being in different planes. The scale edge of the rule should be placed on the part, figure 21-9.

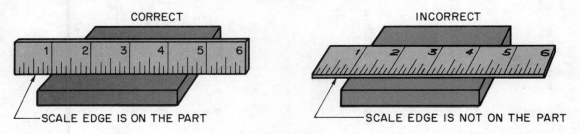

Fig. 21-9

READING FRACTIONAL MEASUREMENTS

An enlarged English rule is shown in figure 21-10. The top scale is graduated in 64ths of an inch. The bottom scale is graduated in 32nds of an inch. The staggered graduations are for halves, quarters, eighths, sixteenths and thirty-seconds.

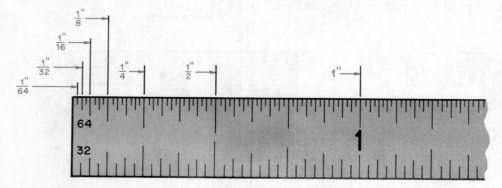

Fig. 21-10 Enlarged English rule with graduations in 32nds and 64ths

Measurements can be read on a rule by noting the last complete inch unit and counting the number of fractional units past the inch unit. For actual on-the-job uses, shortcut methods for reading measurements are used. Refer to the enlarged English rule with graduations in 32nds and 64ths shown in figure 21-11 for these examples. Two methods for reading measurements are shown.

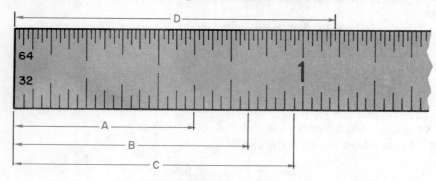

Fig. 21-11

Example 1.   Read the measurement of length A.

METHOD 1

Observe the number of 1-inch graduations.
$0 \times 1'' = 0$

Length A falls on a $\frac{1}{8}$-inch graduation. Count the number of 8ths from zero.

$5 \times \frac{1}{8}'' = \frac{5}{8}''$

$A = \frac{5}{8}'' \ Ans$

METHOD 2

Length A is one $\frac{1}{8}$-inch graduation more than $\frac{1}{2}$ inch.

$A = \frac{1}{2}'' + \frac{1}{8}'' = \frac{4}{8}'' + \frac{1}{8}'' = \frac{5}{8}'' \ Ans$

Example 2.   Read the measurement of length B.

METHOD 1
Observe the number of 1-inch graduations.
$0 \times 1'' = 0$

Length B falls on a $\frac{1}{16}$-inch graduation. Count the number of 16ths from zero.

$13 \times \frac{1}{16}'' = \frac{13}{16}''$

$B = \frac{13}{16}''$ *Ans*

METHOD 2
Length B is one $\frac{1}{16}$-inch graduation more than $\frac{3}{4}$ inch.

$B = \frac{3}{4}'' + \frac{1}{16}'' = \frac{12}{16}'' + \frac{1}{16}'' = \frac{13}{16}''$ *Ans*

Example 3.   Read the measurement of length C.

METHOD 1
Observe the number of 1-inch graduations.
$0 \times 1'' = 0$

Length C falls on a $\frac{1}{32}$-inch graduation. Count the number of 32nds from zero.

$31 \times \frac{1}{32}'' = \frac{31}{32}''$

$C = \frac{31}{32}''$ *Ans*

METHOD 2
Length C is one $\frac{1}{32}$-inch graduation less than 1 inch.

$C = 1'' - \frac{1}{32}'' = \frac{32}{32}'' - \frac{1}{32}'' = \frac{31}{32}''$ *Ans*

Example 4.   Read the measurement of length D.

METHOD 1
Observe the number of 1-inch graduations.
$1 \times 1'' = 1''$

Length D falls on a $\frac{1}{64}$-inch graduation. Count the number of 64ths from 1 inch.

$7 \times \frac{1}{64}'' = \frac{7}{64}''$

$D = 1'' + \frac{7}{64}'' = 1\frac{7}{64}''$ *Ans*

METHOD 2
Length D is one $\frac{1}{64}$-inch graduation less than $1\frac{1}{8}''$.

$D = 1\frac{1}{8}'' - \frac{1}{64}'' = 1\frac{8}{64}'' - \frac{1}{64}'' = 1\frac{7}{64}''$ *Ans*

MEASUREMENTS THAT DO NOT FALL ON RULE GRADUATIONS

Often the end of the object being measured does not fall on a rule graduation. In these cases, read the closer rule graduation. Refer to the enlarged English rule shown in figure 21-12 for these examples.

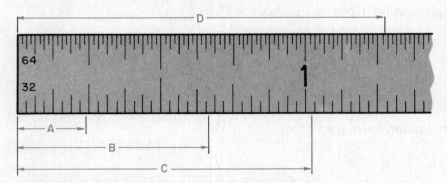

Fig. 21-12 Enlarged English rule with graduations in 32nds and 64ths

Example 1.   Read the measurement of length A.

The measurement is closer to $\frac{1}{4}$ inch than $\frac{7}{32}$ inch.

$A = \frac{1}{4}$ " *Ans*

Example 2.   Read the measurement of length B.

The measurement is closer to $\frac{21}{32}$ inch than $\frac{11}{16}$ inch.

$B = \frac{21}{32}$ " *Ans*

Example 3.   Read the measurement of length C.

The measurement is closer to $1\frac{1}{32}$ inches than 1 inch.

$C = 1\frac{1}{32}$ " *Ans*

Example 4.   Read the measurement of length D.

The measurement is closer to $1\frac{17}{64}$ inches than $1\frac{9}{32}$ inches.

$D = 1\frac{17}{64}$ " *Ans*

Exercise 21-1

1. Read measurements a-p on the enlarged English rule with graduations in 32nds and 64ths shown in figure 21-13.

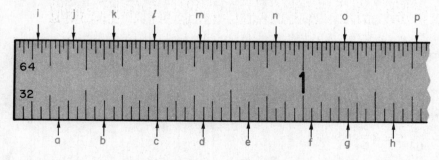

Fig. 21-13

2. Measure the length of each of the line segments a-n to the nearer 32nd inch.

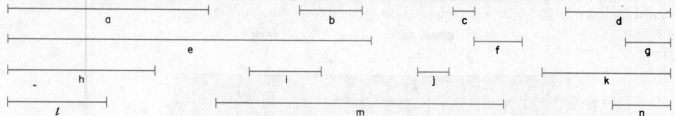

3. Measure the length of dimensions a-n on the template shown in figure 21-14 to the nearer 32nd inch.

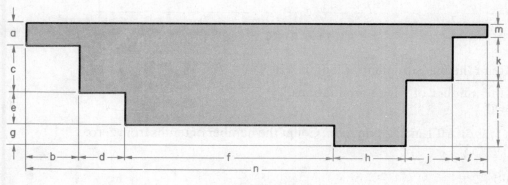

Fig. 21-14

READING DECIMAL-INCH MEASUREMENTS

An enlarged English rule is shown in figure 21-15. The top scale is graduated in 100ths of an inch (0.01 inch). The bottom scale is graduated in 50ths of an inch (0.02 inch). The staggered graduations are for halves, tenths and fiftieths.

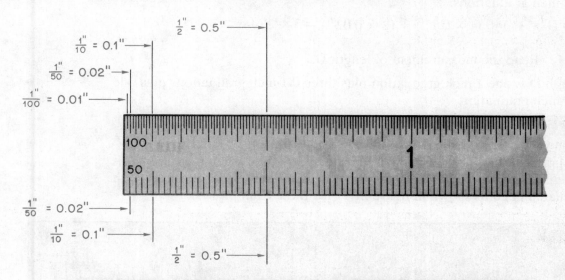

Fig. 21-15 Enlarged English rule with decimal graduations in 50ths and 100ths

Refer to the enlarged English rule with decimal graduations in 50ths and 100ths shown in figure 21-16 for these examples. One method for reading the measurements is shown.

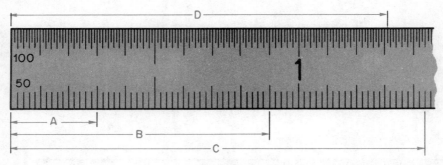

Fig. 21-16

Example 1.   Read the measurement of length A.

Observe the number of 1-inch graduations.
$0 \times 1'' = 0$

Length A falls on a 0.1-inch graduation. Count the number of tenths from zero.
$3 \times 0.1'' = 0.3''$.

A = **0.3″** *Ans*

Example 2.   Read the measurement of length B.

Length B is 0.1-inch graduation less than 1 inch.

B = $1'' - 0.1'' =$ **0.9″** *Ans*

Example 3.   Read the measurement of length C.

Length C is one 1-inch graduation plus four 0.1 inch graduations plus two 0.02-inch graduations.

C = $(1 \times 1'') + (4 \times 0.1'') + (2 \times 0.02'') =$ **1.44″** *Ans*

Example 4.   Read the measurement of length D.

Length D is one 1-inch graduation plus three 0.1-inch graduations plus one 0.01-inch graduation.

D = $(1 \times 1'') + (3 \times 0.1'') + (1 \times 0.01'') =$ **1.31″** *Ans*

Scales graduated in 20ths of an inch (0.05 inch) are used when measurements do not require the precision of 100ths or 50ths of an inch. Refer to the English rule graduated in 20ths shown in figure 21-17 for these examples.

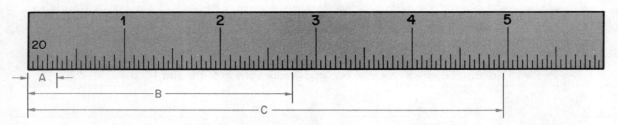

Fig. 21-17 English rule with decimal graduations in 20ths

Example 1. Read the measurement of length A.

Length A falls on a 0.1-inch graduation. Count the number of tenths from zero.
$3 \times 0.1'' = 0.3''$

$A = \textbf{0.3}\,''\, \textit{Ans}$

Example 2. Read the measurement of length B.

Length B is two 1-inch graduations plus one 0.5-inch graduation plus two 0.1-inch graduations plus one 0.05-inch graduation.

$B = (2 \times 1'') + (1 \times 0.5'') + (2 \times 0.1'') + (1 \times 0.05'') = \textbf{2.75}\,''\, \textit{Ans}$

Example 3. Read the measurement of length C.

Length C is one 0.05-inch graduation less than 5 inches.

$C = 5'' - 0.05'' = \textbf{4.95}\,''\, \textit{Ans}$

Exercise 21-2

1. Read measurements a-p on the enlarged English rule with decimal graduations in 50ths and 100ths shown in figure 21-18.

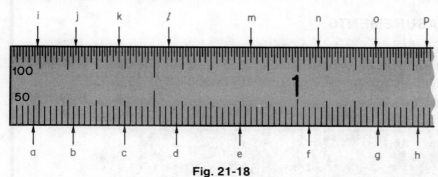

Fig. 21-18

2. Read measurements a-m on the English rule with decimal graduations in 20ths shown in figure 21-19.

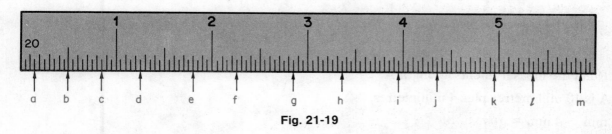

Fig. 21-19

3. Measure the length of each of the line segments a-m to the nearer 20th of an inch (0.05 inch).

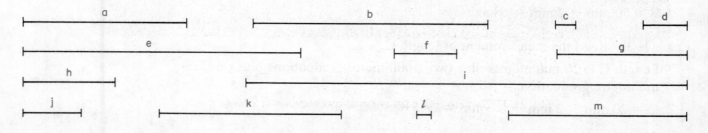

4. Measure the diameters of holes A-I in the plate shown in figure 21-20 to the nearer 20th of an inch.

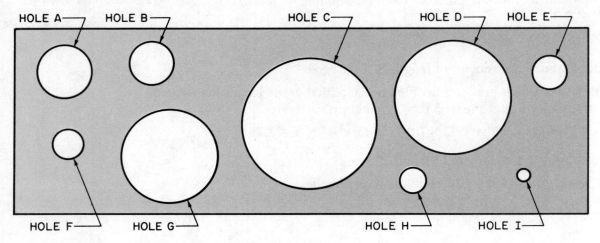

HOLE A— HOLE B—   HOLE C—   HOLE D—   HOLE E—

HOLE F—   HOLE G—   HOLE H—   HOLE I—

Fig. 21-20

READING METRIC MEASUREMENTS

An enlarged metric rule is shown in figure 21-21. The top scale is graduated in one-half millimetres (0.5 mm). The bottom scale is graduated in millimetres (1 mm). Refer to the enlarged metric rule shown for these examples.

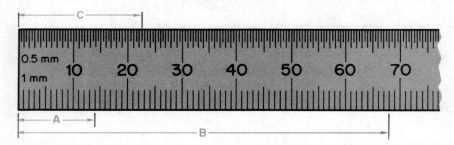

Fig. 21-21 Enlarged metric rule with 1-mm and 0.5-mm graduations

Example 1.   Read the measurement of length A.

Length A is 10 millimetres plus 4 millimetres.

A = 10 mm + 4 mm = 14 mm *Ans*

Example 2.   Read the measurement of length B.

Length B is 2 millimetres less than 70 millimetres.

B = 70 mm − 2 mm = 68 mm *Ans*

Example 3.   Read the measurement of length C.

Length C is 20 millimetres plus two 1-millimetre graduations plus one 0.5-millimetre graduation.

C = 20 mm + 2 mm + 0.5 mm = 22.5 mm *Ans*

Exercise 21-3

1. Read measurements a-p on the enlarged metric rule with 1-millimetre and 0.5-millimetre graduations shown in figure 21-22.

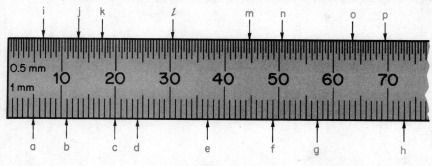

Fig. 21-22

2. Measure the length of each of the line segments a-n to the nearer whole millimetre.

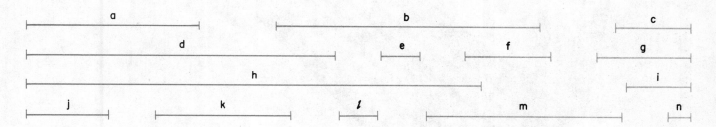

3. Measure dimensions a-j on the shaft shown in figure 21-23 to the nearer whole millimetre.

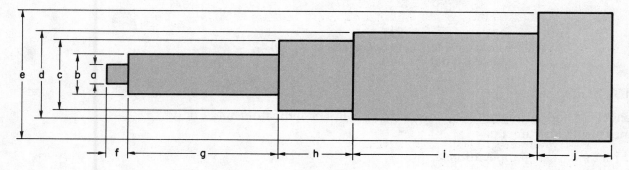

Fig. 21-23

GAGE BLOCKS

Gage blocks are square or rectangular shaped hardened steel blocks which are manufactured to a high degree of accuracy, flatness, and parallelism, figure 21-24. Gage blocks when properly used, provide millionths of an inch accuracy and precision.

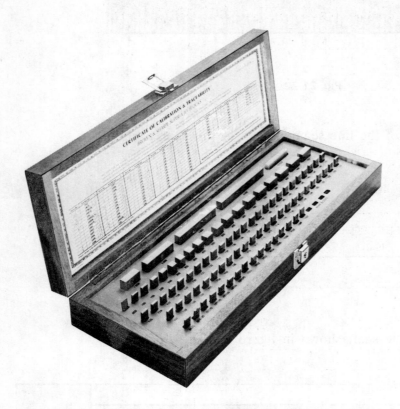

Fig. 21-24 A complete set of gage blocks
(Brown & Sharpe Mfg. Co.)

Gage blocks are used for

- checking and setting micrometers, vernier calipers, indicators, and other measuring instruments.

- direct measuring applications.

- inspection gaging.

- machine set-up, layout, and precision assembly applications.

By *wringing* blocks (slipping blocks one over the other using light pressure), a combination of the proper blocks can be achieved which provides a desired length. Wringing the blocks produces a very thin air gap that is similar to liquid film in holding the blocks together. There are a variety of both English and metric gage block sets available. Figure 21-25 lists the thicknesses of blocks of a frequently used English gage block set. Figure 21-26 lists the thicknesses of blocks of a commonly used metric gage block set.

BLOCK THICKNESSES OF AN ENGLISH GAGE BLOCK SET NOTE: ALL THICKNESSES ARE IN INCHES								
9 BLOCKS 0.000 1″ SERIES								
0.100 1	0.100 2	0.100 3	0.100 4	0.100 5	0.100 6	0.100 7	0.100 8	0.100 9
49 BLOCKS 0.001″ SERIES								
0.101	0.102	0.103	0.104	0.105	0.106	0.107	0.108	0.109
0.110	0.111	0.112	0.113	0.114	0.115	0.116	0.117	0.118
0.119	0.120	0.121	0.122	0.123	0.124	0.125	0.126	0.127
0.128	0.129	0.130	0.131	0.132	0.133	0.134	0.135	0.136
0.137	0.138	0.139	0.140	0.141	0.142	0.143	0.144	0.145
0.146	0.147	0.148	0.149					
19 BLOCKS 0.050″ SERIES								
0.050	0.100	0.150	0.200	0.250	0.300	0.350	0.400	0.450
0.500	0.550	0.600	0.650	0.700	0.750	0.800	0.850	0.900
0.950								
4 BLOCKS 1.000″ SERIES								
1.000	2.000	3.000	4.000					

Fig. 21-25 English gage block set

BLOCK THICKNESSES OF A METRIC GAGE BLOCK SET NOTE: ALL THICKNESSES ARE IN MILLIMETRES								
9 BLOCKS 0.001 mm SERIES								
1.001	1.002	1.003	1.004	1.005	1.006	1.007	1.008	1.009
9 BLOCKS 0.01 mm SERIES								
1.01	1.02	1.03	1.04	1.05	1.06	1.07	1.08	1.09
9 BLOCKS 0.1 mm SERIES								
1.1	1.2	1.3	1.4	1.5	1.6	1.7	1.8	1.9
9 BLOCKS 1 mm SERIES								
1	2	3	4	5	6	7	8	9
9 BLOCKS 10 mm SERIES								
10	20	30	40	50	60	70	80	90

Fig. 21-26 Metric gage block set

DETERMINING GAGE BLOCK COMBINATIONS

Usually there is more than one combination of blocks which gives a desired length. The most efficient procedure for determining block combinations is to eliminate digits of the desired measurement from right to left. This procedure saves time, minimizes the number of blocks, and reduces the chances of error. These examples show how to apply this procedure in determining block combinations.

Example 1.   Determine a combination of gage blocks for 2.946 8 inches. Refer to the gage block sizes given in figure 21-25.

Choose the block which eliminates the last digit to the right, the 8. **Choose the 0.100 8″ block.** Subtract.
2.946 8″ − 0.100 8″ = 2.846 0″

Eliminate the last nonzero digit, 6, of the 2.846 0″. **Choose the 0.146″ block** which eliminates the 4 as well as the 6. Subtract.
2.846 0″ − 0.146″ = 2.700 0″

Eliminate the last nonzero digit, 7 of 2.700 0″. **Choose the 0.700″ block.** Subtract.
2.700 0″ − 0.700″ = 2.000 0″

The 2.000″ block completes the required dimension as shown in figure 21-27.

Check. Add the blocks chosen.
0.100 8″ + 0.146″ + 0.700″ + 2.000″ = 2.946 8″

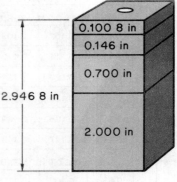

Fig. 21-27

Example 2.   Determine a combination of gage blocks for 10.284 3 inches. Refer to the gage block sizes given in figure 21-25.

Eliminate the 3. **Choose the 0.100 3″ block.** Subtract.
10.284 3″ − 0.100 3″ = 10.184 0″

Eliminate the 4. **Choose the 0.134″ block.** Subtract.
10.184 0″ − 0.134″ = 10.050 0″

Eliminate the 5. **Choose the 0.050″ block.** Subtract.
10.050 0″ − 0.050″ = 10.000 0″

The 1.000″, 2.000″, 3.000″, and 4.000″ blocks complete the required dimension as shown in figure 21-28.

Check.
0.100 3″ + 0.134″ + 0.050″ + 1.000″ + 2.000″ + 3.000″ + 4.000″ = 10.284 3″

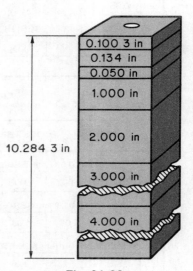

Fig. 21-28

Example 3.   Determine a combination of gage blocks for 157.372 millimetres. Refer to the gage block sizes given in figure 21-26.

Eliminate the 2. **Choose the 1.002 mm block.** Subtract.
157.372 mm − 1.002 mm = 156.370 mm

Eliminate the 7. **Choose the 1.07 mm block.** Subtract.
156.370 mm − 1.07 mm = 155.300 mm

Eliminate the 3. **Choose the 1.3 mm block.** Subtract.
155.300 mm − 1.3 mm = 154.000 mm

Eliminate the 4. **Choose the 4 mm block.** Subtract.
154.000 mm − 4 mm = 150.000 mm

The 60 mm and 90 mm blocks complete the required dimension as shown in figure 21-29.

Check.
1.002 mm + 1.07 mm + 1.3 mm + 4 mm + 60 mm + 90 mm = 157.372 mm

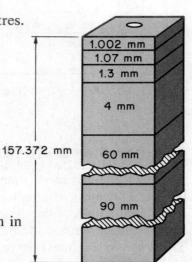

Fig. 21-29

Exercise 21-4

Using the English block sizes given in figure 21-25, determine a combination of gage blocks for each of these dimensions.

Note: Usually more than one combination of blocks gives the desired dimension.

1. 0.632 1 in	8. 8.375 in	15. 5.090 6 in
2. 0.375 6 in	9. 10.050 in	16. 1.978 9 in
3. 4.963 3 in	10. 3.785 7 in	17. 0.874 5 in
4. 2.780 2 in	11. 2.000 1 in	18. 6.666 6 in
5. 5.700 2 in	12. 0.372 1 in	19. 5.434 8 in
6. 6.900 in	13. 4.831 1 in	20. 10.010 2 in
7. 0.999 9 in	14. 6.080 in	

By using the metric block sizes given in Figure 21-26, determine a combination of gage blocks for each of these dimensions.

Note: Usually more than one combination of blocks gives the desired dimension.

21. 26.983 mm	28. 8.888 mm	35. 7.707 mm
22. 56.316 mm	29. 28.98 mm	36. 111.1 mm
23. 43.635 mm	30. 260.1 mm	37. 111.11 mm
24. 125.03 mm	31. 78.08 mm	38. 111.111 mm
25. 211.7 mm	32. 19.19 mm	39. 91.019 mm
26. 50.801 mm	33. 101.01 mm	40. 80.003 mm
27. 77.002 mm	34. 212.792 mm	

UNIT EXERCISE AND PROBLEM REVIEW

Exercise 21-5

READING FRACTIONAL-INCH MEASUREMENTS ON AN ENGLISH RULE

1. Read measurements a-p on the enlarged English rule graduated in 32nds and 64ths shown in figure 21-30.

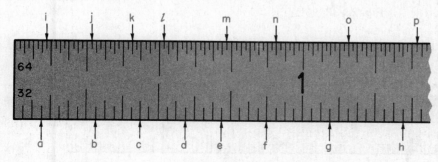

Fig. 21-30

MEASURING FRACTIONAL-INCH LENGTHS WITH AN ENGLISH RULE

2. Measure the length of each of the line segments a-g to the nearer 32nd inch.

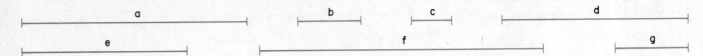

3. Measure dimensions a-*l* of the plate shown in figure 21-31 to the nearer 32nd inch.

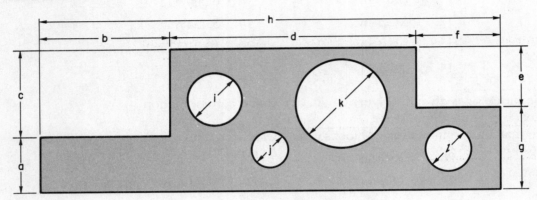

Fig. 21-31

READING DECIMAL-INCH MEASUREMENTS ON AN ENGLISH RULE

4. Read measurements a-p on the enlarged English rule graduated in 50ths and 100ths shown in figure 21-32.

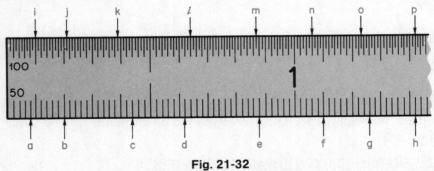

Fig. 21-32

5. Read measurements a-*l* on the English rule graduated in 20ths shown in figure 21-33.

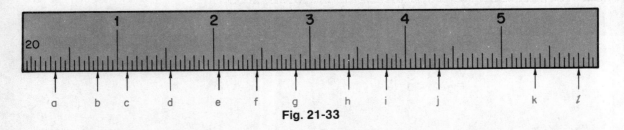

Fig. 21-33

MEASURING DECIMAL-INCH MEASUREMENTS
WITH AN ENGLISH RULE

6. Measure the length of each of the line segments a-g to the nearer 20th inch (0.05″).

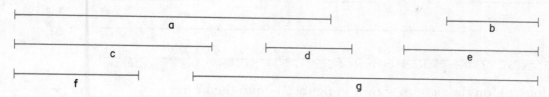

7. Measure dimensions a-i on the support bracket shown in figure 21-34 to the nearer 20th inch.

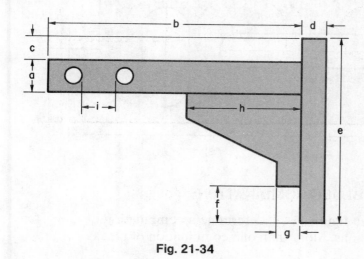

Fig. 21-34

READING MEASUREMENTS WITH A METRIC RULE

8. Read measurements a-p on the enlarged metric rule with 1-mm and 0.5-mm graduations shown in figure 21-35.

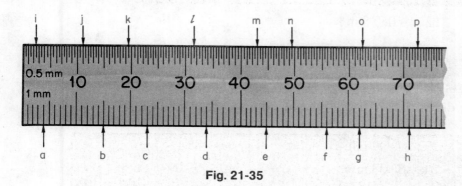

Fig. 21-35

MEASURING LENGTHS WITH A METRIC RULE

9. Measure the length of each of the line segments a-g to the nearer whole millimetre.

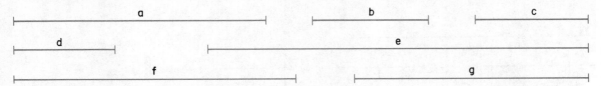

10. Measure dimensions a-k on the pattern shown in figure 21-36 to the nearer whole millimetre.

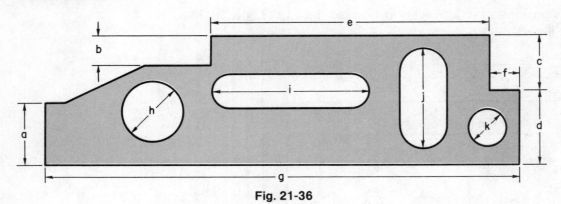

Fig. 21-36

DETERMINING ENGLISH GAGE BLOCK COMBINATIONS

Using the English block sizes given in figure 21-27, determine a combination of gage blocks for each of these dimensions. More than one combination of blocks may be possible.

11. 0.598 7 in	17. 9.060 in	23. 0.799 8 in
12. 0.632 1 in	18. 5.576 7 in	24. 8.888 8 in
13. 5.863 4 in	19. 3.000 2 in	25. 7.384 3 in
14. 1.869 3 in	20. 0.731 1 in	26. 10.002 1 in
15. 7.700 in	21. 6.003 in	
16. 0.375 2 in	22. 4.080 5 in	

DETERMINING METRIC GAGE BLOCK COMBINATIONS

Using the metric block sizes given in figure 21-28, determine a combination of gage blocks for each of these dimensions. More than one combination of blocks may be possible.

27. 63.385 mm	33. 9.999 mm	39. 85.111 mm
28. 14.073 mm	34. 83.38 mm	40. 39.099 mm
29. 34.356 mm	35. 157.08 mm	41. 122.22 mm
30. 146.09 mm	36. 13.86 mm	42. 67.005 mm
31. 213.9 mm	37. 38.727 mm	
32. 43.707 mm	38. 6.071 mm	

UNIT 22
Vernier Instruments:
Calipers and Height Gages

OBJECTIVES

After studying this unit you should be able to

- read English and metric vernier caliper settings.
- determine English and metric vernier caliper scale settings for given lengths.
- read English and metric vernier height gage settings.
- determine English and metric vernier height gage settings.
- determine vernier caliper and vernier height gage English and metric scale settings in practical applied hole location problems.

VERNIER CALIPERS: TYPES AND DESCRIPTION

Vernier calipers are widely used in the manufacturing occupations. They are used for many different applications where precision to thousandths of an inch or hundredths of a millimetre is required. Vernier calipers are commonly used for measuring lengths of objects, determining distances between holes in parts, and measuring inside and outside diameters of cylinders.

Vernier calipers are available in a wide range of lengths with different types of jaws and scale graduations. Three types are shown in figures 22-1 through 22-3.

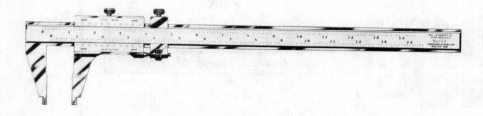

Fig. 22-1 English vernier caliper—50 divisions. The inside measurements are read on the top scale. The outside measurements are read on the bottom scale. (The L.S. Starrett Company)

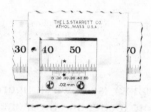

Fig. 22-2 Metric vernier caliper—25 divisions. The outside measurements are read on the front side. The inside measurements are read on the reverse (back) side. (The L.S. Starrett Company)

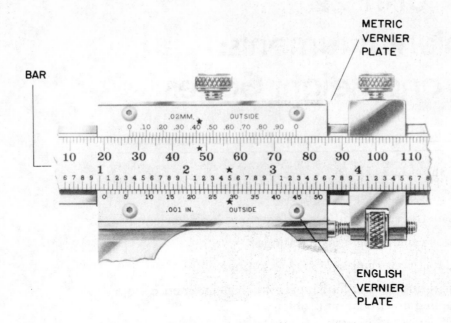

Fig. 22-3 English and metric vernier caliper—50 divisions. Metric measurements are read on the top scale. English measurements are read on the bottom scale. (The L.S. Starrett Company)

There are two basic parts of a vernier caliper. One part is the main scale which is similar to a steel rule with a fixed jaw. The other part is a sliding jaw with a vernier scale. The vernier scale slides parallel to the main scale and provides a degree of precision to 0.001 inch.

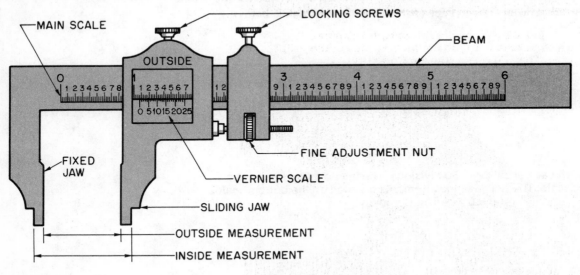

Fig. 22-4

The front side of a commonly used English vernier caliper is shown in figure 22-4. The parts are identified. The main scale is divided into inches and the inches are divided into 10 divisions each equal to 0.1 inch. The 0.1-inch divisions are divided into 4 parts each equal to 0.025 inch. The vernier scale has 25 divisions in a length equal to the length on the main scale that has 24 divisions as shown in figure 22-5. The difference between a main scale division and a vernier scale division is $\frac{1}{25}$ of 0.025 inch or 0.001 inch.

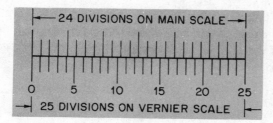

Fig. 22-5

The front side of the English vernier caliper (25 divisions) is used for outside measurements as shown in figure 22-6. The reverse or back side is used for inside measurements as shown in figure 22-7.

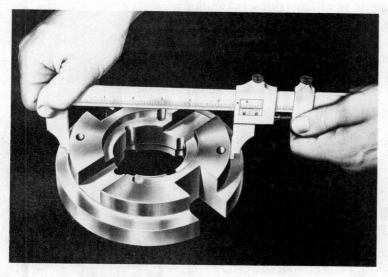

**Fig. 22-6 Measuring an outside diameter.
The measurement is read on the front side of the caliper.
(The L.S. Starrett Company)**

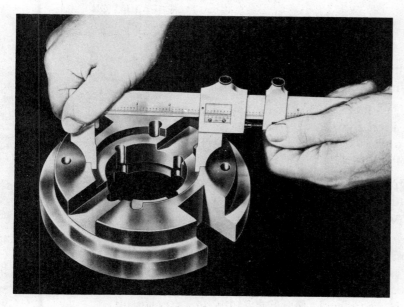

**Fig. 22-7 Measuring an inside diameter.
The measurement is read on the back side of the caliper.
(The L.S. Starrett Company)**

The accuracy of a measurement obtainable with a vernier caliper depends on the user's ability to align the caliper with the part being measured. The line of measurement must be parallel to the beam of the caliper and must lie in the same plane as the caliper. Care must be used to prevent too loose or too tight a caliper setting.

READING AND SETTING MEASUREMENTS ON AN ENGLISH VERNIER CALIPER

A measurement is read by adding the thousandths reading on the vernier scale to the reading from the main scale.

On the main scale read the number of 1-inch divisions, 0.1-inch divisions, and 0.025-inch divisions that are to the left of the zero graduation on the vernier scale. On the vernier scale, find the graduation that most closely coincides with a graduation on the main scale. This vernier graduation indicates the number of thousandths that are added to the main scale reading.

Setting a given measurement is the reverse procedure of reading a measurement on the vernier caliper.

Example 1. Read the measurement set on the English vernier caliper scales shown in figure 22-8.

To the left of the zero graduation on the vernier scale, read the main scale reading: zero 1-inch division, six 0.1-inch divisions, and one 0.025-inch division.
$(0 \times 1'' + 6 \times 0.1'' + 1 \times 0.025'' = 0.625'')$

Observe which vernier scale graduation most closely coincides with a main scale graduation. The sixteenth vernier scale graduation coincides. Add 0.016 inch to the main scale reading.
$(0.625'' + 0.016'' = 0.641'')$

Vernier caliper reading:
0.641" Ans

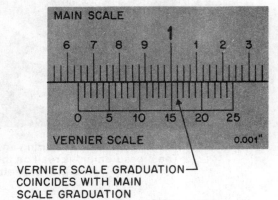

VERNIER SCALE GRADUATION COINCIDES WITH MAIN SCALE GRADUATION

Fig. 22-8

Example 2. Read the measurement set on the English vernier caliper scales shown in figure 22-9.

To the left of the zero graduation on the vernier scale, read the main scale reading: four 1-inch divisions, zero 0.1-inch division, and zero 0.025-inch division.
$(4 \times 1'' + 0 \times 0.1'' + 0 \times 0.025'' = 4'')$

Observe which vernier scale graduation most closely coincides with a main scale graduation. The twenty-first vernier scale graduation coincides. Add 0.021 inch to the main scale reading.
$(4'' + 0.021'' = 4.021'')$

Vernier caliper reading:
4.021" Ans

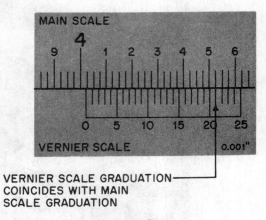

VERNIER SCALE GRADUATION COINCIDES WITH MAIN SCALE GRADUATION

Fig. 22-9

Example 3. Set 1.376 inches on a vernier caliper.

The setting is between 1.375 inches and 1.400 inches. Move the vernier scale zero graduation to 1 inch plus 0.3 inch plus 0.075 inch on the main scale.
$(1 \times 1'' + 3 \times 0.1'' + 3 \times 0.025'' = 1.375'')$

Subtract to find the vernier setting.
$(1.376'' - 1.375'' = 0.001'')$

An additional 0.001 inch is set by carefully adjusting the sliding jaw until the 1 graduation on the vernier scale coincides with a graduation on the main scale.

The 1.376-inch setting is shown in figure 22-10.

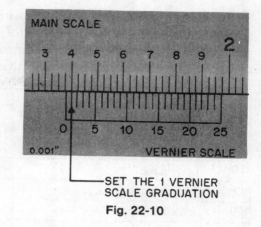

SET THE 1 VERNIER SCALE GRADUATION

Fig. 22-10

Exercise 22-1

Read the English vernier caliper measurements for these settings.

1.
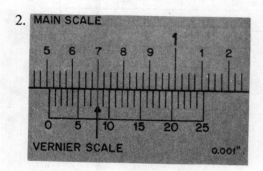

4.
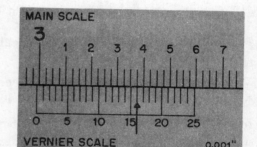

2.
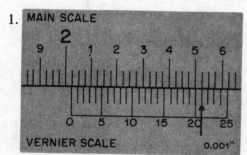

5.
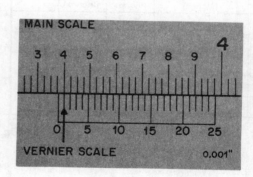

3.
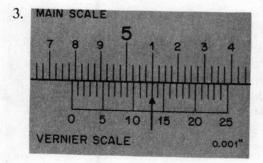

6.
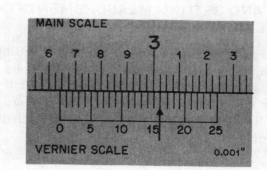

The table in figure 22-11 gives the position of the zero graduation on the vernier scale in reference to the main scale of an English vernier caliper. Also listed is the vernier scale graduation that coincides with a main scale graduation. Determine each vernier caliper setting. The answer to the first exercise is given.

	ZERO VERNIER GRADUATION LIES BETWEEN THESE MAIN SCALE GRADUATIONS (inches)	VERNIER GRADUATION THAT COINCIDES WITH A MAIN SCALE GRADUATION	VERNIER CALIPER SETTING (inches)			ZERO VERNIER GRADUATION LIES BETWEEN THESE MAIN SCALE GRADUATIONS (inches)	VERNIER GRADUATION THAT COINCIDES WITH A MAIN SCALE GRADUATION	VERNIER CALIPER SETTING (inches)
7.	2.725-2.750	17	2.742		13.	5.850-5.875	2	
8.	6.975-7.000	23			14.	0.000-0.025	21	
9.	2.000-2.025	9			15.	2.825-2.850	1	
10.	1.650-1.675	12			16.	3.075-3.100	20	
11.	0.075-0.100	19			17.	1.000-1.025	24	
12.	0.225-0.250	6			18.	5.025-5.050	18	

Fig. 22-11

Refer to this sentence and to the given vernier caliper settings in the table in figure 22-12 to determine the values A, B, and C.

"The zero vernier scale graduation lies between A and B on the main scale, and the vernier graduation C coincides with a main scale graduation."

The answer to the first exercise is given.

	VERNIER CALIPER SETTING (inches)	A (inches)	B (inches)	C			VERNIER CALIPER SETTING (inches)	A (inches)	B (inches)	C
19.	4.963	4.950	4.975	13		24.	7.657			
20.	0.982					25.	3.096			
21.	5.999					26.	2.368			
22.	0.023					27.	0.511			
23.	1.628					28.	4.939			

Fig. 22-12

READING AND SETTING MEASUREMENTS ON A METRIC VERNIER CALIPER

The same principles are used in reading and setting metric vernier calipers as those in English vernier calipers. The main scale is divided in 1-millimetre divisions. Each millimetre division is divided in half or 0.5-millimetre divisions. Every tenth millimetre graduation is numbered in sequence: 10 mm, 20 mm, 30 mm, etc. The vernier scale has 25 divisions. Each division is $\frac{1}{25}$ of 0.5 millimetre or 0.02 millimetre.

A measurement is read by adding the 0.02-millimetre reading on the vernier scale to the reading from the main scale.

On the main scale read the number of millimetre divisions and 0.5-millimetre divisions that are to the left of the zero graduation on the vernier scale. On the vernier scale, find the graduation that most closely coincides with a graduation on the main scale. Multiply the graduation by 0.02 millimetre and add the value obtained to the main scale reading.

Setting a given measurement is the reverse procedure of reading a measurement on the vernier caliper.

Example 1.   Read the measurement set on the metric scales shown in figure 22-13.

To the left of the zero graduation on the vernier scale, read the main scale reading: twenty-one 1-millimetre divisions and one 0.5-millimetre division.
(21×1 mm + 1×0.5 mm = 21.5 mm)

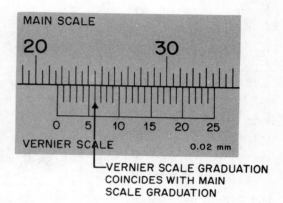

Observe which vernier scale graduation most closely coincides with a main scale graduation. The sixth vernier scale graduation coincides. Each vernier scale graduation represents 0.02 mm. Multiply to find the number of millimetres represented by 6 divisions.
(6×0.02 mm = 0.12 mm)

Fig. 22-13

Add the 0.12 millimetre to the main scale reading.
(21.5 mm + 0.12 mm = 21.62 mm)

Vernier caliper reading:
21.62 mm *Ans*

Example 2.   Set 50.96 millimetres on a vernier caliper.

The setting is between 50.5 millimetres and 51.0 millimetres. Move the vernier scale zero graduation to 50 millimetres plus 0.5 millimetre on the main scale.
(50 mm + 0.5 mm = 50.5 mm)

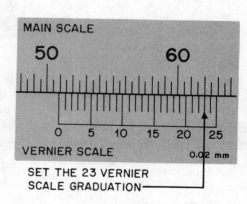

Subtract to find the vernier setting.
(50.96 mm − 50.5 mm = 0.46 mm)

An additional 0.46 millimetre is set by adjusting the sliding jaw. Since each vernier scale graduation represents 0.02 mm, divide to find the number of graduations on the vernier scale.
(0.46 mm ÷ 0.02 mm = 23)

Fig. 22-14

Adjust the sliding jaw until the twenty-third graduation on the vernier scale coincides with a graduation on the main scale.

The 50.96-millimetre setting is shown in figure 22-14.

Exercise 22-2

Read the metric vernier caliper measurements for the following settings.

1.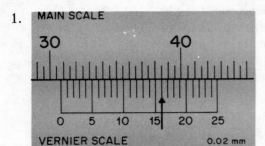

4.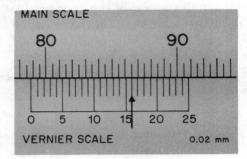

2.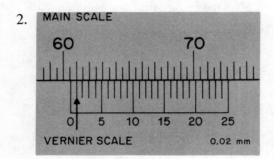

5.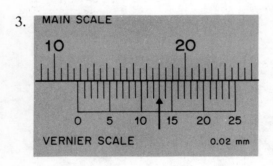

3.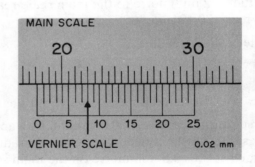

6.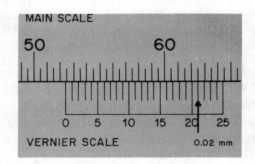

The table in figure 22-15 gives the position of the zero graduation on the vernier scale in reference to the main scale of a metric vernier caliper. Also listed is the vernier scale graduation that coincides with a main scale graduation. Determine each vernier caliper setting. The answer to the first exercise is given.

	ZERO VERNIER GRADUATION LIES BETWEEN THESE MAIN SCALE GRADUATIONS (millimetres)	VERNIER GRADUATION THAT COINCIDES WITH A MAIN SCALE GRADUATION	VERNIER CALIPER SETTING (millimetres)			ZERO VERNIER GRADUATION LIES BETWEEN THESE MAIN SCALE GRADUATIONS (millimetres)	VERNIER GRADUATION THAT COINCIDES WITH A MAIN SCALE GRADUATION	VERNIER CALIPER SETTING (millimetres)
7.	52.5-53.0	14	52.78		13.	48.0-48.5	24	
8.	14.5-15.0	2			14.	77.5-78.0	21	
9.	86.0-86.5	19			15.	16.5-17.0	1	
10.	70.5-71.0	21			16.	98.0-98.5	9	
11.	26.0-26.5	8			17.	41.0-41.5	17	
12.	39.5-40.0	13			18.	56.5-57.0	20	

Fig. 22-15

Refer to this sentence and to the given vernier caliper settings in the table in figure 22-16 to determine the values A, B, and C.

"The zero vernier scale graduation lies between A and B on the main scale and the vernier graduation C coincides with a main scale graduation."

The answer to the first exercise is given.

	VERNIER CALIPER SETTING (millimetres)	A (milli- metres)	B (milli- metres)	C		VERNIER CALIPER SETTING (millimetres)	A (milli- metres)	B (milli- metres)	C
19.	37.68	37.5	38.0	9	24.	20.28			
20.	19.76				25.	43.06			
21.	42.04				26.	77.40			
22.	88.82				27.	81.22			
23.	63.74				28.	96.98			

Fig. 22-16

VERNIER HEIGHT GAGE

The vernier height gage and vernier caliper are similar in operation. The height gage also has a sliding jaw; the fixed jaw is the surface plate with which the height gage is usually used. The gage can be used with a scriber, figure 22-17, a depth gage attachment, figure 22-18, or an indicator. The indicator is the most widely used and, generally, the most accurate attachment. Figure 22-19 shows the parts of a vernier height gage.

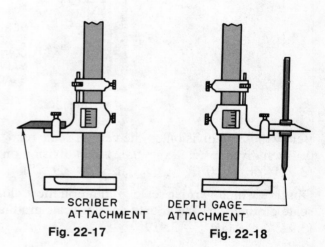

SCRIBER ATTACHMENT
Fig. 22-17

DEPTH GAGE ATTACHMENT
Fig. 22-18

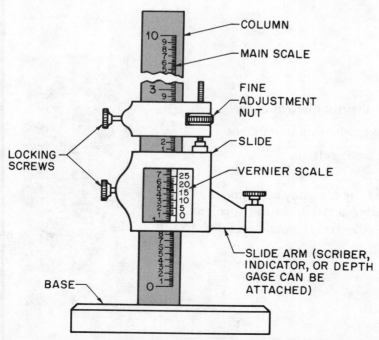

COLUMN

MAIN SCALE

FINE ADJUSTMENT NUT

SLIDE

VERNIER SCALE

LOCKING SCREWS

SLIDE ARM (SCRIBER, INDICATOR, OR DEPTH GAGE CAN BE ATTACHED)

BASE

Fig. 22-19 Vernier height gage

READING AND SETTING MEASUREMENTS ON AN ENGLISH VERNIER HEIGHT GAGE

Measurements on the English vernier height gage are read and set using the same procedure as with the vernier caliper.

Example 1.   Read the measurement set on the English vernier height gage scales shown in figure 22-20.

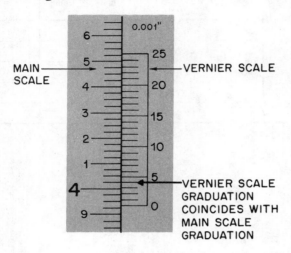

Fig. 22-20

Below the zero division on the vernier scale read three 1-inch divisions, nine 0.1-inch divisions, and one 0.025-inch division on the main scale.
($3 \times 1'' + 9 \times 0.1'' + 1 \times 0.025'' = 3.925''$)

Observe which vernier scale graduation most closely coincides with a main scale graduation. The fourth vernier scale graduation coincides. Add.
($3.925'' + 0.004'' = 3.929''$)

Vernier height gage reading:
3.929 " Ans

Example 2.   Set 6.002 inches on a vernier height gage.

Move the vernier scale zero graduation to 6 inches.

Subtract to find the vernier scale setting.
($6.002'' - 6'' = 0.002''$)

An additional 0.002 inch is set by carefully adjusting the sliding jaw until the second graduation on the vernier scale coincides with a graduation on the main scale.

The 6.002-inch setting is shown in figure 22-21.

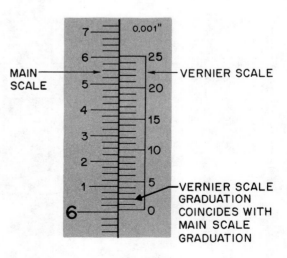

Fig. 22-21

Exercise 22-3

Read the English vernier height gage measurements for the following settings.

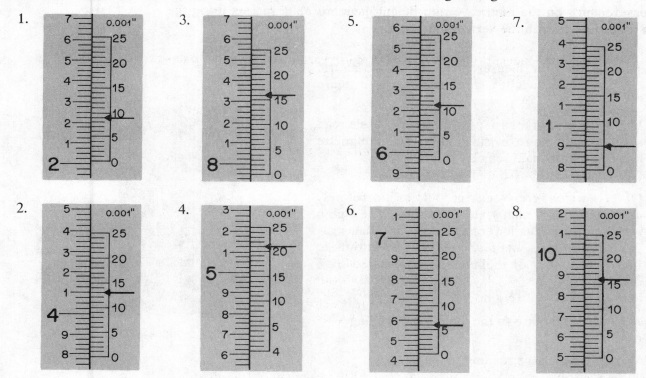

Refer to this sentence and to the given vernier height gage settings in the table in figure 22-22 to determine the values of A, B, and C.

"The zero vernier scale graduation lies between A and B on the main scale and the vernier graduation C coincides with a main scale graduation."

The answer to the first exercise is given.

	VERNIER HEIGHT GAGE SETTING (inches)	A (inches)	B (inches)	C		VERNIER HEIGHT GAGE SETTING (inches)	A (inches)	B (inches)	C
9.	2.687	2.675	2.700	12	14.	5.031			
10.	0.059				15.	4.877			
11.	8.732				16.	1.309			
12.	3.808				17.	9.441			
13.	6.998				18.	7.783			

Fig. 22-22

READING AND SETTING MEASUREMENTS ON A METRIC VERNIER HEIGHT GAGE

Measurements on the metric vernier height gage are read and set using the same procedure as with the vernier caliper.

Example 1.   Read the measurement set on the metric vernier height gage scales shown in figure 22-23.

Below the zero graduation on the vernier scale read seventy 1-millimetre divisions and one 0.5-millimetre division on the main scale.
(70×1 mm $+ 1 \times 0.5$ mm $= 70.5$ mm)

Observe which vernier scale graduation most closely coincides with a main scale graduation. The eighth vernier scale graduation coincides. Each vernier scale graduation represents 0.02 millimetre. Multiply to find the number of millimetres represented by 8 divisions.
(8×0.02 mm $= 0.16$ mm)

Add 0.16 millimetre to the main scale reading.
(70.5 mm $+ 0.16$ mm $= 70.66$ mm)

Vernier height gage reading:
70.66 mm *Ans*

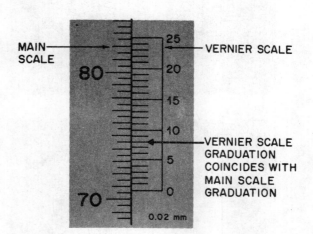

Fig. 22-23

Example 2.   Set 42.74 millimetres on a vernier height gage.

The setting is between 42.5 millimetres and 43.0 millimetres. Move the vernier scale zero graduation to 42 millimetres plus 0.5 millimetre on the main scale.
(42 mm $+ 0.5$ mm $= 42.5$ mm)

Subtract to find the vernier scale setting.
(42.74 mm $- 42.5$ mm $= 0.24$ mm)

An additional 0.24 millimetre is set by carefully adjusting the sliding jaw. Since each vernier scale graduation represents 0.02 mm, divide to find the number of graduations on the vernier scale.
(0.24 mm $\div 0.02$ mm $= 12$)

Adjust the sliding jaw until the twelfth graduation on the vernier scale coincides with a graduation on the main scale.

The 42.74-millimetre-setting is shown in figure 22-24.

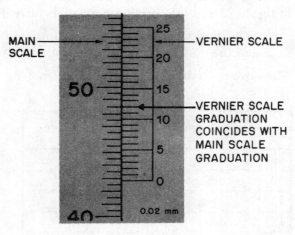

Fig. 22-24

Exercise 22-4

Read the metric vernier height gage measurements for these settings.

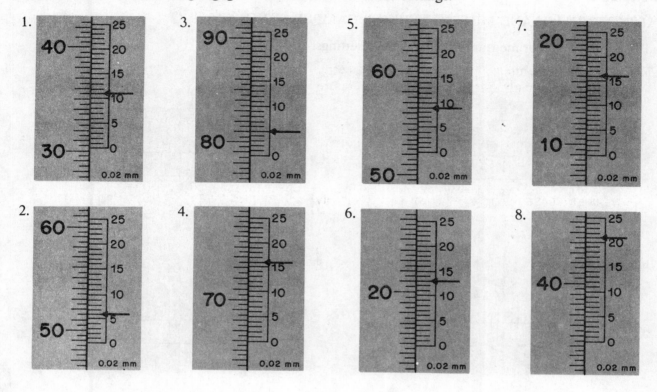

Refer to this sentence and to the given vernier height gage settings in the table in figure 22-25 to determine the values of A, B, and C.

"The zero vernier scale graduation lies between A and B on the main scale, and the vernier graduation C coincides with a main scale graduation."

The answer to the first exercise is given.

	VERNIER HEIGHT GAGE SETTING (millimetres)	A (milli-metres)	B (milli-metres)	C		VERNIER HEIGHT GAGE SETTING (millimetres)	A (milli-metres)	B (milli-metres)	C
9.	53.92	53.5	54.0	21	14.	34.24			
10.	28.64				15.	61.80			
11.	57.08				16.	95.02			
12.	77.94				17.	29.68			
13.	60.66				18.	83.30			

Fig. 22-25

UNIT EXERCISE AND PROBLEM REVIEW

Exercise 22-5

READING ENGLISH AND METRIC VERNIER CALIPER SETTINGS

Read the vernier caliper measurements for these settings.

1. English measurements

a.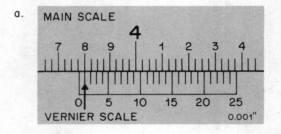

c.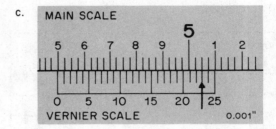

b.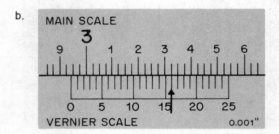

d.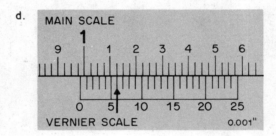

2. Metric measurements

a.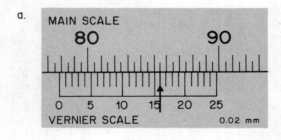

c.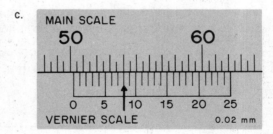

b.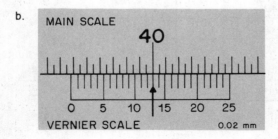

d.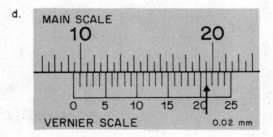

SETTING MEASUREMENTS ON ENGLISH AND METRIC VERNIER CALIPERS

Refer to this sentence and to the given vernier caliper settings in the tables in figures 22-26 and 22-27 to determine the values A, B, and C.

> "The zero vernier scale graduation lies between A and B on the main scale, and the vernier graduation C coincides with a main scale graduation."

3. English settings

	VERNIER CALIPER SETTING (inches)	A (inches)	B (inches)	C
a.	3.864			
b.	0.893			
c.	4.098			
d.	0.057			
e.	5.269			
f.	2.476			
g.	8.974			

Fig. 22-26

4. Metric settings

	VERNIER CALIPER SETTING (millimetres)	A (milli-metres)	B (milli-metres)	C
a.	19.28			
b.	46.82			
c.	60.06			
d.	87.70			
e.	23.64			
f.	98.96			
g.	31.22			

Fig. 22-27

READING ENGLISH AND METRIC VERNIER HEIGHT GAGE SETTINGS

Read the vernier height gage measurements for the following settings.

5. English measurements

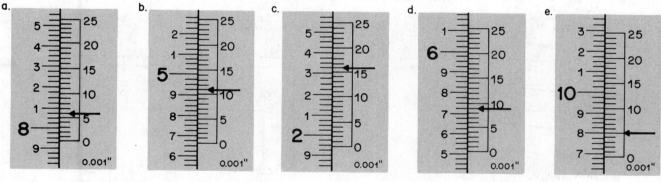

6. Metric measurements

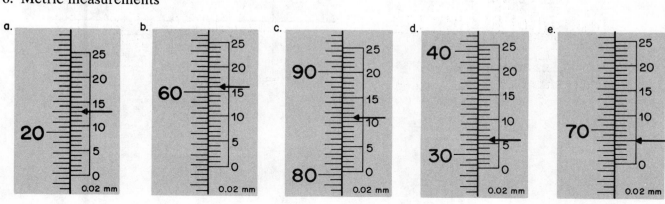

SETTING MEASUREMENTS ON ENGLISH AND METRIC VERNIER HEIGHT GAGES

Refer to this sentence and to the given vernier height gage settings in the tables in figures 22-28 and 22-29 to determine the values A, B, and C.

"The zero scale graduation lies between A and B on the main scale, and the vernier graduation C coincides with a main scale graduation."

7. English settings

	VERNIER HEIGHT GAGE SETTING (inches)	A (inches)	B (inches)	C
a.	5.837			
b.	0.721			
c.	4.039			
d.	9.692			
e.	7.005			
f.	3.567			
g.	2.888			

Fig. 22-28

8. Metric settings

	VERNIER HEIGHT GAGE SETTING (millimetres)	A (milli-metres)	B (milli-metres)	C
a.	18.18			
b.	74.06			
c.	93.84			
d.	21.12			
e.	46.94			
f.	83.48			
g.	55.56			

Fig. 22-29

APPLIED VERNIER CALIPER PROBLEMS

Distances between holes in objects such as the part shown in figure 22-30 are often checked with vernier calipers. The outside distance between two holes is measured. Figure 22-31 shows the position of the caliper in measuring the outside distance between two holes in a part. A sectional view of the part is shown.

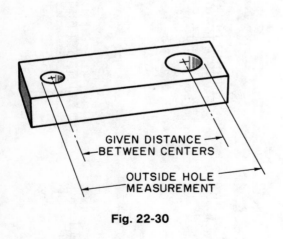

Fig. 22-30

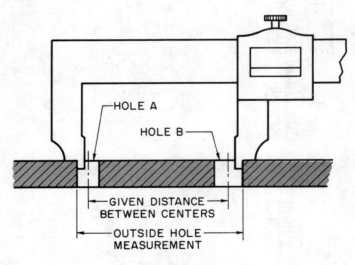

Fig. 22-31

Procedure for Checking Distances Between Holes

- The hole diameters are measured to determine their actual diameters.

- The radius of each hole is computed. A radius is equal to one-half a diameter.

- Each radius is added to the given distance between the centers of the holes considering the given distance tolerances.

- The outside distance between the holes is measured with a vernier caliper to determine whether the holes are located within the center distance high and low limits.

Refer to the data in the tables in figures 22-32 and 22-33. Determine the vernier caliper scale settings for each problem.

9. English measure problems. The answer to the first problem is given.

| | ACTUAL HOLE DIAMETERS | | GIVEN DISTANCE BETWEEN HOLE CENTERS (inches) | VERNIER CALIPER SCALE SETTINGS | | |
	HOLE A (inches)	HOLE B (inches)		MAIN SCALE SETTING (inches)	HIGH LIMIT VERNIER SCALE SETTING	LOW LIMIT VERNIER SCALE SETTING
a.	0.392	0.460	4.340 ± 0.006	4.750-4.775	22	10
b.	0.500	0.632	5.873 ± 0.004			
c.	0.420	0.576	6.190 ± 0.005			
d.	0.750	0.828	8.993 ± 0.002			
e.	0.622	0.736	7.759 ± 0.003			
f.	0.408	0.610	5.322 ± 0.004			

Fig. 22-32

10. Metric measure problems. The answer to the first problem is given.

| | ACTUAL HOLE DIAMETERS | | GIVEN DISTANCE BETWEEN HOLE CENTERS (millimetres) | VERNIER CALIPER SCALE SETTINGS | | |
	HOLE A (millimetres)	HOLE B (millimetres)		MAIN SCALE SETTING (millimetres)	HIGH LIMIT VERNIER SCALE SETTING	LOW LIMIT VERNIER SCALE SETTING
a.	10.52	12.86	56.92 ± 0.07	68.5-69.0	9	2
b.	14.10	17.18	72.08 ± 0.08			
c.	17.34	19.06	95.36 ± 0.04			
d.	9.98	14.80	44.41 ± 0.06			
e.	8.40	11.66	67.33 ± 0.10			
f.	19.36	21.82	86.57 ± 0.012			

Fig. 22-33

APPLIED VERNIER HEIGHT GAGE PROBLEMS

The hole locations of parts such as the block shown in figure 22-34 are checked with a vernier height gage. A dial indicator attachment as shown in figure 22-35 is used on the height gage. The hole locations are checked by placing the block on a surface plate and indicating the bottom of each hole with the dial indicator. A surface plate is a smooth flat plate which is usually made of granite.

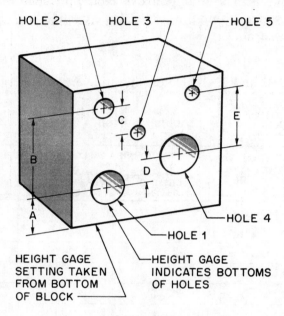

Fig. 22-34

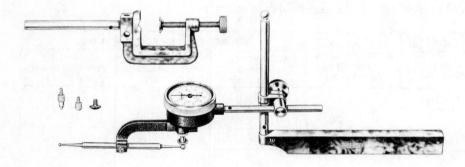

**Fig. 22-35 Dial indicator attachment
(The L.S. Starrett Company)**

The table in figure 22-36 lists given hole diameters and locations for an English dimensioned block. The table in figure 22-37 lists given hole diameters and locations for a metric dimensioned block. Determine the vernier height gage settings from the bottoms of the blocks to the bottom of each hole. Refer to the tables in figures 22-36 and 22-37. Assume that the actual hole diameters and locations are the same as the given dimensions. The setting for the first hole is given.

11. English measure problem

HOLE NUMBER	HOLE DIAMETER (inches)	GIVEN LOCATIONS TO CENTERS OF HOLES (inches)	HEIGHT GAGE SETTINGS	
			MAIN SCALE SETTING (inches)	VERNIER SCALE SETTING
1	0.410	A = 0.725	0.500-0.525	20
2	0.386	B = 1.276		
3	0.178	C = 0.614		
4	0.452	D = 0.320		
5	0.154	E = 0.814		

Fig. 22-36

12. Metric measure problem

HOLE NUMBER	HOLE DIAMETER (millimetres)	GIVEN LOCATIONS TO CENTERS OF HOLES (millimetres)	HEIGHT GAGE SETTINGS	
			MAIN SCALE SETTING (millimetres)	VERNIER SCALE SETTING
1	12.32	A = 15.78	9.5-10.0	6
2	6.38	B = 25.75		
3	4.50	C = 13.26		
4	14.76	D = 8.04		
5	5.84	E = 21.44		

Fig. 22-37

UNIT 23
Micrometers

After studying this unit you should be able to

- read settings on 0.001 decimal-inch micrometer scales.

- determine scale settings for given 0.001 decimal-inch micrometer readings.

- read settings on 0.000 1 decimal-inch vernier micrometer scales.

- determine scale settings for given 0.000 1 decimal-inch vernier micrometer readings.

- read settings on 0.01 millimetre metric micrometer scales.

- determine scale settings for given 0.01 millimetre metric vernier micrometer readings.

- read settings on 0.002 millimetre metric vernier micrometer scales.

- determine scale settings for given 0.002 millimetre metric vernier micrometer readings.

Micrometers are basic measuring instruments which are widely used in the manufacture and inspection of products. Occupations in various technical fields require making measurements with a number of different types of micrometers. Micrometers are commonly used by machinists, pattern makers, sheet metal technicians, inspectors, and automobile mechanics.

TYPES OF MICROMETERS

Micrometers are available in a wide range of sizes and types. Outside micrometers are used to measure lengths between parallel surfaces of objects. Other types of micrometers, such as depth micrometers, inside micrometers, screw-thread micrometers, and wire micrometers have specific applications. Some of the many types of micrometers are shown in figures 23-1 through 23-9.

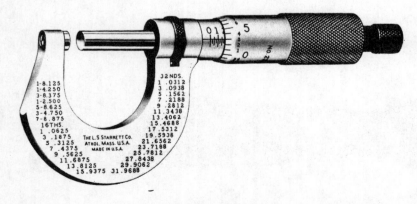

Fig. 23-1 Outside micrometer
(The L.S. Starrett Company)

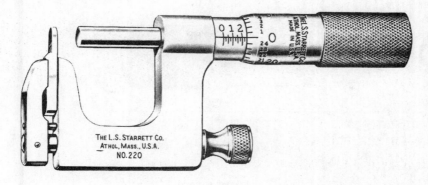

Fig. 23-2
Anvil micrometer
(The L.S. Starrett Company)

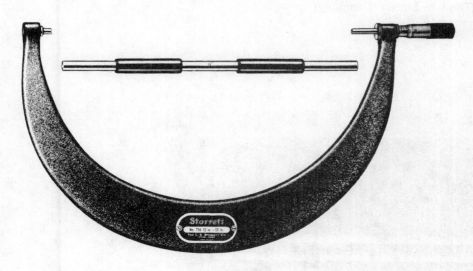

Fig. 23-3
Bow micrometer
(The L.S. Starrett Company)

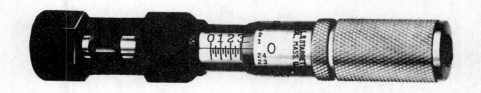

Fig. 23-4
Wire micrometer
(The L.S. Starrett Company)

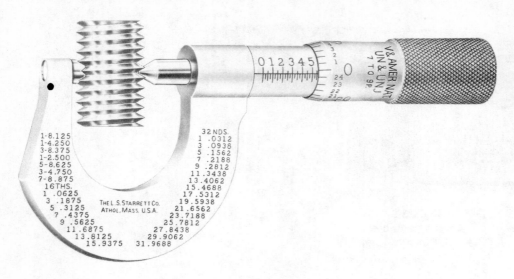

Fig. 23-5
Screw thread micrometer
(The L.S. Starrett Company)

Fig. 23-6
Inside micrometer
(The L.S. Starrett Company)

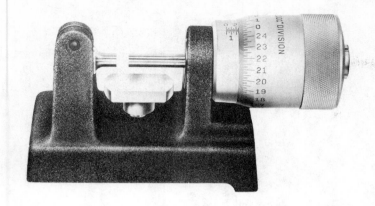

Fig. 23-7
Bench micrometer
(The L.S. Starrett Company)

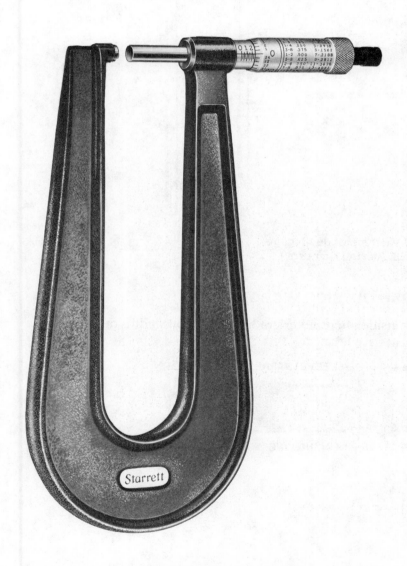

Fig. 23-8
Sheet metal micrometer
(The L.S. Starrett Company)

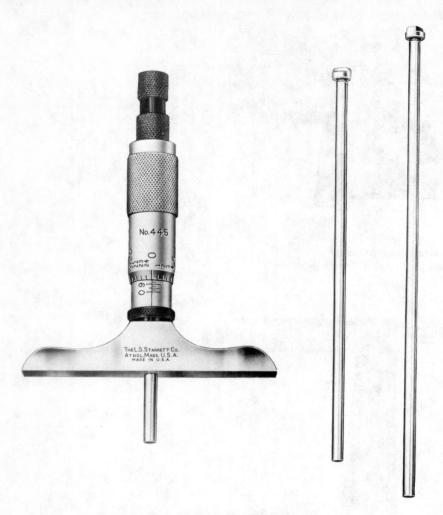

Fig. 23-9 Micrometer depth gage
(The L.S. Starrett Company)

DESCRIPTION OF AN ENGLISH OUTSIDE MICROMETER

Figure 23-10 shows an English outside micrometer graduated in thousandths of an inch (0.001″). The principal parts are labeled.

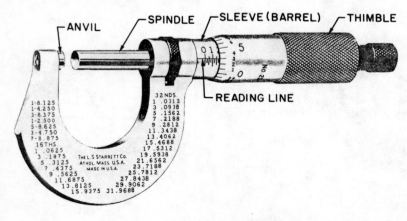

Fig. 23-10 An English outside micrometer
(The L.S. Starrett Company)

The part is placed between the anvil and the spindle. The barrel of a micrometer consists of a scale which is one inch long.

Refer to the barrel and thimble scales shown in figure 23-11. The one-inch barrel scale length is divided into ten divisions each equal to 0.100 inch. The 0.100-inch divisions are further divided into 4 divisions each equal to 0.025 inch.

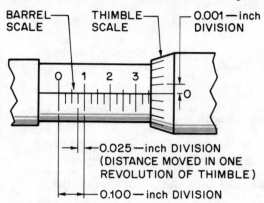

Fig. 23-11 Enlarged barrel and thimble scales

The thimble has a scale which is divided into 25 parts. One revolution of the thimble moves 0.025 inch on the barrel scale. A movement of one graduation on the thimble equals $\frac{1}{25}$ of 0.025 inch or 0.001 inch along the barrel.

READING AND SETTING AN ENGLISH MICROMETER

A micrometer is read by observing the position of the bevel edge of the thimble in reference to the scale on the barrel. The user observes the greatest 0.100-inch division and the number of 0.025-inch divisions on the barrel scale. To this barrel reading, add the number of the 0.001-inch divisions on the thimble that coincide with the horizontal line (reading line) on the barrel scale.

Procedure for Reading a Micrometer

- Observe the greatest 0.100-inch division on the barrel scale.
- Observe the number of 0.025-inch divisions on the barrel scale.
- Add the thimble scale reading (0.001-inch division) that coincides with the horizontal line on the barrel scale.

Example 1.   Read the English micrometer setting shown in figure 23-12.

Observe the greatest 0.100-inch division on the barrel scale. (three 0.100-inch divisions = 0.300 inch)

Observe the number of 0.025-inch divisions between the 0.300 inch mark and the thimble. (two 0.025-inch divisions = 0.050 inch)

Add the thimble scale reading that coincides with the horizontal line on the barrel scale. (eight 0.001-inch divisions = 0.008 inch)

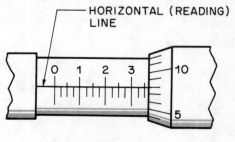

Fig. 23-12

Micrometer reading:
0.300″ + 0.050″ + 0.008″ = **0.358″ Ans**

Example 2.   Read the English micrometer setting shown in figure 23-13.

On the barrel scale, two 0.100-inch divisions = 0.200 inch.

On the barrel scale, zero 0.025-inch division = 0 inch.

On the thimble scale, twenty-three 0.001-inch divisions = 0.023 inch.

Micrometer reading:
0.200″ + 0.023″ = **0.223″** *Ans*

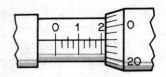
Fig. 23-13

Procedure for Setting a Micrometer to a Given Dimension

- Turn the thimble until the barrel scale indicates the required number of 0.100-inch divisions plus the necessary number of 0.025-inch divisions.
- Turn the thimble until the thimble scale indicates the required additional 0.001-inch divisions.

Example 1.   Set 0.949 inch on a micrometer.

The barrel scale setting is between 0.925″ and 0.950″. Turn the thimble to nine 0.100-inch divisions plus one 0.025-inch division on the barrel scale. (9 × 0.100″ + 0.025″ = 0.925″)

Subtract to find the thimble setting.
(0.949″ − 0.925″ = 0.024″)

Turn the thimble an additional twenty-four 0.001-inch thimble scale divisions.

The 0.949-inch setting is shown in figure 23-14.

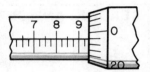
Fig. 23-14

Example 2.   Set 0.520 inch on a micrometer.

The barrel scale setting is between 0.500″ and 0.525″. Turn the thimble to five 0.100-inch divisions on the barrel scale. (5 × 0.100″ = 0.500″)

Subtract to find the thimble setting.
(0.520″ − 0.500″ = 0.020″)

Turn the thimble an additional twenty 0.001-inch divisions.

The 0.520-inch setting is shown in figure 23-15.

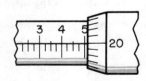
Fig. 23-15

Exercise 23-1

Read the settings on these English micrometer scales graduated in 0.001″.

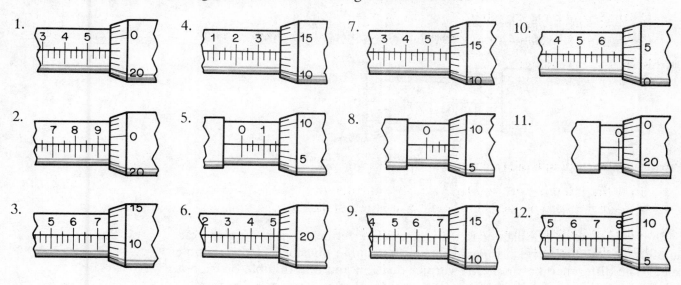

Given the micrometer readings in the tables in figure 23-16, determine the barrel scale and thimble scale settings. The answer to the first problem is given.

	MICROMETER READING (inches)	BARREL SCALE SETTING IS BETWEEN: (inches)	THIMBLE SCALE SETTING (inches)			MICROMETER READING (inches)	BARREL SCALE SETTING IS BETWEEN: (inches)	THIMBLE SCALE SETTING (inches)
13.	0.283	0.275-0.300	0.008	20.	0.579		
14.	0.732			21.	0.007		
15.	0.156			22.	0.416		
16.	0.444			23.	0.138		
17.	0.998			24.	0.967		
18.	0.078			25.	0.880		
19.	0.326			26.	0.796		

Fig. 23-16

THE ENGLISH VERNIER MICROMETER

The addition of a vernier scale on the barrel of a 0.001-inch micrometer increases the degree of precision of the instrument to 0.000 1 inch. The barrel scale and the thimble scale of a vernier micrometer are identical to that of a 0.001-inch micrometer.

Figure 23-17 shows the relative positions of the barrel scale, thimble scale, and vernier scale of a 0.000 1-inch micrometer.

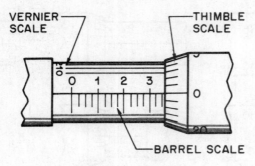

Fig. 23-17

The vernier scale consists of ten divisions. Ten vernier divisions on the circumference of the barrel are equal in length to nine divisions of the thimble scale. The difference between one vernier division and one thimble division is 0.000 1 inch. Figure 23-18 shows a flattened view of a vernier and a thimble scale.

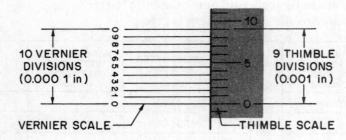

Fig. 23-18

READING AND SETTING AN ENGLISH VERNIER MICROMETER

Reading an English vernier micrometer is the same as reading a 0.001-inch micrometer except for the addition of reading the vernier scale. A particular vernier graduation coincides with a thimble scale graduation. The vernier graduation gives the number of 0.000 1-inch divisions that are added to the barrel and thimble scale readings.

Example 1.   A flattened view of an English vernier micrometer setting is shown in figure 23-19. Read this setting.

Read the barrel scale reading.
$(3 \times 0.100'' + 3 \times 0.025'' = 0.375'')$

Read the thimble scale.
$(9 \times 0.001'' = 0.009'')$

Read the vernier scale.
$(4 \times 0.000\ 1'' = 0.000\ 4'')$

Vernier micrometer reading:
$0.375'' + 0.009'' + 0.000\ 4'' = 0.384\ 4''\ Ans$

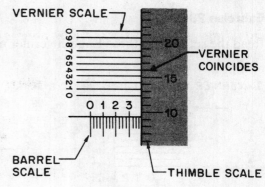

Fig. 23-19

Example 2.   A flattened view of an English vernier micrometer setting is shown in figure 23-20. Read this setting.

On the barrel scale read 0.200 inch.

On the thimble scale read 0.020 inch.

On the vernier scale read 0.000 8 inch.

Vernier micrometer reading:
$0.200'' + 0.020'' + 0.000\ 8'' = 0.220\ 8''\ Ans$

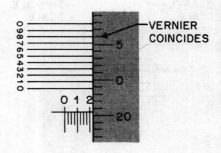

Fig. 23-20

Setting an English vernier micrometer is the same as setting a 0.001-inch micrometer except for the addition of setting the vernier scale.

Example.   Set 0.233 6 inch on a vernier micrometer.

The barrel scale setting is between 0.225'' and 0.250''. Turn the thimble to two 0.100-inch divisions plus one 0.025-inch division on the barrel scale.
$(2 \times 0.100'' + 0.025'' = 0.225'')$

Subtract to find the thimble setting.
$(0.233\ 6'' - 0.225'' = 0.008\ 6'')$

The thimble setting is between 0.008'' and 0.009''. Turn the thimble an additional eight 0.001-inch divisions.
$(2 \times 0.100'' + 0.025'' + 0.008'' = 0.233'')$

Subtract to find the vernier setting.
$(0.233\ 6'' - 0.233'' = 0.000\ 6'')$

Turn the thimble carefully until a graduation on the thimble scale coincides with 0.000 6'' on the vernier scale.

The 0.233 6-inch setting is shown in figure 23-21.

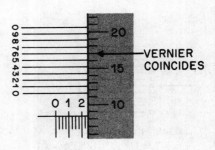

Fig. 23-21

Exercise 23-2

Read the settings on these English vernier micrometer scales graduated in 0.000 1″.

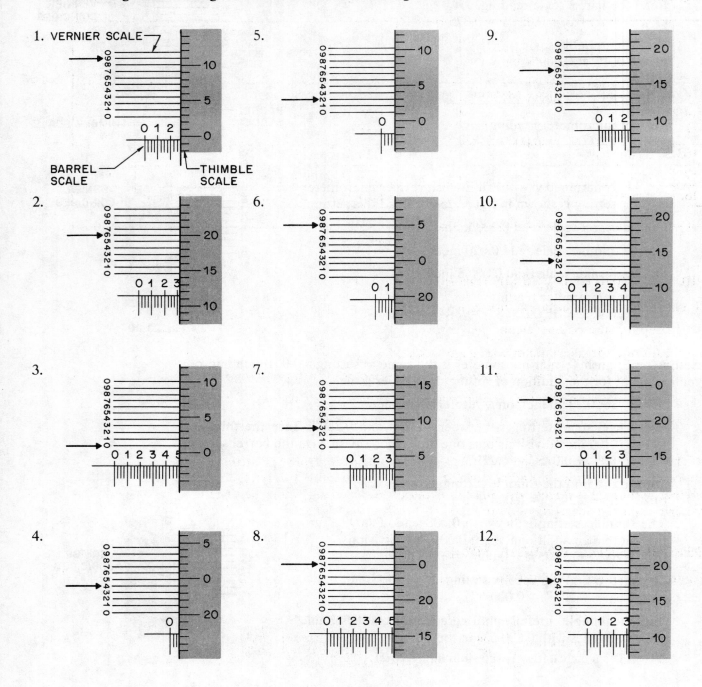

Given the micrometer readings in the table in figure 23-22, determine the barrel scale, thimble scale, and vernier scale settings. The answer to the first problem is given.

	MICROMETER READING (inches)	BARREL SCALE SETTING IS BETWEEN: (inches)	THIMBLE SCALE SETTING IS BETWEEN: (inches)	VERNIER SCALE SETTING (inches)		MICROMETER READING (inches)	BARREL SCALE SETTING IS BETWEEN: (inches)	THIMBLE SCALE SETTING IS BETWEEN: (inches)	VERNIER SCALE SETTING (inches)
13.	0.686 7	0.675-0.700	0.011-0.012	0.000 7	20.	0.603 5			
14.	0.289 3				21.	0.226 4			
15.	0.510 9				22.	0.123 6			
16.	0.111 1				23.	0.005 9			
17.	0.933 2				24.	0.595 1			
18.	0.800 8				25.	0.310 7			
19.	0.398 3				26.	0.881 4			

Fig. 23-22

PROPER CARE AND USE OF THE MICROMETER

To ensure accurate measurements

- keep the micrometer clean.
- calibrate the micrometer with gage blocks.
- take more than one reading and find the average of these measurements.
- hold the micrometer perpendicular to the surface of the part.
- rock across the diameter and along the axis of a cylinder when measuring the diameter of the cylinder.

The technique of adjusting the micrometer to measure a part is extremely important. The micrometer adjustment should not be too loose or too tight. The correct technique is developed through experience. Knowing when the micrometer is adjusted correctly takes practice.

DESCRIPTION OF A METRIC MICROMETER

Figure 23-23 shows a 0.01-millimetre outside micrometer.

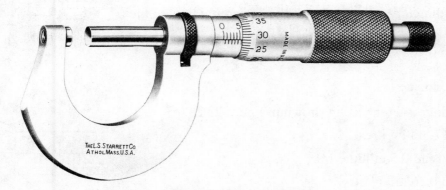

Fig. 23-23 A metric outside micrometer
(The L.S. Starrett Company)

The barrel of a 0.01-millimetre micrometer consists of a scale which is 25 millimetres long. Refer to the barrel and thimble scales shown in figure 23-24. The 25-millimetre barrel scale length is divided into 25 divisions each equal to 1 millimetre. Every fifth millimetre is numbered from 0 to 25 (0, 5, 10, 15, 20, 25). On the lower part of the barrel scale each millimetre is divided in half (0.5 mm).

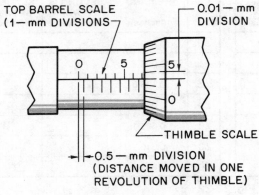

Fig. 23-24

The thimble has a scale which is divided into 50 parts. One revolution of the thimble moves 0.5 millimetre on the barrel scale. A movement of one graduation on the thimble equals $\frac{1}{50}$ of 0.5 millimetre or 0.01 millimetre along the barrel.

READING AND SETTING A METRIC MICROMETER

Procedure for Reading a 0.01 Millimetre Micrometer

- Observe the number of 1-millimetre divisions on the barrel scale.

- Observe the number of 0.5-millimetre divisions (either 0 or 1) on the lower part of the barrel scale.

- Add the thimble scale reading (0.01 division) that coincides with the horizontal line on the barrel scale.

Example 1.   Read the metric micrometer setting shown in figure 23-25.

Observe the number of 1-millimetre divisions on the barrel scale.
(4 × 1 mm = 4 mm)

Observe the number of 0.5-millimetre divisions on the lower barrel scale.
(0 × 0.5 mm = 0)

Add the thimble scale reading that coincides with the horizontal line on the barrel scale.
(33 × 0.01 mm = 0.33 mm)

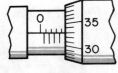

Fig. 23-25

Micrometer reading:
4 mm + 0.33 mm = **4.33 mm** *Ans*

Example 2.   Read the metric micrometer setting shown in figure 23-26.

On the barrel scale read 17 millimetres.

On the lower barrel scale read 0.5 millimetre.

On the thimble scale read 0.26 millimetre.

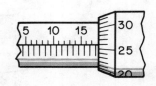

Fig. 23-26

Micrometer reading:
17 mm + 0.5 mm + 0.26 mm = **17.76 mm** *Ans*

Procedure for Setting a Metric Micrometer

- Turn the thimble until the scale indicates the required number of 1-millimetre divisions plus the necessary number of 0.5-millimetre divisions.

- Turn the thimble until the thimble scale indicates the required additional 0.01-millimetre divisions.

Example. Set 14.94 millimetres on a micrometer.

The barrel scale is between 14.5 mm and 15.0 mm. Turn the thimble to fourteen 1-mm divisions plus one 0.5-mm division on the barrel scale.
(14 mm + 0.5 mm = 14.5 mm)

Subtract to find the thimble setting.
(14.94 mm − 14.5 mm = 0.44 mm)

Turn the thimble an additional forty-four 0.01-mm divisions.

The 14.94-millimetre setting is shown in figure 23-27.

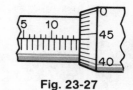

Fig. 23-27

Exercise 23-3

Read the settings on these metric micrometer scales graduated in 0.01 mm.

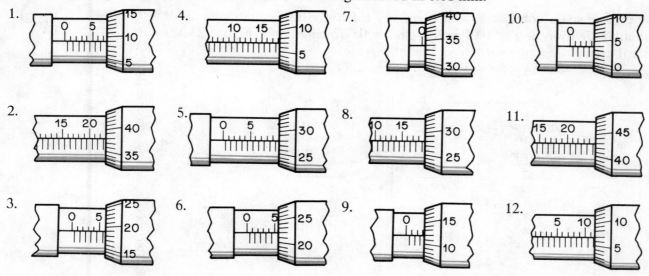

Given the micrometer readings in the table in figure 23-28, determine the barrel scale and thimble scale settings. The answer to the first problem is given.

	MICROMETER READING (millimetres)	BARREL SCALE SETTING IS BETWEEN: (millimetres)	THIMBLE SCALE SETTING (millimetres)		MICROMETER READING (millimetres)	BARREL SCALE SETTING IS BETWEEN: (millimetres)	THIMBLE SCALE SETTING (millimetres)
13.	12.86	12.5-13.0	0.36	20.	6.66		
14.	9.34			21.	8.44		
15.	15.08			22.	19.72		
16.	3.92			23.	23.08		
17.	0.88			24.	5.66		
18.	7.06			25.	21.82		
19.	18.12			26.	13.90		

Fig. 23-28

THE METRIC VERNIER MICROMETER

The addition of a vernier scale on the barrel of a 0.01-millimetre micrometer increases the degree of precision of the instrument to 0.002 millimetre. The barrel scale and the thimble scale of a vernier micrometer are identical to that of a 0.01-millimetre micrometer.

Figure 23-29 shows the relative positions of the barrel scale, thimble scale, and vernier scale of a 0.002-millimetre micrometer.

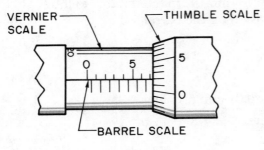

Fig. 23-29

The vernier scale consists of five divisions. Each division equals one-fifth of a thimble division or $\frac{1}{5}$ of 0.01 millimetre or 0.002 millimetre. Figure 23-30 shows a flattened view of a vernier and thimble scale.

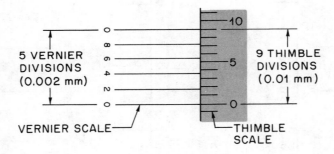

Fig. 23-30

READING AND SETTING A METRIC VERNIER MICROMETER

Reading a metric vernier micrometer is the same as reading a 0.01-millimetre micrometer except for the addition of reading the vernier scale. Observe which division on the vernier scale coincides with a division on the thimble scale. If the vernier division which coincides is marked 2, add 0.002 millimetre to the barrel and thimble scale reading. Add 0.004 millimetre for a coinciding vernier division marked 4, add 0.006 millimetre for a division marked 6, and add 0.008 millimetre for a division marked 8.

Example 1.   A flattened view of a metric vernier micrometer is shown in figure 23-31. Read this setting.

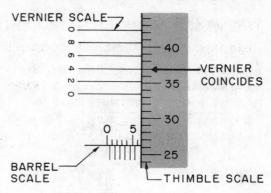

Read the barrel scale.
(6 × 1 mm + 0 × 0.5 mm = 6 mm)

Read the thimble scale.
(26 × 0.01 mm = 0.26 mm)

Read the vernier scale.
(0.004 mm)

Vernier micrometer reading:
6 mm + 0.26 mm + 0.004 mm = **6.264 mm** *Ans*

Fig. 23-31

Example 2.   A flattened view of a metric vernier micrometer is shown in figure 23-32. Read this setting.

On the barrel scale read 9.5 millimetres.

On the thimble scale read 0.43 millimetre.

On the vernier scale read 0.008 millimetre.

Vernier micrometer reading:
9.5 mm + 0.43 mm + 0.008 mm = **9.938 mm** *Ans*

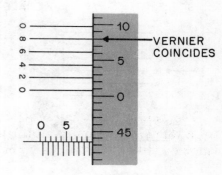

Fig. 23-32

Setting a metric vernier micrometer is the same as setting a 0.01-millimetre micrometer except for the addition of setting the vernier scale.

Example.   Set 1.862 millimetres on a vernier micrometer.

The barrel scale setting is between 1.5 mm and 2.0 mm. Turn the thimble to one 1-mm division plus one 0.5-mm division on the barrel scale.
(1 × 1 mm + 1 × 0.5 mm = 1.5 mm)

Subtract to find the thimble setting.
(1.862 mm − 1.5 mm = 0.362 mm)

The thimble setting is between 0.36 mm and 0.37 mm. Turn the thimble an additional thirty-six 0.01-millimetre divisions.
(1 × 1 mm + 1 × 0.5 mm + 36 × 0.01 mm = 1.86 mm)

Subtract to find the vernier setting.
(1.862 mm − 1.86 mm = 0.002 mm)

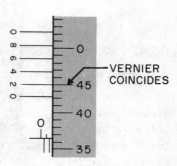

Turn the thimble carefully until a graduation on the thimble coincides with 0.002 mm on the vernier scale.

The 1.862-millimetre setting is shown in figure 23-33.

Fig. 23-33

Exercise 23-4

Read the settings on these metric vernier micrometer scales graduated in 0.002 mm.

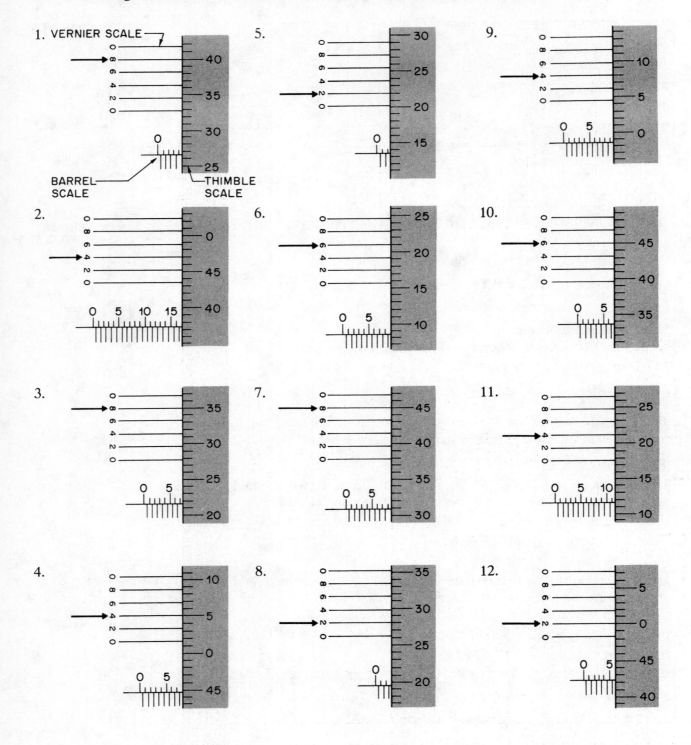

Given the 0.002-millimetre vernier micrometer readings in figure 23-34, determine the barrel scale, thimble scale, and vernier scale settings. The answer to the first problem is given.

	MICROMETER READING (millimetres)	BARREL SCALE SETTING IS BETWEEN: (millimetres)	THIMBLE SCALE SETTING IS BETWEEN: (millimetres)	VERNIER SCALE SETTING (milli-metres)			MICROMETER READING (millimetres)	BARREL SCALE SETTING IS BETWEEN: (millimetres)	THIMBLE SCALE SETTING IS BETWEEN: (millimetres)	VERNIER SCALE SETTING (milli-metres)
13.	14.874	14.5-15.0	0.37-0.38	0.004		20.	20.292			
14.	21.168					21.	5.708			
15.	9.238					22.	13.998			
16.	11.862					23.	8.324			
17.	3.046					24.	0.756			
18.	8.768					25.	14.582			
19.	7.004					26.	9.776			

Fig. 23-34

UNIT EXERCISE AND PROBLEM REVIEW

Exercise 23-5

ENGLISH MICROMETER (0.001″)

1. Read the settings on these English micrometer scales graduated in 0.001″.

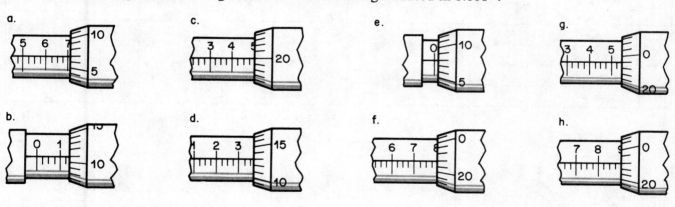

2. Given the micrometer readings in the table in figure 23-35, determine the barrel scale and thimble scale settings.

	MICROMETER READING (inches)	BARREL SCALE SETTING IS BETWEEN: (inches)	THIMBLE SCALE SETTING (inches)			MICROMETER READING (inches)	BARREL SCALE SETTING IS BETWEEN: (inches)	THIMBLE SCALE SETTING (inches)
a.	0.494				e.	0.687		
b.	0.109				f.	0.312		
c.	0.938				g.	0.501		
d.	0.277				h.	0.888		

Fig. 23-35

ENGLISH VERNIER MICROMETER (0.000 1″)

3. Read the settings on these English vernier micrometer scales graduated in 0.000 1″.

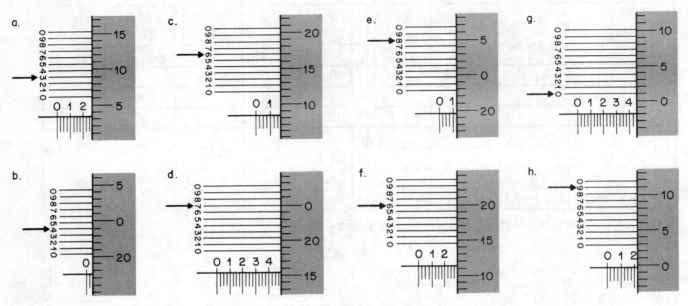

4. Given the micrometer readings in the table in figure 23-36, determine the barrel scale, thimble scale, and vernier scale settings.

	MICROMETER READING (inches)	BARREL SCALE SETTING IS BETWEEN: (inches)	THIMBLE SCALE SETTING IS BETWEEN: (inches)	VERNIER SCALE SETTING (inches)			MICROMETER READING (inches)	BARREL SCALE SETTING IS BETWEEN: (inches)	THIMBLE SCALE SETTING IS BETWEEN: (inches)	VERNIER SCALE SETTING (inches)
a.	0.293 7					e.	0.556 5			
b.	0.806 4					f.	0.035 2			
c.	0.190 3					g.	0.448 4			
d.	0.736 9					h.	0.696 7			

Fig. 23-36

METRIC MICROMETER (0.01 mm)

5. Read the settings on these metric micrometer scales graduated in 0.01 mm.

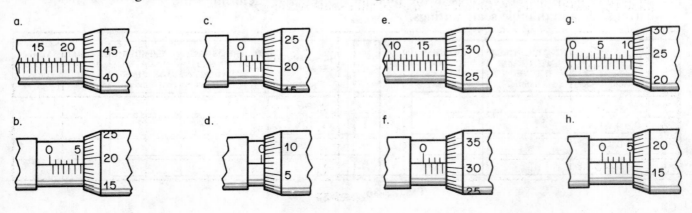

6. Given the micrometer readings in the table in figure 23-37, determine the barrel scale and thimble scale settings.

	MICROMETER READING (millimetres)	BARREL SCALE SETTING IS BETWEEN: (millimetres)	THIMBLE SCALE SETTING (millimetres)			MICROMETER READING (millimetres)	BARREL SCALE SETTING IS BETWEEN: (millimetres)	THIMBLE SCALE SETTING (millimetres)
a.	18.74				e.	8.08		
b.	2.68				f.	15.76		
c.	7.92				g.	9.34		
d.	23.40				h.	16.96		

Fig. 23-37

METRIC VERNIER MICROMETER (0.002 mm)

7. Read the settings on these metric vernier micrometer scales graduated in 0.002 mm.

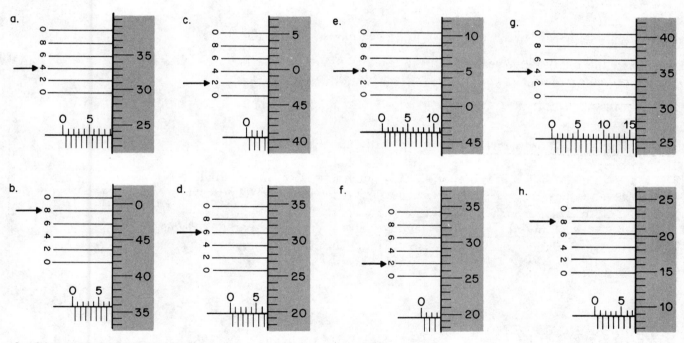

8. Given the 0.002-millimetre vernier micrometer readings in figure 23-38, determine the barrel scale, thimble scale, and vernier scale settings.

	MICROMETER READING (millimetres)	BARREL SCALE SETTING IS BETWEEN: (millimetres)	THIMBLE SCALE SETTING IS BETWEEN: (millimetres)	VERNIER SCALE SETTING (millimetres)			MICROMETER READING (millimetres)	BARREL SCALE SETTING IS BETWEEN: (millimetres)	THIMBLE SCALE SETTING IS BETWEEN: (millimetres)	VERNIER SCALE SETTING (millimetres)
a.	17.736					e.	22.222			
b.	9.088					f.	5.696			
c.	3.872					g.	16.164			
d.	13.704					h.	8.098			

Fig. 23-38

SECTION 5
Computed Measure

UNIT 24
Areas of
Common Polygons

OBJECTIVES

After studying this unit you should be able to

- compute areas of common polygons, given bases and altitudes.
- compute altitudes of common polygons, given bases and areas.
- compute bases of common polygons, given altitudes and areas.
- compute areas of more complex figures which consist of two or more common polygons.
- solve applied problems using principles discussed in this unit.

Many occupations require computation of common polygon areas in finding job materials and costs. It is also sometimes necessary to find unknown lengths, widths, and heights of polygons when the areas are known.

Methods of computing areas, sides, and heights of rectangles, parallelograms, trapezoids, and triangles are presented in this unit. The areas of complex polygons are found by dividing the complex polygons into two or more of these simpler figures.

AREAS OF RECTANGLES

A *rectangle* is a four-sided polygon with opposite sides equal and parallel and with each angle equal to a right angle. The *area of a rectangle* is equal to the product of the length and width.

$A = lw$ 　　　　　　　　where A = area
　　　　　　　　　　　　　　　l = length
　　　　　　　　　　　　　　　w = width

Example 1.　A rectangular platform is 24 feet long and 14 feet wide. Find the area of the platform.

$A = 24 \text{ ft} \times 14 \text{ ft}$

$A = 336 \text{ sq ft } Ans$

380

Example 2. Determine the area, in square metres, of a rectangular strip of sheet stock which is 20 centimetres wide and 3.65 metres long.

To find the area in square metres, express both the length and width in metres.

Length = 3.65 m

Width = 20 cm = 0.20 m

Find the area.

$A = 3.65$ m $\times 0.20$ m

$A = 0.73$ m^2 *Ans*

Example 3. A building floor plan is shown in figure 24-1. Find the area of the floor.

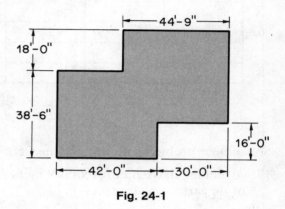

Fig. 24-1

Divide the figure into rectangles. One way of dividing the figure is shown in figure 24-2.

To find the area of the floor, compute the area of each rectangle and add the three areas.

- Area of rectangle ①.

  $A = 42$ ft $\times 16$ ft

  $A = 672$ sq ft

- Area of rectangle ②.

  Length = 42 ft + 30 ft = 72 ft

  Width = 38.5 ft − 16 ft = 22.5 ft

  $A = 72$ ft $\times 22.5$ ft

  $A = 1\ 620$ sq ft

- Area of rectangle ③.

  Length = 44.75 ft

  Width = 18 ft

  $A = 44.75$ ft $\times 18$ ft

  $A = 805.5$ sq ft

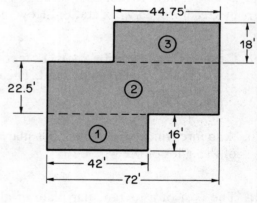

Fig. 24-2

- Total area = 672 sq ft + 1 620 sq ft + 805.5 sq ft = **3 097.5 sq ft** *Ans*

Example 4. A rectangular patio is to have an area of 40.5 square metres. If the length is 9 metres, find the required width.

Substitute values in the formula and solve.

$A = lw$

40.5 m$^2 = 9$ m (w)

$\dfrac{40.5 \text{ m}^2}{9 \text{ m}} = w$

$w = 4.5$ m *Ans*

Exercise 24-1

Use the tables found in the Appendix for equivalent units of measure. Find the unknown area, length or width for each of the rectangles, 1-16, in figure 24-3. Round the answers to 1 decimal place.

	LENGTH	WIDTH	AREA
1.	3 ft	7 ft	
2.	5 m	9 m	
3.	8.5 in	6.0 in	
4.	2.6 yd		11.7 sq yd
5.		23 cm	200.1 cm^2
6.	0.4 km		0.2 km^2
7.	12'-6"	7'-0"	
8.		0.08 mi	0.12 sq mi

	LENGTH	WIDTH	AREA
9.	26.2 mm		366.8 mm^2
10.	5.6 cm	18.8 cm	
11.		42 in	33.6 sq in
12.	64.2 m		3 762 m^2
13.	12'-3"	16'-9"	
14.	2.9 km	0.7 km	
15.	7.4 mi		6.7 sq mi
16.		120 ft	26 160 sq ft

Fig. 24-3

Solve these problems. Round the answers to 2 decimal places.

17. A rectangular strip of steel is 9 inches wide and 6.5 feet long. Find the area of the strip in square feet.

18. A school shop 10 metres wide and 14 metres long is to be built. Allow 5 square metres for each work station. How many work stations can be provided?

19. Carpet is installed in a room 12 feet wide and 24 feet long. The cost of the carpet is $18.75 per square yard. The installation cost is $75.00. Find the total cost of carpeting the room.

20. A square window contains 729 square inches of glass. Find the length of each of the sides of the window.

21. The cost of a rectangular plate of aluminum 3 feet wide and 4 feet long is $45. Find the cost of a rectangular plate 6 feet wide and 8 feet long using this same stock.

22. The walls of a room 14 ft × 18 ft are wallpapered. The height of the walls is 7'-6". The room has a doorway which is 3 ft × 7 ft and 4 windows each 3 ft × 5 ft. Each roll of wallpaper has an area of 60 square feet. An allowance of 20% is made for waste.

    a. Find the wall area to be wallpapered.

    b. How many rolls are required for this job?

23. Find the area of the sheet metal piece shown in figure 24-4.

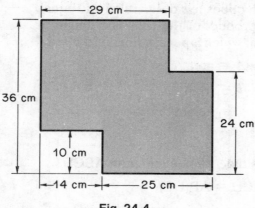

Fig. 24-4

24. The bottom of a rectangular carton is to have an area of 2 400 square centimetres. The length is to be one and one-half times the width. Compute the length and width dimensions.

25. A landscape architect designs a circular patio as shown in figure 24-5. The inscribed square portion of the patio is surfaced with brick and the four outer segments are planted with ground cover. How many square metres of brick are required?

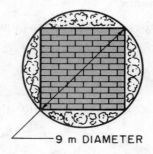

9 m DIAMETER

Fig. 24-5

26. The plot of land shown in figure 24-6 has an area of 6 350 square metres. Find distance x.

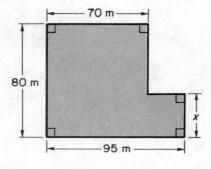

Fig. 24-6

AREAS OF PARALLELOGRAMS

A *parallelogram* is a four-sided polygon with opposite sides parallel and equal. The *area of a parallelogram* is equal to the product of the base and height or altitude. (The height or altitude is a line segment which is perpendicular to a base.)

$$A = bh$$ *where* A = area

b = base

h = height or altitude

In figure 24-7, AB is a base and DE is an altitude of parallelogram ABCD.

Area of parallelogram ABCD = AB(DE)

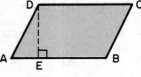

Fig. 24-7

In figure 24-8, BC is a base and DF is an altitude of parallelogram ABCD.

Area of parallelogram ABCD = BC(DF)

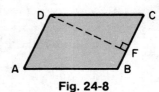

Fig. 24-8

Example 1.   What is the area of a parallelogram with a $1\frac{1}{4}$-foot base and a 4-inch altitude? Express the answer in square inches.

To find the area in square inches, express both the base and altitude in inches.

Base = $1\frac{1}{4}$ ft = 15 in

Altitude = 4 in

A = 15 in × 4 in

A = **60 sq in** *Ans*

Example 2.   The lot shown in figure 24-9 is in the shape of a parallelogram. Find the area of the lot to the nearer metre.

Find the base.

Base = 46 m + 20 m = 66 m

Find the altitude using the Pythagorean Theorem.

$(40 \text{ m})^2 = (20 \text{ m})^2 + h^2$

$1\,600 \text{ m}^2 = 400 \text{ m}^2 + h^2$

$1\,200 \text{ m}^2 = h^2$

$h = \sqrt{1\,200 \text{ m}^2}$

$h = 34.64 \text{ m}$

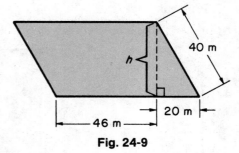

Fig. 24-9

Find the area.

A = 66 m × 34.64 m

A = **2 286 m^2** *Ans*

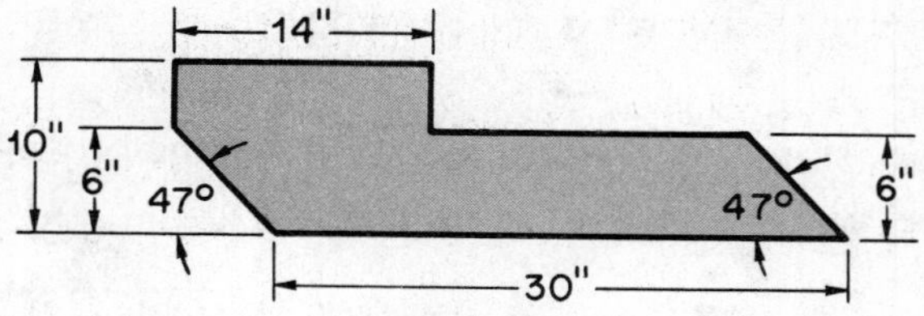

Example 3.   A drawing of a baseplate is shown in figure 24-10. The plate is made of number 2 gage (thickness) aluminum which weighs 3.6 pounds per square foot. Find the weight of the plate.

Fig. 24-10

Fig. 24-11

The area of the plate must be found. By studying the drawing, one method for finding the area is to divide the figure into a rectangle and a parallelogram as shown in figure 24-11.

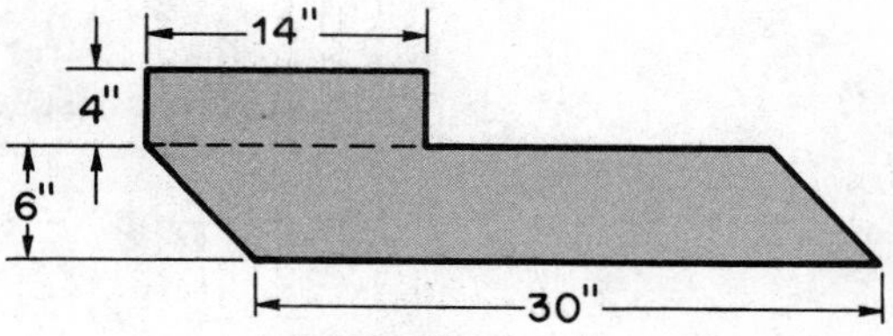

- Find the area of the rectangle.

  $A = 14$ in $\times$ 4 in

  $A = 56$ sq in

- Find the area of the parallelogram.

  $A = 30$ in $\times$ 6 in

  $A = 180$ sq in

- Find the total area of the plate.

  Total area = 56 sq in + 180 sq in = 236 sq in

Compute the weight.

- Find the area in square feet.

  $\dfrac{236 \text{ sq in}}{1} \times \dfrac{1 \text{ sq ft}}{144 \text{ sq in}} = 1.64$ sq ft

- Weight of plate = 1.64 sq ft $\times$ 3.6 lb/sq ft = **5.9 lb** *Ans*

Exercise 24-2

Use the tables found in the Appendix for equivalent units of measure. Find the unknown area, base or altitude for each of the parallelograms 1-16, in figure 24-12. Round the answers to 1 decimal place.

	BASE	ALTITUDE	AREA
1.	20 cm	5.2 cm	
2.	6 yd	9.8 yd	
3.	26 in		486.2 sq in
4.		37.4 mm	2 057 mm²
5.	0.07 mi		0.014 sq mi
6.	2.4 km	4.5 km	
7.	22 m	0.9 m	
8.	19'-6"		331.5 sq ft

	BASE	ALTITUDE	AREA
9.		0.6 km	5.1 km²
10.	56 mm	6.8 mm	
11.	17 mi	18.3 mi	
12.	58.1 cm		5.81 cm²
13.		38 in	1 887.2 sq in
14.	20'-9"		830 sq ft
15.	38 yd	26.6 yd	
16.	7.2 m	0.09 m	

Fig. 24-12

Solve these problems. Round the answers to 2 decimal places.

17. The cross section of the piece of tool steel shown in figure 24-13 is in the shape of a parallelogram. Find the cross-sectional area.

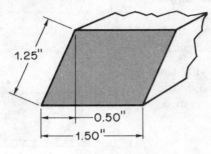

Fig. 24-13

18. A 5-foot wide sidewalk is built around the perimeter of a minipark. The minipark is in the shape of a parallelogram as shown in figure 24-14. Find the total sidewalk area.

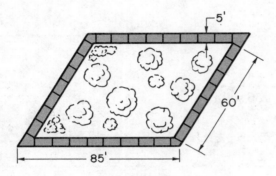

Fig. 24-14

19. Two cutouts in the shape of parallelograms are stamped in a strip of metal as shown in figure 24-15. Segment AB is parallel to segment CD, and dimension E equals dimension F. Compare the areas of the two cutouts.

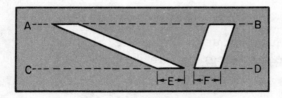

Fig. 24-15

20. An oblique groove is cut in a block as shown in figure 24-16. Before the groove was cut, the top of the block was in the shape of a rectangle. Determine the area of the top after the groove is cut.

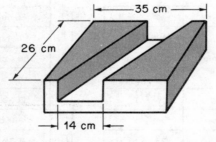

Fig. 24-16

21. Two hundred metres of fencing are to be used to fence in a garden. The garden can be made in the shape of a square, a rectangle, or a parallelogram such as those shown in figure 24-17. Which of the three shapes permits the largest garden?

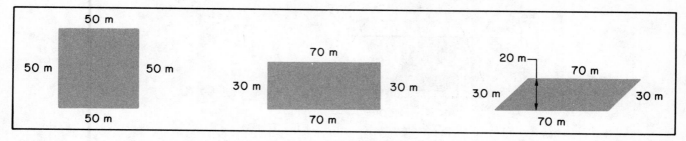

Fig. 24-17

22. In figure 24-18, building floor plans in the shape of a square, a rectangle, and a parallelogram are shown. Each floor plan contains 1 600 square feet. The walls of each building are 10 feet high.

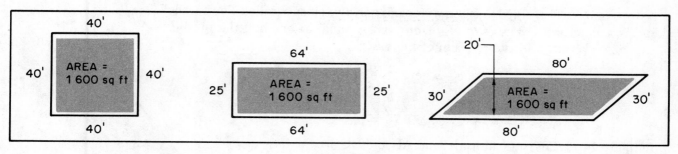

Fig. 24-18

a. Compute the wall area for each building which is required to provide a floor area of 1 600 square feet.

b. Which shape provides the most area for the least amount of material and cost?

23. Find the area of the template shown in figure 24-19.

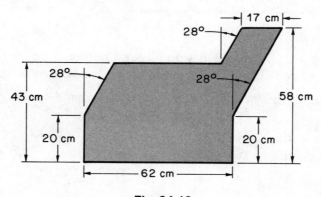

Fig. 24-19

24. A plot of land, ABCD, is in the shape of a parallelogram. The plot is divided into 3 building lots each in the shape of a parallelogram as shown in figure 24-20. Lot 3 has an area of 5 950 square metres.

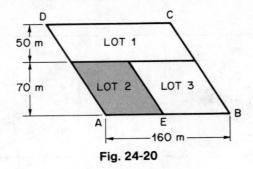

Fig. 24-20

    a. What is the area of lot 2?

    b. How many metres long is distance AE?

AREAS OF TRAPEZOIDS

A *trapezoid* is a four-sided polygon which has only two sides parallel. The parallel sides are called *bases*. The *area of a trapezoid* is equal to one-half the product of the height or altitude and the sum of the bases.

$$A = \tfrac{1}{2}h\,(b_1 + b_2)$$

        where A = area

              h = height or altitude

              b_1 and b_2 = bases

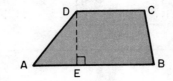

In figure 24-21, DE is the altitude, and AB and DC are the bases of trapezoid ABCD.

    Area of trapezoid ABCD = $\tfrac{1}{2}$DE(AB + DC)

Fig. 24-21

Example 1. Find the area of the stairway wall ABCD, shown in figure 24-22. Round the answer to 1 decimal place.

$$A = \tfrac{1}{2}(4.2 \text{ m})(7.0 \text{ m} + 3.8 \text{ m})$$

$$A = \tfrac{1}{2}(4.2 \text{ m})(10.8 \text{ m})$$

$$A = 22.7 \text{ m}^2 \text{ } Ans$$

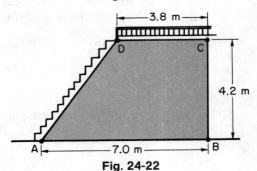

Fig. 24-22

Example 2. The area of a trapezoid is 376 square centimetres. The altitude is 16 centimetres and one base is 35 centimetres. Find the other base.

Substitute values in the formula for the area of a trapezoid and solve.

$$376 \text{ cm}^2 = \tfrac{1}{2}(16 \text{ cm})(35 \text{ cm} + b_2)$$

$$376 \text{ cm}^2 = 8 \text{ cm}(35 \text{ cm} + b_2)$$

$$376 \text{ cm}^2 = 280 \text{ cm}^2 + 8 \text{ cm}(b_2)$$

$$96 \text{ cm}^2 = 8 \text{ cm}(b_2)$$

$$b_2 = 12 \text{ cm } Ans$$

Example 3.   The section of land shown in figure 24-23 is to be graded and paved. The cost is $10.35 per square yard. What is the total cost of grading and paving the section? Express the answer to the nearer dollar.

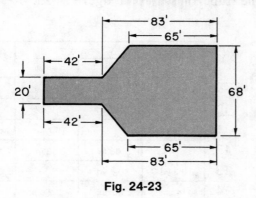

Fig. 24-23

The area of the land must be found. Divide the section of land into two rectangles and a trapezoid as shown in figure 24-24.

- Find area ①.

    $A = 42 \text{ ft} \times 20 \text{ ft}$

    $A = 840 \text{ sq ft}$

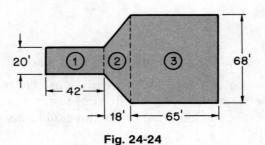

Fig. 24-24

- Find area ②.

    Height $= 83 \text{ ft} - 65 \text{ ft} = 18 \text{ ft}$

    First base $= 68 \text{ ft}$

    Second base $= 20 \text{ ft}$

    $A = \frac{1}{2}(18 \text{ ft})(68 \text{ ft} + 20 \text{ ft})$

    $A = \frac{1}{2}(18 \text{ ft})(88 \text{ ft})$

    $A = 792 \text{ sq ft}$

- Find area ③.

    $A = 65 \text{ ft} \times 68 \text{ ft}$

    $A = 4\,420 \text{ sq ft}$

- Find the total area of the land.

    Total area $= 840 \text{ sq ft} + 792 \text{ sq ft} + 4\,420 \text{ sq ft} = 6\,052 \text{ sq ft}$

Compute the cost.

- Find the area in square yards.

    $\dfrac{6\,052 \text{ sq ft}}{1} \times \dfrac{1 \text{ sq yd}}{9 \text{ sq ft}} = 672.44 \text{ sq yd}$

- Cost $= \$10.35/\text{sq yd} \times 672.44 \text{ sq yd} = $ **\$6 960** *Ans*

Exercise 24-3

Use the tables found in the Appendix for equivalent units of measure. Find the unknown area, altitude, or base for each of the trapezoids, 1-16, in figure 24-25. Round the answer to 1 decimal place.

	HEIGHT (h)	BASES b_1	BASES b_2	AREA (A)
1.	8 in	16 in	10 in	
2.	28 mm	47 mm	38 mm	
3.	0.6 m	6.5 m	2.4 m	
4.		8 ft	4 ft	64 sq ft
5.	1.2 yd		5.5 yd	7.7 sq yd
6.	0.6 km	0.8 km		0.4 km^2
7.		56 cm	48 cm	738.4 cm^2
8.	0.1 mi	1.2 mi	0.6 mi	

	HEIGHT (h)	BASES b_1	BASES b_2	AREA (A)
9.	18.7 m	36 m	28.4 m	
10.	8'-6"	14'-4"	12'-8"	
11.	3.8 km		8.7 km	62.1 km^2
12.		66 in	43 in	2 125.5 sq in
13.	0.3 yd	0.8 yd		0.2 sq yd
14.	14 cm	20 cm	3.2 cm	
15.		19'-9"	13'-3"	132 sq ft
16.	0.9 km	2.2 km	0.8 km	

Fig. 24-25

Solve these problems. Round the answers to 2 decimal places.

17. Dovetail joints, as shown in figure 24-26, are often used to make a tight inter-locking fastening between the sides and front of furniture drawers. Find the cross-sectional area (the shaded area) of the dovetail joints shown.

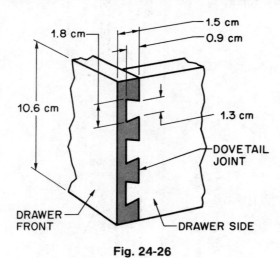

Fig. 24-26

18. A section of land in the shape of a trapezoid has an altitude of 530 feet and bases of 680 feet and 960 feet. How many acres are in the section of land?

19. A wooden ramp form is shown in figure 24-27. The form has an open top and bottom.

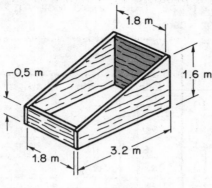

Fig. 24-27

   a. Find the number of square metres of lumber in the form.

   b. The lumber used to construct the form weighs 9.8 kilograms per square metre. Find the total weight of the form.

20. A cross section of a structural steel beam is shown in figure 24-28. The ultimate strength of material is the unit stress that causes the material to break. The ultimate tensile (pulling) strength of the beam is 52 000 pounds per square inch.

   a. Find the cross-sectional area.

   b. What is the total ultimate tensile strength of the beam?

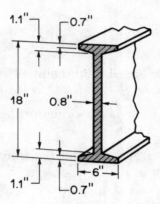

Fig. 24-28

21. A cross section of a concrete retaining wall in the shape of a trapezoid is shown in figure 24-29.

   a. Find the cross-sectional area of this wall in square yards.

   b. Find the length of side AB.

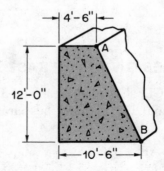

Fig. 24-29

22. A common unit of measure used in carpentry and other woodworking occupations is the board foot. A board foot is equal to one square foot of lumber which is 1 inch thick or less. Oak flooring is installed on the floor shown in figure 24-30. The cost of oak flooring is $965 per 1 000 board feet. An additional 25% must be purchased to allow for waste.

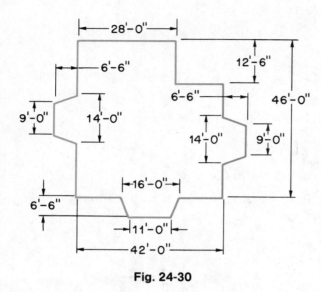

Fig. 24-30

   a. Find, to the nearer board foot, the number of board feet of oak flooring purchased.

   b. What is the cost of the oak flooring for the building?

23. An industrial designer decided that the front plate of an appliance should be in the shape of an isosceles trapezoid with an area of 504 square centimetres. To give the desired appearance, the lower base dimension is to be equal to the altitude dimension, and the upper base dimension is to be equal to three-quarters of the lower base dimension. Compute the dimensions of the altitude and each base.

AREAS OF TRIANGLES GIVEN THE BASE AND ALTITUDE

In parallelogram ABCD shown in figure 24-31, segment DE is the altitude to the base AB. Diagonal DB divides the parallelogram into two congruent triangles.

$$AB = DC \Big\} \quad \text{The opposite sides of a}$$
$$AD = BC \quad \text{parallelogram are equal.}$$

$$DB = DB$$

$$\therefore \triangle ABD \cong \triangle CDB \text{ (SSS)}$$

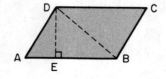

Fig. 24-31

Parallelogram ABCD and triangles ABD and CDE have equal bases and equal altitudes. The area of either triangle is equal to one-half the area of the parallelogram. The area of parallelogram ABCD = AB(DE). Therefore, the area of △ABD or △CDB = $\frac{1}{2}$AB(DE). The *area of a triangle* is equal to one-half the product of the base and altitude.

$$A = \frac{1}{2}bh$$
where A = area

b = base

h = height or altitude

Example 1.   Find the area of the triangle shown in figure 24-32.

$$A = \frac{1}{2}(22 \text{ cm})(19 \text{ cm})$$

$$A = 209 \text{ cm}^2 \; Ans$$

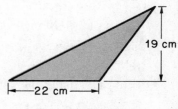

Fig. 24-32

Example 2.   The triangular piece of land shown in figure 24-33 is graded and seeded at a cost of $1 550. What is the grading and seeding cost per square foot?

The area of the land must be found. To find the area the base and altitude must be known. Since two sides of the triangle are the same, the triangle is isosceles. A line segment perpendicular to the base of an isosceles triangle from the vertex opposite the base bisects the base. In figure 24-34, altitude CE bisects base AB.

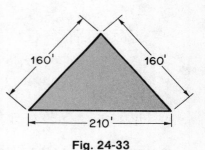

Fig. 24-33

• Find the altitude using the Pythagorean Theorem.

$$(160 \text{ ft})^2 = (105 \text{ ft})^2 + CE^2$$

$$25\,600 \text{ sq ft} = 11\,025 \text{ sq ft} + CE^2$$

$$14\,575 \text{ sq ft} = CE^2$$

$$\sqrt{14\,575 \text{ sq ft}} = CE$$

$$CE = 120.73 \text{ ft}$$

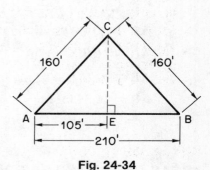

Fig. 24-34

• Find the area of △ABC.

$$A = \frac{1}{2}(210 \text{ ft})(120.73 \text{ ft})$$

$$A = 12\,677 \text{ sq ft}$$

Compute the cost per square foot.

$$\frac{\$1\,550}{12\,677 \text{ sq ft}} = \$0.12/\text{sq ft} \; Ans$$

Example 3. A drafter designs a duct with a triangular cross section as shown in figure 24-35. The specifications require the duct to have a cross-sectional area of the opening equal to 250 square inches and to have sides of 32 inches and 40 inches. Find the length of the third side.

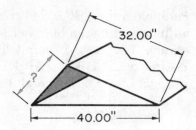

Fig. 24-35

Think the problem through to determine the steps required for the solution. Refer to figure 24-36.

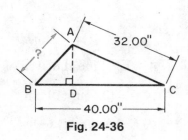

Fig. 24-36

*   Find the altitude.

    $250 \text{ sq in} = \frac{1}{2}(40 \text{ in})(AD)$

    $250 \text{ sq in} = 20 \text{ in}(AD)$

    $AD = 12.5 \text{ in}$

*   Find DC using the Pythagorean Theorem.

    $(32 \text{ in})^2 = DC^2 + (12.5 \text{ in})^2$

    $1\,024 \text{ sq in} = DC^2 + 156.25 \text{ sq in}$

    $867.75 \text{ sq in} = DC^2$

    $\sqrt{867.75 \text{ sq in}} = DC$

    $DC = 29.46 \text{ in}$

*   Find BD.

    $40.00 \text{ in} - 29.46 \text{ in} = 10.54 \text{ in}$

*   Find AB using the Pythagorean Theorem.

    $AB^2 = (10.54 \text{ in})^2 + (12.5 \text{ in})^2$

    $AB^2 = 111.09 \text{ sq in} + 156.25 \text{ sq in}$

    $AB^2 = 267.34 \text{ sq in}$

    $AB = \sqrt{267.34 \text{ sq in}}$

    $AB = \textbf{16.35 in } \textit{Ans}$

AREAS OF TRIANGLES GIVEN THREE SIDES

Sometimes the three sides of a triangle are known but an altitude is not known and cannot be found. A formula, called *Hero's or Heron's Formula*, may be used to compute areas.

$$A = \sqrt{s(s - a)(s - b)(s - c)}$$

where A = Area

a, b, and c = sides

$$s = \frac{1}{2}(a + b + c)$$

Example.   Refer to the triangle shown in figure 24-37.

   a. Find the area of the triangle.

   b. Find the altitude, JK.

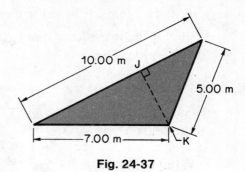

Fig. 24-37

a. Compute the area using Hero's Formula.

$$s = \frac{1}{2}(7 \text{ m} + 5 \text{ m} + 10 \text{ m})$$

$$s = 11 \text{ m}$$

$$A = \sqrt{11 \text{ m}(11 \text{ m} - 7 \text{ m})(11 \text{ m} - 5 \text{ m})(11 \text{ m} - 10 \text{ m})}$$

$$A = \sqrt{11 \text{ m}(4 \text{ m})(6 \text{ m})(1 \text{ m})}$$

$$A = \sqrt{264 \text{ m}^4}$$

$$A = \textbf{16.25 m}^2 \textit{ Ans}$$

b. Compute altitude JK using the formula, $A = \frac{1}{2}bh$.

$$16.25 \text{ m}^2 = \frac{1}{2}(10 \text{ m})(JK)$$

$$16.25 \text{ m}^2 = 5 \text{ m}(JK)$$

$$JK = \textbf{3.25 m} \textit{ Ans}$$

Exercise 24-4

Use the tables found in the Appendix for equivalent units of measure. Find the unknown area, base, or altitude for each of the triangles, 1-16, in figure 24-38. Round the answers to 1 decimal place.

	BASE	ALTITUDE	AREA
1.	21 in	17 in	
2.	43 cm	29 cm	
3.	2.3 m	1.8 m	
4.		7.5 yd	82.5 sq yd
5.	0.2 mi		0.02 sq mi
6.		1.4 km	3.22 km²
7.	0.8 km	0.4 km	
8.	18'-0"	7'-3"	

	BASE	ALTITUDE	AREA
9.	30'-6"		427 sq ft
10.		38 mm	1 919 mm²
11.	63 cm	0.9 cm	
12.	17 m	9.8 m	
13.		0.8 yd	16 sq yd
14.	45.4 in		249.7 sq in
15.	1.1 mi	0.8 mi	
16.		3.4 km	1.7 km²

Fig. 24-38

Given 3 sides of these triangles, find the area of each triangle, 17-24, in figure 24-39. Round the answers to 1 decimal place.

	SIDE a	SIDE b	SIDE c
17.	4 m	6 m	8 m
18.	2 ft	5 ft	6 ft
19.	3'-6"	4'-0"	2'-6"
20.	20 cm	15 cm	25 cm

	SIDE a	SIDE b	SIDE c
21.	3.2 yd	3.6 yd	0.8 yd
22.	9 in	30 in	28 in
23.	7.2 cm	10 cm	9 cm
24.	0.5 m	1.0 m	0.8 m

Fig. 24-39

Solve these problems. Round the answers to 2 decimal places.

25. Find the cross-sectional area of metal in the triangular tubing shown in figure 24-40.

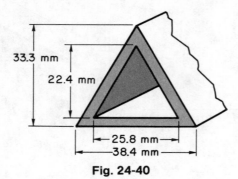

Fig. 24-40

26. Two triangular pieces are cut from the sheet of plywood shown in figure 24-41. After the triangular pieces are cut the sheet is discarded. Find the number of square feet of plywood wasted.

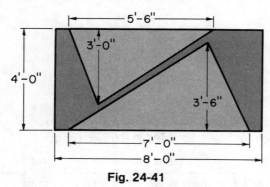

Fig. 24-41

27. A hotel lobby, with a triangular shaped floor, is remodeled. One side of the lobby is 12 metres long and the altitude to the 12-metre side is 9 metres long. At a cost of $38 per square metre, what is the cost of remodeling the lobby?

28. The cross section of a concrete support column is in the shape of an equilateral triangle. Each side of the cross section measures 1'-2". The compressive (crushing) strength of the concrete used for the column is 4 500 pounds per square inch. What is the total compressive strength of the column?

29. The area of the irregularly shaped sheet metal piece shown in figure 24-42 is to be determined. The longest diagonal is drawn on the figure as shown in figure 24-43. Perpendiculars are drawn to the diagonal from each of the other

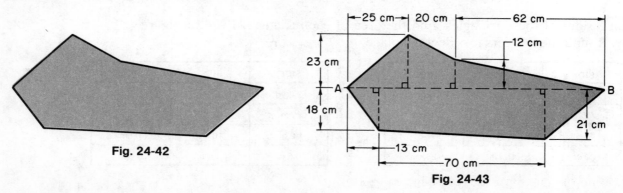

Fig. 24-42   **Fig. 24-43**

vertices. The perpendicular segments are measured as shown. From the measurements the areas of each of the common polygons are computed. This is one method often used to compute areas of irregular figures. Compute the area of the sheet metal piece.

30. Determine the area of the building lot shown in figure 24-44.

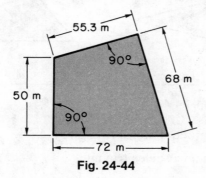

Fig. 24-44

31. A piece with a triangular cross section is to be cut from a block of aluminum as shown in figure 24-45.

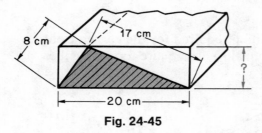

Fig. 24-45

   a. Find the cross-sectional area of the triangular piece.

   b. Determine the minimum thickness block from which the piece can be cut.

32. A hip roof is shown in figure 24-46. The roof front and back are in the shape of congruent isosceles trapezoids. The two sides are in the shape of congruent isosceles triangles.

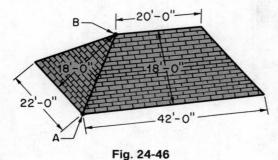

Fig. 24-46

   a. Find the total roof area.

   b. The shingles used on the roof cover 50 square feet per bundle. How many bundles are required to cover the roof?

   c. Find the length of the roof edge AB.

33. In figure 24-47, three playgrounds shaped as equilateral, isosceles, and scalene triangles are shown. Each playground is enclosed by a concrete wall. The inside perimeter of each wall is 300 feet.

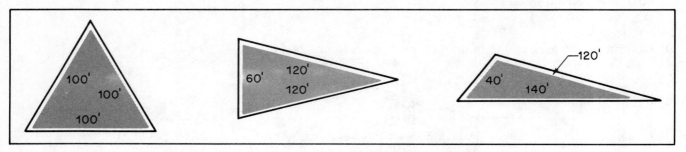

Fig. 24-47

a. Find the area of the playground shaped as an equilateral triangle.

b. Find the area of the playground shaped as an isosceles triangle.

c. Find the area of the playground shaped as a scalene triangle.

d. What general conclusion do you reach as to the type of triangle that provides the most area for the least amount of enclosure cost?

34. Determine the number of board feet of siding required for the garage front shown in figure 24-48. One board foot is equal to one square foot of lumber one inch or less in thickness.

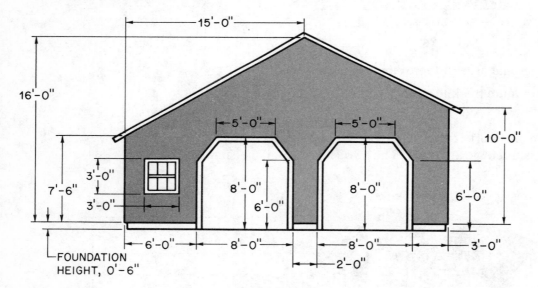

Fig. 24-48

UNIT EXERCISE AND PROBLEM REVIEW

Exercise 24-5

Use the tables found in the Appendix for equivalent units of measure.

RECTANGLES

Find the unknown area, length, or width for each of the rectangles, 1-8, in figure 24-49. Round the answers to 1 decimal place.

	LENGTH	WIDTH	AREA			LENGTH	WIDTH	AREA
1.	17.5 in	9.0 in		5.			0.2 mi	0.12 sq mi
2.	26 cm	18.6 cm		6.		1.2 km	0.9 km	
3.		6.3 m	88.2 m^2	7.		43 mm		851.4 mm^2
4.	15 ft		127.5 sq ft	8.			6'-9''	270 sq ft

Fig. 24-49

PARALLELOGRAMS

Find the unknown area, base, or altitude for each of the parallelograms, 9-16, in figure 24-50. Round the answers to 1 decimal place.

	BASE	ALTITUDE	AREA			BASE	ALTITUDE	AREA
9.	17 m	12 m		13.		0.7 km		1.3 km^2
10.	3 yd		13.8 sq yd	14.		36 cm	19.1 cm	
11.	14.6 in	9.5 in		15.			20'-3''	486 sq ft
12.		3.2 mi	1.6 sq mi	16.		$5\frac{1}{4}$ yd	3 yd	

Fig. 24-50

TRAPEZOIDS

Find the unknown area, altitude, or base for each of the trapezoids, 17-24, in figure 24-51. Round the answers to 1 decimal place.

	ALTITUDE	BASES		AREA			ALTITUDE	BASES		AREA
		b_1	b_2					b_1	b_2	
17.	14 cm	23 cm	17 cm		21.		6'-0''	14'-9''		69 sq ft
18.	6 in	28 in	16 in		22.		0.3 mi	0.5 mi	0.4 mi	
19.		4 yd	5 yd	9 sq yd	23.			36 mm	32 mm	340 mm^2
20.	0.4 km		1 km	0.8 km^2	24.		17.6 m		11.2 m	255.8 m^2

Fig. 24-51

TRIANGLES

Find the unknown area, base, or altitude for each of the triangles, 25-32, in figure 24-52. Round the answers to 1 decimal place.

	BASE	ALTITUDE	AREA
25.	35 in	27 in	
26.	7.6 cm	5.5 cm	
27.	2 m		1.6 m^2
28.		4.3 yd	32.7 sq yd

	BASE	ALTITUDE	AREA
29.	1.2 km		0.36 km^2
30.	0.9 mi	0.7 mi	
31.		22'-9"	819 sq ft
32.	30 mm		2 075 mm^2

Fig. 24-52

Given 3 sides of triangles, find the areas of each triangle, 33-36, in figure 24-53. Round the answers to 1 decimal place.

	SIDE a	SIDE b	SIDE c
33.	5 ft	7 ft	10 ft
34.	12 cm	8 cm	16 cm
35.	1.4 m	1.2 m	0.8 m
36.	24 in	30 in	14 in

Fig. 24-53

APPLIED PROBLEMS

Solve these common polygon problems. Round the answers to 2 decimal places.

37. Find the area, in square feet, of a rectangular piece of lumber 3 inches wide and 7 feet 6 inches long.

38. Pieces in the shape of parallelograms are stamped from rectangular strips of stock as shown in figure 24-54. If 24 pieces are stamped from a strip, how many square inches of strip are wasted?

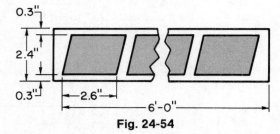

Fig. 24-54

39. The cross section of a dovetail slide is shown in figure 24-55. Before the dovetail was cut, the cross section was rectangular in shape. Find the cross-sectional area of the dovetail slide.

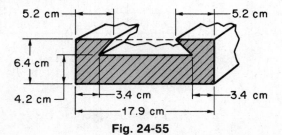

Fig. 24-55

40. A bathroom 2.6 metres long and 2 metres wide is to have four walls covered with tile to a height of 1.5 metres. Deduct 2.3 square metres for door and window openings. How many square metres of wall are covered with tile?

41. Find the area of the side enclosed by the gambrel roof shown in figure 24-56.

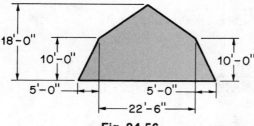

Fig. 24-56

42. A baseplate in the shape of a parallelogram is shown in figure 24-57.

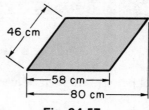

Fig. 24-57

   a. Find the plate area.

   b. Find the weight of the plate if one square metre weighs 68.4 kilograms.

43. An A-frame building has triangular front and rear walls or sides and a roof reaching to the ground. Each of two sides of an A-frame building has a base of 24 feet and an altitude of 30 feet.

   a. Allowing 10% for waste, how many board feet of siding are required for the two sides? One board foot is equal to one square foot of lumber one inch or less in thickness.

   b. At a cost of $740 per 1 000 board feet, what is the total cost of siding for the two sides?

44. The floor of a building is covered with square vinyl tiles. The floor is in the shape of a trapezoid with an altitude of 32 feet and bases of 40 feet and 50 feet. One carton of tiles contains 80 tiles and has a coverage of 45 square feet. Allowing for 5% waste, how many cartons of tiles are purchased for the job?

45. A floor plan of a building is shown in figure 24-58.

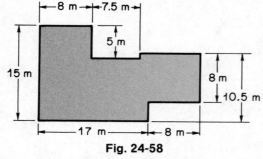

Fig. 24-58

   a. Find the number of square metres of floor area.

   b. Find the number of square metres of exterior wall area of the building disregarding wall thickness. The walls are 4.8 metres high. Make a 20% deduction for windows and doors.

   c. How many litres of paint are required to paint the exterior walls if 1 litre of paint covers 13.5 square metres of wall area?

46. The rectangular bottom of a shipping carton is designed to have an area of 17.5 square feet and a length of 60 inches. Can a thin object 6 feet long be packed in the carton? Show your computations in answering this question.

47. The stairway and platform wall shown in figure 24-59 is faced with brick.

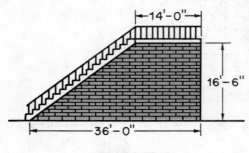

Fig. 24-59

   a. If there are 7 bricks per square foot of area, how many bricks are required for the wall?

   b. Railing, at a cost of $7.20 per foot of length, is used on the stairs and platform. What is the total cost of railing?

48. A concrete support column has a total ultimate compressive strength of 67 200 pounds. The concrete used for the column has an ultimate compressive strength of 4 200 pounds per square inch. If the cross section of the column is a square, what is the length of each side of the cross section?

49. A utility company purchased a power line right-of-way from the owner of a piece of property. The piece is in the shape of the parallelogram shown in figure 24-60. The right-of-way is the area of land between the diagonal broken lines.

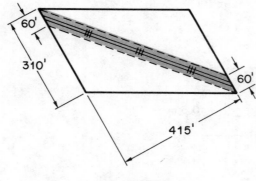

Fig. 24-60

   a. The utility company paid the owner $0.85 per square foot for the land. How much was paid to the owner?

   b. After the right-of-way was acquired, how many acres of land did the owner have left?

50. Compute the area of the pattern shown in figure 24-61.

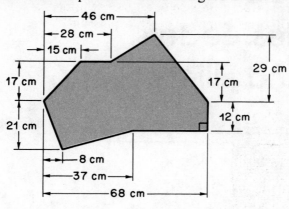

Fig. 24-61

UNIT 25
Areas of Circles, Sectors, Segments, and Ellipses

OBJECTIVES

After studying this unit you should be able to

- compute areas, radii, and diameters of circles.
- compute areas, radii, and central angles of sectors.
- compute areas of segments.
- compute areas, major axes, and minor axes of ellipses.
- solve applied problems using principles discussed in this unit.

Computations of areas of circular objects are often made on-the-job. Material quantities and weights are based on computed areas. Many industrial and construction material strength computations are also based on circular cross-sectional areas of machined parts and structural members.

AREAS OF CIRCLES

The *area of a circle* is equal to the product of pi and the square of the radius.

$$A = \pi r^2 \qquad\qquad\qquad\qquad \text{where } A = \text{area}$$
$$r = \text{radius}$$
$$\pi = 3.14 \text{ or } 3.141\ 6$$

The formula for the area of a circle can be expressed in terms of the diameter. Since the radius is one-half the diameter, $\frac{d}{2}$ can be substituted in the formula for r.

$$A = \pi \left(\frac{d}{2}\right)^2$$
$$A = \frac{\pi d^2}{4}$$
$$A = \frac{3.141\ 6 d^2}{4}$$
$$A = 0.785\ 4 d^2$$

Example 1. Find the area of a circle which has a radius of 6.5 inches.

Substitute values in the formula and solve.

$$A = \pi r^2 = 3.14(6.5 \text{ in})^2 = 3.14(42.25 \text{ sq in}) = \textbf{132.7 sq in } Ans$$

Example 2. Determine the diameter of a circular table top which is to have an area of 1.65 square metres.

METHOD 1

$$A = \pi r^2$$
$$1.65 \text{ m}^2 = 3.141\,6r^2$$
$$r^2 = \frac{1.65 \text{ m}^2}{3.141\,6}$$
$$r^2 = 0.525\,21 \text{ m}^2$$
$$r = \sqrt{0.525\,21 \text{ m}^2}$$
$$r = 0.725 \text{ m}$$
$$d = 2(0.725 \text{ m})$$
$$d = \mathbf{1.45 \text{ m}} \textit{ Ans}$$

METHOD 2

$$A = 0.785\,4d^2$$
$$1.65 \text{ m}^2 = 0.785\,4d^2$$
$$d^2 = \frac{1.65 \text{ m}^2}{0.785\,4}$$
$$d^2 = 2.100\,84 \text{ m}^2$$
$$d = \sqrt{2.100\,84 \text{ m}^2}$$
$$d = \mathbf{1.45 \text{ m}} \textit{ Ans}$$

Example 3. A circular hole is cut in a square metal plate as shown in figure 25-1. The plate weighs 8.3 pounds per square foot. What is the weight of the plate after the hole is cut?

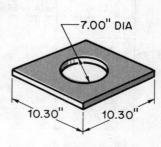

Fig. 25-1

Compute the area of the square:

$$A = (10.30 \text{ in})^2 = 106.09 \text{ sq in}$$

Compute the area of the hole:

$$A = 0.785\,4(7 \text{ in})^2 = 38.48 \text{ sq in}$$

Compute the area of the plate:

$$A = 106.09 \text{ sq in} - 38.48 \text{ sq in} = 67.61 \text{ sq in}$$

Compute the weight of the plate:

$$67.61 \text{ sq in} \div 144 \text{ sq in/sq ft} = 0.47 \text{ sq ft}$$
$$\text{Weight} = 0.47 \text{ sq ft} \times 8.3 \text{ lb/sq ft} = \mathbf{3.9 \text{ lb}} \textit{ Ans}$$

RATIO OF TWO CIRCLES

The areas of two circles have the same ratio as the squares of the radii or diameters.

$$\frac{A_1}{A_2} = \frac{r_1^2}{r_2^2} = \frac{d_1^2}{d_2^2}$$

Example. The radii of two circles are 5 feet and 2 feet. Compare the area of the 5-foot radius circle with the area of the 2-foot radius circle.

Form a ratio of the squares of the radii.

$$\frac{(5 \text{ ft})^2}{(2 \text{ ft})^2} = \frac{25 \text{ sq ft}}{4 \text{ sq ft}} = 6.25$$

The area of the 5-ft radius circle is 6.25 times greater than the area of the 2-ft radius circle. Ans

The radii or diameters of two circles have the same ratio as the square roots of the areas.

$$\frac{r_1}{r_2} = \frac{d_1}{d_2} = \frac{\sqrt{A_1}}{\sqrt{A_2}}$$

Example.   The areas of two circles are 36 cm² and 9 cm². Compare the diameter of the 36-cm² circle with the diameter of the 9-cm² circle.

Form a ratio of the square roots of the areas.

$$\frac{\sqrt{36 \text{ cm}^2}}{\sqrt{9 \text{ cm}^2}} = \frac{6 \text{ cm}}{3 \text{ cm}} = 2$$

The diameter of the circle with an area of 36 cm² is 2 times greater than the diameter of the circle with an area of 9 cm². *Ans*

Exercise 25-1

Use the tables found in the Appendix for equivalent units of measure. Find the unknown area, radius, or diameter for each of the circles, 1-12, in figure 25-2. Use $\pi = 3.141\ 6$. Round the answers to 2 decimal places.

	RADIUS	DIAMETER	AREA			RADIUS	DIAMETER	AREA
1.	7 in	–		7.		–	380 mm²
2.	10.8 cm	–		8.	27.8 in	–	
3.	–	$15\frac{1}{2}$ ft		9.	–	0.2 mi	
4.	–	17.2 m		10.	–		87 cm²
5.	–		34 sq yd	11.	–		3.6 m²
6.	–		0.1 km²	12.	2'-9"	–	

Fig. 25-2

In these exercises, express the areas, radii or diameters of the two circles as ratios, then solve. Round the answers to 2 decimal places.

13. The radii of two circles are 6 inches and 2 inches. Compare the area of the larger circle with the area of the smaller circle.

14. The diameters of two circles are 15 cm and 10 cm. Compare the area of the larger circle with the area of the smaller circle.

15. The areas of two circles are 100 sq ft and 25 sq ft. Compare the radius of the larger circle with the radius of the smaller circle.

16. The areas of two circles are 6.20 m² and 3.60 m². Compare the diameter of the larger circle with the diameter of the smaller circle.

17. The radius of a circle is 5 times greater than the radius of a second circle. Compare the area of the larger circle with the area of the smaller circle.

18. The area of one circle is 12.60 times greater than the area of a second circle. Compare the diameter of the larger circle with the diameter of the smaller circle.

Solve these problems. Use $\pi = 3.141\ 6$. Round the answers to 2 decimal places.

19. How many square yards are contained in a circular pavement with an 85-foot diameter?

20. A sheet metal reducer is shown in figure 25-3. Find the difference in the cross-sectional areas of the two ends.

├─26.8 cm DIA─┤

10.6 cm DIA

Fig. 25-3

21. An electromagnetic brake uses friction discs as shown in figure 25-4. The shaded area shows the brake lining surface of a disc. If 4 brake linings are used in the brake, what is the total brake lining area?

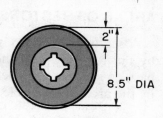

Fig. 25-4

22. Hydraulic pressure of 675 pounds per square inch is exerted on a 2.300-inch diameter piston. Find the total force exerted on the piston.

23. A circular walk has an outside diameter of 56'-6'' and an inside diameter of 47'-6''. Compute the cost of constructing the walk if labor and materials are estimated at a cost of $1.20 per square foot.

24. A force of 62 000 pounds pulls on a steel rod which has a diameter of 1.800 inches. Find the force pulling on one square inch of cross-sectional area.

25. A circular base is shown in figure 25-5. The base is cut from a steel plate which weighs 34 kilograms per square metre of surface area. Find the weight of the circular base.

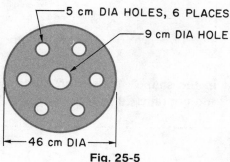

Fig. 25-5

26. Three water pipes, 3.8 cm, 5.0 cm, and 7.5 cm in diameter are connected to a single pipe. The single pipe permits the same amount of water to flow as the total of the three pipes. Find the diameter of the single pipe.

27. Find the area of the template shown in figure 25-6.

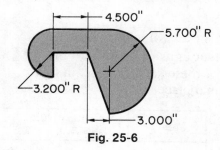

Fig. 25-6

28. A rectangular sheet of plywood 2 metres long and 1.5 metres wide weighs 15.2 kilograms. Find the weight of the sheet after three 0.6-metre diameter holes are cut.

29. A support column is replaced with another column which has 5 times the cross-sectional area of the original column. The diameter of the original column is 20.8 centimetres. Find the diameter of the new column.

30. A landscaper designs a garden area in the square piece of land shown in figure 25-7. The shaded portion is planted with shrubs and ground cover. Find the number of square feet of area planted.

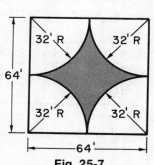

Fig. 25-7

AREAS OF SECTORS

A sector of a circle is a figure formed by two radii and the arc intercepted by the radii. To find the *area of a sector* of a circle, first find the fractional part of a circle represented by the central angle. Then multiply the fraction by the area of the circle.

$$A = \frac{\theta}{360°}(\pi r^2)$$

where A = area

θ = central angle

π = 3.14 or 3.141 6

r = radius

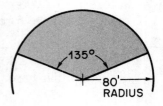

Example 1. The parking area in the shape of a sector as shown in figure 25-8 is graded and paved. At a cost of $0.40 per square foot, find, to the nearer dollar, the total cost of grading and paving the area.

Find the area of the sector:

$$A = \frac{135°}{360°}(3.141\ 6)(80\ \text{ft})^2 = 7\ 539.84\ \text{sq ft}$$

Fig. 25-8

Find the cost:

7 539.84 sq ft × $0.40/sq ft = **$3 016** *Ans*

Example 2. An apartment balcony is designed in the shape of a sector. The balcony has a central angle of 225° and contains 24 square metres of surface area. Find the radius.

Substitute values in the formula and solve.

$$24\ \text{m}^2 = \frac{225°}{360°}(3.141\ 6)r^2$$

$$24\ \text{m}^2 = 1.9635r^2$$

$$r^2 = 12.223\ \text{m}^2$$

$$r = 3.50\ \text{m}\ Ans$$

Exercise 25-2

Use the tables found in the Appendix for equivalent units of measure. Find the unknown area, radius, or central angle for each of these sectors, 1-12, in figure 25-9. Use π = 3.14. Round the answers to 1 decimal place.

	RADIUS	CENTRAL ANGLE	AREA			RADIUS	CENTRAL ANGLE	AREA
1.	10 cm	120°		7.		20'-3''		1 000 sq. ft
2.	3.5 ft	90°		8.		0.2 km	220°	
3.	45 in	40°		9.		54 cm	26°	
4.		65°	300 m²	10.			300°	82 sq in
5.		180°	750 mm²	11.		0.1 mi		0.02 sq in
6.	9.5 yd		94 sq yd	12.		150 m	15°	

Fig 25-9

Solve these problems. Use $\pi = 3.141\ 6$. Round the answers to 2 decimal places.

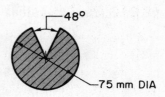

13. A cross section of a piece of round stock with a V-groove cut is shown in figure 25-10. Find the cross-sectional area of the stock.

Fig. 25-10

14. The entrance hall of an office building is constructed in the shape of a sector with a 22-foot radius and a 100° central angle. Compute the cost of carpeting the hall if carpeting costs $21.50 per square yard. Allow an additional 20% for waste.

15. A kitchen counter top is shown in figure 25-11.

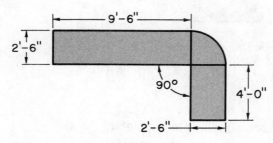

Fig. 25-11

a. Find the surface area of the counter top.

b. The top is covered with laminated plastic which costs $1.35 per square foot. Allowing 15% for waste, find the cost of covering the top.

16. An automobile windshield wiper swings an arc of 140° as shown in figure 25-12. The wiper is 11 inches long with a wiper blade of 8.5 inches. Assuming the windshield is a plane surface, find the area swept by the wiper blade.

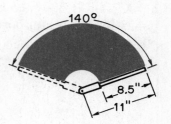

Fig. 25-12

17. Three pieces, each in the shape of a sector, are cut from the rectangular sheet of steel shown in figure 25-13. How many square metres are wasted after the 3 pieces are cut?

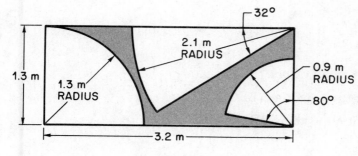

Fig. 25-13

18. A walk around the arc of a sector as shown in figure 25-14 is constructed at a cost of $19 per square metre. Find the cost of constructing the walk.

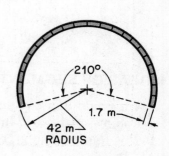

Fig. 25-14

19. A machined guide is shown in figure 25-15.

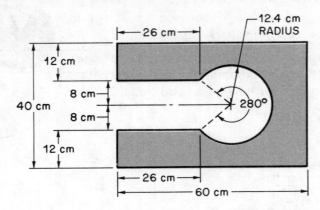

Fig. 25-15

a. Find the surface area of the guide.

b. Before machining, the 40 cm × 60 cm rectangular plate weighed 9.8 kilograms. Find the weight of the guide.

20. A patio is designed in the shape of an isosceles triangle as shown in figure 25-16. The sector portion, ABEC is constructed of concrete. AB, AE, and AC are radii.

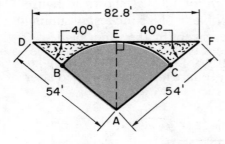

Fig. 25-16

Portions BDE and CFE are planted with flowers.

a. Find the area of the concrete portion (sector ABEC).

b. Find the area of the flower portion (portions BDE and CFE).

AREAS OF SEGMENTS

A *segment* of a circle is a figure formed by an arc and the chord joining the end points of the arc. In the circle shown in figure 25-17, *the area of segment ACB* is found by subtracting the area of triangle AOB from the area of sector OACB.

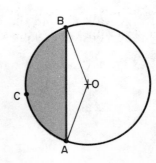

Fig. 25-17

Example.   Segment ACB is cut from the circular plate shown in figure 25-18. Find the area of the segment.

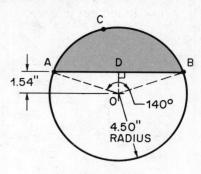

Fig. 25-18

Find the area of sector:

$$A = \frac{140°}{360°}(3.141\ 6)(4.50\ \text{in})^2 = 24.740\ \text{sq in}$$

Find the area of isosceles triangle AOB:

$$c^2 = a^2 + b^2$$

$$(4.50\ \text{in})^2 = (1.54\ \text{in})^2 + AD^2$$

$$20.25\ \text{sq in} = 2.371\ 6\ \text{sq in} + AD^2$$

$$AD^2 = 17.878\ 4\ \text{sq in}$$

$$AD = 4.228\ \text{in}$$

The base AB of isosceles triangle AOB is bisected by altitude DO.

$$AB = 2(AD) = 2(4.228\ \text{in}) = 8.456\ \text{in}$$

$$A = 0.5(8.456\ \text{in})(1.54\ \text{in}) = 6.511\ \text{sq in}$$

Find the area of segment ACB:

$$A = 24.740\ \text{sq in} - 6.511\ \text{sq in} = \textbf{18.23 sq in}\ Ans$$

Exercise 25-3

Use the tables found in the Appendix for equivalent units of measure. Find the area of each of the segments ACB for exercises 1-5 in figure 25-19. Refer to figure 25-20.

	AREA OF ISOSCELES △AOB	AREA OF SECTOR OACB	AREA OF SEGMENT ACB
1.	16.5 sq ft	24.8 sq ft	
2.	6.98 m²	9.35 m²	
3.	156 mm²	213.5 mm²	
4.	85.33 sq in	109.27 sq in	
5.	0.15 km²	0.27 km²	

Fig. 25-19

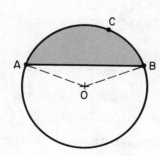

Fig. 25-20

Solve these problems. Use $\pi = 3.141\ 6$. Round the answers to 2 decimal places.

6. Find the area of the shaded segment shown in figure 25-21.

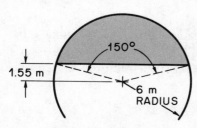

Fig. 25-21

7. Paving cost is $10.30 per square yard. Find the total cost of paving the shaded area shown in figure 25-22.

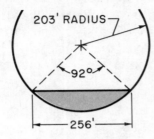

Fig. 25-22

8. A cross section of round stock is shown in figure 25-23. Material is machined from the top of the piece to a depth of 0.562 inch. Find the cross-sectional area of the remaining stock.

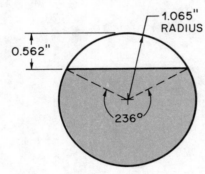

Fig. 25-23

9. A pattern is shown in figure 25-24.

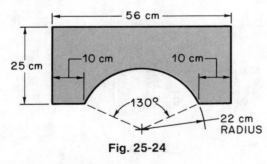

Fig. 25-24

   a. Find the surface area of the pattern.

   b. The metal from which the pattern is made weighs 7.8 kilograms per square metre of surface area. Find the weight of the pattern.

10. The shaded piece shown in figure 25-25 is cut from a circular disc. Find the area of the piece.

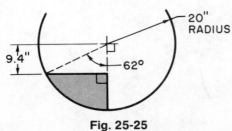

Fig. 25-25

AREAS OF ELLIPSES

The curve of intersection of a plane which diagonally cuts through a cone is an ellipse as shown in figure 25-26. An *ellipse* is a closed oval-shaped curve that is symmetrical to two lines or axes that are perpendicular to each other. The curve shown in figure 25-27 is an ellipse. It is symmetrical to axes AB and CD. The longer axis is called the *major axis* and the shorter axis CD is called the *minor axis*. The *area of an ellipse* is equal to the product of pi and one-half the major axis and one-half the minor axis.

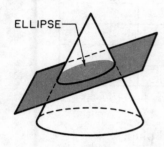

Fig. 25-26

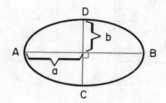

Fig. 25-27

$$A = \pi ab$$

where A = area

$a = \frac{1}{2}$ the major axis

$b = \frac{1}{2}$ the minor axis

Example 1. Find the area of an elliptical swimming pool that is 9 metres long (major axis) and 6 metres wide (minor axis).

$a = 0.5(9 \text{ m}) = 4.5 \text{ m}$

$b = 0.5(6 \text{ m}) = 3 \text{ m}$

$A = 3.14(4.5 \text{ m})(3 \text{ m}) = 42.4 \text{ m}^2$ *Ans*

Example 2. An elliptical platform is designed to have a surface area of 700 square feet. To give the desired form, the major axis must be $1\frac{1}{2}$ times as long as the minor axis. Determine the dimensions of the major and minor axes.

Let x = minor axis $b = 0.5x$

$1.5x$ = major axis $a = 0.75x$

$700 \text{ sq ft} = 3.14(0.75x)(0.5x)$

$700 \text{ sq ft} = 1.177\ 5x^2$

$\quad\quad x^2 = 594.48 \text{ sq ft}$

$\quad\quad x = 24.38 \text{ ft}$

Minor axis = 24.38 ft *Ans*

Major axis = 1.5(24.38 ft) = 36.57 ft *Ans*

Exercise 25-4

Use the tables found in the Appendix for equivalent units of measure. Find the unknown area, major axis, or minor axis of each of the ellipses, 1-10, in figure 25-28. Use $\pi = 3.14$. Round the answers to 1 decimal place.

	MAJOR AXIS	MINOR AXIS	AREA
1.	10 in	7 in	
2.	23.2 cm	15 cm	
3.	8.6 m	4.2 m	
4.	43 ft		1 215 sq ft
5.		4.6 yd	19.5 sq yd

	MAJOR AXIS	MINOR AXIS	AREA
6.	86 mm		4 730 mm^2
7.	36.6 in	25 in	
8.	19'-6''	15'-3''	
9.		0.8 m	0.9 m^2
10.	68.8 cm		2 970 cm^2

Fig. 25-28

Solve these problems. Use $\pi = 3.141\ 6$. Round the answers to 2 decimal places.

11. A concrete wall 3'-6'' wide encloses a courtyard shown in figure 25-29. Find the surface area of the top of the wall.

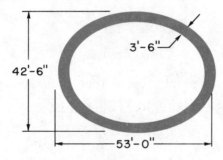

Fig. 25-29

12. A sheet metal reducer is shown in figure 25-30. The top of the reducer is circular and the bottom is elliptical in shape. Find the difference in area between the top and bottom.

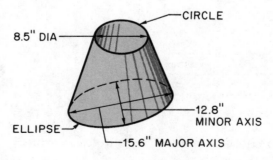

Fig. 25-30

13. A platform was originally designed as a rectangle 10 metres long and 7 metres wide. The rectangular design is replaced with a platform in the shape of an ellipse. The elliptical platform will have the same area as the original rectangular platform and the major axis is 14 metres. Find the minor axis.

14. A room divider panel is made with 8 identical elliptical cutouts as shown in figure 25-31. The panel is made of plywood which weighs 1.4 pounds per square foot. Find the weight of the completed panel.

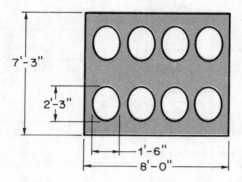

Fig. 25-31

15. An elliptical table top is designed to have a surface area of 2.3 square metres. To give the desired form, the minor axis must be $\frac{3}{4}$ as long as the major axis. Find the dimensions of the major and minor axes.

UNIT EXERCISE AND PROBLEM REVIEW

Exercise 25-5

Use the tables found in the Appendix for equivalent units of measure.

CIRCLES

Find the unknown area, radius, or diameter for each of the circles, 1-5, in figure 25-32. Use $\pi = 3.141\ 6$. Round the answers to 2 decimal places.

	RADIUS	DIAMETER	AREA
1.	14 in	–	
2.	–	28.6 cm	
3.		–	45 sq yd
4.	–		110 m²
5.	–	12'-9"	

Fig. 25-32

In these exercises, express the areas, radii, or diameters of two circles as ratios, then solve. Round the answers to 2 decimal places.

6. The radii of two circles are 12 inches and 3 inches. Compare the area of the larger circle with the area of the smaller circle.

7. The areas of two circles are 2.80 m² and 0.90 m². Compare the radius of the larger circle with the radius of the smaller circle.

8. The diameter of a circle is 9.50 times greater than the diameter of a second circle. Compare the area of the larger circle with the area of the smaller circle.

SECTORS

Determine the unknown area, radius, or central angle for each sector, 9-13, in figure 25-33. Use $\pi = 3.14$. Round the answers to 1 decimal place.

	RADIUS	CENTRAL ANGLE	AREA
9.	5.5 in	120°	
10.	13.4 m	65°	
11.		230°	54 sq in
12.	0.2 km		0.03 km²
13.	18′-9″	78°	

Fig. 25-33

SEGMENTS

Find the area of each of the segments ACB for exercises 14-16 in figure 25-34. Refer to figure 25-35.

	AREA OF ISOSCELES △AOB	AREA OF SECTOR OACB	AREA OF SEGMENT ACB
14.	58 cm²	72.3 cm²	
15.	135.3 sq yd	207.8 sq yd	
16.	587 sq in	719.5 sq in	

Fig. 25-34

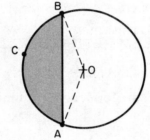

Fig. 25-35

ELLIPSES

Find the unknown area, major axis, or minor axis of each of these ellipses, 17-21, in figure 25-36. Use $\pi = 3.14$. Round the answers to 1 decimal place.

	MAJOR AXIS	MINOR AXIS	AREA
17.	27 yd	19 yd	
18.	9.6 m	7.0 m	
19.	54.6 cm		1 720 cm²
20.		16.6 in	274 sq in
21.	14′-0″	10′-9″	

Fig. 25-36

APPLIED PROBLEMS

Solve these problems. Use $\pi = 3.141\ 6$. Round the answers to 2 decimal places.

22. Find the cross-sectional area of the spacer shown in figure 25-37.

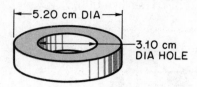

Fig. 25-37

23. A circular wall is 0.5 metre thick and has an inside diameter of 10.20 metres. Find the cross-sectional area of the wall.

24. A minipark is constructed in the shape of a sector with a 70-foot radius and a 130° central angle. The cost of grading and landscaping the park is $7.20 per square yard. Find the total cost of grading and landscaping the park.

25. A compressive force of 2 800 pounds per square inch is exerted on a concrete column. The column has a circular cross section with a 1-foot diameter. Find the total compressive force exerted on the column.

26. An elliptical shaped track is shown in figure 25-38. The cost of resurfacing the track is $0.30 per square foot. Find the total cost of resurfacing the track.

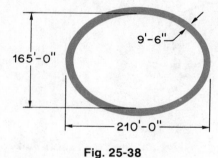

Fig. 25-38

27. Find the area of the shaded segment shown in figure 25-39.

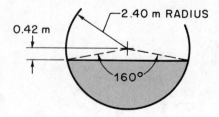

Fig. 25-39

28. A circular plate with a 15-inch radius is cut from a rectangular aluminum piece which is 3 feet wide and 4 feet long. Before the circular plate was cut, the rectangular piece weighed 30 pounds. Find the weight of the circular plate.

29. Two sewer pipes 8 inches and 10 inches in diameter are joined to a single pipe. The single pipe is to carry the same amount of sewage as the combined amount carried by the 8-inch and 10-inch diameter pipes. Find the diameter of the single pipe.

30. Compute the cross-sectional area of the grooved block shown in figure 25-40.

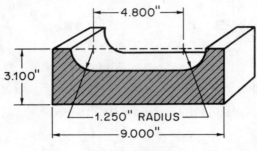

Fig. 25-40

31. A pool designed in the shape of an ellipse has a surface area of 2 550 square feet. The major axis is 1.3 times as long as the minor axis. Find the major and minor axes.

32. Find the area of the pattern shown in figure 25-41.

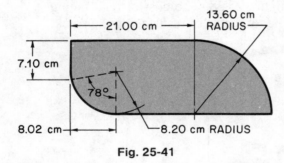

Fig. 25-41

33. A cross section of a die insert is shown in figure 25-42. Find the cross-sectional area of the insert.

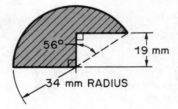

Fig. 25-42

UNIT 26
Prisms and Cylinders: Volumes, Surface Areas, and Weights

OBJECTIVES

After studying this unit you should be able to

- compute volumes of prisms and cylinders.
- compute surface areas of prisms and cylinders.
- compute capacities and weights of prisms and cylinders.
- solve applied problems using principles discussed in this unit.

The ability to compute volumes of prisms and cylinders is required in various occupations. Heating and air conditioning technicians compute the volume of air in a building when determining heating and cooling system requirements. In the construction field, the type and size of structural supports used depend on the volume of the materials being supported. The displacement of an automobile engine is based on the volume of its cylinders. Nurses use volume measure when giving medications to patients.

Surface areas of the faces or sides of prisms and cylinders are often needed. To determine material requirements and costs, a welder computes the surface area of a cylindrical weldment. A packaging designer considers the surface area for the material of a carton when pricing a product.

PRISMS

In practical work, perhaps the most widely used solid is the prism. A *prism* is a solid which has two identical (congruent) parallel polygon faces called *bases* and parallel lateral edges. The other sides or faces of a prism are parallelograms called *lateral faces*. A *lateral edge* is the line segment where two lateral faces meet. The *altitude* of a prism is the perpendicular distance between its two bases.

Prisms are named according to the shape of their bases, such as triangular, rectangular, pentagonal, hexagonal, and octagonal. Some common prisms are shown in figure 26-1. The parts of the prisms are identified. In a *right prism,* the lateral edges are perpendicular to the bases. Prisms A and B in figure 26-1 are examples of right prisms. In an *oblique prism,* the lateral edges are <u>not</u> perpendicular to the bases. Prisms C and D are examples of oblique prisms.

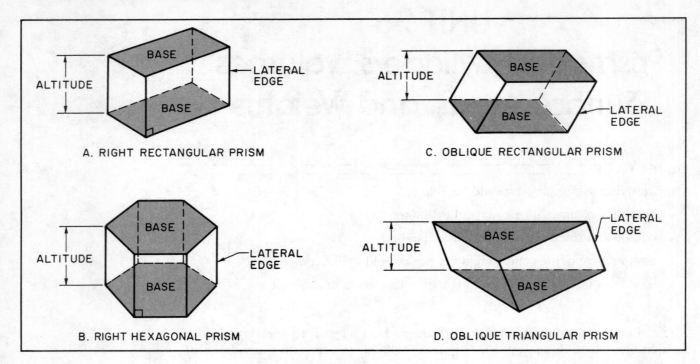

Fig. 26-1

VOLUMES OF PRISMS

The *volume of any prism* (right or oblique) is equal to the product of the base area and altitude.

$$V = A_B h$$

where V = volume

A_B = area of base

h = altitude

Example 1. Compute the volume of a prism which has a base area of 15 square inches and an altitude of 6 inches.

V = 15 sq in × 6 in = **90 cu in** *Ans*

Example 2. A concrete slab with a rectangular base is shown in figure 26-2.

    a. Find the number of cubic yards of concrete required.

    b. One cubic yard of concrete weighs 3 700 pounds. Find the weight of the slab.

a. Find the area of the rectangular base:

    A_B = 40.5 ft × 20 ft = 810 sq ft

Find the volume of the slab:

    V = 810 sq ft × 0.5 ft = 405 cu ft

Find the volume in cubic yards:

    405 cu ft ÷ 27 cu ft/cu yd = **15 cu yd** *Ans*

b. Find the weight of the slab:

    15 cu yd × 3 700 lb/cu yd = **55 500 lb** *Ans*

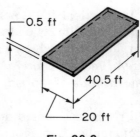

Fig. 26-2

Example 3.   Find the approximate volume of air contained in the building shown in figure 26-3. Disregard the wall and ceiling thicknesses.

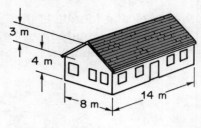

Fig. 26-3

One method of solution is to consider the building as two simple prisms. The roof portion has a triangular base and the remainder of the building has a rectangular base. Find the volume of each portion separately and then add. Find the volume of the triangular base portion:

$A_B = 0.5(8 \text{ m})(3 \text{ m}) = 12 \text{ m}^2$

$V = 12 \text{ m}^2 \times 14 \text{ m} = 168 \text{ m}^3$

Find the volume of the rectangular base portion:

$A_B = 8 \text{ m} \times 4 \text{ m} = 32 \text{ m}^2$

$V = 32 \text{ m}^2 \times 14 \text{ m} = 448 \text{ m}^3$

Find the total volume:

$168 \text{ m}^3 + 448 \text{ m}^3 = \textbf{616 m}^3 \textit{ Ans}$

Exercise 26-1

Use the tables found in the Appendix for equivalent units of measure. Solve these problems. Round the answers to 2 decimal places.

1. Find the volume of a prism with a base area of 125 square inches and an altitude of 8 inches.

2. Compute the volume of a prism with an altitude of 26.5 centimetres and a base of 610 square centimetres.

3. One cubic inch of cast iron weighs 0.26 pound. Find the weight of a block of cast iron with a base area of 48 square inches and an altitude of 5.3 inches.

4. Find the capacity in gallons of a rectangular tank with a base area of 218 square feet and a height of 10 feet.

5. Compute the volume of a wall which is 0.8 metre thick, 7 metres long, and 2 metres high.

6. How many cubic feet of air are heated in a room 28′-6″ long, 22′-0″ wide, and 8′-6″ high?

7. A solid steel wedge is shown in figure 26-4.

   a. Find the volume of the wedge.

   b. The steel used for the wedge weighs 0.008 kilogram per cubic centimetre. Find the weight of the wedge.

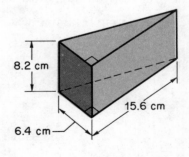

Fig. 26-4

8. An excavation for a building foundation is 60 feet long, 35 feet wide, and 14 feet deep.

   a. How many cubic yards of soil are removed?

   b. How many truck loads are required to haul the soil from the building site if the average truck load is $3\frac{1}{2}$ cubic yards?

9. A pier and footing is shown in figure 26-5. Twenty bricks, including mortar joints, are required per cubic foot. If 15 piers are constructed, how many bricks are required?

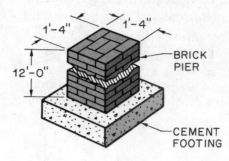

Fig. 26-5

10. A length of angle iron is shown in figure 26-6.

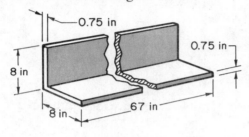

Fig. 26-6

   a. Find the volume of the angle iron.

   b. Find the weight of the angle iron if the material weighs 490 pounds per cubic foot.

11. A rectangular fuel oil storage tank is 10.5 feet long, 8 feet wide, and 6.3 feet high.

   a. How many gallons of fuel oil are contained in the tank when it is 70% full?

   b. Oil is pumped into the tank at a rate of 20 gallons per minute. Starting with a 70% full tank, how long will it take to fill the tank?

12. A concrete retaining wall is shown in figure 26-7.

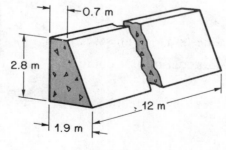

Fig. 26-7

   a. Find the number of cubic metres of concrete required for the wall.

   b. At a cost of $96.50 per cubic metre, what is the total cost of concrete in the wall?

CYLINDERS

Cylinders are used in many industrial and construction applications. Pipes, shafts, support columns, and tanks are a few of the practical uses made of cylinders.

A *circular cylinder* is a solid which has identical circular parallel bases. The surface between the bases is called *lateral surface*. The *altitude* of a circular cylinder is the perpendicular distance between the bases. The *axis* of a circular cylinder is a line which connects the centers of the bases.

In a *right circular cylinder* the axis is perpendicular to the bases. A right circular cylinder with its parts identified is shown in figure 26-8. Only right circular cylinders are considered in this book.

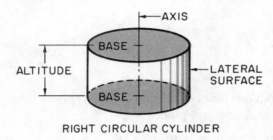

RIGHT CIRCULAR CYLINDER

Fig. 26-8

VOLUMES OF CYLINDERS

As with a prism, a right circular cylinder has a uniform cross-sectional area. The formula for computing volumes of right circular cylinders is the same as that of prisms. The *volume of a right circular cylinder* is equal to the product of the base area and altitude.

$$V = A_B h$$

where V = volume

A_B = area of base

h = height

Example 1. Find the volume of a cylinder with a base area of 30 square centimetres and an altitude of 6 centimetres.

$V = 30 \text{ cm}^2 \times 6 \text{ cm} = \textbf{180 cm}^3 \textit{ Ans}$

Example 2. A cylindrical tank has a 6-foot diameter and a height of 5.5 feet.

 a. Find the volume of the tank.

 b. Find the capacity in gallons.

 a. Find the area of the circular base:

 $A_B = 0.785\ 4(6 \text{ ft})^2 = 28.274\ 4 \text{ sq ft}$

 Find the volume:

 $V = 28.274\ 4 \text{ sq ft} \times 5.5 \text{ ft} = \textbf{155.5 cu ft} \textit{ Ans}$

 b. Find the capacity in gallons:

 $155.5 \text{ cu ft} \times 7.5 \text{ gal/cu ft} = \textbf{1 166.25 gal} \textit{ Ans}$

Example 3.   A length of pipe is shown in figure 26-9. Find the volume of metal in the pipe.

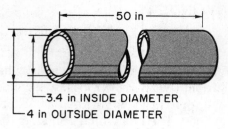

Fig. 26-9

50 in
3.4 in INSIDE DIAMETER
4 in OUTSIDE DIAMETER

Find the area of the outside circle:

$A_B = 0.785\ 4(4\ \text{in})^2 = 12.566\ 4$ sq in

Find the area of the hole:

$A_B = 0.785\ 4(3.4\ \text{in})^2 = 9.079\ 224$ sq in

Find the cross-sectional area:

12.566 4 sq in − 9.079 224 sq in = 3.487 176 sq in

Find the volume:

$V = 3.487\ 176$ sq in × 50 in = **174.4 cu in** *Ans*

Exercise 26-2

Use the tables found in the Appendix for equivalent units of measure. Solve these problems. Use $\pi = 3.14$. Round the answers to 2 decimal places.

1. Find the volume of a right circular cylinder with a base area of 76 square inches and an altitude of 8.60 inches.

2. Compute the volume of a right circular cylinder with an altitude of 0.40 metre and a base area of 0.30 square metre.

3. A cylindrical container has a base area of 154 square inches and a height of 16 inches. Find the capacity, in gallons, of the container.

4. Compute the weight of a cedar post which has a base area of 20.60 square inches and a length of 8 feet. Cedar weighs 23 pounds per cubic foot.

5. Find the volume of a steel shaft which is 59 centimetres long and has a diameter of 3.84 centimetres.

6. Each cylinder of a 6-cylinder engine has a 3.20-inch diameter and a piston stroke of 4.68 inches. Find the total piston displacement of the engine.

7. A cylindrical hot water tank is 1.8 metres high and has a 0.5-metre diameter.

   a. Compute the volume of the tank.

   b. How many litres of water are held in this tank when full?

8. A 0.46-inch diameter brass rod is 8 feet long.

   a. Find the volume, in cubic inches, of the rod.

   b. Compute the total weight of 40 rods. Brass weighs 0.30 pound per cubic inch.

9. A gasoline storage tank has a diameter of 12 metres and a height of 7.5 metres.

   a. Compute the volume of the tank.

   b. How many litres of gasoline are contained in the tank when it is one-third full?

10. A bronze bushing is shown in figure 26-10.

   a. Compute the volume of the bushing.

   b. The bushing weighs 1.50 pounds. Find the weight of 1 cubic inch of bronze.

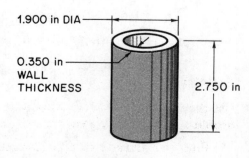

1.900 in DIA
0.350 in WALL THICKNESS
2.750 in

Fig. 26-10

11. Each of two cylindrical vessels is 15 centimetres high. The larger vessel has a diameter of 7.80 centimetres. The smaller vessel has a diameter of 6.12 centimetres. How many more millilitres of liquid does the larger vessel hold?

12. A water pipe has a 5-inch inside diameter. Water flows through the pipe at a rate of 0.6 foot per second. How many gallons of water flow through the pipe in 10 minutes?

COMPUTING ALTITUDES AND BASES OF PRISMS AND CYLINDERS

The altitude of a prism or a right circular cylinder can be determined if the base area and volume are known. Also, the base area can be found if the altitude and volume are known. Substitute the known values in the volume formula and solve for the unknown value.

Example 1.   The volume of a steel shaft 20 inches long is 60 cubic inches. Compute the cross-sectional area.

Substitute the values in the formula and solve.

60 cu in = A_B (20 in)

A_B = **3 sq in** *Ans*

Example 2.   A concrete retaining wall is shown in figure 26-11. Find the length of wall that can be constructed with 50 cubic yards of concrete.

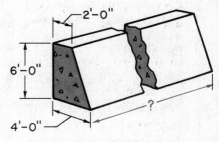

Fig. 26-11

The cross section or base is in the shape of a trapezoid. Find the cross-sectional area:

A_B = 0.5(6 ft)(4 ft + 2 ft) = 18 sq ft

Find the length:

50 cu yd × 27 cu ft/cu yd = 1 350 cu ft

1 350 cu ft = 18 sq ft (h)

h = **75 ft** *Ans*

Example 3.   An engine piston has a height of 10.800 centimetres and a volume of 450 cubic centimetres. Find the piston diameter.

Find the base area:

450 cm³ = A_B (10.800 cm)

A_B = 41.666 7 cm²

Find the piston diameter:

41.666 7 cm² = 0.785 4d^2

d^2 = 53.051 566 cm²

d = **7.284 cm** *Ans*

Exercise 26-3

Use the tables found in the Appendix for equivalent units of measure. Solve these problems. Round the answers to 2 decimal places.

1. Find the altitude of a prism that has a base area of 64 square inches and a volume of 448 cubic inches.

2. A solid right circular cylinder is 15.5 centimetres high and contains 110 cubic centimetres of material. Compute the cross-sectional area of the cylinder.

3. A room with a floor area of 440 square feet contains 3 740 cubic feet of air. Find the height of the room.

4. A solid steel post 28 inches long has a square base. The post has a volume of 112 cubic inches. Compute the length of a side of the base.

5. A cylindrical quart can has a 3.86-inch diameter. What is the height of the can?

6. A rectangular carton is designed to have a volume of 1.632 cubic metres. The carton is 1.20 metres high and 1.60 metres long. Compute the width of the carton.

7. A 20-foot high fuel tank contains 70 000 gallons of fuel when full. Compute the tank diameter.

8. A triangular block of marble is shown in figure 26-12. The block weighs 5 544 pounds. Marble weighs 168 pounds per cubic foot.

   a. Compute the number of cubic feet of marble contained in the block.

   b. Compute the height of the block.

9. A rectangular aluminum plate required for a job is 4 feet wide and 5 feet long. The maximum allowable weight is 505.5 pounds. Aluminum weighs 168.5 pounds per cubic foot. What is the maximum thickness of the plate?

10. Water is pumped into a cylindrical storage tank at the rate of 300 litres per minute for a total of 5 hours. The tank has a base diameter of 6 metres. What is the depth of water in the tank if the tank was empty when the pumping started?

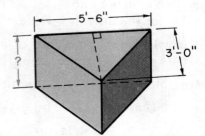

Fig. 26-12

SURFACE AREAS OF RIGHT PRISMS AND CYLINDERS

It is often necessary to determine surface areas of prisms and cylinders. For example, a tradesperson computes the number of square feet of stock for an air duct, the number of bundles of shingles for building siding, or the amount of paint for a cylindrical storage tank.

The *lateral area of a prism* is the sum of the areas of the lateral faces. The *lateral area of a cylinder* is the area of the curved or lateral surface. The lateral area of any prism is determined by computing the area of each lateral face, then adding all of the areas of the faces.

The *lateral area of a right prism* equals the product of the perimeter of the base and altitude.

$$LA = P_B h$$

where LA = lateral area

P_B = perimeter of base

h = altitude

To derive this formula, think of the lateral faces as being spread out on a flat surface or plane. For example, with the triangular prism shown in figure 26-13, imagine that a cut is made along edge E. Then the left face is unfolded back along edge F, and the right face is unfolded back along edge G. The three faces now lie on a flat surface or plane as shown in figure 26-14. It can be seen that the total area of the three prism faces is equal to the area of the rectangle in figure 26-14. Distance A + B + C is the perimeter of the triangular prism base. Distance A + B + C is also the length of the rectangle formed by unfolding the prism faces.

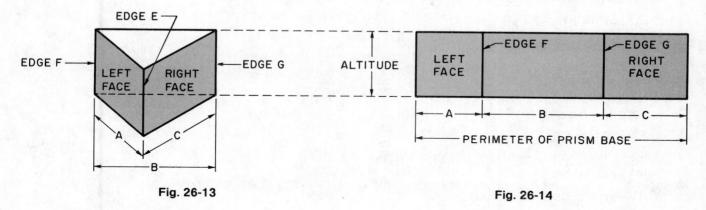

Fig. 26-13   Fig. 26-14

The *lateral area of a right circular cylinder* is equal to the product of the circumference of the base and altitude.

$$LA = C_B h$$

where LA = lateral area

C_B = circumference of base

h = altitude

This formula is developed in much the same way as that of the prism. Imagine that a vertical cut is made along the lateral surface of the cylinder shown in figure 26-15. The lateral surface is then spread out flat as shown in figure 26-16. The length of the rectangle in figure 26-16 is equal to the circumference of the cylinder base in figure 26-15.

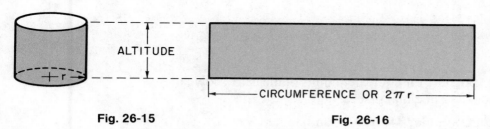

Fig. 26-15   Fig. 26-16

The total surface area of a prism or a cylinder must include the area of both bases as well as the lateral area. The *surface area of a prism or a cylinder* equals the sum of the lateral area and two times the base area.

$$SA = LA + 2A_B$$

where SA = total surface area

LA = lateral area

A_B = area of base

These examples illustrate the method of computing lateral areas and total surface areas of right prisms and right circular cylinders.

Example 1.   A shipping crate is shown in figure 26-17.

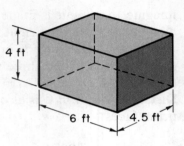

Fig. 26-17

      a. Compute the lateral area.

      b. Compute the total surface area.

a. Find the perimeter of the base:

$P_B = 2(6 \text{ ft}) + 2(4.5 \text{ ft}) = 21 \text{ ft}$

Find the lateral area:

$LA = 21 \text{ ft} \times 4 \text{ ft} = \textbf{84 sq ft } Ans$

b. Find the area of the base:

$A_B = 6 \text{ ft} \times 4.5 \text{ ft} = 27 \text{ sq ft}$

Find the surface area:

$SA = 84 \text{ sq ft} + 2(27 \text{ sq ft}) = \textbf{138 sq ft } Ans$

Example 2.   A cylinder hot water tank has a diameter of 0.6 metre and a height of 1.7 metres.

      a. Find the lateral area.

      b. Find the total surface area.

a. Find the circumference of the circular base:

$C_B = 3.14(0.6 \text{ m}) = 1.884 \text{ m}$

Find the lateral area:

$LA = 1.884 \text{ m} \times 1.7 \text{ m} = \textbf{3.20 m}^2 \, Ans$

b. Find the area of the circular base:

$A_B = 3.14(0.3 \text{ m})^2 = 0.283 \text{ m}^2$

Find the surface area:

$SA = 3.20 \text{ m}^2 + 2(0.283 \text{ m}^2) = \textbf{3.77 m}^2 \, Ans$

Exercise 26-4

Use the tables found in the Appendix for equivalent units of measure. Solve these problems. Round the answers to 2 decimal places.

1. A rectangular crate is $2\frac{1}{2}$ feet wide, 6 feet long, and 3 feet high.

    a. Find the lateral area of the crate.

    b. Find the total surface area of the crate.

2. A 0.46-metre diameter concrete pillar is 4.20 metres high. Compute the lateral area of the pillar.

3. How many square feet of insulation are required to cover a 6-inch outside diameter steam pipe which is 120 feet long?

4. An above ground swimming pool is 2.75 metres high. The base is a regular octagon whose sides are each 2.20 metres long. Compute the lateral area of the pool.

5. A rectangular metal container with an open top is fabricated from 0.072-inch thick aluminum sheet. The container is 18 inches wide, 25 inches long, and 23 inches high. The aluminum sheet weighs 1.045 pounds per square foot. Find the total weight of the container.

6. A room 20 feet wide, 25 feet long, and $7\frac{1}{2}$ feet high is wallpapered. One roll of wallpaper covers 55 square feet. How many rolls are required for the job? Deduct 15% for window and door openings.

7. The sides and top of a cylindrical fuel storage tank are painted with two coats of paint. The tank is 75 feet in diameter and 60 feet high. One gallon of paint covers 550 square feet. How many gallons of paint are required?

8. A firm manufactures sheet metal pipe as shown in figure 26-18. There is a 0.50-inch seam overlap. The material cost is $0.65 per square foot. What is the material cost for 1 200 pieces of pipe?

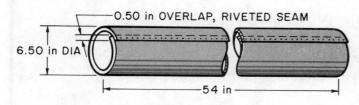

Fig. 26-18

9. A plywood form with bases in the shape of isosceles trapezoids is shown in figure 26-19. Compute the number of square metres of plywood required for the lateral faces of the form.

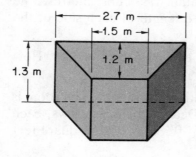

Fig. 26-19

10. A container manufacturer is presently producing one-litre closed cylindrical containers that have a 12.80-centimetre diameter. The manufacturer will replace the present containers with one-litre closed cylindrical containers having a 10.40-centimetre diameter.

   a. Find, in square centimetres, the material per container saved by replacing the 12.80-centimetre diameter containers with the 10.40-centimetre diameter containers.

   b. The cost of material used in making the containers is $2.10 per square metre. Based on an annual production of 5 800 000 containers, find the amount saved in material costs in one year by replacing the present containers.

UNIT EXERCISE AND PROBLEM REVIEW

Exercise 26-5

Use the tables found in the Appendix for equivalent units of measure. Solve these prism and cylinder problems. Round the answers to 2 decimal places.

1. Compute the volume of a prism with a base area of 220 square centimetres and an altitude of 7.6 centimetres.

2. Find the volume of a right circular cylinder which has an altitude of 4.6 inches and a base area of 53 square inches.

3. Compute the altitude of a prism with a base area of 2.7 square feet and a volume of 4.86 cubic feet.

4. A solid right cylinder 0.9 metre high contains 0.8 cubic metre of material. Compute the cross-sectional area of the cylinder.

5. Find the lateral area of a rectangular box 7.3 inches wide, 9.6 inches long, and 5.4 inches high.

6. Each side of a square concrete platform is 8.7 metres long. The platform is 0.2 metre thick. Compute the number of cubic metres of concrete contained in the platform.

7. A circular $2\frac{1}{2}$-inch thick pine table top has a 4-foot diameter. The pine used for the top weighs 25 pounds per cubic foot. What is the weight of the top?

8. Find the capacity, in gallons, of a cylindrical container with a base diameter of 16.6 inches and a height of 18 inches.

9. A carton with a square base is designed to contain 1.80 cubic metres. The carton is 1.15 metres high. What is the required length of each side of the base?

10. A cylindrical one-litre vessel has a base diameter of 5 centimetres. How high is the vessel?

11. The walls and ceiling of a room are covered with plasterboard. The room is 25 feet long, 16 feet wide, and 8 feet high. Deduct for 3 windows, each 3'-0" × 4'-6", and 2 doorways, each 3'-6" × 7'-0". How many square feet of plasterboard are required?

12. An automobile gasoline tank is shown in figure 26-20.

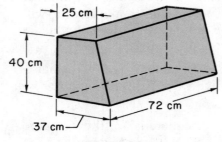

Fig. 26-20

   a. Compute the capacity of the tank in litres.

   b. Compute the number of square metres of tank surface area.

   c. The sheet steel used to fabricate the tank weighs 11.08 kilograms per square metre. Compute the weight of the tank.

13. A length of brass pipe is shown in figure 26-21.

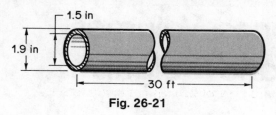

Fig. 26-21

a. Find the number of cubic inches of brass contained in the pipe.

b. Brass weighs 526 pounds per cubic foot. What is the weight of the pipe?

14. The basement of a building is flooded with water to a depth of 18 inches. The basement is 52 feet long and 38 feet wide. Two pumps, each pumping at the rate of 34 gallons per minute, are used to drain the water. How many minutes does it take to completely drain the water from the basement?

15. Topsoil is spread evenly over the entire surface of a rectangular lot which is 200 feet long and 162 feet wide. If 300 cubic yards of topsoil are spread over the lot, find the average thickness, in inches, of the topsoil.

UNIT 27
Pyramids and Cones: Volumes, Surface Areas, and Weights

OBJECTIVES

After studying this unit you should be able to

- compute volumes of pyramids and cones.
- compute surface areas of pyramids and cones.
- compute capacities and weights of pyramids and cones.
- compute volumes of frustums of pyramids and cones.
- compute surface areas of frustums of pyramids and cones.
- compute capacities and weights of frustums of pyramids and cones.
- solve applied problems using principles discussed in this unit.

PYRAMIDS

A *pyramid* is a solid whose base is a polygon and whose sides or faces are triangles. The triangles meet at a point called the *vertex*. The triangular faces which meet at the vertex are called *lateral faces*. A *lateral edge* is the line segment where two lateral faces meet. The *altitude* of a pyramid is the perpendicular distance from the vertex to the base.

Pyramids are named according to the shape of the bases, such as triangular, quadrangular, pentagonal, hexagonal, and octagonal. In a *regular pyramid,* the base is a regular polygon and the lateral edges are all equal in length. Only regular pyramids are considered in this book. Some common regular pyramids are shown in figure 27-1. The parts of the pyramids are identified.

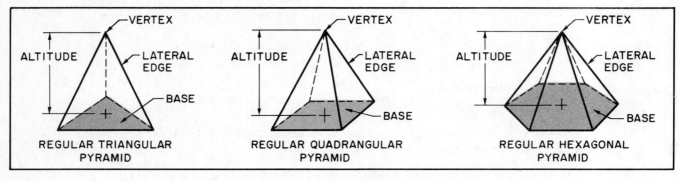

Fig. 27-1

CONES

A *circular cone* is a solid with a circular base and a surface that tapers from the base to a point called the *vertex*. The surface lying between the base and the vertex is called the *lateral surface*. The *altitude* of a circular cone is the perpendicular distance from the vertex to the base. The *axis* of a circular cone is a line which connects the vertex to the center of the circular base.

In a *right circular cone* the axis is perpendicular to the base. A right circular cone with the parts identified is shown in figure 27-2. Only right circular cones are considered in this book.

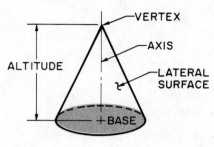

Fig. 27-2

VOLUMES OF REGULAR PYRAMIDS AND RIGHT CIRCULAR CONES

Consider a prism and a pyramid which have identical bases and altitudes. If the volumes of the prism and pyramid are measured, the volume of the pyramid would be one-third the volume of the prism. Also, if the volumes of a cylinder and a cone with identical bases and altitudes are measured, the volume of the cone would be one-third the volume of the cylinder. The formulas for computing volumes of prisms and right circular cylinders are the same. Therefore, the formulas for computing volumes of regular pyramids and right circular cones are the same. The *volume of a regular pyramid or a right circular cone* equals one-third the product of the area of the base and altitude.

$$V = \frac{1}{3}A_B h$$

where V = volume

A_B = area of the base

h = altitude

These examples illustrate the method of computing volumes of regular pyramids and right circular cones.

Example 1. Compute the volume of a pyramid which has a base area of 24 square feet and an altitude of 6 feet.

$$V = \frac{24 \text{ sq ft} \times 6 \text{ ft}}{3} = \textbf{48 cu ft } \textit{Ans}$$

Example 2. A bronze casting in the shape of a right circular cone is 14.5 inches high and has a base diameter of 10 inches.

  a. Find the volume of bronze required for the casting.

  b. Find the weight of the casting. Bronze weighs 547.9 pounds per cubic foot.

  a. $V = \dfrac{(3.14)(5 \text{ in})^2(14.5 \text{ in})}{3} = \textbf{379.4 cu in } \textit{Ans}$

  b. 379.4 cu in ÷ 1 728 cu in/cu ft = 0.22 cu ft

      0.22 cu ft × 547.9 lb/cu ft = **120.5 lb** *Ans*

Example 3.   The roof of the building shown in figure 27-3 is in the shape of a regular pyramid. Find the approximate number of cubic metres of attic space.

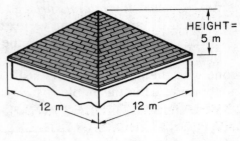

Fig. 27-3

$$A_B = (12 \text{ m})^2 = 144 \text{ m}^2$$

$$V = \frac{(144 \text{ m}^2)(5 \text{ m})}{3} = 240 \text{ m}^3 \text{ } Ans$$

Exercise 27-1

Use the tables found in the Appendix for equivalent units of measure. Solve these problems. Round the answers to 2 decimal places. Use $\pi = 3.14$.

1. Compute the volume of a regular pyramid with a base area of 230 square feet and an altitude of 12 feet.

2. Find the volume of a right circular cone with a base area of 38.6 square centimetres and an altitude of 5 centimetres.

3. Find the volume of a regular pyramid with an altitude of 10.8 inches and a base area of 98 square inches.

4. A container is in the shape of a right circular cone. The base area is 4.8 square feet and the altitude is 1.5 feet. Compute the capacity of the container in gallons.

5. A solid granite monument is in the shape of a regular pyramid. The base area is 60 square feet and the height is 10'-3". Find the weight of the monument. Granite weighs 168 pounds per cubic foot.

6. A brass casting is in the shape of a right circular cone with a base diameter of 7.8 centimetres and a height of 16.4 centimetres. Find the volume.

7. Compute the number of cubic feet of attic space in a building which has a roof in the shape of a regular pyramid. Each of the 4 outside walls of the building is 42 feet long and the roof is 18 feet high.

8. Two solid pieces of aluminum in the shape of right circular cones with different base diameters are machined. The altitudes of both pieces are 6 inches. The base of the smaller piece is 2 inches in diameter. The base of the larger piece is twice as large or 4 inches in diameter. How many times heavier is the larger piece than the smaller?

9. A vessel is in the shape of a right circular cone. This vessel contains liquid to a depth of 12.8 centimetres as shown in figure 27-4. How many litres of liquid must be added in order to fill the vessel?

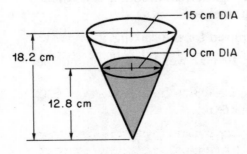

Fig. 27-4

10. The steeple of a building is in the shape of a regular pyramid with a triangular base. Each of the 3 base sides is 4.60 metres long and the steeple is 7 metres high. Compute the number of cubic metres of air space contained in the steeple.

COMPUTING ALTITUDES AND BASES OF REGULAR PYRAMIDS AND RIGHT CIRCULAR CONES

As with prisms and cylinders, altitudes and base areas of regular pyramids and right circular cones are readily determined. Substitute known values in the volume formula and solve for the unknown value.

Example 1.   The volume of a regular pyramid is 270 cubic centimetres and the height (altitude) is 18 centimetres. Compute the base area.

Substitute the values in the formula and solve.

$$270 \text{ cm}^3 = \frac{A_B(18 \text{ cm})}{3}$$

$$A_B = 45 \text{ cm}^2 \text{ } Ans$$

Example 2.   A disposable plastic drinking cup is designed in the shape of a right circular cone. The cup holds $\frac{1}{3}$ pint (9.63 cubic inches) of liquid when full. The rim (base) diameter is 3.60 inches. Find the cup depth (altitude).

Substitute the values in the formula and solve.

$$9.63 \text{ cu in} = \frac{3.14(1.80 \text{ in})^2 \text{ } (h)}{3}$$

$$h = 2.84 \text{ in } Ans$$

Exercise 27-2

Use the tables found in the Appendix for equivalent units of measure. Solve these problems. Round the answers to 2 decimal places. Use $\pi = 3.14$.

1. Compute the altitude of a regular pyramid with a base area of 32 square feet and a volume of 152 cubic feet.

2. A right circular cone 1.2 metres high contains 0.80 cubic metre of material. Find the cone base area.

3. The base area of a wooden form in the shape of a regular pyramid is 28 square feet. The form contains 21 cubic feet of air space. How high is the form?

4. A container with a capacity of 6 gallons is in the shape of a right circular cone. The container is 1.5 feet high. Find the container base area.

5. A tent in the shape of a regular pyramid is designed to contain 5.6 cubic metres of air space. The base of the tent is square with each side 2.5 metres long. What is the height of the tent?

6. Find the base diameter of a right circular cone which has a volume of 920 cubic centimetres and an altitude of 14 centimetres.

7. A concrete monument in the shape of a regular pyramid with a square base weighs 13 400 pounds. The monument is 7.30 feet high. Compute the length of a base side. Concrete weighs 137 pounds per cubic foot.

SURFACE AREAS OF REGULAR PYRAMIDS AND RIGHT CIRCULAR CONES

To determine material requirements and weights of pyramids and conical shaped objects, surface areas are computed. These types of computations have wide application in the industrial and construction fields.

Slant heights are used in determining lateral areas of pyramids and cones. The *slant height of a regular pyramid* is the altitude of any of the lateral faces. The slant height of a regular pyramid is shown in figure 27-5. The *slant height of a right circular cone* is a straight line segment which connects the vertex to any point on the circular base. The slant height of a right circular cone is shown in figure 27-6. The lateral area of a pyramid is the sum of the areas of the lateral faces. The *lateral area of a regular pyramid* equals one-half the product of the perimeter of the base and the slant height.

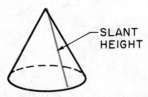

Fig. 27-5   Fig. 27-6

$$LA = \tfrac{1}{2}P_B h_s$$

where LA = lateral area

P_B = perimeter of base

h_s = slant height

The lateral area of a circular cone is the area of the lateral surface. The *lateral area of a right circular cone* equals one-half the product of the circumference of the base and the slant height.

$$LA = \tfrac{1}{2}C_B h_s$$

where LA = lateral area

C_B = circumference of base

h_s = slant height

The total surface area of a pyramid or cone includes the base as well as the lateral area. The *total surface area of a pyramid or cone* equals the sum of the lateral area and the base area.

$$SA = LA + A_B$$

where SA = total surface area

LA = lateral area

A_B = area of base

These examples illustrate the procedure for computing lateral areas and total surface areas of regular pyramids and right circular cones.

Example 1. Refer to the right circular cone shown in figure 27-7.

a. Compute the lateral area.

b. Compute the total surface area.

a. Find the lateral area:

$LA = 0.5(3.14)(14 \text{ in})(16 \text{ in}) = \textbf{351.68 sq in } Ans$

b. Find the total surface area:

$A_B = 3.14(7 \text{ in})^2 = 153.86 \text{ sq in}$

$SA = 351.68 \text{ sq in} + 153.86 \text{ sq in} = \textbf{505.5 sq in } Ans$

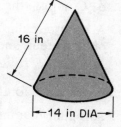

Fig. 27-7

Example 2. The pyramid shown in figure 27-8 has a square base with each base side 20 centimetres long. The pyramid altitude, 25 centimetres, is given. Find the lateral area of the pyramid.

The slant height is not known and must be computed. In figure 27-9, right triangle ACB is formed within the pyramid.

The triangle is formed by altitude CB, slant height AB, and triangle base CA. Slant height AB is computed by applying the Pythagorean Theorem.

$c^2 = a^2 + b^2$

$AB^2 = (10 \text{ cm})^2 + (25 \text{ cm})^2$

$AB^2 = 100 \text{ cm}^2 + 625 \text{ cm}^2$

$AB^2 = 725 \text{ cm}^2$

$AB = 26.93 \text{ cm}$

Find the lateral area:

$P_B = 4(20 \text{ cm}) = 80 \text{ cm}$

$LA = 0.5(80 \text{ cm})(26.93 \text{ cm}) = \textbf{1 077.2 cm}^2 \text{ } Ans$

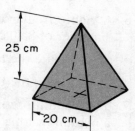

Fig. 27-8

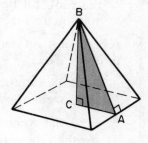

Fig. 27-9

Exercise 27-3

Use the tables found in the Appendix for equivalent units of measure. Solve these problems. Round the answers to 2 decimal places.

1. Find the lateral area of a regular pyramid which has a base perimeter of 92 inches and a slant height of 20 inches.

2. Find the lateral area of a right circular cone with a slant height of 1.8 metres and a base perimeter of 6.4 metres.

3. A regular pyramid has a base perimeter of 58.4 centimetres, a slant height of 17.8 centimetres, and a base area of 213.16 square centimetres.

   a. Compute the lateral area of the pyramid.

   b. Compute the total surface area of the pyramid.

4. A right circular cone has a slant height of 4.25 feet, a base circumference of 18.84 feet, and a base area of 28.26 square feet.

   a. Find the lateral area of the cone.

   b. Find the total surface area of the cone.

5. A regular pyramid with a square base has a slant height of 10 inches. Each side of the base is 8 inches long.

   a. Find the lateral area of the pyramid.

   b. Find the total surface area of the pyramid.

6. A right circular cone with a slant height of 13.52 centimetres has a base diameter of 8.40 centimetres.

   a. Compute the lateral area of the cone.

   b. Compute the total surface area of the cone.

7. The building roof shown in figure 27-10 is in the shape of a pyramid with a square base.

   a. Find the surface area of the roof.

   b. Find the number of bundles of shingles required to cover the roof if 4 bundles of shingles are required for each 100 square feet of roof area.

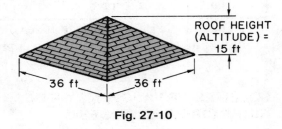

ROOF HEIGHT (ALTITUDE) = 15 ft

36 ft   36 ft

Fig. 27-10

8. A conical sheet copper cover with an open bottom is shown in figure 27-11.

   a. Find the number of square feet of copper contained in the cover. Allow 5% for the overlapping seam.

   b. Find the weight of the cover. The sheet copper used for the fabrication weighs 2.65 pounds per square foot.

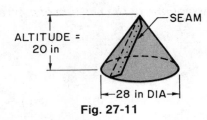

ALTITUDE = 20 in

SEAM

28 in DIA

Fig. 27-11

9. A plywood form in the shape of a right pyramid with a regular hexagon base is constructed. Each side of the base is 1.2 metres long and the form is 2.7 metres high. Allow 20% for waste. Find the number of square metres of plywood required for the lateral area of the form.

10. The conical spire of a building has a 10-metre diameter. The altitude is 18 metres.

   a. Find the lateral area of the spire.

   b. How many litres of paint are required to apply 2 coats of paint to the spire? One litre of paint covers 12.3 square metres of surface area.

FRUSTUMS OF PYRAMIDS AND CONES

When a pyramid or a cone is cut by a plane parallel to the base, the part that remains is called a *frustum*. Frustums of pyramids and cones are often found in architecture. As well as architectural applications, containers, tapered shafts, funnels, and lamp shades are a few familiar examples of frustums of pyramids and cones.

The *larger base* is the base of the cone or pyramid. The *smaller base* is the circle or polygon formed by the parallel cutting plane. The smaller base of the pyramid has the same shape as the larger base. The two bases are similar. The *altitude* is the perpendicular distance between the larger and smaller bases. A frustum of a pyramid and a frustum of a cone with their parts identified are shown in figure 27-12.

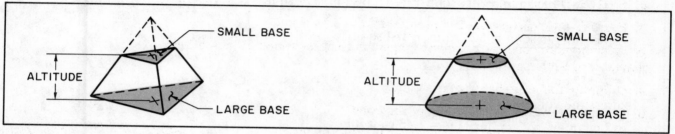

Fig. 27-12

VOLUMES OF FRUSTUMS OF REGULAR PYRAMIDS AND RIGHT CIRCULAR CONES

The *volume of the frustum of a pyramid or cone* is computed using this formula.

$$V = \frac{1}{3}h(A_B + A_b + \sqrt{A_B A_b})$$

where V = volume of the frustum of a pyramid or cone

h = altitude

A_B = area of larger base

A_b = area of smaller base

The formula for the volume of a frustum of a right circular cone is expressed in this form.

$$V = \frac{1}{3}\pi h(R^2 + r^2 + Rr)$$

where V = volume of a right circular cone

h = altitude

R = radius of larger base

r = radius of smaller base

These examples illustrate the method of computing volumes of frustums of regular pyramids and right circular cones.

Example 1.   A waste basket is designed in the shape of a frustum of a pyramid with a square base as shown in figure 27-13. Find the volume of the basket in cubic feet.

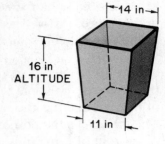

Fig. 27-13

Find the larger base area:

$A_B = (14 \text{ in})^2 = 196$ sq in

Find the smaller base area:

$A_b = (11 \text{ in})^2 = 121$ sq in

Find the volume:

$$V = \frac{(16 \text{ in})\left[196 \text{ sq in} + 121 \text{ sq in} + \sqrt{(196 \text{ sq in})(121 \text{ sq in})}\right]}{3}$$

$$V = \frac{(16 \text{ in})(196 \text{ sq in} + 121 \text{ sq in} + 154 \text{ sq in})}{3}$$

$V = 2\,512$ cu in

Express the volume in cubic feet:

$2\,512$ cu in $\div\ 1\,728$ cu in/cu ft $= \mathbf{1.45}$ **cu ft** *Ans*

Example 2.   A tapered steel shaft is shown in figure 27-14.

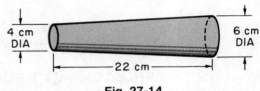

Fig. 27-14

   a. Find the number of cubic centimetres of steel contained in the shaft.

   b. Find the weight of the shaft. The steel in the shaft weighs 0.007 8 kilogram per cubic centimetre.

   a. Find the volume:

$$V = \frac{(3.14)(22 \text{ cm})[(3 \text{ cm})^2 + (2 \text{ cm})^2 + (3 \text{ cm})(2 \text{ cm})]}{3}$$

$V = \mathbf{437.51} \text{ cm}^3 \ Ans$

   b. Compute the weight:

437.51 cm^3 × 0.007 8 kg/cm^3 = **3.41 kg** *Ans*

Exercise 27-4

Use the tables found in the Appendix for equivalent units of measure. Solve these problems. Round the answers to 2 decimal places.

1. Compute the volume of the frustum of a regular pyramid with an altitude of 18 feet. The larger base area is 150 square feet, and the smaller base area is 90 square feet.

2. The frustum of a right circular cone has the larger base area equal to 32 square inches, and the smaller base area equal to 15 square inches. The altitude is 16 inches. Compute the volume.

3. A pail is in the shape of a frustum of a right circular cone. The smaller base area is 450 square centimetres, and the larger base area is 900 square centimetres. The altitude is 30 centimetres. Compute the capacity of the pail in litres.

4. A solid oak trophy base is in the shape of a frustum of a regular pyramid. It has a larger base area of 175 square inches, and a smaller base area of 120 square inches. The height is 8.5 inches. Compute the weight of the trophy base. Oak weighs 47 pounds per cubic foot.

5. A concrete platform is in the shape of a frustum of a regular pyramid with square bases as shown in figure 27-15. Compute the number of cubic metres of concrete in the platform.

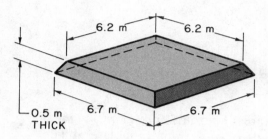

Fig. 27-15

6. A tapered maple table leg is shown in figure 27-16. Maple weighs 38 pounds per cubic foot. Compute the weight of 4 legs.

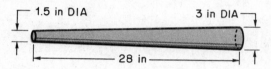

Fig. 27-16

7. The bottom of a drinking glass is 2.3 inches in diameter. The top is 2.8 inches in diameter. The height is 3.5 inches.

   a. Compute the volume of space contained in the glass.

   b. Compute the capacity of the glass in ounces.

8. The side view of a tapered steel shaft is shown in figure 27-17. The length of the shaft is reduced from 18.4 inches to 13.6 inches. How many cubic inches of stock are removed?

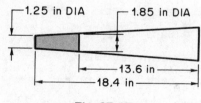

Fig. 27-17

9. A sand storage bin in the shape of a frustum of a regular pyramid with square bases is shown in figure 27-18.

   a. Find the maximum number of cubic yards of sand that can be stored in the bin.

   b. Find the weight of sand in the bin when it is full. Sand weighs 100 pounds per cubic foot.

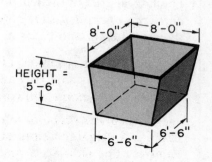

Fig. 27-18

10. A solid bronze casting in the shape of a frustum of a pyramid is shown in figure 27-19. The bases of the casting are equilateral triangles.

   a. Find the number of cubic centimetres of bronze contained in the casting.

   b. Find the weight of the casting. Bronze weighs 0.009 kilogram per cubic centimetre.

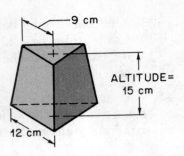

ALTITUDE= 15 cm

9 cm

12 cm

Fig. 27-19

SURFACE AREAS OF FRUSTUMS OF REGULAR PYRAMIDS AND RIGHT CIRCULAR CONES

All lateral faces of frustums of pyramids are trapezoids. The *slant height* of the frustum of a regular pyramid is the altitude of each trapezoidal lateral face. The slant height of the frustum of a regular pyramid is shown in figure 27-20. The slant height of the frustum of a right circular cone is the shortest distance between the bases on the lateral surface. The slant height of the frustum of a right circular cone is shown in figure 27-21.

SLANT HEIGHT (ALTITUDE OF A TRAPEZOIDAL FACE)

Fig. 27-20

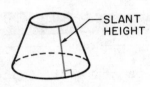

SLANT HEIGHT

Fig. 27-21

The lateral area of the frustum of a pyramid is the sum of the areas of the lateral faces. The lateral area can be determined by computing the area of each trapezoidal face and adding the face areas. However, it is easier to compute lateral areas by using altitudes and base perimeters. The *lateral area of the frustum of a regular pyramid* equals one-half the product of the slant height and the sum of the two base perimeters.

$$LA = \frac{1}{2}h_s(P_B + P_b)$$

where LA = lateral area

h_s = slant height

P_B = perimeter of larger base

P_b = perimeter of smaller base

The lateral area of the frustum of a cone is the area of the lateral surface. The *lateral area of the frustum of a right circular cone* equals one-half the product of the slant height and the sum of the two base circumferences.

$$LA = \frac{1}{2}h_s(C_B + C_b)$$

where LA = lateral area

h_s = slant height

C_B = circumference of larger base

C_b = circumference of smaller base

The formula for the lateral area of the frustum of a right circular cone is simplified to this form.

$$LA = \pi h_s(R + r)$$

where LA = lateral area

h_s = slant height

R = radius of larger base

r = radius of smaller base

The total surface area of the frustum of a pyramid or cone must include the area of both bases as well as the lateral area. The *total surface area of the frustum of a pyramid or cone* equals the sum of the lateral area, the larger base area, and the smaller base area.

$$SA = LA + A_B + A_b$$

where SA = total surface area

LA = lateral area

A_B = area of larger base

A_b = area of smaller base

These examples illustrate the procedure for computing lateral areas and total areas of frustums of regular pyramids and right circular cones.

Example 1.   A plywood pedestal has the shape of the frustum of a square based regular pyramid. Each side of the larger base is 4′-6″ long. Each side of the smaller base is 3′-3″ long. The slant height is 3′-0″.

   a. Compute the lateral area of the pedestal.

   b. Compute the total surface area of the pedestal.

 a. Compute the lateral area:

   $P_B = 4 \times 4.5$ ft = 18 ft

   $P_b = 4 \times 3.25$ ft = 13 ft

   $LA = 0.5(3$ ft$)(18$ ft + 13 ft$) =$ **46.5 sq ft** *Ans*

 b. Compute the total surface area:

   $A_B = (4.5$ ft$)^2 = 20.25$ sq ft

   $A_b = (3.25$ ft$)^2 = 10.56$ sq ft

   $SA = 46.5$ sq ft + 20.25 sq ft + 10.56 sq ft = **77.31 sq ft** *Ans*

Example 2.   Compute the number of square centimetres of fabric contained in the lamp shade shown in figure 27-22.

The slant height must be found. In figure 27-23, right triangle ACB is formed by the altitude CB, the slant height AB, and triangle base AC.

   $c^2 = a^2 + b^2$

 $AB^2 = (36$ cm$)^2 + (9$ cm$)^2$

 $AB^2 = 1\ 377$ cm^2

  $AB = 37.11$ cm

Find the lateral area:

   $LA = 3.14(37.11$ cm$)(20$ cm + 11 cm$) =$ **3 612 cm²** *Ans*

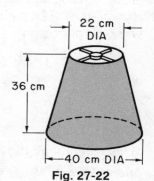

Fig. 27-22

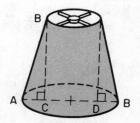

Fig. 27-23

Exercise 27-5

Use the tables found in the Appendix for equivalent units of measure. Solve these problems. Round the answers to 2 decimal places.

1. The frustum of a regular pyramid has a larger base perimeter of 60 feet, and a smaller base perimeter of 44 feet. The slant height is 16 feet. Compute the lateral area.

2. A frustum of a right circular cone has a slant height of 5.6 inches. The larger base circumference is 4.8 inches, and the smaller base circumference is 3.2 inches. Find the lateral area.

3. The frustum of a regular pyramid has square bases. The length of a side of the larger base is 3.6 metres, and the length of a side of the smaller base is 2.7 metres. The slant height is 4.2 metres.

    a. Find the lateral area of the pyramid.

    b. Find the total surface area of the pyramid.

4. The frustum of a right circular cone has a smaller base diameter of 24.2 centimetres, and a larger base diameter of 36.4 centimetres. The slant height is 29.3 centimetres.

    a. Compute the lateral area of the cone.

    b. Compute the total surface area of the cone.

5. A redwood planter in the shape of a frustum of a regular pyramid is shown in figure 27-24. The bases are regular hexagons. Find the number of square feet of redwood required for the lateral surface of the planter.

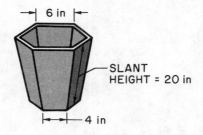

Fig. 27-24

6. A wooden platform in the shape of a frustum of a regular pyramid is constructed. The platform bases are equilateral triangles. Each side of the bottom base is 4.8 metres long, and each side of the top base is 4 metres long. The slant height is 0.7 metre. The bottom of the platform is open. Allow 15% for waste. Find the number of square metres of lumber required to construct the platform.

7. A support column in the shape of a frustum of a right circular cone has a slant height of 16 feet. The smaller base is 15 inches in diameter, and the larger base is 21 inches in diameter. Find, in square feet, the lateral area of the column.

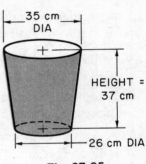

Fig. 27-25

8. An open top pail is shown in figure 27-25.

   a. Compute the lateral area of the pail.

   b. Compute the total number of square metres of metal contained in the pail.

   c. The pail is made of galvanized sheet steel which weighs 11.20 kilograms per square metre. Compute the weight of the pail.

9. A metal hopper is shown in figure 27-26. The hopper is in the shape of a frustum of a pyramid with square bases. Compute the lateral area in square feet.

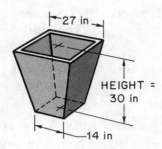

Fig. 27-26

10. A granite monument in the shape of a frustum of a regular pyramid with regular octagonal bases is shown in figure 27-27. The sides and the top of the monument are ground and polished. Find the number of square metres of surface area ground and polished.

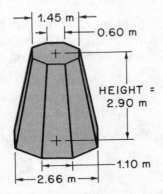

Fig. 27-27

UNIT EXERCISE AND PROBLEM REVIEW

Exercise 27-6

Use the tables found in the Appendix for equivalent units of measure. Solve these problems. Round the answers to 2 decimal places.

1. Find the volume of a right circular cone with a base area of 0.80 square metre and an altitude of 1.24 metres.

2. Compute the volume of a regular pyramid which has an altitude of 2.6 feet and a base area of 2.8 square feet.

3. A regular pyramid with a base area of 54 square feet contains 210 cubic feet of material. Find the altitude of the pyramid.

4. Compute the base area of a right circular cone which is 16.3 centimetres high and has a volume of 1 280 cubic centimetres.

5. A regular pyramid has a base perimeter of 56 inches and a slant height of 14 inches. Find the lateral area of the pyramid.

6. A right circular cone has a slant height of 3.76 feet. The base circumference is 17.58 feet, and the base area is 24.62 square feet.

   a. Compute the lateral area of the cone.

   b. Compute the total surface area of the cone.

7. The frustum of a right circular cone has a larger base area of 40 square centimetres, and a smaller base area of 19 square centimetres. The altitude is 22 centimetres. Find the volume.

8. The frustum of a regular pyramid has a smaller base perimeter of 18 metres, and a larger base perimeter of 26 metres. The slant height is 5.6 metres. Find the lateral area.

9. A building has a roof in the shape of a regular pyramid. Each of the 4 outside walls of the building is 38 feet long, and the roof is 16 feet high. Compute the number of cubic feet of attic space in the building.

10. A solid brass casting in the shape of a right circular cone has a base diameter of 4.36 inches and a height of 3.94 inches. Find the weight of the casting. Brass weighs 0.302 pound per cubic inch.

11. A vessel in the shape of a right circular cone has a capacity of 0.5 litre. The base diameter is 10 centimetres. What is the height of the vessel?

12. A plywood form is constructed in the shape of a right pyramid with a square base. Each side of the base is 7'-6" long and the form is 5'-3" high. Compute the number of square feet of plywood required for the lateral surface of the form. Allow 15% for waste.

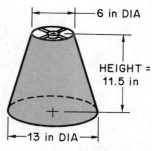

Fig. 27-28

13. A container in the shape of a frustum of a right pyramid with square bases is shown in figure 27-28. Compute the capacity of the container in litres.

14. Compute the number of square inches of fabric contained in the lamp shade shown in figure 27-29.

15. A decorative copper piece in the shape of a regular pyramid with an equilateral triangle base is shown in figure 27-30. The lateral faces and base are covered with sheet copper which weighs 1.87 pounds per square foot.

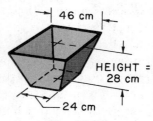

Fig. 27-29

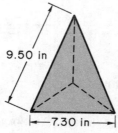

Fig. 27-30

   a. Compute the total number of square feet of copper contained in the piece.

   b. Compute the weight of the piece.

UNIT 28
Spheres and Composite Objects: Volumes, Surface Areas, and Weights

OBJECTIVES

After studying this unit you should be able to

- compute surface areas and volumes of spheres.
- compute capacities and weights of spheres.
- solve applied sphere problems using the principles discussed in this unit.
- solve applied composite solid figures using principles discussed in Section 5.

SPHERES

A *sphere* is a solid bounded by a curved surface such that every point on the surface is equally distant from a point called the *center*. A round ball, such as a baseball or basketball, is an example of a sphere.

The *radius* of a sphere is a straight line segment from the center to any point on the surface. A *diameter* is a straight line segment through the center with its endpoints on the curved surface. The diameter of a sphere is twice the radius.

If a plane cuts through a sphere and does <u>not</u> go through the center, the section is called a *small circle*. As intersecting planes move closer to the center, the circular sections get larger. A plane that cuts through the center of a sphere is called a great circle. A *great circle* is the largest circle that can be cut by an intersecting plane. If a plane is passed through the center of a sphere, the sphere is cut in two equal parts. Each part is a half sphere called a *hemisphere*. A sphere with its parts identified is shown in figure 28-1.

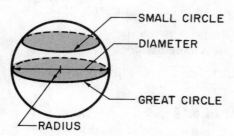

SMALL CIRCLE
DIAMETER
GREAT CIRCLE
RADIUS

Fig. 28-1

SURFACE AREA OF A SPHERE

The *surface area of a sphere* equals four times the area of the great circle.

$$SA = 4\pi r^2$$

where SA = surface area of the sphere

r = radius of the sphere

Example. A spherical gas storage tank, which has a 96-foot diameter, will be painted.

  a. Compute the surface area of the tank to the nearer square foot.

  b. Compute, to the nearer gallon, the amount of paint required. One gallon of paint covers 530 square feet.

 a. Find the surface area:

  $SA = 4(3.14)(48 \text{ ft})^2 = 28\,938 \text{ sq ft } Ans$

 b. Find the number of gallons of paint required:

  $28\,938 \text{ sq ft} \div 530 \text{ sq ft/gal} = 55 \text{ gal } Ans$

Exercise 28-1

Use the tables found in the Appendix for equivalent units of measure. Find the surface area for each sphere. Use $\pi = 3.14$ and round the answers to 2 decimal places.

1. 3-inch diameter

2. 20'-6" diameter

3. 1.4-metre radius

4. 26-centimetre radius

5. 7.9-foot radius

6. 6.38-inch diameter

7. 0.74-metre diameter

8. 39.2-centimetre radius

Solve these problems. Use $\pi = 3.14$ and round the answers to 2 decimal places.

9. A spherical storage tank has an 80-foot diameter. The storage tank will be repainted and the cost of preparation, priming, and applying a finish coat of paint is estimated at $0.20 per square foot. Compute the total cost of repainting the tank.

10. A company manufactures plastic covers in the shape of hemispheres. The diameter of each cover is 38 centimetres. The material expense for the covers is based on a cost of $3.40 per square metre. What is the material cost for a production run of 55 000 covers?

11. A spherical copper float with a diameter of 1.4 inches weighs 0.8 ounce. Another spherical float made of the same material is twice the diameter, or 2.8 inches. What is the weight of the 2.8-inch diameter float?

12. Compute the surface area of a basketball which has a circumference (great circle) of 29.75 inches.

13. A spherical fuel storage tank has a diameter of 6.12 metres. A cylindrical fuel storage tank has the same diameter, 6.12 metres, and a height of 4.08 metres. Both tanks have the same fuel capacity of approximately 120 000 litres.

  a. Which of the two tanks requires more surface area material?

  b. How much more material is required by the larger tank?

VOLUME OF A SPHERE

The *volume of a sphere* equals the surface area multiplied by one-third the radius. Since the surface area of a sphere equals $4\pi r^2$, the volume equals $\frac{1}{3}r(4\pi r^2)$. The formula for the volume of a sphere is simplified to this form.

$$V = \frac{4}{3}\pi r^3$$

where V = volume of the sphere

r = radius of the sphere

Example.   A stainless steel ball bearing contains balls which are 1.80 centimetres in diameter.

a. Find the volume of a ball.

b. Find the weight of a ball. Stainless steel weighs 7.88 grams per cubic centimetre.

a. Find the volume:

$$V = \frac{4(3.14)(0.90 \text{ cm})^3}{3} = 3.05 \text{ cm}^3 \text{ Ans}$$

b. Find the weight:

$3.05 \text{ cm}^3 \times 7.88 \text{ g/cm}^3 = 24.03 \text{ g } \text{Ans}$

Exercise 28-2

Use the tables found in the Appendix for equivalent units of measure. Compute the volume of each sphere. Use $\pi = 3.14$ and round the answers to 2 decimal places.

1. 2-metre radius
2. 28-centimetre diameter
3. 7.6-inch diameter
4. 6-foot radius

5. 4.2-inch radius
6. 0.8-metre diameter
7. 16.20-centimetre diameter
8. 25'-6" diameter

Solve these problems. Use $\pi = 3.14$ and round the answers to 2 decimal places.

9. A thrust bearing contains 18 steel balls. The steel used weighs 0.283 pound per cubic inch. The diameter of each ball is 0.24 inch. Compute the total weight of the balls in the bearing.

10. A vat in the shape of a hemisphere with an 18-inch diameter contains liquid. What is the capacity of the vat in gallons?

11. An empty spherical tank which has a diameter of 8.6 metres is filled with water. Water is pumped into the tank at a rate of 800 litres per minute. How many hours of pumping are required to fill the tank?

12. Spheres are formed from molten bronze. The diameter of the mold in which the spheres are formed is 6.26 centimetres. When the bronze spheres solidify (turn solid) they shrink by 6% of the molten-state volume. Compute the volume of a sphere after the bronze solidifies.

13. A truck will deliver a shipment of solid concrete spheres. The concrete weighs 137 pounds per cubic foot. The diameter of the spheres is 22 inches. The maximum load weight limit of the truck is 6 short tons. What is the maximum number of spheres that can be carried by the truck?

VOLUMES AND SURFACE AREAS OF COMPOSITE SOLIDS

Practical volume and surface area applications often require working with objects that are a combination of two or more simple solid shapes. For example, a shaft or a container may be a combination of a cylinder and the frustum of a cone. A round head rivet is a combination of a cylinder and a hemisphere. Objects of this kind are called composite solids.

To compute *volumes and surface areas of composite solids,* it is necessary to determine the volume or surface area of each simple solid separately. The individual volumes or areas are then added or subtracted.

Example 1. An aluminum weldment is shown in figure 28-2.

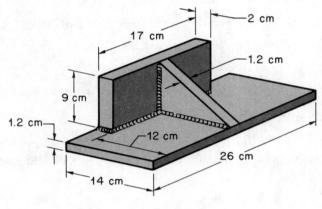

    a. Find the total volume of the weldment.

    b. Find the weight of the weldment. Aluminum weighs 0.002 7 kilogram per cubic centimetre.

a. Find the volume of the bottom plate:

$$V_1 = (14 \text{ cm})(26 \text{ cm})(1.2 \text{ cm}) = 436.8 \text{ cm}^3$$

Find the volume of the top plate:

$$V_2 = (9 \text{ cm})(17 \text{ cm})(2 \text{ cm}) = 306 \text{ cm}^3$$

Find the volume of the triangular plate:

$$V_3 = 0.5(12 \text{ cm})(9 \text{ cm})(1.2 \text{ cm}) = 64.8 \text{ cm}^3$$

Find the total volume:

$$V = 436.8 \text{ cm}^3 + 306 \text{ cm}^3 + 64.8 \text{ cm}^3 = \textbf{807.6 cm}^3 \textit{ Ans}$$

Fig. 28-2

b. Find the weight:

$$0.002\ 7 \text{ kg/cm}^3 \times 807.6 \text{ cm}^3 = \textbf{2.18 kg } \textit{Ans}$$

Example 2. The side view of a flanged shaft is shown in figure 28-3. Find the volume of metal in the shaft.

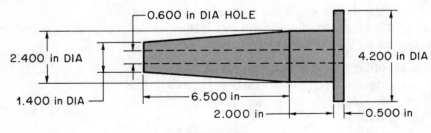

Fig. 28-3

Find the volume of the 6.500-inch long frustum of a cone:

$R = 0.5(2.400 \text{ in}) = 1.200 \text{ in}$

$r = 0.5(1.400 \text{ in}) = 0.700 \text{ in}$

$$V_1 = \frac{(3.14)(6.500 \text{ in})[(1.200 \text{ in})^2 + (0.700 \text{ in})^2 + (1.200 \text{ in})(0.700 \text{ in})]}{3}$$

$$V_1 = \frac{(3.14)(6.500 \text{ in})(1.440 \text{ sq in} + 0.490 \text{ sq in} + 0.840 \text{ sq in})}{3}$$

$V_1 = 18.845 \text{ cu in}$

Find the volume of the 2.400-inch diameter cylinder:

$r = 0.5(2.400 \text{ in}) = 1.200 \text{ in}$

$V_2 = 3.14(1.200 \text{ in})^2(2.000 \text{ in}) = 9.043 \text{ cu in}$

Find the volume of the 4.200-inch diameter cylinder:

$V_3 = 3.14(2.100 \text{ in})^2(0.500 \text{ in}) = 6.924 \text{ cu in}$

Find the volume of the 0.600-inch diameter through hole:

$r = 0.5(0.600 \text{ in}) = 0.300 \text{ in}$

$h = 6.500 \text{ in} + 2.000 \text{ in} + 0.500 \text{ in} = 9.000 \text{ in}$

$V_4 = 3.14(0.300 \text{ in})^2(9.000 \text{ in}) = 2.543 \text{ cu in}$

Find the volume of the metal:

$V = (18.845 \text{ cu in} + 9.043 \text{ cu in} + 6.924 \text{ cu in}) - 2.543 \text{ cu in}$

$V = \textbf{32.27 cu in } \textit{Ans}$

Example 3. Compute the surface area of the sheet metal elbow shown in figure 28-4.

Find the lateral area of the rectangular bottom section:

$LA = [2(8 \text{ in}) + 2(10 \text{ in})] \times 9 \text{ in} = 324 \text{ sq in}$

Find the lateral area of the triangular section:

The section consists of two triangular faces and one rectangular back face.

$A_1 = 0.5(3 \text{ in})(7.4 \text{ in}) = 11.1 \text{ sq in}$

$A_2 = 3 \text{ in} \times 10 \text{ in} = 30 \text{ sq in}$

$LA = 2(11.1 \text{ sq in}) + 30 \text{ sq in} = 52.2 \text{ sq in}$

Find the lateral area of the rectangular top section:

$LA = [2(10 \text{ in}) + 2(7.4 \text{ in})] \times 7 \text{ in} = 243.6 \text{ sq in}$

Find the total surface area of the elbow:

$SA = 324 \text{ sq in} + 52.2 \text{ sq in} + 243.6 \text{ sq in} = \textbf{619.8 sq in } \textit{Ans}$

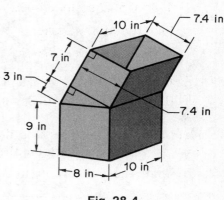

Fig. 28-4

Exercise 28-3

Use the tables found in the Appendix for equivalent units of measure. Solve these problems. Use $\pi = 3.14$ and round the answers to 2 decimal places.

1. Compute the number of cubic yards of concrete required to construct the steps shown in figure 28-5.

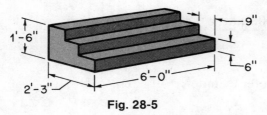

Fig. 28-5

2. Find the weight of the steel baseplate shown in figure 28-6. Steel weighs 490 pounds per cubic foot.

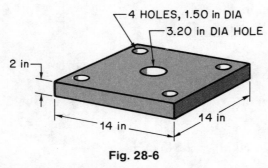

Fig. 28-6

3. What is the total number of cubic metres of air space in the building shown in figure 28-7? Disregard wall and floor volumes.

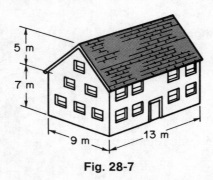

Fig. 28-7

4. Compute the capacity, in litres, of the container shown in figure 28-8.

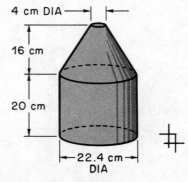

Fig. 28-8

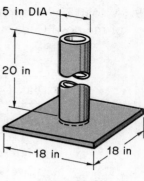

Fig. 28-9

5. A sheet copper pipe and flange are shown in figure 28-9. The pipe fits into a 5-inch diameter hole in the flange.

   a. Find the total surface area of the pipe and flange.

   b. Find the weight of the pipe and flange. The copper sheet weighs 2.355 pounds per square foot.

6. Compute the weight of the steel V-block shown in figure 28-10. Steel weighs 0.008 kilogram per cubic centimetre.

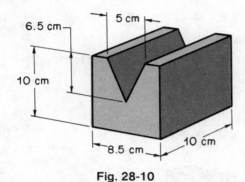

Fig. 28-10

7. Find the number of cubic centimetres of material contained in the jig bushing shown in figure 28-11.

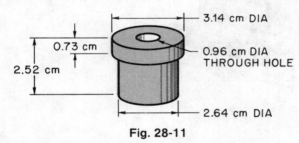

Fig. 28-11

8. A sheet metal reducer is shown in figure 28-12. The top and the bottom sections are in the shape of rectangular prisms with square bases. The middle section is in the shape of a frustum of a regular pyramid with square bases. Allow 10% for waste and seam overlaps. Find the total number of square feet of material required for the lateral surface of the reducer.

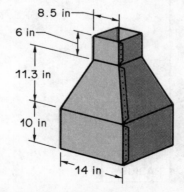

Fig. 28-12

9. A solid cedar support post is shown in figure 28-13. Compute the weight of the post. Cedar weighs 33 pounds per cubic foot.

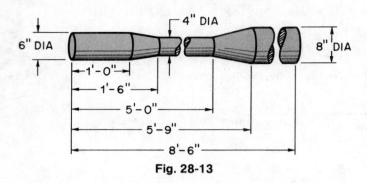

Fig. 28-13

10. Compute the number of cubic centimetres of material contained in the locating saddle shown in figure 28-14.

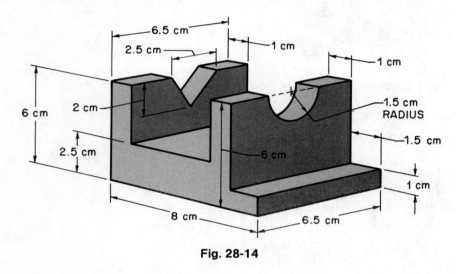

Fig. 28-14

11. Find the number of cubic metres of topsoil required for the plot of land shown in figure 28-15. The topsoil will be spread to an average thickness of 15 centimetres.

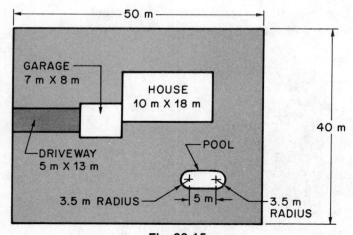

Fig. 28-15

12. Compute the number of cubic yards of concrete required for the 3-inch thick concrete patio shown in figure 28-16.

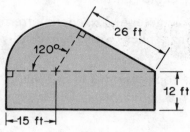

Fig. 28-16

UNIT EXERCISE AND PROBLEM REVIEW

Exercise 28-4

Use the tables found in the Appendix for equivalent units of measure. Use $\pi = 3.14$ and round the answers to 2 decimal places.

For each sphere in exercises 1-4 find the following:

a. Compute the surface area.

b. Compute the volume.

1. 6.4-inch diameter
2. 26.8-centimetre diameter
3. 0.4-metre radius
4. 7'-6'' radius

Solve each of these problems.

5. A firm manufactures lamp shades in the shape of hemispheres with a 14-inch diameter. The cost of the shade material is $0.60 per square foot. Compute the total material expense of 2 500 lamp shades.

6. The side view of a steel round-head rivet is shown in figure 28-17. What is the weight of the rivet? Steel weighs 0.283 pound per cubic inch.

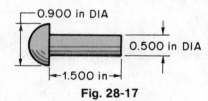

Fig. 28-17

7. Find the number of cubic metres of concrete required for the retaining wall shown in figure 28-18.

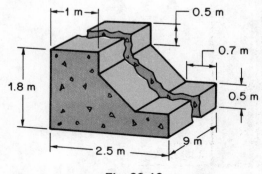

Fig. 28-18

8. A hollow glass sphere has an outside circumference (great circle) of 23.80 centimetres. The wall thickness of the sphere is 0.50 centimetre. Compute the weight of the sphere. Glass weighs 1.5 grams per cubic centimetre.

9. The material cost of a solid bronze sphere with a diameter of 3.80 centimetres is $1.05. Compute the material cost of a solid bronze sphere with a 5.70 centimetre diameter.

10. A wooden planter is shown in figure 28-19. The top section is in the shape of a prism with a square base. The bottom section is in the shape of a frustum of a pyramid with square bases.

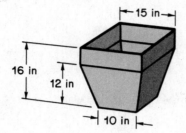

Fig. 28-19

   a. Compute the number of cubic feet of soil that can be held by the planter when full. Disregard the thickness of the lumber.

   b. Compute the total number of square feet of lumber required in the construction. Disregard the thickness of the lumber. Allow 15% for waste.

11. A spherical tank has a diameter of 35 feet. The tank is $\frac{1}{4}$ full of water. The water will be drained from the tank at a rate of 250 gallons per minute. How long will it take to empty the tank?

12. Compute the number of cubic yards of asphalt required to pave the section of land shown in figure 28-20. The average thickness of the asphalt is 3 inches.

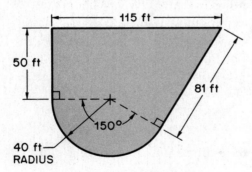

Fig. 28-20

SECTION 6
Fundamentals of Trigonometry

UNIT 29
Introduction to Trigonometric Functions

OBJECTIVES

After studying this unit you should be able to

- identify the sides of a right triangle with reference to any angle.
- state the ratios of the 6 trigonometric functions in relation to given triangles.
- find functions of given angles using both the degree-10 minute and decimal-degree trigonometric function tables.
- find angles of given functions using both the degree-10 minute and decimal-degree trigonometric function tables.
- interpolate angles and functions using both the degree-10 minute and decimal trigonometric function tables.

Trigonometry is the branch of mathematics which is used to compute unknown angles and sides of triangles. The word trigonometry is derived from the Greek words for triangle and measurement. Trigonometry is based on the principles of geometry. Many problems require the use of both geometry and trigonometry.

As with geometry, much in our lives is dependent upon trigonometry. The methods of trigonometry are used in constructing buildings, roads, and bridges. Trigonometry is used in the design of automobiles, trains, airplanes, and ships. The machines which produce the manufactured products we need could not be made without the use of trigonometry.

A knowledge of trigonometry and the ability to apply the knowledge in actual occupational uses is required in many skilled trades. Machinists, surveyors, drafters, electricians, and electronics technicians are a few of the many occupations in which trigonometry is a requirement.

Practical problems are often solved by using a combination of elements of algebra, geometry, and trigonometry. It is essential that you develop the ability to analyze a problem in order to determine the mathematical principles which are involved in the solution. The solution is done in orderly steps based on mathematical facts.

When solving a problem, it is important that you understand the trigonometric operations involved rather than to mechanically plug in values. To solve more complex problems, such as those found later in this section, an understanding of the principles involved is essential.

RATIO OF RIGHT TRIANGLE SIDES

In a right triangle, the ratio of two sides of the triangle determines the sizes of the angles, and the angles determine the ratio of the sides. For example, in figure 29-1, the size of angle A is determined by the ratio of side a to side b. When side $a = 1$ inch and side $b = 2$ inches, the ratio of a to b is 1:2. If side a is increased to 2 inches and side b remains 2 inches, as shown in figure 29-2, the ratio of a to b is 1:1. Figure 29-3 compares the two ratios and shows the change in angle A.

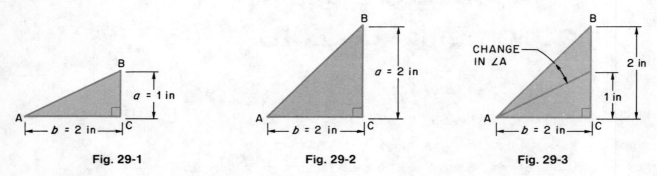

Fig. 29-1   Fig. 29-2   Fig. 29-3

IDENTIFYING RIGHT TRIANGLE SIDES BY NAME

The sides of a right triangle are named the opposite side, adjacent side, and hypotenuse. The *hypotenuse* is the longest side of a right triangle and is always the side opposite the right angle. The positions of the opposite and adjacent sides depend on the reference angle. The *opposite side* is opposite the reference angle. The *adjacent side* is next to the reference angle.

For example, in figure 29-4, the hypotenuse (c) is opposite the right angle. In reference to angle A, b is the adjacent side and a is the opposite side. In figure 29-5, the hypotenuse (c) is opposite the right angle. In reference to angle B, side b is the opposite side and side a is the adjacent side. It is important to be able to identify the opposite and adjacent sides of right triangles in reference to any angle regardless of the positions of the triangles.

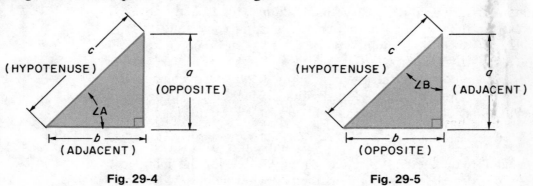

Fig. 29-4   Fig. 29-5

Exercise 29-1

With reference to ∠1, name the sides of each of these right triangles as opposite, adjacent, or hypotenuse.

1. Name sides *r*, *x*, and *y*.

2. Name sides *r*, *x*, and *y*.

3. Name sides *a*, *b*, and *c*.

4. Name sides *a*, *b*, and *c*.

5. Name sides *a*, *b*, and *c*.

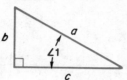

6. Name sides *d*, *m*, and *p*.

7. Name sides *d*, *m*, and *p*.

8. Name sides *e*, *f*, and *g*.

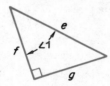

9. Name sides *h*, *k*, and *l*.

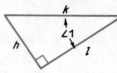

10. Name sides *h*, *k*, and *l*.

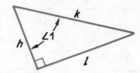

11. Name sides *m*, *p*, and *s*.

12. Name sides *m*, *p*, and *s*.

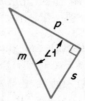

13. Name sides *m*, *r*, and *t*.

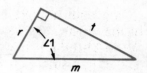

14. Name sides *m*, *r*, and *t*.

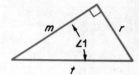

15. Name sides *f*, *g*, and *h*.

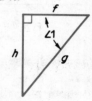

16. Name sides *f*, *g*, and *h*.

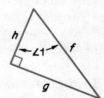

TRIGONOMETRIC FUNCTIONS: RATIO METHOD

There are two methods of defining trigonometric functions: the unity or unit circle method and the ratio method. Only the ratio method is presented in this book. Since a triangle has three sides and a ratio is the comparison of any two sides, there are six different ratios. The names of the ratios are the sine, cosine, tangent, cotangent, secant, and cosecant.

The six trigonometric functions are defined in the table shown in figure 29-7. They are defined in relation to the triangle shown in figure 29-6, where the reference angle is A, the adjacent side is *b,* the opposite side is *a,* and the hypotenuse is *c.*

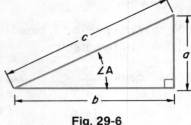

Fig. 29-6

FUNCTION	SYMBOL	DEFINITION OF FUNCTION
sine of Angle A	sin A	$\sin A = \dfrac{\text{opposite side}}{\text{hypotenuse}} = \dfrac{a}{c}$
cosine of Angle A	cos A	$\cos A = \dfrac{\text{adjacent side}}{\text{hypotenuse}} = \dfrac{b}{c}$
tangent of Angle A	tan A	$\tan A = \dfrac{\text{opposite side}}{\text{adjacent side}} = \dfrac{a}{b}$
cotangent of Angle A	cot A	$\cot A = \dfrac{\text{adjacent side}}{\text{opposite side}} = \dfrac{b}{a}$
secant of Angle A	sec A	$\sec A = \dfrac{\text{hypotenuse}}{\text{adjacent side}} = \dfrac{c}{b}$
cosecant of Angle A	csc A	$\csc A = \dfrac{\text{hypotenuse}}{\text{opposite side}} = \dfrac{c}{a}$

Fig. 29-7

To properly use trigonometric functions, you must understand that the function of an angle depends upon the ratio of the sides and <u>not the size</u> of the triangle. The functions of similar triangles are the same regardless of the sizes of the triangles since the sides of similar triangles are proportional. For example, in the 3 similar triangles shown in figure 29-8, the functions of angle A are the same for the three triangles. The equality of the tangent function is shown. Each of the other five functions have equal values for the 3 similar triangles.

In $\triangle$ACB, $\tan A = \dfrac{0.500}{1.000} = 0.500$

In $\triangle$AED, $\tan A = \dfrac{0.800}{1.600} = 0.500$

In $\triangle$AGF, $\tan A = \dfrac{1.200}{2.400} = 0.500$

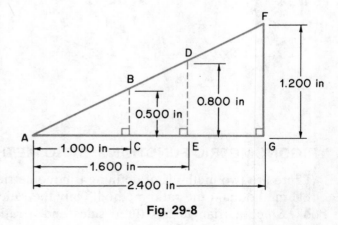

Fig. 29-8

Exercise 29-2

The sides of each of these triangles are labeled with different letters. State the ratio of each of the 6 functions in relation to ∠1 for each of the triangles. For example, for the triangle in exercise number 1, $\sin \angle 1 = \frac{y}{r}$, $\cos \angle 1 = \frac{x}{r}$, $\tan \angle 1 = \frac{y}{x}$, $\cot \angle 1 = \frac{x}{y}$, $\sec \angle 1 = \frac{r}{x}$, $\csc \angle 1 = \frac{r}{y}$.

1.

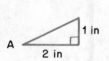

3.

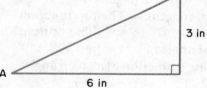

5.

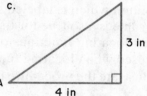

2.

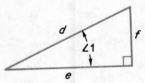

4.

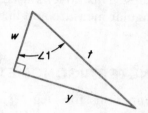

6.

These exercises show three groups of triangles. Each group consists of four triangles. Within each group name the triangles, a, b, c, or d, in which angles A are equal.

7. a.

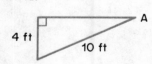

b.

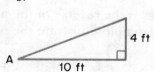

c.

d.

8. a.

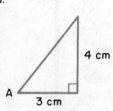

b.

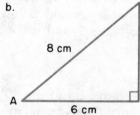

c.

d.

9. a.

b.

c.

d.

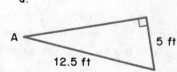

USE OF TRIGONOMETRIC FUNCTION TABLES

Angular measure in the English system is generally expressed in degrees and minutes. Precise angular measurements are expressed in degrees, minutes, and seconds such as $12°42'15''$. In the metric system, the decimal degree is the preferred unit of measure. The English measure $12°42'$ is expressed as $12.7°$ in the metric system.

Two separate trigonometric function tables are given in the Appendix of this book. The functions listed in the tables are the decimal equivalents of the ratios of two sides of a right triangle. One table lists functions of angles from $0°$ to $90°$ in 10-minute increments or steps. This table is used when working with English units of degrees and minutes of angular measure and linear measures such as inches and feet. The second table lists functions of angles from $0°$ to $90°$ in 0.1-degree increments or steps. This table is used when working with metric units of decimal degrees of angular measure and linear measures such as millimetres, centimetres, and metres.

THE DEGREE-10 MINUTE TRIGONOMETRIC FUNCTION TABLE

The Trigonometric Functions for Degrees and Minutes Table found in the Appendix should be used when computing English units of measure. Observe that the angles are listed in $10'$ increments. Angles from $0°$ to $45°$ are located in the left column and increase in value reading from the top to the bottom of a page. Angles from $45°$ to $90°$ are located in the right column and increase in value reading from the bottom to the top of a page.

Observe that a column which is labeled sin on the top of a page is labeled cos on the bottom. The same is also true for the other cofunctions. The top function names are used when locating functions of angles from $0°$ to $45°$. The bottom function names are used when locating functions of angles from $45°$ to $90°$.

These examples illustrate the procedure for locating a function of a given angle.

Example 1.   Find the sine of $23°40'$.

Procedure: Locate $23°$ in the left column and move down to the $40'$ row. Locate the sin function on top of the page and move down the sin column to the $23°40'$ row. The value found is 0.401 41. **The sine of $23°40'$ is 0.401 41** *Ans.*

Example 2.   Find the tangent of $58°20'$.

Procedure: Locate $58°$ in the right column and move up to the $20'$ row. Locate the tan function on the bottom of the page and move up the tan column to the $58°20'$ row. The value found is 1.621 3. **The tangent of $58°20'$ is 1.621 3** *Ans.*

The procedure for locating angles of given functions is the reverse of the procedure for locating functions of given angles. These examples illustrate the procedure for locating an angle of a given function:

Example 1.   Find the angle whose cosine is 0.960 46.

Procedure: Locate the cos column in the table and read down the column until 0.960 46 is located.

Since the cos function listed on top of the table is used, the corresponding angle, $16°10'$, is located in the left column directly across from 0.960 46. **The angle whose cosine is 0.960 46 is $16°10'$** *Ans.*

Example 2.   Find the angle whose cosine is 0.311 78.

Procedure: In reading from the top, the value 0.311 78 cannot be found. In the column with the cos function on the bottom, read up until 0.311 78 is located.

Since the cos function listed on the bottom is used, the corresponding angle, 71°50', is located in the right column directly across from 0.311 78. The angle whose cosine is 0.311 78 is 71°50' Ans.

Exercise 29-3

Use the degree-10 minute trigonometric function table found in the Appendix to determine the functions of these angles.

1.	sin 30°	9.	cos 10°20'	17.	csc 53°20'
2.	cos 16°	10.	cot 26°40'	18.	sec 12°40'
3.	tan 25°	11.	sin 66°30'	19.	sin 89°10'
4.	cot 50°	12.	cos 79°10'	20.	tan 0°50'
5.	sin 73°	13.	tan 5°50'	21.	cos 0°10'
6.	tan 80°	14.	cot 18°30'	22.	cot 89°50'
7.	csc 14°	15.	sec 80°10'	23.	sec 1°20'
8.	sec 72°	16.	cos 47°50'	24.	csc 45°10'

Use the degree-10 minute trigonometric function table found in the Appendix to determine the values of Angle A that correspond to these functions.

25.	tan A = 0.122 78	33.	tan A = 0.604 83	41.	tan A = 0.099 23
26.	cot A = 19.081	34.	sec A = 1.230 9	42.	sin A = 0.985 31
27.	sin A = 0.156 43	35.	cos A = 0.696 75	43.	csc A = 1.031 4
28.	cos A = 0.906 31	36.	csc A = 1.529 4	44.	cot A = 0.337 83
29.	sec A = 2.062 7	37.	sin A = 0.878 82	45.	tan A = 0.498 58
30.	csc A = 1.094 6	38.	cos A = 0.935 65	46.	sin A = 0.377 30
31.	cot A = 2.747 5	39.	cot A = 0.505 87	47.	cot A = 0.011 64
32.	sin A = 0.601 82	40.	sec A = 1.089 1	48.	cos A = 0.999 89

THE DECIMAL-DEGREE TRIGONOMETRIC FUNCTION TABLE

The Trigonometric Functions for Decimal Fractions of a Degree Table found in the Appendix should be used when computing metric units of measure. Observe that the angles are listed in 0.1° increments. As with the degree-minute table, angles from 0° to 45° are located in the left column and increase in value reading from the top to the bottom of a page. Angles from 45° to 90° are located in the right column and increase in value reading from the bottom to the top of a page.

The table columns are labeled the same as the labeling of the degree-minute table. The top function names are used when locating functions of angles from 0° to 45°. The bottom function names are used when locating functions of angles from 45° to 90°.

The procedure for locating a function of a given angle or an angle of a given function is the same as with using the decimal-minute table.

Example 1.   Find the tangent of 39.7°.

Procedure: Locate 39° in the left column and move down to the 0.7° row. Locate the tan function on top of the page and move down the tan column to the 39.7° row. The value found is 0.830 2. The tangent of 39.7° is 0.830 2 *Ans.*

Example 2.   Find the angle whose cotangent is 1.718 2.

Procedure: Locate the cot column in the table and read down the column until 1.718 2 is located.

Since the cot function listed on top of the table is used, the corresponding angle, 30.2° is located in the left column directly across from 1.718 2. The angle whose cotangent is 1.718 2 is 30.2° *Ans.*

Exercise 29-4

Use the decimal-degree trigonometric function table found in the Appendix to determine the functions of these angles.

1. tan 35°	8. cot 48.6°	15. cos 0.2°
2. cot 18°	9. cos 67.8°	16. cot 44.9°
3. sin 57°	10. sin 80.7°	17. tan 45.1°
4. cos 64°	11. csc 5.3°	18. csc 37.8°
5. csc 10°	12. sec 8.9°	19. sec 50.2°
6. sec 23°	13. tan 73.1°	20. sin 89.9°
7. tan 17.4°	14. sin 55.5°	

Use the decimal-degree trigonometric function table found in the Appendix to determine the values of Angle A that correspond to these functions.

21. cot A = 1.366 3	28. cos A = 0.964 1	35. tan A = 0.568 1
22. sin A = 0.661 3	29. cot A = 0.154 81	36. cos A = 0.703 4
23. tan A = 3.024	30. sec A = 1.503 2	37. sec A = 22.926
24. sec A = 1.039 8	31. tan A = 17.886	38. tan A = 0.993 0
25. cos A = 0.446 2	32. sin A = 0.657 4	39. sin A = 0.001 75
26. csc A = 1.128 4	33. csc A = 5.647 0	40. cot A = 0.003 49
27. sin A = 0.166 77	34. cot A = 1.331 9	

INTERPOLATION USING TRIGONOMETRIC FUNCTION TABLES

To determine the function of an angle or the angle of a function not listed in the trigonometric function tables, a method called interpolation is used. Interpolation is a method of finding values between two known values.

When interpolating values, it is important to consider whether the function of an angle increases or decreases as an angle increases. Functions that do <u>not</u> begin with "co" (sine, tangent, secant) increase as the angle increases. Functions that begin with "co" (cosine, cotangent, cosecant) decrease as the angle increases. When interpolating functions of given angles, whether the function increases or decreases must be kept in mind. The type of function determines whether an obtained value is added or subtracted in the final interpolation computation. This fact is illustrated in the interpolation examples which follow.

Observe the following rules when using the tables in this book in solving problems which require interpolation. When interpolating functions from given angles or angles from given functions, do <u>not</u> use the cotangent, secant, or cosecant functions for angles less than 15°. Do <u>not</u> use the tangent, secant or cosecant functions for angles greater than 75°. The trigonometric functions which are listed in 10′ and 0.1°, in the respective tables, produce changes which are either too small or too large to always obtain accurate interpolated values.

INTERPOLATION USING DEGREE-10 MINUTE TABLES

These two examples illustrate interpolation of functions of given angles.

Example 1.   Determine the tangent of 37°23′.

   Procedure: The angle 37°23′ lies between 37°20′ and 37°30′. Therefore, the tangent function of 37°23′ lies between the tangent of 37°20′ and the tangent of 37°30′.

- Determine a ratio using the given angles: The difference between 37°20′ and 37°30′ is 10′ and the difference between 37°20′ and 37°23′ is 3′. The resulting ratio is $\frac{3}{10}$.

- Look up the tangent of 37°20′ and the tangent 37°30′. The tangent of 37°20′ is 0.762 72. The tangent of 37°30′ is 0.767 33. Compute the difference between the two functions: 0.767 33 − 0.762 72 = 0.004 61.

- Multiply the function difference by the ratio: $\frac{3}{10}$ × 0.004 61 = 0.001 38. Add 0.001 38 to the function 0.762 72 of the smaller angle 37°20′: 0.762 72 + 0.001 38 = 0.764 10. **The tangent of 37°23′, to 4 decimal places, is 0.764 1** *Ans.* Note: The value 0.001 38 was added to 0.762 72 because the tangent is an increasing function.

$$10' \left\{ \ 3' \left\{ \begin{array}{l} \tan 37°20' = 0.762\ 72 \\ \tan 37°23' = 0.764\ 10 \end{array} \right\} 0.001\ 38 \right\} 0.004\ 61$$
$$\tan 37°30' = 0.767\ 33$$

Example 2.   Determine the cosine of 62°46′.

Procedure: The angle of 62°46′ lies between 62°40′ and 62°50′. Therefore the cosine function of 62°46′ lies between the cosine of 62°40′ and the cosine of 62°50′.

- Determine a ratio using the given angles: The difference between 62°40′ and 62°50′ is 10′. The difference between 62°40′ and 62°46′ is 6′. The resulting ratio is $\frac{6}{10}$.

- Look up the cosine of 62°40′ and the cosine of 62°50′. The cosine of 62°40′ is 0.459 17. The cosine of 62°50′ is 0.456 58. Compute the difference between the two functions: 0.459 17 − 0.456 58 = 0.002 59.

- Multiply the function difference by the ratio: $\frac{6}{10}$ × 0.002 59 = 0.001 55. Subtract 0.001 55 from the function 0.459 17 of the smaller angle 62°40′: 0.459 17 − 0.001 55 = 0.457 62. The cosine of 62°46′, to 4 decimal places, is 0.457 6 Ans. Note: The value 0.001 55 was subtracted from 0.459 17 because the cosine is a decreasing function.

$$10' \left\{ 6' \left\{ \begin{array}{l} \cos 62°40' = 0.459\ 17 \\ \cos 62°46' = 0.457\ 62 \\ \cos 62°50' = 0.456\ 58 \end{array} \right\} 0.001\ 55 \right\} 0.002\ 59$$

This example illustrates interpolation of an angle of a given function.

Example: Determine the angle whose sine is 0.362 16.

Procedure: • Look up the two nearest sine functions that 0.362 16 lies between: 0.362 16 lies between the sine function 0.361 08 whose angle is 21°10′ and the sine function 0.363 79 whose angle is 21°20′.

- Determine a ratio using the obtained functions: The difference between 0.361 08 and 0.363 79 is 0.002 71. The difference between 0.361 08 and 0.362 16 is 0.001 08. The resulting ratio is $\frac{0.001\ 08}{0.002\ 71}$ or $\frac{108}{271}$.

- The difference between 21°10′ and 21°20′ is 10′. Multiply the angle difference by the ratio: $\frac{108}{271}$ × 10′ = $\frac{1\ 080}{271}$ = 3.99 = 4′. Add: 21°10′ + 4′ = 21°14′. The angle whose sine is 0.362 16 is 21°14′ Ans.

$$10' \left\{ 4' \left\{ \begin{array}{l} \sin 21°10' = 0.361\ 08 \\ \sin 21°14' = 0.362\ 16 \\ \sin 21°20' = 0.363\ 79 \end{array} \right\} 0.001\ 08 \right\} 0.002\ 71$$

Note: In this example, the numerator 0.001 08 of the ratio $\frac{0.001\ 08}{0.002\ 71}$ was determined in reference to the sine function of the smaller angle 21°10′. Always compute the numerator of the ratio in reference to the function of the smaller angle whether the function is increasing or decreasing. In so doing, the final interpolation computation always involves adding the computed minute value to the smaller angle.

Exercise 29-5

Use the degree-10 minute trigonometric function table found in the Appendix to determine the functions of these angles.

1. sin 25°13′
2. tan 36°26′
3. cos 8°44′
4. cot 60°12′
5. sec 29°55′
6. csc 52°47′
7. sin 76°9′
8. cos 4°24′
9. cot 37°18′
10. tan 49°51′

11. sin 2°34′
12. csc 26°33′
13. cos 88°46′
14. sec 46°2′
15. sin 63°28′
16. cos 31°41′
17. tan 19°15′
18. cot 50°7′
19. sec 38°53′
20. csc 56°44′

Use the degree-10 minute trigonometric function table found in the Appendix to determine the values of angle A to the nearer minute that correspond to these functions.

21. tan A = 0.583 84
22. cot A = 0.817 52
23. sin A = 0.644 7
24. cos A = 0.487 5
25. csc A = 2.035 4
26. sec A = 1. 666 6
27. cot A = 1.134 0
28. tan A = 0.510 65
29. cos A = 0.908 62
30. sin A = 0.946 8

31. tan A = 0.089 3
32. cos A = 0.164 4
33. csc A = 1.326 0
34. sin A = 0.781 77
35. sec A = 1.639 5
36. cot A = 0.663 64
37. tan A = 0.426 6
38. sin A = 0.321 1
39. sec A = 1.575 3
40. csc A = 1.976 2

INTERPOLATION USING DECIMAL-DEGREE TABLES

The procedure for interpolation using the decimal-degree trigonometric function table is the same as when using the degree-10 minute table. The only difference is that 0.1° table increments are used rather than 10′ increments. Angles are computed to the nearer 0.01 degree rather than to the nearer minute.

This example illustrates interpolation of a function of a given angle.

Example.   Determine the sine of 14.86°.

Procedure: The angle 14.86° lies between 14.8° and 14.9°. Therefore, the sine function of 14.86° lies between the sine of 14.8° and the sine of 14.9°.

- Determine a ratio using the given angles: The difference between 14.8° and 14.9° is 0.1° and the difference between 14.8° and 14.86° is 0.06°. The resulting ratio is $\frac{0.06}{0.1}$ or $\frac{6}{10}$.

- Look up the sine of 14.8° and the sine of 14.9°. The sine of 14.8° is 0.255 4. The sine of 14.9° is 0.257 1. Compute the difference between the two functions: $0.257\ 1 - 0.255\ 4 = 0.001\ 7$.

- Multiply the function difference by the ratio: $\frac{6}{10} \times 0.001\ 7 = 0.001\ 0$. Add 0.001 0 to the function 0.255 4 of the smaller angle 14.8°: $0.255\ 4 + 0.001\ 0 = 0.256\ 4$. **The sine of 14.86° is 0.256 4** *Ans.* Note: The value 0.001 0 was added to 0.255 4 because the sine is an increasing function.

$$0.1° \left\{ 0.06° \left\{ \begin{array}{l} \sin 14.8° = 0.255\ 4 \\ \sin 14.86° = 0.256\ 4 \\ \sin 14.9° = 0.257\ 1 \end{array} \right. \right. \left. \begin{array}{l} \\ \end{array} \right\} 0.001\ 0 \right\} 0.001\ 7$$

This example illustrates the interpolation of an angle of a given function.

Example: Determine the angle whose cotangent is 0.953 4.

Procedure:
- Look up the two nearest cotangent functions that 0.953 4 lies between: 0.953 4 lies between the cotangent function 0.955 6 whose angle is 46.3° and the cotangent function 0.952 3 whose angle is 46.4°.

- Determine a ratio using the obtained functions: The difference between 0.955 6 and 0.952 3 is 0.003 3. The difference between 0.955 6 and 0.953 4 is 0.002 2. The resulting ratio is $\frac{0.002\ 2}{0.003\ 3}$ or $\frac{22}{33}$.

- The difference between 46.3° and 46.4° is 0.1°. Multiply the angle difference by the ratio: $\frac{22}{33} \times 0.1° = \frac{2.2}{33} = 0.067 = 0.07°$. Add: $46.3° + 0.07° = 46.37°$. **The angle whose cotangent is 0.953 4 is 46.37°** *Ans.*

$$0.1° \left\{ 0.07° \left\{ \begin{array}{l} \cot 46.3° = 0.955\ 6 \\ \cot 46.37° = 0.953\ 4 \\ \cot 46.4° = 0.952\ 3 \end{array} \right. \right. \left. \begin{array}{l} \\ \end{array} \right\} 0.002\ 2 \right\} 0.003\ 3$$

Note: In this example, the numerator 22 of the ratio $\frac{22}{33}$ was determined in reference to the cotangent function of the smaller angle 46.3°. Always compute the numerator of the ratio in reference to the function of the smaller angle whether the function is increasing or decreasing. In so doing, the final interpolation computation always involves adding the computed hundredth of a degree value to the smaller angle.

Exercise 29-6

Use the decimal-degree trigonometric function table found in the Appendix to determine the functions of these angles.

1. sin 34.62°
2. cos 51.86°
3. tan 47.35°
4. cot 29.93°
5. sin 50.14°
6. sec 41.67°
7. csc 52.89°

8. cos 87.51°
9. tan 12.58°
10. cot 37.05°
11. sin 89.72°
12. sec 30.94°
13. cos 4.47°
14. cot 61.33°

15. csc 53.08°
16. tan 4.59°
17. cos 11.82°
18. cot 89.06°
19. csc 37.14°
20. sec 49.23°

Use the decimal-degree trigonometric function table found in the Appendix to determine the values of Angle A, to the nearer hundredth of a degree, that correspond to these functions.

21. tan A = 0.335 2
22. cot A = 0.506 5
23. cos A = 0.787 2
24. sin A = 0.826 8
25. sec A = 2.021 3
26. csc A = 3.796 1
27. cot A = 0.107 0

28. tan A = 0.029 1
29. cos A = 0.712 9
30. sin A = 0.775 2
31. tan A = 0.510 0
32. cos A = 0.646 4
33. sec A = 1.237 5
34. sin A = 0.592 3

35. csc A = 1.400 6
36. cos A = 0.800 0
37. tan A = 0.459 5
38. sin A = 0.272 7
39. cot A = 0.084 8
40. sec A = 1.305 1

UNIT EXERCISE AND PROBLEM REVIEW

Exercise 29-7

NAMING RIGHT TRIANGLE SIDES

With reference to ∠1, name the sides of each of the following right triangles as opposite, adjacent, or hypotenuse.

1. Name sides *a, b,* and *c.*

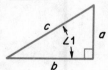

2. Name sides *r, x,* and *y.*

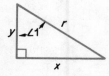

3. Name sides *e, f,* and *g.*

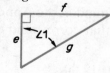

4. Name sides *m, n,* and *p.*

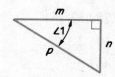

5. Name sides *h, j,* and *k.*

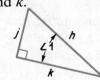

6. Name sides *s, t,* and *w.*

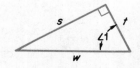

7. Name sides *a, d,* and *p.*

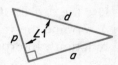

8. Name sides *b, f,* and *m.*

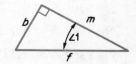

RATIOS OF RIGHT TRIANGLE SIDES

The sides of each of these triangles are labeled with different letters. State the ratio of each of the 6 functions in relation to ∠1 for each of the triangles.

9.

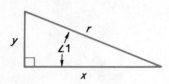

10.

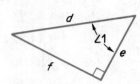

11.

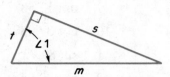

12. Of the five triangles shown, name the triangles, a, b, c, d, or e, in which angles A are equal.

a.

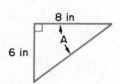

b.

c.

d.

e.

DETERMINING FUNCTIONS OF ANGLES USING THE DEGREE-10 MINUTE TABLE

Use the degree-10 minute trigonometric function table found in the Appendix to determine the functions of these angles. Interpolate where necessary.

13. sin 25°

14. cos 58°

15. tan 13°20′

16. cot 37°40′

17. sec 55°10′

18. csc 41°50′

19. sin 67°26′

20. tan 18°53′

21. cos 75°45′

22. cot 39°47′

23. csc 70°32′

24. sec 26°8′

DETERMINING ANGLES OF FUNCTIONS USING THE DEGREE-10 MINUTE TABLE

Use the degree-10 minute trigonometric function table found in the Appendix to determine the values of angle A, to the nearer minute, that correspond to these functions. Interpolate where necessary.

25. tan A = 0.704 55

26.   sin A = 0.827 41

27. cos A = 0.935 65

28. cot A = 0.167 34

29. csc A = 1.715 1

30. sec A = 1.321 7

31. sin A = 0.412 90

32. tan A = 2.894 3

33. cot A = 1.380 3

34. cos A = 0.782 53

35. sec A = 1.108 2

36. csc A = 1.407 0

DETERMINING FUNCTIONS OF ANGLES USING THE DECIMAL-DEGREE TABLE

Use the decimal-degree trigonometric function table found in the Appendix to determine the functions of the following angles. Interpolate where necessary.

37. cos 47°

38. tan 23°

39. sin 36.8°

40. cot 77.8°

41. sec 19.2°

42. csc 89.1°

43. tan 14.53°

44. sin 68.05°

45. cos 22.44°

46. csc 36.12°

47. cot 89.86°

48. sec 48.97°

DETERMINING ANGLES OF FUNCTIONS USING THE DECIMAL-DEGREE TABLE

Use the decimal-degree trigonometric function table found in the Appendix to determine the values of angle A that correspond to these functions. Interpolate to the nearer hundredth of a degree where necessary.

49. sin A = 0.236 8

50. tan A = 6.691

51. cot A = 0.935 8

52. cos A = 0.142 63

53. csc A = 1.542 9

54. sec A = 1.747 8

55. cos A = 0.643 7

56. tan A = 0.905 0

57. cot A = 1.090 2

58. csc A = 1.140 9

59. sin A = 0.826 3

60. sec A = 1.252 9

UNIT 30
Trigonometric Functions with Right Triangles

OBJECTIVES

After studying this unit you should be able to

- determine the variations of functions as angles change.
- compute cofunctions of complementary angles.
- compute unknown angles of right triangles when two sides are known.
- compute unknown sides of a right triangle when an angle and a side are known.

VARIATION OF FUNCTIONS

As the size of an angle increases the sine, tangent, and secant functions increase while the cofunctions (cosine, cotangent, cosecant) decrease. As the reference angles approach 0° or 90°, the function variation can be shown. These examples illustrate variations of an increasing function and a decreasing function for a reference angle which is increasing in size. Use figure 30-1 for these examples.

Example 1. Variation of an increasing function; the sine function. Refer to figure 30-1.

OP_1 and OP_2 are radii of the arc of a circle. $OP_1 = OP_2 = r$

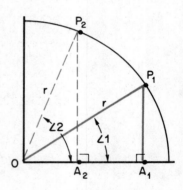

Fig. 30-1

The sine of an angle $= \dfrac{\text{opposite side}}{\text{hypotenuse}}$

$$\sin \angle 1 = \frac{A_1P_1}{r}$$

$$\sin \angle 2 = \frac{A_2P_2}{r}$$

A_2P_2 is greater than A_1P_1, therefore, $\sin \angle 2$ is greater than $\sin \angle 1$.

Conclusion: **As the angle is increased from $\angle 1$ to $\angle 2$, the sine of the angle increases.** Observe that if $\angle 1$ decreases to 0°, side $A_1P_1 = 0$.

$$\sin 0° = \frac{0}{r} = 0$$

If $\angle 2$ increases to 90°, side $A_2P_2 = r$.

$$\sin 90° = \frac{r}{r} = 1$$

Example 2.   Variation of a decreasing function; the cosine function. Refer to figure 30-1.

The cosine of an angle $= \dfrac{\text{adjacent side}}{\text{hypotenuse}}$

$$\cos \angle 1 = \frac{OA_1}{r}$$

$$\cos \angle 2 = \frac{OA_2}{r}$$

OA_2 is less than OA_1, therefore, $\cos \angle 2$ is less than $\cos \angle 1$.

Conclusion: **As the angle is increased from $\angle 1$ to $\angle 2$, the cosine of the angle decreases.** Observe that if $\angle 1$ decreases to $0°$, side $OA_1 = r$.

$$\cos 0° = \frac{r}{r} = 1$$

If $\angle 2$ increases to $90°$, side $OA_2 = 0$.

$$\cos 90° = \frac{0}{r} = 0$$

Study the tables of trigonometric functions found in the Appendix and observe the changes in functions as angles increase or decrease. It is also helpful to sketch figures similar to figure 30-1 for all functions in order to further develop an understanding of the relationship of angles and their functions. Particular attention should be given to functions of angles close to $0°$ and $90°$.

A summary of the variations taken from the table of trigonometric functions is shown for an angle increasing from $0°$ to $90°$.

As an angle increases from 0° to 90°	
sin increases from 0 to 1	cos decreases from 1 to 0
tan increases from 0 to ∞	cot decreases from ∞ to 0
sec increases from 1 to ∞	csc decreases from ∞ to 1

The symbol ∞ means infinity. Infinity is the quality of existing beyond or being greater than any countable value. It cannot be used for computations at this level of mathematics.

Rather than to attempt to treat ∞ as a value, think of the tangent and secant functions not at an angle of $90°$, but at angles very close to $90°$. Observe that as an angle approaches $90°$, the tangent and secant functions get very large. Think of the cotangent and cosecant functions not at an angle of $0°$, but as very small angles close to $0°$. Observe that as an angle approaches $0°$ the cotangent and cosecant functions get very large.

Exercise 30-1

Refer to figure 30-2 in answering these questions. It may be helpful to sketch figures.

1. When ∠1 is almost 90°:

   a. how does side y compare to side r?

   b. how does side x compare to side r?

   c. how does side x compare to side y?

2. When ∠1 is 90°:

   a. what is the value of side x?

   b. how does side y compare to side r?

3. When ∠1 is slightly greater than 0°:

   a. how does side y compare to side r?

   b. how does side x compare to side r?

   c. how does side x compare to side y?

4. When ∠1 is 0°:

   a. what is the value of side y?

   b. how does side x compare to side r?

5. When side x = side y:

   a. what is the value of ∠1?

   b. what is the value of the tangent function?

   c. what is the value of the cotangent function?

6. When side x = side r:

   a. what is the value of the cosine function?

   b. what is the value of the secant function?

   c. what is the value of the sine function?

   d. what is the value of the tangent function?

7. When side y = side r:

   a. what is the value of the sine function?

   b. what is the value of the cosecant function?

   c. what is the value of the cosine function?

   d. what is the value of the cotangent function?

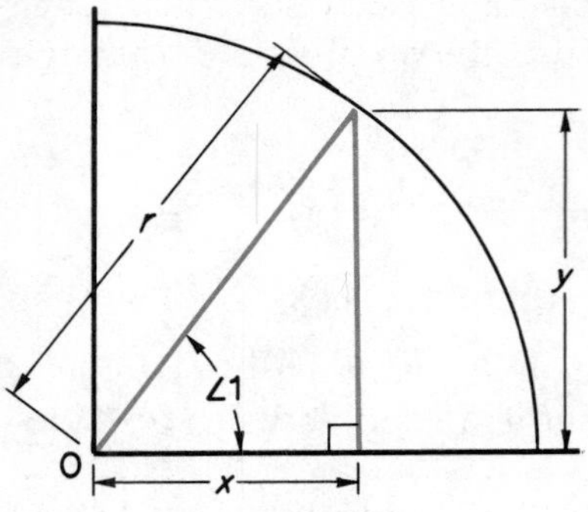

Fig. 30-2

For each exercise, functions of two angles are given. Which of the functions of the two angles is greater? Do not use the tables of trigonometric functions.

8. sin 38°; sin 43°

9. tan 17°; tan 18°

10. cos 76°; cos 80°

11. cot 40°; cot 36°

12. sec 5°; sec 8°

13. csc 22°; csc 25°

14. tan 19°20'; tan 16°40'

15. cos 81°19'; cos 81°20'

16. sin 0.42°; sin 0.37°

17. csc 39.30°; csc 39.25°

18. cot 27°23'; cot 87°0'

19. sec 55°; sec 54°50'

FUNCTIONS OF COMPLEMENTARY ANGLES

Two angles are complementary when their sum is 90°. For example, 20° is the complement of 70° and 70° is the complement of 20°. In figure 30-3, ∠A is the complement of ∠B and ∠B is the complement of ∠A. The six functions of the angle and the cofunctions of the complementary angle are shown.

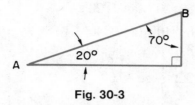

Fig. 30-3

sin 20° = cos 70° = 0.342 02	cos 20° = sin 70° = 0.939 69
tan 20° = cot 70° = 0.363 97	cot 20° = tan 70° = 2.747 5
sec 20° = csc 70° = 1.064 2	csc 20° = sec 70° = 2.923 8

A function of an angle is equal to the cofunction of the complement of the angle.

The complement of an angle equals 90° minus the angle. The relationships of the six functions of angles and the cofunctions of the complementary angles are shown.

sin A = cos (90° − A)	cos A = sin (90° − A)
tan A = cot (90° − A)	cot A = tan (90° − A)
sec A = csc (90° − A)	csc A = sec (90° − A)

Examples. For each function of an angle, write the cofunction of the complement of the angle.

1. sin 30° = cos (90° − 30°) = **cos 60°** *Ans*
2. cot 10° = tan (90° − 10°) = **tan 80°** *Ans*
3. tan 72.53° = cot (90° − 72.53°) = **cot 17.47°** *Ans*
4. sec 40°20′ = csc (90° − 40°20′) = csc (89°60′ − 40°20′) = **csc 49°40′** *Ans*
5. cos 90° = sin (90° − 90°) = **sin 0°** *Ans*

Exercise 30-2

For each function of an angle, write the cofunction of the complement of the angle.

1. tan 17°	8. sin 0°	15. cos 5.89°
2. sin 49°	9. tan 66.5°	16. cot 0°
3. cos 26°	10. cos 12.2°	17. tan 90°
4. sec 87°	11. cot 7°10′	18. sec 44°29′
5. cot 35°	12. sec 31°26′	19. cos 0.01°
6. csc 51°	13. csc 0°38′	20. sin 89°59′
7. cos 90°	14. sin 5.89°	

For each exercise, functions and cofunctions of two angles are given. Which of the functions or cofunctions of the two angles is greater? Do not use the tables of trigonometric functions.

21. cos 55°; sin 20°
22. cos 55°; sin 40°
23. tan 30°; cot 65°
24. tan 30°; cot 45°
25. sec 43°; csc 56°
26. sec 43°; csc 58°

27. sin 12°; cos 80°
28. sin 12°; cos 75°
29. cot 89°10'; tan 1°20'
30. cot 89°10'; tan 0°40'
31. sec 0.2°; csc 89.9°
32. sec 0.2°; csc 89.0°

DETERMINING AN UNKNOWN ANGLE WHEN TWO SIDES OF A RIGHT TRIANGLE ARE KNOWN

In order to solve for an unknown angle of a right triangle where neither acute angle is known, at least two sides must be known. The following procedure outlines the steps required in computing an angle:

Procedure for Determining an Unknown Angle When Two Sides Are Given

- In relation to the desired angle, identify two given sides as adjacent, opposite, or hypotenuse.

- Determine the functions that are ratios of the sides identified in relation to the desired angle.

  NOTE: Two of the six trigonometric functions are ratios of the two known sides. Either of the two functions can be used. Both produce the same value for the unknown, except for cotangents, secants, and cosecants of angles less than 15° and tangents, secants, and cosecants of angles greater than 75°.

- Choose one of the two functions, substitute the given sides in the ratio, and divide.

- Using the tables of trigonometric functions found in the Appendix, determine the angle that corresponds to the quotient obtained. It is often necessary to interpolate. Use the degree-10 minute table when computing with English units. Use the decimal-degree table when computing with metric units.

Example 1.   Determine ∠A of the right triangle shown in figure 30-4 to the nearer minute.

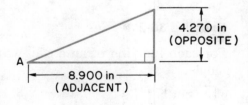

Fig. 30-4

Solution: In relation to ∠A, the 8.900-inch side is the adjacent side and the 4.270-inch side is the opposite side.

Determine the two functions whose ratios consist of the adjacent and opposite sides. The tan ∠A = $\frac{\text{opposite side}}{\text{adjacent side}}$, and the cot ∠A = $\frac{\text{adjacent side}}{\text{opposite side}}$. Either the tangent or cotangent function can be used.

Choosing the tangent function, tan ∠A = $\frac{4.270}{8.900}$, tan ∠A = 0.479 78.

Interpolate from the degree-10 minute function table to determine the angle whose tangent function is nearer 0.479 78. The angle interpolated to the nearer minute is 25°38'. **Angle A = 25°38' Ans**

Example 2.   Determine ∠B of the right triangle shown in figure 30-5 to the nearer hundredth degree.

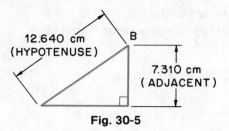

Fig. 30-5

Solution: In relation to ∠B, the 12.640-centimetre side is the hypotenuse and the 7.310-centimetre side is the adjacent side.

Determine the two functions whose ratios consist of the adjacent side and the hypotenuse. The cos ∠B = $\frac{\text{adjacent side}}{\text{hypotenuse}}$ and the sec ∠B = $\frac{\text{hypotenuse}}{\text{adjacent side}}$. Either the cosine or secant function can be used. Choosing the cosine function, cos ∠B = $\frac{7.310}{12.640}$, cos ∠B = 0.578 3.

Interpolate from the decimal-degree function table to determine the angle whose cosine function is nearest 0.578 3. The angle interpolated to the nearer hundredth degree is 54.67°.
Angle B = 54.67° Ans

Example 3.   Determine ∠1 and ∠2 of the triangle shown in figure 30-6 to the nearer minute.

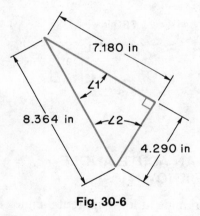

Fig. 30-6

Solution: Compute either ∠1 or ∠2. Choose any two of the three given sides for a ratio. In relation to ∠1, the 4.290-inch side is the opposite side and the 8.364-inch side is the hypotenuse.

Determine the two functions whose ratios consist of the opposite side and the hypotenuse. The sin of ∠1 = $\frac{\text{opposite side}}{\text{hypotenuse}}$, and the csc of ∠1 = $\frac{\text{hypotenuse}}{\text{opposite}}$. Either the sine or cosecant can be used.

Choosing the sine function, sin ∠1 = $\frac{4.290}{8.364}$, sin ∠1 = 0.512 91.

Interpolate from the degree-10 minute function table to determine the angle whose sine function is nearer 0.512 91. The angle interpolated to the nearer minute is 30°51'. **Angle 1 = 30°51'. Ans**
Since ∠1 + ∠2 = 90°, ∠2 = 90° − 30°51' = 89°60' − 30°51' = 59°9'. **Angle 2 = 59°9' Ans**

Exercise 30-3

Tables of trigonometric functions are found in the Appendix. Determine the unknown angles of these right triangles. Compute angles to the nearer minute in triangles with English unit sides. Compute angles to the nearer hundredth degree in triangles with metric unit sides.

1. Determine ∠A.

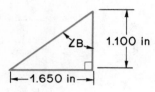

4. Determine ∠x.

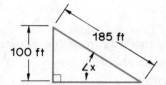

7. Determine ∠y.

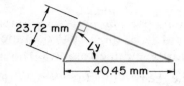

10. Determine ∠A and ∠B.

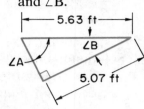

2. Determine ∠B.

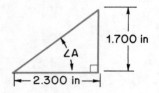

5. Determine ∠1.

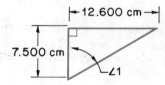

8. Determine ∠B.

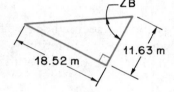

11. Determine ∠x and ∠y.

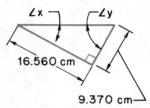

3. Determine ∠1.

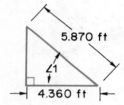

6. Determine ∠A.

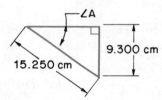

9. Determine ∠1 and ∠2.

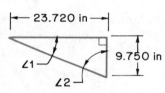

12. Determine ∠C and ∠D.

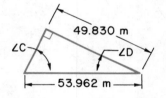

DETERMINING AN UNKNOWN SIDE WHEN AN ACUTE ANGLE AND ONE SIDE OF A RIGHT TRIANGLE ARE KNOWN

In order to solve for an unknown side of a right triangle at least an acute angle and one side must be known. The following procedure outlines the steps required in computing the unknown side.

Procedure for Determining an Unknown Side When an Angle and a Side Are Given

- In relation to the given angle, identify the given side and the unknown side as adjacent, opposite, or hypotenuse.

- Determine the trigonometric functions that are ratios of the sides identified in relation to the given angle.

NOTE: Two of the six functions will be found as ratios of the two identified sides. Either of the two functions can be used. Both produce the same value for the unknown except for cotangents, secants, and cosecants of angles less than 15° and tangents, secants, and cosecants of angles greater than 75°. If the unknown side is made the numerator of the ratio, the problem is solved by multiplication. If the unknown side is made the denominator of the ratio, the problem is solved by division.

• Choose one of the two functions and substitute the given side and given angle.

• Using the trigonometric function table found in the Appendix, look up the function of the given angle and substitute this value. If the angle is not given in the table, interpolate the function of the angle. Use the degree-10 minute table when computing with English units. Use the decimal-degree table when computing with metric units.

• Solve as a proportion for the unknown side.

Example 1.   Determine side x of the right triangle shown in figure 30-7.

Solution: In relation to the 61°50' angle, the 5.410-inch side is the adjacent side and side x is the opposite side.

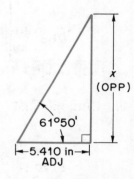

Fig. 30-7

Determine the two functions whose ratios consist of the adjacent and opposite sides. The $\tan 61°50' = \frac{\text{opposite side}}{\text{adjacent side}}$ and the $\cot 61°50' = \frac{\text{adjacent side}}{\text{opposite side}}$. Either the tangent or cotangent function can be used.

Choosing the tangent function, $\tan 61°50' = \frac{x}{5.410}$. Look up the tangent of 61°50' in the function table: $\tan 61°50' = 1.867\,6$. Substitute 1.867 6 for $\tan 61°50'$: $1.867\,6 = \frac{x}{5.410}$.

Solve as a proportion: $\frac{1.867\,6}{1} = \frac{x}{5.410}$, $x = 1.867\,6(5.410)$, $x = 10.104$ in *Ans*

Example 2.   Determine side r of the right triangle shown in figure 30-8.

Solution: In relation to the 28.76° angle, the 15.775-centimetre side is the opposite side and side r is the hypotenuse.

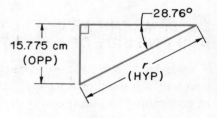

Fig. 30-8

Determine the two functions whose ratios consist of the opposite side and the hypotenuse. The $\sin 28.76° = \frac{\text{opposite side}}{\text{hypotenuse}}$ and the $\csc 28.76° = \frac{\text{hypotenuse}}{\text{opposite side}}$. Either the sine or cosecant function can be used.

Choosing the sine function, $\sin 28.76° = \frac{15.775}{r}$. Interpolate the sine of 28.76°: $\sin 28.76° = 0.481\,2$. Substitute 0.481 2 for $\sin 28.76°$: $0.481\,2 = \frac{15.775}{r}$.

Solve as a proportion: $\frac{0.481\,2}{1} = \frac{15.775}{r}$, $0.481\,2\,r = 15.775$, $r = \frac{15.775}{0.481\,2}$, $r = 32.783$ cm *Ans*

Example 3.   Determine side x, side y, and $\angle 1$ of the right triangle shown in figure 30-9.

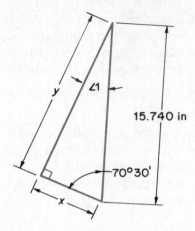

Fig. 30-9

Solution: Compute either side x or side y. Choosing side x, in relation to the $70°30'$ angle, side x is the adjacent side. The 15.740-inch side is the hypotenuse.

Determine the two functions whose ratios consist of the adjacent side and the hypotenuse. Either the cosine or secant function can be used.

Choosing the cosine function, $\cos 70°30' = \frac{x}{15.740}$. Look up the cosine of $70°30'$ in the function table: $\cos 70°30' = 0.333\,81$. Substitute $0.333\,81$ for $\cos 70°30'$: $0.333\,81 = \frac{x}{15.740}$.

Solve as a proportion: $\frac{0.333\,81}{1} = \frac{x}{15.740}$, $x = 0.333\,81(15.740)$, $x = \mathbf{5.254}$ **in** *Ans*

Solve for side y by using either a trigonometric function or the Pythagorean Theorem. If the Pythagorean Theorem is used to determine y, then $y^2 = 15.740^2 - 5.254^2$ and $y = \sqrt{15.740^2 - 5.254^2}$. In cases like this, it is generally more convenient to solve for the side using a trigonometric function. In relation to the $70°30'$ angle, side y is the opposite side. The 15.740-inch side is the hypotenuse.

Determine the two functions whose ratios consist of the opposite side and the hypotenuse. Either the sine or cosecant function can be used.

Choosing the sine function, $\sin 70°30', = \frac{y}{15.740}$. Look up the sine of $70°30'$ in the function table: $\sin 70°30' = 0.942\,64$. Substitute $0.942\,64$ for $\sin 70°30'$. $0.942\,64 = \frac{y}{15.740}$.

Solve as a proportion: $\frac{0.942\,64}{1} = \frac{y}{15.740}$, $y = 0.942\,64(15.740)$, $y = \mathbf{14.837}$ **in** *Ans*

Determine $\angle 1$; $\angle 1 = 90° - 70°30'$, $\angle 1 = \mathbf{19°30'}$ *Ans*

Exercise 30-4

Tables of trigonometric functions are found in the Appendix. Determine the unknown sides in these right triangles. Compute sides to three decimal places.

1. Determine side *b*.

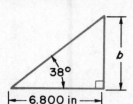

2. Determine side *c*.

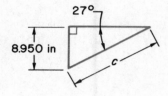

3. Determine side *x*.

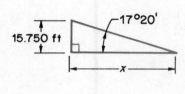

4. Determine side *d*.

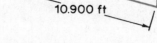

5. Determine side *y*.

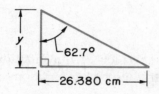

6. Determine side *f*.

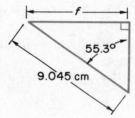

7. Determine side *p*.

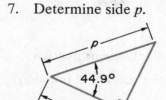

8. Determine side *y*.

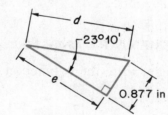

9. Determine sides *d* and *e*.

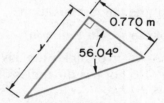

10. Determine sides *s* and *t*.

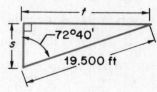

11. Determine sides *x* and *y*.

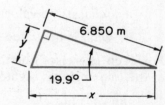

12. Determine sides *p* and *n*.

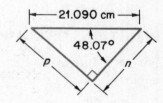

UNIT EXERCISE AND PROBLEM REVIEW

Exercise 30-5

Tables of trigonometric functions are found in the Appendix.

VARIATION OF FUNCTIONS

Refer to figure 30-10 in answering these questions. It may be helpful to sketch figures.

1. When ∠1 = 0°:

   a. what is the value of side *y*?

   b. how does side *x* compare to side *r*?

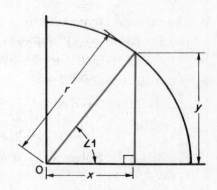

Fig. 30-10

2. When $\angle 1 = 90°$:

    a. what is the value of side x?

    b. how does side y compare to side r?

3. When side $x =$ side y:

    a. what is the value of $\angle 1$?

    b. what is the value of the tangent function?

    c. what is the value of the cotangent function?

4. When side $y =$ side r:

    a. what is the value of the cosine function?

    b. what is the value of the sine function?

5. When side $x =$ side r:

    a. what is the value of the tangent function?

    b. what is the value of the secant function?

For each exercise, functions of two angles are given. Which of the functions of the two angles is greater? Do not use the tables of trigonometric functions.

6. $\tan 28°$; $\tan 31°$

7. $\cot 43°$; $\cot 48°$

8. $\cos 86°$; $\cos 37°$

9. $\sin 28°12'$; $\sin 14°50'$

10. $\sec 47.85°$; $\sec 40.36°$

11. $\csc 81.66°$; $\csc 79.12°$

FUNCTIONS OF COMPLEMENTARY ANGLES

For each function of an angle, write the cofunction of the complement of the angle.

12. $\sin 39°$

13. $\cos 66°$

14. $\tan 77°$

15. $\sec 25°$

16. $\cot 9°26'$

17. $\csc 0°$

18. $\tan 90°$

19. $\sin 51.88°$

20. $\cos 89°59'$

For each exercise, functions and cofunctions of two angles are given. Which of the functions or cofunctions of the two angles is greater? Do not use the tables of trigonometric functions.

21. $\tan 40°$; $\cot 60°$

22. $\tan 42°$; $\cot 47°$

23. $\cos 44°$; $\sin 41°$

24. $\sin 39°$; $\cos 63°$

25. $\csc 54°$; $\sec 45°$

26. $\csc 68°$; $\sec 50°$

DETERMINING ANGLES AND SIDES OF RIGHT TRIANGLES

Determine the unknown angles or sides of these right triangles. Compute angles to the nearer minute in triangles with English unit sides. Compute angles to the nearer hundredth degree in triangles with metric unit sides. Compute sides to three decimal places.

27. Determine ∠A.

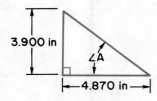

28. Determine ∠B.

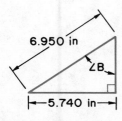

29. Determine side x.

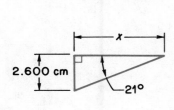

30. Determine side b.

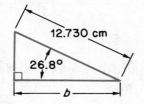

31. Determine ∠B.

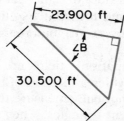

32. Determine side c.

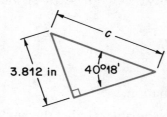

33. Determine ∠1.

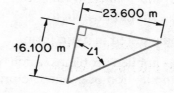

34. Determine side y.

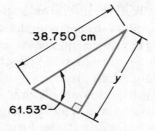

35. Determine ∠B, side x, and side y.

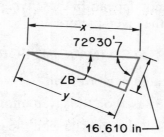

36. Determine ∠1, ∠2, and side a.

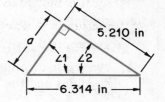

37. Determine side a, side b, and ∠2.

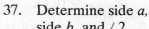
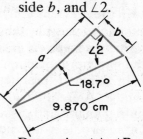

38. Determine ∠A, ∠B, and side r.

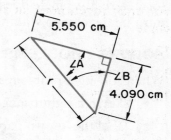

UNIT 31
Practical Applications with Right Triangles

After studying this unit you should be able to

- solve applied problems stated in word form.

- solve relatively simple applied problems which require the projection of auxiliary lines and the application of geometric principles.

- solve more complex applied problems which require forming two or more right triangles by the projection of auxiliary lines.

In the previous unit, you solved for unknown angles and sides of right triangles. Emphasis was placed on developing an understanding and the ability to apply proper procedures in solving for angles and sides. No attempt was made to show the many practical applications of right angle trigonometry.

In this unit, practical applications from various occupational fields are presented. A great advantage of trigonometry is that it provides a method of computing angles and distances without actually having to physically measure them. Often problems are not given directly in the form of right triangles. They may be given in word form, which may require expressing word statements as pictures by sketching right triangles. Also, often when a problem is given in picture form, a right triangle does not appear. In these types of problems, right triangles must be developed within the given picture.

SOLVING PROBLEMS STATED IN WORD FORM

When solving a problem stated in word form

- sketch a right triangle based on the given information.

- label the known parts of the triangle with the given values. Label the angle or side which is to be found.

- follow the procedure for determining an unknown angle or side of a right triangle.

Example 1.   A brace 15 feet long is to support a wall. One end of the brace is fastened to the floor at an angle of 40° with the floor. At what height from the floor will the brace be fastened to the wall?

Solution: Sketch and label a right triangle as shown in figure 31-1.
Let h represent the unknown height.

Compute h:

$$\sin 40° = \frac{h}{15}$$

$$0.642\ 79 = \frac{h}{15}$$

$$h = 9.64 \text{ ft } Ans$$

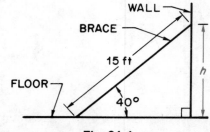

Fig. 31-1

Example 2: The sides of a sheet metal piece in the shape of a right triangle measure 25.50 cm, 12.00 cm, and 28.18 cm. What are the measures of the two acute angles of the piece?

Solution: Sketch and label a right triangle as shown in figure 31-2. Let $\angle 1$ and $\angle 2$ represent the unknown angles.

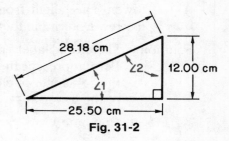

Fig. 31-2

Compute $\angle 1$: Choose any two sides for a ratio. Choose the 12.00-cm side and the 25.50-cm side.

$$\tan \angle 1 = \frac{12.00}{25.50}$$

$$\tan \angle 1 = 0.470\ 6$$

$$\angle 1 = \textbf{25.2° } \textit{Ans}$$

Compute $\angle 2$:

$$\angle 2 = 90° - 25.2° = \textbf{64.8° } \textit{Ans}$$

Surveying and navigation computations are based on right angle trigonometry. A surveyor uses a transit to measure angles between locations. By a combination of angle and distance measurements, distances which cannot be measured directly can be computed.

When a surveyor sights a point which is either above or below the horizontal, the measured angle is read on the transit vertical protractor. When a point above eye level is sighted, the transit telescope is pointed upward. The angle formed by the line of sight and the horizontal is called the *angle of elevation*. An angle of elevation is shown in figure 31-3. When a point below eye level is sighted, the transit telescope is pointed downward. The angle formed by the line of sight and the horizontal is called the *angle of depression*. An angle of depression is shown in Figure 31-4.

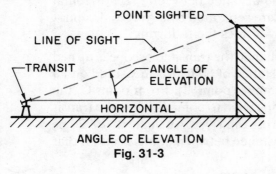

ANGLE OF ELEVATION
Fig. 31-3

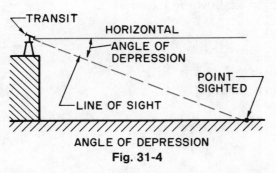

ANGLE OF DEPRESSION
Fig. 31-4

When measuring angles of elevation or depression, computed vertical distances must be corrected by adding or subtracting the height of the transit from the ground to the telescope. This type of problem is illustrated by the following example.

Example.   A surveyor is to determine the height of a tower. The transit is positioned at a horizontal distance of 35 metres from the foot of the tower. An angle of elevation of 58° is read in sighting the top of the tower. The height from the ground to the transit telescope is 1.70 metres. Determine the height of the tower.

Solution: Sketch and label a right triangle as shown in figure 31-5. Let x represent the side of the right triangle opposite the 58° angle of elevation. Let h represent the height of the tower; $h = x$ + transit height.

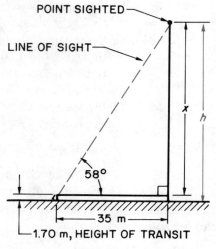

Compute x:

$$\tan 58° = \frac{x}{35}$$

$$1.600\ 3 = \frac{x}{35}$$

$$x = 56.01 \text{ m}$$

Compute h:

$$h = x + \text{transit height}$$

$$h = 56.01 \text{ m} + 1.70 \text{ m} = \textbf{57.71 m } Ans$$

Fig. 31-5

When surveying a section of land, horizontal distances which cannot be measured directly are computed by determining angles between horizontal points. From a horizontal line of sight, the surveyor turns the transit telescope to the left or right in sighting a point. The angle between lines of sight is read on the transit horizontal protractor. This type of problem is illustrated by this example.

Example.   A surveyor wishes to measure the distance between two horizontal points. The two points, A and B, are separated by a river and cannot be directly measured. The surveyor does the following:

From point A, point B is sighted, then the transit telescope is turned 90°. Along the 90° sighting, a distance of 80 feet is measured and a stake is driven at the 80-foot distance (point C). From point C, the surveyor points the transit telescope back to point A. Then the transit telescope is turned to point B across the river. An angle of 70°20′ is read on the transit. What is the distance between points A and B that could not be directly measured?

Solution: Sketch and label a right triangle as shown in figure 31-6.

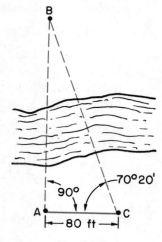

Compute distance AB:

$$\tan 70°20′ = \frac{AB}{AC}$$

$$2.7980 = \frac{AB}{80}$$

$$AB = \textbf{223.84 ft } Ans$$

Fig. 31-6

Vector quantities have magnitude and direction. Magnitude means size or amount. Vectors are widely applied in the fields of mechanics, construction, electronics, and navigation. They are used for computing amounts and directions of forces, velocities, voltages, and distances.

The magnitude of a vector is indicated by the length of the vector line segment and the direction is indicated by the arrowhead on the endpoint of the line segment. The result of two vectors is called the resultant vector. The following two examples illustrate uses of vectors.

Example 1. A force of 100 pounds pulls vertically up on an object. A second force of 150 pounds pulls horizontally to the right on the object. Compute the force and the direction of the resultant vector.

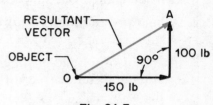

Fig. 31-7

Solution: Sketch and label a right triangle as shown in figure 31-7. From the object or origin (point 0), the horizontal vector is drawn and labeled. From the arrowhead of the horizontal vector, the vertical vector is drawn. Remember the vectors show both the magnitude and direction of the forces. The resultant vector is OA.

Compute the magnitude of the resultant vector, OA:

Applying the Pythagorean Theorem,

$$OA^2 = 150^2 + 100^2$$
$$OA^2 = 22\,500 + 10\,000$$
$$OA^2 = 32\,500$$
$$OA = 180.28 \text{ lb}$$

Compute $\angle O$:

$$\cot \angle O = \frac{150}{100}$$
$$\cot \angle O = 1.500\,0$$
$$\angle O = 33°41'$$

The resultant vector pulls on the object with a force of 180.28 pounds in a direction up and to the right at an angle of 33°41′ from the horizontal. A force of 180.28 pounds pulling in a direction 33°41′ from the horizontal produces the same result as the combination of a 100-pound vertical force and a 150-pound horizontal force.

Example 2. What is the instantaneous value (e) of an alternating emf when it has reached 45° of its cycle if the maximum value (E_{max}) is 600 volts?

Vector diagrams are often used for alternating current applications in electricity. One type of application of vectors is in representing electromotive force (emf) and determining its value at various instants.

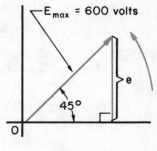

Fig. 31-8

Solution: The problem is sketched and labeled as follows: (Refer to figure 31-8). From the horizontal (0°), the maximum voltage (E_{max}) is rotated 45° in a counterclockwise direction. The instantaneous voltage (e) is the value of the vertical projection to the horizontal from the end of the E_{max} vector.

Compute the instantaneous value (e):

$$\sin 45° = \frac{e}{E_{max}}$$
$$\sin 45° = \frac{e}{600}$$
$$0.707\,11 = \frac{e}{600}$$
$$e = \textbf{424.3 volts } Ans$$

Exercise 31-1

Sketch and label each of the following problems. Compute the unknown linear values to 2 decimal places unless otherwise noted, English angular values to the nearer minute, and metric angular values to the nearer hundredth of a degree.

1. The sides of a pattern, which is in the shape of a right triangle, measure 10.600 inches, 23.500 inches, and 25.780 inches. What are the measures of the two acute angles of the pattern?

2. A highway entrance ramp rises 35 feet in a horizontal distance of 160 feet. What is the measure of the angle that the ramp makes with the horizontal?

3. The roof of a building slopes at an angle of 32° from the horizontal. The horizontal distance (run) of the roof is 6 metres. Compute the rafter length of the roof.

4. The centers of two diagonal holes in a locating plate are 22.600 centimetres apart. The angle between the centerline of the 2 holes and a vertical line is 53.60°. Compute distances to 3 decimal places.

   a. What is the vertical distance between the centers of the 2 holes?

   b. What is the horizontal distance between the centers of the 2 holes?

5. A wall brace is to be positioned so that it makes an angle of 40° with the floor. It is to be fastened to the floor at a distance of 12 feet from the foot of the wall. Compute the length of the brace.

6. A surveyor wishes to determine the height of a building. The transit is positioned on level land at a distance of 160 feet from the foot of the building. An angle of 41°30′ is read in sighting the top of the building. The height from the ground to the transit telescope is 5.5 feet. What is the height of the building?

7. A force of 180 pounds pulls vertically up on an object. A second force of 120 pounds pulls horizontally to the left of the object. Compute the force and the direction of the resultant vector.

8. A 4′ × 8′ rectangular sheet of plywood is to be cut into 2 pieces of equal size using a diagonal cut made from the lower left corner to the upper right corner of the sheet. What is the measure of the angle that the diagonal cut makes with the 4-foot side?

9. What is the instantaneous value (e) of an alternating emf when it has reached 60° of its cycle? The maximum value (E_{max}) is 450 volts.

10. From a centerpunched starting point on a sheet of steel, a horizontal line segment 32.40 centimetres long is scribed and the endpoint is centerpunched. From this centerpunched point, a vertical line segment 27.80 centimetres is scribed and the endpoint is centerpunched. A line segment is scribed between the starting point and the last centerpunched point. What are the measures of the 2 acute angles of the scribed triangle?

11. A surveyor determines the horizontal distance between two locations. The transit is positioned at the first location which is 18 metres higher in elevation than the second location. The second location is sighted and a 34° angle of

depression is read. The height from the ground to the transit telescope is 1.7 metres. Determine the horizontal distance between the two locations.

12. A hole is drilled through the entire thickness of a rectangular metal block at an angle of 46°20′ with the horizontal top surface. The block is 2.750 inches thick. What is the length of the drilled hole? Compute the answer to 3 decimal places.

13. A drain pipe is to be laid between two points. One point is 10 feet higher in elevation than the second point. The pipe is to slope at an angle of 12° with the horizontal. Compute the length of the drain pipe.

14. The rectangular bottom of a carton is designed so the length is one and one-half times as long as the width. What is the measure of the angle made by a diagonal across corners and the length of the bottom?

15. What is the instantaneous value (e) of an alternating emf when it has reached 30° of its cycle? The maximum value (E_{max}) is 800 volts.

16. A surveyor determines the distance between two horizontal points on a piece of land. The two points, A and B, are separated by an obstruction and cannot be directly measured. The surveyor does the following:

    From point A, point B is sighted, then the transit telescope is turned 90°. Along the 90° sighting, a distance of 30 metres is measured and a stake is driven at the 30 metre distance (point C). From point C, the surveyor points the transit telescope back to point A. The telescope is then turned to point B and an angle of 66° is read on the horizontal protractor. Compute the distance between point A and point B.

17. An airplane flies in a direction 28° north of east at an average speed of 380 miles per hour. At the end of $2\frac{1}{2}$ hours of flying, how far due east is the airplane from its starting point?

18. A force of 15 000 pounds is exerted down and to the right on a steel beam at an angle of 65° with the horizontal. Compute the force of the horizontal and vertical vectors (components) of the given force. Compute answers to the nearer whole pound of force.

SOLVING PROBLEMS GIVEN IN PICTURE FORM WHICH REQUIRE AUXILIARY LINES

The following examples are practical applications of right angle trigonometry, although they do not appear in the form of right triangles. To solve the problems, it is necessary to project auxiliary lines to produce right triangles. The unknown value, and the given or computed values are parts of the produced right triangle.

The auxiliary lines may be projected between given points or from given points. Also, they may be projected parallel or perpendicular to centerlines, tangents, or other reference lines.

A knowledge of both geometric and trigonometric principles and the ability to apply the principles to specific situations are required in solving these problems. It is important to carefully study the procedures and use of auxiliary lines as they are applied in the solutions of these examples.

Example 1.   Compute ∠1 in the pattern shown in figure 31-9.

Solution: Angle 1 must be computed by forming a right triangle which contains ∠1. Refer to figure 31-10.

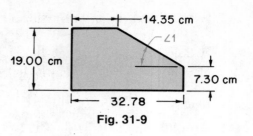

Fig. 31-9

Project line segment AB parallel to the base of the pattern.
Project vertical segment CB. Right △ABC is formed.

Compute sides AB and CB:

AB = 32.78 cm − 14.35 cm = 18.43 cm

CB = 19.00 cm − 7.30 cm = 11.70 cm

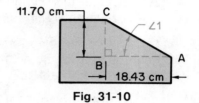

Fig. 31-10

Solve for ∠1:

$$\tan \angle 1 = \frac{CB}{AB} = \frac{11.70}{18.43} = 0.634\,8$$

$$\angle 1 = 32.4° \; Ans$$

Example 2.   Determine the included taper angle, ∠T, of the shaft
shown in figure 31-11.

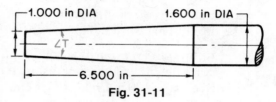

Fig. 31-11

Solution: Refer to figure 31-12. Project line segment AB
parallel to the shaft centerline. Right △ABC is
formed in which ∠1 is equal to one-half the
included taper angle, ∠T.

Determine sides AB and BC:

AB = 6.500 in

BC = (1.600 in − 1.000 in) ÷ 2 = 0.300 in

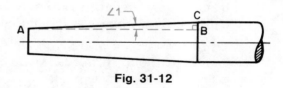

Fig. 31-12

Solve for ∠1:

$$\tan \angle 1 = \frac{BC}{AB} = \frac{0.300}{6.500} = 0.046\,15$$

$$\angle 1 = 2°39'$$

Compute ∠T:

$$\angle T = 2(\angle 1) = 2(2°39') = 5°18' \; Ans$$

The solutions to many practical trigonometry problems are based on recognizing
figures as isosceles triangles. A perpendicular projected from the vertex to the
base of an isosceles triangle bisects the vertex angle and the base. This fact
is illustrated by the following two problems.

Example 1. Determine the rafter length, AD, of the roof section shown in figure 31-13.

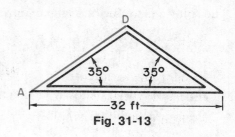

Fig. 31-13

Solution: Since both base angles equal 35°, the roof section is in the form of an isosceles triangle.

Refer to figure 31-14. Project line segment DB perpendicular to base AC. Base AC is bisected by DB.

$AB = AC \div 2 = 32$ ft $\div 2 = 16$ ft

In right $\triangle ABD$, $AB = 16$ ft, $\angle C = 35°$.

Solve for side AD:

$$\cos 35° = \frac{AB}{AD}$$

$$0.819\ 15 = \frac{16}{AD}$$

$$AD = 19.53 \text{ ft } Ans$$

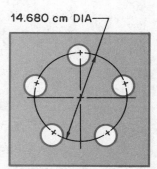

Fig. 31-14

Example 2. In figure 31-15, 5 holes are equally spaced on a 14.680-centimetre diameter circle. Determine the straight line distance between the centers of any two consecutive holes.

Solution: Refer to figure 31-16.

Choosing any two consecutive holes, such as A and B, project radii from center O to hole centers A and B. Project a line segment from A to B. Since OA = OB, $\triangle AOB$ is isosceles.

Compute central $\angle AOB$:

$\angle AOB = 360° \div 5 = 72°$

Project line segment OC perpendicular to AB from point O. Line segment OC bisects $\angle AOB$ and side AB.

In right $\triangle AOC$,

$\angle AOC = 72° \div 2 = 36°$

$AO = 14.680$ cm $\div 2 = 7.340$ cm

Compute side AC:

$$\sin 36° = \frac{AC}{AO}$$

$$0.587\ 8 = \frac{AC}{7.340}$$

$$AC = 4.314\ 5 \text{ cm}$$

Compute side AB:

$AB = 2(AC) = 2\ (4.314\ 5 \text{ cm}) = 8.629$ cm Ans

14.680 cm DIA

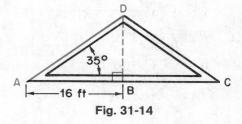

Fig. 31-15

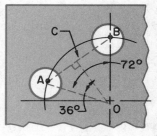

Fig. 31-16

The solutions to the following two examples are based on the geometric theorem that a tangent is perpendicular to the radius of a circle at the tangent point. The solutions to applied trigonometry problems in many fields, such as construction and manufacturing, are based on this principle.

Example 1. A park is shown in figure 31-17. A fence is to be built from point T to point R. Line segment TR is tangent to the circle at point T. Compute the required length of fencing.

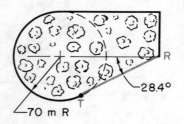

Fig. 31-17

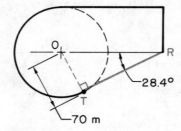

Fig. 31-18

Solution: Refer to figure 31-18.

Connect a line segment from the center of the circle O to tangent point T. Segment OT is a radius.

OT = 70 m

∠OTR = 90°

(A tangent is perpendicular to a radius at its tangent point).

In right △OTR, OT = 70 m and ∠R = 28.4°.

Solve for side TR:

$$\tan 28.4° = \frac{OT}{TR}$$

$$0.540\,7 = \frac{70}{TR}$$

$$TR = \textbf{129.46 m } Ans$$

Example 2. The front view of the internal half of a dovetail slide is shown in figure 31-19. Two pins or balls are used to check the dovetail slide for both location and angular accuracy. Compute check dimension x.

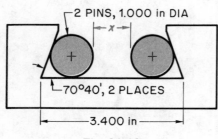

Fig. 31-19

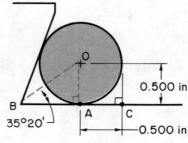

Fig. 31-20

Solution: Refer to figure 31-20. Only the left side of the dovetail slide is shown. The left and right sides are congruent.

Project vertical line segment OA from pin center O to tangent point A. The angle at A equals 90°. (A tangent is perpendicular to a radius at its tangent point.)

Project line segment OB from pin center O to point B. Segment OB bisects the 70°40′ angle. (The angle formed by two tangents meeting at a point outside a circle is bisected by a segment drawn from the point to the center of the circle.)

In right △ABO,

$\angle B = 70°40′ \div 2 = 35°20′$

$OA = 1.000 \text{ in} \div 2 = 0.500 \text{ in}$

Compute side AB:

$$\cot 35°20′ = \frac{AB}{OA}$$

$$1.410\ 6 = \frac{AB}{0.500}$$

$$AB = 0.705\ 3 \text{ in}$$

$AC = \text{pin radius} = 0.500 \text{ in}$

$BC = AB + AC = 0.705\ 3 \text{ in} + 0.500 \text{ in} = 1.205\ 3 \text{ in}$

Check dimension x:

$x = 3.400 \text{ in} - 2(1.205\ 3 \text{ in}) = $ **0.989 in** *Ans*

Exercise 31-2

Compute the unknown values in each of these problems. Compute linear values to 2 decimal places, unless otherwise noted, English angular values to the nearer minute, and metric angular values to the nearer hundredth of a degree.

1. Compute ∠A in the template shown in figure 31-21.

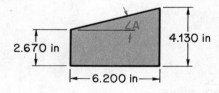

Fig. 31-21

2. A plot of land is shown in figure 31-22.

   a. Compute distance AB.

   b. Compute distance BC.

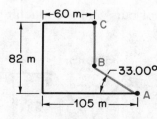

Fig. 31-22

3. Compute the included taper angle, ∠T, of the shaft shown in figure 31-23.

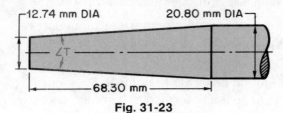

Fig. 31-23

4. Compute diameter B of the tapered support column shown in figure 31-24.

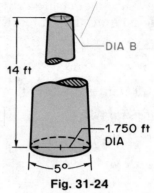

Fig. 31-24

5. Compute the rafter length of the roof section shown in figure 31-25.

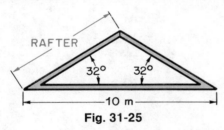

Fig. 31-25

6. Compute the distance across the centers, dimension *x*, of two consecutive holes in the baseplate shown in figure 31-26. Compute the answer to 3 decimal places.

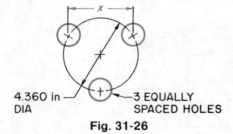

Fig. 31-26

7. Compute the depth of cut, *y*, in the machined block shown in figure 31-27, Distance AC = BC.

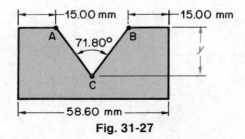

Fig. 31-27

8. A sidewalk is constructed from point A to point B in the minipark shown in figure 31-28. Point B is a tangent point. What is required length of sidewalk?

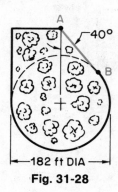

Fig. 31-28

9. Two sections of a brick wall, AB and AC, meet at point A as shown in figure 31-29. A circular patio is to be constructed so that it is tangent to the wall at points D and E.

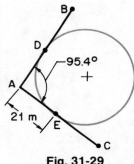

Fig. 31-29

   a. What is the required diameter of the patio?

   b. At what distance must the center of the patio be located from point A?

10. Compute check dimension x of the internal half of the dovetail slide shown in figure 31-30.

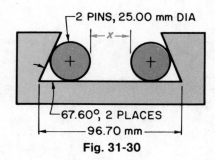

Fig. 31-30

11. A gambrel roof is shown in figure 31-31.

   a. Compute ∠1.

   b. Compute ∠2.

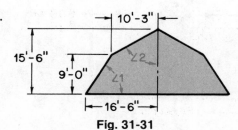

Fig. 31-31

12. A plumber is to install a water pipe assembly as shown in figure 31-32.

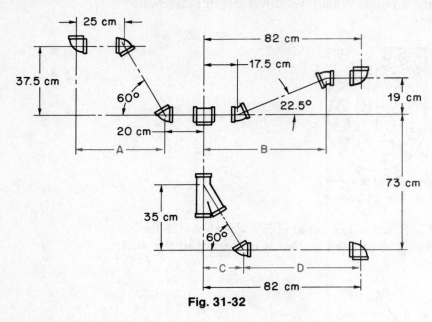

Fig. 31-32

   a. Compute dimension A.

   b. Compute dimension B.

   c. Compute dimension C.

   d. Compute dimension D.

13. The top view of a platform is shown in figure 31-33. Compute ∠A.

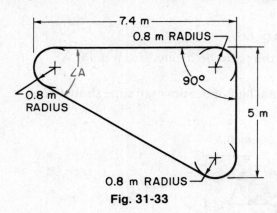

Fig. 31-33

14. Determine gage dimension *y* of the V-Block shown in figure 31-34. Compute the answer to 3 decimal places. Dimension EF = GF.

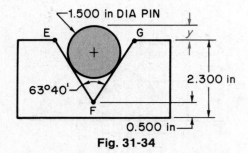

Fig. 31-34

15. Eight circular columns located in a circular pattern as shown in figure 31-35, are proposed to support the roof of a structure. Compute the inside distance *x* between two adjacent columns.

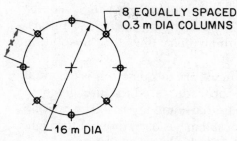

8 EQUALLY SPACED
0.3 m DIA COLUMNS

16 m DIA

Fig. 31-35

16. The side view of a sheet metal pipe and flange is shown in figure 31-36.

   a. Compute dimension A.

   b. Compute dimension B.

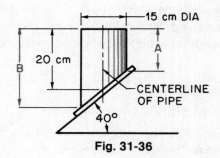

15 cm DIA

20 cm

B

A

CENTERLINE
OF PIPE

40°

Fig. 31-36

17. A portion of the framework for a building is shown in figure 31-37.

   a. Compute distance AB.

   b. Compute distance BC.

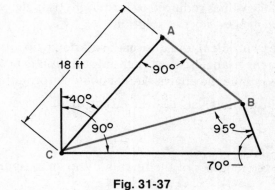

18 ft

A

90°

40°

90°

C

B

95°

70°

Fig. 31-37

18. A plot of land was surveyed as shown in figure 31-38. The distance between points A and B, and the distance between points C and B could not be measured directly because of obstructions.

   a. Compute distance AB.

   b. Compute distance BC.

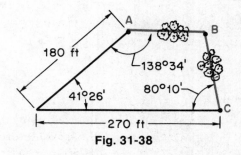

A

B

180 ft

138°34'

41°26'

80°10'

C

270 ft

Fig. 31-38

SOLVING MORE COMPLEX PROBLEMS WHICH REQUIRE AUXILIARY LINES

The following examples and problems are more challenging than those previously presented. These problems are also practical applications which require a combination of principles from geometry and trigonometry in their solutions. Two or more right triangles must be formed with auxiliary lines for the solution of each problem.

Typical examples from various occupational fields are discussed. It is essential that you study and, if necessary, restudy the procedures which are given in detail for solving the examples. There is a common tendency to begin writing computations before the complete solution to a problem has been thought through. This tendency must be avoided.

As problems become more complex, a greater proportion of time and effort is required in analyzing the problems. After a problem has been completely analyzed, the written computations must be developed in clear and orderly steps.

Apply the following procedures when solving complex problems.

Method of Solution

Analyze the problem before writing computations.

- Relate given dimensions to the unknown and determine whether other dimensions in addition to the given dimensions are required in the solution.

- Determine the auxiliary lines required to form right triangles which contain dimensions that are needed for the solution.

- Determine whether sufficient dimensions are known to obtain required values within the right triangles. If enough information is not available for solving a triangle, continue the analysis until enough information is obtained.

- Check each step in the analysis to verify that there are no gaps or false assumptions.

Write the computations.

Example 1.   Determine the length x of the template shown in figure 31-39.

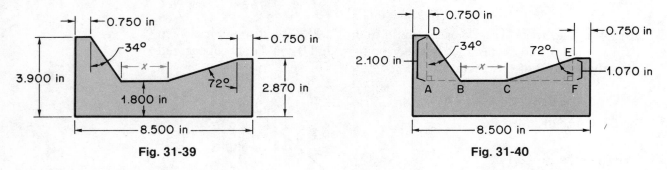

Fig. 31-39   Fig. 31-40

Analyze the problem:

Refer to figure 31-40. Project auxiliary line segments to form right △ABD and right △CEF. If distance AB and CF can be determined, length x can be computed. Length $x = 8.500$ in $- (0.750$ in $+$ AB $+$ CF $+ 0.750$ in$)$

Determine whether enough information is given to solve for AB. In right △ABD, ∠D $= 34°$ and AD $= 2.100$ inches. There is enough information to determine AB.

Determine whether enough information is given to solve for CF. In right △CEF, ∠E = 72° and EF = 1.070 inches. There is enough information to determine CF.

Computations:

Solve for AB:

$$\tan \angle D = \frac{AB}{AD}$$

$$\tan 34° = \frac{AB}{2.100}$$

$$0.674\ 51 = \frac{AB}{2.100}$$

$$AB = 1.416\ 5 \text{ in}$$

Solve for CF:

$$\tan \angle E = \frac{CF}{EF}$$

$$\tan 72° = \frac{CF}{1.070}$$

$$3.077\ 7 = \frac{CF}{1.070}$$

$$CF = 3.293\ 1$$

Solve for x:

$$x = 8.500 \text{ in} - (0.750 \text{ in} + AB + CF + 0.750 \text{ in})$$

$$x = 8.500 \text{ in} - (0.750 \text{ in} + 1.416\ 5 \text{ in} + 3.293\ 1 \text{ in} + 0.750 \text{ in})$$

$$x = \mathbf{2.290 \text{ in}} \ Ans$$

Example 2. A plaza is to be constructed in a city redevelopment area. The shaded area shown in figure 31-41 represents the proposed plaza. Determine ∠y.

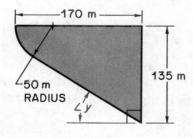

Fig. 31-41

Analyze the problem:

Generally, when solving problems which involve an arc which is tangent to one or more lines, it is necessary to project the radius of the arc to the tangent point and to project a line from the vertex of the unknown angle to the center of the arc.

Refer to figure 31-42. Project auxiliary line segments between points A and O and from point O to tangent point B. Right △ACO and right △ABO are formed.

If ∠1 and ∠2 can be determined, ∠y can be computed.

Determine whether enough information is given to solve for ∠1. In right △ACO, AC = 135 m and OC = 120 m. There is enough information to determine ∠1.

Determine whether enough information is given to solve for ∠2. In right △ABO, OB = 50 m. Side OA is also a side of right △ACO and can be computed by the Pythagorean Theorem or after ∠1 is computed. There is enough information given to determine ∠2.

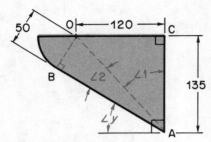

Fig. 31-42

Computations:

Solve for ∠1:

$$\tan \angle 1 = \frac{OC}{AC} = \frac{120}{135} = 0.888\ 9$$

$$\angle 1 = 41.65°$$

Solve for side OA:

$$OA^2 = OC^2 + AC^2$$
$$OA^2 = 120^2 + 135^2$$
$$OA^2 = 14\ 400 + 18\ 225$$
$$OA^2 = 32\ 625$$
$$OA = 180.624\ m$$

Solve for ∠2:

$$\sin \angle 2 = \frac{OB}{OA} = \frac{50}{180.624} = 0.276\ 8$$

$$\angle 2 = 16.07°$$

Solve for ∠y:

$$\angle y = 90° - (\angle 1 + \angle 2)$$
$$\angle y = 90° - (41.65° + 16.07°) = \textbf{32.28°} \textit{ Ans}$$

Example 3.   The front view of a metal piece with a V-groove cut is shown in figure 31-43. A 1.200-inch diameter pin is used to check the groove for depth and angular accuracy. Compute check dimension y.

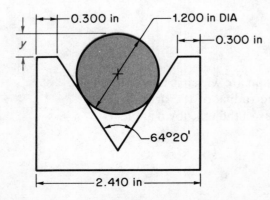

Fig. 31-43

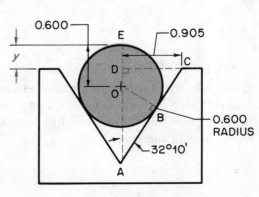

Fig. 31-44

Analyze the problem:

Check dimension y is determined by the pin diameter, the points of tangency where the pin touches the groove, the angle of the V-groove, and the depth of the groove. Therefore, these dimensions and locations must be included in the calculations for y.

Refer to figure 31-44. Project auxiliary line segments from point A through the center O of the pin, from point O to the tangent point B, and, from point C, horizontally intersect vertical segment AE at point D. Right $\triangle$ABO and right $\triangle$ADC are formed.

If AO and AD can be determined, check dimension y can be computed.

$y = (AO + OE) - AD$

Determine whether enough information is given to solve for AO. In right $\triangle$ABO, OB = 0.600 inches and $\angle A = 32°10'$. (The angle formed by two tangents at a point outside a circle is bisected by a line drawn from the point to the center of the circle.) There is enough information to determine AO.

Determine whether enough information is given to solve for AD. In right $\triangle$ADC, DC = 0.905 inches and $\angle A = 32°10'$. There is enough information to determine AD.

Computations:

Solve for AO:

$$\csc \angle A = \frac{AO}{OB}$$

$$\csc 32°10' = \frac{AO}{0.600}$$

$$1.878\,3 = \frac{AO}{0.600}$$

$$AO = 1.127\,0 \text{ in}$$

Solve for AD:

$$\cot \angle A = \frac{AD}{DC}$$

$$\cot 32°10' = \frac{AD}{0.905}$$

$$1.590\,0 = \frac{AD}{0.905}$$

$$AD = 1.439\,0 \text{ in}$$

Solve for check dimension y:

$y = (AO + OE) - AD = (1.127\,0 \text{ in} + 0.600 \text{ in}) - 1.439\,0 \text{ in} = $ **0.288 in** *Ans*

Example 4. Two proposed circular landscaped sections of a park are shown in figure 31-45. A fence is to be constructed between points A and B. In laying out the plot, a drafter is required to compute ∠x. What is the value of ∠x?

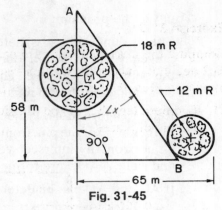

Fig. 31-45

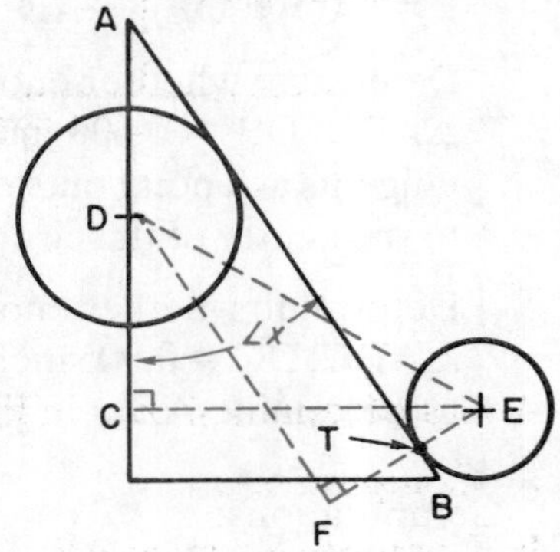

Analyze the problem:

Refer to figure 31-46. Project an auxiliary line segment between centers D and E of the two circles. From center point E, project a horizontal auxiliary line segment which meets the vertical centerline at point C. Right △CDE is formed.

Project an auxiliary line segment from point D parallel to segment AB. Project an auxiliary line segment from point E through tangent point T. The two line segments meet at right angles at point F. Right △FDE is formed.

If ∠CDE and ∠FDE can be determined, ∠x can be computed. ∠CDF = ∠CDE − ∠FDE. Angle x = ∠CDF. (If 2 parallel lines are intersected by a transversal, the corresponding angles are equal.)

Determine whether enough information is given to solve for ∠CDE. In right △CDE, CD = 58 m − (12 m + 18 m) = 28 m and CE = 65 m − 12 m = 53 m. There is enough information to determine ∠CDE.

Determine whether enough information is given to solve for ∠FDE. In right △FDE, FE = FT + TE = 18 m + 12 m = 30 m. Referring back to right △CDE, DE can be computed by the Pythagorean Theorem. $DE^2 = CD^2 + CE^2$. There is enough information to determine ∠FDE.

Fig. 31-46

Computations:

Solve for ∠CDE:

$$\tan \angle CDE = \frac{CE}{CD} = \frac{53}{28} = 1.893$$

$$\angle CDE = 62.15°$$

Solve for ∠FDE:

$$DE^2 = CD^2 + CE^2$$

$$DE^2 = 28^2 + 53^2$$

$$DE^2 = 784 + 2\ 809$$

$$DE^2 = 3\ 593$$

$$DE = 59.942 \text{ m}$$

$$\sin \angle FDE = \frac{FE}{DE} = \frac{30}{59.942} = 0.500\ 5$$

$$\angle FDE = 30.03°$$

Solve for ∠x:

∠CDF = ∠CDE − ∠FDE = 62.15° − 30.03° = 32.12°

Angle x = ∠CDF = **32.12°** *Ans*

Exercise 31-3

Compute the unknown values in each of these problems. Compute linear values to 2 decimal places unless otherwise noted, English angular values to the nearer minute, and metric angular values to the nearer hundredth of a degree.

1. Compute length x of the pin shown in figure 31-47. Compute the answer to 3 decimal places.

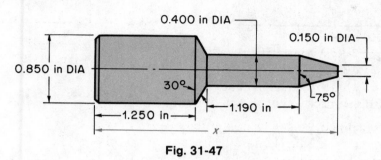

Fig. 31-47

2. A plot of land is shown in figure 31-48.

   a. Compute ∠A.

   b. Compute distance AB.

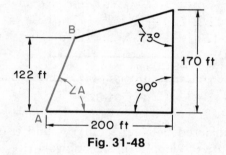

Fig. 31-48

3. A roof truss is shown in figure 31-49.

   a. Compute the length of cross member DE.

   b. Compute ∠E.

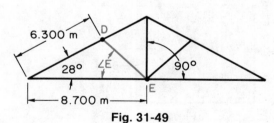

Fig. 31-49

4. Compute ∠x of the pattern shown in figure 31-50.

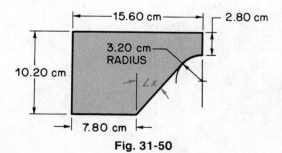

Fig. 31-50

5. Compute ∠y of the gage shown in figure 31-51.

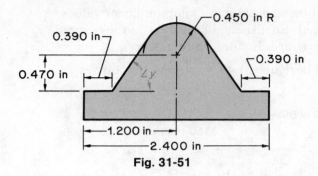

Fig. 31-51

6. Compute check dimension y of the V-groove cut shown in figure 31-52.

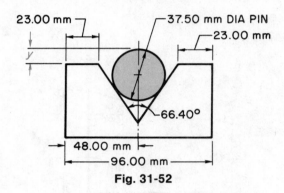

Fig. 31-52

7. A sidewalk is constructed between points A and B of a mall as shown in figure 31-53. Compute the length of the sidewalk.

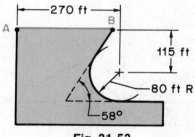

Fig. 31-53

8. Compute the angular hole location ∠x, in the guide plate shown in figure 31-54.

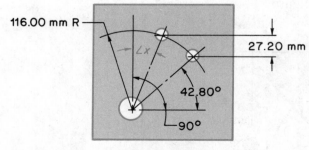

Fig. 31-54

9. A traffic rotary is designed as shown in figure 31-55. Compute distance *d*.

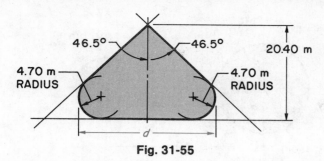

Fig. 31-55

10. In surveying a piece of land, a surveyor made the measurements shown in figure 31-56. Compute ∠1.

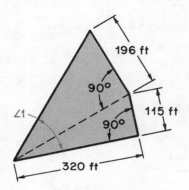

Fig. 31-56

11. Compute dimension *x* of the template shown in figure 31-57. Compute the answer to 3 decimal places.

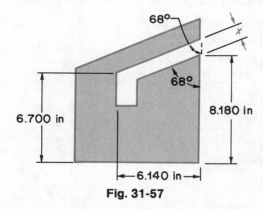

Fig. 31-57

12. Determine ∠*y* made by the vertical and the tangent line of the two pins shown in figure 31-58.

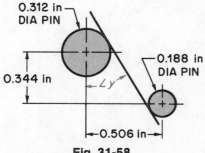

Fig. 31-58

13. A section of a park in the shape shown in figure 31-59, is designed as a botanical garden.

    a. Determine ∠1.

    b. Determine ∠2.

    c. Determine distance AB.

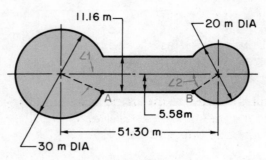

Fig. 31-59

14. A curved driveway is shown in figure 31-60. Compute ∠y.

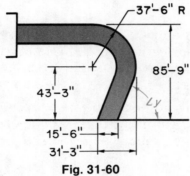

Fig. 31-60

15. Compute hole location check dimension x shown in the piece in figure 31-61.

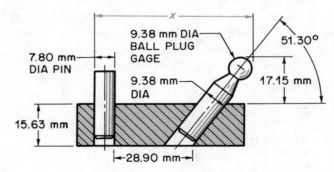

Fig. 31-61

UNIT EXERCISE AND PROBLEM REVIEW

Exercise 31-4

PROBLEMS STATED IN WORD FORM

Sketch and label each of these problems. Compute unknown linear values to 2 decimal places unless otherwise noted, English angular values to the nearer minute, and metric angular values to the nearer hundredth of a degree.

1. A piece of sheet metal is sheared in the shape of a right triangle. The hypotenuse measures 17.48 inches and one of the acute angles measures 37°30′. What is the length of the side opposite the 37°30′ angle?

2. A road rises uniformly along a horizontal distance of 450 metres. The rise at the end of the 450 metres is 95 metres.

   a. What is the measure of the angle that the road makes with the horizontal?

   b. What is the length of the road? Compute the answer to the nearer whole metre.

3. A surveyor wishes to determine the height of a tower. The transit is positioned at a distance of 200 feet from the foot of the tower. An angle of elevation of 46°50′ is read in sighting the top of the tower. The height from the ground to the transit telescope is 5′-6″. What is the height of the tower?

4. A force of 260 pounds pushes vertically downward on an object. A second force of 400 pounds pulls horizontally to the right of the object. Compute the force and the direction of the resultant vector. Compute the force to the nearer pound.

5. What is the instantaneous value (e) of an alternating emf when it has reached 45° of its cycle? The maximum value (E_{max}) is 400 volts.

6. A machinist drills three holes in a plate as follows: The first hole is drilled 20 millimetres from the left edge of the plate. The second hole is located and drilled at a distance of 58 millimetres from the left edge of the plate, directly to the right of the first hole. The third hole is located and drilled at a distance of 75 millimetres from the second hole, directly above the second hole. Compute the two acute angles of the triangle made by line segments connecting the centers of the 3 holes.

7. The horizontal distance between two points which are located at different elevations is to be determined. A surveyor positions the transit at a point which is 24.50 metres lower than the second point. The height from the ground to the transit telescope is 1.8 metres. The second point is sighted and 42.6° angle of elevation is read. What is the horizontal distance between the two points?

8. A surveyor wishes to determine the distance between two horizontal points on a flat piece of land. The two points, A and B, are separated by an obstruction and cannot be directly measured. The surveyor does the following:

   From point A, point B is sighted, then the transit telescope is turned 90°. Along the 90° sighting, a distance of 150 feet is measured and a stake is driven at the 150 foot distance (point C). From point C, the surveyor points the transit telescope back to point A. The telescope is then turned to point B and an angle of 57° is read on the horizontal protractor.

   Compute the distance between point A and point B.

PROBLEMS WHICH REQUIRE AUXILIARY LINES

Each of these problems requires forming a right triangle by projecting auxiliary lines. Compute linear values to 2 decimal places unless otherwise noted, English angular values to the nearer minute, and metric angular values to the nearer hundredth of a degree.

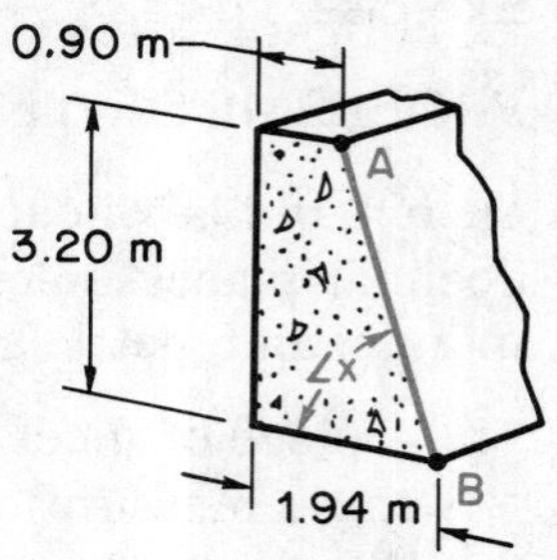

9. Compute ∠x and the length of edge AB of the retaining wall shown in figure 31-62.

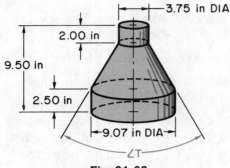

Fig. 31-62

10. Compute ∠T of the sheet metal reducer shown in figure 31-63.

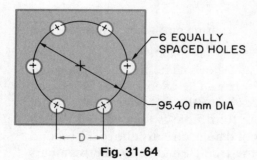

Fig. 31-63

11. Compute the distance across centers, dimension *D*, of the holes in the locating plate shown in figure 31-64.

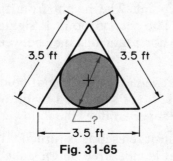

Fig. 31-64

12. What is the diameter of the largest circular piece that can be cut from the triangular sheet of plywood shown in figure 31-65?

Fig. 31-65

13. Compute check dimension x of the external half of a dovetail slide shown in figure 31-66. Compute the answer to 3 decimal places.

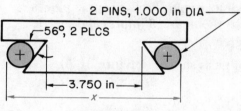

Fig. 31-66

14. A patio is to be constructed as shown in figure 31-67. Compute the straight line distance between point A and point B.

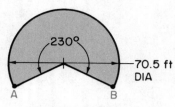

Fig. 31-67

15. A platform is laid out as shown in figure 31-68. Compute $\angle x$.

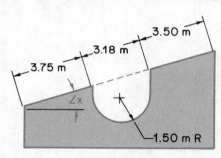

Fig. 31-68

16. A positioning fixture is shown in figure 31-69. Compute distance y.

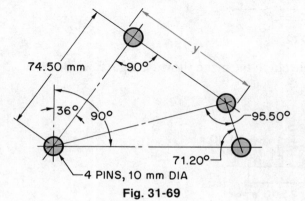

Fig. 31-69

MORE COMPLEX PROBLEMS WHICH REQUIRE AUXILIARY LINES

In the solution, each of these problems require forming two or more right triangles by projecting auxiliary lines. Compute linear values to 2 decimal places unless otherwise noted, English angular values to the nearer minute, and metric angular values to the nearer hundredth of a degree.

17. Compute the length of piece AB of the roof truss shown in figure 31-70.

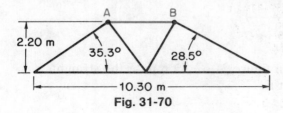

Fig. 31-70

18. Determine ∠x of the pattern shown in figure 31-71.

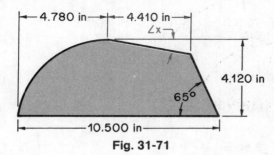

Fig. 31-71

19. A section of a road is laid out as shown in figure 31-72. Compute ∠y.

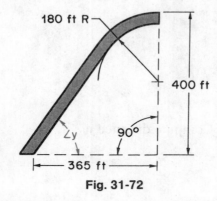

Fig. 31-72

20. Compute check dimension x of the angle cut in the piece shown in figure 31-73.

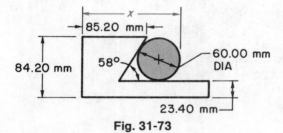

Fig. 31-73

21. A wall is to be constructed along distance *d* in the courtyard shown in figure 31-74. Compute the length of the wall.

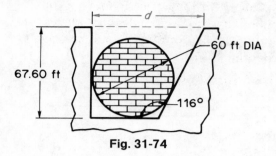

Fig. 31-74

22. Compute ∠*x* of the gage shown in figure 31-75.

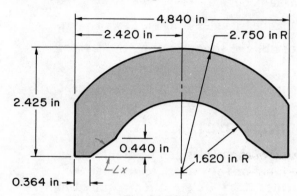

Fig. 31-75

UNIT 32
Law of Sines and Law of Cosines

OBJECTIVES

After studying this unit you should be able to

- determine functions of angles in any quadrant.

- determine functions of angles greater than 360°.

- compute unknown angles and sides of oblique triangles using the Law of Sines.

- compute unknown angles and sides of oblique triangles using the Law of Cosines.

- solve applied problems by using principles of right and oblique triangles.

CARTESIAN (RECTANGULAR) COORDINATE SYSTEM

In a triangle that is not a right triangle, one of the angles can be greater than 90°. It is sometimes necessary to determine functions of angles greater than 90°. Computations using functions of angles greater than 90° are often required in solving obtuse triangle problems. In the fields of electricity and electronics, functions of angles greater than 90° are used when solving certain problems in alternating current.

A function of any angle is described by the Cartesian Coordinate System shown in figure 32-1. A fixed point (O) called the *origin* is located at the intersection of a vertical and a horizontal axis. The horizontal axis is the *x*-axis and the vertical axis is the *y*-axis. The *x* and *y* axes divide a plane into four parts which are called *quadrants*. Quadrant I is the upper right section. Quadrants II, III, and IV are located going in a counterclockwise direction from Quadrant I.

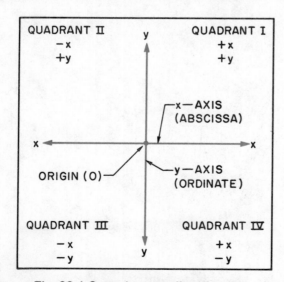

Fig. 32-1 Cartesian coordinate system

All points located to the right of the *y*-axis have positive (+) *x* values; all points to the left of the *y*-axis have negative (−) *x* values. All points above the *x*-axis have positive (+) *y* values; all points below the *x*-axis have negative (−) *y* values. The *x* value is called the abscissa and the *y* value is called the ordinate.

The *x* and *y* values for each quadrant are listed.

QUADRANT I	QUADRANT II	QUADRANT III	QUADRANT IV
+x	−x	−x	+x
+y	+y	−y	−y

DETERMINING FUNCTIONS OF ANGLES IN ANY QUADRANT

As a ray is rotated through any of the four quadrants, functions of an angle are determined as follows:

- The ray is rotated in a counterclockwise direction with its vertex at the origin (O). Zero degrees is on the *x*-axis.

- From a point on the rotated ray, a line segment is projected perpendicular to the *x*-axis. A right triangle is formed of which the rotated side (ray) is the hypotenuse, the projected line segment is the opposite side, and the side on the *x*-axis is the adjacent side. The *reference angle* is the acute angle of the triangle which has the vertex at the origin (O).

- The sign of the functions of a reference angle is determined by noting the signs (+ or −) of the opposite and adjacent sides of the right triangle. The hypotenuse (*r*) is always positive in all four quadrants.

These examples illustrate the method of determining functions of angles greater than 90° in the various quadrants.

Example 1.   Determine the sine and cosine functions of 120°. Refer to figure 32-2.

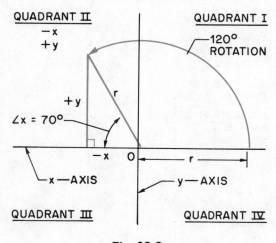

Fig. 32-2

With the endpoint of the ray (*r*) at the origin (O), the ray is rotated 120° in a counterclockwise direction.

From a point on r, side y is projected perpendicular to the x-axis. In the right triangle formed, in relation to the reference angle ($\angle x$), r is the hypotenuse, y is the opposite side, and x is the adjacent side.

$$\angle x = 180° - 120° = 70°$$

Sin $\angle x = \frac{\text{opposite side}}{\text{hypotenuse}}$. In Quadrant II, y is positive and r is always positive. Therefore, $\sin \angle x = \frac{+y}{+r}$. In Quadrant II, the sine is a positive ($+$) function.

$$\text{Sin } 120° = \sin (180° - 120°) = \sin 70° = \mathbf{0.939\ 69}\ \textit{Ans}$$

Cos $\angle x = \frac{\text{adjacent side}}{\text{hypotenuse}}$. Side x is negative ($-$), therefore, $\cos \angle x = \frac{-x}{+r}$. Since the quotient of a negative value divided by a positive value is negative, in Quadrant II, the cosine is a negative ($-$) function.

$$\text{Cos } 120° = -\cos (180° - 120°) = -\cos 70°$$

Look up the cosine of $70°$ in the function table and prefix a negative sign.

$$\cos 70° = 0.342\ 02$$
$$-\cos 70° = -0.342\ 02$$
$$\cos 120° = -\cos 70° = \mathbf{-0.342\ 02}\ \textit{Ans}$$

NOTE: A negative function of an angle does <u>not</u> mean that the angle is negative; it is a negative function of a positive angle. For example, $-\cos 70°$ does <u>not</u> mean $\cos (-70°)$.

Example 2.   Determine the tangent and secant functions of $220°$. Refer to figure 32-3.

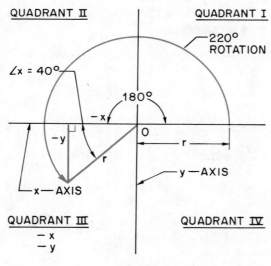

Fig. 32-3

Rotate r $220°$ in a counterclockwise direction.

From a point on r, project side y perpendicular to the x-axis.

$$\angle x = 220° - 180° = 40°$$

Tan $\angle x = \frac{\text{opposite side}}{\text{adjacent side}}$. In Quadrant III, y is negative and x is negative. Therefore, $\tan \angle x = \frac{-y}{-x}$. Since the quotient of a negative value divided by a negative value is positive, in Quadrant III, the tangent is a positive ($+$) function.

$$\text{Tan } 220° = \tan (220° - 180°) = \tan 40° = \mathbf{0.839\ 10}\ \textit{Ans}$$

Sec $\angle x = \frac{\text{hypotenuse}}{\text{adjacent side}}$. In Quadrant III, x is negative and r is always positive. Therefore, sec $\angle x = \frac{+r}{-x}$. Since the quotient of a positive value divided by a negative value is negative, in Quadrant III, the secant is a negative $(-)$ function.

Sec $220° = -\sec(220° - 180°) = -\sec 40° = $ **−1.305 4** *Ans*

Example 3.   Determine the cotangent and cosecant functions of 305°. Refer to figure 32-4.

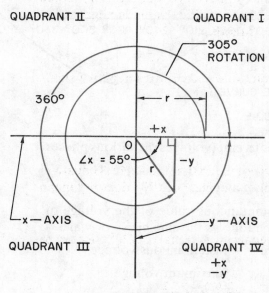

Fig. 32-4

Rotate r 305° in a counterclockwise direction. From a point on r, project side y perpendicular to the x-axis.

$\angle x = 360° - 305° = 55°$

cot $\angle x = \frac{\text{adjacent side}}{\text{opposite side}}$. In Quadrant IV, y is negative and x is positive. Therefore, cot $\angle x = \frac{+x}{-y}$. Since the quotient of a positive value divided by a negative value is negative, in Quadrant IV, the cotangent is a negative $(-)$ function.

Cot $305° = -\cot(360° - 305°) = -\cot 55° = $ **−0.700 21** *Ans*

Csc $\angle x = \frac{\text{hypotenuse}}{\text{opposite side}}$. In Quadrant IV, y is negative and r is always positive. Therefore, csc $\angle x = \frac{+r}{-y}$. The cosecant is a negative $(-)$ function.

Csc $305° = -\csc(360° - 305°) = -\csc 55° = $ **−1.220 8** *Ans*

ALTERNATING CURRENT APPLICATIONS

An electric current which flows back and forth at regular intervals in a circuit is called an alternating current. The current and voltage each rise from zero to a maximum value and return to zero; then current and voltage increase to a maximum in the opposite direction and return to zero. This process is called a cycle.

The cycle is divided into 360 degrees. Current and electromotive force (voltage) are continuously changing during the cycle, therefore, their values must be stated at a given instant. A curve, such as the one shown in figure 32-5, is called a sine curve. This curve generally approximates the curves of electromotive force (emf) values of most alternating current generators.

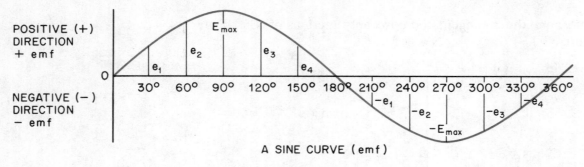

A SINE CURVE (emf)

Fig. 32-5

NOTE: e_1 through $-e_4$ represent instantaneous emf (voltages) at various phases in a cycle.

E_{max} represents the maximum emf (voltage) of a cycle.

This is the formula for computing the instantaneous value of the voltage of an alternating circuit current when the voltage follows the sine curve or wave.

$$e = E_{max} \text{ sine } \theta$$

where e = instantaneous voltage

E_{max} = maximum voltage

θ = angle in degrees

NOTE: θ is a Greek letter called theta.

Since the cycle is divided into 360°, θ may be any angle from 0° to 360°. Therefore, the sine function of θ may be either positive (+) or negative (−) depending on which of the 4 quadrants θ lies in when determining voltage at a certain instant.

Refer to the Cartesian Coordinate System shown in figure 32-6. Observe that the sine function is positive (+) for the range of angles greater than 0° and less than 180°. The sine function is negative (−) for the range of angles greater than 180° and less than 360°. These positive and negative sine functions compare directly to the positive and negative signs of the instantaneous voltages (+e and −e) from 0° to 360° in the sine curve shown in figure 32-5.

In the formula e = E_{max} sin θ, sin θ is computed using the procedure given for determining functions of angles in any of the four quadrants.

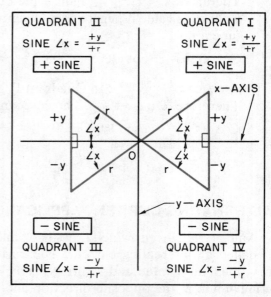

Fig. 32-6

Example 1.   What is the instantaneous voltage (e) of an alternating emf when it has reached 160° of the cycle? The maximum voltage (E_{max}) is 600 volts.

Compute $\sin \theta$:

$\sin 160° = \sin(180° - 160°) = \sin 20° = 0.342\ 02$

Compute e:

$e = E_{max} \sin \theta = 600\ \text{V}(0.342\ 02) = $ **205.2 V** *Ans*

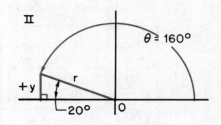

Example 2.   What is the instantaneous voltage (e) of an alternating emf when it has reached 320° of the cycle? The maximum voltage (E_{max}) is 550 volts.

Compute $\sin \theta$:

$\sin 320° = -\sin(360° - 320°) = -\sin 40° = -0.642\ 79$

Compute e:

$e = E_{max} \sin \theta = 550\ \text{V}(-0.642\ 79) = $ **−353.5 V** *Ans*

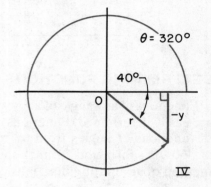

Exercise 32-1

Determine the sine, cosine, tangent, cotangent, secant, and cosecant for each of these angles. For each angle, sketch a right triangle similar to those shown in figures 32-2, 32-3 and 32-4. Label the sides of the triangles + or −. Determine the reference angles and look up the functions of the angles. Keep in mind that a function of an angle greater than 90° may be a negative value.

1. 125°
2. 207°
3. 260°
4. 168°
5. 300°
6. 350°

7. 216°20′
8. 96°50′
9. 146°10′
10. 202.6°
11. 313.2°
12. 179.9°

Compute the instantaneous voltage (e), in volts, of an alternating electromotive force (emf) for each of these problems. Compute the answer to 1 decimal place.

	NUMBER OF DEGREES REACHED IN CYCLE (θ)	MAXIMUM VOLTAGE (E_{max})	INSTANTANEOUS VOLTAGE (e)
13.	120°	600 volts	
14.	165°	320 volts	
15.	210°	240 volts	
16.	255°	550 volts	
17.	300°	120 volts	
18.	330°	800 volts	
19.	90°	300 volts	
20.	180°	240 volts	
21.	270°	550 volts	
22.	360°	600 volts	

DETERMINING FUNCTIONS OF ANGLES GREATER THAN 360°

Functions of any angle of a ray which is rotated more than 360° or one revolution are easily determined. Functions of an angle greater than 360° are computed just as functions of angles from 0° to 360° are computed after 360° or a multiple of 360° is subtracted from the given angle. These two examples illustrate the method of computing functions of angles greater than 360°.

Example 1.   Determine the tangent of 472°.

Subtract one complete revolution.

Tan 472° = tan (472° − 360°) = tan 112°

Ray *r* is rotated one complete revolution plus an additional 112°. Reference ∠x lies in Quadrant II as shown in Figure 32-7.

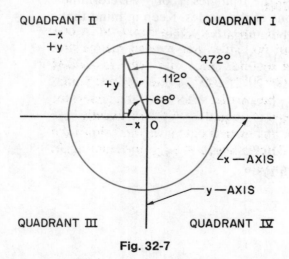

Fig. 32-7

In Quadrant II, tan ∠$x = \frac{+y}{-x}$, therefore, the tangent function is negative (−).

Tan 112° = −tan (180° − 112°) = −tan 68° = −2.475 1.

Tan 472° = −2.475 1 *Ans*

Example 2.   Determine the cosine of 1 055°.

Divide by 360° to find the number of complete rotations.

1 055° ÷ 360° = 2 complete revolutions plus 335°

Cos 1 055° = cos [1 055° − 2(360°)] = cos 335°

Ray r is rotated 2 complete revolutions plus an additional 335°. Reference $\angle x$ lies in Quadrant IV as shown in Figure 32-8. In Quadrant IV, cos $\angle x = \frac{+x}{+r}$, therefore, the cosine function is positive (+).

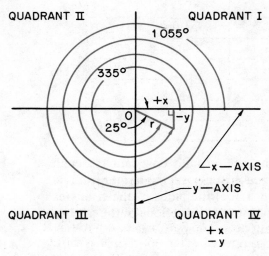

Fig. 32-8

Cos 335° = cos (360° − 335°) = cos 25° = 0.906 31

Cos 1 055° = **0.906 31** *Ans*

ALTERNATING CURRENT APPLICATIONS

The frequency of current is the number of times a cycle is repeated in one second of time. The standard frequency of 60 cycles per second means that the current makes 60 complete cycles in a second. Since one cycle is divided into 360°, the current goes through 60 × 360° or 21 600° in one second. Stated in terms of an alternating current generator, the angular velocity of the generator is 21 600° per second. The angle in degrees (θ) equal 21 600° at exactly one second in time. Therefore, the value of θ at any instant equals 21 600° times the number of seconds at that instant. After θ is determined, e = E_{max} sin θ, may again be used to compute an instantaneous voltage (e).

Example.   In a 60 cycle alternating emf the angular velocity is 21 600° per second. What is the instantaneous voltage (e) at the end of exactly 0.03 seconds? The maximum voltage (E_{max}) is 120 volts.

Compute θ:

$\theta = (21\ 600°/s)(0.03\ s) = 648°$

Subtract one complete revolution from 648°.

$\text{Sin } 648° = \sin (648° - 360°) = \sin 288°$

Compute sin 288°:

$\sin 288° = -\sin (360° - 288°) = -\sin 72° = -0.951\ 06$

$\sin \theta = -0.951\ 06$

Compute e:

$e = (120\ V)(-0.951\ 06) = -114.1\ \text{volts } Ans$

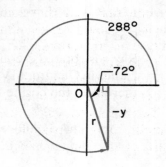

Exercise 32-2

Determine the sine, cosine, tangent, cotangent, secant, and cosecant for each of these angles which are greater than 360°. For each angle, sketch a right triangle similar to those shown in figures 32-7 and 32-8. Label the sides of the triangles + or −. Determine the reference angles and look up the functions of the angles. Remember that a function may be either a positive or a negative value.

1. 510°
2. 405°
3. 555°
4. 680°
5. 531°

6. 743°
7. 937°
8. 1 036°30′
9. 1 248.4°
10. 1 440°

Each of these problems has a 60 cycle alternating electromotive force (emf); the angular velocity is 21 600° per second. Compute the instantaneous voltage (e), in volts, for each problem. Compute the answer to 1 decimal place.

	TIME	MAXIMUM VOLTAGE (E_{max})	INSTANTANEOUS VOLTAGE (e)
11.	0.02 second	240 volts	
12.	0.016 second	550 volts	
13.	0.03 second	320 volts	
14.	0.027 second	600 volts	
15.	0.035 second	120 volts	
16.	0.01 second	300 volts	
17.	0.022 second	800 volts	
18.	0.08 second	240 volts	
19.	0.04 second	600 volts	
20.	0.096 second	550 volts	

SOLVING OBLIQUE TRIANGLES

An *oblique triangle* is a triangle that does not have a right angle. An oblique triangle may be either acute or obtuse. In an acute triangle, each of the three angles is acute or less than 90°. In an obtuse triangle, one of the angles is obtuse or greater than 90°.

Angles and sides must be computed in practical problems which involve oblique triangles. These problems can be solved as a series of right triangles, but the process is time consuming.

Two formulas, called the Law of Sines and the Law of Cosines, are used to simplify oblique triangle computations. In order to use either formula, three parts of an oblique triangle must be known and at least one part must be a side.

LAW OF SINES

In any triangle the sides of a triangle are proportional to the sines of their opposite angles.

In reference to the triangle shown in figure 32-9,

$$\frac{a}{\sin A} = \frac{b}{\sin B} = \frac{c}{\sin C}$$

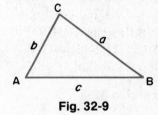

Fig. 32-9

The Law of Sines is used to solve these two kinds of oblique triangle problems.

- Problems where any two angles and any side of an oblique triangle are known.

- Problems where any two sides and an angle opposite one of the given sides of an oblique triangle are known.

NOTE: Since an angle of an oblique triangle may be greater than 90°, you must often determine the sine of an angle greater than 90° and less than 180°. Recall that the angle lies in Quadrant II of the Cartesian Coordinate System. The sine of an angle between 90° and 180° equals the sine of the supplement of the angle. For example, the sine of 120°40′ = sin (180° − 120°40′) = sin 59°20′ = 0.860 15.

SOLVING PROBLEMS GIVEN TWO ANGLES AND A SIDE USING THE LAW OF SINES

Example 1. Given two angles and a side, determine side x of the oblique triangle shown in figure 32-10.

Since side x is opposite the 39° angle and the 5.700-inch side is opposite the 62° angle, the proportion is set up as: $\frac{x}{\sin 39°} = \frac{5.700}{\sin 62°}$

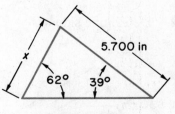

Fig. 32-10

Look up the sines of 39° and 62° and solve:

$$\frac{x}{0.629\ 32} = \frac{5.700}{0.882\ 95}$$

$$0.882\ 95x = 3.587\ 12$$

$$x = \textbf{4.063 in } Ans$$

Example 2.   Given two angles and a side, determine ∠A, side *a*, and
side *b* of the oblique triangle shown in figure 32-11.

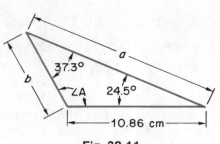

Fig. 32-11

Solve for ∠A: The sum of the three angles of a triangle equals 180°.
∠A = 180° − (37.3° + 24.5°) = **118.2°** *Ans*

Solve for side *a*:

Sin 118.2° = sin (180° − 118.2°) = sin 61.8° = 0.881 3

$$\frac{a}{\sin 118.2°} = \frac{10.86}{\sin 37.3°}$$

$$\frac{a}{0.881\ 3} = \frac{10.86}{0.606\ 0}$$

$$0.606\ 0a = 9.570\ 9$$

$$a = \textbf{15.79 cm } \textit{Ans}$$

Solve for side *b*:

$$\frac{b}{\sin 24.5°} = \frac{10.86}{\sin 37.3°}$$

$$\frac{b}{0.414\ 7} = \frac{10.86}{0.606\ 0}$$

$$0.606\ 0b = 4.503\ 6$$

$$b = \textbf{7.43 cm } \textit{Ans}$$

Exercise 32-3

In each of these problems, two angles and a side are given. Determine the required values. Compute side lengths to 3 decimal places.

1. Determine side *x*.

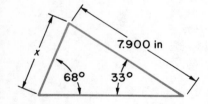

3. Determine side *d*.

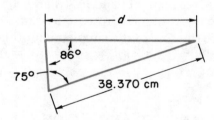

5. Determine side *b*.

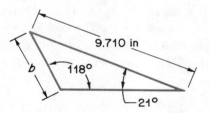

2. Determine side *a*.

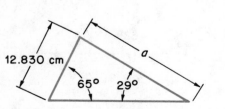

4. Determine side *y*.

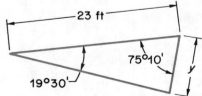

6. Determine side *c*.

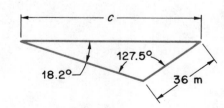

7. a. Determine ∠A.
    b. Determine side *a*.

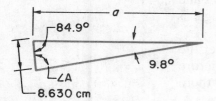

9. a. Determine ∠A.
    b. Determine side *a*.

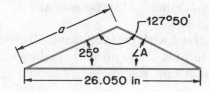

11. a. Determine ∠A.
     b. Determine side *a*.
     c. Determine side *b*.

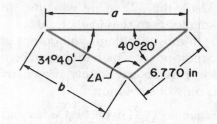

8. a. Determine ∠C.
    b. Determine side *c*.

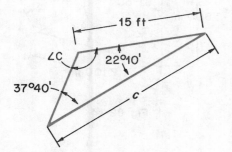

10. a. Determine ∠D.
     b. Determine side *d*.
     c. Determine side *e*.

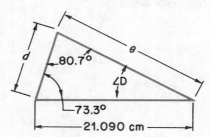

12. a. Determine ∠E.
     b. Determine side *f*.
     c. Determine side *g*.

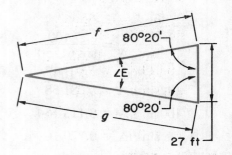

SOLVING PROBLEMS GIVEN TWO SIDES AND AN ANGLE OPPOSITE ONE OF THE GIVEN SIDES USING THE LAW OF SINES

A special condition exists when solving certain problems in which two sides and an angle opposite one of the sides is given. If triangle data are given in word form or if a triangle is inaccurately sketched, there may be two solutions to a problem.

It is possible to have two different triangles with the same two sides and the same angle opposite one of the given sides. A situation of this kind is called an ambiguous case. The following example illustrates the ambiguous case or a problem with two solutions.

Example (the Ambiguous Case or 2 solutions). A triangle has a 1.5 inch side, a 2.5 inch side and an angle of 32° which is opposite the 1.5 inch side. Using the given data, figure 32-12 is accurately drawn. Observe that two different triangles are constructed using identical given data. Both triangle BCA and triangle DCA have a 1.5 inch side, a 2.5 inch side, and a 32° angle opposite the 1.5 inch side. The triangles are shown separately in figure 32-13.

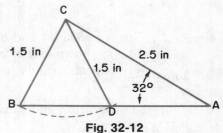

Fig. 32-12

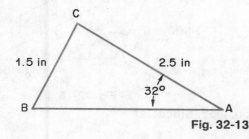
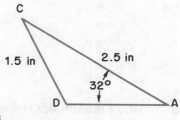

Fig. 32-13

The only conditions under which a problem can have two solutions is when the given angle is acute and the given side opposite the given angle is smaller than the other given side. For example, in the problem illustrated by figures 32-12 and 32-13, the 32° angle is acute, and the 1.5-inch side opposite the 32° angle is smaller than the 2.5-inch side.

In most problems you do not get involved with two solutions. Even under the conditions in which there can be two solutions, if the problem is shown in picture form as an accurately drawn triangle, it can readily be observed that there is only one solution.

Example 1.   Given two sides and an angle opposite one of the given sides, determine ∠A, ∠C, and side c of the oblique triangle shown in figure 32-14.

The 7.100-inch side opposite the 61°50′ angle is larger than the 5.800-inch side, therefore there is only one solution.

Solve for ∠A:

$$\frac{5.800}{\sin \angle A} = \frac{7.100}{\sin 61°50′}$$

$$\frac{5.800}{\sin \angle A} = \frac{7.100}{0.881\ 58}$$

$$7.100\sin \angle A = 5.113\ 16$$

$$\sin \angle A = 0.720\ 16$$

$$\angle A = 46°4′\ \textit{Ans}$$

Solve for ∠C:

$$\angle C = 180° - (61°50′ + 46°4′) = 72°6′\ \textit{Ans}$$

Solve for side c:

$$\frac{c}{\sin 72°6′} = \frac{7.100}{\sin 61°50′}$$

$$\frac{c}{0.951\ 59} = \frac{7.100}{0.881\ 58}$$

$$0.881\ 58c = 6.756\ 29$$

$$c = 7.664\ \text{in}\ \textit{Ans}$$

Fig. 32-14

Example 2.   Given two sides and an angle opposite one of the given sides as shown in figure 32-15, determine ∠D. Figure 32-15 is drawn accurately to scale. Observe that ∠D is greater than 90°.

Set up the proportion and solve:

$$\frac{6.870}{\sin \angle D} = \frac{3.500}{\sin 27.6°}$$

$$\frac{6.870}{\sin \angle D} = \frac{3.500}{0.463\ 3}$$

$$3.500\sin \angle D = 3.182\ 87$$

$$\sin \angle D = 0.909\ 4$$

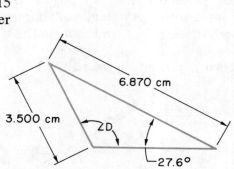

Fig. 32-15

The angle that corresponds to the sine function 0.909 4 is 65.43°. Since ∠D is greater than 90°, ∠D is the supplement of 65.43°.

$$\angle D = 180° - 65.43° = 114.57°\ \textit{Ans}$$

Exercise 32-4

Two sides and an angle opposite one of the sides of triangles are given in these problems. Identify each problem as to whether it has one or two solutions. <u>Do not</u> solve the problems for angles and sides.

1. A 3″ side, a 5″ side, a 37° angle opposite the 3″ side.

2. A 9.5-cm side, a 9.8-cm side, a 75° angle opposite the 9.5-cm side.

3. A 21-m side, a 29-m side, a 41° angle opposite the 29-m side.

4. A 0.943″ side, a 1.612″ side, and a 82°15′ angle opposite the 1.612″ side.

5. A 210-ft side, a 305-ft side, a 29°30′ angle opposite the 305-ft side.

6. A 16.35-cm side, a 23.86-cm side, a 115° angle opposite the 23.86-cm side.

7. An 87.6-m side, a 124.8-m side, a 12.9° angle opposite the 87.6-m side.

8. A 33.86″ side, a 34.09″ side, a 46°18′ angle opposite the 33.86″ side.

In each of these problems, two sides and an angle opposite one of the sides are given. Compute side lengths to 3 decimal places, English angular values to the nearer minute, and metric angular values to the nearer hundredth of a degree. The triangles are drawn accurately to scale.

9. Determine ∠A.

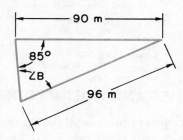

11. Determine ∠B.

13. Determine ∠A.

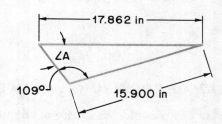

10. Determine ∠E.

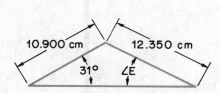

12. Determine ∠C.

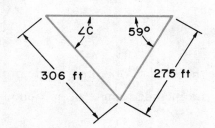

14. Determine ∠D.

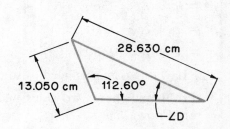

15. a. Determine ∠A.
    b. Determine ∠B.

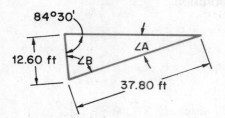

17. a. Determine ∠A.
    b. Determine ∠B.

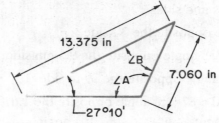

19. a. Determine ∠A.
    b. Determine ∠B.
    c. Determine side b.

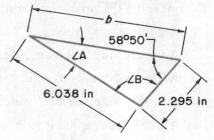

16. a. Determine ∠D.
    b. Determine ∠E.

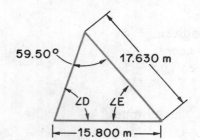

18. a. Determine ∠C.
    b. Determine ∠D.
    c. Determine side d.

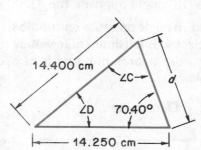

20. a. Determine ∠E.
    b. Determine ∠F.
    c. Determine side f.

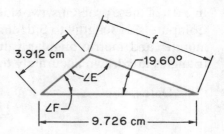

LAW OF COSINES (GIVEN TWO SIDES AND THE INCLUDED ANGLE)

In any triangle, the square of any side is equal to the sum of the squares of the other two sides minus twice the product of these two sides multiplied by the cosine of their included angle.

In reference to the triangle shown in figure 32-16,

$$a^2 = b^2 + c^2 - 2bc(\cos A)$$
$$b^2 = a^2 + c^2 - 2ac(\cos B)$$
$$c^2 = a^2 + b^2 - 2ab(\cos C)$$

The Law of Cosines is used to solve this kind of oblique triangle problem.

• Problems where two sides and the included angle of an oblique triangle are known.

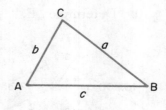

Fig. 32-16

NOTE: An angle of an oblique triangle may be greater than 90°. Therefore, you must often determine the cosine of an angle greater than 90° and less than 180°. These angles lie in Quadrant II of the Cartesian Coordinate System. Recall that the cosine of an angle between 90° and 180° equals the negative (−) cosine of the supplement of the angle. For example, the cosine of 118°10′ = −cos (180° − 118°10′) = −cos 61°50′ = −0.472 04.

SOLVING PROBLEMS GIVEN TWO SIDES AND THE INCLUDED ANGLE USING THE LAW OF COSINES

Example 1. Given two sides and the included angle, determine side x of the oblique triangle shown in figure 32-17. Observe that 34.6° is included between the 8.700-cm and 9.100-cm sides.

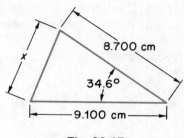

Fig. 32-17

Substitute the given values in their appropriate places in the formula and solve for side x:

$x^2 = 8.700^2 + 9.100^2 - 2(8.700)(9.100)(\cos 34.6°)$

$x^2 = 75.690 + 82.810 - 2(8.700)(9.100)(0.823\ 1)$

$x^2 = 158.500 - 130.330$

$x^2 = 28.170$

$x = \textbf{5.308 cm } Ans$

Example 2. Given two sides and the included angle, determine side a, $\angle$B, and $\angle$C of the oblique triangle shown in figure 32-18.

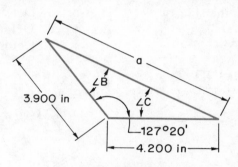

Fig. 32-18

Solve for a using the Law of Cosines:

$\text{Cos } 127°20' = -\cos (180° - 127°20') = -\cos 52°40' = -0.606\ 45$

$a^2 = 3.900^2 + 4.200^2 - 2(3.900)(4.200)(\cos 127°20')$

$a^2 = 15.210 + 17.640 - 2(3.900)(4.200)(-0.606\ 45)$

$a^2 = 32.850 - (-19.867)$

$a^2 = 52.717$

$a = \textbf{7.261 in } Ans$

Solve for $\angle$B using the Law of Sines:

$\text{Sin } 127°20' = \sin (180° - 127°20') = \sin 52°40' = 0.795\ 12$

$$\frac{4.200}{\sin \angle B} = \frac{7.261}{\sin 127°20'}$$

$$\frac{4.200}{\sin \angle B} = \frac{7.261}{0.795\ 12}$$

$7.261\sin \angle B = 3.339\ 5$

$\sin \angle B = 0.459\ 92$

$\angle B = \textbf{27°23' } Ans$

Solve for $\angle$C:

$\angle C = 180° - (127°20' + 27°23') = \textbf{25°17' } Ans$

Exercise 32-5

In each of these problems, two sides and the included angle of a triangle are given. Compute side lengths to 3 decimal places, English angular values to the nearer minute, and metric angular values to the nearer hundredth of a degree.

1. Determine side x.

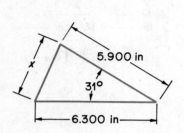

2. Determine side a.

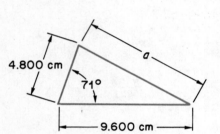

3. Determine side b.

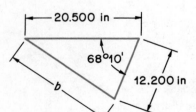

4. Determine side y.

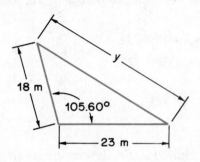

5. Determine side x.

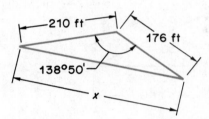

6. Determine side c.

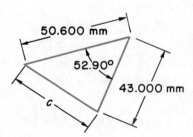

7. a. Determine side c.
    b. Determine $\angle A$.
    c. Determine $\angle B$.

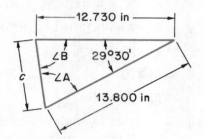

8. a. Determine side e.
    b. Determine $\angle F$.
    c. Determine $\angle G$.

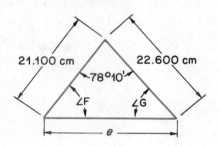

9. a. Determine side c.
    b. Determine $\angle B$.
    c. Determine $\angle C$.

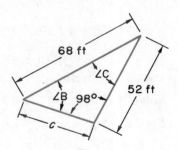

10. a. Determine side *n*.
     b. Determine ∠M.
     c. Determine ∠P.

11. a. Determine side *a*.
     b. Determine ∠B.
     c. Determine ∠C.

12. a. Determine side *c*.
     b. Determine ∠D.
     c. Determine ∠E.

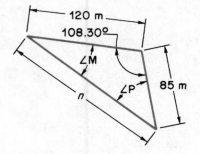

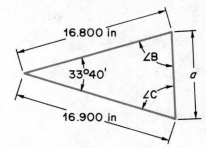

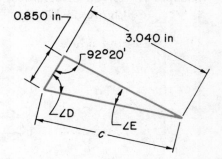

LAW OF COSINES (GIVEN THREE SIDES)

   In any triangle, the cosine of an angle is equal to the sum of the squares of the two adjacent sides minus the square of the opposite side, divided by twice the product of the two adjacent sides.

   In reference to the triangle shown in figure 32-19,

$$\cos A = \frac{b^2 + c^2 - a^2}{2bc}$$

$$\cos B = \frac{a^2 + c^2 - b^2}{2ac}$$

$$\cos C = \frac{a^2 + b^2 - c^2}{2ab}$$

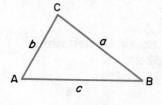

Fig. 32-19

The Law of Cosines is used to solve this kind of oblique triangle problem.

• Problems where three sides of an oblique triangle are known.

NOTE: When solving for an unknown angle, the cosine function of the angle may be a negative value. A negative cosine function means that the angle being computed is greater than 90°. Look up the positive cosine function in the trigonometric function table and find its corresponding angle. The angle to be determined is equal to the supplement of the angle found in the table. For example, if the cosine of an angle is computed as −0.844 95, look up the cosine of 0.844 95. The corresponding angle is 32°20′. Compute the supplement of 32°20′; 180° − 32°20′ = 147°40′. The angle whose cosine is −0.844 95 is 147°40′.

SOLVING PROBLEMS GIVEN THREE SIDES USING THE LAW OF COSINES

Example 1. Given three sides, determine ∠A of the oblique triangle shown in figure 32-20.

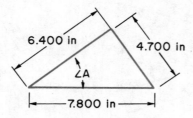

6.400 in   4.700 in
∠A
7.800 in

Fig. 32-20

$$\cos \angle A = \frac{6.400^2 + 7.800^2 - 4.700^2}{2(6.400)(7.800)}$$

$$\cos \angle A = \frac{40.960 + 60.840 - 22.090}{99.840}$$

$$\cos \angle A = \frac{79.710}{99.840}$$

$$\cos \angle A = 0.798\ 38$$

$$\angle A = 37°1'\ Ans$$

Example 2. Given three sides, determine ∠P of the oblique triangle shown in figure 32-21.

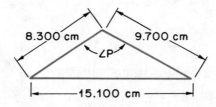

8.300 cm   9.700 cm
∠P
15.100 cm

Fig. 32-21

$$\cos \angle P = \frac{8.300^2 + 9.700^2 - 15.100^2}{2(8.300)(9.700)}$$

$$\cos \angle P = \frac{68.890 + 94.090 - 228.010}{161.020}$$

$$\cos \angle P = \frac{-65.030}{161.020}$$

$$\cos \angle P = -0.403\ 9$$

Since cos ∠P is a negative value, ∠P is equal to the supplement of the angle that corresponds to the cosine of 0.403 9. The cosine of 0.403 9 is 66.18°. Therefore, the angle whose cosine function is −0.403 9 = 180° − 66.18° = 113.82°.

$$\angle P = 113.82°\ Ans$$

Example 3.   Given three sides, determine $\angle A$, $\angle B$, and $\angle C$ of the oblique triangle shown in figure 32-22.

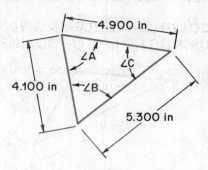

Solve for $\angle A$:

$$\cos \angle A = \frac{4.100^2 + 4.900^2 - 5.300^2}{2(4.100)(4.900)}$$

$$\cos \angle A = \frac{16.810 + 24.010 - 28.090}{40.180}$$

$$\cos \angle A = \frac{12.730}{40.180}$$

$$\cos \angle A = 0.316\ 82$$

$$\angle A = 71°32'\ Ans$$

Fig. 32-22

Solve for $\angle B$: Angle B may also be computed using the Law of Cosines formula, but it is simpler to use the Law of Sines formula. Use the Law of Sines.

$$\frac{4.900}{\sin \angle B} = \frac{5.300}{\sin \angle A}$$

$$\frac{4.900}{\sin \angle B} = \frac{5.300}{\sin 71°32'}$$

$$\frac{4.900}{\sin \angle B} = \frac{5.300}{0.948\ 51}$$

$$5.300\sin \angle B = 4.647\ 7$$

$$\sin \angle B = 0.876\ 92$$

$$\angle B = 61°16'\ Ans$$

Solve for $\angle C$:

$$\angle C = 180° - (71°32' + 61°16') = 47°12'\ Ans$$

Exercise 32-6

In each of these problems, three sides of a triangle are given. Compute English angular values to the nearer minute and metric angular values to the nearer hundredth of a degree.

1. Determine $\angle A$.   2. Determine $\angle B$.   3. Determine $\angle C$.

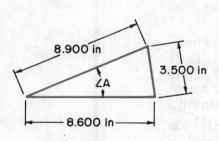

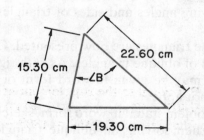

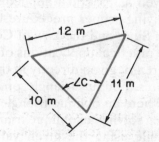

4. Determine ∠F.

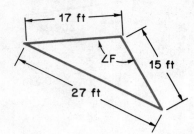

7. a. Determine ∠B.
    b. Determine ∠C.
    c. Determine ∠D.

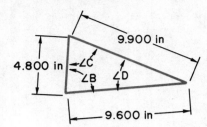

10. a. Determine ∠A.
    b. Determine ∠B.
    c. Determine ∠C.

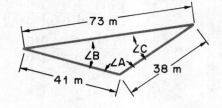

5. Determine ∠A.

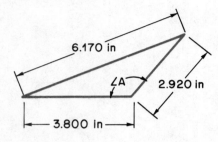

8. a. Determine ∠F.
    b. Determine ∠G.
    c. Determine ∠H.

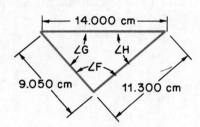

11. a. Determine ∠M.
    b. Determine ∠R.
    c. Determine ∠T.

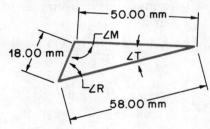

6. Determine ∠M.

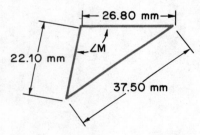

9. a. Determine ∠A.
    b. Determine ∠B.
    c. Determine ∠C.

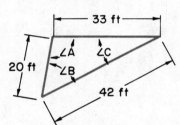

12. a. Determine ∠D.
    b. Determine ∠E.
    c. Determine ∠F.

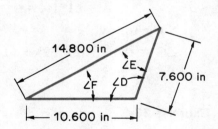

PRACTICAL APPLICATIONS OF OBLIQUE TRIGONOMETRY

The oblique triangle examples and problems which have been presented were not given as practical applied problems. They were intended to develop skills in applying proper procedures in solving angles and sides of triangles using the Law of Sines and the Law of Cosines.

The practical applications of oblique triangles are now presented. Often problems are not given directly in the form of oblique triangles. As with right triangle problems, oblique triangle problems may be given in word form or in picture form where an oblique triangle does not appear.

When solving an oblique triangle problem stated in word form, sketch and label a triangle using the given values. When solving an oblique triangle problem where an oblique triangle is not directly given, it may be necessary to project auxiliary lines to form triangles. In addition, oblique triangle problems sometimes require a combination of right triangles and oblique triangles in the solution.

These examples illustrate the methods of solving practical word type and picture type problems.

Example 1.   A metal frame in the shape of an oblique triangle is to be fabricated. One side of the frame is 2.40 metres long. One end of the second side which is 1.80 metres long is to be fastened to an end of the 2.40-metre side at an angle of 58°. Compute the required length of the third side of the frame.

Solution: Sketch and label an oblique triangle as shown in figure 32-23. Let c represent the third side.

Compute side c:

Two sides and the included angle are known. Apply the Law of Cosines.

$c^2 = 1.80^2 + 2.40^2 - 2(1.80)(2.40)(\cos 58°)$

$c^2 = 3.24 + 5.76 - 2(1.80)(2.40)(0.529\ 9)$

$c^2 = 9.00 - 4.578$

$c^2 = 4.42$

$c = 2.10\ \text{m}\ Ans$

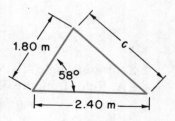

1.80 m c 58°   2.40 m

Fig. 32-23

Example 2.   A surveyor wishes to measure the distance between two horizontal points. The two points, A and B, are separated by a pond and the distance cannot be directly measured. The surveyor does the following:

On the same side of the pond as point A, a third point (point C) is measured at a distance of 150 feet toward the pond from point A. From point A, point C is sighted, then the transit telescope is turned to point B across the pond. An angle of 29°30′ is read on the transit. The surveyor moves to point C. From point C, point A is sighted, then the transit telescope is turned to point B across the pond. An angle of 138° is recorded. Determine the distance between point A and point B.

Solution: Sketch and label an oblique triangle as shown in figure 32-24. Compute AB: Two angles and a side are known. Apply the Law of Sines. Since ∠B lies opposite the known side, 150 feet, ∠B must first be determined.

∠B = 180° − (29°30′ + 138°) = 12°30′

Applying the Law of Sines, $\dfrac{AB}{\sin \angle C} = \dfrac{AC}{\sin \angle B}$

$$\frac{AB}{\sin 138°} = \frac{150}{\sin 12°30′}$$

$\sin 138° = \sin (180° - 138°) = \sin 42° = 0.669\ 13$

$$\frac{AB}{0.669\ 13} = \frac{150}{0.216\ 44}$$

$$0.216\ 44 AB = 100.369\ 5$$

$$AB = 463.73\ \text{ft}\ Ans$$

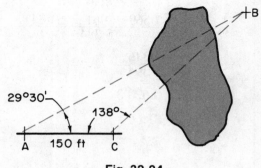

29°30′   138°   A   150 ft   C   B

Fig. 32-24

Example 3.   A piece of land is measured off as shown in figure 32-25. Sides AB and DC are parallel. Compute ∠A.

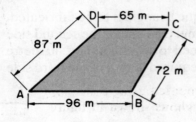

Fig. 32-25

Solution: Angle A is computed by forming an oblique triangle which contains ∠A. Refer to figure 32-26.

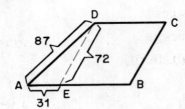

Fig. 32-26

Project line segment DE parallel to side BC. Oblique triangle AED is formed.

In triangle AED, AD = 87 m, ED = BC = 72 m
(EDCB is a parallelogram).

EB = DC = 65 m

AE = 96 m − 65 m = 31 m

Solve for ∠A: Three sides of triangle AED are known. Apply the Law of Cosines.

$$\cos \angle A = \frac{87^2 + 31^2 - 72^2}{2(87)(31)}$$

$$\cos \angle A = \frac{7\,569 + 961 - 5\,184}{5\,394}$$

$$\cos \angle A = \frac{3\,346}{5\,394}$$

$$\cos \angle A = 0.620\,3$$

$$\angle A = \mathbf{51.66°}\ Ans$$

Example 4. A metal plate is to be machined to the dimensions shown in figure 32-27. Compute dimension x.

Analyze the problem:

Refer to figure 32-28. Project an auxiliary line segment from point A to point C. Two oblique triangles are formed, $\triangle ABC$ and $\triangle ACD$.

If AC can be determined, side x can be computed using the Law of Sines, since AD, AC, and $\angle D$ would be known in $\triangle ACD$.

Determine whether enough information is given to solve for AC. In oblique $\triangle ABC$, AB = 12.300 in , BC = 8.900 in, and $\angle B = 72°$. Side AC can be computed using the Law of Cosines.

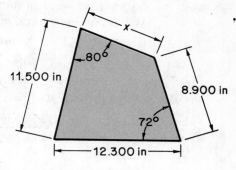

Fig. 32-27

Computations:

In $\triangle ABC$, solve for AC: Use the Law of Cosines.

$AC^2 = 12.300^2 + 8.900^2 - 2(12.300)(8.900)(\cos 72°)$

$AC^2 = 151.290 + 79.210 - 2(12.300)(8.900)(0.309\ 02)$

$AC^2 = 230.500 - 67.657$

$AC^2 = 162.843$

$AC = 12.761$ in

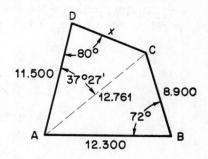

Fig. 32-28

In $\triangle ACD$ solve for dimension x: Angle ACD must first be computed using the Law of Sines.

$$\frac{AD}{\sin\angle ACD} = \frac{AC}{\sin 80°}$$

$$\frac{11.500}{\sin\angle ACD} = \frac{12.761}{0.984\ 81}$$

$12.761\sin\angle ACD = 11.325$

$\sin\angle ACD = 0.887\ 47$

$\angle ACD = 62°33'$

Compute $\angle DAC$:

$\angle DAC = 180° - (80° + 62°33') = 37°27'$

Compute dimension x: Use the Law of Sines.

$$\frac{x}{\sin 37°27'} = \frac{12.761}{\sin 80°}$$

$$\frac{x}{0.608\ 07} = \frac{12.761}{0.984\ 81}$$

$0.984\ 81x = 7.759\ 6$

$x = $ **7.879 in** *Ans*

Example 5. Two forces are pulling on a structure at point O as shown in figure 32-29. Compute the force and direction of the resultant vector.

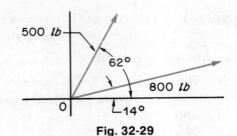

Fig. 32-29

An accurate method of solving problems of this type is by forming a parallelogram and solving for the resultant vector applying the principles of oblique trigonometry.

Form parallelogram OABC by projecting line segments parallel to the given vectors as shown in figure 32-30. The resultant vector is the line segment made by connecting points O and B.

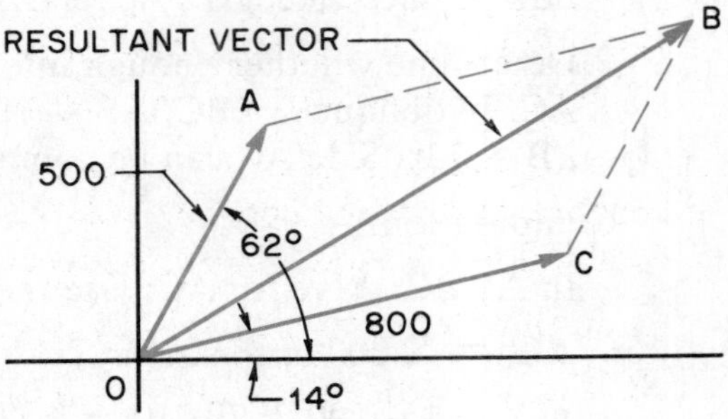

Recall that opposite sides and opposite angles of a parallelogram are equal and the sum of the 4 interior angles of a parallelogram equals $360°$. In parallelogram OABC,

$\angle AOC = \angle ABC = 62° - 14° = 48°$

$\angle OCB = \angle OAB = [360° - 2(48°)] \div 2 = 132°$

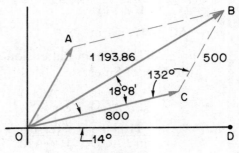

Fig. 32-30

Compute the force of resultant vector OB: (Refer to figure 32-31). In oblique $\triangle OCB$, OB is computed using the Law of Cosines.

$\cos 132° = -\cos (180° - 132°) = -\cos 48° = -0.669\,13$

$OB^2 = 800^2 + 500^2 - 2(800)(500)(\cos 132°)$

$OB^2 = 800^2 + 500^2 - 2(800)(500)(-0.669\,13)$

$OB^2 = 640\,000 + 250\,000 - (-535\,304)$

$OB^2 = 640\,000 + 250\,000 + 535\,304$

$OB^2 = 1\,425\,304$

$OB = 1\,193.86$ lb

Fig. 32-31

Compute $\angle BOC$ using the Law of Sines:

$\sin 132° = \sin (180° - 132°) = \sin 48° = 0.743\,14$

$$\frac{500}{\sin \angle BOC} = \frac{1\,193.86}{\sin 132°}$$

$$\frac{500}{\sin \angle BOC} = \frac{1\,193.86}{0.743\,14}$$

$1\,193.86 \sin \angle BOC = 371.57$

$\sin \angle BOC = 0.311\,23$

$\angle BOC = 18°8'$

Compute resultant vector $\angle BOD$:

$\angle BOD = \angle BOC + \angle COD = 18°8' + 14° = 32°8'$

The resultant vector pulls on the structure at point O with a force of 1 193.86 pounds in a direction up and to the right at an angle of 32°8′ with the horizontal. *Ans*

Exercise 32-7

Solve these problems. Compute unknown linear values to 2 decimal places unless otherwise stated, English angular values to the nearer minute, and metric angular values to the nearer hundredth of a degree.

1. Two sides of a triangular shaped template are 9.300 inches and 8.600 inches. An angle of 57° lies opposite the 9.300-inch side. Compute the angle which lies opposite the 8.600-inch side.

2. A triangular shaped piece of land is to be fenced in. Two sides of the property are 120 feet and 160 feet. The included angle between these two sides is 62°. What is the length of fencing required for the third side?

3. Center locations of three holes are laid out on a piece of sheet metal. The centerline distance between hole #1 and hole #2 is 5.60 cm, between hole #1 and hole #3 is 6.50 cm, and between hole #2 and hole #3 is 6.10 cm.

   a. Compute the angle made by the centerlines at hole #1.

   b. Compute the angle made by the centerlines at hole #2.

   c. Compute the angle made by the centerlines at hole #3.

4. Sides AB and CD of the baseplate shown in figure 32-32 are parallel. Compute ∠A.

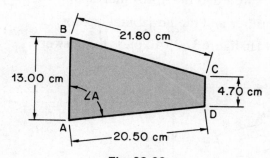

Fig. 32-32

5. Three circles are to be cut out of the plywood panel shown in figure 32-33. The 8-inch diameter and 11-inch diameter circles are each tangent to the 15-inch diameter circle. Determine the distance from the center of the 8-inch diameter circle to the center of the 11-inch diameter circle.

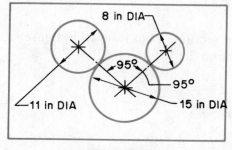

Fig. 32-33

6. A cabinetmaker is to make a counter top to the dimensions given in figure 32-34. Compute the length of side AB.

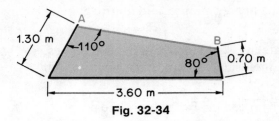

Fig. 32-34

7. In laying out an acute oblique triangle, a drafter draws a line segment 5 inches long. From one endpoint of the 5-inch segment, a line segment is drawn at an angle of 48°. From the other endpoint of the 5-inch segment, another line segment is drawn at an angle of 59°.

a. Find the length of the side opposite the 48° angle.

b. Find the length of the side opposite the 59° angle.

8. An unequally pitched roof has a front rafter 4.500 metres long and a rear rafter 7.000 metres long. The horizontal distance (span) between the front and rear endpoints of the rafters is 8.500 metres.

a. Compute the angle made by the front rafter and the horizontal (span).

b. Compute the angle made by the rear rafter and the horizontal (span).

9. Compute dimension b of the drill jig shown in figure 32-35. Express the answer to 3 decimal places.

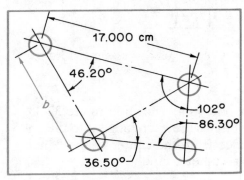

Fig. 32-35

10. A wall is built from point A to point B in the section of land shown in figure 32-36. Sides AC and BD are parallel. Determine the length of AB.

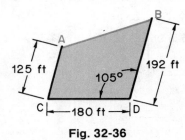

Fig. 32-36

11. Compute ∠B of the template shown in figure 32-37.

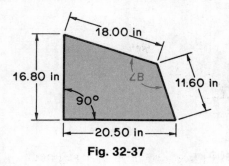

Fig. 32-37

12. A frame in the shape of a parallelogram is to be strengthened by the addition of a diagonal brace fastened on opposite corners of the frame. The frame has two sides, each 2.30 metres long and two sides, each 3.70 metres long. The brace is to lie opposite an included angle of 115° which is made by two sides of the frame. Compute the required length of the brace.

13. A structural section in the shape of an oblique triangle with 30-foot, 22-foot, and 16-foot sides is to be fabricated.

    a. Compute the angle opposite the 22-foot side.

    b. Compute the angle opposite the 16-foot side.

    c. A brace is to be made which extends from the midpoint of the 30-foot side to the vertex where the 16-foot and 22-foot sides meet. What is the required length of the brace?

14. In a proposed housing development plan, 4 streets meet as shown in figure 32-38. Compute ∠A.

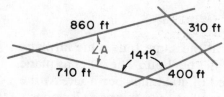

Fig. 32-38

15. Determine ∠x of the pattern shown in figure 32-39.

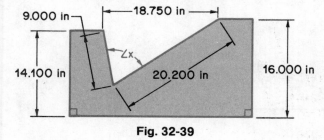

Fig. 32-39

16. A concrete platform is shown in figure 32-40. Compute ∠A.

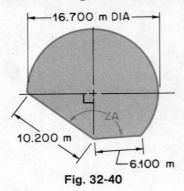

Fig. 32-40

17. A surveyor wishes to measure the distance between two horizontal points. The two points, A and B, are separated by a river and cannot be directly measured. The surveyor does the following:

    On the same side of the river as point A, a third point (point C) is measured at a distance of 120 feet toward the river from point A. From point A, point C is sighted, then the transit telescope is turned to point B across the river. An angle of 33°20′ is read on the transit. The surveyor moves to point C. From point C, point A is sighted, then the transit telescope is turned to point B across the river. An angle of 132° is recorded.

    Determine the distance between point A and point B.

18. A length of sidewalk is to be constructed in a square lot. Each side of the lot is 130 feet long. The sidewalk is laid out as follows:

    Stakes are driven at two opposite corners of the lot and a string is stretched between the two stakes. From one of the staked corners, a distance of 60 feet is measured along the string and a third stake is driven. From this stake, a measurement is made to one of the corners of the lot where a stake has not been driven.

    What is the length of this measurement?

19. Two airplanes start from the same location at the same time. One airplane travels due south at an average speed of 370 miles per hour. The other airplane travels 25° north of west at an average speed of 400 miles per hour. At the end of 2 hours what is the straight-line distance between the two airplanes?

20. Two forces are pulling on a structure at point O as shown in figure 32-41. Compute the force and direction of the resultant vector.

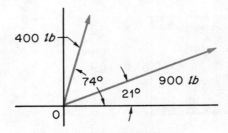

Fig. 32-41

21. Compute ∠x of the fixture hole location shown in figure 32-42.

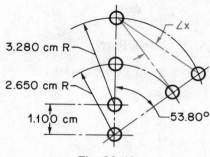

3.280 cm R

2.650 cm R

1.100 cm

53.80°

∠x

Fig. 32-42

22. In determining the height of a tower, a surveyor made the distance and angular measurements shown in figure 32-43. What is the height of the tower?

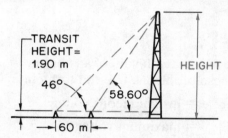

TRANSIT
HEIGHT=
1.90 m

46°

58.60°

HEIGHT

60 m

Fig. 32-43

23. Two forces are pulling on an object at point O as shown in figure 32-44. Compute the force and direction of the resultant vector.

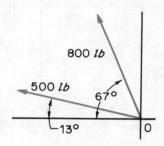

800 *lb*

500 *lb*

67°

13°

O

Fig. 32-44

24. Compute ∠D of the template shown in figure 32-45.

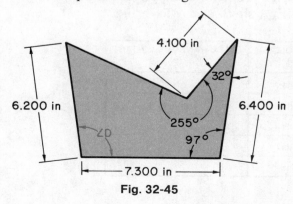

4.100 in

32°

6.200 in

6.400 in

255°

97°

∠D

7.300 in

Fig. 32-45

UNIT EXERCISE AND PROBLEM REVIEW

Exercise 32-8

DETERMINING FUNCTIONS OF ANGLES IN ANY QUADRANT

Determine the sine, cosine, tangent, cotangent, secant, and cosecant of these angles.

1. 115°
2. 220°
3. 290°20′
4. 95.6°

5. 580°
6. 490°
7. 755.3°
8. 1 060°50′

DETERMINING INSTANTANEOUS VOLTAGES

9. Compute the instantaneous voltage (e) to the nearer tenth volt, of an alternating electromotive force (emf) for each of these problems. Use the formula

    $e = E_{max} \sin \theta$ where e = instantaneous voltage

    E_{max} = maximum voltage

    θ = angle in degrees

	NUMBER OF DEGREES REACHED IN CYCLE (θ)	MAXIMUM VOLTAGE (E_{max})	INSTANTANEOUS VOLTAGE (e)
a.	140°	240 volts	
b.	235°	600 volts	
c.	310°	120 volts	
d.	180°	800 volts	
e.	340°	300 volts	

10. Each of these problems has a 60 cycle alternating electromotive force (emf). The angular velocity is 21 600° per second. Compute the instantaneous voltage (e), to the nearer tenth volt, for each problem. Compute the angle in degrees (θ), then apply the formula $e = E_{max} \sin \theta$.

	TIME	MAXIMUM VOLTAGE (E_{max})	INSTANTANEOUS VOLTAGE (e)
a.	0.015 second	550 volts	
b.	0.02 second	120 volts	
c.	0.026 second	600 volts	
d.	0.007 second	240 volts	
e.	0.033 second	800 volts	

SOLVING OBLIQUE TRIANGLE PROBLEMS USING THE LAW OF SINES

Solve these problems using the Law of Sines. Compute side lengths to 3 decimal places, English angular values to the nearer minute, and metric angular values to the nearer hundredth of a degree.

11. Determine side *a*.

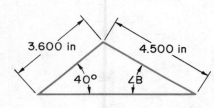

15. Determine side *c*.

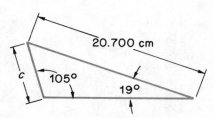

19. a. Determine ∠A.
    b. Determine side *a*.

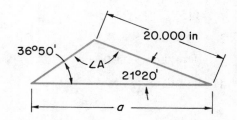

12. Determine ∠B.

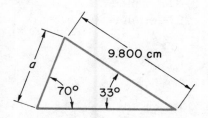

16. Determine ∠M.

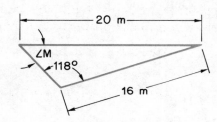

20. a. Determine ∠A.
    b. Determine ∠B.
    c. Determine side *b*.

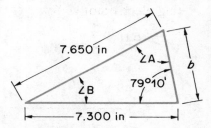

13. Determine side *x*.

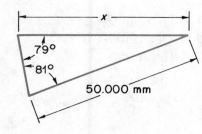

17. a. Determine ∠B.
    b. Determine side *b*.

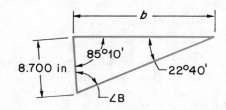

21. a. Determine ∠E.
    b. Determine side *e*.
    c. Determine side *f*.

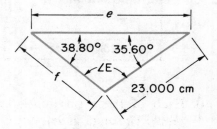

14. Determine ∠A.

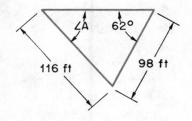

18. a. Determine ∠F.
    b. Determine ∠G.

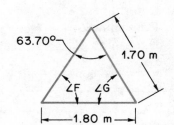

22. a. Determine ∠N.
    b. Determine ∠P.
    c. Determine side *p*.

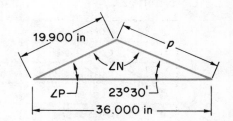

SOLVING OBLIQUE TRIANGLE PROBLEMS USING THE LAW OF COSINES

Solve these problems using the Law of Cosines. Also, apply the Law of Sines in the solution of certain problems. Compute side lengths to 3 decimal places, English angular values to the nearer minute, and metric angular values to the nearer hundredth of a degree.

23. Determine side *a*.

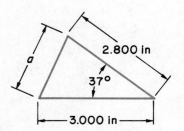

27. Determine side *a*.

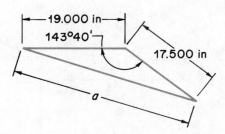

31. a. Determine side *d*.
    b. Determine ∠E.
    c. Determine ∠F.

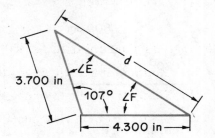

24. Determine ∠B.

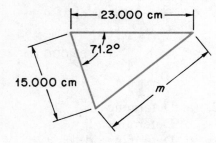

28. Determine ∠B.

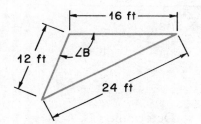

32. a. Determine ∠B.
    b. Determine ∠C.
    c. Determine ∠D.

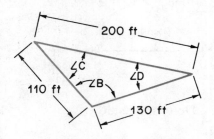

25. Determine side *m*.

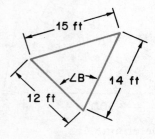

29. a. Determine side *d*.
    b. Determine ∠E.
    c. Determine ∠F.

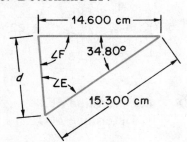

33. a. Determine side *a*.
    b. Determine ∠B.
    c. Determine ∠C.

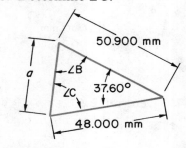

26. Determine ∠C.

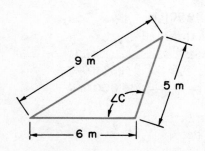

30. a. Determine ∠A.
    b. Determine ∠B.
    c. Determine ∠C.

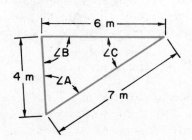

34. a. Determine ∠M.
    b. Determine ∠R.
    c. Determine ∠T.

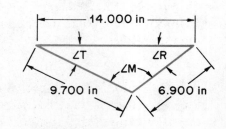

SOLVING APPLIED OBLIQUE TRIANGLE PROBLEMS

Solve these problems. Compute unknown linear values to 2 decimal places unless otherwise noted, English angular values to the nearer minute, and metric angular values to the nearer hundredth of a degree.

35. A triangular shaped panel is to be machined. Two sides are given as 14.200 inches and 11.700 inches with an included angle of 70°20′. Determine the length of the third side. Compute the answer to 3 decimal places.

36. A triangular roof truss has sides of 9 metres, 7 metres, and 6 metres.
    a. Compute the angle opposite the 6-metre side.
    b. Compute the angle opposite the 7-metre side.
    c. Compute the angle opposite the 9-metre side.

37. Determine ∠A of the structural frame shown in figure 32-46.

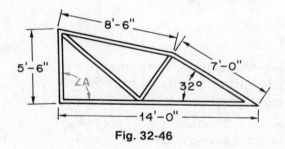

Fig. 32-46

38. Determine side x of the assembly cover plate shown in figure 32-47.

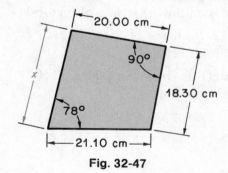

Fig. 32-47

39. Three externally tangent holes are to be bored in a casting. The hole diameters are 3.400 inches, 2.800 inches, and 2.200 inches. Compute the three angles of a triangle made by connecting line segments between the centers of the three holes.

40. A building lot in the shape of a parallelogram has 2 sides, each 65 metres long and 2 sides, each 40 metres long. A measurement of 90 metres across opposite acute angle corners of the lot is made. What are the values of the two pairs of opposite angles of the lot?

41. Compute dimension x of the template shown in figure 32-48.

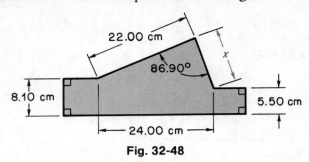

Fig. 32-48

42. A piece of stock is to be machined as shown in figure 32-49. Determine dimension b. Compute the answer to 3 decimal places.

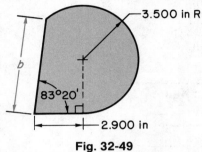

Fig. 32-49

43. A surveyor wishes to measure the distance between two horizontal points. The two points, A and B, are separated by an obstruction and cannot be directly measured. The surveyor does the following:

   On the same side of the obstruction as point A, a third point (point C) is measured at a distance of 50 metres toward the obstruction from point A. From point A, point C is sighted, then the transit telescope is turned to point B on the other side of the obstruction. An angle of 40.50° is read on the transit. The surveyor moves to point C. From point C, point A is sighted, then the transit telescope is turned to point B on the other side of the obstruction. An angle of 121.30° is recorded.

   Determine the distance between point A and point B.

44. Two forces are pulling on an object at point O as shown in figure 32-50. Compute the force and direction of the resultant vector.

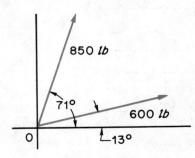

Fig. 32-50

APPENDIX

LINEAR MEASURE

ENGLISH UNITS OF LINEAR MEASURE

1 foot (ft)	=	12 inches (in)
1 yard (yd)	=	3 feet (ft)
1 yard (yd)	=	36 inches (in)
1 rod (rd)	=	16.5 feet (ft)
1 furlong	=	220 yards (yd)
1 mile (mi)	=	5 280 feet (ft)
1 mile (mi)	=	1 760 yards (yd)
1 mile (mi)	=	320 rods (rd)
1 mile (mi)	=	8 furlongs

METRIC UNITS OF LINEAR MEASURE

10 millimetres (mm)	=	1 centimetre (cm)
10 centimetres (cm)	=	1 decimetre (dm)
10 decimetres (dm)	=	1 metre (m)
10 metres (m)	=	1 dekametre (dam)
10 dekametres (dam)	=	1 hectometre (hm)
10 hectometres (hm)	=	1 kilometre (km)

METRIC TO ENGLISH UNITS

1 millimetre (mm)	=	0.039 37 inch (in)
1 centimetre (cm)	=	0.393 7 inch (in)
1 metre (m)	=	39.37 inches (in)
1 metre (m)	=	3.280 8 feet (ft)
1 kilometre (km)	=	0.621 4 mile (mi)

ENGLISH TO METRIC UNITS

1 inch (in)	=	25.4 millimetres (mm)
1 inch (in)	=	2.54 centimetres (cm)
1 foot (ft)	=	0.304 8 metre (m)
1 yard (yd)	=	0.914 4 metre (m)
1 mile (mi)	=	1.609 kilometres (km)

AREA MEASURE

ENGLISH UNITS OF AREA MEASURE

1 square foot (sq ft)	=	144 square inches (sq in)
1 square yard (sq yd)	=	9 square feet (sq ft)
1 square rod (sq rd)	=	30.25 square yards (sq yd)
1 acre (A)	=	160 square rods (sq rd)
1 acre (A)	=	43 560 square feet (sq ft)
1 square mile (sq mi)	=	640 acres (A)

METRIC UNITS OF AREA MEASURE

100 square millimetres (mm^2)	=	1 square centimetre (cm^2)
100 square centimetres (cm^2)	=	1 square decimetre (dm^2)
100 square decimetres (dm^2)	=	1 square metre (m^2)
100 square metres (m^2)	=	1 square dekametre (dam^2)
100 square dekametres (dam^2)	=	1 square hectometre (hm^2)
100 square hectometres (hm^2)	=	1 square kilometre (km^2)

METRIC TO ENGLISH UNITS

1 square millimetre (mm^2)	=	0.001 55 square inch (sq in)
1 square centimetre (cm^2)	=	0.155 square inch (sq in)
1 square metre (m^2)	=	10.764 square feet (sq ft)
1 square metre (m^2)	=	1.196 square yards (sq yd)
1 square kilometre (km^2)	=	0.386 1 square mile (sq mi)

ENGLISH TO METRIC UNITS

1 square inch (sq in)	=	645.2 square millimetres (mm^2)
1 square inch (sq in)	=	6.452 square centimetres (cm^2)
1 square foot (sq ft)	=	0.092 9 square metre (m^2)
1 square yard (sq yd)	=	0.836 square metre (m^2)
1 square mile (sq mi)	=	2.589 9 square kilometres (km^2)

VOLUME MEASURE

```
┌─────────────────────────────────────────────────────────┐
│        ENGLISH UNITS OF VOLUME MEASURE                    │
│  ┌──────────────────────────────────────────────────┐    │
│  │  1 cubic foot (cu ft)    =   1 728 cubic inches (cu in)│
│  │  1 cubic yard (cu yd)    =   27 cubic feet (cu ft) │    │
│  └──────────────────────────────────────────────────┘    │
└─────────────────────────────────────────────────────────┘
```

ENGLISH UNITS OF VOLUME MEASURE

1 cubic foot (cu ft)	=	1 728 cubic inches (cu in)
1 cubic yard (cu yd)	=	27 cubic feet (cu ft)

METRIC UNITS OF VOLUME MEASURE

1 000 cubic millimetres (mm^3)	=	1 cubic centimetre (cm^3)
1 000 cubic centimetres (cm^3)	=	1 cubic decimetre (dm^3)
1 000 cubic decimetres (dm^3)	=	1 cubic metre (m^3)
1 000 cubic metres (m^3)	=	1 cubic dekametre (dam^3)
1 000 cubic dekametres (dam^3)	=	1 cubic hectometre (hm^3)
1 000 cubic hectometres (hm^3)	=	1 cubic kilometre (km^3)

METRIC TO ENGLISH UNITS

1 cubic centimetre (cm^3)	=	0.061 cubic inch (cu in)
1 cubic metre (m^3)	=	35.314 cubic feet (cu ft)
1 cubic metre (m^3)	=	1.308 cubic yards (cu yd)

ENGLISH TO METRIC UNITS

1 cubic inch (cu in)	=	16.387 2 cubic centimetres (cm^3)
1 cubic foot (cu ft)	=	0.028 3 cubic metre (m^3)
1 cubic yard (cu yd)	=	0.764 5 cubic metre (m^3)

CAPACITY MEASURE

ENGLISH UNITS OF CAPACITY MEASURE

16 ounces (oz)	=	1 pint (pt)
2 pints (pt)	=	1 quart (qt)
4 quarts (qt)	=	1 gallon (gal)

COMMONLY USED CAPACITY — CUBIC MEASURE EQUIVALENTS

1 gallon (gal)	=	231 cubic inches (cu in)
7.5 gallons (gal)	=	1 cubic foot (cu ft)

METRIC UNITS OF CAPACITY MEASURE

10 millilitres (mL)	=	1 centilitre (cL)
10 centilitres (cL)	=	1 decilitre (dL)
10 decilitres (dL)	=	1 litre (L)
10 litres (L)	=	1 dekalitre (daL)
10 dekalitres (daL)	=	1 hectolitre (hL)
10 hectolitres (hL)	=	1 kilolitre (kL)

COMMONLY USED CAPACITY—CUBIC MEASURE EQUIVALENTS

1 millilitre (mL)	=	1 cubic centimetre (cm^3)
1 litre (L)	=	1 cubic decimetre (dm^3)
1 litre (L)	=	1 000 cubic centimetres (cm^3)
1 000 litres (L)	=	1 cubic metre (m^3)

METRIC TO ENGLISH UNITS

1 millilitre (mL)	=	0.034 ounce (oz)
1 litre (L)	=	1.057 quarts (qt)
1 litre (L)	=	0.264 gallon (gal)

ENGLISH TO METRIC UNITS

1 ounce (oz)	=	29.563 millilitres (mL)
1 quart (qt)	=	0.946 litre (L)
1 gallon (gal)	=	3.785 litres (L)

WEIGHT (MASS) MEASURE

ENGLISH UNITS OF WEIGHT MEASURE

16 ounces (oz)	=	1 pound (lb)
2 000 pounds (lb)	=	1 net or short ton
2 240 pounds (lb)	=	1 gross or long ton

METRIC UNITS OF WEIGHT (MASS) MEASURE

10 milligrams (mg)	=	1 centigram (cg)
10 centigrams (cg)	=	1 decigram (dg)
10 decigrams (dg)	=	1 gram (g)
10 grams (g)	=	1 dekagram (dag)
10 dekagrams (dag)	=	1 hectogram (hg)
10 hectograms (hg)	=	1 kilogram (kg)
1 000 kilograms (kg)	=	1 metric ton (t)

METRIC TO ENGLISH UNITS

1 gram (g)	=	0.035 ounce (oz)
1 kilogram (kg)	=	2.205 pounds (lb)
1 metric ton (t)	=	1.102 short tons
1 metric ton (t)	=	0.984 long ton

ENGLISH TO METRIC UNITS

1 ounce (oz)	=	28.348 grams (g)
1 pound (lb)	=	0.454 kilogram (kg)
1 short ton	=	0.907 metric ton (t)
1 long ton	=	1.016 metric tons (t)

TRIGONOMETRIC FUNCTIONS FOR DEGREES AND MINUTES

Deg	Sin	Cos	Tan	Cot	Sec	Csc	Deg
0° 00′	0.000 00	1.000 0	0.000 00	Infin	1.000 0	Infin	90° 00′
10′	0.002 91	1.000 0	0.002 91	343.77	1.000 0	343.77	50′
20′	0.005 82	0.999 98	0.005 82	171.88	1.000 0	171.89	40′
30′	0.008 73	0.999 96	0.008 73	114.59	1.000 0	114.59	30′
40′	0.011 64	0.999 93	0.011 64	85.940	1.000 1	85.946	20′
50′	0.014 54	0.999 89	0.014 55	68.750	1.000 1	68.757	10′
1° 00′	0.017 45	0.999 85	0.017 46	57.290	1.000 1	57.299	89° 00′
10′	0.020 36	0.999 79	0.020 36	49.104	1.000 2	49.114	50′
20′	0.023 27	0.999 73	0.023 28	42.964	1.000 3	42.976	40′
30′	0.026 18	0.999 66	0.026 19	38.189	1.000 3	38.201	30′
40′	0.029 08	0.999 58	0.029 10	34.368	1.000 4	34.382	20′
50′	0.031 99	0.999 49	0.032 01	31.242	1.000 5	31.257	10′
2° 00′	0.034 90	0.999 39	0.034 92	28.636	1.000 6	28.654	88° 00′
10′	0.037 81	0.999 29	0.037 83	26.432	1.000 7	26.450	50′
20′	0.040 71	0.999 17	0.040 75	24.542	1.000 8	24.562	40′
30′	0.043 62	0.999 05	0.043 66	22.904	1.000 9	22.925	30′
40′	0.046 53	0.998 92	0.046 58	21.470	1.001 1	21.494	20′
50′	0.049 43	0.998 78	0.049 49	20.206	1.001 2	20.230	10′
3° 00′	0.052 34	0.998 63	0.052 41	19.081	1.001 4	19.107	87° 00′
10′	0.055 24	0.998 47	0.055 33	18.075	1.001 5	18.103	50′
20′	0.058 14	0.998 31	0.058 24	17.169	1.001 7	17.198	40′
30′	0.061 05	0.998 13	0.061 16	16.350	1.001 9	16.380	30′
40′	0.063 95	0.997 95	0.064 08	15.605	1.002 0	15.637	20′
50′	0.066 85	0.997 76	0.067 00	14.924	1.002 2	14.958	10′
4° 00′	0.069 76	0.997 56	0.069 93	14.301	1.002 4	14.335	86° 00′
10′	0.072 66	0.997 36	0.072 85	13.727	1.002 6	13.763	50′
20′	0.075 56	0.997 14	0.075 78	13.197	1.002 9	13.235	40′
30′	0.078 46	0.996 92	0.078 70	12.706	1.003 1	12.745	30′
40′	0.081 36	0.996 68	0.081 63	12.251	1.003 3	12.291	20′
50′	0.084 26	0.996 44	0.084 56	11.826	1.003 6	11.868	10′
5° 00′	0.087 16	0.996 19	0.087 49	11.430	1.003 8	11.474	85° 00′
10′	0.090 05	0.995 94	0.090 42	11.059	1.004 1	11.104	50′
20′	0.092 95	0.995 67	0.093 35	10.712	1.004 3	10.758	40′
30′	0.095 85	0.995 40	0.096 29	10.385	1.004 6	10.433	30′
40′	0.098 74	0.995 11	0.099 23	10.078	1.004 9	10.127	20′
50′	0.101 64	0.994 82	0.102 16	9.788 2	1.005 2	9.839 1	10′
6° 00′	0.104 53	0.994 52	0.105 10	9.514 4	1.005 5	9.566 8	84° 00′
10′	0.107 42	0.994 21	0.108 05	9.255 3	1.005 8	9.309 2	50′
20′	0.110 31	0.993 90	0.110 99	9.009 8	1.006 1	9.065 1	40′
30′	0.113 20	0.993 57	0.113 94	8.776 9	1.006 5	8.833 7	30′
40′	0.116 09	0.993 24	0.116 88	8.555 6	1.006 8	8.613 8	20′
50′	0.118 98	0.992 90	0.119 83	8.345 0	1.007 1	8.404 6	10′
7° 00′	0.121 87	0.992 55	0.122 78	8.144 4	1.007 5	8.205 5	83° 00′
10′	0.124 76	0.992 19	0.125 74	7.953 0	1.007 9	8.015 6	50′
20′	0.127 64	0.991 82	0.128 69	7.770 4	1.008 2	7.834 4	40′
30′	0.130 53	0.991 44	0.131 65	7.595 8	1.008 6	7.661 3	30′
40′	0.133 41	0.991 06	0.134 61	7.428 7	1.009 0	7.495 7	20′
50′	0.136 29	0.990 67	0.137 58	7.268 7	1.009 4	7.337 2	10′
8° 00′	0.139 17	0.990 27	0.140 54	7.115 4	1.009 8	7.185 3	82° 00′
10′	0.142 05	0.989 86	0.143 51	6.968 2	1.010 2	7.039 6	50′
20′	0.144 93	0.989 44	0.146 48	6.826 9	1.010 7	6.899 8	40′
30′	0.147 81	0.989 02	0.149 45	6.691 2	1.011 1	6.765 5	30′
40′	0.150 69	0.988 58	0.152 43	6.560 6	1.011 5	6.636 3	20′
50′	0.153 56	0.988 14	0.155 40	6.434 8	1.012 0	6.512 1	10′
9° 00′	0.156 43	0.987 69	0.158 38	6.313 8	1.012 5	6.392 4	81° 00′
10′	0.159 31	0.987 23	0.161 37	6.197 0	1.012 9	6.277 2	50′
20′	0.162 18	0.986 76	0.164 35	6.084 4	1.013 4	6.166 1	40′
30′	0.165 05	0.986 29	0.167 34	5.975 8	1.013 9	6.058 8	30′
40′	0.167 92	0.985 80	0.170 33	5.870 8	1.014 4	5.955 4	20′
50′	0.170 78	0.985 31	0.173 33	5.769 4	1.014 9	5.855 4	10′
10° 00′	0.173 65	0.984 81	0.176 33	5.671 3	1.015 4	5.758 8	80° 00′
10′	0.176 51	0.984 30	0.179 33	5.576 4	1.015 9	5.665 3	50′
20′	0.179 37	0.983 78	0.182 33	5.484 5	1.016 5	5.574 9	40′
30′	0.182 24	0.983 25	0.185 34	5.395 5	1.017 0	5.487 4	30′
40′	0.185 09	0.982 72	0.188 35	5.309 3	1.017 6	5.402 6	20′
50′	0.187 95	0.982 18	0.191 36	5.225 7	1.018 1	5.320 5	10′
11° 00′	0.190 81	0.981 63	0.194 38	5.144 6	1.018 7	5.240 8	79° 00′
10′	0.193 66	0.981 07	0.197 40	5.065 8	1.019 3	5.163 6	50′
20′	0.196 52	0.980 50	0.200 42	4.989 4	1.019 9	5.088 6	40′
30′	0.199 37	0.979 92	0.203 45	4.915 2	1.020 5	5.015 8	30′
40′	0.202 22	0.979 34	0.206 48	4.843 0	1.021 1	4.945 2	20′
50′	0.205 07	0.978 75	0.209 52	4.772 9	1.021 7	4.876 5	10′
12° 00′	0.207 91	0.978 15	0.212 56	4.704 6	1.022 3	4.809 7	78° 00′
10′	0.210 76	0.977 54	0.215 60	4.638 3	1.023 0	4.744 8	50′
20′	0.213 60	0.976 92	0.218 64	4.573 6	1.023 6	4.681 7	40′
30′	0.216 44	0.976 30	0.221 69	4.510 7	1.024 3	4.620 2	30′
40′	0.219 28	0.975 66	0.224 75	4.449 4	1.024 9	4.560 4	20′
50′	0.222 12	0.975 02	0.227 81	4.389 7	1.025 6	4.502 1	10′
13° 00′	0.224 95	0.974 37	0.230 87	4.331 5	1.026 3	4.445 4	77° 00′
10′	0.227 78	0.973 71	0.233 93	4.274 7	1.027 0	4.391 0	50′
20′	0.230 62	0.973 04	0.237 00	4.219 3	1.027 7	4.336 2	40′
30′	0.233 45	0.972 37	0.240 08	4.165 3	1.028 4	4.283 6	30′
40′	0.236 27	0.971 69	0.243 16	4.112 6	1.029 1	4.232 4	20′
50′	0.239 10	0.971 00	0.246 24	4.061 1	1.029 9	4.182 4	10′
14° 00′	0.241 92	0.970 30	0.249 33	4.010 8	1.030 6	4.133 6	76° 00′
10′	0.244 74	0.969 59	0.252 42	3.961 7	1.031 4	4.085 9	50′
20′	0.247 56	0.968 87	0.255 52	3.913 6	1.032 1	4.039 4	40′
30′	0.250 38	0.968 15	0.258 62	3.866 7	1.032 9	3.993 9	30′
40′	0.253 20	0.967 42	0.261 72	3.820 8	1.033 7	3.949 5	20′
50′	0.256 01	0.966 67	0.264 83	3.776 0	1.034 5	3.906 1	10′
Deg	Cos	Sin	Cot	Tan	Csc	Sec	Deg

Deg	Sin	Cos	Tan	Cot	Sec	Csc	Deg
15° 00′	0.258 82	0.965 93	0.267 95	3.732 1	1.035 3	3.863 7	75° 00′
10′	0.261 63	0.965 17	0.271 07	3.689 1	1.036 1	3.822 2	50′
20′	0.264 43	0.964 40	0.274 19	3.647 1	1.036 9	3.781 6	40′
30′	0.267 24	0.963 63	0.277 32	3.605 9	1.037 7	3.742 0	30′
40′	0.270 04	0.962 85	0.280 46	3.565 6	1.038 6	3.703 1	20′
50′	0.272 84	0.962 06	0.283 60	3.526 1	1.039 4	3.665 1	10′
16° 00′	0.275 64	0.961 26	0.286 75	3.487 4	1.040 3	3.627 9	74° 00′
10′	0.278 43	0.960 46	0.289 90	3.449 5	1.041 2	3.591 5	50′
20′	0.281 23	0.959 64	0.293 05	3.412 4	1.042 0	3.555 9	40′
30′	0.284 02	0.958 82	0.296 21	3.375 9	1.042 9	3.520 9	30′
40′	0.286 80	0.957 99	0.299 38	3.340 2	1.043 8	3.486 7	20′
50′	0.289 59	0.957 15	0.302 55	3.305 2	1.044 8	3.453 2	10′
17° 00′	0.292 37	0.956 30	0.305 73	3.270 9	1.045 7	3.420 3	73° 00′
10′	0.295 15	0.955 45	0.308 91	3.237 1	1.046 6	3.388 1	50′
20′	0.297 93	0.954 59	0.312 10	3.204 1	1.047 6	3.356 5	40′
30′	0.300 71	0.953 72	0.315 30	3.171 6	1.048 5	3.325 5	30′
40′	0.303 48	0.952 84	0.318 50	3.139 7	1.049 5	3.295 1	20′
50′	0.306 25	0.951 95	0.321 71	3.108 4	1.050 5	3.265 3	10′
18° 00′	0.309 02	0.951 06	0.324 92	3.077 7	1.051 5	3.236 1	72° 00′
10′	0.311 78	0.950 15	0.328 14	3.047 5	1.052 5	3.207 4	50′
20′	0.314 54	0.949 24	0.331 36	3.017 8	1.053 5	2.179 2	40′
30′	0.317 30	0.948 32	0.334 60	2.988 7	1.054 5	3.151 5	30′
40′	0.320 06	0.947 40	0.337 83	2.960 0	1.055 5	3.124 4	20′
50′	0.322 82	0.946 46	0.341 08	2.931 9	1.056 6	3.097 7	10′
19° 00′	0.325 57	0.945 52	0.344 33	2.904 2	1.057 6	3.071 5	71° 00′
10′	0.328 32	0.944 57	0.347 58	2.877 0	1.058 7	3.045 8	50′
20′	0.331 06	0.943 61	0.350 85	2.850 2	1.059 8	3.020 6	40′
30′	0.333 81	0.942 64	0.354 12	2.823 9	1.060 8	2.995 7	30′
40′	0.336 55	0.941 67	0.357 40	2.798 0	1.061 9	2.971 3	20′
50′	0.339 29	0.940 68	0.360 68	2.772 5	1.063 0	2.947 4	10′
20° 00′	0.342 02	0.939 69	0.363 97	2.747 5	1.064 2	2.923 8	70° 00′
10′	0.344 75	0.938 69	0.367 27	2.722 8	1.065 3	2.900 6	50′
20′	0.347 48	0.937 69	0.370 57	2.698 5	1.066 4	2.877 8	40′
30′	0.350 21	0.936 67	0.373 88	2.674 6	1.067 6	2.855 4	30′
40′	0.352 93	0.935 65	0.377 20	2.651 1	1.068 8	2.833 4	20′
50′	0.355 65	0.934 62	0.380 53	2.627 9	1.069 9	2.811 7	10′
21° 00′	0.358 37	0.933 58	0.383 86	2.605 1	1.071 1	2.790 4	69° 00′
10′	0.361 08	0.932 53	0.387 21	2.582 6	1.072 3	2.769 4	50′
20′	0.363 79	0.931 48	0.390 55	2.560 5	1.073 6	2.748 8	40′
30′	0.366 50	0.930 42	0.393 91	2.538 7	1.074 8	2.728 5	30′
40′	0.369 21	0.929 35	0.397 27	2.517 2	1.076 0	2.708 5	20′
50′	0.371 91	0.928 27	0.400 65	2.496 0	1.077 3	2.688 8	10′
22° 00′	0.374 61	0.927 18	0.404 03	2.475 1	1.078 5	2.669 5	68° 00′
10′	0.377 30	0.926 09	0.407 41	2.454 5	1.079 8	2.650 4	50′
20′	0.379 99	0.924 99	0.410 81	2.434 2	1.081 1	2.631 6	40′
30′	0.382 68	0.923 88	0.414 21	2.414 2	1.082 4	2.613 1	30′
40′	0.385 37	0.922 76	0.417 63	2.394 5	1.083 7	2.594 9	20′
50′	0.388 05	0.921 64	0.421 05	2.375 0	1.085 0	2.577 0	10′
23° 00′	0.390 73	0.920 50	0.424 47	2.355 9	1.086 4	2.559 3	67° 00′
10′	0.393 41	0.919 36	0.427 91	2.336 9	1.087 7	2.541 9	50′
20′	0.396 08	0.918 22	0.431 36	2.318 3	1.089 1	2.524 7	40′
30′	0.398 75	0.917 06	0.434 81	2.299 8	1.090 4	2.507 8	30′
40′	0.401 41	0.915 90	0.438 28	2.281 7	1.091 8	2.491 2	20′
50′	0.404 08	0.914 72	0.441 75	2.263 7	1.093 2	2.474 8	10′
24° 00′	0.406 74	0.913 55	0.445 23	2.246 0	1.094 6	2.458 6	66° 00′
10′	0.409 39	0.912 36	0.448 72	2.228 6	1.096 1	2.442 6	50′
20′	0.412 04	0.911 16	0.452 22	2.211 3	1.097 5	2.426 9	40′
30′	0.414 69	0.909 96	0.455 73	2.194 3	1.098 9	2.411 4	30′
40′	0.417 34	0.908 75	0.459 24	2.177 5	1.100 4	2.396 1	20′
50′	0.419 98	0.907 53	0.462 77	2.160 9	1.101 9	2.381 1	10′
25° 00′	0.422 62	0.906 31	0.466 31	2.144 5	1.103 4	2.366 2	65° 00′
10′	0.425 25	0.905 07	0.469 85	2.128 3	1.104 9	2.351 5	50′
20′	0.427 88	0.903 83	0.473 41	2.112 3	1.106 4	2.337 1	40′
30′	0.430 51	0.902 59	0.476 98	2.096 5	1.107 9	2.322 8	30′
40′	0.433 13	0.901 33	0.480 55	2.080 9	1.109 5	2.308 7	20′
50′	0.435 75	0.900 07	0.484 14	2.065 5	1.111 0	2.294 9	10′
26° 00′	0.438 37	0.898 79	0.487 73	2.050 3	1.112 6	2.281 2	64° 00′
10′	0.440 98	0.897 52	0.491 34	2.035 3	1.114 2	2.267 6	50′
20′	0.443 59	0.896 23	0.494 95	2.020 4	1.115 8	2.254 3	40′
30′	0.446 20	0.894 93	0.498 58	2.005 7	1.117 4	2.241 1	30′
40′	0.448 80	0.893 63	0.502 22	1.991 2	1.119 0	2.228 2	20′
50′	0.451 40	0.892 32	0.505 87	1.976 8	1.120 7	2.215 3	10′
27° 00′	0.453 99	0.891 01	0.509 53	1.962 6	1.122 3	2.202 7	63° 00′
10′	0.456 58	0.889 68	0.513 19	1.948 6	1.124 0	2.190 2	50′
20′	0.459 17	0.888 35	0.516 88	1.934 7	1.125 7	2.177 8	40′
30′	0.461 75	0.887 01	0.520 57	1.921 0	1.127 4	2.165 7	30′
40′	0.464 33	0.885 66	0.524 27	1.907 4	1.129 1	2.153 6	20′
50′	0.466 90	0.884 31	0.527 98	1.894 0	1.130 8	2.141 8	10′
28° 00′	0.469 47	0.882 95	0.531 71	1.880 7	1.132 6	2.130 0	62° 00′
10′	0.472 04	0.881 58	0.535 45	1.867 6	1.134 3	2.118 5	50′
20′	0.474 60	0.880 20	0.539 20	1.854 6	1.136 1	2.107 0	40′
30′	0.477 16	0.878 82	0.542 96	1.841 8	1.137 9	2.095 7	30′
40′	0.479 71	0.877 43	0.546 73	1.829 1	1.139 7	2.084 6	20′
50′	0.482 26	0.876 03	0.550 51	1.816 5	1.141 5	2.073 5	10′
29° 00′	0.484 81	0.874 62	0.554 31	1.804 1	1.143 3	2.062 7	61° 00′
10′	0.487 35	0.873 21	0.558 12	1.791 7	1.145 2	2.051 9	50′
20′	0.489 89	0.871 78	0.561 94	1.779 6	1.147 1	2.041 3	40′
30′	0.492 42	0.870 36	0.565 77	1.767 5	1.148 9	2.030 8	30′
40′	0.494 95	0.868 92	0.569 62	1.755 6	1.150 8	2.020 4	20′
50′	0.497 48	0.867 48	0.573 48	1.743 8	1.152 8	2.010 1	10′
Deg	Cos	Sin	Cot	Tan	Csc	Sec	Deg

TRIGONOMETRIC FUNCTIONS FOR DEGREES AND MINUTES (Cont'd)

Deg	Sin	Cos	Tan	Cot	Sec	Csc	Deg
30° 00'	0.500 00	0.866 03	0.577 35	1.732 1	1.154 7	2.000 0	60° 00'
10'	0.502 52	0.864 57	0.581 24	1.720 5	1.156 6	1.990 0	50'
20'	0.505 03	0.863 10	0.585 13	1.709 0	1.158 6	1.980 1	40'
30'	0.507 54	0.861 63	0.589 04	1.697 7	1.160 6	1.970 3	30'
40'	0.510 04	0.860 15	0.592 97	1.686 4	1.162 6	1.960 6	20'
50'	0.512 54	0.858 66	0.596 91	1.675 3	1.164 6	1.951 0	10'
31° 00'	0.515 04	0.857 17	0.600 86	1.664 3	1.166 6	1.941 6	59° 00'
10'	0.517 53	0.855 67	0.604 83	1.653 4	1.168 7	1.932 2	50'
20'	0.520 02	0.854 16	0.608 81	1.642 6	1.170 7	1.923 0	40'
30'	0.522 50	0.852 64	0.612 80	1.631 9	1.172 8	1.913 9	30'
40'	0.524 98	0.851 12	0.616 81	1.621 3	1.174 9	1.904 8	20'
50'	0.527 45	0.849 59	0.620 83	1.610 7	1.177 0	1.895 9	10'
32° 00'	0.529 92	0.848 05	0.624 87	1.600 3	1.179 2	1.887 1	58° 00'
10'	0.532 38	0.846 50	0.628 92	1.590 0	1.181 3	1.878 3	50'
20'	0.534 84	0.844 95	0.632 99	1.579 8	1.183 5	1.869 7	40'
30'	0.537 30	0.843 39	0.637 07	1.569 7	1.185 7	1.861 1	30'
40'	0.539 75	0.841 82	0.641 17	1.559 7	1.187 9	1.852 7	20'
50'	0.542 20	0.840 25	0.645 28	1.549 7	1.190 1	1.844 3	10'
33° 00'	0.544 64	0.838 67	0.649 41	1.539 9	1.192 4	1.836 1	57° 00'
10'	0.547 08	0.837 08	0.653 55	1.530 1	1.194 6	1.827 9	50'
20'	0.549 51	0.835 49	0.657 71	1.520 4	1.196 9	1.819 8	40'
30'	0.551 94	0.833 89	0.661 89	1.510 8	1.199 2	1.811 8	30'
40'	0.554 36	0.832 28	0.666 08	1.501 3	1.201 5	1.803 9	20'
50'	0.556 78	0.830 66	0.670 28	1.491 9	1.203 9	1.796 0	10'
34° 00'	0.559 19	0.829 04	0.674 51	1.482 6	1.206 2	1.788 3	56° 00'
10'	0.561 60	0.827 41	0.678 75	1.473 3	1.208 6	1.780 6	50'
20'	0.564 01	0.825 77	0.683 01	1.464 1	1.211 0	1.773 0	40'
30'	0.566 41	0.824 13	0.687 28	1.455 0	1.213 4	1.765 5	30'
40'	0.568 80	0.822 48	0.691 57	1.446 0	1.215 8	1.758 1	20'
50'	0.571 19	0.820 82	0.695 88	1.437 0	1.218 3	1.750 7	10'
35° 00'	0.573 58	0.819 15	0.700 21	1.428 2	1.220 8	1.743 4	55° 00'
10'	0.575 96	0.817 48	0.704 55	1.419 3	1.223 3	1.736 2	50'
20'	0.578 33	0.815 80	0.708 91	1.410 6	1.225 8	1.729 1	40'
30'	0.580 70	0.814 12	0.713 29	1.402 0	1.228 3	1.722 0	30'
40'	0.583 07	0.812 42	0.717 69	1.393 4	1.230 9	1.715 1	20'
50'	0.585 43	0.810 72	0.722 11	1.384 8	1.233 5	1.708 1	10'
36° 00'	0.587 79	0.809 02	0.726 54	1.376 4	1.236 1	1.701 3	54° 00'
10'	0.590 14	0.807 30	0.731 00	1.368 0	1.238 7	1.694 5	50'
20'	0.592 48	0.805 58	0.735 47	1.359 7	1.241 3	1.687 8	40'
30'	0.594 82	0.803 86	0.739 96	1.351 4	1.244 0	1.681 2	30'
40'	0.597 16	0.802 12	0.744 47	1.343 2	1.246 7	1.674 6	20'
50'	0.599 49	0.800 38	0.749 00	1.335 1	1.249 4	1.668 1	10'
37° 00'	0.601 82	0.798 64	0.753 55	1.327 0	1.252 1	1.661 6	53° 00'
10'	0.604 14	0.796 88	0.758 12	1.319 0	1.254 9	1.655 2	50'
20'	0.606 45	0.795 12	0.762 72	1.311 1	1.257 7	1.648 9	40'
30'	0.608 76	0.793 35	0.767 33	1.303 2	1.260 5	1.642 7	30'
40'	0.611 07	0.791 58	0.771 96	1.295 4	1.263 3	1.636 5	20'
50'	0.613 37	0.789 80	0.776 61	1.287 6	1.266 1	1.630 3	10'
Deg	Cos	Sin	Cot	Tan	Csc	Sec	Deg

Deg	Sin	Cos	Tan	Cot	Sec	Csc	Deg
38° 00'	0.615 66	0.788 01	0.781 29	1.279 9	1.269 0	1.624 3	52° 00'
10'	0.617 95	0.786 22	0.785 98	1.272 3	1.271 9	1.618 2	50'
20'	0.620 24	0.784 42	0.790 70	1.264 7	1.274 8	1.612 3	40'
30'	0.622 51	0.782 61	0.795 44	1.257 2	1.277 8	1.606 4	30'
40'	0.624 79	0.780 79	0.800 20	1.249 7	1.280 7	1.600 5	20'
50'	0.627 06	0.778 97	0.804 98	1.242 3	1.283 7	1.594 7	10'
39° 00'	0.629 32	0.777 15	0.809 78	1.234 9	1.286 7	1.589 0	51° 00'
10'	0.631 58	0.775 31	0.814 61	1.227 6	1.289 8	1.583 3	50'
20'	0.633 83	0.773 47	0.819 46	1.220 3	1.292 9	1.577 7	40'
30'	0.636 08	0.771 62	0.824 34	1.213 1	1.296 0	1.572 1	30'
40'	0.638 32	0.769 77	0.829 23	1.205 9	1.299 1	1.566 6	20'
50'	0.640 56	0.767 91	0.834 15	1.198 8	1.302 2	1.561 1	10'
40° 00'	0.642 79	0.766 04	0.839 10	1.191 8	1.305 4	1.555 7	50° 00'
10'	0.645 01	0.764 17	0.844 07	1.184 7	1.308 6	1.550 3	50'
20'	0.647 23	0.762 29	0.849 06	1.177 8	1.311 8	1.545 0	40'
30'	0.649 45	0.760 41	0.854 08	1.170 9	1.315 1	1.539 8	30'
40'	0.651 66	0.758 51	0.859 12	1.164 0	1.318 4	1.534 5	20'
50'	0.653 86	0.756 61	0.864 19	1.157 2	1.321 7	1.529 4	10'
41° 00'	0.656 06	0.754 71	0.869 29	1.150 4	1.325 0	1.524 2	49° 00'
10'	0.658 25	0.752 80	0.874 41	1.143 6	1.328 4	1.519 2	50'
20'	0.660 44	0.750 88	0.879 55	1.136 9	1.331 8	1.514 1	40'
30'	0.662 62	0.748 96	0.884 73	1.130 3	1.335 2	1.509 2	30'
40'	0.664 80	0.747 03	0.889 92	1.123 7	1.338 6	1.504 2	20'
50'	0.666 97	0.745 09	0.895 15	1.117 1	1.342 1	1.499 3	10'
42° 00'	0.669 13	0.743 14	0.900 40	1.110 6	1.345 6	1.494 5	48° 00'
10'	0.671 29	0.741 20	0.905 69	1.104 1	1.349 2	1.489 7	50'
20'	0.673 44	0.739 24	0.910 99	1.097 7	1.352 7	1.484 9	40'
30'	0.675 59	0.737 28	0.916 33	1.091 3	1.356 3	1.480 2	30'
40'	0.677 73	0.735 31	0.921 70	1.085 0	1.360 0	1.475 5	20'
50'	0.679 87	0.733 33	0.927 09	1.078 6	1.363 6	1.470 9	10'
43° 00'	0.682 00	0.731 35	0.932 52	1.072 4	1.367 3	1.466 3	47° 00'
10'	0.684 12	0.729 37	0.937 97	1.066 1	1.371 0	1.461 7	50'
20'	0.686 24	0.727 37	0.943 45	1.059 9	1.374 8	1.457 2	40'
30'	0.688 35	0.725 37	0.948 96	1.053 8	1.378 6	1.452 7	30'
40'	0.690 46	0.723 37	0.954 51	1.047 7	1.382 4	1.448 3	20'
50'	0.692 56	0.721 36	0.960 08	1.041 6	1.386 3	1.443 9	10'
44° 00'	0.694 66	0.719 34	0.965 69	1.035 5	1.390 2	1.439 5	46° 00'
10'	0.696 75	0.717 32	0.971 32	1.029 5	1.394 1	1.435 2	50'
20'	0.698 83	0.715 29	0.977 00	1.023 6	1.398 0	1.431 0	40'
30'	0.700 91	0.713 25	0.982 70	1.017 6	1.402 0	1.426 7	30'
40'	0.702 98	0.711 21	0.988 43	1.011 7	1.406 0	1.422 5	20'
50'	0.705 05	0.709 16	0.994 20	1.005 8	1.410 1	1.418 3	10'
45° 00'	0.707 11	0.707 11	1.000 0	1.000 0	1.414 2	1.414 2	45° 00'
Deg	Cos	Sin	Cot	Tan	Csc	Sec	Deg

TRIGONOMETRIC FUNCTIONS FOR DECIMAL-DEGREES

Deg	Sin	Cos	Tan	Cot	Sec	Csc	Deg	Deg	Sin	Cos	Tan	Cot	Sec	Csc	Deg
0.0	0.000 00	1.000 0	0.000 00	Infin	1.000 0	Infin	90.0	8.0	0.139 17	0.990 3	0.140 54	7.115	1.009 8	7.185 3	82.0
.1	0.001 75	1.000 0	0.001 75	573.0	1.000 0	572.96	.9	.1	0.140 90	0.990 0	0.142 32	7.026	1.010 1	7.097 2	.9
.2	0.003 49	1.000 0	0.003 49	286.5	1.000 0	286.48	.8	.2	0.142 63	0.989 8	0.144 10	6.940	1.010 3	7.011 2	.8
.3	0.005 24	1.000 0	0.005 24	191.0	1.000 0	190.99	.7	.3	0.144 36	0.989 5	0.145 88	6.855	1.010 6	6.927 3	.7
.4	0.006 98	1.000 0	0.006 98	143.24	1.000 0	143.24	.6	.4	0.146 08	0.989 3	0.147 67	6.772	1.010 8	6.845 4	.6
.5	0.008 73	1.000 0	0.008 73	114.59	1.000 0	114.59	.5	.5	0.147 81	0.989 0	0.149 45	6.691	1.011 1	6.765 5	.5
.6	0.010 47	0.999 9	0.010 47	95.49	1.000 1	95.495	.4	.6	0.149 54	0.988 8	0.151 24	6.612	1.011 4	6.687 4	.4
.7	0.012 22	0.999 9	0.012 22	81.85	1.000 1	81.853	.3	.7	0.151 26	0.988 5	0.153 02	6.535	1.011 6	6.611 1	.3
.8	0.013 96	0.999 9	0.013 96	71.62	1.000 1	71.622	.2	.8	0.152 99	0.988 2	0.154 81	6.460	1.011 9	6.536 6	.2
.9	0.015 71	0.999 9	0.015 71	63.66	1.000 1	63.665	.1	.9	0.154 71	0.988 0	0.156 60	6.386	1.012 2	6.463 7	.1
1.0	0.017 45	0.999 8	0.017 46	57.29	1.000 2	57.299	89.0	9.0	0.156 43	0.987 7	0.158 38	6.314	1.012 5	6.392 5	81.0
.1	0.019 20	0.999 8	0.019 20	52.08	1.000 2	52.090	.9	.1	0.158 16	0.987 4	0.160 17	6.243	1.012 7	6.322 8	.9
.2	0.020 94	0.999 8	0.020 95	47.74	1.000 2	47.750	.8	.2	0.159 88	0.987 1	0.161 96	6.174	1.013 0	6.254 6	.8
.3	0.022 69	0.999 7	0.022 69	44.07	1.000 3	44.077	.7	.3	0.161 60	0.986 9	0.163 76	6.107	1.013 3	6.188 0	.7
.4	0.024 43	0.999 7	0.024 44	40.92	1.000 3	40.930	.6	.4	0.163 33	0.986 6	0.165 55	6.041	1.013 6	6.122 7	.6
.5	0.026 18	0.999 7	0.026 19	38.19	1.000 3	38.202	.5	.5	0.165 05	0.986 3	0.167 34	5.976	1.013 9	6.058 9	.5
.6	0.027 92	0.999 6	0.027 93	35.80	1.000 4	35.815	.4	.6	0.166 77	0.986 0	0.169 14	5.912	1.014 2	5.996 3	.4
.7	0.029 67	0.999 6	0.029 68	33.69	1.000 4	33.708	.3	.7	0.168 49	0.985 7	0.170 93	5.850	1.014 5	5.935 1	.3
.8	0.031 41	0.999 5	0.031 41	31.82	1.000 5	31.836	.2	.8	0.170 21	0.985 4	0.172 73	5.789	1.014 8	5.875 1	.2
.9	0.033 16	0.999 5	0.033 17	30.14	1.000 6	30.161	.1	.9	0.171 93	0.985 1	0.174 53	5.730	1.015 1	5.816 4	.1
2.0	0.034 90	0.999 4	0.034 92	28.64	1.000 6	28.654	88.0	10.0	0.173 6	0.984 8	0.176 3	5.671	1.015 4	5.758 8	80.0
.1	0.036 64	0.999 3	0.036 67	27.27	1.000 7	27.290	.9	.1	0.175 4	0.984 5	0.178 1	5.614	1.015 7	5.702 3	.9
.2	0.038 39	0.999 3	0.038 42	26.03	1.000 7	26.050	.8	.2	0.177 1	0.984 2	0.179 9	5.558	1.016 1	5.647 0	.8
.3	0.040 13	0.999 2	0.040 16	24.90	1.000 8	24.918	.7	.3	0.178 8	0.983 9	0.181 7	5.503	1.016 4	5.592 8	.7
.4	0.041 88	0.999 1	0.041 91	23.86	1.000 9	23.880	.6	.4	0.180 5	0.983 6	0.183 5	5.449	1.016 7	5.539 6	.6
.5	0.043 62	0.999 0	0.043 66	22.90	1.001 0	22.926	.5	.5	0.182 2	0.983 3	0.185 3	5.396	1.017 0	5.487 4	.5
.6	0.045 36	0.999 0	0.045 41	22.02	1.001 0	22.044	.4	.6	0.184 0	0.982 9	0.187 1	5.343	1.017 4	5.436 2	.4
.7	0.047 11	0.998 9	0.047 16	21.20	1.001 1	21.229	.3	.7	0.185 7	0.982 6	0.189 0	5.292	1.017 7	5.386 0	.3
.8	0.048 85	0.998 8	0.048 91	20.45	1.001 2	20.471	.2	.8	0.187 4	0.982 3	0.190 8	5.242	1.018 0	5.336 7	.2
.9	0.050 59	0.998 7	0.050 66	19.74	1.001 3	19.766	.1	.9	0.189 1	0.982 0	0.192 6	5.193	1.018 4	5.288 3	.1
3.0	0.052 34	0.998 6	0.052 41	19.081	1.001 4	19.107	87.0	11.0	0.190 8	0.981 6	0.194 4	5.145	1.018 7	5.240 8	79.0
.1	0.054 08	0.998 5	0.054 16	18.464	1.001 5	18.492	.9	.1	0.192 5	0.981 3	0.196 2	5.097	1.019 1	5.194 2	.9
.2	0.055 82	0.998 4	0.055 91	17.886	1.001 6	17.914	.8	.2	0.194 2	0.981 0	0.198 0	5.050	1.019 4	5.148 4	.8
.3	0.057 56	0.998 3	0.057 66	17.343	1.001 7	17.372	.7	.3	0.195 9	0.980 6	0.199 8	5.005	1.019 8	5.103 4	.7
.4	0.059 31	0.998 2	0.059 41	16.832	1.001 8	16.862	.6	.4	0.197 7	0.980 3	0.201 6	4.959	1.020 1	5.059 3	.6
.5	0.061 05	0.998 1	0.061 16	16.350	1.001 9	16.380	.5	.5	0.199 4	0.979 9	0.203 5	4.915	1.020 5	5.015 9	.5
.6	0.062 79	0.998 0	0.062 91	15.895	1.002 0	15.926	.4	.6	0.201 1	0.979 6	0.205 3	4.872	1.020 9	4.973 2	.4
.7	0.064 53	0.997 9	0.064 67	15.464	1.002 1	15.496	.3	.7	0.202 8	0.979 2	0.207 1	4.829	1.021 2	4.931 3	.3
.8	0.066 27	0.997 8	0.066 42	15.056	1.002 2	15.089	.2	.8	0.204 5	0.978 9	0.208 9	4.787	1.021 6	4.890 1	.2
.9	0.068 02	0.997 7	0.068 17	14.669	1.002 3	14.703	.1	.9	0.206 2	0.978 5	0.210 7	4.745	1.022 0	4.849 6	.1
4.0	0.069 76	0.997 6	0.069 93	14.301	1.002 4	14.336	86.0	12.0	0.207 9	0.978 1	0.212 6	4.705	1.022 3	4.809 7	78.0
.1	0.071 50	0.997 4	0.071 68	13.951	1.002 6	13.987	.9	.1	0.209 6	0.977 8	0.214 4	4.665	1.022 7	4.770 6	.9
.2	0.073 24	0.997 3	0.073 44	13.617	1.002 7	13.654	.8	.2	0.211 3	0.977 4	0.216 2	4.625	1.023 1	4.732 1	.8
.3	0.074 98	0.997 2	0.075 19	13.300	1.002 8	13.337	.7	.3	0.213 0	0.977 0	0.218 0	4.586	1.023 5	4.694 2	.7
.4	0.076 27	0.997 1	0.076 95	12.996	1.003 0	13.035	.6	.4	0.214 7	0.976 7	0.219 9	4.548	1.023 9	4.656 9	.6
.5	0.078 46	0.996 9	0.078 70	12.706	1.003 1	12.745	.5	.5	0.216 4	0.976 3	0.221 7	4.511	1.024 3	4.620 2	.5
.6	0.080 20	0.996 8	0.080 46	12.429	1.003 3	12.469	.4	.6	0.218 1	0.975 9	0.223 5	4.474	1.024 7	4.584 1	.4
.7	0.081 94	0.996 6	0.082 21	12.163	1.003 4	12.204	.3	.7	0.219 8	0.975 5	0.225 4	4.437	1.025 1	4.548 6	.3
.8	0.083 68	0.996 5	0.083 97	11.909	1.003 5	11.951	.2	.8	0.221 5	0.975 1	0.227 2	4.402	1.025 5	4.513 7	.2
.9	0.085 42	0.996 3	0.085 73	11.664	1.003 7	11.707	.1	.9	0.223 3	0.974 8	0.229 0	4.366	1.025 9	4.479 3	.1
5.0	0.087 16	0.996 2	0.087 49	11.430	1.003 8	11.474	85.0	13.0	0.225 0	0.974 4	0.230 9	4.331	1.026 3	4.445 4	77.0
.1	0.088 89	0.996 0	0.089 25	11.205	1.004 0	11.249	.9	.1	0.226 7	0.974 0	0.232 7	4.297	1.026 7	4.412 1	.9
.2	0.090 63	0.995 9	0.091 01	10.988	1.004 1	11.034	.8	.2	0.228 4	0.973 6	0.234 5	4.264	1.027 1	4.379 2	.8
.3	0.092 37	0.995 7	0.092 77	10.780	1.004 3	10.826	.7	.3	0.230 0	0.973 2	0.236 4	4.230	1.027 6	4.346 9	.7
.4	0.094 11	0.995 6	0.094 53	10.579	1.004 5	10.626	.6	.4	0.231 7	0.972 8	0.238 2	4.198	1.028 0	4.315 0	.6
.5	0.095 85	0.995 4	0.096 29	10.385	1.004 6	10.433	.5	.5	0.233 4	0.972 4	0.240 1	4.165	1.028 4	4.283 7	.5
.6	0.097 58	0.995 2	0.098 05	10.199	1.004 8	10.248	.4	.6	0.235 1	0.972 0	0.241 9	4.134	1.028 8	4.252 7	.4
.7	0.099 32	0.995 1	0.099 81	10.019	1.005 0	10.068	.3	.7	0.236 8	0.971 5	0.243 8	4.102	1.029 3	4.222 3	.3
.8	0.101 06	0.994 9	0.101 58	9.845	1.005 1	9.895 5	.2	.8	0.238 5	0.971 1	0.245 6	4.071	1.029 7	4.192 3	.2
.9	0.102 79	0.994 7	0.103 34	9.677	1.005 3	9.728 3	.1	.9	0.240 2	0.970 7	0.247 5	4.041	1.030 2	4.162 7	.1
6.0	0.104 53	0.994 5	0.105 10	9.514	1.005 5	9.566 8	84.0	14.0	0.241 9	0.970 3	0.249 3	4.011	1.030 6	4.133 6	76.0
.1	0.106 26	0.994 3	0.106 87	9.357	1.005 7	9.410 5	.9	.1	0.243 6	0.969 9	0.251 2	3.981	1.031 1	4.104 8	.9
.2	0.108 00	0.994 2	0.108 63	9.205	1.005 9	9.259 3	.8	.2	0.245 3	0.969 4	0.253 0	3.952	1.031 5	4.076 5	.8
.3	0.109 73	0.994 0	0.110 40	9.058	1.006 1	9.112 9	.7	.3	0.247 0	0.969 0	0.254 9	3.923	1.032 0	4.048 6	.7
.4	0.111 47	0.993 8	0.112 17	8.915	1.006 3	8.971 1	.6	.4	0.248 7	0.968 6	0.256 8	3.895	1.032 4	4.021 1	.6
.5	0.113 20	0.993 6	0.113 94	8.777	1.006 5	8.833 7	.5	.5	0.250 4	0.968 1	0.258 6	3.867	1.032 9	3.993 9	.5
.6	0.114 94	0.993 4	0.115 70	8.643	1.006 7	8.700 4	.4	.6	0.252 1	0.967 7	0.260 5	3.839	1.033 4	3.967 2	.4
.7	0.116 67	0.993 2	0.117 47	8.513	1.006 9	8.571 1	.3	.7	0.253 8	0.967 3	0.262 3	3.812	1.033 8	3.940 8	.3
.8	0.118 40	0.993 0	0.119 24	8.386	1.007 1	8.445 7	.2	.8	0.255 4	0.966 8	0.264 2	3.785	1.034 3	3.914 7	.2
.9	0.120 14	0.992 8	0.121 01	8.264	1.007 3	8.323 8	.1	.9	0.257 1	0.966 4	0.266 1	3.758	1.034 8	3.889 0	.1
7.0	0.121 87	0.992 5	0.122 78	8.144	1.007 5	8.205 5	83.0	15.0	0.258 8	0.965 9	0.267 9	3.732	1.035 3	3.863 7	75.0
.1	0.123 60	0.992 3	0.124 56	8.028	1.007 7	8.090 5	.9	.1	0.260 5	0.965 5	0.269 8	3.706	1.035 8	3.838 7	.9
.2	0.125 33	0.992 1	0.126 33	7.916	1.007 9	7.978 7	.8	.2	0.262 2	0.965 0	0.271 7	3.681	1.036 3	3.814 0	.8
.3	0.127 06	0.991 9	0.128 10	7.806	1.008 2	7.870 0	.7	.3	0.263 9	0.964 6	0.273 6	3.655	1.036 7	3.789 7	.7
.4	0.128 80	0.991 7	0.129 88	7.700	1.008 4	7.764 2	.6	.4	0.265 6	0.964 1	0.275 4	3.630	1.037 2	3.765 7	.6
.5	0.130 53	0.991 4	0.131 65	7.596	1.008 6	7.661 3	.5	.5	0.267 2	0.963 6	0.277 3	3.606	1.037 7	3.742 0	.5
.6	0.132 26	0.991 2	0.133 43	7.495	1.008 9	7.561 1	.4	.6	0.268 9	0.963 2	0.279 2	3.582	1.038 2	3.718 6	.4
.7	0.133 99	0.991 0	0.135 21	7.396	1.009 1	7.463 5	.3	.7	0.270 6	0.962 7	0.281 1	3.558	1.038 8	3.695 5	.3
.8	0.135 72	0.990 7	0.136 98	7.300	1.009 3	7.368 4	.2	.8	0.272 3	0.962 2	0.283 0	3.534	1.039 3	3.672 7	.2
.9	0.137 44	0.990 5	0.138 76	7.207	1.009 6	7.275 7	.1	.9	0.274 0	0.961 7	0.284 9	3.511	1.039 8	3.650 2	.1
Deg	Cos	Sin	Cot	Tan	Csc	Sec	Deg	Deg	Cos	Sin	Cot	Tan	Csc	Sec	Deg

TRIGONOMETRIC FUNCTIONS FOR DECIMAL-DEGREES (Cont'd)

Deg	Sin	Cos	Tan	Cot	Sec	Csc	Deg
16.0	0.275 6	0.961 3	0.286 7	3.487	1.040 3	3.628 0	74.0
.1	0.277 3	0.960 8	0.288 6	3.465	1.040 8	3.606 0	.9
.2	0.279 0	0.960 3	0.290 5	3.442	1.041 3	3.584 3	.8
.3	0.280 7	0.959 8	0.292 4	3.420	1.041 9	3.562 9	.7
.4	0.282 3	0.959 3	0.294 3	3.398	1.042 4	3.541 8	.6
.5	0.284 0	0.958 8	0.296 2	3.376	1.042 9	3.520 9	.5
.6	0.285 7	0.958 3	0.298 1	3.354	1.043 5	3.500 3	.4
.7	0.287 4	0.957 8	0.300 0	3.333	1.044 0	3.479 9	.3
.8	0.289 0	0.957 3	0.301 9	3.312	1.044 6	3.459 8	.2
.9	0.290 7	0.956 8	0.303 8	3.291	1.045 1	3.439 9	.1
17.0	0.292 4	0.956 3	0.305 7	3.271	1.045 7	3.420 3	73.0
.1	0.294 0	0.955 8	0.307 6	3.251	1.046 3	3.400 9	.9
.2	0.295 7	0.955 3	0.309 6	3.230	1.046 8	3.381 7	.8
.3	0.297 4	0.954 8	0.311 5	3.211	1.047 4	3.362 8	.7
.4	0.299 0	0.954 2	0.313 4	3.191	1.048 0	3.344 0	.6
.5	0.300 7	0.953 7	0.315 3	3.172	1.048 5	3.325 5	.5
.6	0.302 4	0.953 2	0.317 2	3.152	1.049 1	3.307 2	.4
.7	0.304 0	0.952 7	0.319 1	3.133	1.049 7	3.289 1	.3
.8	0.305 7	0.952 1	0.321 1	3.115	1.050 3	3.271 2	.2
.9	0.307 4	0.951 6	0.323 0	3.096	1.050 9	3.253 5	.1
18.0	0.309 0	0.951 1	0.324 9	3.078	1.051 5	3.236 1	72.0
.1	0.310 7	0.950 5	0.326 9	3.060	1.052 1	3.218 8	.9
.2	0.312 3	0.950 0	0.328 8	3.042	1.052 7	3.201 7	.8
.3	0.314 0	0.949 4	0.330 7	3.024	1.053 3	3.184 8	.7
.4	0.315 6	0.948 9	0.332 7	3.006	1.053 9	3.168 1	.6
.5	0.317 3	0.948 3	0.334 6	2.989	1.054 5	3.151 5	.5
.6	0.319 0	0.947 8	0.336 5	2.971	1.055 1	3.135 2	.4
.7	0.320 6	0.947 2	0.338 5	2.954	1.055 7	3.119 0	.3
.8	0.322 3	0.946 6	0.340 4	2.937	1.056 4	3.103 0	.2
.9	0.323 9	0.946 1	0.342 4	2.921	1.057 0	3.087 2	.1
19.0	0.325 6	0.945 5	0.344 3	2.904	1.057 6	3.071 6	71.0
.1	0.327 2	0.944 9	0.346 3	2.888	1.058 3	3.056 1	.9
.2	0.328 9	0.944 4	0.348 2	2.872	1.058 9	3.040 7	.8
.3	0.330 5	0.943 8	0.350 2	2.856	1.059 5	3.025 6	.7
.4	0.332 2	0.943 2	0.352 2	2.840	1.060 2	3.010 6	.6
.5	0.333 8	0.942 6	0.354 1	2.824	1.060 8	2.995 7	.5
.6	0.335 5	0.942 1	0.356 1	2.808	1.061 5	2.981 1	.4
.7	0.337 1	0.941 5	0.358 1	2.793	1.062 2	2.966 5	.3
.8	0.338 7	0.940 9	0.360 0	2.778	1.062 8	2.952 1	.2
.9	0.340 4	0.940 3	0.362 0	2.762	1.063 5	2.937 9	.1
20.0	0.342 0	0.939 7	0.364 0	2.747	1.064 2	2.923 8	70.0
.1	0.343 7	0.939 1	0.365 9	2.733	1.064 9	2.909 9	.9
.2	0.345 3	0.938 5	0.367 9	2.718	1.065 5	2.896 0	.8
.3	0.346 9	0.937 9	0.369 9	2.703	1.066 2	2.882 4	.7
.4	0.348 6	0.937 3	0.371 9	2.689	1.066 9	2.868 8	.6
.5	0.350 2	0.936 7	0.373 9	2.675	1.067 6	2.855 5	.5
.6	0.351 8	0.936 1	0.375 9	2.660	1.068 3	2.842 2	.4
.7	0.353 5	0.935 4	0.377 9	2.646	1.069 0	2.829 1	.3
.8	0.355 1	0.934 8	0.379 9	2.633	1.069 7	2.816 1	.2
.9	0.356 7	0.934 2	0.381 9	2.619	1.070 4	2.803 2	.1
21.0	0.358 4	0.933 6	0.383 9	2.605	1.071 1	2.790 4	69.0
.1	0.360 0	0.933 0	0.385 9	2.592	1.071 9	2.777 8	.9
.2	0.361 6	0.932 3	0.387 9	2.578	1.072 6	2.765 3	.8
.3	0.363 3	0.931 7	0.389 9	2.565	1.073 3	2.752 9	.7
.4	0.364 9	0.931 1	0.391 9	2.552	1.074 0	2.740 7	.6
.5	0.366 5	0.930 4	0.393 9	2.539	1.074 8	2.728 5	.5
.6	0.368 1	0.929 8	0.395 9	2.526	1.075 5	2.716 5	.4
.7	0.369 7	0.929 1	0.397 9	2.513	1.076 3	2.704 6	.3
.8	0.371 4	0.928 5	0.400 0	2.500	1.077 0	2.692 7	.2
.9	0.373 0	0.927 8	0.402 0	2.488	1.077 8	2.681 1	.1
22.0	0.374 6	0.927 2	0.404 0	2.475	1.078 5	2.669 5	68.0
.1	0.376 5	0.926 5	0.406 1	2.463	1.079 3	2.658 0	.9
.2	0.377 8	0.925 9	0.408 1	2.450	1.080 1	2.646 6	.8
.3	0.379 5	0.925 2	0.410 1	2.438	1.080 8	2.635 4	.7
.4	0.381 1	0.924 5	0.412 2	2.426	1.081 6	2.624 2	.6
.5	0.382 7	0.923 9	0.414 2	2.414	1.082 4	2.613 1	.5
.6	0.384 3	0.923 2	0.416 3	2.402	1.083 2	2.602 2	.4
.7	0.385 9	0.922 5	0.418 3	2.391	1.084 0	2.591 3	.3
.8	0.387 5	0.921 9	0.420 4	2.379	1.084 8	2.580 5	.2
.9	0.389 1	0.921 2	0.422 4	2.367	1.085 6	2.569 9	.1
23.0	0.390 7	0.920 5	0.424 5	2.356	1.086 4	2.559 3	67.0
.1	0.392 3	0.919 8	0.426 5	2.344	1.087 2	2.548 8	.9
.2	0.393 9	0.919 1	0.428 6	2.333	1.088 0	2.538 4	.8
.3	0.395 5	0.918 4	0.430 7	2.322	1.088 8	2.528 2	.7
.4	0.397 1	0.917 8	0.432 7	2.311	1.089 6	2.518 0	.6
.5	0.398 7	0.917 1	0.434 8	2.300	1.090 4	2.507 8	.5
.6	0.400 3	0.916 4	0.436 9	2.289	1.091 3	2.497 8	.4
.7	0.401 9	0.915 7	0.439 0	2.278	1.092 1	2.487 9	.3
.8	0.403 5	0.915 0	0.441 1	2.267	1.092 9	2.478 0	.2
.9	0.405 1	0.914 3	0.443 1	2.257	1.093 8	2.468 3	.1
Deg	Cos	Sin	Cot	Tan	Csc	Sec	Deg

Deg	Sin	Cos	Tan	Cot	Sec	Csc	Deg
24.0	0.406 7	0.913 5	0.445 2	2.246	1.094 6	2.458 6	66.0
.1	0.408 3	0.912 8	0.447 3	2.236	1.095 5	2.449 0	.9
.2	0.409 9	0.912 1	0.449 4	2.225	1.096 3	2.439 5	.8
.3	0.411 5	0.911 4	0.451 5	2.215	1.097 2	2.430 0	.7
.4	0.413 1	0.910 7	0.453 6	2.204	1.098 1	2.420 7	.6
.5	0.414 7	0.910 0	0.455 7	2.194	1.098 9	2.411 4	.5
.6	0.416 3	0.909 2	0.457 8	2.184	1.099 8	2.402 2	.4
.7	0.417 9	0.908 5	0.459 9	2.174	1.100 7	2.393 1	.3
.8	0.419 5	0.907 8	0.462 1	2.164	1.101 6	2.384 1	.2
.9	0.421 0	0.907 0	0.464 2	2.154	1.102 5	2.375 1	.1
25.0	0.422 6	0.906 3	0.466 3	2.145	1.103 4	2.366 2	65.0
.1	0.424 2	0.905 6	0.468 4	2.135	1.104 3	2.357 4	.9
.2	0.425 8	0.904 8	0.470 6	2.125	1.105 2	2.348 6	.8
.3	0.427 4	0.904 1	0.472 7	2.116	1.106 1	2.340 0	.7
.4	0.428 9	0.903 3	0.474 8	2.106	1.107 0	2.331 4	.6
.5	0.430 5	0.902 6	0.477 0	2.097	1.107 9	2.322 8	.5
.6	0.432 1	0.901 8	0.479 1	2.087	1.108 9	2.314 4	.4
.7	0.433 7	0.901 1	0.481 3	2.078	1.109 8	2.306 0	.3
.8	0.435 2	0.900 3	0.483 4	2.069	1.110 7	2.297 6	.2
.9	0.436 8	0.899 6	0.485 6	2.059	1.111 7	2.289 4	.1
26.0	0.438 4	0.898 8	0.487 7	2.050	1.112 6	2.281 2	64.0
.1	0.439 9	0.898 0	0.489 9	2.041	1.113 6	2.273 0	.9
.2	0.441 5	0.897 3	0.492 1	2.032	1.114 5	2.265 0	.8
.3	0.443 1	0.896 5	0.494 2	2.023	1.115 5	2.257 0	.7
.4	0.444 6	0.895 7	0.496 4	2.014	1.116 4	2.249 0	.6
.5	0.446 2	0.894 9	0.498 6	2.006	1.117 4	2.241 2	.5
.6	0.447 8	0.894 2	0.500 8	1.997	1.118 4	2.233 3	.4
.7	0.449 3	0.893 4	0.502 9	1.988	1.119 4	2.225 6	.3
.8	0.450 9	0.892 6	0.505 1	1.980	1.120 3	2.217 9	.2
.9	0.452 4	0.891 8	0.507 3	1.971	1.121 3	2.210 3	.1
27.0	0.454 0	0.891 0	0.509 5	1.963	1.122 3	2.202 7	63.0
.1	0.455 5	0.890 2	0.511 7	1.954	1.123 3	2.195 2	.9
.2	0.457 1	0.889 4	0.513 9	1.946	1.124 3	2.187 7	.8
.3	0.458 6	0.888 6	0.516 1	1.937	1.125 3	2.180 3	.7
.4	0.460 2	0.887 8	0.518 4	1.929	1.126 4	2.173 0	.6
.5	0.461 7	0.887 0	0.520 6	1.921	1.127 4	2.165 7	.5
.6	0.463 3	0.886 2	0.522 8	1.913	1.128 4	2.158 4	.4
.7	0.464 8	0.885 4	0.525 0	1.905	1.129 4	2.151 3	.3
.8	0.466 4	0.884 6	0.527 2	1.897	1.130 5	2.144 1	.2
.9	0.467 9	0.883 8	0.529 5	1.889	1.131 5	2.137 1	.1
28.0	0.469 5	0.882 9	0.531 7	1.881	1.132 6	2.130 1	62.0
.1	0.471 0	0.882 1	0.534 0	1.873	1.133 6	2.123 1	.9
.2	0.472 6	0.881 3	0.536 2	1.865	1.134 7	2.116 2	.8
.3	0.474 1	0.880 5	0.538 4	1.857	1.135 7	2.109 3	.7
.4	0.475 6	0.879 6	0.540 7	1.849	1.136 8	2.102 5	.6
.5	0.477 2	0.878 8	0.543 0	1.842	1.137 9	2.095 7	.5
.6	0.478 7	0.878 0	0.545 2	1.834	1.139 0	2.089 0	.4
.7	0.480 2	0.877 1	0.547 5	1.827	1.140 1	2.082 4	.3
.8	0.481 8	0.876 3	0.549 8	1.819	1.141 2	2.075 7	.2
.9	0.483 3	0.875 5	0.552 0	1.811	1.142 3	2.069 2	.1
29.0	0.484 8	0.874 6	0.554 3	1.804	1.143 4	2.062 7	61.0
.1	0.486 3	0.873 8	0.556 6	1.797	1.144 5	2.056 2	.9
.2	0.487 9	0.872 9	0.558 9	1.789	1.145 6	2.049 8	.8
.3	0.489 4	0.872 1	0.561 2	1.782	1.146 7	2.043 4	.7
.4	0.490 9	0.871 2	0.563 5	1.775	1.147 8	2.037 1	.6
.5	0.492 4	0.870 4	0.565 8	1.767	1.149 0	2.030 8	.5
.6	0.493 9	0.869 5	0.568 1	1.760	1.150 1	2.024 5	.4
.7	0.495 5	0.868 6	0.570 4	1.753	1.151 2	2.018 3	.3
.8	0.497 0	0.867 8	0.572 7	1.746	1.152 4	2.012 2	.2
.9	0.498 5	0.866 9	0.575 0	1.739	1.153 5	2.006 1	.1
30.0	0.500 0	0.866 0	0.577 4	1.732 1	1.154 7	2.000 0	60.0
.1	0.501 5	0.865 2	0.579 7	1.725 1	1.155 9	1.994 0	.9
.2	0.503 0	0.864 3	0.582 0	1.718 2	1.157 0	1.988 0	.8
.3	0.504 5	0.863 4	0.584 4	1.711 3	1.158 2	1.982 1	.7
.4	0.506 0	0.862 5	0.586 7	1.704 5	1.159 4	1.976 2	.6
.5	0.507 5	0.861 6	0.589 0	1.697 7	1.160 6	1.970 3	.5
.6	0.509 0	0.860 7	0.591 4	1.690 9	1.161 8	1.964 5	.4
.7	0.510 5	0.859 9	0.593 8	1.684 2	1.163 0	1.958 7	.3
.8	0.512 0	0.859 0	0.596 1	1.677 5	1.164 2	1.953 0	.2
.9	0.513 5	0.858 1	0.598 5	1.670 9	1.165 4	1.947 3	.1
31.0	0.515 0	0.857 2	0.600 9	1.664 3	1.166 6	1.941 6	59.0
.1	0.516 5	0.856 3	0.603 2	1.657 7	1.167 9	1.936 0	.9
.2	0.518 0	0.855 4	0.605 6	1.651 2	1.169 1	1.930 4	.8
.3	0.519 5	0.854 5	0.608 0	1.644 7	1.170 3	1.924 9	.7
.4	0.521 0	0.853 6	0.610 4	1.638 3	1.171 6	1.919 4	.6
.5	0.522 5	0.852 6	0.612 8	1.631 9	1.172 8	1.913 9	.5
.6	0.524 0	0.851 7	0.615 2	1.625 5	1.174 1	1.908 4	.4
.7	0.525 5	0.850 8	0.617 6	1.619 1	1.175 3	1.903 1	.3
.8	0.527 0	0.849 9	0.620 0	1.612 8	1.176 6	1.897 7	.2
.9	0.528 4	0.849 0	0.622 4	1.606 6	1.177 9	1.892 4	.1
Deg	Cos	Sin	Cot	Tan	Csc	Sec	Deg

TRIGONOMETRIC FUNCTIONS FOR DECIMAL-DEGREES (Cont'd)

Deg	Sin	Cos	Tan	Cot	Sec	Csc	Deg
32.0	0.5299	0.8480	0.6249	1.6003	1.1792	1.8871	58.0
.1	0.5314	0.8471	0.6273	1.5941	1.1805	1.8818	.9
.2	0.5329	0.8462	0.6297	1.5880	1.1818	1.8766	.8
.3	0.5344	0.8453	0.6322	1.5818	1.1831	1.8714	.7
.4	0.5358	0.8443	0.6346	1.5757	1.1844	1.8663	.6
.5	0.5373	0.8434	0.6371	1.5697	1.1857	1.8612	.5
.6	0.5388	0.8425	0.6395	1.5637	1.1870	1.8561	.4
.7	0.5402	0.8415	0.6420	1.5577	1.1883	1.8510	.3
.8	0.5417	0.8406	0.6445	1.5517	1.1897	1.8460	.2
.9	0.5432	0.8396	0.6469	1.5458	1.1910	1.8410	.1
33.0	0.5446	0.8387	0.6494	1.5399	1.1924	1.8361	57.0
.1	0.5461	0.8377	0.6519	1.5340	1.1937	1.8312	.9
.2	0.5476	0.8368	0.6544	1.5282	1.1951	1.8263	.8
.3	0.5490	0.8358	0.6569	1.5224	1.1964	1.8214	.7
.4	0.5505	0.8348	0.6594	1.5166	1.1978	1.8166	.6
.5	0.5519	0.8339	0.6619	1.5108	1.1992	1.8118	.5
.6	0.5534	0.8329	0.6644	1.505·1	1.2006	1.8070	.4
.7	0.5548	0.8320	0.6669	1.4994	1.2020	1.8023	.3
.8	0.5563	0.8310	0.6694	1.4938	1.2034	1.7976	.2
.9	0.5577	0.8300	0.6720	1.4882	1.2048	1.7929	.1
34.0	0.5592	0.8290	0.6745	1.4826	1.2062	1.7883	56.0
.1	0.5606	0.8281	0.6771	1.4770	1.2076	1.7837	.9
.2	0.5621	0.8271	0.6796	1.4715	1.2091	1.7791	.8
.3	0.5635	0.8261	0.6822	1.4659	1.2105	1.7745	.7
.4	0.5650	0.8251	0.6847	1.4605	1.2120	1.7700	.6
.5	0.5664	0.8241	0.6873	1.4550	1.2134	1.7655	.5
.6	0.5678	0.8231	0.6899	1.4496	1.2149	1.7610	.4
.7	0.5693	0.8221	0.6924	1.4442	1.2163	1.7566	.3
.8	0.5707	0.8211	0.6950	1.4388	1.2178	1.7522	.2
.9	0.5721	0.8202	0.6976	1.4335	1.2193	1.7478	.1
35.0	0..5736	0.8192	0.7002	1.4281	1.2208	1.7434	55.0
.1	0.5750	0.8181	0.7028	1.4229	1.2223	1.7391	.9
.2	0.5764	0.8171	0.7054	1.4176	1.2238	1.7348	.8
.3	0.5779	0.8161	0.7080	1.4124	1.2253	1.7305	.7
.4	0.5793	0.8151	0.7107	1.4071	1.2268	1.7263	.6
.5	0.5807	0.8141	0.7133	1.4019	1.2283	1.7221	.5
.6	0.5821	0.8131	0.7159	1.3968	1.2299	1.7179	.4
.7	0.5835	0.8121	0.7186	1.3916	1.2314	1.7137	.3
.8	0.5850	0.8111	0.7212	1.3865	1.2329	1.7095	.2
.9	0.5864	0.8100	0.7239	1.3814	1.2345	1.7054	.1
36.0	0.5878	0.8090	0.7265	1.3764	1.2361	1.7013	54.0
.1	0.5892	0.8080	0.7292	1.3713	1.2376	1.6972	.9
.2	0.5906	0.8070	0.7319	1.3663	1.2392	1.6932	.8
.3	0.5920	0.8059	0.7346	1.3613	1.2408	1.6892	.7
.4	0.5934	0.8049	0.7373	1.3564	1.2424	1.6852	.6
.5	0.5948	0.8039	0.7400	1.3514	1.2440	1.6812	.5
.6	0.5962	0.8028	0.7427	1.3465	1.2456	1.6772	.4
.7	0.5976	0.8018	0.7454	1.3416	1.2472	1.6733	.3
.8	0.5990	0.8007	0.7481	1.3367	1.2489	1.6694	.2
.9	0.6004	0.7997	0.7508	1.3319	1.2505	1.6655	.1
37.0	0.6018	0.7986	0.7536	1.3270	1.2521	1.6616	53.0
.1	0.6032	0.7976	0.7563	1.3222	1.2538	1.6578	.9
.2	0.6046	0.7965	0.7590	1.3175	1.2554	1.6540	.8
.3	0.6060	0.7955	0.7618	1.3127	1.2571	1.6502	.7
.4	0.6074	0.7944	0.7646	1.3079	1.2588	1.6464	.6
.5	0.6088	0.7934	0.7673	1.3032	1.2605	1.6427	.5
.6	0.6101	0.7923	0.7701	1.2985	1.2622	1.6390	.4
.7	0.6115	0.7912	0.7729	1.2938	1.2639	1.6353	.3
.8	0.6129	0.7902	0.7757	1.2892	1.2656	1.6316	.2
.9	0.6143	0.7891	0.7785	1.2846	1.2673	1.6279	.1
38.0	0.6157	0.7880	0.7813	1.2799	1.2690	1.6243	52.0
.1	0.6170	0.7869	0.7841	1.2753	1.2708	1.6207	.9
.2	0.6184	0.7859	0.7869	1.2708	1.2725	1.6171	.8
.3	0.6198	0.7848	0.7898	1.2662	1.2742	1.6135	.7
.4	0.6211	0.7837	0.7926	1.2617	1.2760	1.6099	.6
.5	0.6225	0.7826	0.7954	1.2572	1.2778	1.6064	.5
.6	0.6239	0.7815	0.7983	1.2527	1.2796	1.6029	.4
.7	0.6252	0.7804	0.8012	1.2482	1.2813	1.5994	.3
.8	0.6266	0.7793	0.8040	1.2437	1.2831	1.5959	.2
.9	0.6280	0.7782	0.8069	1.2393	1.2849	1.5925	.1

Deg	Sin	Cos	Tan	Cot	Sec	Csc	Deg
39.0	0.6293	0.7771	0.8098	1.2349	1.2868	1.5890	51.0
.1	0.6307	0.7760	0.8127	1.2305	1.2886	1.5856	.9
.2	0.6320	0.7749	0.8156	1.2261	1.2904	1.5822	.8
.3	0.6334	0.7738	0.8185	1.2218	1.2923	1.5788	.7
.4	0.6347	0.7727	0.8214	1.2174	1.2941	1.5755	.6
.5	0.6361	0.7716	0.8243	1.2131	1.2960	1.5721	.5
.6	0.6374	0.7705	0.8273	1.2088	1.2978	1.5688	.4
.7	0.6388	0.7694	0.8302	1.2045	1.2997	1.5655	.3
.8	0.6401	0.7683	0.8332	1.2002	1.3016	1.5622	.2
.9	0.6414	0.7672	0.8361	1.1960	1.3035	1.5590	.1
40.0	0.6428	0.7660	0.8391	1.1918	1.3054	1.5557	50.0
.1	0.6441	0.7649	0.8421	1.1875	1.3073	1.5525	.9
.2	0.6455	0.7638	0.8451	1.1833	1.3093	1.5493	.8
.3	0.6468	0.7627	0.8481	1.1792	1.3112	1.5461	.7
.4	0.6481	0.7615	0.8511	1.1750	1.3131	1.5429	.6
.5	0.6494	0.7604	0.8541	1.1708	1.3151	1.5398	.5
.6	0.6508	0.7593	0.8571	1.1667	1.3171	1.5366	.4
.7	0.6521	0.7581	0.8601	1.1626	1.3190	1.5335	.3
.8	0.6534	0.7570	0.8632	1.1585	1.3210	1.5304	.2
.9	0.654.7	0.7559	0.8662	1.1544	1.3230	1.5273	.1
41.0	0.6561	0.7547	0.8693	1.1504	1.3250	1.5243	49.0
.1	0.6574	0.7536	0.8724	1.1463	1.3270	1.5212	.9
.2	0.6587	0.7524	0.8754	1.1423	1.3291	1.5182	.8
.3	0.6600	0.7513	0.8785	1.1383	1.3311	1.5151	.7
.4	0.6613	0.7501	0.8816	1.1343	1.3331	1.5121	.6
.5	0.6626	0.7490	0.8847	1.1303	1.3352	1.5092	.5
.6	0.6639	0.7478	0.8878	1.1263	1.3373	1.5062	.4
.7	0.6652	0.7466	0.8910	1.1224	1.3393	1.5032	.3
.8	0.6665	0.7455	0.8941	1.1185	1.3414	1.5003	.2
.9	0.6678	0.7443	0.8972	1.1145	1.3435	1.4974	.1
42.0	0.6691	0.7431	0.9004	1.1106	1.3456	1.4945	48.0
.1	0.6704	0.7420	0.9036	1.1067	1.3478	1.4916	.9
.2	0.6717	0.7408	0.9067	1.1028	1.3499	1.4887	.8
.3	0.6730	0.7396	0.9099	1.0990	1.3520	1.4859	.7
.4	0.6743	0.7385	0.9131	1.0951	1.3542	1.4830	.6
.5	0.6756	0.7373	0.9163	1.0913	1.3563	1.4802	.5
.6	0.6769	0.7361	0.9195	1.0875	1.3585	1.4774	.4
.7	0.6782	0.7349	0.9228	1.0837	1.3607	1.4746	.3
.8	0.6794	0.7337	0.9260	1.0799	1.3629	1.4718	.2
.9	0.6807	0.7325	0.9293	1.0761	1.3651	1.4690	.1
43.0	0.6820	0.7314	0.9325	1.0724	1.3673	1.4663	47.0
.1	0.6833	0.7302	0.9358	1.0686	1.3696	1.4635	.9
.2	0.6845	0.7290	0.9391	1.0649	1.3718	1.4608	.8
.3	0.6858	0.7278	0.9424	1.0612	1.3741	1.4581	.7
.4	0.6871	0.7266	0.9457	1.0575	1.3763	1.4554	.6
.5	0.6884	0.7254	0.9490	1.0538	1.3786	1.4527	.5
.6	0.6896	0.7242	0.9523	1.0501	1.3809	1.4501	.4
.7	0.6909	0.7230	0.9556	1.0464	1.3832	1.4474	.3
.8	0.6921	0.7218	0.9590	1.0428	1.3855	1.4448	.2
.9	0.6934	0.7206	0.9623	1.0392	1.3878	1.4422	.1
44.0	0.6947	0.7193	0.9657	1.0355	1.3902	1.4396	46.0
.1	0.6959	0.7181	0.9691	1.0319	1.3925	1.4370	.9
.2	0.6972	0.7169	0.9725	1.0283	1.3949	1.4344	.8
.3	0.6984	0.7157	0.9759	1.0247	1.3972	1.4318	.7
.4	0.6997	0.7145	0.9793	1.0212	1.3996	1.4293	.6
.5	0.7009	0.7133	0.9827	1.0176	1.4020	1.4267	.5
.6	0.7022	0.7120	0.9861	1.0141	1.4044	1.4242	.4
.7	0.7034	0.7108	0.9896	1.0105	1.4069	1.4217	.3
.8	0.7046	0.7096	0.9930	1.0070	1.4093	1.4192	.2
.9	0.7059	0.7083	0.9965	1.0035	1.4118	1.4167	.1
45.0	0.7071	0.7071	1.0000	1.0000	1.4142	1.4142	45.0

Deg	Cos	Sin	Cot	Tan	Csc	Sec	Deg

ANSWERS TO ODD-NUMBERED EXERCISES

Answers may vary slightly due to rounding within the solution.

UNIT 1

Exercise 1-1
1. 97
3. 12 909
5. 10 008

Exercise 1-2
1. 64
3. 7 207
5. 409 012

Exercise 1-3
1. 122 in

3. a. 9 423
   b. 6 727
   c. 8 759
   d. 7 197
   e. 32 106
5. a. 60 mm
   b. 80 mm

Exercise 1-4
1. 6 384
3. 2 670 580
5. 193 996 043

Exercise 1-5
1. 73
3. 9 375 R2
5. 69 R534

Exercise 1-6
1. 588 ft
3. a. 15 cm
   b. 13 cm
   c. 17 cm
5. 4:00 PM

Exercise 1-7
1. 16
3. 13
5. 800

Exercise 1-8
1. A: hp = 3
   B: hp = 4
   C: hp = 6
   D: hp = 3
   E: hp = 6
3. 39 700 sq ft

UNIT 2

Exercise 2-1
1. $\frac{6}{16}$
3. $\frac{54}{78}$

Exercise 2-2
1. $\frac{1}{2}$
3. $\frac{3}{8}$
5. $\frac{3}{7}$

Exercise 2-3
1. $\frac{5}{2}$
3. $\frac{49}{5}$
5. $\frac{871}{16}$

Exercise 2-4
1. $3\frac{1}{2}$

3. $21\frac{3}{4}$
5. $12\frac{27}{32}$

Exercise 2-5
1. 16
3. 30

Exercise 2-6
1. $\frac{5}{8}$
3. $2\frac{1}{4}$
5. $\frac{71}{96}$

Exercise 2-7
1. $7\frac{7}{8}$
3. $16\frac{9}{16}$

Exercise 2-8
1. $\frac{2}{5}$
3. $\frac{13}{48}$
5. $\frac{7}{48}$

Exercise 2-9
1. $20\frac{7}{16}$
3. $14\frac{5}{12}$
5. $9\frac{1}{4}$
7. $41\frac{5}{28}$

Exercise 2-10
1. $10\frac{3}{8}$ lb
3. $3\ 462\frac{3}{4}$ ft

Exercise 2-11
1. $\frac{1}{16}$
3. $\frac{7}{10}$
5. $\frac{11}{72}$
7. $\frac{2}{5}$
9. $\frac{19}{99}$

Exercise 2-12
1. $4\frac{1}{2}$
3. $11\frac{2}{3}$
5. $1\frac{2}{15}$
7. $21\frac{7}{10}$
9. $168\frac{13}{36}$

UNIT 2 (Cont'd)

Exercise 2-13

1. $1\frac{1}{4}$

3. $\frac{2}{3}$

5. $1\frac{22}{27}$

7. $3\frac{1}{3}$

9. $1\frac{1}{2}$

Exercise 2-14

1. 21

3. $\frac{1}{18}$

5. $\frac{14}{81}$

7. $55\frac{1}{3}$

9. $2\frac{41}{75}$

Exercise 2-15

1. a. (1) $5\frac{1}{4}$ T

   (2) 9 T

(3) $3\frac{3}{4}$ T

(4) $13\frac{1}{2}$ T

(5) $2\frac{1}{4}$ T

(6) $3\frac{3}{4}$ T

(7) 3 T

b. (1) $8\frac{3}{4}$ T

(2) 15 T

(3) $6\frac{1}{4}$ T

(4) $22\frac{1}{2}$ T

(5) $3\frac{3}{4}$ T

(6) $6\frac{1}{4}$ T

(7) 5 T

3. a. (1) $3\,712\frac{1}{2}$ lb

(2) 2 700 lb

(3) $202\frac{1}{2}$ lb

(4) 54 lb

(5) 27 lb

(6) 0

(7) 54 lb

b. (1) 6 000 lb

(2) $37\frac{1}{2}$ lb

(3) 0

(4) 750 lb

(5) 675 lb

(6) $18\frac{3}{4}$ lb

(7) $18\frac{3}{4}$ lb

c. (1) 4 620 lb

(2) 105 lb

(3) 0

(4) $472\frac{1}{2}$ lb

(5) $10\frac{1}{2}$ lb

(6) 0

(7) 42 lb

Exercise 2-16

1. $\frac{7}{16}$

3. $2\frac{5}{9}$

5. $5\frac{4}{9}$

7. $11\frac{37}{40}$

9. $4\frac{53}{140}$

Exercise 2-17

1. a. $343\,809\frac{37}{48}$ sq ft

   b. 38 201 sq ft

3. a. $14\frac{1}{4}$ bd ft

   b. 8 bd ft

   c. $8\frac{7}{9}$ bd ft

   d. $31\frac{1}{36}$ bd ft

UNIT 3

Exercise 3-1

1. 0.78

3. 0.01

5. 3.81

7. 139.01

Exercise 3-2

1. 0.875

3. 0.95

5. 0.810

Exercise 3-3

1. $\frac{4}{5}$

3. $\frac{31}{500}$

5. $\frac{67}{200}$

Exercise 3-4

1. 0.63

3. 0.11

Exercise 3-5

1. 0.346

3. 118.768

5. 12.040

Exercise 3-6

1. 0.573

3. 0.000 4

5. 12.388

Exercise 3-7

1. $4.95

3. 8.50 in

Exercise 3-8

1. 0.45

3. 0.100 8

5. 0.002 3

7. 7.236

Exercise 3-9

1. 3.1

3. 373 700

5. 0.017 023

Exercise 3-10

1. 4

3. 18

5. 0.002

7. 0.003

Exercise 3-11

1. 0.037

3. 0.298 05

5. 260

Exercise 3-12

1. 131.4 brake hp

3. a. $252.51

   b. $197.35

Exercise 3-13

1. 121

3. 0.25

5. 74.088

7. 0.512

9. 0.057 6

Exercise 3-14

1. 9

3. 1

5. 3

7. 7

9. 8

11. 4

Exercise 3-15

1. 19.80

3. 0.965 2

5. 22.47

7. 0.03

9. 1.762

UNIT 3 (Cont'd)

Exercise 3-16

1. a. A: 10.24 sq ft
        V: 32.77 cu ft
   b. A: 349.69 mm^2
       V: 6 539.20 mm^3
   c. A: 0.25 m^2
       V: 0.13 m^3
   d. A: 96.04 sq in
       V:941.19 cu in
3. 2 m

Exercise 3-17

1. 11.51
3. 171.68

Exercise 3-18

1. 0.077 cm
3. 13.91 ft

UNIT 4

Exercise 4-1

1. a. 0.23
   b. 0.059
   c. 2.187
   d. 0.035
   e. 1.103

Exercise 4-2

1. 83%
3. 315.8%
5. 175%

Exercise 4-3

1. 20
3. 117.14
5. 27.75
7. 35.79
9. 4.2
11. 41.24%
13. 119.6
15. 140.94%
17. 73.91%
19. 32.75%

Exercise 4-4

1. 82.5 bd ft
3. 95 pieces
5. 92.31%
7. 56.67%
9. 180 ft
11. 1 440 units
13. 1 734 ft
15. 8 lb
17. 60 m^3
19. 122 units

Exercise 4-5

1. 24
3. 34.7
5. Mean: 0.502 5
    Median: 0.502
    Mode: 0.502

Exercise 4-6

1. 31.1 mi/gal
3. a. Mean: 21.7° C
   b. Median: 22.4° C

Exercise 4-7

1. a. Range: 4
       Mean Deviation: 1
   b. Range: 0.009
       Mean Deviation: 0.003
3. Range: 1.1 lb/sq in
    Mean Deviation: 0.3 lb/sq in

Exercise 4-8

1. a. $10 600 000
   b. $2 350 000
   c. 22.2%
   d. 22.6%
3. a. 1 900 r/min
   b. (1)   190 ft-lb
       (2)   205 ft-lb
       (3)   185 ft-lb
       (4)   160 ft-lb
   c. 70%

Exercise 4-9

1. (See Instructor's Guide)
3. (See Instructor's Guide)

UNIT 5

Exercise 5-1

1. 2.125 ft
3. 0.75 mi
5. 15 yd 2 ft
7. 38 ft
9. 81 in
11. 146 yd 2 ft

Exercise 5-2

1. 12 ft 3 in
3. 10 ft $1\frac{3}{4}$ in
5. 2 yd $1\frac{1}{2}$ ft
7. 20 ft 10 in
9. 15 yd 1 ft 4 in
11. 3 yd $2\frac{2}{3}$ ft

Exercise 5-3

1. A = 49′-6″
    B = 4′-0″
    C = 26′-10″
    D = 12′-10″
3. Distance A = 300 ft
    Distance B = 375 ft

UNIT 5 (Cont'd)

Exercise 5-4
1. 3 cm
3. 2.46 m
5. 0.65 km
7. 750 mm
9. 0.372 5 km

Exercise 5-5
1. 76.6 mm
3. 77.4 m
5. 2 240 m
7. 118.87 dm

Exercise 5-6
1. A = 24 mm
   B = 38.67 mm
   C = 32.4 mm
   D = 30 mm
3. 48 km

Exercise 5-7
1. 15.748 in
3. 14.764 ft
5. 2.461 ft
7. 5.031 yd
9. 3.858 in

Exercise 5-8
1. 203.2 mm
3. 1.77 m

5. 82.30 cm
7. 1.18 km
9. 2.50 m

Exercise 5-9
1. 3.5 sq ft
3. 604.8 sq in
5. 5 A
7. 47.7 sq ft
9. 103.68 sq in

Exercise 5-10
1. 5.30 cm^2
3. 1.460 m^2
5. 600 dm^2
7. $9 000 \text{ m}^2$
9. 0.028 m^2

Exercise 5-11
1. 48 pieces
3. 0.55 m^2

Exercise 5-12
1. 3.1 sq in
3. 0.961 sq in

Exercise 5-13
1. 90.328 cm^2
3. 6.475 km^2

Exercise 5-14
1. 2.72 cu ft
3. 1 209.6 cu in
5. 1 088.64 cu in
7. 0.43 cu yd

Exercise 5-15
1. 2.40 cm^3
3. $7 000 \text{ cm}^3$
5. $3 800 \text{ dm}^3$
7. 0.06 m^3

Exercise 5-16
1. 222.478 cu ft
3. 139.291 cm^3
5. 10.736 cu in

Exercise 5-17
1. 27.78 cu ft
3. 12.52 cm^3
5. 6.61 cu yd

Exercise 5-18
1. 60 qt
3. 3.25 qt
5. 415.8 cu in
7. 1.6 pt

Exercise 5-19
1. 1 300 mL
3. 93.4 cm^3

5. 0.54 m^3
7. 60 mL

Exercise 5-20
1. 10.993 qt
3. 30.28 L
5. 1.656 L
7. 1.416 pt

Exercise 5-21
1. 2.13 lb
3. 21.43 long tons
5. 1 320 lb

Exercise 5-22
1. 1.88 kg
3. 2 700 kg
5. 210 g

Exercise 5-23
1. 339.57 lb
3. 7.7 oz
5. 6 769.35 lb

Exercise 5-24
1. 1.7 L
3. 2.5 qt
5. 24 holes
7. 6.03 long tons

UNIT 6

Exercise 6-1
1. a + 3
3. 7 − d
5. xy
7. b ÷ 25
9. e + 12
11. 20 ÷ n
13. y − 75
15. $a + b^2$
17. 3V − 12
19. $\frac{1}{2}x - 4y$

21. 9 m + 2 n
23. x ÷ 25y
25. a. a + 6″ + b
    b. 6″ + b + 3a
    c. b + 3a + 5″
    d. a + 5″ + 3a + b =
       4a + b + 5″
27. L ÷ N
29. B − C + D
31. $0.785 \ 4D^2LN$
33. $\sqrt{x^2 + R^2}$

Exercise 6-2
1. a. 18
   b. 3
   c. 10
   d. 24
   e. 8
3. a. 105
   b. 52
   c. 48
   d. 7
   e. 9.6

5. a. 138
   b. 11
   c. 8
   d. 5
   e. 50
7. 0.5 min
9. 30 mils
11. 54° F
13. 77.1 hp
15. 5 500 sq ft
17. 131.59 cm
19. 11.1 m

UNIT 6 (Cont'd)

Exercise 6-3
1. $6x + 12$
3. $\frac{1}{4}mR$
5. $d \div 14f$
7. $2M - \frac{1}{3}R$

9. $(F^2 + G) \div H$
11. $M \div C$
13. $3GH$
15. $S + S + S + S - 2G$
   or $4S - 2G$
17. a. 7
   b. 55

c. 5
d. 4
19. a. 66
   b. 51
   c. 12
   d. 25
21. 163.2 gal
23. 15.1 mm

UNIT 7

Exercise 7-1
1. -8 mi/h
3. $-\$18$
5. $-\$48\,000$
7. $+9$ volts
9. $-\$280$

Exercise 7-2
1. $+6$
3. $+2$
5. $+8$
7. -11
9. $+6$
11. -20
13. -11
15. -4
17. $+6$
19. $+11$
21. $+5\frac{1}{2}$
23. -3.5
25. -7.25
27. $-2\frac{3}{4}$
29. -2.25
31. -4.25
33. $+3; 5$
35. $+1; 6$
37. $-28; 45$
39. $-14; 4$
41. $+2.5; 5$
43. $+18.3; 38.9$
45. $+1\frac{1}{16}; 2\frac{15}{16}$
47. $+\frac{3}{16}; \frac{15}{32}$
49. $-22, -18, -1, 0, +2,$
   $+4, +16$

51. $-15, -8, -3, 0, +3,$
   $+15, +17$
53. $-1.1, -1, -0.4, +1,$
   $+2.3, +17.8$
55. $-6\frac{1}{4}, -6\frac{5}{32}, -1\frac{1}{2},$
   $-1\frac{15}{32}, -1\frac{7}{16}, 0$

Exercise 7-3
1. 5
3. 4
5. 9
7. 1
9. 0
11. $2\frac{1}{2}$
13. 2.9
15. 0.023

Exercise 7-4
1. 15
3. 24
5. 25
7. -23
9. -29
11. 7
13. -3
15. -6
17. -22
19. -35
21. -18.8
23. -19.1
25. -13
27. $-13\frac{3}{16}$
29. -14.47

31. 1
33. 18
35. 30.1

Exercise 7-5
1. -2
3. 18
5. -8
7. 22
9. 0
11. -80
13. -7
15. -5
17. 44
19. 2.2
21. -2.2
23. 101.2
25. $3\frac{1}{4}$
27. 10
29. 15
31. -1
33. 11.15
35. -10

Exercise 7-6
1. -24
3. 24
5. -20
7. -35
9. 0
11. -13
13. -11.2
15. $-\frac{3}{4}$
17. 0
19. -8

21. 8
23. 0
25. -1
27. 1
29. $-2\frac{3}{8}$

Exercise 7-7
1. 2
3. -2
5. -7
7. 6
9. 8
11. 4
13. -3
15. -6
17. 120
19. -0.75
21. $-\frac{1}{4}$
23. -12
25. $-1\frac{5}{8}$
27. -5.6
29. -4.08

Exercise 7-8
1. 4
3. 8
5. -27
7. 16
9. -32
11. -125
13. 64
15. -1.728
17. -0.027
19. $\frac{1}{4}$

UNIT 7 (Cont'd)

Exercise 7-8 (Cont'd)

21. $\frac{1}{8}$

23. $-\frac{27}{64}$

25. $-\frac{1}{2}$

27. $-\frac{1}{27}$

29. $-\frac{1}{125}$

31. $\frac{1}{32}$

33. $-\frac{1}{9.261}$ or
    -0.108 (rounded)

Exercise 7-9

1. 3
3. -4
5. -3
7. 3
9. -5
11. -2
13. 1
15. -1
17. 1
19. 3
21. $\frac{2}{3}$
23. $-\frac{2}{3}$
25. $-\frac{1}{2}$

27. 1

29. $-\frac{3}{8}$

Exercise 7-10

1. 2
3. 12
5. 3
7. 2
9. -5
11. 4
13. $\frac{1}{2}$
15. $\frac{1}{4}$

Exercise 7-11

1. -28
3. 33
5. 3
7. -64
9. 0
11. -35
13. 2 928
15. 2
17. 1
19. 964

Exercise 7-12

1. $-\$20\ 000$
3. $+18\%$

5. a. $+9$
   b. $+5.4$
   c. -9.2
   d. $+0.8$
   e. -2.4
   f. -2.8
   g. $+11.6$
   h. -5.8
7. -19
9. -7
11. 0
13. -4.7
15. 11
17. -6
19. 23
21. 11.5
23. -18
25. 9.4
27. 11
29. 5.47
31. -15
33. 27
35. -16.8
37. -0.15
39. 81
41. $7\frac{7}{8}$
43. -5.4
45. 4
47. 8
49. -25
51. 0

53. -4.2
55. 16
57. 64
59. -32
61. -0.008
63. $\frac{1}{8}$
65. $\frac{1}{100}$
67. -4
69. -3
71. 3
73. -5
75. $\frac{1}{2}$
77. -32
79. 145
81. 85
83. 4 896
85. -0.125
87. 43
89. $+\frac{1}{4}$
91. a. (1) $+\$40\ 000$
       (2) $-\$50\ 000$
       (3) $-\$40\ 000$
       (4) $-\$15\ 000$
       (5) $+\$50\ 000$
       (6) $+\$50\ 000$
    b. (1) $+\$3\ 000$
       (2) $-\$26\ 250$
       (3) $-\$5\ 625$

UNIT 8

Exercise 8-1

1. 11a
3. $-4x$
5. 21y
7. $-22xy$
9. 0
11. $-8pt$
13. $15.2a^2b$
15. $1\frac{1}{4}xy$
17. $-2.91gh^3$
19. 6P
21. $-1\frac{7}{8}xy$
23. 6.666M

25. $13x + 18Y$
27. $10x + 7xy + 4y$
29. $4x + (-xy)$
31. $x^2y + (-xy^2) + (-15x^2y^2)$
33. $-0.4c + 3.6cd + 2.9d$
35. $6b^4 + (-6b^2c)$
37. $6.4x$
39. $4\frac{1}{2}B$
41. $A = 2.3x$
    $B = 3.8x$
    $C = 6.1x$
    $D = 4.0x$

$E = 7.2x$
$F = 3.1x$
$G = 1.1x$

Exercise 8-2

1. $2x$
3. $-8a$
5. $-8y^2$
7. 0
9. $-11c^2$
11. 16M
13. $-6.1P$
15. 0.1D
17. c^2d

19. $1\frac{3}{8}H$
21. $-6.1xy$
23. g^2h
25. $-3P^2 + 5P$
27. 4
29. $-N + 11NS$
31. $-ab + a^2b - ab^2$
33. $5x^3 + x^2 - 3x$
35. $-\frac{1}{4}x + \frac{1}{4}x^2 - \frac{3}{8}x^3$
37. $10.09e + 15.76f + 10.03$

UNIT 8 (Cont'd)

39. $A = 1\frac{3}{4}x$

$B = \frac{7}{8}x$

$C = \frac{1}{4}x$

$D = \frac{7}{8}x$

$E = 1\frac{1}{8}x$

$F = 2\frac{1}{4}x$

41. $0.5x$

Exercise 8-3

1. $2x^3$
3. $-10c^5$
5. $27a^3b^3c^5$
7. $12c^5d^3$
9. $12P^8N^4$
11. $1.25x^4y^4$
13. 0
15. $\frac{15}{32}x^5y^3$
17. a^2b^2cd
19. $1.8F^3G^3$
21. $80x^2y^4P$
23. x^6y^3
25. $6x^2 + 2xy$
27. $3M^3 - 3M^2N$
29. $30c^3d^4 - 40c^2d^2$
31. $-r^4t^3s^3 + r^2t^3s^2 - r^5t^4s$
33. $-f^2g + 9fg^2 - 12fh$
35. $x^2 + xy + xy + y^2 =$
$x^2 + 2xy + y^2$
37. $x^2 - xy - xy + y^2 =$
$x^2 - 2xy + y^2$
39. $4a^4 + 24a + 5a^3 + 30$
41. $21a^3x^5 - 3ac^2x^2 +$
$7a^2cx^4 - c^3x$
43. $16x^4y^6 - 36x^2y^2$
45. a. $15N$
b. 6.5 min $(N - 20$ r/min$)$
47. a. $0.6xy$
b. $1.25xy$
c. $3xy$
d. $5xy$
e. $8xy$
49. a. $0.392\ 7x^3$
b. $0.785\ 4(x^2)(0.5x - 6$ m$)$

Exercise 8-4

1. $2x$
3. 2
5. $5xy^4$
7. 1
9. $6a^3$
11. $-DM^2$
13. 2.6
15. $5cd$
17. $8g^2h$
19. xz^3
21. $4P^2V$
23. $8xyz$
25. $3x^2 + 5x$
27. $3x^2y^2 - 2xy$
29. $-14M + 12MN$
31. $4ab + 3a^2$
33. $0.3xy^3 + 0.1y^2$
35. $xy^3z - z^4 - xy$
37. $4a - 6a^2c - 8c^2$
39. $-3G - 7EG^2 + 9E^2H$
41. a. $2x$
b. $0.5x$
c. $1.2x$
d. $9\ 600x^2$
e. $1\ 500x^2$
f. $4\ 000x^2$
43. a. $0.1x + 0.8$ in
b. $0.2x + 0.4$ in
45. $A = 0.5x + 2$ mm
$B = 0.4y + 1$ mm
$C = 0.4x + 1$ mm
$D = 0.65\ y + 0.5$ mm

Exercise 8-5

1. a^2b^2
3. $9a^2b^2$
5. $8x^6y^3$
7. $-27c^9d^6e^{12}$
9. $49x^8y^{10}$
11. $a^6b^3c^9$
13. $-x^{12}y^{15}z^3$
15. $0.064x^9y^3$
17. $10.24M^6N^2P^4$
19. $\frac{27}{64}a^3b^3c^9$
21. $-27x^6y^{12}z^9$
23. $\frac{25}{64}a^8b^4c^{12}$

25. $a^2 + 2ab + b^2$
27. $x^4 + 2x^2y + y^2$
29. $4x^4 - 12x^2y^3 + 9y^6$
31. $x^4y^6 + 2x^3y^5 + x^2y^4$
33. $20.25M^2P^2 - 9M^2P^5 + P^8$
35. $a^{12} - 2a^6b^6 + b^{12}$
37. a. $49x^2$
b. $0.062\ 5x^2$
c. $10\frac{9}{16}x^2$
d. $(x + 3\ m)^2$
e. $(2x + 6\ in)^2$
39. a. $50.24x^2$
b. $0.125\ 6x^2$
c. $158.287\ 4x^2$
d. $3.14(x + 2\ ft)^2$
e. $3.14(3x + 1\ mm)^2$

Exercise 8-6

1. $2abc$
3. $4cd^3$
5. $-4xy^3$
7. $5fg^4$
9. $7cd^3e^5$
11. $-3x^2y^4$
13. $0.8a^3c^4f$
15. $10\sqrt{xy}$
17. $12p^2\sqrt{ms}$
19. $\frac{1}{4}y^2\sqrt{x}$
21. $-4d^2t^3$
23. $3f^2\sqrt[3]{d^2e}$
25. $2h^2$
27. $t^2\sqrt[3]{c^2d}$
29. $\frac{2}{3}a^2c^3\sqrt{b}$
31. a. $10x$
b. $0.6x$
c. $1.2x$
d. $\frac{1}{2}x$
33. a. $2x$
b. $4x$
c. $0.2x$
d. $0.3x$

UNIT 8 (Cont'd)

Exercise 8-7

1. $7a - 2a^2 + a^3$
3. $9b - 15b^2 + c - d$
5. $4y^2 + 5$
7. $-xy$
9. $-2c^3 + d - 12$
11. $-16 - xy$
13. 0
15. $34 - c^2d$

Exercise 8-8

1. $14 + 13a$
3. $20 - 49x^2y^2$
5. $7c^2 - 9d$
7. $6 + 5H^2 - 3H^4$
9. $y - xy + 5x$
11. $b^6 + 12$
13. $4D$
15. $-80a + 5a^4b^6$
17. $20c - c^5d^2 + 4c^2$
19. $-16x^2y$

Exercise 8-9

1. $-3x$
3. $8MP$
5. $14.7a^2c$
7. $\frac{5}{8}x^2y^3$
9. $6x$
11. $1\frac{3}{8}ab$
13. $9a + 14b$
15. $6m + 3mn$
17. $-4.3F + (-4.9G)$
19. $-6P$
21. 0

23. $-0.7x^2$
25. $0.24H$
27. $\frac{5}{16}B$
29. $-cd^2$
31. $2R + 3R^2$
33. $T + 8TW$
35. $-y^3 + 4y^2 - 4y$
37. $-\frac{3}{8}c - \frac{1}{4}d + 4\frac{1}{4} - cd$
39. $60x^3y^3$
41. $-20c^3d^3e^5$
43. $2.58x^4y^3$
45. $\frac{9}{32}a^4b^3c$
47. $c^3b^2d^3$
49. $-\frac{1}{10}P^4S^3$
51. $7D^5 - 7D^3H$
53. $-a^4b^3c^6 + a^2b^4c^4 - a^2b^5c^5$
55. $-20m^4 + 43m^2n^3 - 21n^6$
57. $0.64P^3S^3 + 0.4P^4S + 9.6S^2 + 6P$
59. $2y$
61. $-c$
63. $7m^3$
65. $5.2a^2b$
67. $12EF$
69. $\frac{1}{8}ab^2$
71. $3x^2 - 2x$
73. $5CD^4 + 4C^2D^3$
75. $0.2FG^2 + 0.1F^2G$
77. $2x - 3x^2y - 8y^2$
79. $25a^2b^2$
81. $9M^8p^4$
83. $81M^{12}P^8T^{16}$
85. $37.21d^6f^2h^4$
87. $49x^8b^{12}c^2$

89. $0.16m^6n^6s^{12}$
91. $x^4 + 2x^2y + y^2$
93. $9a^4 + 12a^2b + 4b^2$
95. $0.64P^4T^6 - 0.64P^2T^4 + 0.16T^2$
97. $F^{12} - 2F^6H^6 + H^{12}$
99. $3xy^2z$
101. $2MP^2T^3$
103. $0.4F^2H$
105. $10y\sqrt{x}$
107. $-4\sqrt[3]{d^2e}$
109. $-2a^2b\sqrt[5]{c^2}$
111. $-3a^2 - b + c^2$
113. $-xy$
115. $13 - P$
117. $25 - m^2r + 2r$
119. $18 + 31x$
121. $2M^2 - 3P$
123. $6 - 3D + 3D^2$
125. $6x - x^5y^2 + 2x^2 + 4y$
127. $-12m^2t$
129. a. $0.75x$
　　b. $0.15x$
　　c. $0.25x$
131. a. (1) $x + \$90$
　　　(2) $2x + \$40$
　　　(3) $2x + \$50$
　　b. $27x + \$560$
　　c. $5.4x + \$112$
133. a. $\frac{1}{2}(2x + 4\text{ in})(x + 10\text{ in})$
　　b. $\frac{1}{2}(2x + 6\text{ in})(x + 10\text{ in})$
　　c. $\frac{1}{2}(2x + 4\text{ in})(x + 6\text{ in})$
　　d. $\frac{1}{2}(4x + 8\text{ in})(2x + 20\text{ in})$

UNIT 9

Exercise 9-1

1. 15
3. 10
5. 4
7. 6
9. 6
11. 7
13. 10
15. a. 3 ft
　　b. 9 ft

17. a. 10 000 sq ft
　　b. 20 000 sq ft
　　c. 20 000 sq ft
　　d. 15 000 sq ft
19. a. 400 cal
　　b. 800 cal
　　c. 1 200 cal
21. 3 in
23. 2 cm
25. 6°

27. a. 20 V
　　b. 16 V
　　c. 26 V
　　d. 40 V
　　e. 18 V
29. a. 24°
　　b. 48°
　　c. 52°
　　d. 56°
　　e. 72°
　　f. 156°

Exercise 9-2

1. 10
3. 19
5. 4
7. 36
9. -22
11. -53
13. 34
15. -50
17. 18.8
19. 24.09

UNIT 9 (Cont'd)

21. 0

23. $-1\frac{5}{8}$

25. $-3\frac{1}{4}$

27. $-23\frac{1}{8}$

29. -17.101

31. 2.3

33. $\frac{7}{16}$ in

35. $61\frac{1}{2}°$

37. $194.75

39. 7.22 cm

41. 75 W

43. 4.428 6 in

45. 3.48 cm

Exercise 9-3

1. 40

3. 13

5. 3

7. -14

9. 20

11. 9

13. 49

15. 1.3

17. 8.00

19. 105.70

21. 109.861

23. 1

25. $18\frac{1}{2}$

27. 0

29. $-\frac{1}{32}$

31. 58.37 mm

33. $17' -10''$

35. 8.048 in

37. 53.3 mm

39. $25.75

41. 80.6 cm

Exercise 9-4

1. 8

3. 4

5. -9

7. 0.08

9. -3.5

11. 0

13. 6

15. -8.8

17. 0

19. 7

21. -7.2

23. 64

25. 5

27. 1

29. $-2\ 469$

31. 25.7 mm

33. 8''

35. 15.8 ft

37. 230 V

39. 10.5 A

41. 3.5 yr

Exercise 9-5

1. 20

3. 63

5. 27

7. 0

9. 36

11. 18

13. 23.4

15. -6

17. 0

19. 0.001

21. 0.083 2

23. $3\frac{3}{4}$

25. 2

27. $\frac{3}{8}$

29. 0.9

31. 150°

33. 259 sq ft

35. 44 mi

37. 12 V

39. 1 125 ft-lb

Exercise 9-6

1. 4

3. 9

5. 3

7. 12

9. 5

11. 100

13. $\frac{2}{3}$

15. $\frac{3}{5}$

17. $-\frac{1}{2}$

19. $\frac{4}{5}$

21. 0.3

23. 1.5

25. 0.4

27. 2.8

29. 0.3

31. a.   7 ft

    b.   9 mm

    c. $\frac{5}{8}$

    d.   2.5 m

    e.   0.6 yd

Exercise 9-7

1. 64

3. 1.44

5. 0.672 4

7. 12.167

9. -0.001

11. 0

13. -32

15. -0.216

17. 0.001

19. $\frac{9}{16}$

21. $\frac{1}{16}$

23. $\frac{25}{64}$

25. $15\frac{5}{8}$

27. $5\frac{23}{64}$

29. $\frac{-27}{1\ 000}$

31. a.   12.96 cm²

    b.   0.705 6 m²

    c. $30\frac{1}{4}$ sq in

    d. $\frac{9}{16}$ sq ft

    e.   0.008 1 m²

Exercise 9-8

1. 6

3. 3

5. $350 000

7. 60 V

9. 4

11. -13

13. 33

15. -2

17. -12

19. 1

21. -1.1

23. 10

25. 4.64

27. $3\frac{3}{4}$

29. $\frac{1}{8}$

31. $-25\frac{11}{16}$

33. -7

35. 32

37. -324

39. 0

41. -17

43. 2.2

45. 2.28

47. 3.4

49. 57.68

51. 12

53. $-\frac{3}{32}$

55. $-2\frac{5}{8}$

57. 4

59. 121

61. 5

63. 0

65. 0.49

67. -0.5

69. 0.3

71. 0.3

73. -1

75. $-\frac{1}{3}$

77. $\frac{8}{125}$

79. $-20\frac{51}{64}$

81. 2.8 in

83. 2.5 cm

85. $5 200

87. 120 V

89. 5 cm

91. $1 134

UNIT 10

Exercise 10-1

1. 8
3. 7
5. 2
7. 0.2
9. 9
11. −0.67
13. 4.8
15. 7
17. 31.3
19. 3
21. 4
23. −1
25. 36
27. 3
29. 6

Exercise 10-2

1. 6 ft
3. 750 turns
5. 15 ft
7. 45
9. 46.771 A

Exercise 10-3

1. $b = \dfrac{A}{a}$
3. $E = IR$

5. $\angle C = 180° - \angle A - \angle B$
7. $S + \dfrac{1.732}{N} = T$
9. $\dfrac{C_a + SF}{S} = C$
11. $\dfrac{1\,000P}{E} = I$
13. $IR + E_c = E_x$
15. $\sqrt{PR} = E$
17. $\dfrac{D_o + d - 2a}{2} = c$
19. $I^2R = P$
21. $M + 0.866P - 3W = E$
23. $\dfrac{L - 1.57D - 2x}{1.57} = d$
25. a. $\dfrac{FR}{r} = W$
    b. $\dfrac{FR}{W} = r$
27. a. $\dfrac{2A - a(H + h) - cH}{h} = b$
    b. $\dfrac{2A - bh - cH}{H + h} = a$

Exercise 10-4

1. 4
3. 7
5. −6.5
7. 7.5
9. 12.6
11. 8
13. −2
15. 0.25
17. 2.069
19. 248.200
21. a. $\dfrac{R}{1.155} = r$
    b. $\sqrt{\dfrac{A}{2.598}} = R$
23. a. $\sqrt{d^2 - b^2} = a$
    b. $\sqrt{d^2 - a^2} = b$
25. a. $\dfrac{D_o - 2C + d}{2} = a$
    b. $\dfrac{D_o + d - 2a}{2} = C$
27. a. $\dfrac{6V - 2abh}{bh} = c$
    b. $\dfrac{6V - cbh}{2bh} = a$

UNIT 11

Exercise 11-1

1. $\dfrac{3}{7}$
3. $\dfrac{1}{2}$
5. $\dfrac{4}{15}$
7. $\dfrac{6}{23}$
9. $\dfrac{9}{22}$
11. $\dfrac{13}{4}$
13. $\dfrac{1}{x}$
15. $\dfrac{5}{7}$
17. $\dfrac{2}{1}$
19. $\dfrac{4}{3}$
21. $\dfrac{32}{3}$

23. $\dfrac{c}{b}$
25. $\dfrac{1}{6}$
27. $\dfrac{30}{23}$
29. $\dfrac{1}{2}$
31. $\dfrac{2}{5}$
33. $\dfrac{3}{4}$
35. $\dfrac{1}{2}$
37. a. $\dfrac{11}{15}$
    b. $\dfrac{8}{13}$
    c. $\dfrac{13}{15}$
    d. $\dfrac{8}{11}$

39. a. $\dfrac{2}{5}$
    b. $\dfrac{1}{3}$
    c. $\dfrac{2}{5}$
    d. $\dfrac{1}{3}$
    e. $\dfrac{3}{8}$
    f. $\dfrac{5}{12}$
    g. $\dfrac{3}{7}$
    h. $\dfrac{1}{3}$

Exercise 11-2

1. 1
3. 35
5. 12

7. 17.5
9. 2.2
11. 8.2
13. 4
15. $\dfrac{5}{6}$
17. $-31\dfrac{1}{2}$
19. 5.25
21. 0.5
23. 6
25. a. 16 ft
    b. 4 ft
    c. 10 m
    d. 4.4 m
    e. 13 ft
27. 4.0 m
29. 0.665 in

UNIT 11 (Cont'd)

Exercise 11-3
1. 8 gal
3. a. 3 m
   b. 23 mL
   c. 15 mL
   d. 0.5 pt
   e. 3.5 g
   f. 5.33 . . .3
   g. 22.5 g
5. 8 bakers
7. a. 2 400 L
   b. 4 080 L
   c. 2 232 L
9. 2 214.5 r/min
11. a. Pulley B
        846 r/min
        Pulley C
        270 r/min
    b. Pulley A
        14.4 cm
        Pulley C
        24 cm

c. Pulley A
    600 r/min
    Pulley B
    7.5 cm
d. Pulley A
    16.8 cm
    Pulley B
    875 r/min

Exercise 11-4

1. $\dfrac{15}{32}$

3. $\dfrac{6}{23}$

5. $\dfrac{7}{16}$

7. $\dfrac{5x}{1}$

9. $\dfrac{1}{2}$

11. $\dfrac{H}{F}$

13. $\dfrac{5}{1}$

15. $\dfrac{3}{2}$

17. $\dfrac{3}{4}$

19. a. $\dfrac{15}{24}$

        $\dfrac{5}{3}$

    b. $\dfrac{7}{12}$

        $\dfrac{7}{5}$

    c. $\dfrac{6}{11}$

        $\dfrac{6}{5}$

    d. $\dfrac{51}{110}$

        $\dfrac{51}{59}$

21. 2
23. 24

25. −4.5
27. 56
29. 1.5
31. 15
33. a. 45 lb/sq in
    b. 90 lb/sq in
    c. 1 cu ft
    d. 0.2 cu ft
35. $132.30
37. a. 7.2 mm
    b. 2.7 mm
    c. 5.4 mm
    d. 8.1 mm
    e. 6.3 mm

39. $\dfrac{3}{8}$ oz

UNIT 12

Exercise 12-1
1. Geometry is the branch of mathematics in which the properties of points, lines, surfaces, and solids are studied.
3. a. Quantities equal to the same quantities or to equal quantities are equal to each other.
    b. If equals are subtracted from equals, the remainders are equal.
    c. The whole is equal to the sum of all its parts.
    d. If equals are added to equals, the sums are equal.
    e. If equals are multiplied by equals, the products are equal.
    f. If equals are subtracted from equals, the remainders are equal.
    g. Quantities equal to the same quantities or to equal quantities are equal to each other.
5. a.

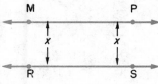
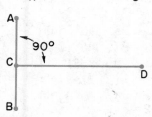

b.

c.

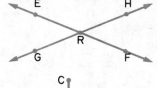
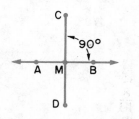

d.

e.

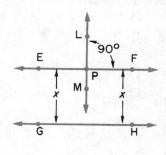

UNIT 13

Exercise 13-1

1. 82°
3. 26°49′
5. 85°14′
7. 75°29′39″
9. 20°13′34″
11. 132°49′15″
13. 102°12′06″
15. 97°12′09″
17. 17°
19. 16°08′
21. 53°54′
23. 2°47′41″
25. 3°02′01″
27. 1°57′41″
29. 31°57′39″
31. 53°42′
33. 38°54′
35. 73°45′35″
37. 74°27′41″

Exercise 13-2

1. 108°
3. 30°38′
5. 73°48′
7. 56°06′
9. 84°24′48″
11. 94°49′14″
13. 41°24′48″
15. 275°16′54″
17. 9°06′
19. 18°17′
21. 11°33′
23. 8°06′03″
25. 48°45′25″
27. 92°41′59″
29. 22°12′22″
31. 130°52′
33. 48°42′
35. 244°36′50″
37. 56°24′
39. a. 48°30′
   b. 18°21′
   c. 106°12′
   d. 57°03′
   e. 5°45′
   f. 29°54′
   g. 66°06′
   h. 72°52′

i. 93°05′
j. 2°50′
k. 134°40′
l. 19°17′
m. 7°01′
n. 31°46′
o. 25°05′

Exercise 13-3

1. A = 25°
   B = 42°
   C = 54°
   D = 77°
   E = 93°
   F = 11°
   G = 23°
   H = 46°
   I = 81°
   J = 87°

3.

5.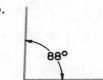

7.

9.

11.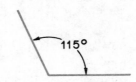

13.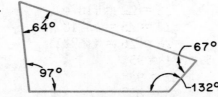

The fourth angle measures 67°.

Exercise 13-4

1. See Instructor's Guide
3. See Instructor's Guide
5. See Instructor's Guide

Exercise 13-5

1. 10°30′
3. 29°25′
5. 59°25′
7. 10°20′
9. 50°15′
11. 78°
13. 89°
15. 45°01′
17. 89°16′41″
19. 0°0′01″
21. 161°
23. 51°
25. 0°01′
27. 90°02′10″
29. 179°56′48″

Exercise 13-6

1. 131°
3. 60°29′
5. 19°23′44″
7. 81°29′35″
9. 14°09′
11. 36°19′11″
13. 3°11′48″
15. 30°01′03″
17. 108°42′
19. 159°57′36″
21. 108°48′27″
23. 26°45′
25. 10°41′36″
27. 29°52′14″
29. 5°15′23″
31. 42°01′30″
33. 248°
35. 96°55′06″
37. 66°12′
39. 8°51′
41. 216°49′48″
43. 60°04′59″

UNIT 13 (Cont'd)

45. a.

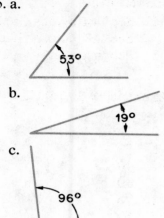

b.

c.

d.

e.

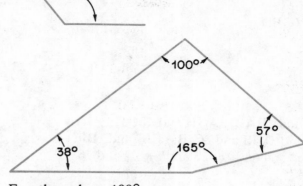

129°

47.

100°

38°   165°   57°

Fourth angle = 100°.

49. See Instructor's Guide
51. 4°30′
53. a. 27°
    b. 71°33′
    c. 3°40′12″
    d. 44°57′53″
    e. 45°56′56″

UNIT 14

Exercise 14-1

1.   ∠A, ∠BAF, ∠FAB
3.   ∠3, ∠CDE, ∠EDC
5.   ∠5, ∠EFA, ∠AFE
7. · ∠2, ∠FBC
9.   ∠4, ∠BCE
11. ∠6, ∠DCB
13. Acute
15. Right
17. Obtuse
19. Acute
21. Right
23. a. 330°
    b. Reflex
25. a. 180°
    b. Straight
27. a. 72°
    b. Acute
29. a. 180°
    b. Straight
31. ∠1 and ∠8; ∠2 and ∠4; ∠3 and ∠9
33. ∠GCB and ∠HBA; ∠HBC and ∠DCG; ∠FCB and ∠EBA; ∠EBC and ∠FCD

Exercise 14-2

1.   ∠1 = 36°
     ∠2 = 60°40′
     ∠3 = 83°20′
     ∠4 = 104°
     ∠5 = 159°20′
3. a.   ∠2 = 180° − 59° = 121°
         ∠3 = ∠1 = 59°
         ∠4 = ∠2 = 121°
         ∠5 = ∠3 = 59°
         ∠6 = ∠2 = 121°
         ∠7 = ∠5 = 59°
         ∠8 = ∠6 = 121°
   b.   ∠2 = 179°60′ − 63°18′ = 116°42′
         ∠3 = ∠1 = 63°18′
         ∠4 = ∠2 = 116°42′
         ∠5 = ∠3 = 63°18′
         ∠6 = ∠2 = 116°42′
         ∠7 = ∠5 = 63°18′
         ∠8 = ∠6 = 116°42′
5.   ∠1 = 95°
     ∠2 = 95°
     ∠3 = 85°
     ∠4 = 85°

∠5 = 85°
∠6 = 95°
∠7 = 85°
∠8 = 95°
∠9 = 85°
∠10 = 95°
∠11 = 85°
∠12 = 95°
∠13 = 95°
∠14 = 85°
∠15 = 53°
∠16 = 85°
∠17 = 53°
∠18 = 51°
∠19 = 76°
∠20 = 53°
∠21 = 76°
∠22 = 76°
7. a. ∠F = 94°
       ∠G = 86°
       ∠H = 86°
   b. ∠F = 100°41′
       ∠G = 79°19′
       ∠H = 79°19′

Exercise 14-3

1. ∠6, ∠ABC
3. ∠2, ∠DFH
5. ∠DFG, ∠GFD
7. Obtuse
9. Acute
11. Reflex
13. Acute
15. Straight
17. ∠GAH and ∠HAB; ∠AGH and ∠FGH; ∠GHA and ∠JHA; ∠HJB and ∠CJB; ∠EJC and ∠BJC
19. ∠1 and ∠5; ∠4 and ∠8; ∠3 and ∠7; ∠2 and ∠6
21. ∠1 = 97°
     ∠2 = 97°
     ∠3 = 83°
     ∠4 = 48°

∠5 = 35°
∠6 = 145°
∠7 = 82°
∠8 = 98°
∠9 = 117°
∠10 = 63°

23. ∠1 = 92°20′
     ∠2 = 87°40′
     ∠3 = 92°20′
     ∠4 = 87°40′
     ∠5 = 87°40′
     ∠6 = 87°40′
     ∠7 = 37°
     ∠8 = 82°45′
     ∠9 = 60°15′
     ∠10 = 82°45′

UNIT 15

Exercise 15-1

1. See Instructor's Guide
3. a. Isosceles
   b. Scalene
   c. Isosceles
   d. Equilateral
   e. Scalene
   f. Isosceles
   g. Equilateral
   h. Isosceles

Exercise 15-2

1. 180°
3. a. 26°21′
   b. 27°48′
5. a. 83°
   b. 9°16′
7. a. 45°
9. a. 24°43′
   b. 68°14′
11. a. 47°
    b. 28°

Exercise 15-3

1. a. BC and EF, AC and DF, AB and DE
   b. OM and OG, OK and OH, KM and GH
   c. PT and PR, ST and SR, SP and SP
3. a. ASA   d. AAS
   b. SSS   e. ASA
   c. HL   f. SAS

5. Drive a stake at a convenient point C. Sight along AC and extend AC. Measure off CE equal to AC and drive a stake at point E. Sight along BC and extend BC. Measure off CD equal to BC and drive a stake at point D.
∠DCE = ∠ACB
  AC = CE
  BC = DC
△ACB ≅ △DCE (SAS)
Since AB and DE are corresponding sides of ≅ △'s, AB = DE. Measure DE, AB = DE.

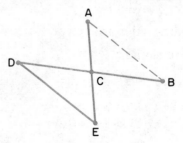

Exercise 15-4

1. 25 in
3. 24 mm
5. 60 mm
7. a. 8 cm
   b. 51°
9. 14.32 m

UNIT 15 (Cont'd)

11. The wall is square if the hypotenuse squared is equal to the sum of the squares of the legs.
$AB^2 = (4.5\ ft)^2 + (6\ ft)^2$
$AB^2 = 20.25\ sq\ ft + 36\ sq\ ft$
$AB^2 = 56.25\ sq\ ft$
$AB = \sqrt{56.25\ sq\ ft}$
$AB = 7.5\ ft\ or\ 7'\text{-}6''$
The wall and floor are not square.
$7'\text{-}6'' \neq 7'\text{-}9''$
13. 117.2 km
15. 26.59 cm

7. $\angle B$ and $\angle D$; $\angle BAC$ and $\angle DAC$; $\angle BCA$ and $\angle DCA$; AB and AD; BC and DC; AC and AC
9. HC and CD; FC and CE; FH and DE; $\angle F$ and $\angle E$; $\angle H$ and $\angle D$; $\angle FCH$ and $\angle ECD$
11. 23.7 in
13. 72°
15. $c^2 = (9\ ft)^2 + (12\ ft)^2$
$c^2 = 81\ sq\ ft + 144\ sq\ ft$
$c^2 = 225\ sq\ ft$
$c = \sqrt{225\ sq\ ft}$
$c = 15\ ft$
Since both the computed measurement and the actual measurement are 15 ft, the wall is square.
17. Beam length = 35 ft
19. 37.5 mi/h

Exercise 15-5

1. See Instructor's Guide
3. a. 140°46′
   b. 18°42′
5. a. 123°; 16°
   b. 109°43′; 50°25′

UNIT 16

Exercise 16-1

1. a. Polygons are similar: $\frac{1.8}{2.7} = \frac{2}{3} = \frac{1}{1.5} = \frac{1.5}{2.25} = 0.66\ldots$

   Corresponding sides are proportional, corresponding angles are equal, and the number of sides is the same.

   b. Polygons are not similar: $\frac{10}{8} = 1.25$; $\frac{14}{10} = 1.14$.

   Corresponding sides are not proportional.

   c. Polygons are not similar: $\frac{6.6}{3} = 2.2$; $\frac{9.6}{4} = 2.4$.

   Corresponding sides are not proportional.

   d. Polygons are similar: $\frac{HJ}{NS} = \frac{JK}{NP} = \frac{KM}{PR} = \frac{MH}{SR}$

   $\frac{5.2}{9.36} = \frac{5}{9} = \frac{3.1}{5.58} = \frac{5.4}{9.72} = 0.555\ldots$

   Corresponding sides are proportional, corresponding angles are equal, and the number of sides is the same.

   e. Polygons are similar: $\frac{AB}{GH} = \frac{BC}{HK} = \frac{CD}{KM} = \frac{DE}{MN} = \frac{EF}{NP} = \frac{FA}{PG}$

   $\frac{10}{8} = \frac{3.75}{3} = \frac{2.5}{2} = \frac{5}{4} = \frac{2.5}{2} = \frac{8.75}{7} = 1.25$

   Corresponding sides are proportional, corresponding angles are equal, and the number of sides is the same.

   f. Polygons are similar: $\frac{AB}{EF} = \frac{BC}{FG} = \frac{CD}{GH} = \frac{DA}{HE}$

   $\frac{6}{3} = \frac{8}{4} = \frac{10}{5} = \frac{4}{2} = 2$

   Corresponding sides are proportional, corresponding angles are equal, and the number of sides is the same.
3. a. 21.6 cm   c. 18.4 cm   e. 90.4 cm
   b. 20 cm   d. 14.4 cm

UNIT 16 (Cont'd)

Exercise 16-2

1. a. If the corresponding sides of two triangles are proportional, the triangles are similar.
   b. Within a triangle, if a line is parallel to one side and intersects the other two sides, the triangle formed and the given triangle are similar.
   c. If two angles of a triangle are equal to two angles of another triangle, the triangles are similar.
   d. If the corresponding sides of two triangles are respectively parallel or perpendicular, the triangles are similar.
   e. If two sides of a triangle are proportional to two sides of another triangle and if the angles included between these sides are equal, the triangles are similar.
   f. If the altitude is drawn to the hypotenuse of a right triangle, the two triangles formed are similar to each other and to the given triangle.
   g. If the corresponding sides of two triangles are respectively parallel or perpendicular, the triangles are similar.
   h. If two angles of a triangle are equal to two angles of another triangle, the triangles are similar.

3. $x = 3.03$ cm   5. 13 ft
    $y = 4.20$ cm   7. 19.2 mm

Exercise 16-3   3. a. 21.07 in   5. a. 60°
  1. a. 4.6 in   b. 22.72 in   b. 60°
     b. 38°46′   c. 4.2 m

Exercise 16-4

1. Polygons in b. are similar.
3. a. (1) If the altitude is drawn to the hypotenuse of a right triangle, the two triangles formed are similar to each other and to the given triangle. $\triangle ABC \sim \triangle ADC \sim \triangle CDB$
       (2) $\angle 1 = 59°$ $\angle 2 = 31°$ $\angle 3 = 31°$
   b. (1) If two angles of a triangle are equal to two angles of another triangle, the triangles are similar. $\triangle FGK \sim \triangle HJM$
       (2) Side FK $= 8.8$ cm   Side JM $= 4.5$ cm
   c. (1) $\angle A = \angle DCE$ (alternate interior $\angle$'s)
            $\dfrac{AC}{DC} = \dfrac{AB}{EC}$ $\dfrac{11.2}{8} = \dfrac{6.3}{4.5}$ $1.4 = 1.4$
            If two sides of a triangle are proportional to two sides of another triangle and if the angles included between these sides are equal, the triangles are similar. $\triangle CDE \sim \triangle ABC$
       (2) DE $= 6$ in
   d. (1) $\angle A = \angle A$ $\angle B = \angle ADE$
            If two angles of a triangle are equal to two angles of another triangle, the triangles are similar. $\triangle ADE \sim \triangle ABC$
       (2) DE $= 1.5$ ft   AD $= 2.09$ ft
5. E $= 5'\text{-}3''$ 7. a. $\angle 1 = 57°30'$
    F $= 8'\text{-}9''$ b. $\angle 2 = 32°30'$
    G $= 5'\text{-}7\frac{1}{2}''$
    H $= 7'\text{-}6''$

UNIT 17

Exercise 17-1

1. a. Concave polygon
   b. Convex polygon
   c. Convex polygon
   d. Convex polygon
   e. Not a polygon
   f. Convex polygon
   g. Convex polygon
   h. Not a polygon
   i. Not a polygon
   j. Concave polygon

Exercise 17-2

1. Yes. All parallelograms have four sides.
3. Yes. All rectangles have opposite sides parallel and equal.
5. Yes. All squares have equal and parallel opposite sides.
7. No. All the sides of a rectangle do not have to be equal.
9. a. 14 in
   b. 8 in
   c. 82°
   d. 98°
11. a. 3 ft
    b. 115°
    c. 65°

Exercise 17-3

1. a. 360°
   b. 540°

c. 720°
d. 1 080°
3. a. 108°
   b. 120°
   c. 135°
   d. 150°
5. a. 72°
   b. 60°
   c. 45°
   d. 22°30'
7. a. 6
   b. 8
   c. 5
   d. 9
9. 56°

Exercise 17-4

1. a. AP = 11.5 cm
      DP = 14.7 cm
   b. AP = 2'-3"
      DP = 2'-10"
3. a. Median = 17 cm
   b. Median = 16'-6"
   c. Median = 36.6 m
5. y = 19.70 mm
   x = 35.21 mm
7. 8.75 in

Exercise 17-5

1. a. Convex polygon
   b. Convex polygon

c. Not a polygon
d. Concave polygon
e. Convex polygon
3. a. CB = 3.7 in
   b. ∠B = 64°
   c. ∠C = 116°
5. a. 81°
   b. 27°
   c. 99°
7. a. 720°
   b. 1 260°
   c. 1 800°
9. a. 122°
   b. 118°
11. a. 30
    b. 16
    c. 96
13. a. 315°
    b. 60°
15. a. 4.5 m
    b. $4'-1\frac{1}{2}''$
17. a. $b = 7\frac{5}{16}$ in
    b. b = 15.94 m
19. A = 113.0 mm

UNIT 18

Exercise 18-1

1. a. Chord
   b. Diameter
   c. Radius
   d. Center
3. a. Sector
   b. Segment
   c. Radius
   d. Chord
   e. Arc

Exercise 18-2

1. a. 87.9 in
   b. 103.0 cm

c. 23.6 ft
d. 19.5 m
e. 111.2 in
f. 223.6 mm
3. 6.1 in
5. 7.2 in
7. 19.9 m
9. 747.3
11. 3 014.4 m
13. 145.2 ft

Exercise 18-3

1. a. 2.5 in
   b. 2.5 in

3. a. 5.0 in
   b. 3.3 in
5. a. 1.2 m
   b. 1.35 m
7. a. 2.2 ft
   b. 216.7°
9. 32.2 ft
11. 3.7 m

Exercise 18-4

1. a. ∠E = 45°42'
      ∠F = 24°52'
   b. ∠2 = 43°40'

3. a. ∠2 = 32°
   b. ∠3 = 125°31'
5. 1.91 in
7. 165.79 ft

Exercise 18-5

1. a. 35°
   b. 145°
3. a. 42°
   b. 52°30'
5. a. 61°
   b. 90°
   c. 58°
7. 98°

UNIT 18 (Cont'd)

Exercise 18-5 (Cont'd)

9. A rectangle is formed.
11. $\angle 1 = 25°$
    $\angle 2 = 67°$
    $\angle 3 = 48°$
    $\angle 4 = 29°$
    $\angle 5 = 48°$
    $\angle 6 = 86°$
    $\angle 7 = 94°$
    $\angle 8 = 126°$
    $\angle 9 = 54°$
    $\angle 10 = 88°$

Exercise 18-6

1. a. $13°$
  b. $17°30'$
  c. $32°$
  d. $104°$
  e. $13°30'$
  f. $105°$
3. a. $25°$
  b. $23°30'$
  c. $108°$
  d. $11°$
  e. $12°$
  f. $35°$
5. a. $\overset{\frown}{DH} = 13°$
    $\overset{\frown}{EDH} = 26°$

b. $156°$
7. a. 15.40 cm
  b. 32.26 cm
9. a. 19.10 m
  b. 6.62 m
11. $A = 0.400$ in
    $B = 1.362$ in

Exercise 18-7

1. a. Chord
  b. Diameter
  c. Radius
  d. Arc
  e. Tangent
  f. Tangent point
3. a. 100.5 cm
  b. 16.3 in
  c. 5.0 m
5. $r = 2.4$ m
7. 9.7 in
9. 224.2

11. a. $\overset{\frown}{MH} = 2.9$ m
  b. $\overset{\frown}{EF} = 1.7$ m
13. a. $EH = 11.5$ cm
    $\overset{\frown}{EGF} = 28$ cm
  b. $\overset{\frown}{EGF} = 40$ cm
    $HF = 17.5$ cm

15. $x = 8.0$
17. a. $\angle 1 = 39°$
  b. $\angle 2 = 42°$
19. $x = 5.7$ in
21. a. $59°30'$
  b. $34°$
23. a. $120°$
  b. $60°$
  c. $44°$
25. a. $16°$
  b. $88°$
  c. $31°$
27. a. $25°$
  b. $198°$
  c. $40°$
29. $\angle 1 = 32°$
    $\angle 2 = 58°$
    $\angle 3 = 17°$
    $\angle 4 = 15°$
    $\angle 5 = 32°$
    $\angle 6 = 20°$
    $\angle 7 = 38°$
    $\angle 8 = 21°$
    $\angle 9 = 69°$
    $\angle 10 = 122°$
31. a. 15.30 m
  b. 9.40 m
33. 8.79 in

UNIT 19

(See Instructor's Guide)

UNIT 20

Exercise 20-1

1. a. 0.1″
  b. The range includes all numbers equal to or greater than 3.55″ and less than 3.65″.
3. a. 0.1″
  b. The range includes all numbers equal to or greater than 4.25″ and less than 4.35″.
5. a. 0.001″
  b. The range includes all numbers equal to or greater than 15.884 5″ and less than 15.885 5″.
7. a. 0.001″
  b. The range includes all numbers equal to or greater than 12.001 5″ and less than 12.002 5″.
9. a. 0.01″.
  b. The range includes all numbers equal to or greater than 7.005″ and less than 7.015″.
11. a. 0.1″
  b. The range includes all numbers equal to or greater than 9.05″ and less than 9.15″.

UNIT 20 (Cont'd)

Exercise 20-2

	GREATEST POSSIBLE ERROR (inches)	ACTUAL LENGTH	
		SMALLEST POSSIBLE (inches)	LARGEST POSSIBLE (inches)
1.	$\frac{1}{32}$	$23\frac{13}{32}$	$23\frac{15}{32}$
3.	0.01	15.67	15.69
5.	0.000 5	0.752 5	0.753 5

	GREATEST POSSIBLE ERROR (millimetres)	ACTUAL LENGTH	
		SMALLEST POSSIBLE (millimetres)	LARGEST POSSIBLE (millimetres)
7.	1	74	76
9.	0.5	361.5	362.5
11.	0.01	58.25	58.27

Exercise 20-3

1. Tolerance $= \frac{1}{32}''$

3. Minimum Limit $= 16.74''$

5. Tolerance $= 0.000\ 3''$

7. Tolerance $= 0.9$ mm

9. Maximum Limit $= 258.07$ mm

11. Maximum Limit $= 12.737$ cm

Exercise 20-4

		BASIC DIMENSION (inches)	MAXIMUM DIAMETER (inches)	MINIMUM DIAMETER (inches)	MAXIMUM CLEARANCE (inches)	MINIMUM CLEARANCE (inches)
1.	DIA A	1.458 0	1.458 0	1.455 0	0.009 0	0.003 0
	DIA B	1.461 0	1.464 0	1.461 0		
3.	DIA A	2.105 3	2.105 3	2.102 3	0.008 5	0.002 5
	DIA B	2.107 8	2.110 8	2.107 8		
5.	DIA A	0.999 6	0.999 6	0.996 6	0.007 1	0.001 1
	DIA B	1.000 7	1.003 7	1.000 7		

		BASIC DIMENSION (millimetres)	MAXIMUM DIMENSION (millimetres)	MINIMUM DIMENSION (millimetres)	MAXIMUM CLEARANCE (millimetres)	MINIMUM CLEARANCE (millimetres)
7.	DIM A	40.12	40.12	40.06	0.18	0.06
	DIM B	40.18	40.24	40.18		
9.	DIM A	56.73	56.73	56.67	0.14	0.02
	DIM B	56.75	56.81	56.75		

Exercise 20-5

		BASIC DIMENSION (inches)	MAXIMUM DIMENSION (inches)	MINIMUM DIMENSION (inches)	MAXIMUM CLEARANCE (inches)	MINIMUM CLEARANCE (inches)
1.	DIM A	0.839 2	0.840 0	0.838 4	0.003 6	0.000 4
	DIM B	0.841 2	0.842 0	0.840 4		
3.	DIM A	0.999 5	1.000 3	0.998 7	0.004 1	0.000 9
	DIM B	1.002 0	1.002 8	1.001 2		
5.	DIM A	1.439 2	1.440 0	1.438 4	0.003 6	0.000 4
	DIM B	1.441 2	1.442 0	1.440 4		

UNIT 20 (Cont'd)

Exercise 20-5 (Cont'd)

		BASIC DIMENSION (millimetres)	MAXIMUM DIAMETER (millimetres)	MINIMUM DIAMETER (millimetres)	MAXIMUM INTERFERENCE (millimetres)	MINIMUM INTERFERENCE (millimetres)
7.	DIA A	32.07	32.09	32.05	0.10	0.02
	DIA B	32.01	32.03	31.99		
9.	DIA A	47.02	47.04	47.00	0.09	0.01
	DIA B	46.97	46.99	46.95		

Exercise 20-6

1. 3.779″

3. $9\frac{55}{64}$″

5. $7'\text{-}5\frac{7}{16}$″

7. 16.5 mm

9. 1.006 0 mm

11. 7.315 5 cm

13. 0.743″ ± 0.005″

15. 1.999″ ± 0.001″

17. 0.194 5″ ± 0.001 5″

19. 1.000 7″ ± 0.000 9″

21. 4.466 8″ ± 0.000 5″

23. 0.385 8″ ± 0.001 5″

25. 38.7 mm ± 0.1 mm

27. 10.02 mm ± 0.04 mm

29. 104 mm ± 0.1 mm

31. 38.43 mm ± 0.45 mm

33. 66.71 mm ± 0.05 mm

35. 43.076 mm ± 0.015 mm

Exercise 20-7

1. a. 0.1″
   b. The range includes all numbers equal to or greater than 5.25″ and less than 5.35″.

3. a. 0.001″
   b. The range includes all numbers equal to or greater than 1.833 5″ and less than 1.834 5 ″.

5. a. 0.001″
   b. The range includes all numbers equal to or greater than 19.000 5″ and less than 19.001 5″.

7. a. 0.1″
   b. The range includes all numbers equal to or greater than 28.95″ and less than 29.05″.

9.

	GREATEST POSSIBLE ERROR (inches)	ACTUAL LENGTH	
		SMALLEST POSSIBLE (inches)	LARGEST POSSIBLE (inches)
a.	$\frac{1}{32}$	$18\frac{23}{32}$	$18\frac{25}{32}$
b.	0.025	3.225	3.275
c.	0.000 5	11.027 5	11.028 5
d.	0.000 05	0.803 05	0.803 15

11. a. Tolerance = $\frac{1}{16}$″
    b. Minimum Limit = $18\frac{15}{64}$″
    c. Maximum Limit = 2.781″
    d. Tolerance = 0.001 1″

13.

		BASIC DIMENSION (inches)	MAXIMUM DIAMETER (inches)	MINIMUM DIAMETER (inches)	MAXIMUM CLEARANCE (inches)	MINIMUM CLEARANCE (inches)
a.	DIA A	1.712 0	1.712 0	1.710 6	0.004 4	0.001 6
	DIA B	1.713 6	1.715 0	1.113 6		
b.	DIA A	0.296 2	0.296 2	0.294 8	0.003 6	0.000 8
	DIA B	0.297 0	0.298 4	0.297 0		
c.	DIA A	2.806 4	2.806 4	2.805 0	0.003 9	0.001 1
	DIA B	2.807 5	2.808 9	2.807 5		

15.

		BASIC DIMENSION (inches)	MAXIMUM DIMENSION (inches)	MINIMUM DIMENSION (inches)	MAXIMUM CLEARANCE (inches)	MINIMUM CLEARANCE (inches)
a.	DIM A	3.142 5	3.143 5	3.141 5	0.007 0	0.003 0
	DIM B	3.147 5	3.148 5	3.146 5		
b.	DIM A	5.903 5	5.904 5	5.902 5	0.004 9	0.000 9
	DIM B	5.906 4	5.907 4	5.905 4		
c.	DIM A	8.076 0	8.077 0	8.075 0	0.006 6	0.002 6
	DIM B	8.080 6	8.081 6	8.079 6		

17. a. 6.048″

b. 2.322 5″

c. $10\frac{25}{64}$″

d. 5′-3″

19. a. 1.907″ ± 0.004″

b. 1.899″ ± 0.004″

c. 0.880″ ± 0.005″

d. 0.064 0″ ± 0.001 5″

e. 5.00 4″ ± 0.000 6″

f. 1.008″ ± 0.009″

g. 12.560 8″ ± 0.000 5″

h. 0.600 7″ ± 0.000 3″

i. 3.999 7″ ± 0.000 7″

21. Defective spacers: 0.379″, 0.370″, 0.380″

23. Maximum value Length A = $35\frac{23}{32}$″

Minimum value Length A = $35\frac{17}{32}$″

25. $8\frac{9}{16}$″

27. Holes 5 and 6 are drilled out of tolerance.

UNIT 21

Exercise 21-1

1. a = $\frac{5}{32}$″

b = $\frac{5}{16}$″

c = $\frac{1}{2}$″

d = $\frac{21}{32}$″

e = $\frac{13}{16}$″

f = $1\frac{1}{32}$″

g = $1\frac{5}{32}$″

h = $1\frac{5}{16}$″

i = $\frac{5}{64}$″

j = $\frac{13}{64}$″

k = $\frac{11}{32}$″

l = $\frac{31}{64}$″

m = $\frac{41}{64}$″

n = $\frac{29}{32}$″

o = $1\frac{9}{64}$″

p = $1\frac{25}{64}$″

Exercise 21-1 (Cont'd)

3. $a = \dfrac{1}{4}''$ $e = \dfrac{11}{32}''$ $i = \dfrac{23}{32}''$ $m = \dfrac{1}{8}''$

   $b = \dfrac{9}{16}''$ $f = 2\dfrac{3}{16}''$ $j = \dfrac{1}{2}''$ $n = 4\dfrac{13}{16}''$

   $c = \dfrac{1}{2}''$ $g = \dfrac{7}{32}''$ $k = \dfrac{15}{32}''$

   $d = \dfrac{15}{32}''$ $h = \dfrac{3}{4}''$ $l = \dfrac{3}{8}''$

Exercise 21-2

1. $a = 0.08''$ $e = 0.8''$ $i = 0.09''$ $m = 0.84''$
   $b = 0.22''$ $f = 1.04''$ $j = 0.23''$ $n = 1.07''$
   $c = 0.4''$ $g = 1.28''$ $k = 0.38''$ $o = 1.27''$
   $d = 0.58''$ $h = 1.42''$ $l = 0.55''$ $p = 1.45''$

3. $a = 1.7''$ $e = 2.9''$ $i = 4.6''$ $m = 1.85''$
   $b = 2.45''$ $f = 0.65''$ $j = 0.6''$
   $c = 0.2''$ $g = 1.35''$ $k = 1.9''$
   $d = 0.45''$ $h = 0.95''$ $l = 0.15''$

Exercise 21-3

1. $a = 5$ mm $e = 37$ mm $i = 6.5$ mm $m = 44.5$ mm
   $b = 11$ mm $f = 49$ mm $j = 13$ mm $n = 50.5$ mm
   $c = 20$ mm $g = 57$ mm $k = 17.5$ mm $o = 63.5$ mm
   $d = 24$ mm $h = 73$ mm $l = 30.5$ mm $p = 69.5$ mm

3. $a = 5$ mm $e = 35$ mm $i = 49$ mm
   $b = 11$ mm $f = 6$ mm $j = 20$ mm
   $c = 19$ mm $g = 40$ mm
   $d = 24$ mm $h = 20$ mm

Exercise 21-4

1. 0.100 1″, 0.132″, 0.400″
3. 0.100 3″, 0.113″, 0.750″, 4.000″
5. 0.100 2″, 0.600″, 1.000″, 4.000″
7. 0.100 9″, 0.149″, 0.750″
9. 0.050″, 1.000″, 2.000″, 3.000″, 4.000″
11. 0.100 1″, 0.900″, 1.000″
13. 0.100 1″, 0.131″, 0.600″, 4.000″
15. 0.100 6″, 0.140″, 0.850″, 4.000″
17. 0.100 5″, 0.124″, 0.650″
19. 0.100 8″, 0.134″, 0.200″, 1.000″, 4.000″

21. 1.003 mm, 1.08 mm, 1.9 mm, 3 mm, 20 mm
23. 1.005 mm, 1.03 mm, 1.6 mm, 40 mm
25. 1.7 mm, 40 mm, 80 mm, 90 mm
27. 1.002 mm, 6 mm, 70 mm
29. 1.08 mm, 1.9 mm, 6 mm, 20 mm
31. 1.08 mm, 7 mm, 70 mm
33. 1.01 mm, 10 mm, 90 mm
35. 1.007 mm, 1.7 mm, 5 mm
37. 1.01 mm, 1.1 mm, 9 mm, 10 mm, 90 mm
39. 1.009 mm, 1.01 mm, 9 mm, 80 mm

UNIT 21 (Cont'd)

Exercise 21-5

1. a $= \dfrac{3}{32}''$ e $= \dfrac{23}{32}''$ i $= \dfrac{7}{64}''$ m $= \dfrac{47}{64}''$

   b $= \dfrac{9}{32}''$ f $= \dfrac{7}{8}''$ j $= \dfrac{17}{64}''$ n $= \dfrac{29}{32}''$

   c $= \dfrac{7}{16}''$ g $= 1\dfrac{3}{32}''$ k $= \dfrac{13}{32}''$ o $= 1\dfrac{5}{32}''$

   d $= \dfrac{19}{32}''$ h $= 1\dfrac{11}{32}''$ l $= \dfrac{33}{64}''$ p $= 1\dfrac{25}{64}''$

3. a $= \dfrac{19}{32}''$ d $= 2\dfrac{9}{16}''$ g $= \dfrac{7}{8}''$ j $= \dfrac{3}{8}''$

   b $= 1\dfrac{11}{32}''$ e $= \dfrac{21}{32}''$ h $= 4\dfrac{13}{16}''$ k $= \dfrac{15}{16}''$

   c $= \dfrac{15}{16}''$ f $= \dfrac{29}{32}''$ i $= \dfrac{9}{16}''$ l $= \dfrac{15}{32}''$

5. a $= 0.35''$ d $= 1.55''$ g $= 2.85''$ j $= 4.35''$
   b $= 0.8''$ e $= 2.05''$ h $= 3.4''$ k $= 5.35''$
   c $= 1.1''$ f $= 2.45''$ i $= 3.8''$ l $= 5.8''$

7. a $= 0.35''$ d $= 0.25''$ g $= 0.25''$
   b $= 2.65''$ e $= 2''$ h $= 1.2''$
   c $= 0.25''$ f $= 0.4''$ i $= 0.35''$

9. a $= 67$ mm   d $= 27$ mm
   b $= 31$ mm   e $= 101$ mm
   c $= 30$ mm   f $= 75$ mm   g $= 62$ mm

11. 0.100 7″, 0.148″, 0.350″
13. 0.100 4″, 0.163″, 0.600″, 1.000″, 4.000″
15. 0.700″, 3.000″, 4.000″
17. 0.110″, 0.950″, 1.000″, 3.000″, 4.000″
19. 0.100 2″, 0.900″, 2.000″
21. 0.103″, 0.900″, 1.000″, 4.000″
23. 0.100 8″, 0.149″, 0.550″
25. 0.100 3″, 0.134″, 0.150″, 3.000″, 4.000″
27. 1.005 mm, 1.08 mm, 1.3 mm, 60 mm
29. 1.006 mm, 1.05 mm, 1.3 mm, 1 mm, 30 mm
31. 1.9 mm, 2 mm, 40 mm, 80 mm, 90 mm
33. 1.009 mm, 1.09 mm, 1.9 mm, 6 mm
35. 1.08 mm, 6 mm, 60 mm, 90 mm
37. 1.007 mm, 1.02 mm, 1.7 mm, 5 mm, 30 mm
39. 1.001 mm, 1.01 mm, 1.1 mm, 2 mm, 80 mm
41. 1.02 mm, 1.2 mm, 30 mm, 90 mm

UNIT 22

Exercise 22-1

1. 2.021″	11. 0.094″
3. 4.788″	13. 5.852″
5. 3.376″	15. 2.826″
7. 2.742″	17. 1.024″
9. 2.009″	

	A (inches)	B (inches)	C
19.	4.950	4.975	13
21.	5.975	6.000	24
23.	1.625	1.650	3
25.	3.075	3.100	21
27.	0.500	0.525	11

Exercise 22-2

1. 30.82 mm	11. 26.16 mm
3. 11.76 mm	13. 48.48 mm
5. 52.42 mm	15. 16.52 mm
7. 52.78 mm	17. 41.34 mm
9. 86.38 mm	

	A (millimetres)	B (millimetres)	C
19.	37.5	38.0	9
21.	42.0	42.5	2
23.	63.5	64.0	12
25.	43.0	43.5	3
27.	81.0	81.5	11

Exercise 22-3

1. 2.009″
3. 7.941″
5. 5.961″
7. 0.780″

	A (inches)	B (inches)	C
9.	2.675	2.700	12
11.	8.725	8.750	7
13.	6.975	7.000	23
15.	4.875	4.900	2
17.	9.425	9.450	16

Exercise 22-4

1. 30.22 mm
3. 78.60 mm
5. 52.18 mm
7. 8.82 mm

	A (millimetres)	B (millimetres)	C
9.	53.5	54.0	21
11.	57.0	57.5	4
13.	60.5	61.0	8
15.	61.5	62.0	15
17.	29.5	30.0	9

Exercise 22-5

1. a. 3.776″
   b. 2.941″
   c. 4.498″
   d. 0.981″

3.

	A (inches)	B (inches)	C
a.	3.850	3.875	14
b.	0.875	0.900	18
c.	4.075	4.100	23
d.	0.050	0.075	7
e.	5.250	5.275	19
f.	2.475	2.500	1
g.	8.950	8.975	24

5. a. 7.931″
   b. 4.661″
   c. 1.941″
   d. 5.509″
   e. 9.680″

7.

	A (inches)	B (inches)	C
a.	5.825	5.850	12
b.	0.700	0.725	21
c.	4.025	4.050	14
d.	9.675	9.700	17
e.	7.000	7.025	5
f.	3.550	3.575	17
g.	2.875	2.900	13

UNIT 22 (Cont'd)

9. a. $0.392'' \div 2 = 0.196''$
$0.460'' \div 2 = 0.230''$
$0.196'' + 0.230'' = 0.426''$

    High limit $= 4.340'' + 0.006'' + 0.426'' = 4.772''$
    Low limit $= 4.340'' - 0.006'' + 0.426'' = 4.760''$

   b. $0.500'' \div 2 = 0.250''$
$0.632'' \div 2 = 0.316''$
$0.250'' + 0.316'' = 0.566''$

    High limit $= 5.873'' + 0.004'' + 0.566'' = 6.443''$
    Low limit $= 5.873'' - 0.004'' + 0.566'' = 6.435''$

   c. $0.420'' \div 2 = 0.210''$
$0.576'' \div 2 = 0.288''$
$0.210'' + 0.288'' = 0.498''$

    High limit $= 6.190'' + 0.005'' + 0.498'' = 6.693''$
    Low limit $= 6.190'' - 0.005'' + 0.498'' = 6.683''$

   d. $0.750'' \div 2 = 0.375''$
$0.828'' \div 2 = 0.414''$
$0.375'' + 0.414'' = 0.789''$

    High limit $= 8.993'' + 0.002'' + 0.789'' = 9.784''$
    Low limit $= 8.993'' - 0.002'' + 0.789'' = 9.780''$

   e. $0.622'' \div 2 = 0.311''$
$0.736'' \div 2 = 0.368''$
$0.311'' + 0.368'' = 0.679''$

    High limit $= 7.759'' + 0.003'' + 0.679'' = 8.441''$
    Low limit $= 7.759'' - 0.003'' + 0.679'' = 8.435''$

   f. $0.408'' \div 2 = 0.204''$
$0.610'' \div 2 = 0.305''$
$0.204'' + 0.305'' = 0.509''$

    High limit $= 5.322'' + 0.004'' + 0.509'' = 5.835''$
    Low limit $= 5.322'' - 0.004'' + 0.509'' = 5.827''$

	VERNIER CALIPER SCALE SETTINGS		
	MAIN SCALE SETTING (inches)	HIGH LIMIT VERNIER SCALE SETTING	LOW LIMIT VERNIER SCALE SETTING
a.	4.750 - 4.775	22	10
b.	6.425 - 6.450	18	10
c.	6.675 - 6.700	18	8
d.	9.775 - 9.800	9	5
e.	8.425 - 8.450	16	10
f.	5.825 - 5.850	10	2

11.   Hole 1: $0.725'' - (0.410'' \div 2) = 0.725'' - 0.205'' = 0.520''$
     Hole 2: $0.725'' + 1.276'' - (0.386'' \div 2) = 2.001'' - 0.193'' = 1.808''$
     Hole 3: $0.725'' + 1.276'' - 0.614'' - (0.178'' \div 2) = 2.001'' - 0.703'' = 1.298''$
     Hole 4: $0.725'' + 0.320'' - (0.452'' \div 2) = 1.045'' - 0.226'' = 0.819''$
     Hole 5: $0.725'' + 0.320'' + 0.814'' - (0.154'' \div 2) = 1.859'' - 0.077'' = 1.782''$

HOLE NUMBER	HEIGHT GAGE SETTINGS	
	MAIN SCALE SETTING (inches)	VERNIER SCALE SETTING
1	0.500 - 0.525	20
2	1.800 - 1.825	8
3	1.275 - 1.300	23
4	0.800 - 0.825	19
5	1.775 - 1.800	7

UNIT 23

Exercise 23-1

1. 0.598″   7. 0.589″
3. 0.736″   9. 0.738″
5. 0.157″   11. 0.022″

	BARREL SCALE SETTING IS BETWEEN (inches)	THIMBLE SCALE SETTING (inches)
13.	0.275 - 0.300	0.008
15.	0.150 - 0.175	0.006
17.	0.975 - 1.000	0.023
19.	0.325 - 0.350	0.001
21.	0.000 - 0.025	0.007
23.	0.125 - 0.150	0.013
25.	0.875 - 0.900	0.005

Exercise 23-2

1. 0.274 9″   7. 0.328 3″
3. 0.498 0″   9. 0.233 6″
5. 0.098 2″   11. 0.363 7″

	BARREL SCALE SETTING IS BETWEEN (inches)	THIMBLE SCALE SETTING IS BETWEEN (inches)	VERNIER SCALE SETTING (inches)
13.	0.675 - 0.700	0.011 - 0.012	0.000 7
15.	0.500 - 0.525	0.010 - 0.011	0.000 9
17.	0.925 - 0.950	0.008 - 0.009	0.000 2
19.	0.375 - 0.400	0.023 - 0.024	0.000 3
21.	0.225 - 0.250	0.001 - 0.002	0.000 4
23.	0.000 - 0.025	0.005 - 0.006	0.000 9
25.	0.300 - 0.325	0.010 - 0.011	0.000 7

Exercise 23-3

1. 7.09 mm   7. 0.34 mm
3. 5.69 mm   9. 3.12 mm
5. 9.78 mm   11. 24.93 mm

	BARREL SCALE SETTING IS BETWEEN (millimetres)	THIMBLE SCALE SETTING (millimetres)
13.	12.5 - 13.0	0.36
15.	15.0 - 15.5	0.08
17.	0.5 - 1.0	0.38
19.	18.0 - 18.5	0.12
21.	8.0 - 8.5	0.44
23.	23.0 - 23.5	0.08
25.	21.5 - 22.0	0.32

Exercise 23-4

1. 4.268 mm   7. 8.308 mm
3. 7.218 mm   9. 9.484 mm
5. 2.132 mm   11. 11.114 mm

	BARREL SCALE SETTING IS BETWEEN (millimetres)	THIMBLE SCALE SETTING IS BETWEEN (millimetres)	VERNIER SCALE SETTING (millimetres)
13.	14.5 - 15.0	0.37 - 0.38	0.004
15.	9.0 - 9.5	0.23 - 0.24	0.008
17.	3.0 - 3.5	0.04 - 0.05	0.006
19.	7.0 - 7.5	0.00 - 0.01	0.004
21.	5.5 - 6.0	0.20 - 0.21	0.008
23.	8.0 - 8.5	0.32 - 0.33	0.004
25.	14.5 - 15.0	0.08 - 0.09	0.002

UNIT 23 (Cont'd)

Exercise 23-5

1. a. 0.707"
   b. 0.136"
   c. 0.495"
   d. 0.363"
   e. 0.008"
   f. 0.797"
   g. 0.549"
   h. 0.898"

3. a. 0.253 3"
   b. 0.042 4"
   c. 0.158 6"
   d. 0.490 7"
   e. 0.119 8"
   f. 0.286 6"
   g. 0.448 0"
   h. 0.224 9"

5. a. 22.93 mm
   b. 5.69 mm
   c. 3.71 mm
   d. 0.07 mm
   e. 18.78 mm
   f. 3.81 mm
   g. 10.74 mm
   h. 5.17 mm

7. a. 9.234 mm
   b. 7.358 mm
   c. 3.902 mm
   d. 6.696 mm
   e. 11.464 mm
   f. 3.192 mm
   g. 15.754 mm
   h. 7.088 mm

UNIT 24

Exercise 24-1

1. 21 sq ft
3. 51 sq in
5. 8.7 cm
7. 87.5 sq ft
9. 14 mm
11. 0.8 in
13. 205.2 sq ft
15. 0.9 mi
17. 4.88 sq ft
19. $675
21. $180
23. 1 144 cm^2
25. 40.5 m^2

Exercise 24-2

1. 104 cm^2
3. 18.7 in
5. 0.2 mi
7. 19.8 m^2
9. 8.5 km
11. 311.1 sq mi
13. 49.7 in
15. 1 010.8 sq yd
17. 1.72 sq in
19. The two cutouts have equal areas.
21. The square has the greatest area and permits the largest garden.
23. 2 921 cm^2

Exercise 24-3

1. 104 sq in
3. 2.67 m^2
5. 7.3 yd
7. 14.2 cm
9. 602.1 m^2
11. 24.0 km
13. 0.5 yd
15. 8 ft
17. 11.72 cm^2
19. a. 10.50 m^2
    b. 102.9 kg
21. a. 10 sq yd
    b. 13.42 ft
23. h = 24 cm
     b_1 = 24 cm
     b_2 = 18 cm

Exercise 24-4

1. 178.5 sq in
3. 2.1 m^2
5. 0.2 mi
7. 0.2 km^2
9. 28 ft
11. 28.4 cm^2
13. 40 yd
15. 0.4 mi
17. 11.6 m^2
19. 4.3 sq ft
21. 1.2 sq yd
23. 31.3 cm^2

25. 350.40 mm^2
27. $2 052
29. (1) 117 cm^2
    (2) 287.5 cm^2
    (3) 372 cm^2
    (4) 252 cm^2
    (5) 1 365 cm^2
    (6) 350 cm^2
    Total area = 2 743.5 cm^2
31. a. 66.98 cm^2
    b. 6.70 cm
33. a. 4 330.13 sq ft
    b. 3 485.69 sq ft
    c. 2 224.86 sq ft
    d. An equilateral triangle provides the most area for the least amount of enclosure (perimeter) cost.

Exercise 24-5

1. 157.5 sq in
3. 14 m
5. 0.6 mi
7. 19.8 mm
9. 204 m^2
11. 138.7 sq in
13. 1.9 km
15. 24 ft
17. 280 cm^2
19. 2 yd

21. 8.3 ft
23. 10 mm
25. 472.5 sq in
27. 1.6 m
29. 0.6 km
31. 72 ft
33. 16.2 sq ft
35. 0.5 m^2
37. 1.88 sq ft
39. 94.10 cm^2
41. 365 sq ft
43. a. 792 bd ft
    b. $586.08
45. a. 274.75 m^2
    b. 311.04 m^2
    c. 23.04 L
47. a. 2 888 bricks
    b. $298.80
49. a. $21 165
    b. 2.38 acres

UNIT 25

Exercise 25-1
1. 153.94 sq in
3. 188.69 sq ft
5. 3.29 yd
7. 11.00 mm
9. 0.03 sq mi
11. 1.07 m
13. 9 times greater
15. 2 times greater
17. 25 times greater
19. 630.50 sq yd
21. 163.36 sq in
23. $882.16
25. 5.03 kg
27. 103.42 sq in
29. 46.51 cm

Exercise 25-2
1. 104.7 cm
3. 706.5 sq in
5. 21.9 mm
7. 279.6°
9. 661.3 cm^2
11. 229.3°

13. 3 828.83 mm^2
15. a. 38.66 sq ft
    b. $60.02
17. 1.04 m^2
19. a. 1 532.50 cm^2
    b. 6.26 kg

Exercise 25-3
1. 8.3 sq ft
3. 57.5 mm^2
5. 0.12 km^2
7. $14 782.97
9. a. 1 078.60 cm^2
   b. 0.84 kg

Exercise 25-4
1. A = 55.0 sq in
3. A = 28.4 m^2
5. Major axis = 5.4 yd
7. A = 718.3 sq in
9. Major axis = 1.4 m
11. 486.56 sq ft

13. Minor axis = 6.37 m
15. Major axis = 1.98 m
    Minor axis = 1.48 m

Exercise 25-5
1. 615.75 sq in
3. 3.78 yd
5. 127.68 sq ft
7. 1.76 times greater
9. 31.7 sq in
11. 5.2 in
13. 239.2 sq ft
15. 72.5 sq yd
17. A = 402.7 sq yd
19. Minor axis = 40.1 cm
21. A = 118.1 sq ft
23. 16.81 m^2
25. 316 673.28 lb
27. 7.05 m^2
29. 12.81 in
31. Minor axis = 49.98 ft
    Major axis = 64.97 ft
33. 1 204.99 mm^2

UNIT 26

Exercise 26-1
1. 1 000 cu in
3. 66.14 lb
5. 11.2 m^3
7. a. 409.34 cm^3
   b. 3.27 kg
9. 6 400 bricks
11. a. 2 778.3 gal
    b. 59.54 min

Exercise 26-2
1. 653.6 cu in
3. 10.67 gal
5. 682.94 cm^3
7. a. 0.35 m^3
   b. 350 L

9. a. 847.8 m^3
   b. 282 600 L
11. 275.37 mL

Exercise 26-3
1. 7 in
3. 8.5 ft
5. 4.94 in
7. 24.38 ft
9. 1.8 in

Exercise 26-4
1. a. 51 sq ft
   b. 81 sq ft
3. 188.4 sq ft

5. 17.62 lb
7. 68 gal
9. 8.95 m^2

Exercise 26-5
1. 1 672 cm^3
3. 1.8 ft
5. 182.52 sq in
7. 65.4 lb
9. 1.25 m
11. 966.5 sq ft
13. a. 384.34 cu in
    b. 116.98 lb
15. 3 in

UNIT 27

Exercise 27-1
1. 920 cu ft
3. 352.8 cu in
5. 34 440 lb
7. 10 584 cu ft
9. 0.74 L

Exercise 27-2
1. 14.25 ft
3. 2.25 m
5. 2.69 m
7. 6.34 ft

Exercise 27-3
1. 920 sq in
3. a. 519.76 cm^2
   b. 732.92 cm^2
5. a. 160 sq in
   b. 224 sq in
7. a. 1 687.03 sq ft
   b. 68 bundles
9. 12.48 m^2

Exercise 27-4
1. 2 137.14 cu ft
3. 19.86 L

5. 20.81 m^3
7. a. 17.92 cu in
   b. 9.93 oz
9. a. 10.75 cu yd
   b. 29 012.5 lb

Exercise 27-5
1. 832 sq ft
3. a. 52.92 m^2
   b. 73.17 m^2
5. 4.17 sq ft
7. 75.36 sq ft
9. 17.48 sq ft

Exercise 27-6
1. 0.33 m^3
3. 11.67 ft
5. 392 sq in
7. 634.83 cm^3
9. 7 701.33 cu ft
11. 19.11 cm
13. 35.43 L
15. a. 0.83 sq ft
    b. 1.55 lb

UNIT 28

Exercise 28-1
1. 28.26 sq in
3. 24.62 m^2
5. 783.87 sq ft
7. 1.72 m^2
9. $4 019.20
11. 3.20 oz
13. a. The cylindrical tank requires more surface area material.
    b. 19.60 m^2

Exercise 28-2
1. 33.49 m^3
3. 229.73 cu in
5. 310.18 cu in
7. 2 224.97 cm^3
9. 0.04 lb
11. 6.93 h
13. 27 spheres

Exercise 28-3
1. 0.5 cu yd
3. 1 111.5 m^3
5. a. 618.38 sq in
   b. 10.11 lb
7. 13.62 cm^3
9. 55.54 lb
11. 243.83 m^3

Exercise 28-4
1. a. 128.61 sq in
   b. 137.19 cu in
3. a. 2.01 m^2
   b. 0.27 m^3
5. $3 205.42
7. 25.83 m^3
9. $3.55
11. 168.28 min

UNIT 29

Exercise 29-1
1. r is hypotenuse
   x is adjacent
   y is opposite
3. a is opposite
   b is adjacent
   c is hypotenuse
5. a is hypotenuse
   b is opposite
   c is adjacent
7. d is hypotenuse
   m is opposite
   p is adjacent
9. h is opposite
   k is hypotenuse
   l is opposite
11. m is opposite
    p is hypotenuse
    s is adjacent

13. m is hypotenuse
    r is adjacent
    t is opposite
15. f is adjacent
    g is hypotenuse
    h is opposite

Exercise 29-2
1. $\sin \angle 1 = \dfrac{y}{r}$

   $\cos \angle 1 = \dfrac{x}{r}$

   $\tan \angle 1 = \dfrac{y}{x}$

   $\cot \angle 1 = \dfrac{x}{y}$

   $\sec \angle 1 = \dfrac{r}{x}$

   $\csc \angle 1 = \dfrac{r}{y}$

3. $\sin \angle 1 = \dfrac{h}{g}$

   $\cos \angle 1 = \dfrac{k}{g}$

   $\tan \angle 1 = \dfrac{h}{k}$

   $\cot \angle 1 = \dfrac{k}{h}$

   $\sec \angle 1 = \dfrac{g}{k}$

   $\csc \angle 1 = \dfrac{g}{h}$

5. $\sin \angle 1 = \dfrac{r}{s}$

   $\cos \angle 1 = \dfrac{p}{s}$

   $\tan \angle 1 = \dfrac{r}{p}$

   $\cot \angle 1 = \dfrac{p}{r}$

   $\sec \angle 1 = \dfrac{s}{p}$

   $\csc \angle 1 = \dfrac{s}{r}$

Exercise 29-3
1. 0.500 0
3. 0.466 31
5. 0.956 30
7. 4.133 6
9. 0.983 78
11. 0.916 06
13. 0.102 16
15. 5.855 4
17. 1.246 7
19. 0.999 89
21. 1.000 0
23. 1.000 3
25. 7°0′
27. 9°0′

UNIT 29 (Cont'd)

Exercise 29-3 (Cont'd)

29. 61°0′
31. 20°0′
33. 31°10′
35. 45°50′
37. 61°30′
39. 63°10′
41. 5°40′
43. 75°50′
45. 26°30′
47. 89°20′

Exercise 29-4

1. 0.700 2
3. 0.838 7
5. 5.758 8
7. 0.313 4
9. 0.377 8
11. 10.826
13. 3.291
15. 1.000 0
17. 1.003 5
19. 1.562 2
21. 36.2°
23. 71.7°
25. 63.5°
27. 9.6°
29. 81.2°
31. 86.8°
33. 10.2°
35. 29.6°
37. 87.5°
39. 0.1°

Exercise 29-5

1. 0.426 04
3. 0.988 40

5. 1.153 8
7. 0.970 93
9. 1.312 7
11. 0.044 78
13. 0.021 52
15. 0.894 67
17. 0.349 22
19. 1.284 6
21. 30°17′
23. 40°9′
25. 29°26′
27. 41°24′
29. 24°41′
31. 5°6′
33. 48°57′
35. 52°25′
37. 23°6′
39. 50°36′

Exercise 29-6

1. 0.568 1
3. 1.085 6
5. 0.767 6
7. 1.254 0
9. 0.223 1
11. 1.000 0
13. 0.997 0
15. 1.250 8
17. 0.978 8
19. 1.656 3
21. 18.53°
23. 38.07°
25. 60.35°
27. 83.89°
29. 44.53°
31. 27.02°

33. 36.09°
35. 45.56°
37. 24.68°
39. 85.15°

Exercise 29-7

1. a is opposite
   b is adjacent
   c is hypotenuse
3. e is adjacent
   f is opposite
   g is hypotenuse
5. h is hypotenuse
   j is opposite
   k is adjacent
7. a is opposite
   d is hypotenuse
   p is adjacent
9. $\sin \angle 1 = \dfrac{y}{r}$

   $\cos \angle 1 = \dfrac{x}{r}$

   $\tan \angle 1 = \dfrac{y}{x}$

   $\cot \angle 1 = \dfrac{x}{y}$

   $\sec \angle 1 = \dfrac{r}{x}$

   $\csc \angle 1 = \dfrac{r}{y}$

11. $\sin \angle 1 = \dfrac{s}{m}$

    $\cos \angle 1 = \dfrac{t}{m}$

    $\tan \angle 1 = \dfrac{s}{t}$

    $\cot \angle 1 = \dfrac{t}{s}$

$\sec \angle 1 = \dfrac{m}{t}$

$\csc \angle 1 = \dfrac{m}{s}$

13. 0.422 62
15. 0.237 00
17. 1.750 7
19. 0.923 43
21. 0.246 15
23. 1.060 6
25. 35°10′
27. 20°40′
29. 35°40′
31. 24°23′
33. 35°55′
35. 25°32′
37. 0.682 0
39. 0.599 0
41. 1.058 9
43. 0.259 2
45. 0.924 3
47. 0.002 45
49. 13.7°
51. 46.9°
53. 40.4°
55. 49.93°
57. 42.53°
59. 55.72°

UNIT 30

Exercise 30-1

1. a. side y and side r are almost the same length
   b. side x is very small compared to side r
   c. side x is very small compared to side y
3. a. side y is very small compared to side r
   b. side x and side r are almost the same length
   c. side x is very large compared to side y
5. a. $\angle 1 = 45°$
   b. $\tan \angle 1 = \dfrac{\text{opp side}}{\text{adj side}} = \dfrac{y}{x} = 1.000\ldots$

   c. $\cot \angle 1 = \dfrac{\text{adj side}}{\text{opp side}} = \dfrac{x}{y} = 1.000\ldots$

7. a. $\sin \angle 1 = \dfrac{y}{r} = 1.000\ldots$

   b. $\csc \angle 1 = \dfrac{r}{y} = 1.000\ldots$

   c. $\cos \angle 1 = \dfrac{x}{r} = \dfrac{0}{r} = 0$

   d. $\cot \angle 1 = \dfrac{x}{y} = \dfrac{0}{y} = 0$

UNIT 30 (Cont'd)

9. tan 18°
11. cot 36°
13. csc 22°
15. cos 81°19′
17. csc 39.25°
19. sec 55°

23. tan 30°
25. sec 43°
27. sin 12°
29. tan 1°20′
31. sec 0.2°

5. $y = 13.615$ cm
7. $p = 6.878$ m
9. $d = 2.229$ in
    $e = 2.049$ in
11. $x = 7.285$ m
    $y = 2.480$ m

15. csc 65°
17. sec 90°
19. cos 38.12°
21. tan 40°
23. cos 44°
25. sec 45°
27. $\angle A = 38°41′$
29. $x = 6.773$ cm
31. $\angle B = 38°24′$
33. $\angle 1 = 55°42′$
35. $\angle B = 17°30′$
    $x = 55.237$ in
    $y = 52.680$ in
37. $a = 9.349$ cm
    $b = 3.164$ cm
    $\angle 2 = 71.3°$

Exercise 30-2

1. cot 73°
3. sin 64°
5. tan 55°
7. sin 0°
9. cot 23.5°
11. tan 82°50′
13. sec 89°22′
15. sin 84.11°
17. cot 0°
19. sin 89.99°
21. cos 55°

Exercise 30-3

1. $\angle A = 36°28′$
3. $\angle 1 = 42°2′$
5. $\angle 1 = 59.24°$
7. $\angle y = 54.10°$
9. $\angle 1 = 22°21′$
    $\angle 2 = 67°39′$
11. $\angle x = 29.50°$
    $\angle y = 60.10°$

Exercise 30-4

1. $b = 5.313$ in
3. $x = 50.465$ ft

Exercise 30-5

1. a. $y = 0$
   b. $x = $ side r
3. a. $\angle 1 = 45°$
   b. $1.000 \ldots$
   c. $1.000 \ldots$
5. a. 0
   b. $1.000 \ldots$
7. cot 43°
9. sin 28°12′
11. csc 79.12°
13. sin 24°

UNIT 31

Exercise 31-1

1. $\angle A = 24°17′$
    $\angle B = 65°43′$
3. 7.08 m
5. 15.67 ft
7. The resultant vector pulls on the object with a force of 216.33 lb in a direction up and to the left at an angle of 56°19′ from the horizontal.
9. 389.71 V
11. 29.21 m
13. 48.10 ft
15. 400 V
17. 838.80 mi

Exercise 31-2

1. 13°15′
3. 6.75°

5. 5.90 m
7. 19.75 mm
9. a. 46.16 m
   b. 31.20 m
11. a. 55°13′
    b. 57°37′
13. 30.38°
15. 5.82 m
17. a. 12.60 ft
    b. 21.97 ft

Exercise 31-3

1. 3.036 in
3. a. 4.31 m
   b. 43.31°
5. 58°50′
7. 247.52 ft
9. 28.83 m

11. 928 in
13. a. 21.84°
    b. 33.92°
    c. 29.08 m
15. 57.89 mm

Exercise 31-4

1. 10.64 in
3. 218.72 ft
5. 282.84 V
7. 24.69 m
9. 3.36 m
11. 47.70 mm
13. 6.631 in
15. 19.37°
17. 3.14 m
19. 56°4′
21. 81.72 ft

UNIT 32

Exercise 32-1

1. sin 125° = sin 55° = 0.819 15
    cos 125° = −cos 55° = −0.573 58
    tan 125° = −tan 55° = −1.428 2
    cot 125° = −cot 55° = −0.700 21
    sec 125° = −sec 55° = −1.743 4
    csc 125° = csc 55° = 1.220 8

3. sin 260° = −sin 80° = −0.984 81
    cos 260° = −cos 80° = −0.173 65
    tan 260° = tan 80° = 5.671 3
    cot 260° = cot 80° = 0.176 33
    sec 260° = −sec 80° = −5.758 8
    csc 260° = −csc 80° = −1.015 4

Exercise 32-1 (Cont'd)

5. $\sin 300° = -\sin 60° = -0.866\ 03$
    $\cos 300° = \cos 60° = 0.500\ 00$
    $\tan 300° = -\tan 60° = -1.732\ 1$
    $\cot 300° = -\cot 60° = -0.577\ 35$
    $\sec 300° = \sec 60° = 2.000\ 0$
    $\csc 300° = -\csc 60° = -1.154\ 7$

7. $\sin 216°20' = -\sin 36°20' = -0.592\ 48$
    $\cos 216°20' = -\cos 36°20' = -0.805\ 58$
    $\tan 216°20' = \tan 36°20' = 0.735\ 47$
    $\cot 216°20' = \cot 36°20' = 1.359\ 7$
    $\sec 216°20' = -\sec 36°20' = -1.241\ 3$
    $\csc 216°20' = -\csc 36°20' = -1.687\ 8$

9. $\sin 146°10' = \sin 33°50' = 0.556\ 78$
    $\cos 146°10' = -\cos 33°50' = -0.830\ 66$
    $\tan 146°10' = -\tan 33°50' = -0.670\ 28$
    $\cot 146°10' = -\cot 33°50' = -1.491\ 9$
    $\sec 146°10' = -\sec 33°50' = -1.203\ 9$
    $\csc 146°10' = \csc 33°50' = 1.796\ 0$

11. $\sin 313.2° = -\sin 46.8° = -0.729\ 0$
    $\cos 313.2° = \cos 46.8° = 0.684\ 5$
    $\tan 313.2° = -\tan 46.8° = -1.064\ 9$
    $\cot 313.2° = -\cot 46.8° = -0.939\ 1$
    $\sec 313.2° = \sec 46.8° = 1.460\ 8$
    $\csc 313.2° = -\csc 46.8° = -1.371\ 8$

13. 519.6 V
15. −120 V
17. −103.9 V
19. 300 V
21. −550 V

Exercise 32-2

1. $\sin 510° = \sin 150° = \sin 30° = 0.500\ 00$
    $\cos 510° = \cos 150° = -\cos 30° = -0.866\ 03$
    $\tan 510° = \tan 150° = -\tan 30° = -0.577\ 35$
    $\cot 510° = \cot 150° = -\cot 30° = -1.732\ 1$
    $\sec 510° = \sec 150° = -\sec 30° = -1.154\ 7$
    $\csc 510° = \csc 150° = \csc 30° = 2.000\ 0$

3. $\sin 555° = \sin 195° = -\sin 15° = -0.258\ 82$
    $\cos 555° = \cos 195° = -\cos 15° = -0.965\ 93$
    $\tan 555° = \tan 195° = \tan 15° = 0.267\ 95$
    $\cot 555° = \cot 195° = \cot 15° = 3.732\ 1$
    $\sec 555° = \sec 195° = -\sec 15° = -1.035\ 3$
    $\csc 555° = \csc 195° = -\csc 15° = -3.863\ 7$

5. $\sin 531° = \sin 171° = \sin 9° = 0.156\ 43$
    $\cos 531° = \cos 171° = -\cos 9° = -0.987\ 69$
    $\tan 531° = \tan 171° = -\tan 9° = -0.158\ 38$
    $\cot 531° = \cot 171° = -\cot 9° = -6.313\ 8$
    $\sec 531° = \sec 171° = -\sec 9° = -1.012\ 5$
    $\csc 531° = \csc 171° = \csc 9° = 6.392\ 4$

7. $\sin 937° = \sin 217° = -\sin 37° = -0.601\ 82$
    $\cos 937° = \cos 217° = -\cos 37° = -0.798\ 64$
    $\tan 937° = \tan 217° = \tan 37° = 0.753\ 55$
    $\cot 937° = \cot 217° = \cot 37° = 1.327\ 0$
    $\sec 937° = \sec 217° = -\sec 37° = -1.252\ 1$
    $\csc 937° = \csc 217° = -\csc 37° = -1.661\ 6$

9. $\sin 1\ 248.4° = \sin 168.4° = \sin 11.6° = 0.201\ 1$
    $\cos 1\ 248.4° = \cos 168.4° = -\cos 11.6° = -0.979\ 6$
    $\tan 1\ 248.4° = \tan 168.4° = -\tan 11.6° = -0.205\ 3$
    $\cot 1\ 248.4° = \cot 168.4° = -\cot 11.6° = -4.872$
    $\sec 1\ 248.\ 4° = \sec 168.4° = -\sec 11.6° = -1.020\ 9$
    $\csc 1\ 248.4° = \csc 168.4° = \csc 11.6° = 4.973\ 2$

11. 228.3 V
13. −304.3 V
15. 70.5 V
17. 723.8 V
19. 352.7 V

Exercise 32-3

1. 4.641 in
3. 37.151 cm
5. 3.941 in
7. a. 85.3°
    b. 50.530 cm
9. a. 27°10'
    b. 15.059 in
11. a. 108°
    b. 12.265 in
    c. 8.347 in

Exercise 32-4

1. two solutions
3. one solution
5. one solution
7. two solutions
9. 51°30'
11. 69.05°
13. 57°19'
15. a. 19°23'
    b. 76°7'
17. a. 120°7'
    b. 32°43'

UNIT 32 (Cont'd)

19. a. 18°59'
    b. 102°11'
    c. 6.898 in

Exercise 32-5

1. 3.283 in
3. 19.572 in
5. 361.556 ft
7. a. 6.833 in
   b. 66°33'
   c. 83°57'
9. a. 91.171 ft
   b. 49°13'
   c. 32°47'
11. a. 9.760 in
    b. 73°43'
    c. 72°37'

Exercise 32-6

1. 22°59'
3. 69.52°
5. 132°53'
7. a. 79°15'
   b. 72°18'
   c. 28°27'
9. a. 102°1'
   b. 50°13'
   c. 27°46'
11. a. 107.46°
    b. 55.32°
    c. 17.22°

Exercise 32-7

1. 50°51'
3. a. 60°

b. 67.34°
c. 52.66°
5. 18.09 in
7. a. 3.89 in
   b. 4.48 in
9. 11.981 cm
11. 125°44'
13. a. 45°34'
    b. 31°17'
    c. 12.04 ft
15. 68°24'
17. 352.20 ft
19. 1 299.22 mi
21. 18.03°
23. The resultant vector pulls on the object at point 0 with a force of 1 166.29 pounds in a direction up and to the left at an angle of 46°42' with the horizontal.

Exercise 32-8

1. sin 115° = sin 65° = 0.906 31
    cos 115° = −cos 65° = −0.422 62
    tan 115° = −tan 65° = −2.144 5
    cot 115° = −cot 65° = −0.466 31
    sec 115° = −sec 65° = −2.366 2
    csc 115° = csc 65° = 1.103 4
3. sin 290°20' = −sin 69°40' = −0.937 69
    cos 290°20' = cos 69°40' = 0.347 48
    tan 290°20' = −tan 69°40' = −2.698 5
    cot 290°20' = −cot 69°40' = −0.370 57
    sec 290°20' = sec 69°40' = 2.877 8
    csc 290°20' = −csc 69°40' = −1.066 4
5. sin 580° = sin 220° = −sin 40° = −0.642 79
    cos 580° = cos 220° = −cos 40° = −0.766 04
    tan 580° = tan 220° = tan 40° = 0.839 10
    cot 580° = cot 220° = cot 40° = 1.191 8
    sec 580° = sec 220° = −sec 40° = −1.305 4
    csc 580° = csc 220° = −csc 40° = −1.555 7
7. sin 755.3° = sin 35.3° = 0.577 9
    cos 755.3° = cos 35.3° = 0.816 1
    tan 755.3° = tan 35.3° = 0.708 0
    cot 755.3° = cot 35.3° = 1.412 4
    sec 755.3° = sec 35.3° = 1.225 3
    csc 755.3° = csc 35.3° = 1.730 5
9. a. 154.3 V
   b. −491.5 V
   c. −91.9 V
   d. 0 V
   e. −102.6 V

11. 5.680 cm
13. 50.311 mm
15. 6.978 cm
17. a. 72°10'
    b. 21.491 in
19. a. 121°50'
    b. 28.344 in
21. a. 105.60°
    b. 35.355 cm
    c. 21.367
23. 1.850 in
25. 23.057 cm
27. 34.684 in
29. a. 8.967 cm
    b. 68.31°
    c. 76.89°
31. a. 6.441 in
    b. 39°41'
    c. 33°19'
33. a. 31.989 mm
    b. 66.27°
    c. 76.13°
35. 15.06 in
37. 92°34'
39. 49°49'
     58°50'
     71°21'
41. 11.20 cm
43. 136.81 m

ACKNOWLEDGMENTS

Brown & Sharpe Mfg. Co.
Industrial Products Division
Precision Park
North Kingston, RI   02852

Lufkin Measuring Tools
THE COOPER GROUP
P.O. Box 728
Apex, NC   27502

L. S. Starrett Company
Athol, MA   01331

INDEX